Revenue Statistics

2016

SPECIAL FEATURE: CURRENT ISSUES ON REPORTING TAX REVENUES

Statistiques des recettes publiques

2016

ÉTUDE SPÉCIALE : QUESTIONS ACTUELLES SUR LA COMPTABILISATION DES RECETTES FISCALES

OECD
BETTER POLICIES FOR BETTER LIVES

This work is published on the responsibility of the Secretary-General of the OECD. The opinions expressed and arguments employed herein do not necessarily reflect the official views of the Organisation or of the governments of its member countries.

Cet ouvrage est publié sous la responsabilité du Secrétaire général de l'OCDE. Les opinions et les interprétations exprimées ne reflètent pas nécessairement les vues de l'OCDE ou des gouvernements de ses pays membres.

This document and any map included herein are without prejudice to the status of or sovereignty over any territory, to the delimitation of international frontiers and boundaries and to the name of any territory, city or area.

Ce document et toute carte qu'il peut comprendre ne préjugent en rien du statut de tout territoire, de la souveraineté s'exerçant sur ce dernier, du tracé des frontières et limites internationales, et du nom de tout territoire, ville ou région.

Please cite this publication as:
OECD (2016), *Revenue Statistics 2016*, OECD Publishing.
http://dx.doi.org/10.1787/10.1787/rev_stats-2016-en-fr

Merci de citer cet ouvrage comme suit :
OCDE (2016), *Statistiques des recettes publiques 2016*, Éditions OCDE.
http://dx.doi.org/10.1787/10.1787/rev_stats-2016-en-fr

ISBN 978-92-64-26510-3 (print/*imprimé*)
ISBN 978-92-64-26511-0 (PDF)

Annual/*Annuel* : Revenue Statistics/Statistiques des recettes publiques
ISSN 1560-3660 (print/*imprimé*)
ISSN 1996-3726 (on line/*en ligne*)

The statistical data for Israel are supplied by and under the responsibility of the relevant Israeli authorities. The use of such data by the OECD is without prejudice to the status of the Golan Heights, East Jerusalem and Israeli settlements in the West Bank under the terms of international law.

Les données statistiques concernant Israël sont fournies par et sous la responsabilité des autorités israéliennes compétentes. L'utilisation de ces données par l'OCDE est sans préjudice du statut des hauteurs du Golan, de Jérusalem-Est et des colonies de peuplement israéliennes en Cisjordanie aux termes du droit international.

Corrigenda to OECD publications may be found on line at: *www.oecd.org/publishing/corrigenda*.
Les corrigenda des publications de l'OCDE sont disponibles sur : *www.oecd.org/editions/corrigenda*.

Foreword

This annual publication provides information on tax levels and tax structures in OECD countries. It was prepared under the auspices of the Working Party on Tax Policy Analysis and Tax Statistics of the Committee on Fiscal Affairs and is published under the responsibility of the Secretary-General of the OECD.

Avant-propos

Cette publication annuelle fournit des informations sur les niveaux d'imposition et la structure de la fiscalité dans les pays de l'OCDE. Elle a été préparée sous les auspices du Groupe de travail sur l'analyse des politiques et des statistiques fiscales du Comité des affaires fiscales ; elle est publiée sous la responsabilité du Secrétaire général de l'OCDE.

Table of contents

Figures

Table des matières

Tableaux

Graphiques

Follow OECD Publications on:

http://twitter.com/OECD_Pubs

http://www.facebook.com/OECDPublications

http://www.linkedin.com/groups/OECD-Publications-4645871

http://www.youtube.com/oecdilibrary

http://www.oecd.org/oecddirect/

This book has...

StatLinks

A service that delivers Excel® files from the printed page!

Look for the *StatLinks* at the bottom of the tables or graphs in this book. To download the matching Excel® spreadsheet, just type the link into your Internet browser, starting with the *http://dx.doi.org* prefix, or click on the link from the e-book edition.

Executive summary

Tax revenues in OECD countries, measured as a percentage of GDP, increased again in 2015 to a new high of 34.3% on average. This continues the trend of steady increases in tax levels in the period after the financial crisis. Prior to the financial crisis, tax revenues had risen from 33.1% of GDP in 2004 to a pre-crisis peak of 33.8% in 2007, before falling to a low of 32.4% in 2009.

Taxes are defined in this publication as compulsory, unrequited payments to general government. Taxes are unrequited in that benefits provided by governments to taxpayers are not normally allocated in proportion to their payments. Taxes are classified by their base: income, profits and capital gains; payroll; property; goods and services; and other taxes. Compulsory social security contributions paid to general government are also treated as taxes. Revenues are also analysed by level of government: federal or central; state; local; and social security funds. Detailed information on the classifications can be found in the Interpretative Guide in Annex A of this report.

Tax levels in 2015

Between 2014 and 2015, the OECD average tax to GDP ratio increased from 34.2% in 2014 to 34.3% in 2015, despite large falls in the tax to GDP ratio in two countries. This is the sixth consecutive increase, and means that the OECD average tax to GDP level is, again, the highest in the fifty-year period covered by *Revenue Statistics*. OECD average tax levels have now exceeded pre-crisis levels since 2012.

An increase in tax to GDP ratios from 2014 to 2015 is also observed in 25 of the 32 countries for which preliminary 2015 data is available. In 23 countries, tax revenues increased at a faster rate than GDP, but in Greece and Switzerland, GDP growth was negative. The increase was largest in Mexico, due to higher revenues from taxes on income and on goods and services, and increases were above one percentage point in five other countries. Only seven countries experienced a decrease in tax to GDP ratios in 2015, relative to 2014. The decrease was sharpest in Ireland, where exceptional nominal GDP growth of over 30% led to a decrease of tax to GDP levels of over 5 percentage points. The tax to GDP ratio in Denmark decreased by 3.0 percentage points , driven by a correction from unusually high income tax revenues in 2014. Decreases of more than one percentage point were also seen in Iceland and in Luxembourg. In 2015, eighteen OECD countries reported tax to GDP ratios higher than those in 2007; among the remaining 14 countries that provided provisional information for 2015, all but Iceland, Ireland and Norway saw increased tax to GDP levels between 2014 and 2015.

Tax structure in 2015

The tax structure continues to evolve slowly after the global financial crisis. Revenues from income taxes have increased since 2010 (the lowest point following the crisis) to 11.6% of GDP but have not again reached their high point of 12.2% of GDP in 2007, prior to the crisis. Within this category, corporate income tax revenues have not grown at the same rate as personal income tax revenues, shifting more of the burden of income taxation toward households. Since 2011, the share of corporate income taxes to GDP has remained relatively steady at around 2.9%, while the share of personal income taxes has increased from 7.8 to 8.5% of GDP.

Following a notable increase between 2007 and 2009, social security contributions remained relatively constant in 2014 and 2015 at just over 26% of total tax revenue and 9.1% of GDP on average. Similarly, the OECD average shares of property, payroll and unspecified taxes also remained stable.

Revenues from taxes on goods and services were 10.8% of GDP from 2002 to 2005 and decreased to 10.3% in 2009, their lowest point following the crisis. Since then, revenues from taxes on goods and services have returned to pre-crisis levels, notwithstanding a small decline 2014 and 2015 from 11% to 10.9%. Revenues from VAT are increasing since 2009 and were 6.8% of GDP on average in 2015. At the same time, revenues from taxes on specific goods and services, notably excises, have been decreasing as a share of GDP and represented 3.2% on average in the OECD in 2015.

Intra-country deviations from the OECD average were typically small in the latest years covered by this report (changes from 2013 to 2015). Among the 32 countries who reported provisional data for 2015:

- Twenty-two countries had higher shares of personal income tax revenues to GDP in 2015 relative to 2013, with an average increase across the OECD of 0.2 percentage points. Only Ireland had a decrease of more than one percentage point, owing to the large increase in its GDP in 2015.
- Eighteen countries experienced an increase in corporate income tax revenues as a percentage of GDP, with changes in all countries, except for Norway, falling within the range of -0.5 to 0.8 percentage points. Corporate income tax levels in Norway decreased by nearly 4 percentage points. The OECD average did not change.
- VAT increased as a share of GDP in 20 countries and on average across the OECD by 0.2 percentage points. The strongest increase in VAT revenues was seen in Japan (1.6 percentage points, following their VAT rate increase) and the greatest fall, except for Ireland, was in Luxembourg, of 0.7 percentage points.
- The share of social security contributions and property taxes each increased by less than 0.1 percentage point on average, with a similar decrease for other goods & services taxes, with no significant outlying countries.

Changes by level of government

Tax revenues at different levels of government remained relatively stable in 2014 relative to 2013, both on an OECD average basis and in individual countries. The federal share of revenues in 2014 remained at 53% of general government revenue in federal countries and at 64% in unitary countries. In federal countries, 24% of revenues were received at subnational level on average (ranging from 5% in Austria to 40% in Switzerland), with on average two-thirds of revenues being received by state governments and one-third by local governments. In unitary countries, the share of local government revenues was 12%, ranging from 1% in the Czech Republic and Estonia to 37% in Sweden.

Résumé

Les recettes fiscales dans les pays de l'OCDE, mesurées en pourcentage du PIB, ont de nouveau augmenté en 2015 pour atteindre 34.3 % en moyenne, niveau sans précédent. Cette augmentation est dans la continuité de l'évolution de la pression fiscale dans la période qui a suivi la crise financière. Avant la crise, les recettes fiscales étaient passées de 33.1 % du PIB en 2004 à un niveau record de 33.8 % en 2007, avant de retomber à un point bas de 32.4 % en 2009.

Dans cette publication, les impôts désignent les versements obligatoires sans contrepartie aux administrations publiques. Les impôts sont sans contrepartie car les prestations fournies par les administrations aux contribuables ne sont pas normalement proportionnelles à leurs paiements. Les impôts sont ventilés en fonction de l'assiette : revenu, bénéfices et gains en capital ; salaires ; patrimoine ; biens et services ; et autres impôts. Les cotisations obligatoires de sécurité sociale versées aux administrations publiques sont aussi traitées comme des impôts. Les recettes sont également analysées par niveau d'administration : État fédéral ou administration centrale, administration d'un État fédéré, administrations locales et caisses de sécurité sociale. Le Guide d'interprétation à l'Annexe A du présent rapport contient des informations plus détaillées sur la classification des impôts.

Niveaux d'imposition en 2015

Entre 2014 et 2015, le ratio moyen des recettes fiscales rapportées au PIB dans la zone OCDE a progressé de 34.2 % à 34.3 %, malgré une forte baisse de ce ratio dans deux pays. Il s'agit de la sixième hausse consécutive, avec pour conséquence que le ratio moyen dans les pays de l'OCDE n'a jamais été aussi élevé au cours des cinquante années couvertes par les *Statistiques des recettes publiques*. Depuis 2012, les niveaux moyens d'imposition dans la zone OCDE dépassent ceux d'avant la crise.

On constate également une augmentation du ratio des recettes fiscales au PIB entre 2014 et 2015 dans 25 des 32 pays pour lesquels des données préliminaires pour 2015 sont disponibles. Dans 23 pays, les recettes fiscales ont augmenté plus vite que le PIB, mais en Grèce et en Suisse, le PIB a diminué. C'est au Mexique que la hausse a été la plus forte, sous l'effet de la progression des recettes générées par les impôts sur le revenu et sur les biens et services, tandis que les hausses ont dépassé un point de pourcentage dans cinq autres pays. Sept pays seulement ont vu leur ratio des recettes fiscales au PIB diminuer en 2015 par rapport à 2014. La baisse a été la plus marquée en Irlande, où la croissance exceptionnelle du PIB nominal, de plus de 30 %, a entraîné un recul du ratio de plus de 5 points de pourcentage. Au Danemark, le ratio des recettes fiscales au PIB a cédé 3.0 points de pourcentage, sous l'effet d'une correction de recettes de l'impôt sur le revenu inhabituellement élevées en 2014. Des baisses de plus d'un point se sont également produites en Islande et au Luxembourg. En 2015, 18 pays de l'OCDE affichaient des taux d'imposition supérieurs à ceux de 2007 ; tous les 14 pays restants qui ont communiqué des informations provisoires pour 2015, sauf l'Irlande, l'Islande et la Norvège, ont vu ce taux augmenter entre 2014 et 2015.

Composition des recettes fiscales en 2015

La structure fiscale change progressivement après la crise financière mondiale. Les recettes provenant des impôts sur le revenu ont augmenté depuis 2010 (le point bas après la crise) pour s'établir à 11.6 % du PIB, mais n'ont pas renoué avec leur point haut de 12.2 % du GDP en 2007, avant la crise. Dans cette catégorie, les recettes de l'impôt sur les bénéfices des sociétés n'ont pas progressé au même rythme que celles de l'impôt sur le revenu des personnes physiques, entraînant un alourdissement de la charge fiscale supportée par les ménages. Depuis 2011, la part des impôts sur les bénéfices des sociétés dans le PIB est restée relativement stable à environ 2.9 %, tandis que celle des impôts sur le revenu des personnes physiques est passée de 7.8 % à 8.5 % du PIB.

Après une forte augmentation entre 2007 et 2009, les cotisations de sécurité sociale sont restées relativement constantes en 2014 et 2015, à un peu plus de 26 % du total des recettes fiscales et 9.1 % du PIB en moyenne. De même, en moyenne dans les pays de l'OCDE, les parts des impôts sur le patrimoine, sur les salaires et des autres impôts sont également restées stables.

Les recettes des impôts sur les biens et services représentaient 10.8 % du PIB de 2002 à 2005, avant de se replier à 10.3 % en 2009, leur point bas après la crise. Depuis lors, elles ont retrouvé leur niveau d'avant la crise, malgré une légère baisse de 11 % à 10.9 % entre 2014 et 2015. Les recettes de TVA augmentent depuis 2009, et s'établissaient à 6.8 % du PIB en moyenne en 2015. Dans le même temps, les recettes des impôts sur les biens et services déterminés, notamment les accises, ont reculé en pourcentage du PIB, et représentaient 3.2 % en moyenne dans l'OCDE en 2015.

Les écarts propres aux différents pays par rapport à la moyenne de l'OCDE étaient généralement faibles au cours des dernières années couvertes par ce rapport (variations entre 2013 et 2015). Parmi les 32 pays qui ont communiqué des données provisoires pour 2015 :

- La part des recettes de l'impôt sur le revenu des personnes physiques dans le PIB était plus élevée en 2015 qu'en 2013 dans 22 pays, avec une hausse moyenne de 0.2 point dans la zone OCDE. Seule l'Irlande a enregistré une baisse supérieure à un point, sous l'effet de la forte progression de son PIB en 2015.
- La part des recettes de l'impôt sur les bénéfices des sociétés dans le PIB s'est accrue dans 18 pays avec une variation de -0.5 à 0.8 point dans tous les pays sauf la Norvège, qui a enregistré une diminution de cette part de près de 4 points. La moyenne de la zone OCDE n'a pas changé.
- La part des recettes de TVA dans le PIB a augmenté dans 20 pays et de 0.2 point dans la zone OCDE en moyenne. La plus forte hausse des recettes de TVA s'est produite au Japon (1.6 point, sous l'effet du relèvement du taux de TVA intervenu dans ce pays), tandis que la baisse la plus marquée, hormis l'Irlande, a concerné le Luxembourg (-0.7 point).
- Les parts respectives des cotisations de sécurité sociale et des impôts sur le patrimoine dans le total des recettes fiscales ont progressé de moins 0.1 point en moyenne, tandis que la part des autres impôts sur les biens et services a diminué dans des proportions similaires, aucun pays ne se démarquant sensiblement de cette tendance.

Variations par niveau d'administration

La répartition des impôts par niveaux d'administration est restée relativement stable en 2014 par rapport à 2013, à la fois en moyenne dans l'OCDE et dans les différents pays. En 2014, la part des recettes de l'administration fédérale représentait 53 % du total des recettes des administrations publiques dans les pays fédéraux, et 64 % dans les pays unitaires. Dans les pays fédéraux, 24 % des recettes étaient perçues par les administrations infranationales en moyenne (dans un intervalle compris entre 5 % en Autriche et 40 % en Suisse), les deux tiers des recettes en moyenne revenant aux administrations des états fédérés et un tiers aux collectivités locales. Dans les pays unitaires, la part des recettes perçues par les collectivités locales s'établissait à 12 %, l'éventail allant de 1 % en République tchèque et en Estonie à 37 % en Suède.

Introduction

The purpose of this annual publication is to provide internationally comparative data on tax levels and tax structures in member countries of the OECD. The taxes imposed in each country are presented in a standardised framework based upon the OECD classification of taxes and its Interpretative Guide as contained in Annex A to this Report.

Starting in 2004, the data for recent years in this publication are mainly reported on an accrual basis, rather than the cash basis that has been used in previous editions. The reasons for this change were discussed in Special Feature S.2 of the 2003 edition. Details of the practical implementation of this change were given in Special Feature S.1 of the 2004 edition.

The criteria followed for the grouping of taxes are not affected by this change to accrual reporting and are primarily the basis on which a tax is charged and secondly whether households or other entities pay the tax. Borderline classification cases, where definitional issues and other difficulties arise, are noted in the Interpretative Guide. Footnotes which accompany the country tables in Chapter 4 record where countries deviate from the guidelines.

The data for the Report has, for the most part, been provided by Delegates to Working Party No. 2 on Tax Policy Analysis and Tax Statistics of the Committee on Fiscal Affairs. The OECD acknowledges the co-operation of the International Monetary Fund, whose classification of tax revenues – although in a number of respects less detailed – is in many respects similar to that of the OECD.[1] The most important of the other classifications currently in use is the System of National Accounts (henceforth referred to as SNA) and the European System of Integrated Economic Accounts of EU member states (henceforth referred to as ESA), which is primarily an elaboration of SNA, though differing from it in certain respects. Subject to a few exceptions, SNA/ESA figures can be reconciled with the figures in the present Report, since SNA criteria and definitions have been adopted unless the contrary is specifically indicated.

The material is organised in five chapters. Chapter 1 summarises tax trends of the past 50 years focusing in turn on tax levels (Section 1.1), tax structures (Section 1.2) and taxes by level of government (Section 1.3). Section 1.4 discusses the impact of GDP revisions. This year's issue also carries in Chapter 2 a special feature on "Current issues on reporting tax revenues". Chapter 3 contains a set of comparative statistical tables for years 1965-2014 (Section 3.1) and a series of comparative graphs which show the differences between countries as regards tax levels and tax structures (Section 3.2). Estimates of 2015 tax revenues are presented in Section 3.3 for all countries for which such data are available. Chapter 4 provides statistical tables with a detailed breakdown of tax revenues by country for years between 1965 and 2014 (Section 4.1).[2] A second series of tables shows how countries finance their social benefits (Section 4.2), followed by a series of tables detailing taxes and social security contributions paid by general government (Section 4.3). Chapter 5 attributes tax revenues to general government by the following sub-sectors: central, state; local and social security funds. It contains a series of comparative graphs which show the differences between countries as regards tax structures (Section 5.1), a set of comparative statistical tables for years 1975-2014 (Section 5.2) and a second series of tables with a detailed breakdown of tax revenues by country for years between 1975 and 2014 (Section 5.3).

Notes

1. See IMF (2014), *Government Finance Statistics Manual 2014*, International Monetary Fund, Washington, DC.
2. Because of space limitations, data are shown for selected years between 1965 and 2014. Data for years not shown are available online.

Introduction

Le but de cette publication annuelle est de présenter des données permettant d'effectuer des comparaisons internationales sur les niveaux d'imposition et la structure de la fiscalité dans les différents pays membres de l'OCDE. Les impôts perçus dans chaque pays sont présentés sous une forme normalisée selon le modèle de classification des impôts de l'OCDE et son guide d'interprétation qui figure à l'Annexe A de ce rapport.

À partir de l'année 2004, les données de cette publication concernant les années récentes sont surtout enregistrées sur la base des droits constatés et non plus sur la base des décaissements qui était utilisée pour les éditions précédentes. Les motifs de ce changement ont été examinés dans l'Étude spéciale S.2 de l'édition de 2003. On trouvera des précisions sur l'application pratique de ce changement dans l'Étude spéciale S.1 de l'édition 2004.

Les critères retenus pour la classification des impôts ne sont pas affectés par cette adoption de l'enregistrement sur la base des droits constatés et sont constitués essentiellement par l'assiette de l'impôt et en second lieu par la question de savoir si les ménages ou autres entités paient l'impôt. Les cas particuliers de la classification, dans lesquels des questions de définition ainsi que d'autres problèmes se posent, sont mentionnés dans le Guide d'interprétation. Les notes de bas de page qui accompagnent les tableaux par pays du chapitre 4 enregistrent les cas dans lesquels les pays s'écartent des principes directeurs.

Les données utilisées ont été fournies pour la plupart par les Délégués du Groupe de travail n° 2 du Comité des affaires fiscales sur l'analyse des politiques et les statistiques fiscales. L'OCDE remercie de sa coopération le Fonds monétaire international dont la classification des recettes publiques – bien qu'elle soit, à certains égards, moins détaillée – est à bien des égards semblable à celle de l'OCDE[1]. Parmi les autres classifications actuellement utilisées, les plus importantes sont le Système de comptabilité nationale (appelé ci-après SCN) et le Système européen de comptes économiques intégrés des États membres de l'Union européenne (appelé ci-après SEC) qui constitue essentiellement un approfondissement du SCN bien qu'il en diffère à certains égards. Sous réserve de quelques exceptions mineures, les chiffres du SCN ou du SEC peuvent être rattachés directement à ceux de la présente étude car les critères et définitions du SCN ont été adoptées sauf mention contraire expresse.

Cette publication comprend cinq chapitres. Le chapitre 1 indique succinctement l'évolution de la fiscalité au cours des 50 dernières années en mettant l'accent successivement sur les niveaux d'imposition (section 1.1), sur les structures fiscales (section 1.2) et sur la répartition des impôts par niveau d'administration (section 1.3). La section 1.4 discute l'impact de la révision des données du PIB. La publication de cette année comporte également dans son chapitre 2 une étude spéciale sur les « Questions actuelles sur la comptabilisation des recettes fiscales ». Le chapitre 3 contient une série de tableaux statistiques comparatifs pour les années 1965-2014 (section 3.1) et une série de graphiques comparatifs qui indiquent les différences entre les pays quant au niveau d'imposition et aux structures fiscales (section 3.2). Des estimations des recettes fiscales pour 2015 sont présentées à la section 3.3 pour tous les pays dans lesquels de telles données sont disponibles. Le chapitre 4 contient des tableaux statistiques comportant une ventilation détaillée des recettes fiscales par pays pour les années comprises entre 1965 et 2014 (section 4.1)[2] et elle indique en outre comment les pays financent leurs régimes de prestations sociales (section 4.2) ainsi que les cotisations sociales versées par les administrations (section 4.3). Le chapitre 5 ventile les recettes publiques entre les sous-secteurs ci-après : administration fédérale ou centrale, administration des États, administrations locales et de sécurité sociale. Il contient une série de graphiques comparatifs qui indiquent les différences entre les pays quant aux structures fiscales (section 5.1), une série de tableaux statistiques comparatifs pour les années 1975-2014 (section 5.2) et une deuxième série de tableaux statistiques comportant une ventilation détaillée des recettes fiscales par pays pour les années comprises entre 1975 et 2014 (section 5.3).

Notes

1. Voir FMI (2014), *Government Finance Statistics Manual 2014*, Fonds Monétaire International, Washington, DC.
2. En raison du manque de place, les données indiquées concernent une sélection d'années entre 1965 et 2014. Les données portant sur les autres années sont disponibles en ligne.

Revenue Statistics 2016
Statistiques des recettes publiques 2016

Chapter 1

Tax revenue trends, 1965-2015

Introduction

This annual Report presents detailed internationally comparable data on tax revenues of OECD countries for all levels of government. The latest edition provides outturn (i.e. final) data on tax revenues in 1965-2014. In addition, provisional estimates of tax revenues in 2015 are included for almost all OECD countries.

In this Report, taxes are defined as compulsory, unrequited payments to general government. Taxes are unrequited in the sense that benefits provided by government are not normally in proportion to their payments.

In the OECD classification, taxes are classified by the base of the tax:

- Income and profits (heading 1000)
- compulsory social security contributions paid to general government, which are treated as taxes (heading 2000);
- payroll and workforce (heading 3000);
- property (heading 4000);
- goods and services (heading 5000);
- other (heading 6000).

Much greater detail on the tax concept, the classification of taxes and the accrual basis of reporting is set out in the *OECD Interpretative Guide* at Annex A of this Report.

All of the averages presented in this Report are unweighted.

1.1. Tax ratio

a. Provisional data on tax ratios for 2015

New OECD data in the annual *Revenue Statistics* publication show that tax revenues as a percentage of GDP continue to recover gradually from the falls in almost all countries in 2008 and 2009 that stemmed from the financial and economic crisis. The average tax to GDP ratio in OECD countries was 34.3%[1] in 2015 compared with 34.2% in 2014 and 33.8% in 2013. The 2015 figure is the highest recorded OECD average tax to GDP ratio since records began in 1965 (Tables 1.1 and 1.2).

- Denmark had the highest tax to GDP ratio in 2015 (46.6%) and Mexico the lowest (17.4%).
- Of the 32 countries for which data for 2015 are available, the ratio of tax revenues to GDP compared to 2014 rose in 25 and fell in 7.
- Between 2014 and 2015, the largest tax ratio increases were in Mexico (2.3 percentage points explained by an increase in taxes on income and profits and in taxes on goods and services as a percentage of GDP) and in Turkey (1.3 due to higher revenues from taxes on goods and services and higher social security contribution revenues). Other countries with increases in their tax to GDP ratio between 2014 and 2015 of more than one percentage point were Estonia, Greece, Hungary and the Slovak Republic.

Table 1.1. **Total tax revenue as % of GDP**

	1965	1975	1985	1995	2000	2007	2009	2012	2014	2015p
Australia	20.6	25.4	27.8	28.2	30.4	29.7	25.8	27.4	27.8	..
Austria	33.6	36.4	40.5	41.1	42.1	40.5	41.0	41.7	42.8	43.5
Belgium	30.6	38.7	43.5	42.6	43.5	42.7	42.4	44.2	45.0	44.8
Canada	25.2	31.4	31.7	34.8	34.8	32.1	32.0	31.0	31.2	31.9
Chile	..	..	..	18.4	18.8	22.8	17.4	21.5	19.8	20.7
Czech Republic	..	..	..	34.9	32.5	34.3	32.4	33.7	33.1	33.5
Denmark[1]	29.1	37.0	43.9	46.5	46.9	46.4	45.2	45.8	49.6	46.6
Estonia	..	..	..	36.0	31.1	31.3	34.9	31.5	32.4	33.6
Finland	30.0	36.1	39.1	44.5	45.8	41.5	40.9	42.7	43.8	44.0
France[1]	33.6	34.9	41.9	41.9	43.1	42.4	41.3	44.3	45.5	45.5
Germany[2]	31.6	34.3	36.1	36.2	36.2	34.9	36.1	36.3	36.6	36.9
Greece[1]	17.1	18.7	24.6	27.8	33.4	31.2	30.9	35.5	35.8	36.8
Hungary	..	..	..	41.0	38.6	39.6	39.2	38.6	38.2	39.4
Iceland	25.5	29.3	27.5	30.5	36.3	39.0	31.9	35.3	38.9	37.1
Ireland	24.5	27.9	33.6	31.7	30.8	30.4	27.4	27.5	28.7	23.6
Israel[3]	..	..	..	35.6	34.8	34.0	29.7	29.7	31.2	31.4
Italy	24.7	24.5	32.5	38.6	40.6	41.7	42.1	43.9	43.7	43.3
Japan	17.8	20.4	26.7	26.4	26.6	28.5	27.0	29.4	32.0	..
Korea	..	14.9	15.8	19.1	21.5	24.8	23.8	24.8	24.6	25.3
Latvia	..	..	..	29.7	29.1	28.2	27.9	28.5	28.9	29.0
Luxembourg	26.4	31.5	37.9	34.9	37.2	36.5	38.9	38.8	38.4	37.0
Mexico[4]	..	..	15.2	11.4	13.6	13.2	13.6	13.9	15.2	17.4
Netherlands	30.9	38.2	39.8	37.7	37.2	36.0	35.4	36.0	37.5	37.8
New Zealand	23.2	27.5	29.5	35.6	32.5	33.9	30.3	32.0	32.5	32.8
Norway	29.4	38.8	41.9	40.0	41.9	42.1	41.2	41.5	38.7	38.1
Poland	..	..	..	37.7	32.9	34.6	31.4	31.9	32.1	..
Portugal	15.7	18.9	24.1	29.3	31.1	31.8	29.9	31.8	34.2	34.5
Slovak Republic	..	..	..	39.6	33.6	29.2	28.9	28.4	31.2	32.3
Slovenia	..	..	..	38.4	36.6	37.1	36.2	36.9	36.5	36.6
Spain[1]	14.3	18.0	26.8	31.3	33.4	36.5	30.0	32.4	33.8	33.8
Sweden	31.4	38.9	44.8	45.6	49.0	45.0	44.1	42.6	42.8	43.3
Switzerland	16.6	22.5	23.9	25.4	27.4	26.1	27.0	26.8	27.0	27.9
Turkey	10.6	11.9	11.5	16.8	24.2	24.1	24.6	27.6	28.8	30.0
United Kingdom	29.3	34.2	35.1	29.8	32.8	33.0	31.5	32.7	32.1	32.5
United States	23.5	24.6	24.6	26.5	28.2	26.7	23.0	24.1	25.9	26.4
Unweighted average										
OECD Average[5]	**24.8**	**28.6**	**31.5**	**33.3**	**34.0**	**33.8**	**32.4**	**33.4**	**34.2**	**34.3**

.. indicates not available; p: provisional.

1. The total tax revenues have been reduced by the amount of any capital transfer that represents uncollected taxes.
2. Unified Germany beginning in 1991.
3. The data for Israel are supplied by and under the responsibility of the relevant Israeli authorities. The use of such data by the OECD is without prejudice to the status of the Golan Heights, East Jerusalem and Israeli settlements in the West Bank under the terms of international law.
4. Secretariat estimate, including expected revenues collected by state and local governments.
5. Calculated by applying the unweighted average percentage change for 2015 in the 32 countries providing data for that year to the overall average tax to GDP ratio in 2014.

StatLink http://dx.doi.org/10.1787/888933416165

- The largest falls in the tax ratio between 2014 and 2015 were in Ireland (5.1 percentage points, due to exceptionally high GDP growth in 2015), Denmark (3 percentage points, due to a fall in revenues from taxes on income and profits) and Iceland (1.8 percentage point). Luxembourg also showed a fall of more than one percentage point.
- Compared with 2007 (pre-recession) tax to GDP ratios, the ratio in 2015 was still down by more than 3 percentage points in two countries (Ireland and Norway). The biggest fall has been in Ireland, from 30.4% in 2007 to 23.6% of GDP in 2015. Excluding Ireland, the largest fall has been in Norway, from 42.1% of GDP in 2007 to 38.1% in 2015.
- The tax burden in Turkey increased from 24.1% to 30.0% between 2007 and 2015. Two other countries (Greece and Mexico) showed increases of 4 percentage points or more over the same period.

Table 1.2. **Taxes on income and profits as % of GDP**

	1965	1975	1985	1995	2000	2007	2009	2012	2014	2015p
Australia	10.5	14.2	15.2	15.6	17.7	17.7	14.4	15.9	16.1	..
Austria	8.6	9.5	10.7	10.8	12.0	12.2	11.5	12.0	12.6	13.2
Belgium	8.5	15.3	17.6	16.2	16.8	15.3	14.4	15.3	16.1	16.0
Canada	9.7	14.8	14.0	16.1	17.4	15.7	15.3	14.7	15.0	15.2
Chile	..	..	..	4.6	4.4	10.4	5.4	8.4	6.5	7.5
Czech Republic	..	..	..	8.7	7.4	8.5	6.9	6.9	7.1	7.2
Denmark[1]	13.6	21.8	25.7	29.3	28.8	27.9	27.7	28.4	32.2	29.2
Estonia	..	..	..	10.8	7.7	7.4	7.4	6.6	7.4	7.9
Finland	12.4	15.6	16.0	16.1	19.7	16.3	14.6	14.6	15.3	15.5
France[1]	5.3	5.5	6.7	6.8	10.7	10.1	8.6	10.6	10.8	10.7
Germany[2]	10.7	11.8	12.6	11.0	10.9	10.9	10.4	11.0	11.4	11.6
Greece[1]	1.6	2.5	4.3	6.2	9.0	7.3	7.5	8.5	8.5	8.7
Hungary	..	..	..	8.6	9.4	9.9	9.5	7.0	6.8	6.9
Iceland	5.5	6.7	6.2	10.4	14.5	17.7	15.1	16.0	18.1	17.5
Ireland	6.3	8.4	11.6	12.8	13.4	12.4	10.6	11.2	11.6	10.2
Israel	..	..	..	12.4	13.8	12.4	8.9	9.1	9.7	9.9
Italy	4.4	5.3	12.0	13.6	13.5	14.1	13.7	14.3	14.0	13.9
Japan	7.8	9.1	12.2	10.1	9.3	10.4	8.0	9.1	10.2	10.4
Korea	..	3.6	4.2	5.8	6.2	7.9	6.8	7.4	7.2	7.6
Latvia	..	..	..	6.5	7.0	8.2	6.9	7.4	7.5	7.5
Luxembourg	9.5	13.6	16.4	14.0	13.6	12.7	13.8	13.7	13.3	13.4
Mexico	..	..	3.4	3.7	4.5	4.9	4.9	5.1	5.7	6.8
Netherlands	11.0	13.3	10.5	10.3	9.7	10.2	10.0	9.1	9.6	10.5
New Zealand	14.1	18.3	20.5	21.8	19.5	21.3	17.2	17.8	18.0	18.1
Norway	12.8	13.4	16.6	14.1	18.8	20.2	18.9	20.0	16.4	15.0
Poland	..	..	..	10.9	6.7	7.9	6.8	6.5	6.3	..
Portugal	3.9	3.3	6.2	7.7	9.1	8.8	8.3	8.7	10.5	10.5
Slovak Republic	..	..	..	10.1	6.9	6.1	5.5	5.5	6.5	6.9
Slovenia	..	..	..	6.4	6.8	8.7	7.5	6.9	6.5	6.6
Spain[1]	3.5	4.0	6.7	9.1	9.5	12.2	9.0	9.7	9.7	9.7
Sweden	17.2	19.6	18.9	17.9	20.0	17.4	15.5	14.5	14.9	15.5
Switzerland	6.8	10.7	11.0	11.1	12.2	12.1	12.6	12.2	12.3	13.0
Turkey	3.1	5.0	4.3	4.8	7.1	5.7	5.9	6.0	6.1	6.1
United Kingdom	10.8	15.3	13.6	11.0	12.8	13.0	12.1	11.6	11.2	11.5
United States	11.3	11.3	11.2	12.1	14.1	12.9	9.3	11.3	12.3	12.9
Unweighted average										
OECD Average[3]	**8.7**	**10.9**	**11.8**	**11.4**	**12.0**	**12.2**	**10.9**	**11.2**	**11.5**	**11.6**

.. indicates not available; p: provisional.

1. The total tax revenues have been reduced by the amount of any capital transfer that represents uncollected taxes.
2. Unified Germany beginning in 1991.
3. Calculated by applying the unweighted average percentage change for 2015 in the 33 countries providing data for that year to the overall average tax to GDP ratio in 2014.

StatLink http://dx.doi.org/10.1787/888933416170

Between 2014 and 2015, Ireland experienced unusually high GDP growth, at 32.4% in nominal terms (26.3% in real terms). This exceptionally high GDP growth was driven by transfers of intangible assets (including licences and patents) into the Irish jurisdiction by a number of multinational enterprises. The increase in the stock of intangible assets, used in supporting contract manufacturing arrangements, resulted in higher production that was attributable to Ireland, as well as to higher exports, depreciation and consumption of fixed capital. Together with increased aircraft imports into Ireland in 2015, this has led to the unusually high GDP growth.

Although the nominal amount of tax revenues increased by 8.8% from 2014 to 2015 (measured in national currency), the higher GDP growth during this period caused the tax to GDP ratio in Ireland to fall sharply, decreasing from 28.7% in 2014 to 23.6% in 2015. The fall in the tax to GDP ratio in Ireland lowered the unweighted OECD average tax to GDP ratio in 2015. Inclusive of Ireland, the unweighted OECD tax to GDP ratio in 2015 was 34.3%, a 0.1 percentage point increase since 2014. Excluding Ireland, the average tax to GDP ratio for the remaining OECD countries is 34.6% in 2015, an increase of 0.3 percentage points since 2014 for the remaining 34 countries.

b. Final data on tax ratios for 2014

The latest year for which tax to GDP ratios are based on final revenue data and available for all OECD countries is 2014 (Figure 1.1). These data show that tax ratios vary considerably across countries.

- In 2014, Denmark had the highest tax to GDP ratio (49.6%), followed by France, Belgium and Finland.
- In contrast, nine countries – Australia, Chile, Ireland, Korea, Latvia, Mexico, Switzerland, Turkey and the United States – had tax ratios of below 30%.
- Mexico had the lowest ratio at 15.2% followed by Chile at 19.8%.
- The tax ratio in the OECD area as a whole (unweighted average) rose by 0.4 percentage points from 2013 to 34.2% in 2014 (see Table 1.1).
- Relative to 2013, overall tax ratios rose in 26 OECD member countries and fell in 9.
- The largest increases in the ratio were in Iceland (2.9 percentage points), Denmark (2.8) and Japan (1.7) and New Zealand (1.3).
- Three countries – Estonia, Netherlands and Slovak Republic – saw increases between 0.9 and 1.0 percentage points from 2013 to 2014.
- The largest reductions were in Norway (1.2 percentage point) and the Czech Republic (1.0).

The key changes in the tax to GDP ratio of the main tax headings between 2013 and 2014 were as follows:

- Revenues from taxes on income (personal and corporate income taxes together) as a percentage of GDP increased from 11.4% in 2013 to 11.5% in 2014 on average. The largest increase was in Denmark (2.9 percentage points) and Iceland (1.3 percentage point). Norway and Italy reported the largest falls in this ratio (by 1.7 and 0.6 percentage point of GDP respectively) (Table 1.2).
- The corresponding ratios were largely unchanged between 2013 and 2014:
  - social security contributions remained at 9.1% (Table 3.13);
  - payroll taxes remained at 0.4% (Table 3.19);
  - property taxes remained at 1.9% (Table 3.21);
  - taxes on goods and services increased from 10.8 to 11.0% (Table 3.23).

Aggregate tax ratios often figure prominently in policy debates and they are sometimes linked directly to the economic performance of nations. A special feature included in Section S.2 of the 1999 edition of this Report explained why figures on tax revenues measured as a percentage of GDP should generally be interpreted with caution. More specifically, the revised guidelines set out in the 2008 System of National Accounts (SNA) that have been used to estimate the value of GDP for 32 of the 35 OECD countries, have resulting in higher GDP levels. As a consequence, the revised tax ratios reported in this publication are lower than tax to GDP ratios before these revisions. To limit any distortionary impact over the reporting period, the present edition of the Report employs revised GDP estimates for 1965 and later years in those cases where OECD countries have not reported revised GDP figures. The scale of the GDP revisions is considered in greater detail in the "Methodology issues" section below.

Figure 1.1. **Total tax revenue as % of GDP, 2014**

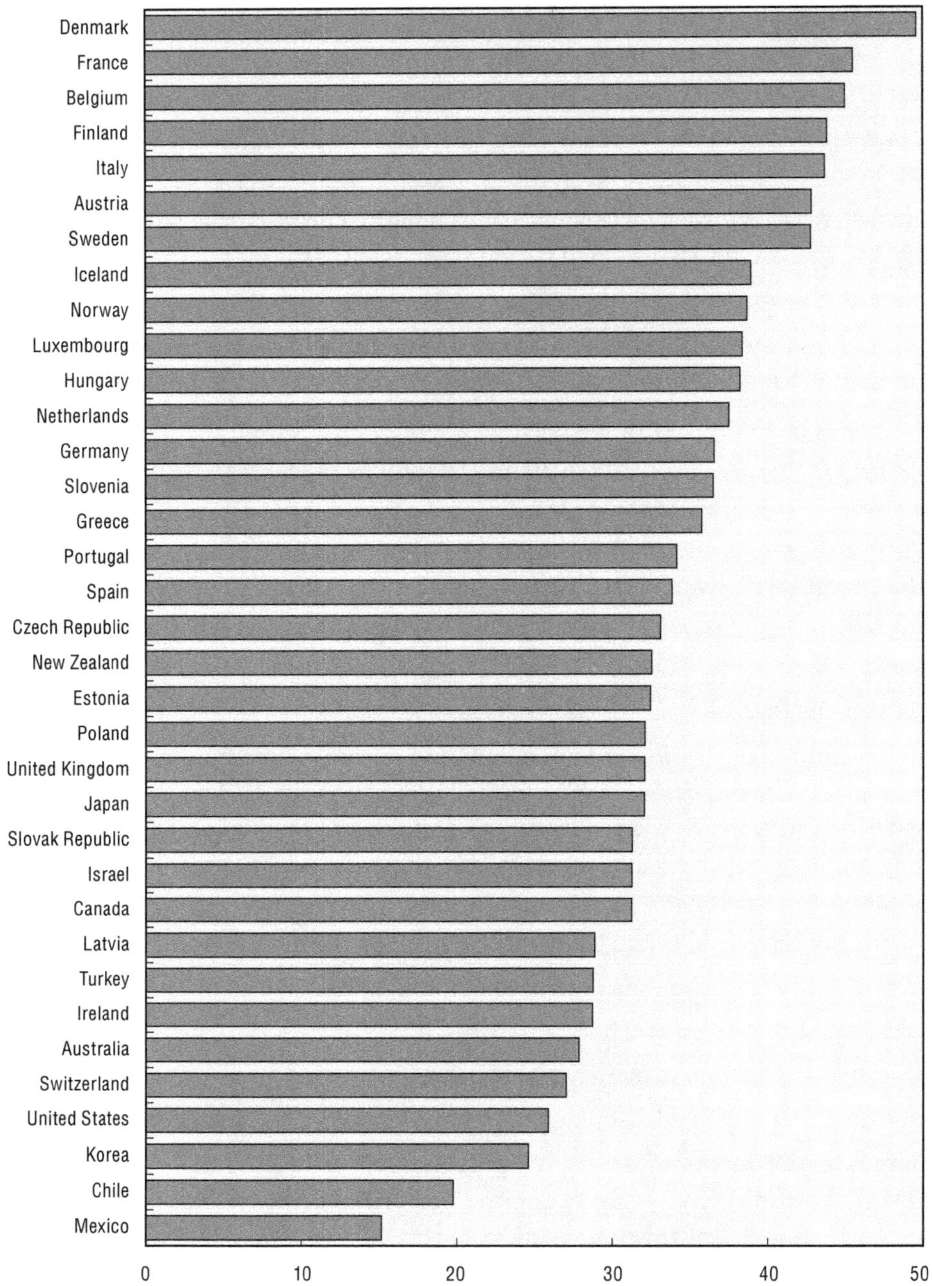

Note: Countries have been ranked by their total tax revenue to GDP ratios.
Source: Table 3.1.

StatLink http://dx.doi.org/10.1787/888933416001

c. *Tax ratios changes between 1965 and 2014*

The evolution of the changes in tax ratios between 1965 and 2014 is as follows:

- The average tax to GDP ratio in the OECD area increased from 24.8% to 34.2% (9.4 percentage points) between 1965 and 2014 (Table 3.2).
- The historical development of tax ratios for individual OECD countries varies greatly, as shown in Figures 1.2, 1.3, 1.4 and 1.5. Each figure relates national changes in the tax ratio to the OECD average, for the periods 1965-75, 1975-85, 1985-95 and 1995-2014,

Figure 1.2. **Changes in tax to GDP ratio (in % points)**

1965-1975

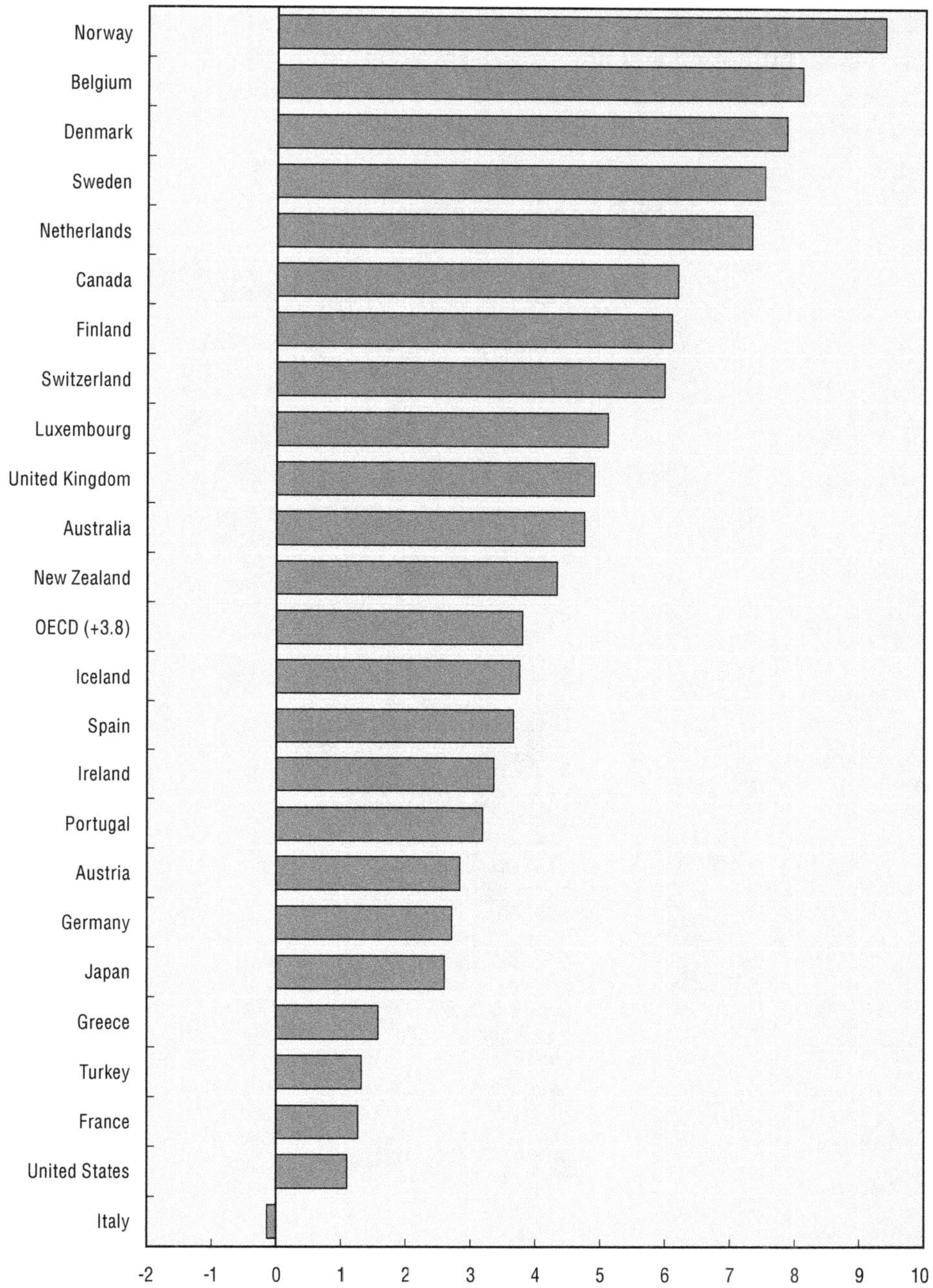

Source: Table 3.2.

Information on data for Israel: *http://oe.cd/israel-disclaimer*.

StatLink http://dx.doi.org/10.1787/888933416014

respectively. Despite the increase, on average across the OECD countries total tax revenues as a percentage of GDP have fallen in some countries.

- Between 1965 and 1975, the tax burden in the OECD area increased by 3.8 percentage points (Figure 1.2). Until the first oil shock (1973 to 1974), strong, almost uninterrupted income growth enabled tax levels to rise in all OECD countries. In part, tax levels rose automatically through the effect of fiscal drag on personal income tax schedules.

- Between 1975 and 1985, the tax burden in the OECD area increased by 2.9 percentage points (Figure 1.3). After the mid-1970s, the combination of slower real income growth and higher levels of unemployment apparently limited the revenue raising capacity of governments. But during and after the deep recession following the second oil shock (1980), countries in Europe saw tax levels rise further, to finance higher spending on social security and rein in budget deficits.

Figure 1.3. **Changes in tax to GDP ratio (in % points)**

1975-85

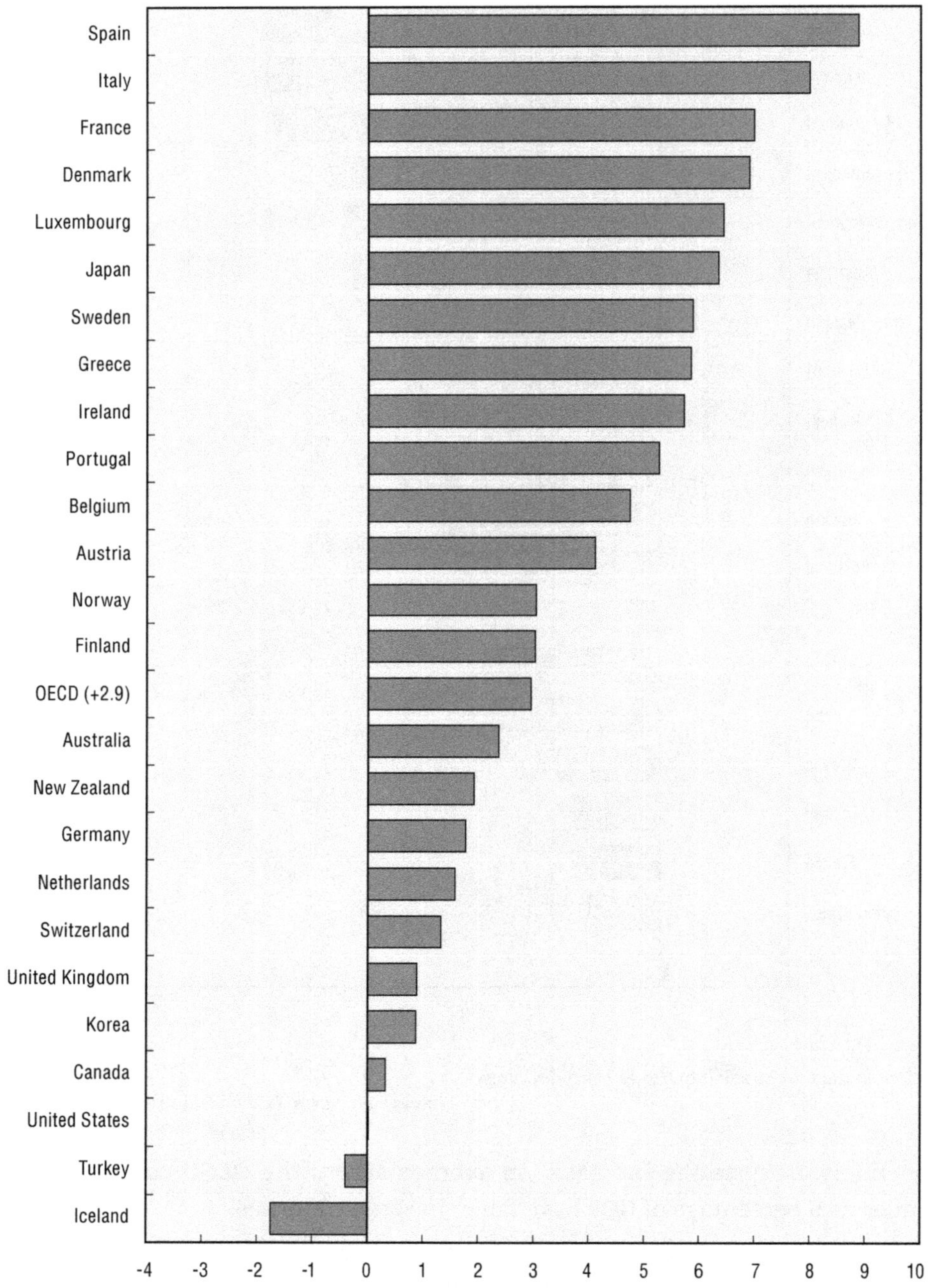

Source: Table 3.2.
Information on data for Israel: *http://oe.cd/israel-disclaimer*.

StatLink http://dx.doi.org/10.1787/888933416028

- Between 1985 and 1995, the tax burden in the OECD area increased by a further 1.8 percentage point (Figure 1.4). After the mid-1980s, most OECD countries substantially reduced the statutory rates of their personal and corporate income tax, but the negative revenue impact of widespread tax reforms was often offset by reducing or abolishing tax reliefs.

Figure 1.4. **Changes in tax to GDP ratio (in % points)**

1985-95

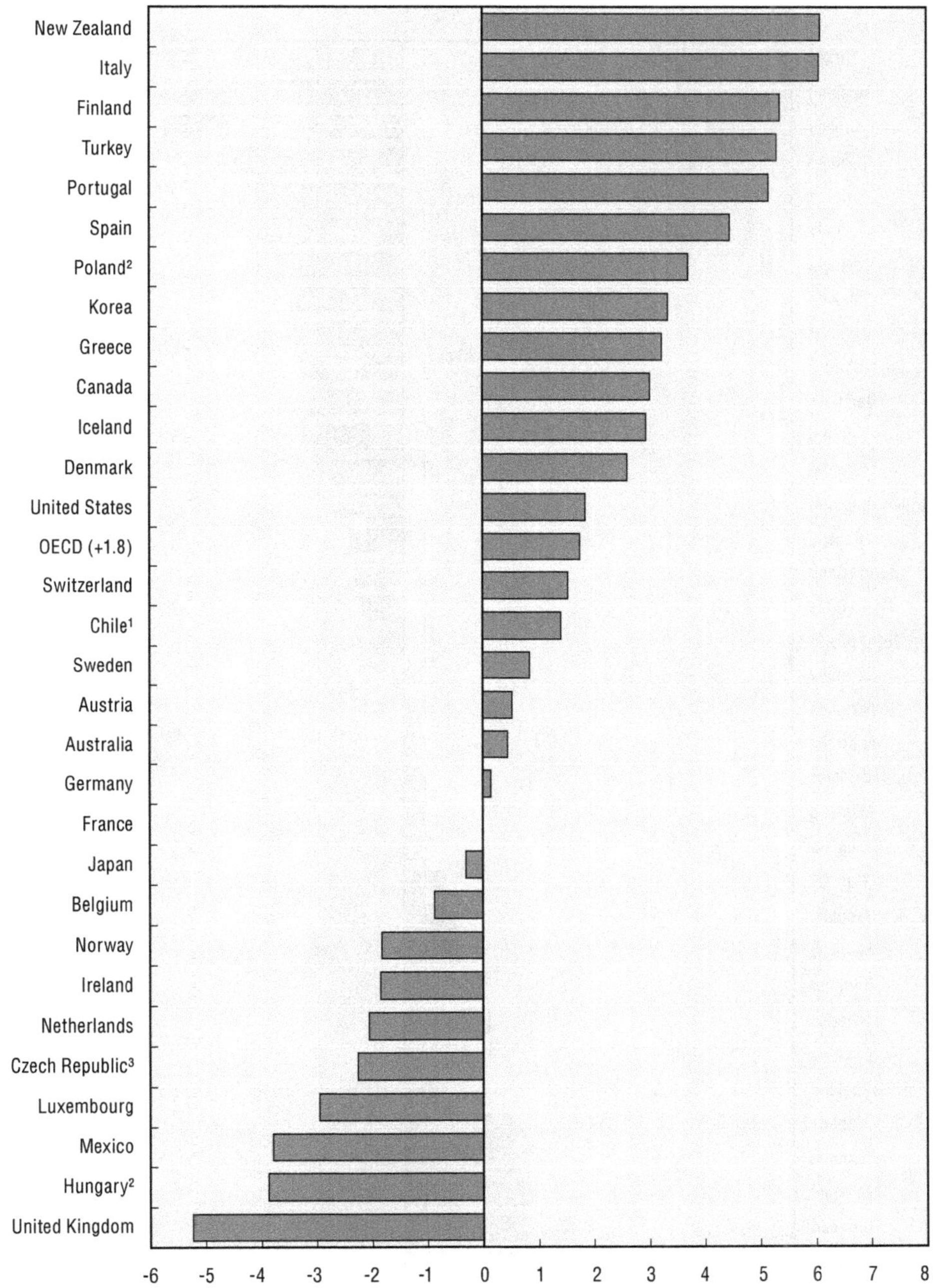

1. 1990-95.
2. 1991-95.
3. 1993-95.

Source: Table 3.2.

Information on data for Israel: *http://oe.cd/israel-disclaimer*.

StatLink http://dx.doi.org/10.1787/888933416039

- Between 1995 and 2000, the average OECD tax to GDP ratio rose to 34.0%, its highest recorded level at that time. It fell back slightly between 2001 and 2004, but then rose again between 2005 and 2007 before falling back following the crisis. Taking these changes together the average tax level in the OECD area increased by 0.9 percentage point between 1995 and 2014 (Figure 1.5).

Figure 1.5. **Changes in tax to GDP ratio (in % points)**

1995-2014

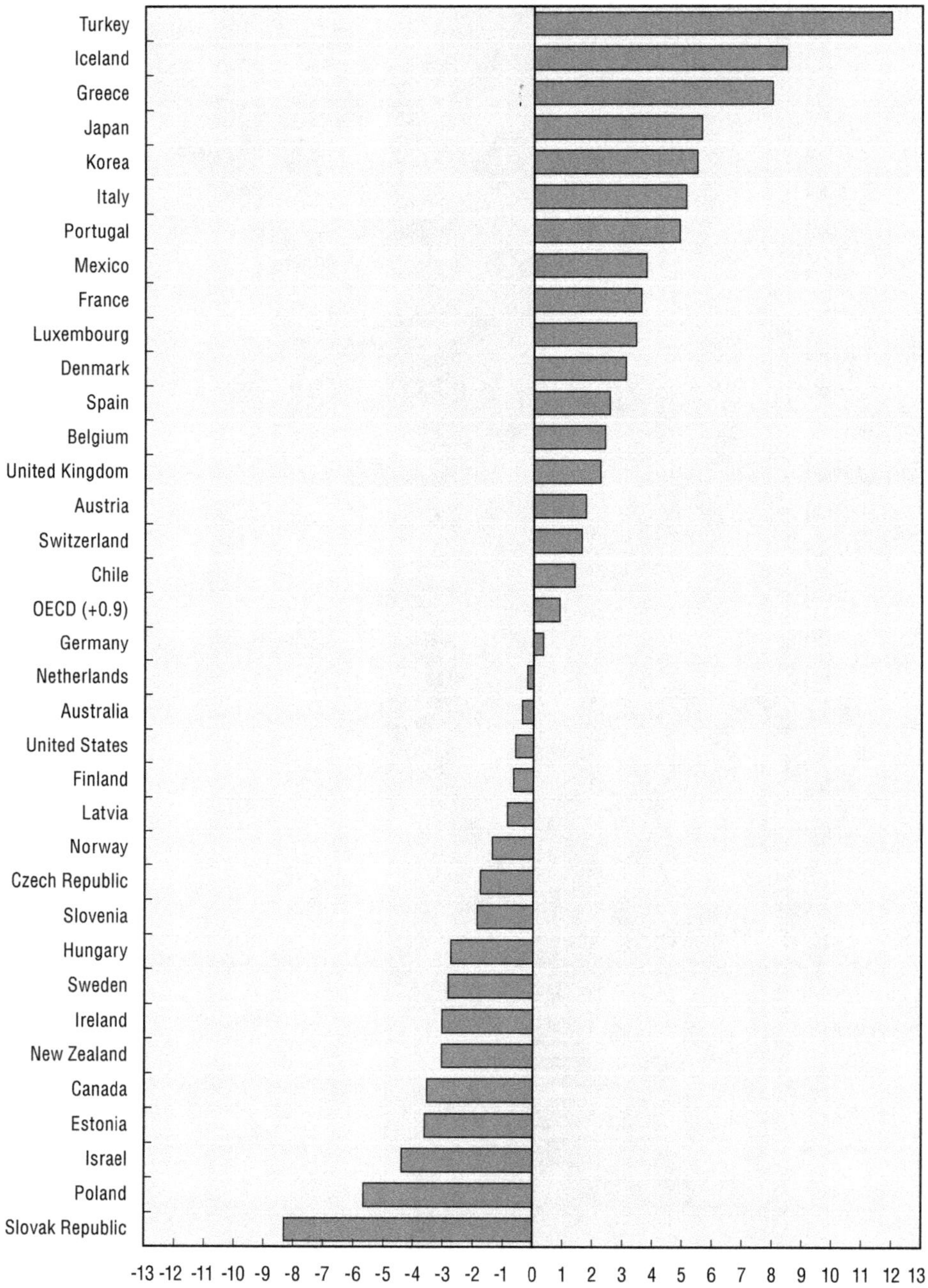

Source: Table 3.2.
Information on data for Israel: *http://oe.cd/israel-disclaimer*.

StatLink http://dx.doi.org/10.1787/888933416041

- Such averages for the OECD area as a whole conceal the great variety in national tax burdens. In 1965, measures of tax to GDP ratios in OECD countries ranged from 10.6% in Turkey to 33.6% in France. By 2014, the corresponding range was from 15.2% in Mexico to 49.6% in Denmark. The trend towards higher tax levels over this period reflects the need to finance sizeable increase of public sector outlays in almost all OECD countries.

1.2. Tax structures

Tax structures are measured by the share of major taxes in total tax revenue. While, on average, tax levels have generally been rising, the share of main taxes in total revenues – the tax structure or tax "mix" – has been remarkably stable over time. Nevertheless, several trends have emerged up to 2014 (the latest year for which data is available for all 35 OECD countries) (Table 1.3).

Table 1.3. **Tax structures in the OECD area**

Per cent

	1965	1975	1985	1995	2005	2010	2014
Total tax revenue	**100**	**100**	**100**	**100**	**100**	**100**	**100**
1100 Taxes on income, profits and capital gains of individuals	26	30	30	25	23	23	24
1200 Taxes on income, profits and capital gains of corporates	9	8	8	8	10	9	9
2000 Social security contributions (SSC)[1]	18	22	22	25	25	27	26
of which:							
2100 Employees SSC	6	7	7	8	9	9	10
2200 Employers SSC	10	14	13	15	15	15	15
3000 Taxes on payroll and workforce	1	1	1	1	1	1	1
4000 Taxes on property	8	6	5	5	6	5	6
5110 General taxes on goods and services	12	13	16	20	21	21	21
5120 Taxes on specific goods and services	24	18	16	12	10	10	10
Other Taxes[2]	2	2	2	3	4	4	4

Note: Percentage share of major tax categories in total tax revenue. Data are included from 1965 onwards for Australia, Austria, Belgium, Canada, Denmark, Finland, France, Germany, Greece, Iceland, Ireland, Italy, Japan, Luxembourg, the Netherlands, New Zealand, Norway, Portugal, Spain, Sweden, Switzerland, Turkey, United Kingdom and United States; from 1972 for Korea; from 1980 for Mexico; from 1990 for Chile; from 1991 for Hungary and Poland; from 1993 for the Czech Republic and from 1995 for Estonia, Israel, Latvia, the Slovak Republic and Slovenia.

1. Including social security contributions paid by the self-employed and benefit recipients (heading 2300) that are not shown in the breakdown.
2. Including certain taxes on goods and services (heading 5200) and stamp taxes.

Source: OECD (2016), "Revenue Statistics: Comparative Tables", *OECD Tax Statistics (database)*, DOI: *http://dx.doi.org/10.1787/data-00262-en*.

StatLink http://dx.doi.org/10.1787/888933416186

Taxes on income and profits

- On average, OECD countries collected 33.7% of their tax revenues through taxes on income and profits (personal and corporate income taxes taken together) (Table 3.8). Taxes on personal and corporate incomes remain the most important source of revenues used to finance public spending in sixteen OECD countries, and in nine of them – Australia, Canada, Denmark, Iceland, Ireland, New Zealand, Norway, Switzerland and the United States – the share of income taxes in the tax mix exceeds 40% (Table 3.6).
- Revenues from personal income taxes are 24% of total taxes on average in 2014 compared with around 30% in the 1980s (Table 3.10). About two percentage points of this reduction can be attributed to the impact on the average of a number of relatively new entrants to the OECD from Eastern Europe for which tax revenue data is only available from the 1990s onwards. These countries tend to have relatively low personal income tax revenues and high revenues from social security contributions, but this impact is observed on the post 1990 data only.

- The variation in the share of the personal income tax between countries is considerable. In 2014, it ranged from a low of 7% and 10% in Chile and the Slovak Republic, respectively, to 41% in Australia and 54% in Denmark (Table 3.10).
- The sharp fall in the share of revenues from corporate income taxes in total taxation in 2008 and 2009 did not continue into 2011 and 2012, but the share of these taxes in total revenues remains, at 9% in 2014, below its 11% share in 2007 (Table 3.12).
- The share of the corporate income tax in total tax revenues shows a considerable spread, from around 4% (Finland, Hungary and Slovenia) to 17% (Norway) and 21% (Chile). Apart from the spread in statutory rates of the corporate income tax, these differences are at least partly explained by institutional factors or the exploitation of mineral deposits, for example:
  - the degree to which firms in a country are incorporated;
  - taxation of oil revenues;
  - the erosion of the corporate income tax base, for example as a consequence of generous depreciation schemes; and
  - other instruments to postpone the taxation of earned profits.

Social security contributions

- Social security contributions as a share of total tax revenues were 26% in 2014. They were highest in the Czech Republic and the Slovak Republic (43-44%). In contrast, Australia and New Zealand do not have social security contributions (Table 3.14). OECD countries also show a wide variety in the relative proportions of social security contributions paid by employees and employers (Tables 3.16 and 3.18).

Property taxes

- Between 1965 and 2014, the share of taxes on property fell from 8% to 6% of total tax revenues on average.
- In relative terms, property taxes have a share exceeding 10% of total tax revenue – in five countries (Australia, Canada, Korea, the United Kingdom and the United States) (Table 3.22).

Consumption taxes

- The share of taxes on consumption (general consumption taxes plus specific consumption taxes) fell from 36% to 31% between 1965 and 2014 (Table 3.26).
- During this period, the composition of taxes on goods and services has fundamentally changed. A fast-growing revenue source has been general consumption taxes, especially the value-added tax (VAT) which is now found in thirty-four of the thirty-five OECD countries.
- General consumption taxes presently produce 21% of total tax revenue, compared with only 12% in the mid-1960s (Table 3.28).
- In fact, the substantially increased importance of the value-added tax has served to counteract the diminishing share of specific consumption taxes, such as excises and custom duties:
  - between 1965 and 2014, the share of specific taxes on consumption (mostly on tobacco, alcoholic drinks and fuels, including some newly introduced environment-related taxes) was more than halved;
  - rates of taxes on imported goods were considerably reduced everywhere, reflecting a global trend to remove trade barriers;

- nevertheless, countries such as Estonia (around 14%), Slovenia (around 15%) and Turkey (around 22%) still collect a relatively large part of their tax revenues by way of taxes on specific goods and services (Table 3.30).

1.3. Taxes by level of government

Table 1.4 shows the relative share of tax revenues attributed to the various sub-sectors of general government and how it has changed between 1975 and 2014.

Table 1.4. **Attribution of tax revenues to sub-sectors of general government as % of total tax revenue**

	Supranational			Central government			State or Regional government			Local government			Social Security Funds		
	1975	1995	2014	1975	1995	2014	1975	1995	2014	1975	1995	2014	1975	1995	2014
Federal countries															
Australia	..	..	..	80.1	77.5	80.0	15.7	19.0	16.5	4.2	3.4	3.5	0.0	0.0	0.0
Austria	..	0.0	0.3	51.7	64.8	66.5	10.6	1.8	1.6	12.4	4.1	3.2	25.3	29.3	28.5
Belgium	1.4	1.0	0.7	65.3	60.1	57.4	..	1.8	5.3	4.4	4.8	4.6	28.8	32.2	31.9
Canada	..	..	..	47.6	39.1	41.4	32.5	37.1	39.1	9.9	9.8	10.3	10.0	14.0	9.2
Germany	1.2	0.6	0.4	33.5	31.4	31.2	22.3	21.6	22.0	9.0	7.4	8.2	34.0	39.0	38.1
Mexico	..	..	..	..	73.9	73.3	..	2.8	4.4	..	1.5	1.6	..	21.8	20.6
Switzerland	..	..	..	30.7	31.6	35.2	27.0	23.8	24.7	20.3	17.6	15.3	22.0	27.0	24.9
United States	..	..	..	45.4	41.4	42.1	19.5	20.0	19.7	14.7	13.3	14.1	20.5	25.2	24.1
Unweighted average	1.3	0.6	0.5	50.6	52.5	53.4	21.3	16.0	16.7	10.7	7.7	7.6	20.1	23.6	22.2
Regional country															
Spain[1,2]	..	0.5	0.4	48.2	50.4	42.3	..	4.8	13.6	4.3	8.5	10.0	47.5	35.8	33.6
Unitary countries															
Chile	..	..	..	..	89.9	86.7	..	..	..	..	6.5	7.6	..	3.6	5.8
Czech Republic	..	..	0.5	..	57.7	54.5	..	..	..	..	0.9	1.2	..	41.4	43.8
Denmark[2]	1.1	0.5	0.3	68.9	68.2	74.6	..	..	..	30.0	31.3	25.0	0.1	0.0	0.1
Estonia	..	..	0.5	..	84.3	82.0	..	..	..	..	0.8	1.1	..	14.9	16.5
Finland	..	0.4	0.2	56.0	46.6	47.4	..	..	..	23.5	22.3	23.5	20.4	30.8	28.9
France[2]	0.7	0.4	0.2	51.2	42.3	33.1	..	..	..	7.6	11.0	13.0	40.6	46.3	53.7
Greece[2]	..	0.6	0.2	67.1	66.8	68.6	..	..	..	3.4	0.9	3.0	29.5	31.7	28.2
Hungary	..	..	0.3	..	63.8	60.8	..	..	..	..	2.5	5.7	..	33.6	33.2
Iceland	..	..	..	81.3	79.2	75.5	..	..	..	18.7	20.8	24.5	0.0	0.0	0.0
Ireland	2.3	1.5	0.5	77.4	83.1	82.4	..	..	..	7.3	2.7	2.8	13.1	12.7	14.3
Israel	..	..	..	..	79.7	75.6	..	..	..	..	6.4	8.0	..	13.9	16.4
Italy	..	0.4	0.3	53.2	62.7	53.4	..	..	..	0.9	5.4	16.5	45.9	31.5	29.8
Japan	..	..	..	45.4	41.2	36.9	..	..	..	25.6	25.3	23.5	29.0	33.5	39.7
Korea	..	..	..	89.0	69.2	56.2	..	..	..	10.1	18.7	16.9	0.9	12.1	26.9
Latvia	..	..	0.5	..	43.5	50.8	..	..	..	..	19.5	19.5	..	36.9	29.1
Luxembourg	0.8	0.4	0.1	63.6	66.5	68.8	..	..	..	6.7	6.5	3.3	29.0	26.6	27.8
Netherlands	1.5	1.3	1.0	58.9	56.0	55.6	..	..	..	1.2	3.1	3.8	38.4	39.5	39.6
New Zealand	..	..	..	92.3	94.7	93.3	..	..	..	7.7	5.3	6.7	0.0	0.0	0.0
Norway	..	..	..	50.6	58.4	86.1	..	..	..	22.4	19.6	13.9	27.0	22.0	0.0
Poland	..	..	0.3	..	61.9	48.2	..	..	..	..	8.3	13.4	..	29.8	38.1
Portugal	..	0.8	0.3	65.4	72.3	67.8	..	..	..	0.0	5.4	7.2	34.6	21.5	24.7
Slovak Republic	..	..	0.5	..	62.5	54.6	..	..	..	..	1.3	2.7	..	36.2	42.1
Slovenia	..	..	0.4	..	51.8	50.0	..	..	..	..	6.3	10.6	..	41.9	39.0
Sweden	..	0.4	0.3	51.3	46.9	50.0	..	..	..	29.2	30.9	36.9	19.5	21.8	12.7
Turkey	..	..	..	..	75.1	62.0	..	..	..	..	12.8	9.4	..	12.1	28.5
United Kingdom	1.0	1.0	0.6	70.5	77.5	75.8	..	..	..	11.1	3.7	5.0	17.5	17.8	18.7
Unweighted average	1.2	0.7	0.4	65.1	65.5	63.5	..	..	..	12.8	10.7	11.7	21.6	23.5	24.5

1. Spain is constitutionally a non-federal country with a highly decentralised political structure.
2. The total tax revenue has been reduced by the amount of any capital transfer that represents uncollected taxes.

StatLink http://dx.doi.org/10.1787/888933416193

Federal and regional countries

- In 2014, the share of central government receipts in the eight federal OECD countries varied from 31% in Germany to 80% in Australia.
- In 2014, the share of the states varied from 2% in Austria, 4% in Mexico and 5% in Belgium to 39% in Canada. The share of local government varied from 2% in Mexico to 15% in Switzerland.

- Between 1975 and 2014, the share of federal government revenues declined by about eight percentage points in Belgium and less rapidly in Canada, Germany and the United States.
- The share of federal government revenues increased in Austria and Switzerland by 15 and five percentage points respectively. There was little change in Australia and Mexico.
- Of the seven federal countries with social security funds the share increased in five, the exceptions being Canada and Mexico where it slightly declined.
- Spain is now classified as a regional rather than a unitary country because of its highly decentralised political structure. In 2014, the share of central government receipts was 42% compared with 14% for the regional government. Between 1975 and 2014, the share of local government receipts increased from 4% to 10% and the share of social security funds declined from 48% to 34%.

Unitary countries

- In unitary OECD countries, the share of central government receipts in 2014 varied from 34% in France and 37% in Japan to 93% in New Zealand.
- The local government share varied from 1% in Estonia and in the Czech Republic to 37% in Sweden.
- Between 1975 and 2014, there have been shifts to local government of 5 percentage points or more in six countries – France, Iceland, Italy, Korea, Portugal and Sweden and smaller increase in the Netherlands. Shifts of 5 percentage points or more in the other direction occurred in two countries – Norway and the United Kingdom.
- Between 1975 and 2014, there were increases in the share of social security funds of 7 or more percentage points in four countries – Finland, France, Japan and Korea – and corresponding decreases in three others – Italy, Norway and Portugal. In two other countries – Poland and Turkey – the data showed an increase of 7 percentage points or more between 1995 and 2014.
- The guidelines for attributing these revenue shares to the different levels of government are based on the final version of the 2008 System of National Accounts. These guidelines are discussed in the Special feature S.1 in the 2011 edition of *OECD Revenue Statistics*.

EU member states in the OECD

- The "supranational" column of Table 1.4 reports taxes collected on behalf of the European Union (EU) by the twenty-one EU member states that are members of the OECD. For years prior 1998, custom duties collected on behalf of the EU by national tax administrations of the EU member states are included under heading 5123. From 1998 onwards, these custom duties are shown as a "memorandum" item since they represent a tax imposed by the EU and collected by national administrations. However, they continue to be part of the aggregate revenue figures which represent all taxes imposed within the territory of EU member states. This approach ensures consistency of the time series, and ensures that the tax to GDP ratio measures are immune to changes in the relative share of customs duties in: 1) the composition of EU financing resources; and 2) national tax mixes of EU member states. The amounts of customs duties concerned are shown in Table 1.5.

Table 1.5. **Customs duties collected on behalf of the European Union**

Millions of national currency

	2000	2008	2009	2011	2012	2013	2014	2015p
Austria[1]	356	371	320	378	344	328	369	414
Belgium[1]	960	1 420	1 147	1 285	1 247	1 185	1 257	1 364
Czech Republic	..	6 323	5 548	6 961	6 172	5 544	6 968	7 859
Denmark	2 325	3 106	2 647	3 177	2 962	2 824	3 001	3 285
Estonia[1]	..	33	20	29	29	29	30	34
Finland[1]	129	205	152	189	184	166	170	165
France[1]	1 513	1 615	1 461	1 866	1 883	1 842	1 827	1 931
Germany[1]	3 394	4 036	3 778	4 556	4 417	4 251	4 608	5 195
Greece[1]	210	305	252	186	162	148	148	..
Hungary	..	26 689	25 657	27 462	27 206	26 337	31 927	38 960
Ireland[1]	208	245	208	240	242	247	275	327
Italy[1]	1 536	2 200	2 008	2 319	2 077	1 890	2 022	2 246
Latvia[1]	..	35	21	31	32	28	36	40
Luxembourg[1]	27	18	13	17	15	15	19	23
Netherlands[1]	1 310	1 800	1 518	1 889	1 780	1 756	2 046	2 441
Poland	..	1 572	1 308	1 447	1 611	1 613	1 791	..
Portugal[1]	204	177	154	168	155	144	149	158
Slovak Republic[1]	..	156	111	157	129	115	127	119
Slovenia[1]	..	77	57	62	54	52	52	52
Spain[1]	970	1 578	1 328	1 554	1 436	1 316	1 512	1 754
Sweden	3 450	5 212	4 764	5 399	4 995	4 976	5 737	6 243
United Kingdom	1 800	2 297	2 435	2 925	2 885	2 914	2 949	3 077

.. indicates not available; p: provisional.

1. For euro area countries, the figures are in euros for all years.

StatLink http://dx.doi.org/10.1787/888933416209

1.4. The impact of GDP revisions on reported tax levels

The tax ratios shown in this Report express aggregate tax revenues as a percentage of GDP. It is important to recognise that the value of this ratio depends on its denominator (GDP) as well as its numerator (tax revenue), and that the denominator is subject to historical revision.

The numerator (tax revenue)

- For the numerator, the OECD Secretariat uses revenue figures that are submitted annually by correspondents from national Ministries of Finance, Tax Administrations or National Statistics Offices. Although provisional figures for most countries become available with a lag of about six months, finalised data become available with a lag of around one and a half years. Final revenue data for 2014 were received during the period May-August 2016.
- In thirty-one OECD countries, the reporting year coincides with the calendar year. Four countries – Australia, Canada, Japan and New Zealand – have different reporting years. Reporting year 2013 includes Q2/2013–Q1/2014 (Canada, Japan) and Q3/2013–Q2/2014 (Australia, New Zealand) respectively (Q = quarter).

The denominator (GDP)

- For the denominator, the GDP figures used for this Report are the most recently available on 1 September 2016. By that time, the 2014 and 2015 GDP figures were available for all OECD countries.
- Using these GDP figures ensures a maximum of consistency and international comparability for the reported tax to GDP ratios.

- The GDP figures are based on the OECD Annual National Accounts (ANA-SNA) for the thirty-one OECD countries where the reporting year is the actual calendar year.
- Where the reporting year differs from the calendar year, the annual GDP estimates are obtained by aggregating quarterly GDP estimates provided by the OECD Statistics Directorate for those quarters corresponding to each country's fiscal (tax) year. For example, in the case of Canada Q2/2013-Q1/2014.

Revisions to the numerator and denominator

Both the numerator (tax revenues) and the denominator (the GDP figure) are subject to revisions, as more accurate estimates of the amounts involved become available. Such revisions will directly impact on published tax ratios.

- If the tax figure rises and the GDP figure remains unchanged, the tax ratio will increase.
- If the GDP figure is revised downward, the tax ratio will also go up, even though aggregate tax revenues have not increased.
- Conversely, a higher GDP estimate implies a lower tax ratio, even if the amount collected in taxes has not changed.
- Revenue data, especially for recent years, can be subject to infrequent and usually minor revisions. GDP figures are revised and updated more frequently, though not necessarily for all countries at the same time, reflecting better data sources and improved estimation procedures. Generally these revisions have a rather limited impact on tax ratios.
- Occasionally, however, GDP figures may change in a more fundamental way when internationally agreed guidelines to measure the value of GDP are changed. The latest such change relates to the System of National Accounts 2008 (2008 SNA) which has now largely replaced its predecessor, the System of National Accounts 1993 (1993 SNA). An earlier version of the System of National Accounts was set up in 1968.
- The twenty-two OECD countries that are member states of the EU have to adhere to the European System of Integrated Economic Accounts (ESA) for computing their GDP figures. The ESA is primarily an elaboration of SNA, though differing from it in several minor aspects which are not pertinent to this Report. Following the 2008 revision to the System of National Accounts, the 1995 ESA was replaced by the 2010 ESA.
- So far, the 2008 SNA applies to the GDP figures presented in this publication for 32 countries. The exceptions are Chile, Japan, and Turkey which will follow over the next few months. The GDP figures for these thirty-two countries are, with the exception of odd figures in particular years, higher following the application of the new SNA because of both methodological changes and the impact of improved data sources.
- The tax revenue figures reported in *Revenue Statistics* have hardly been affected by the changes to the definitions and standards in the SNA/ESA but in some countries there have been some adjustments as the opportunity has been taken to improve data sources and methodologies for compiling the national accounts figures (including tax revenues). However these changes have been generally relatively smaller than the changes to the GDP figures and tax ratios have generally fallen for those countries that have implemented the revised statistical framework.

- One particular problem raised by the 2008 SNA/2010 ESA revisions is that countries have varied in the period for which they have revised their GDP figures. To limit this distortionary impact, the OECD Statistics Directorate/Centre for Tax Policy and Administration have estimated revised GDP estimates for 1965 and later years in those cases where OECD countries have not reported revised GDP figures.

Note

1. Calculated by applying the unweighted average percentage change for 2015 in the 32 countries providing data for that year to the overall average tax to GDP ratio in 2014.

Revenue Statistics 2016
Statistiques des recettes publiques 2016

Chapitre 1

Tendances des recettes fiscales, 1965-2015

Introduction

Les *Statistiques des recettes publiques* sont une publication annuelle qui présente des données détaillées permettant de comparer, à l'échelle internationale, les recettes fiscales perçues par tous les niveaux d'administration dans les pays de l'OCDE. La dernière édition fournit des informations sur les recettes fiscales au cours de la période 1965-2014. En outre, des estimations provisoires relatives aux recettes fiscales pour l'année 2015 sont indiquées pour la plupart des pays de l'OCDE.

Dans ce rapport, les impôts désignent les versements obligatoires sans contrepartie aux administrations publiques. Les impôts sont sans contrepartie en ce sens que les prestations fournies par les administrations ne sont pas normalement proportionnelles à leurs paiements.

Dans la classification de l'OCDE, les impôts sont ventilés en fonction de leur base :

- revenus et bénéfices (rubrique 1000) ;
- les cotisations obligatoires de sécurité sociale versées aux administrations publiques, qui sont traitées comme des impôts (rubrique 2000) ;
- salaire et main-d'œuvre (rubrique 3000) ;
- patrimoine (rubrique 4000) ;
- biens et services (rubrique 5000) ;
- autres impôts (rubrique 6000).

On trouvera des précisions sur la notion d'impôt, la classification des impôts et l'enregistrement sur la base des droits constatés dans le *Guide d'interprétation de l'OCDE* qui figure à l'Annexe A du présent Rapport.

Les moyennes présentées dans ce Rapport ne sont pas pondérées.

1.1. Niveau d'imposition

a. Données provisoires relatives aux ratios fiscaux pour 2015

Les nouvelles données de l'OCDE qui figurent dans la publication annuelle *Statistiques des recettes publiques* montrent que les recettes fiscales exprimées en pourcentage du PIB continuent de se rétablir progressivement, après les baisses enregistrées dans pratiquement tous les pays en 2008 et 2009 sous l'effet de la crise économique et financière. Le ratio moyen des recettes fiscales rapportées au PIB dans les pays de l'OCDE était de 34.3 %[1] en 2015, contre 34.2 % en 2014 et 33.8 % en 2013. Le chiffre de 2015 est le plus élevé obtenu depuis le début de l'enregistrement des données en 1965 (tableaux 1.1 et 1.2).

- En 2015, le Danemark enregistrait le ratio le plus élevé (46.6 %) et le Mexique celui le plus faible (17.4%).
- Sur les 32 pays pour lesquels on dispose de données se rapportant à 2015, le ratio des recettes fiscales au PIB a augmenté depuis 2014 dans 25 pays et diminué dans 7 pays.

Tableau 1.1. **Total des recettes fiscales en % du PIB**

	1965	1975	1985	1995	2000	2007	2009	2012	2014	2015p
Australie	20.6	25.4	27.8	28.2	30.4	29.7	25.8	27.4	27.8	..
Autriche	33.6	36.4	40.5	41.1	42.1	40.5	41.0	41.7	42.8	43.5
Belgique	30.6	38.7	43.5	42.6	43.5	42.7	42.4	44.2	45.0	44.8
Canada	25.2	31.4	31.7	34.8	34.8	32.1	32.0	31.0	31.2	31.9
Chili	..	..	..	18.4	18.8	22.8	17.4	21.5	19.8	20.7
République tchèque	..	..	..	34.9	32.5	34.3	32.4	33.7	33.1	33.5
Danemark[1]	29.1	37.0	43.9	46.5	46.9	46.4	45.2	45.8	49.6	46.6
Estonie	..	..	..	36.0	31.1	31.3	34.9	31.5	32.4	33.6
Finlande	30.0	36.1	39.1	44.5	45.8	41.5	40.9	42.7	43.8	44.0
France[1]	33.6	34.9	41.9	41.9	43.1	42.4	41.3	44.3	45.5	45.5
Allemagne[2]	31.6	34.3	36.1	36.2	36.2	34.9	36.1	36.3	36.6	36.9
Grèce[1]	17.1	18.7	24.6	27.8	33.4	31.2	30.9	35.5	35.8	36.8
Hongrie	..	..	..	41.0	38.6	39.6	39.2	38.6	38.2	39.4
Islande	25.5	29.3	27.5	30.5	36.3	39.0	31.9	35.3	38.9	37.1
Irlande	24.5	27.9	33.6	31.7	30.8	30.4	27.4	27.5	28.7	23.6
Israël[3]	..	..	..	35.6	34.8	34.0	29.7	29.7	31.2	31.4
Italie	24.7	24.5	32.5	38.6	40.6	41.7	42.1	43.9	43.7	43.3
Japon	17.8	20.4	26.7	26.4	26.6	28.5	27.0	29.4	32.0	..
Corée	..	14.9	15.8	19.1	21.5	24.8	23.8	24.8	24.6	25.3
Lettonie	..	..	..	29.7	29.1	28.2	27.9	28.5	28.9	29.0
Luxembourg	26.4	31.5	37.9	34.9	37.2	36.5	38.9	38.8	38.4	37.0
Mexique[4]	..	..	15.2	11.4	13.6	13.2	13.6	13.9	15.2	17.4
Pays-Bas	30.9	38.2	39.8	37.7	37.2	36.0	35.4	36.0	37.5	37.8
Nouvelle-Zélande	23.2	27.5	29.5	35.6	32.5	33.9	30.3	32.0	32.5	32.8
Norvège	29.4	38.8	41.9	40.0	41.9	42.1	41.2	41.5	38.7	38.1
Pologne	..	..	..	37.7	32.9	34.6	31.4	31.9	32.1	..
Portugal	15.7	18.9	24.1	29.3	31.1	31.8	29.9	31.8	34.2	34.5
République slovaque	..	..	..	39.6	33.6	29.2	28.9	28.4	31.2	32.3
Slovénie	..	..	..	38.4	36.6	37.1	36.2	36.9	36.5	36.6
Espagne[1]	14.3	18.0	26.8	31.3	33.4	36.5	30.0	32.4	33.8	33.8
Suède	31.4	38.9	44.8	45.6	49.0	45.0	44.1	42.6	42.8	43.3
Suisse	16.6	22.5	23.9	25.4	27.4	26.1	27.0	26.8	27.0	27.9
Turquie	10.6	11.9	11.5	16.8	24.2	24.1	24.6	27.6	28.8	30.0
Royaume-Uni	29.3	34.2	35.1	29.8	32.8	33.0	31.5	32.7	32.1	32.5
États-Unis	23.5	24.6	24.6	26.5	28.2	26.7	23.0	24.1	25.9	26.4
Moyenne non pondérée										
Moyenne OCDE[5]	**24.8**	**28.6**	**31.5**	**33.3**	**34.0**	**33.8**	**32.4**	**33.4**	**34.2**	**34.3**

.. signifie non disponible ; p : provisoire.

1. Le total des recettes fiscales a été diminué du montant de tout transfert en capital représentant les recettes non collectées.
2. Allemagne unifiée à partir de 1991.
3. Les données statistiques concernant Israël sont fournies par et sous la responsabilité des autorités israéliennes compétentes. L'utilisation de ces données par l'OCDE est sans préjudice du statut des hauteurs du Golan, de Jérusalem Est et des colonies de peuplement israéliennes en Cisjordanie aux termes du droit international.
4. Estimation du Secrétariat, incluant les recettes escomptées collectées par les administrations d'État et locales.
5. Calculé en appliquant le pourcentage moyen non pondéré de variation pour 2015 dans les 32 pays qui ont communiqué des données pour cette année au ratio moyen global impôts/PIB en 2014.

StatLink http://dx.doi.org/10.1787/888933416211

- Entre 2014 et 2015, les hausses les plus prononcées du ratio ont été constatées au Mexique (2.3 points de pourcentage, en raison de la hausse des impôts sur le revenu et des impôts sur les biens et services en pourcentage du PIB) et en Turquie (1.3 point, principalement causée par la hausse des recettes provenant des impôts sur les biens et services et l'augmentation des cotisations de sécurité sociale). Les autres pays dont le ratio impôts/PIB a connu une augmentation entre 2014 et 2015 sont l'Estonie, la Grèce, la Hongrie et la République slovaque (1.0 point).
- Entre 2014 et 2015, les diminutions les plus importantes du ratio concernent l'Irlande (5.1 points de pourcentage, à cause de la croissance exceptionnelle du PIB en 2015), le Danemark (3 points de pourcentage, en raison de la baisse des recettes issues des impôts sur le revenu) et l'Islande (1.8 point de pourcentage). Le Luxembourg a vu son ratio décliner de plus d'un point de pourcentage.

Tableau 1.2. **Impôts sur le revenu et les bénéfices en % du PIB**

	1965	1975	1985	1995	2000	2007	2009	2012	2014	2015p
Australie	10.5	14.2	15.2	15.6	17.7	17.7	14.4	15.9	16.1	..
Autriche	8.6	9.5	10.7	10.8	12.0	12.2	11.5	12.0	12.6	13.2
Belgique	8.5	15.3	17.6	16.2	16.8	15.3	14.4	15.3	16.1	16.0
Canada	9.7	14.8	14.0	16.1	17.4	15.7	15.3	14.7	15.0	15.2
Chili	..	..	..	4.6	4.4	10.4	5.4	8.4	6.5	7.5
République tchèque	..	..	..	8.7	7.4	8.5	6.9	6.9	7.1	7.2
Danemark[1]	13.6	21.8	25.7	29.3	28.8	27.9	27.7	28.4	32.2	29.2
Estonie	..	..	..	10.8	7.7	7.4	7.4	6.6	7.4	7.9
Finlande	12.4	15.6	16.0	16.1	19.7	16.3	14.6	14.6	15.3	15.5
France[1]	5.3	5.5	6.7	6.8	10.7	10.1	8.6	10.6	10.8	10.7
Allemagne[2]	10.7	11.8	12.6	11.0	10.9	10.9	10.4	11.0	11.4	11.6
Grèce[1]	1.6	2.5	4.3	6.2	9.0	7.3	7.5	8.5	8.5	8.7
Hongrie	..	..	..	8.6	9.4	9.9	9.5	7.0	6.8	6.9
Islande	5.5	6.7	6.2	10.4	14.5	17.7	15.1	16.0	18.1	17.5
Irlande	6.3	8.4	11.6	12.8	13.4	12.4	10.6	11.2	11.6	10.2
Israël	..	..	..	12.4	13.8	12.4	8.9	9.1	9.7	9.9
Italie	4.4	5.3	12.0	13.6	13.5	14.1	13.7	14.3	14.0	13.9
Japon	7.8	9.1	12.2	10.1	9.3	10.4	8.0	9.1	10.2	10.4
Corée	..	3.6	4.2	5.8	6.2	7.9	6.8	7.4	7.2	7.6
Lettonie	..	..	..	6.5	7.0	8.2	6.9	7.4	7.5	7.5
Luxembourg	9.5	13.6	16.4	14.0	13.6	12.7	13.8	13.7	13.3	13.4
Mexique	..	..	3.4	3.7	4.5	4.9	4.9	5.1	5.7	6.8
Pays-Bas	11.0	13.3	10.5	10.3	9.7	10.2	10.0	9.1	9.6	10.5
Nouvelle-Zélande	14.1	18.3	20.5	21.8	19.5	21.3	17.2	17.8	18.0	18.1
Norvège	12.8	13.4	16.6	14.1	18.8	20.2	18.9	20.0	16.4	15.0
Pologne	..	..	..	10.9	6.7	7.9	6.8	6.5	6.3	..
Portugal	3.9	3.3	6.2	7.7	9.1	8.8	8.3	8.7	10.5	10.5
République slovaque	..	..	..	10.1	6.9	6.1	5.5	5.5	6.5	6.9
Slovénie	..	..	..	6.4	6.8	8.7	7.5	6.9	6.5	6.6
Espagne[1]	3.5	4.0	6.7	9.1	9.5	12.2	9.0	9.7	9.7	9.7
Suède	17.2	19.6	18.9	17.9	20.0	17.4	15.5	14.5	14.9	15.5
Suisse	6.8	10.7	11.0	11.1	12.2	12.1	12.6	12.2	12.3	13.0
Turquie	3.1	5.0	4.3	4.8	7.1	5.7	5.9	6.0	6.1	6.1
Royaume-Uni	10.8	15.3	13.6	11.0	12.8	13.0	12.1	11.6	11.2	11.5
États-Unis	11.3	11.3	11.2	12.1	14.1	12.9	9.3	11.3	12.3	12.9
Moyenne non pondérée										
Moyenne OCDE[3]	**8.7**	**10.9**	**11.8**	**11.4**	**12.0**	**12.2**	**10.9**	**11.2**	**11.5**	**11.6**

n.d. signifie non disponible.

1. Le total des recettes fiscales a été diminué du montant de tout transfert en capital représentant les recettes non collectées.
2. Allemagne unifiée à partir de 1991.
3. Calculé en appliquant le pourcentage moyen non pondéré de variation pour 2015 dans les 33 pays qui ont communiqué des données pour cette année au ratio moyen global impôts/PIB en 2014.

StatLink http://dx.doi.org/10.1787/888933416224

- Le ratio fiscal en 2015 était encore inférieur de plus de 3 points de pourcentage à son niveau de 2007 (avant la récession) dans deux pays : Irlande et Norvège. La baisse la plus forte s'est produite en Irlande, où le ratio est passé de 30.4 % du PIB en 2007 à 23.6 % en 2015. En excluant l'Irlande, la baisse la plus importante a été constatée en Norvège, de 42.1 % du PIB en 2007 à 38.1 % en 2015.
- La charge fiscale en Turquie a augmenté de 24.1 % à 30.0 % entre 2007 et 2015. Deux autres pays – Grèce et Mexique – ont enregistré des hausses de quatre points de pourcentage, voire plus, au cours de la même période.

Entre 2014 et 2015, l'Irlande a enregistré une croissance inhabituelle du PIB de 32.4 % en valeur (26.3 % en volume). Cette croissance résulte des transferts d'actifs intangibles (incluant les licences et les brevets) effectués par diverses entreprises multi-nationales vers la juridiction irlandaise. L'augmentation du stock d'actifs intangibles utilisés dans les accords de sous-traitance à la production manufacturière a fait croître la production attribuable à l'Irlande, ainsi que les exportations, la consommation de capital fixe et sa dépréciation. En conjonction avec l'augmentation des importations d'avions, ces facteurs ont contribué à la croissance inhabituelle du PIB en Irlande pour l'année 2015.

Bien que le montant des recettes en valeur (exprimées en monnaie nationale) ait augmenté de 8.8 % entre 2014 et 2015, la croissance encore plus rapide du PIB durant cette période a provoqué une forte diminution du ratio impôts sur PIB, de 28.7 % en 2014 à 23.6 % en 2015. La diminution du ratio impôts sur PIB en Irlande a également affecté la moyenne non-pondérée des ratios pour les pays de l'OCDE en 2015. En incluant l'Irlande, le ratio moyen s'élevait à 34.3% en 2015, avec une augmentation de 0.1 point de pourcentage depuis 2014. En excluant l'Irlande, le ratio moyen serait de 34.6 % en 2015, avec une augmentation de 0.3 points depuis 2014 pour les 34 pays restants.

b. Données définitives relatives aux ratios fiscaux pour 2014

La dernière année pour laquelle on dispose de ratios des recettes fiscales rapportées au PIB fondés sur des recettes fiscales définitives pour tous les pays de l'OCDE est 2014 (graphique 1.1). Les chiffres montrent que ces ratios diffèrent fortement selon les pays.

- En 2014, le Danemark avait le ratio des recettes fiscales rapportées au PIB le plus élevé (49.6 %), suivi par la France, la Belgique et la Finlande.
- Au contraire, neuf pays – l'Australie, le Chili, la Corée, les États-Unis, l'Irlande, la Lettonie, le Mexique, la Suisse et la Turquie – enregistraient des niveaux d'imposition inférieurs à 30 %.
- Le Mexique avait le ratio le plus faible (15.2 %), suivi du Chili (19.8 %).
- Depuis 2013, le ratio des recettes fiscales rapportées au PIB dans la zone OCDE (moyenne non pondérée) a augmenté de 0.4 point pour atteindre 34.2 % en 2014 (voir le tableau 1.1).
- Par rapport à 2013, la charge fiscale a augmenté dans 26 pays membres de l'OCDE et a diminué dans 9 pays.
- Les augmentations les plus importantes ont été constatées en Islande (2.9 points de pourcentage), au Danemark (2.8 points), au Japon (1.7 point), et en Nouvelle-Zélande (1.3 point).
- Trois pays – Estonie, Pays-Bas et République slovaque – ont enregistré des augmentations comprises entre 0.9 et 1.0 point de pourcentage entre 2013 et 2014.
- Les diminutions les plus marquées ont été constatées en Norvège (1.2 point de pourcentage) et la République tchèque (1.0 point).

Les principaux changements affectant le ratio des recettes fiscales rapportées au PIB pour les grandes rubriques d'impôt entre 2013 et 2014 sont les suivants :

- Les recettes des impôts sur le revenu des personnes physiques et sur les bénéfices des sociétés exprimées en pourcentage du PIB ont en moyenne augmenté de 11.4 % en 2013 à 11.5 % en 2014. Les augmentations les plus importantes ont eu lieu au Danemark (2.9 points de pourcentage) et en Islande (1.3 point). La Norvège et l'Italie ont enregistré la diminution la plus forte de ce taux, respectivement de 1.7 et 0.6 point de PIB (tableau 1.2).
- Les ratios suivants sont pour l'essentiel restés stables entre 2013 et 2014 :
  - cotisations de sécurité sociale : 9.1 % (Table 3.13) ;
  - impôts sur les salaires : 0.4% (Table 3.19) ;
  - impôts sur le patrimoine : 1.9 % (Table 3.21) ;
  - impôts sur les biens et services : augmentation de 10.8 % à 11.0 % (Table 3.23).

Graphique 1.1. **Total des recettes fiscales en pourcentage du PIB, 2014**

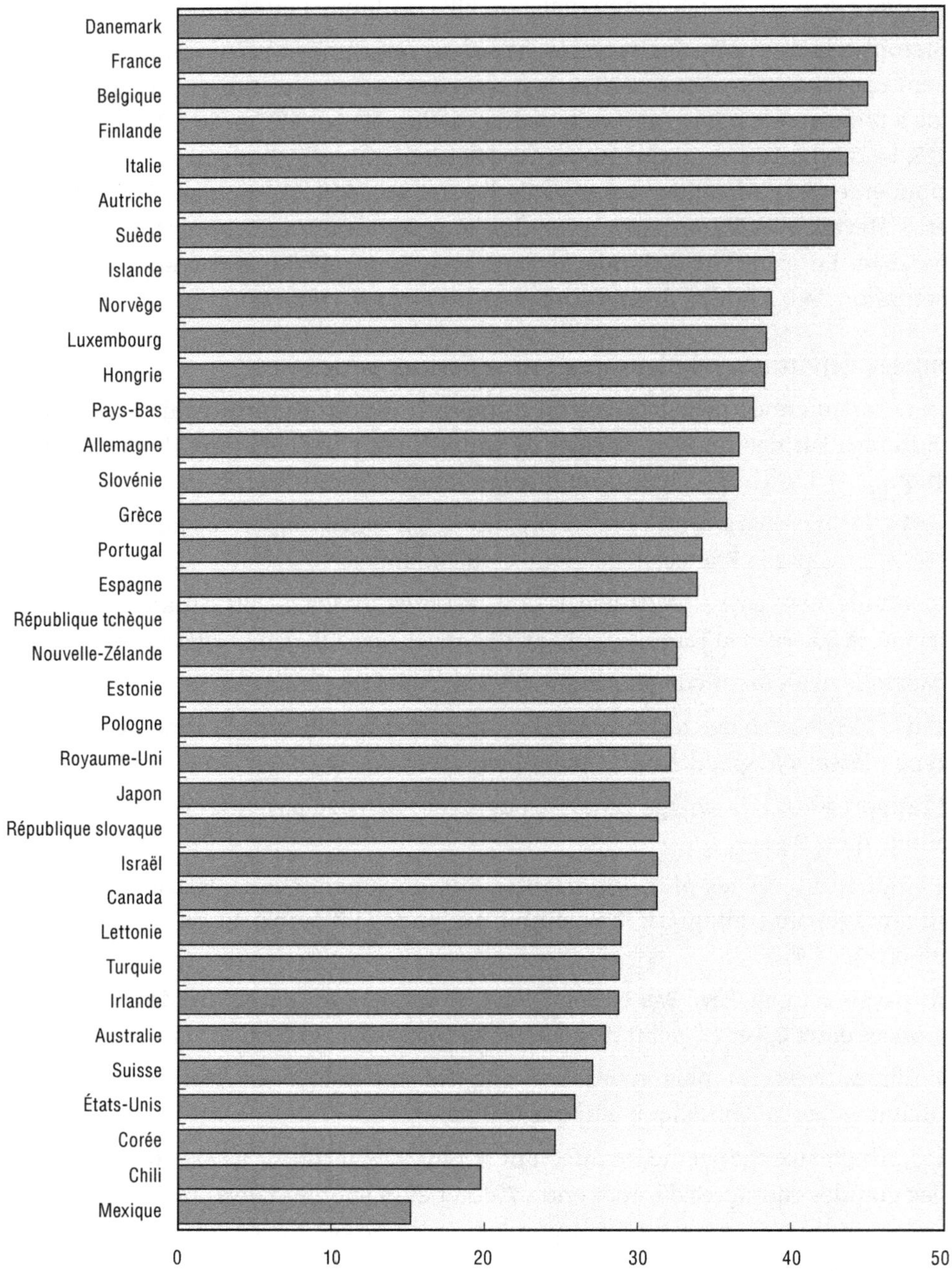

Note : Les pays sont classés en fonction du total des recettes fiscales par rapport au PIB.
Source : Table 3.1.

StatLink http://dx.doi.org/10.1787/888933416058

Les niveaux globaux d'imposition tiennent souvent une place essentielle dans les débats politiques et sont parfois directement associés à l'efficacité économique des nations. Une Étude spéciale qui figurait dans la Section S.2 de l'édition 1999 de ce Rapport expliquait pourquoi les chiffres relatifs aux niveaux d'imposition doivent être interprétés avec prudence. Plus précisément, les directives révisées énoncées dans le Système des comptes nationaux (SCN) de 2008 qui sont utilisées pour estimer le PIB de 32 des 35 pays membres de l'OCDE ont eu pour effet d'accroître son niveau. En conséquence, les ratios impôts/PIB révisés présentés dans cette publication sont systématiquement inférieurs aux ratios rapportés avant ces changements. Afin de limiter cet effet de distorsion pour la période concernée, on a utilisé dans la présente édition du rapport des estimations du PIB révisé pour 1965 et les années suivantes quand les pays de l'OCDE n'ont pas fourni de chiffres révisés du PIB. La section « Questions méthodologiques » ci-dessous examine plus en détail l'ampleur des révisions du PIB.

c. *Variations de la pression fiscale entre 1965 et 2014*

L'évolution des coefficients de pression fiscale entre 1965 et 2014 est la suivante :

- Le coefficient moyen dans la zone OCDE a augmenté de 24.8 % à 34.2 % (9.4 points) entre 1965 et 2014 (Table 3.2).
- L'évolution historique des ratios d'imposition dans les différents pays de l'OCDE varie fortement, comme le montrent les graphiques 1.2, 1.3, 1.4 et 1.5. Chaque graphique rapproche les évolutions observées dans les différents pays du niveau d'imposition moyen de la zone OCDE respectivement pour les périodes 1965-75, 1975-85, 1985-95 et 1995-2014. Bien que les recettes fiscales totales exprimées en pourcentage du PIB aient augmenté en moyenne dans les pays de l'OCDE, le ratio d'imposition a baissé dans certains pays.
- Entre 1965 et 1975, la charge fiscale dans la zone OCDE a augmenté de 3.8 points (graphique 1.2). Jusqu'au premier choc pétrolier (1973-74), une croissance des revenus forte et presque ininterrompue a permis aux niveaux d'imposition d'augmenter dans tous les pays de l'OCDE. Les niveaux d'imposition ont augmenté automatiquement sous l'effet de la progressivité des barèmes de l'impôt sur le revenu des personnes physiques.
- Entre 1975 et 1985, la charge fiscale dans la zone OCDE a augmenté de 2.9 points (graphique 1.3). Après le milieu des années 70, le ralentissement de la croissance des revenus réels, combiné à l'augmentation du chômage, ont limité la capacité des pouvoirs publics à prélever des recettes. Cependant, à partir de la profonde récession qui a suivi le second choc pétrolier (1980), les pays européens ont été amenés à augmenter leurs impôts pour financer la hausse des dépenses de sécurité sociale et s'efforcer de maîtriser les déficits budgétaires.
- Entre 1985 et 1995, la charge fiscale dans la zone OCDE a de nouveau augmenté de 1.8 point (graphique 1.4). Après le milieu des années 80, la plupart des pays de l'OCDE ont sensiblement réduit les taux de leurs impôts sur le revenu des personnes physiques et sur les bénéfices des sociétés, mais l'incidence sur les recettes publiques des vastes réformes fiscales qui ont été engagées est restée limitée dans la mesure où, en même temps, la base de ces impôts était élargie par une réduction ou une suppression des déductions fiscales.
- Entre 1995 et 2000, le taux moyen d'imposition dans la zone OCDE a atteint 34.0 %, soit le niveau le plus élevé enregistré à cette époque. Il s'est ensuite légèrement replié entre 2001 et 2004, avant de repartir à la hausse entre 2005 et 2007, puis de retomber sous l'effet de la crise. En résumé, la charge fiscale moyenne dans la zone OCDE a augmenté de 0.9 point entre 1995 et 2014 (graphique 1.5).
- Ces moyennes concernant l'ensemble de la zone OCDE dissimulent la grande variété des charges fiscales nationales. En 1965, les niveaux d'imposition étaient compris entre 10.6 % en Turquie et 33.6 % en France. En 2014, ces niveaux oscillaient entre 15.2 % au Mexique et 49.6 % au Danemark. La tendance continue à l'augmentation des niveaux d'imposition reflète le besoin de financer la hausse marquée des dépenses du secteur public dans presque tous les pays de l'OCDE.

Graphique 1.2. **Variations du niveau d'imposition (en points de %)**

1965-1975

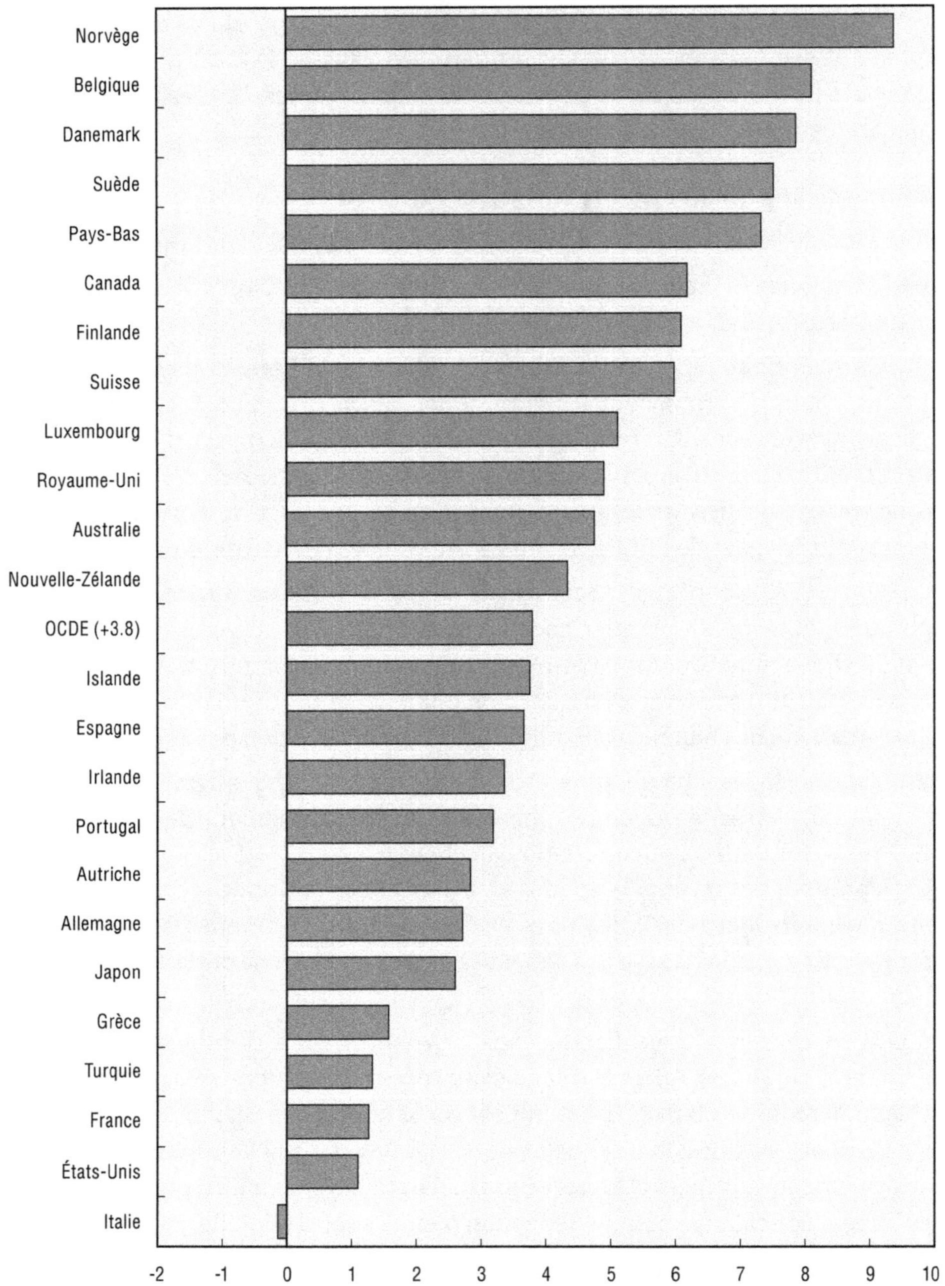

Source : Table 3.2.

Information sur les données concernant Israël : *http://oe.cd/israel-disclaimer.*

StatLink http://dx.doi.org/10.1787/888933416062

Graphique 1.3. **Variations du niveau d'imposition (en points de %)**

1975-85

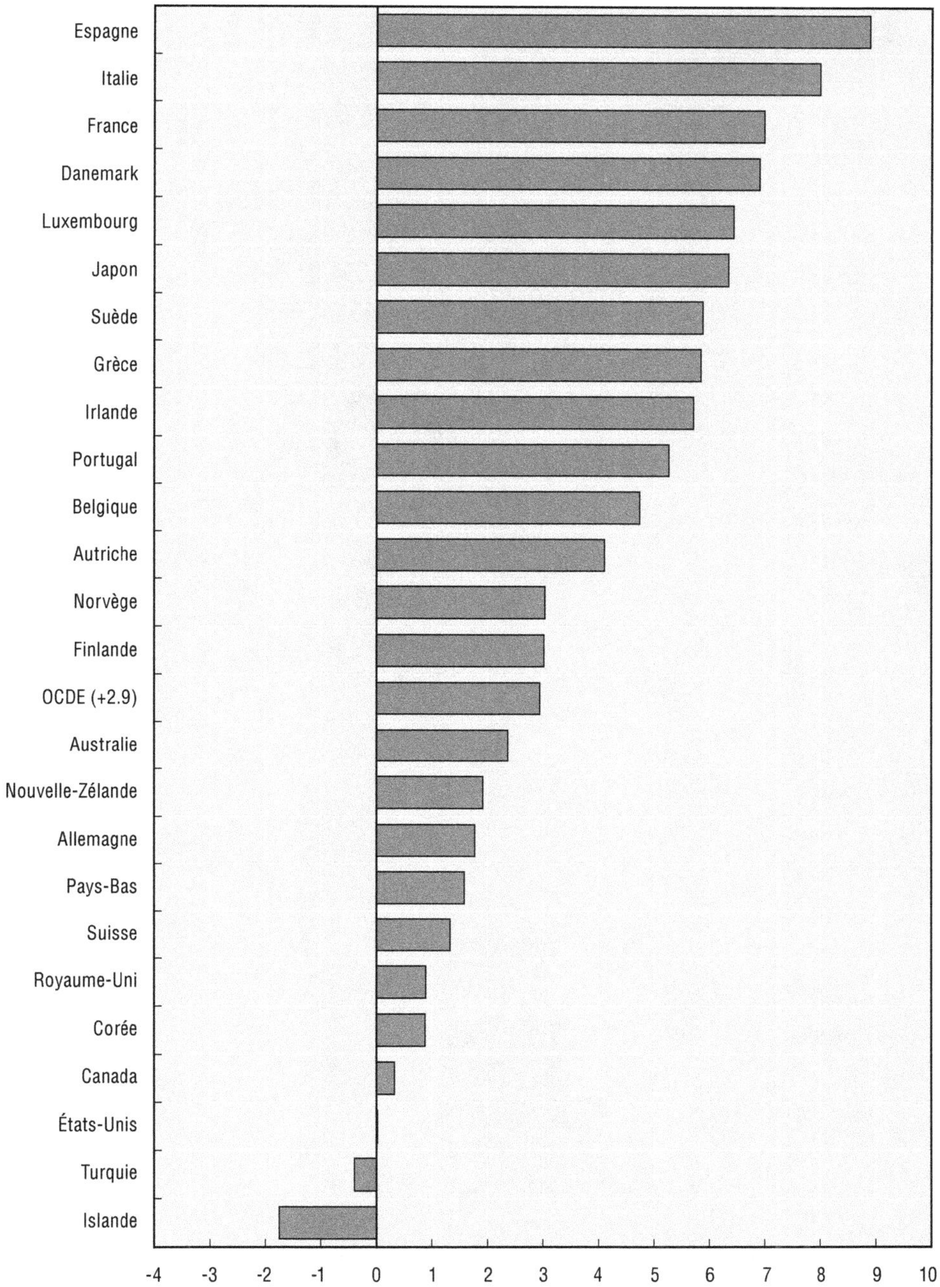

Source : Table 3.2.

Information sur les données concernant Israël : *http://oe.cd/israel-disclaimer*.

StatLink *http://dx.doi.org/10.1787/888933416079*

Graphique 1.4. **Variations du niveau d'imposition (en points de %)**

1985-95

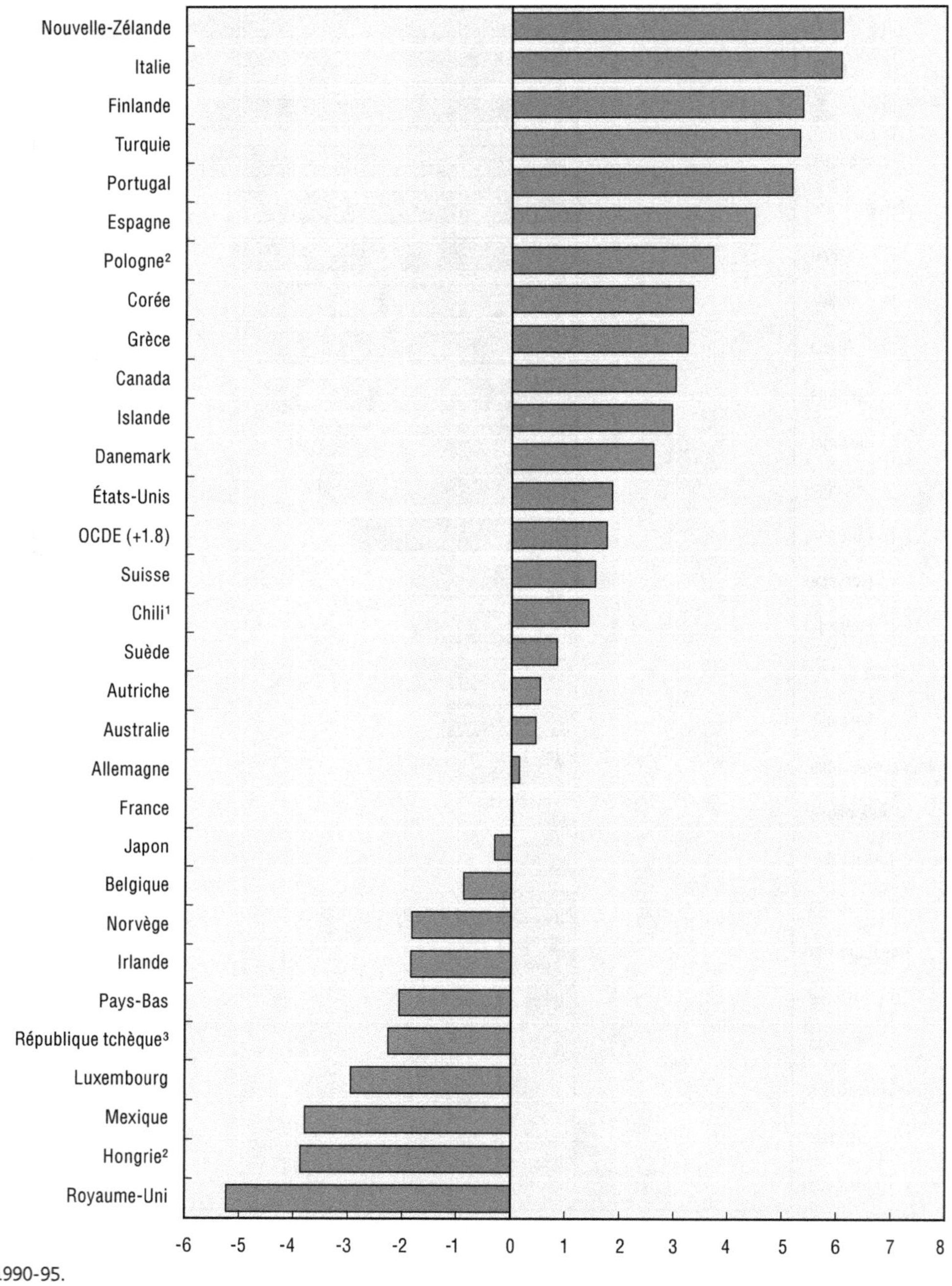

1. 1990-95.
2. 1991-95.
3. 1993-95.

Source : Table 3.2.

Information sur les données concernant Israël : *http://oe.cd/israel-disclaimer.*

StatLink http://dx.doi.org/10.1787/888933416085

Graphique 1.5. **Variations du niveau d'imposition (en points de %)**

1995-2014

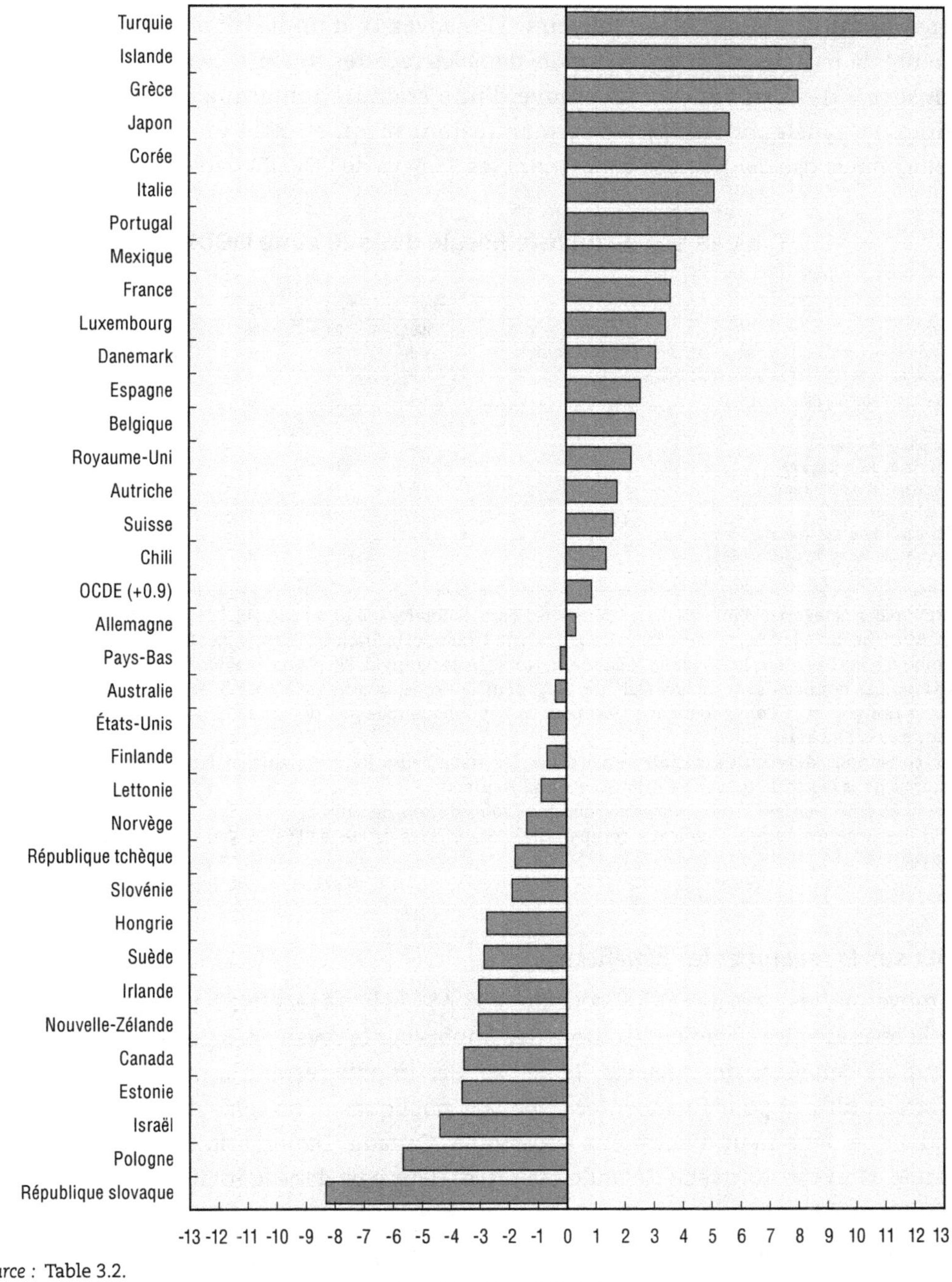

Source : Table 3.2.

Information sur les données concernant Israël : *http://oe.cd/israel-disclaimer.*

StatLink http://dx.doi.org/10.1787/888933416094

1.2. Structures fiscales

Les structures fiscales sont mesurées par la part des principaux impôts dans les recettes fiscales totales. Si, en moyenne, les niveaux d'imposition ont généralement augmenté, la part des principaux impôts dans les recettes totales – la structure fiscale ou le « dosage » des impôts – a fait preuve d'une stabilité remarquable dans le temps. Néanmoins, plusieurs tendances se manifestent jusqu'en 2014 (dernière année pour laquelle on dispose de données concernant les 35 pays de l'OCDE) (tableau 1.3).

Tableau 1.3. **Structure fiscale dans la zone OCDE**

Pour cent

	1965	1975	1985	1995	2005	2010	2014
Recettes fiscales totales	**100**	**100**	**100**	**100**	**100**	**100**	**100**
1100 Impôts sur le revenu, les bénéfices et les gains en capital des personnes physiques	26	30	30	25	23	23	24
1200 Impôts sur le revenu, les bénéfices et les gains en capital des sociétés	9	8	8	8	10	9	9
2000 Cotisations de sécurité sociale (CSS)[1]	18	22	22	25	25	27	26
dont :							
2100 CSS à la charge des salariés	6	7	7	8	9	9	10
2200 CSS à la charge des employeurs	10	14	13	15	15	15	15
3000 Impôts sur les salaires et la main-d'oeuvre	1	1	1	1	1	1	1
4000 Impôts sur le patrimoine	8	6	5	5	6	5	6
5110 Impôts généraux sur les biens et services	12	13	16	20	21	21	21
5120 Impôts sur des biens et des services déterminés	24	18	16	12	10	10	10
Autres impôts[2]	2	2	2	3	4	4	4

Note : Part des principales catégories d'impôts dans les recettes fiscales totales (en pourcentage). Les données sont incluses depuis 1965 pour l'Australie, l'Autriche, la Belgique, le Canada, le Danemark, la Finlande, la France, l'Allemagne, la Grèce, l'Islande, l'Irlande, l'Italie, le Japon, le Luxembourg, les Pays-Bas, la Nouvelle-Zélande, la Norvège, le Portugal, l'Espagne, la Suède, la Suisse, la Turquie, le Royaume-Uni et les États-Unis. Les données sont incluses depuis 1972 pour la Corée, depuis 1980 pour le Mexique, depuis 1990 pour le Chili, depuis 1991 pour la Hongrie et la Pologne, depuis 1993 pour la République tchèque, depuis 1995 pour l'Estonie, Israël, la Lettonie, la République slovaque et la Slovénie.

1. Y compris les cotisations de sécurité sociale versées par les travailleurs indépendants et les bénéficiaires (rubrique 2300) qui n'apparaissent pas dans la ventilation entre salariés et employeurs.
2. Y compris certaines taxes sur les biens et services (rubrique 5200) et droits de timbre.

Source : OCDE (2016), « Recettes fiscales : Tableaux comparatifs », *Statistiques fiscales de l'OCDE* (base de données) DOI: *http://dx.doi.org/10.1787/data-00262-fr.*

StatLink *http://dx.doi.org/10.1787/888933416230*

Impôts sur le revenu et les bénéfices

- En moyenne, les pays de l'OCDE collectent 33.7 % de leurs recettes fiscales via les impôts sur le revenu et les bénéfices (somme des impôts sur le revenu des personnes physiques et sur les bénéfices des sociétés, Table 3.8). Ces impôts restent la principale source de recettes utilisées pour financer les dépenses publiques dans seize des pays de l'OCDE, tandis que dans neuf d'entre eux – Australie, Canada, Danemark, États-Unis, Irlande, Islande, Norvège, Nouvelle-Zélande et Suisse – leur part dans le total des impôts excède 40 % (Table 3.6).
- En 2014, les recettes issues de l'impôt sur le revenu des personnes physiques représentent en moyenne 24 % du total des recettes, contre 30 % environ au cours des années 80 (Table 3.10). Dans cette baisse, deux points environ peuvent être attribués à l'inclusion dans la zone OCDE de pays d'Europe de l'Est pour lesquels les données relatives aux recettes fiscales ne sont disponibles qu'à partir des années 90. Dans ces pays, les recettes générées par l'impôt sur le revenu sont relativement faibles, alors que celles liées aux cotisations de sécurité sociale sont plus élevées, mais l'effet de l'inclusion de ces pays concerne seulement les données postérieures à l'année 1990.

- Les différences observées entre les pays sont considérables pour ce qui est de l'importance de l'impôt sur le revenu des personnes physiques. En 2014, la part de cet impôt allait d'un minimum de 7 % à 10 % respectivement au Chili et en République slovaque, à 41 % en Australie et 54 % au Danemark (Table 3.10).
- La forte baisse de la part des recettes tirées des impôts sur les bénéfices des sociétés dans le total des recettes fiscales constatée en 2008 et 2009 ne s'est pas poursuivie en 2011 et 2012, mais la part de ces impôts dans le total des prélèvements en 2014, soit 9 %, reste inférieure à leur niveau de 2007, lorsqu'elle s'établissait à 11 % (Table 3.12).
- La part des impôts sur les bénéfices des sociétés dans les recettes fiscales totales affiche une dispersion considérable, de 4 % environ (Finlande, Hongrie et Slovénie) à 17 % (Norvège) et 21 % (Chili). Hormis la dispersion des taux légaux d'imposition des sociétés, ces différences sont au moins partiellement imputables à des facteurs institutionnels ou à l'exploitation des gisements de minerai, par exemple :
  - la proportion des entreprises constituées sous forme de sociétés ;
  - la taxation des recettes pétrolières ;
  - l'érosion de la base d'imposition des sociétés consécutive, par exemple, à des méthodes généreuses de calcul de l'amortissement ;
  - d'autres instruments permettant de différer l'imposition des bénéfices.

Cotisations de sécurité sociale

- En 2014, les cotisations de sécurité sociale représentaient 26 % du total des recettes fiscales. Elles étaient les plus élevées en République tchèque et en République slovaque (43-44 %). En revanche, l'Australie et la Nouvelle-Zélande ne collectent pas de cotisations de sécurité sociale (Table 3.14). On observe par ailleurs de grandes différences entre les pays de l'OCDE pour ce qui est des parts relatives des cotisations de sécurité sociale versées par les salariés et par les employeurs (voir les Tablex 3.16 et 3.18).

Impôts sur le patrimoine

- Entre 1965 et 2014, la part des impôts sur le patrimoine a été ramenée en moyenne de 8 % à 6 % du total des recettes fiscales.
- En termes relatifs, la part des impôts sur le patrimoine est supérieure à 10 % du total des recettes fiscales dans cinq pays : Australie, Canada, Corée, États-Unis et Royaume-Uni (Table 3.22).

Impôts sur la consommation

- La part des impôts sur la consommation (impôts généraux sur la consommation plus impôts spécifiques sur la consommation) a diminué de 36 % à 31 % entre 1965 et 2014 (Table 3.26).
- Pendant cette période, la composition des taxes sur les biens et services s'est profondément modifiée. Les impôts généraux sur la consommation ont vu leur importance en tant que source de recettes s'affirmer rapidement, notamment pour la taxe sur la valeur ajoutée (TVA) qui est désormais appliquée dans 34 des 35 pays de l'OCDE.
- Les impôts généraux sur la consommation représentent actuellement 21 % des recettes fiscales totales, contre seulement 12 % au milieu des années 60 (Table 3.28).

- En fait, la montée en puissance de la taxe sur la valeur ajoutée a contribué à compenser la diminution de la part des impôts spécifiques sur la consommation, tels que les droits d'accise et les droits de douane.
  - Entre 1965 et 2014, la part des impôts spécifiques sur la consommation (surtout sur le tabac, les boissons alcoolisées et le carburant, y compris certaines taxes environnementales récemment instaurées) a été réduite de plus de la moitié.
  - Les taux des impôts sur les produits importés ont fortement baissé dans tous les pays, ce qui s'explique par la tendance générale à la suppression des obstacles aux échanges.
  - Néanmoins, l'Estonie (environ 14 %), la Slovénie (environ 15 %) et la Turquie (environ 22 %) collectent encore une part relativement importante de leurs recettes fiscales totales sous forme de taxes sur des biens et services spécifiques (Table 3.30).

1.3. Répartition des impôts par niveaux d'administration

Le tableau 1.4 indique la part relative des recettes fiscales attribuées aux différents sous-secteurs des administrations publiques et son évolution au cours de la période 1975-2014.

Pays fédéraux et régionaux

- En 2014, dans les huit pays fédéraux de l'OCDE, la part des recettes de l'administration centrale variait de 31 % en Allemagne à 80 % en Australie.
- En 2014, la part des collectivités régionales ou provinciales s'échelonnait entre 2 % en Autriche, 4 % au Mexique, 5 % en Belgique et 39 % au Canada. La part des collectivités locales était comprise entre 2 % au Mexique et 15 % en Suisse.
- Entre 1975 et 2014, la part des recettes de l'administration fédérale a reculé d'environ huit points de pourcentage en Belgique, tandis qu'elle a décliné moins rapidement en Allemagne, au Canada et aux États-Unis.
- La part des recettes de l'administration fédérale a augmenté en Autriche et en Suisse respectivement de 15 et 5 points. Il y a eu peu de changement en Australie et au Mexique.
- La part des caisses de sécurité sociale a augmenté dans cinq des sept pays fédéraux, à l'exception du Canada et du Mexique où elle a légèrement diminué.
- L'Espagne est maintenant classée dans la catégorie « pays régional » plutôt que dans celle des « pays unitaires » à cause de sa structure politique fortement décentralisée. En 2014, la part des recettes de l'administration centrale était de 42 %, contre 14 % pour les collectivités régionales. Entre 1975 et 2014, la part des recettes des collectivités locales a augmenté de 4 % à 10 % et la part des caisses de sécurité sociale a baissé de 48 % à 34 %.

Pays unitaires

- Dans les pays unitaires de l'OCDE, la part des recettes de l'administration centrale en 2014 se situait entre 34 % en France et 37 % au Japon, et 93 % en Nouvelle-Zélande.
- La part des collectivités locales variait de 1 % en Estonie et en République tchèque à 37 % en Suède.
- Entre 1975 et 2014, les transferts aux collectivités locales ont augmenté de 5 points ou plus dans six pays – Corée, France, Islande, Italie, Portugal et Suède – mais ont moins progressé aux Pays-Bas. Une diminution des transferts de 5 points ou plus s'est produite dans deux pays – Norvège et Royaume-Uni.

Tableau 1.4. Répartition des recettes fiscales entre les sous-secteurs de l'Administration en % du total des recettes fiscales

	Supranationale			Administration centrale			Administration d'un État/Région			Administrations locales			Administrations de sécurité sociale		
	1975	1995	2014	1975	1995	2014	1975	1995	2014	1975	1995	2014	1975	1995	2014
Pays fédéraux															
Australie	..	..	..	80.1	77.5	80.0	15.7	19.0	16.5	4.2	3.4	3.5	0.0	0.0	0.0
Autriche	..	0.0	0.3	51.7	64.8	66.5	10.6	1.8	1.6	12.4	4.1	3.2	25.3	29.3	28.5
Belgique	1.4	1.0	0.7	65.3	60.1	57.4	..	1.8	5.3	4.4	4.8	4.6	28.8	32.2	31.9
Canada	..	..	..	47.6	39.1	41.4	32.5	37.1	39.1	9.9	9.8	10.3	10.0	14.0	9.2
Allemagne	1.2	0.6	0.4	33.5	31.4	31.2	22.3	21.6	22.0	9.0	7.4	8.2	34.0	39.0	38.1
Mexique	..	..	..	..	73.9	73.3	..	2.8	4.4	..	1.5	1.6	..	21.8	20.6
Suisse	..	..	..	30.7	31.6	35.2	27.0	23.8	24.7	20.3	17.6	15.3	22.0	27.0	24.9
États-Unis	..	..	..	45.4	41.4	42.1	19.5	20.0	19.7	14.7	13.3	14.1	20.5	25.2	24.1
Moyenne non pondérée	1.3	0.6	0.5	50.6	52.5	53.4	21.3	16.0	16.7	10.7	7.7	7.6	20.1	23.6	22.2
Pays régional															
Espagne[1,2]	..	0.5	0.4	48.2	50.4	42.3	..	4.8	13.6	4.3	8.5	10.0	47.5	35.8	33.6
Pays unitaires															
Chili	..	..	..	..	89.9	86.7	..	..	..	..	6.5	7.6	..	3.6	5.8
République tchèque	..	..	0.5	..	57.7	54.5	..	..	..	..	0.9	1.2	..	41.4	43.8
Danemark[2]	1.1	0.5	0.3	68.9	68.2	74.6	..	..	..	30.0	31.3	25.0	0.1	0.0	0.1
Estonie	..	..	0.5	..	84.3	82.0	..	..	..	..	0.8	1.1	..	14.9	16.5
Finlande	..	0.4	0.2	56.0	46.6	47.4	..	..	..	23.5	22.3	23.5	20.4	30.8	28.9
France[2]	0.7	0.4	0.2	51.2	42.3	33.1	..	..	..	7.6	11.0	13.0	40.6	46.3	53.7
Grèce[2]	..	0.6	0.2	67.1	66.8	68.6	..	..	..	3.4	0.9	3.0	29.5	31.7	28.2
Hongrie	..	..	0.3	..	63.8	60.8	..	..	..	..	2.5	5.7	..	33.6	33.2
Islande	..	..	..	81.3	79.2	75.5	..	..	..	18.7	20.8	24.5	0.0	0.0	0.0
Irlande	2.3	1.5	0.5	77.4	83.1	82.4	..	..	..	7.3	2.7	2.8	13.1	12.7	14.3
Israël	..	..	..	..	79.7	75.6	..	..	..	..	6.4	8.0	..	13.9	16.4
Italie	..	0.4	0.3	53.2	62.7	53.4	..	..	..	0.9	5.4	16.5	45.9	31.5	29.8
Japon	..	..	..	45.4	41.2	36.9	..	..	..	25.6	25.3	23.5	29.0	33.5	39.7
Corée	..	..	..	89.0	69.2	56.2	..	..	..	10.1	18.7	16.9	0.9	12.1	26.9
Lettonie	..	..	0.5	..	43.5	50.8	..	..	..	..	19.5	19.5	..	36.9	29.1
Luxembourg	0.8	0.4	0.1	63.6	66.5	68.8	..	..	..	6.7	6.5	3.3	29.0	26.6	27.8
Pays-Bas	1.5	1.3	1.0	58.9	56.0	55.6	..	..	..	1.2	3.1	3.8	38.4	39.5	39.6
Nouvelle-Zélande	..	..	..	92.3	94.7	93.3	..	..	..	7.7	5.3	6.7	0.0	0.0	0.0
Norvège	..	..	..	50.6	58.4	86.1	..	..	..	22.4	19.6	13.9	27.0	22.0	0.0
Pologne	..	..	0.3	..	61.9	48.2	..	..	..	..	8.3	13.4	..	29.8	38.1
Portugal	..	0.8	0.3	65.4	72.3	67.8	..	..	..	0.0	5.4	7.2	34.6	21.5	24.7
République slovaque	..	..	0.5	..	62.5	54.6	..	..	..	..	1.3	2.7	..	36.2	42.1
Slovénie	..	..	0.4	..	51.8	50.0	..	..	..	..	6.3	10.6	..	41.9	39.0
Suède	..	0.4	0.3	51.3	46.9	50.0	..	..	..	29.2	30.9	36.9	19.5	21.8	12.7
Turquie	..	..	..	..	75.1	62.0	..	..	..	..	12.8	9.4	..	12.1	28.5
Royaume-Uni	1.0	1.0	0.6	70.5	77.5	75.8	..	..	..	11.1	3.7	5.0	17.5	17.8	18.7
Moyenne non pondérée	1.2	0.7	0.4	65.1	65.5	63.5	..	..	..	12.8	10.7	11.7	21.6	23.5	24.5

1. L'Espagne est constitutionnellement un pays non fédéral mais avec une structure politique très décentralisée.
2. Le total des recettes fiscales a été diminué du montant de tout transfert en capital représentant les impôts non perçus.

StatLink http://dx.doi.org/10.1787/888933416240

- Entre 1975 et 2014, la part des caisses de sécurité sociale a progressé de 7 points ou plus dans quatre pays – Corée, Finlande, France et Japon - tandis qu'elle enregistrait des baisses du même ordre de grandeur dans trois pays – Italie, Norvège et Portugal. Entre 1995 et 2014, cette part a augmenté de 7 points ou plus dans deux autres pays (Pologne et Turquie).
- Les directives suivies pour attribuer ces parts des recettes aux différents niveaux d'administration s'appuient sur la version finale du Système des comptes nationaux de 2008. Ces directives sont examinées dans l'Étude spéciale S.1 de l'édition 2011 des *Statistiques des recettes publiques de l'OCDE*.

États membres de l'UE dans l'OCDE

- Dans le tableau 1.4, la colonne « supranationale » donne le montant des impôts collectés pour le compte de l'Union européenne par les 21 États membres de l'UE qui sont membres de l'OCDE. Pour les années antérieures à 1998, les droits de douane collectés pour le compte de l'Union européenne par les administrations fiscales des États membres de l'UE figurent dans la rubrique 5123. À partir de 1998, ces droits de douane sont indiqués en tant que poste « pour mémoire », car ils sont en fait imposés par l'Union européenne et collectés pour son compte par les administrations fiscales nationales. Toutefois, ils continuent de faire partie du total des recettes fiscales collectées dans les États membres de l'UE. Cette approche permet d'assurer la cohérence des séries chronologiques et évite que les ratios des recettes fiscales aux PIB subissent les effets des changements de la part relative des droits de douane dans : 1) la composition des ressources de financement de l'UE ; et 2) la composition des différents impôts des États membres de l'UE. Le tableau 1.5 résume les montants de ces droits de douane.

Tableau 1.5. **Droits de douanes collectés pour le compte de l'Union européenne**

Millions de monnaie nationale

	2000	2008	2009	2011	2012	2013	2014	2015p
Autriche[1]	356	371	320	378	344	328	369	414
Belgique[1]	960	1 420	1 147	1 285	1 247	1 185	1 257	1 364
République tchèque	..	6 323	5 548	6 961	6 172	5 544	6 968	7 859
Danemark	2 325	3 106	2 647	3 177	2 962	2 824	3 001	3 285
Estonie[1]	..	33	20	29	29	29	30	34
Finlande[1]	129	205	152	189	184	166	170	165
France[1]	1 513	1 615	1 461	1 866	1 883	1 842	1 827	1 931
Allemagne[1]	3 394	4 036	3 778	4 556	4 417	4 251	4 608	5 195
Grèce[1]	210	305	252	186	162	148	148	..
Hongrie	..	26 689	25 657	27 462	27 206	26 337	31 927	38 960
Irlande[1]	208	245	208	240	242	247	275	327
Italie[1]	1 536	2 200	2 008	2 319	2 077	1 890	2 022	2 246
Lettonie[1]	..	35	21	31	32	28	36	40
Luxembourg[1]	27	18	13	17	15	15	19	23
Pays-Bas[1]	1 310	1 800	1 518	1 889	1 780	1 756	2 046	2 441
Pologne	..	1 572	1 308	1 447	1 611	1 613	1 791	..
Portugal[1]	204	177	154	168	155	144	149	158
République slovaque[1]	..	156	111	157	129	115	127	119
Slovénie[1]	..	77	57	62	54	52	52	52
Espagne[1]	970	1 578	1 328	1 554	1 436	1 316	1 512	1 754
Suède	3 450	5 212	4 764	5 399	4 995	4 976	5 737	6 243
Royaume-Uni	1 800	2 297	2 435	2 925	2 885	2 914	2 949	3 077

.. signifie non disponible ; p : provisoire.

1. Pour les pays de la zone euro, les montants sont exprimés en euros pour toutes les années.

StatLink http://dx.doi.org/10.1787/888933416252

1.4. Impact de la révision des données du PIB sur les niveaux d'imposition déclarés

Les coefficients de pression fiscale qui figurent dans ce Rapport expriment les recettes fiscales globales en pourcentage du PIB. Il est important de tenir compte du fait que la valeur de ce ratio dépend de son dénominateur (PIB) et de son numérateur (recettes fiscales), le dénominateur étant sujet à des révisions historiques.

Le numérateur (recettes fiscales)

- En ce qui concerne le numérateur, le Secrétariat de l'OCDE utilise pour ce Rapport les données relatives aux recettes fiscales qui lui sont fournies annuellement par les correspondants des ministères des Finances, des administrations fiscales nationales ou des services nationaux de statistiques. Bien que pour la plupart des pays, des chiffres provisoires soient disponibles avec un décalage d'environ six mois, les données finalisées le sont dans un délai d'environ dix-huit mois. Ainsi, les données définitives pour 2014 ont été reçues entre mai et août 2016.

- Dans trente et un pays de l'OCDE, l'année fiscale coïncide avec l'année civile. Elle en diffère dans quatre pays : Australie, Canada, Japon et Nouvelle-Zélande. Les déclarations pour l'année 2013 couvrent respectivement T2/2013-T1/2014 (Canada, Japon) et T3/2013-T2/2014 (Australie, Nouvelle-Zélande) (T = trimestre).

Le dénominateur (PIB)

- En ce qui concerne le dénominateur, ce Rapport utilise les chiffres du PIB les plus récents dont on disposait au 1er septembre 2016. À cette date, les chiffres du PIB pour 2014 et 2015 étaient disponibles pour tous les pays de l'OCDE.
- L'utilisation de ces PIB harmonisés assure un maximum de cohérence et de comparabilité internationale aux ratios impôts/PIB.
- Les chiffres du PIB proviennent des Comptes nationaux annuels des pays membres de l'OCDE (CNA-SCN) pour les trente et un pays où l'année fiscale coïncide avec l'année civile.
- Lorsque l'année fiscale diffère de l'année civile, les estimations annuelles du PIB sont obtenues par l'agrégation des données fournies par la Direction des statistiques de l'OCDE pour les trimestres correspondants aux années fiscales de chacun des pays. Par exemple, dans le cas du Canada : T2/2013-T1/2014.

Révisions du numérateur et du dénominateur

Le numérateur (recettes fiscales) et le dénominateur du ratio (PIB) sont tous deux sujets à révision lorsque des données plus récentes sont disponibles. Une telle révision influe directement sur les coefficients de pression fiscale publiés.

- Si les recettes fiscales augmentent alors que le PIB demeure inchangé, le coefficient augmente.
- Si le montant du PIB est révisé à la baisse, le coefficient augmente aussi, même si les recettes fiscales n'ont pas augmenté.
- À l'inverse, un PIB plus élevé entraîne un coefficient plus faible, même si le montant des impôts collectés n'a pas varié.
- Pour les années les plus récentes en particulier, les montants des recettes ont pu faire l'objet de révisions peu fréquentes et de faible ampleur. Les données concernant le PIB sont révisées et mises à jour plus fréquemment, mais pas nécessairement pour tous les pays en même temps, reflétant l'utilisation de sources et de procédures d'estimation plus fiables. En général, ces révisions ont une incidence assez limitée sur les ratios impôts/PIB.
- Toutefois, les chiffres du PIB peuvent parfois changer de façon plus fondamentale lorsque sont introduites, au plan international, de nouvelles procédures de calcul du PIB. Le changement le plus récent est la mise en œuvre du Système de comptabilité nationale de 2008 (SCN 2008) qui a maintenant largement remplacé son prédécesseur, le Système de comptabilité nationale de 1993 (SCN 1993). Une version plus ancienne du Système de comptabilité nationale a été mise en place en 1968.
- Les 22 pays de l'OCDE qui sont membres de l'UE sont tenus de se conformer au Système européen de comptes économiques intégrés (SEC) pour le calcul de leur PIB. Le SEC constitue essentiellement un approfondissement du SCN, bien qu'il en diffère sur certains points mineurs sans importance pour ce rapport. À la suite de la révision du SCN en 2008, le SEC de 1995 a été remplacé par le SEC de 2010.

- Jusqu'à présent, les chiffres du PIB présentés dans cette publication se fondent sur le SCN 2008 pour 32 pays. Les exceptions sont le Chili, le Japon et la Turquie, qui suivront lors des prochains mois. À l'exception de quelques chiffres concernant certaines années, les montants du PIB pour ces trente-deux pays sont plus élevés suite à l'application du nouveau SCN. Ceci s'explique par les changements méthodologiques et aussi par l'amélioration des sources des données.
- Les chiffres des recettes fiscales publiés dans les *Statistiques des recettes publiques* ont été peu affectés par les changements de définitions et de normes intervenus dans le SCN/SEC. Néanmoins, il y a eu des ajustements dans certains pays qui ont saisi l'occasion d'améliorer les sources des données et les méthodologies de compilation des chiffres de comptabilité nationale (incluant les recettes fiscales). Ces changements dans les recettes fiscales ont le plus souvent été moins marqués que ceux associés aux chiffres du PIB et les ratios ont en règle générale diminué pour les pays qui ont appliqué le système révisé.
- Un problème particulier soulevé par la révision des systèmes SCN 2008/SEC 2010 est que la période couverte par les révisions du PIB varie selon les pays. Afin de limiter cet effet de distorsion, la Direction des statistiques de l'OCDE et le Centre de politique et d'administration fiscales ont calculé des estimations du PIB révisées pour 1965 et les années suivantes quand les pays de l'OCDE n'ont pas fourni de chiffres révisés du PIB.

Note

1. Calculé en appliquant le pourcentage moyen non pondéré de variation pour 2015 dans les 32 pays qui ont communiqué des données pour cette année au ratio moyen global impôts/PIB en 2014.

Revenue Statistics 2016
Statistiques des recettes publiques 2016

Chapter 2

Special feature: Current issues on reporting tax revenues

2.1. Introduction

The release of the final version of the *IMF Government Finance Statistics Manual* 2014 (IMF GFSM 2014) completed the releases of the revised versions of the three classification systems which historically have had, in the area of government revenues, a very strong overlap with the *OECD Tax Classification and Interpretative Guide*:

- the *IMF GFSM 2014;*
- the *2008 System of National Accounts (SNA);*
- the *2010 European System of Accounts (ESA)*.

The degree of overlap is illustrated by a "bridge" table, contained in the *OECD Interpretative Guide*, which maps how the list of taxes in the *OECD Tax Classification* links to the corresponding lists in the other classification systems. The latest version of this table is shown in Annex A of this Report.

These latest editions of the three classification systems contain some revisions to the definitions and classification of government revenues compared with the previous versions. It has therefore been necessary to review certain sections of the *Interpretative Guide* in those areas where either the methodology for defining tax revenues has been altered or there have been substantial changes to the explanatory drafting in the other classification systems.

This report considers the following issues relating to the methodology in the *OECD Interpretative Guide*:

- payable or non-wastable tax credits;
- the VAT based third EU own resource in the ESA 2010;
- the classification of revenues from fines or penalties;
- profits of fiscal monopolies;
- imputed taxes and subsidies arising from the operation of multiple exchange rate systems;
- imputed taxes and subsidies arising from central banks imposing a rate of interest other than market rates;
- taxes on financial and capital transactions.

2.2. Payable or non-wastable tax credits

2.a. Two kinds of tax credits

There are two kinds of tax credit systems:

- Non-payable or wastable tax credits are those which can only ever be used to reduce or eliminate a tax liability. They cannot be paid out to either tax-payers or non-tax payers as a benefit. They are therefore the same as a tax allowance or relief.
- In contrast, payable or non-wastable tax credits can be partitioned into two parts. One part is used to reduce or eliminate a tax liability in the same way as a wastable tax credit.

The other part can be paid directly to recipients as a benefit payment, when the benefit exceeds the tax liability.

2.b. The OECD methodology for classifying non-wastable tax credits and two alternatives

The OECD methodology for classifying non-wastable tax credits is set out in paragraphs 19 and 20 of the *Interpretative Guide*. This states that only the part of a non-wastable tax credit that is used to reduce or eliminate a taxpayer's tax liability should be deducted in the reporting of tax revenues. This is referred to as the "tax expenditure component" of the credit. In contrast, the part of the tax credit that exceeds the taxpayer's tax liability and is paid to that taxpayer is treated as an expenditure item and not deducted in the reporting of tax revenues. This part is referred to as the "transfer component". This approach was also followed in the previous versions of the *IMF GFSM, SNA and ESA*.

Table 2.1 provides information on the non-wastable tax credits in 2014 for those countries reporting them in the Revenue Statistics 2016 (though it may be that some countries with non-wastable tax credits do not appear in the table). It shows the amounts of the non-wastable tax credits and their two components together with the results of using the figures to calculate tax revenue values and the associated tax-to-GDP ratios. This table has the same construction as one that has appeared in the "Part I – Commentary on revenues and trends" in the Revenue Statistics 2014. The treatment consistent with the Interpretative Guide is referred to as the "split basis" as shown in columns 5 and 8. Two alternative treatments to the split basis are also shown:

- the "net basis" which treats non-wastable tax credits entirely as tax provisions, so that the full value of the tax credit reduces reported tax revenues, as shown in columns 4 and 7;
- the "gross basis" is the exact opposite, treating non-wastable tax credits entirely as expenditure provisions, with neither the transfer component nor the tax expenditure component being deducted from tax revenue, as shown in columns 6 and 9.

Historically, there have been some practical difficulties in implementing these paragraphs of the *Interpretative Guide*, resulting in some lack of uniformity of reporting. In addition, distinguishing between tax and expenditure provisions can be conceptually difficult and so there are valid arguments for the alternative treatments. This issue was examined in Special Features appearing in both the 2000 and the 2001 editions of the *Revenue Statistics*. Consequently there is no ideal solution to the problem of how these tax credits should be treated. However, any comparison with the tax-to-GDP ratio results based on the two alternative treatments of these tax credits should take into account their potential drawbacks.

- While the "gross basis" provides comparability between the treatment of public expenditure on in-work income related benefits and non-wastable tax credits, it does not provide comparability between wastable and non-wastable credits. For example, changing a wastable tax credit into a non-wastable tax credit, even if it involves minimal fiscal cost or impact on taxpayers, could produce a large increase in reported revenue. This is because amounts previously deducted from tax revenues would be treated as an expenditure provision and no longer be deducted.
- The most serious drawback of the "net basis" is that it does not ensure comparability between countries with and without non-wastable tax credits. This is because it reduces tax revenues for countries with non-wastable tax credits by amounts that would be

Table 2.1. **Effect of alternative treatments of non-wastable tax credits, 2014**

	Non-wastable tax credits in millions of national currency			Total tax revenues in millions of national currency			Total tax revenues as a percentage of GDP		
	Total value	Transfer component	Tax expenditure component	Net basis	Split basis (per current guidance)	Gross basis	Net basis	Split basis (per current guidance)	Gross basis
	(1)	(2)	(3)	(4) = (5) – (2)	(5)	(6) = (5) + (3)	(7)	(8)	(9)
Australia	8 280	4 936	3 344	441 891	**446 827**	450 171	27.5	**27.8**	28.1
Austria	560	245	315	141 232	**41 477**	141 792	42.7	**42.8**	42.9
Belgium	1 052	317	735	179 863	**180 180**	180 915	44.9	**45.0**	45.2
Canada	11 519	10 489	1 030	607 728	**618 217**	619 247	30.7	**31.2**	31.3
Chile	..	..	..	**29 145 219**	..	..	**19.8**	..	..
Czech Republic	28 969	8 258	20 711	1 419 016	**1 427 274**	1 447 984	32.9	**31.1**	33.6
Denmark	5 495	275	5 220	962 909	**963 184**	968 404	49.6	**49.6**	49.9
France	21 243	8 375	12 868	965 005	**973 380**	986 248	45.1	**45.5**	46.1
Germany	41 514	14 541	26 974	1 054 718	**1 069 259**	1 096 233	36.1	**36.6**	37.5
Iceland	1 162	1 000	162	773 263	**774 263**	774 425	38.9	**38.9**	38.9
Ireland	..	..	667	..	**55 453**	56 120	..	**28.7**	29.1
Israel	625	587	38	341 127	**341 714**	341 752	31.2	**31.2**	31.2
Italy	12 611	7 585	5 027	696 633	**704 217**	709 244	43.2	**43.7**	44.0
Luxembourg	217	..	..	..	..	**18 761**	..	..	**38.4**
Mexico	43 716	2 423	41 293	2 605 273	**2 607 696**	2 648 989	15.1	**15.2**	15.4
New Zealand	2 555	1 686	869	76 225	**77 911**	78 780	31.8	**32.5**	32.9
Norway	1 467	1 275	380	1 218 594	**1 219 869**	1 220 249	38.6	**38.7**	38.7
Slovak Republic	263	..	..	..	..	**23 612**	..	..	**31.2**
Spain	582	..	..	..	..	**352 394**	..	..	**33.8**
United Kingdom	31 432	28 005	3 427	556 464	**584 469**	587 896	30.5	**32.1**	32.3
United States	144 640	99 810	44 830	4 400 720	**4 500 530**	4 545 360	25.3	**25.9**	26.1

Notes: The Austrian children's tax credit is not regarded as a tax credit in the OECD *Revenue Statistics* and is treated entirely as an expenditure provision.

For Denmark, France and Spain, the total tax revenues have been reduced by the amount of any capital transfer that represents uncollected taxes.

Some non-wastable tax credits in Canada cannot be split into the transfer and tax expenditure components. Their total values have been added to the transfer component.

".." not available.

treated as expenditure in countries that use comparable expenditure programmes to deliver transfers to those who do not pay taxes. Even between countries with non-wastable tax credits, reporting on a net basis would produce lower tax revenues (everything else being the same) for countries that are giving greater assistance to non-taxpayers with these credits. Arguably, this may give a misleading impression of the extent of the tax system.

However, Table 2.1 does show that, with some exceptions, the choice of method for reporting non-wastable tax credits has only a small impact on the ratio of total tax revenue to GDP. For the countries with available data, the differences between the ratios on a net basis and on a gross basis are one percentage point or more in only France, Germany, New Zealand and the United Kingdom, and half a percentage point or more in Australia, Canada, Czech Republic, Italy and the United States.

2.c. *A new methodology adopted by IMF GFSM, SNA and ESA*

SNA *2008* was the first of the revisions of the three "associated" classification systems to be published. This document contained a change in the rules for classifying the taxes and benefits associated with non-wastable tax credit systems. Now, the whole amount of the payable tax credits is registered as a "tax expense" or in other words a subsidy or social benefit, irrespective of how much is used to reduce tax liability, and how much is paid direct to beneficiaries. The taxes and benefits are now shown in the national accounts on the "gross basis" – i.e. the revenues will show the full liability before the non-wastable tax credits are allowed for, and the whole of the credits under the non-wastable tax credits system will be shown as subsidies or social benefits.

The *IMF GFSM 2014* and *ESA 2010* replicated the changes made in the *2008 SNA* in this respect.

The catalyst for the decision to revise the classification of non-wastable tax credits in *SNA 2008* was contained in a paper written by the International Public Sector Accounting Standards (IPSAS) Board. "IPSAS 23 – Revenue from non-exchange transactions taxes and transfers", which was released in December 2006, contained the following extract titled "Expenses paid through the tax system and tax expenditures". The clearly expressed view that the whole amount of these tax credits should be accounted for totally as expenditure was discussed by the Inter-Secretariat Working Group on National Accounts (ISWGNA) and the SNA's Advisory Expert Group (AEG) in the context of drafting *SNA 2008*. As a result, the principle to treat these tax credits totally as expenses was adopted for the new version.

Expenses Paid Through the Tax System and Tax Expenditures

Taxation revenue shall be determined at a gross amount. It shall not be reduced for expenses paid through the tax system.

In some jurisdictions, the government uses the tax system as a convenient method of paying to taxpayers benefits, which would otherwise be paid using another payment method, such as writing a check, directly depositing the amount in a taxpayer's bank account, or settling another account on behalf of the taxpayer. For example, a government may pay part of residents' health insurance premiums, to encourage the uptake of such insurance, either by reducing the individual's tax liability, making a payment by check or by paying an amount directly to the insurance company. In these cases, the amount is payable irrespective of whether the individual pays taxes. Consequently this amount is an expense of the government and should be recognized separately in the statement of financial performance. Tax revenue should be increased for the amount of any of these expenses paid through the tax system.

Taxation revenue shall not be grossed up for the amount of tax expenditures

In most jurisdictions, governments use the tax system to encourage certain financial behaviour and discourage other behaviour. For example, in some jurisdictions, home owners are permitted to deduct mortgage interest and property taxes from their gross income when calculating tax assessable income. These types of concessions are available only to taxpayers. If an entity (including a natural person) does not pay tax, it cannot access the concession. These types of concessions are called tax expenditures. Tax expenditures are foregone revenue, not expenses, and do not give rise to inflows or outflows of resources – that is, they do not give rise to assets, liabilities, revenue or expenses of the taxing government.

The key distinction between expenses paid through the tax system and tax expenditures is that for expenses paid through the tax system, the amount is available to recipients irrespective of whether they pay taxes, or use a particular mechanism to pay their taxes. IPSAS 1, "Presentation of Financial Statements," prohibits the offsetting of items of revenue and expense unless permitted by another Standard. The offsetting of tax revenue and expenses paid through the tax system is not permitted.

2.d. The classification of non-wastable tax credits remains unchanged in the OECD Interpretative Guide

The OECD Tax Policy and Tax Statistics Working Party No. 2 (WP2) has decided to retain the existing guidelines for reporting non-wastable tax credits as opposed to changing them to align with the revised versions of the other statistical sources. The following paragraphs contain some of the points that were taken into account in the discussion.

There are obvious advantages in opting for and maintaining consistency between the guidelines for presenting information in different statistical sources just to avoid the confusion that can arise when different approaches are adopted. Other things being equal, one option was therefore to revise the *Interpretative Guide* to be consistent with the revisions made to the *IMF GFSM, SNA* and *ESA*.

However, on the other hand, there are also some compelling reasons for retaining the existing guidelines which can be set out as follows:

- These issues were previously discussed in WP2 meetings held in 1999 and 2000. The discussions concluded that, from the perspective of tax policy makers and tax administrators, the current OECD guidelines reflect the most appropriate way to report the non-wastable tax credits. The topic was discussed in Special Features in both the 2000 and the 2001 editions of the *Revenue Statistics*.
- It is often the case in tax systems containing non-wastable tax credits that the payable element represents a relatively small element (sometimes a very small element) of the total value of the credit. The "gross-basis" of reporting dictates that the rules for reporting the whole value of the credit would be based on the existence of this smaller element. Additionally, in some cases, a move from a wastable to a non-wastable tax credit could be the result of a minor administrative change. In such cases, the "gross-basis" of reporting could create undesirable situations where a substantial change in reported tax revenues results from an administrative change having a minimal impact on taxpayers or fiscal cost. This is because amounts previously treated as a deduction from tax revenues would be treated as an expenditure provision and no longer deducted.
- The adoption of the "gross-basis" of reporting would create inconsistencies between the reporting in the *Revenue Statistics* and some of the indicators reported in the *Taxing Wages* publication. In the latter, the calculations of both the average personal income tax rate (defined as personal income tax divided by gross earnings) and the average personal tax rate (defined as personal income tax plus employee social security contributions divided by gross earnings) deduct the full value of any non-wastable tax credit from the income tax liability.
- The new guidelines are inconsistent in their application to tax expenditures in general given their application to non-wastable tax credits is different to that of other tax expenditures.
- The "gross-basis" of reporting would also produce inconsistencies between the *Revenue Statistics* and the reporting of tax expenditures. Normally, the full value of any existing non-wastable tax credit would be included in a report on tax expenditures. If the "gross-basis" of reporting were applied to the latter then a wide range of both personal income and corporate income tax credits would have to be excluded.

- There are other provisions in tax systems that are deducted from tax revenues (i.e. tax allowances or wastable tax credits) that could also be seen as a substitute for expenditure programmes. The "gross basis" does not provide comparability between these and the non-wastable tax credits.
- The consequences of these issues are likely to grow as the total value of non-wastable tax credits is increasing over time in a number of OECD countries.

These issues were once again discussed in WP2 meetings in 2015 and 2016. On the basis of the arguments presented in Section 2.d of this chapter, it was decided that from the perspective of tax policy makers and tax economists it would be appropriate to retain the existing OECD guidelines on the presentation of non-wastable tax credits in the *Revenue Statistics* and not to move to the new guidelines adopted in the *IMF GFSM 2014*, the 2008 SNA and the 2010 ESA.

2.3. The VAT based third EU own resource in ESA 2010

There has been a change in the recording of the VAT based third EU own resource in ESA 2010. These are amounts of VAT that are collected by the governments of the EU member states and then re-mitted to the Institutions of the EU. The level of the contribution of each member state is based on the levels of their particular VAT base.

In the ESA 1995, these tax receipts were recorded as "taxes on production and imports" (category D2) directly paid to the rest of the world. However, in the *Revenue Statistics*, these receipts have always been recorded as tax receipts in the EU member states as opposed to receipts of the EU. They have therefore been included in the overall tax to GDP ratio figures of the member states. This is confirmed by the text of paragraphs 102 to 105 of the OECD *Interpretative Guide* in *Revenue Statistics 2015* set out in italics below.

Levies paid by member states of the European Union (EU)

102. *The levies paid by the member states of the EU take the form:*

- VAT own resources; and
- Specific levies which include:
  1. custom duties and levies on agricultural goods (5123);
  2. gross monetary compensation accounts (5123 if relating to imports and 5124 if relating to exports); and
  3. steel, coal, sugar and milk levies (5128).

103. *The custom duties collected by member states on behalf of the EU are recorded:*

- on a gross of collection fee basis;
- using figures adjusted so that duties are shown on a "final destination" as opposed to a "country of first entry" basis where such adjustments can be made. These adjustments concern in particular duties collected at important (sea) ports. Although the EU duties are collected by the authorities of the country of first entry, when possible these duties should be excluded from the revenue of the collecting country and be included in the revenue of the country of final destination.

104. *This is the specific EU levy that most clearly conforms to the attribution criterion described in §96 above. Consequently as from 1998, these amounts are footnoted as a memorandum item to the EU member state country tables in Chapter 3 and no longer shown under heading 5123. However,*

the figures are included in the total tax revenue figures on the top line for all the relevant years shown in the tables.

105. *The VAT own resources, which are determined by applying a rate not exceeding 1 per cent to an assessment basis specified in the Sixth Directive are more of a borderline case. They have some of the characteristics of a transfer (they are not derived from a clearly identifiable source of funds that are actually collected) and some of a tax (the amount of the transfer is determined by the receiving sub-sector of government). In this publication, they are not shown as a tax of the European Union (but as a tax of the EU member states), though the amounts involved are footnoted in the tables contained in Part IV.*

In ESA 2010, the VAT based third EU own resource is now recorded as a current transfer paid by the government of each member state to the Institutions of the EU. This contribution to the budget of the Institutions of the EU is now recorded under the heading "VAT and Gross National Income (GNI) based EU own resources" (category D76). The VAT-based third EU own resource (D761) and the GNI-based fourth EU own resource (D762) both represent contributions to the budget of the EU. The level of the contribution of each member state is based on the levels of their VAT base and their GNI respectively. The heading D76 also includes miscellaneous other contributions of the governments to the institutions of the EU (D763).

The consequence of this change is that the recording of the VAT based budget contribution no longer has any impact on the recording of tax revenues in the National Accounts. The change in the recording of the transfer means that the amounts of taxes on production and imports (D2) payable to the rest of the world will decrease.

There is no impact on the tax revenues recorded in the *Revenue Statistics* because the amount of the transfer was previously recorded as tax receipts in the EU member states. However the change does mean that any link between the VAT based third EU own resource and the presentation of the VAT revenues in the *Revenue Statistics 2016* publication has been removed. As a result:

- the references to VAT own resources have been deleted from the paragraph 102 of the *Interpretative Guide* in *Revenue Statistics 2015* shown above;
- paragraph 105 of the *Interpretative Guide* in *Revenue Statistics 2015* has been deleted entirely; and
- the VAT based third EU resource figures will no longer be shown in the footnotes to the individual country tables in Chapter 5 "Tax revenues by subsectors of general government" of the 2016 publication (i.e. the EU country tables among tables 5.13-5.47).

2.4. The treatment of revenues from fines and penalties

In the *Revenue Statistics*, "fines and penalties" paid in relation to the assessment and payment of taxes have traditionally been recorded as tax receipts. This topic is covered as follows in paragraph 15 of the *Interpretative Guide* in *Revenue Statistics 2015*.

"15. Receipts from fines and penalties paid for the infringement of regulations identified as relating to a particular tax and interest due on payments overdue in respect of a particular tax are recorded together with receipts from that tax. Other kinds of fines identifiable as relating to tax offences are classified in the residual heading 6000. Fines not relating to tax offences (e.g. for parking offences), or not identifiable as relating to tax offences, are not treated as taxes."

This approach was mirrored in the previous versions of the *GFSM, SNA, and ESA*. However, the revised versions adopt a different approach and state that, in principle, fines and penalties charged on tax offences should not be treated as taxes. They are instead considered to be compulsory current transfers. There is an exception in the case where it may not be possible to separate payments of fines or other penalties from the tax revenues to which they relate. In this case the fines and penalties are recorded together with the tax revenues. This topic is covered as follows in paragraph 5143 of the new *GFSM*.

"5143 In principle, fines and penalties charged on overdue taxes or penalties imposed for the attempted evasion of taxes should not be recorded as taxes. However, it may not be possible to separate payments of fines or other penalties from the taxes to which they relate. In this case, the fines and penalties relating to a particular tax are recorded together with that tax, and fines and penalties relating to unidentifiable taxes are classified as "other taxes (116)".

WP2 discussed at a meeting in 2016 whether to retain the existing classification in the *Interpretative Guide* or to move to the revised approach adopted by the other classifications. At this meeting, the following arguments were considered:

- it could be argued that the current draft of the *Interpretative Guide* would lead to better comparative statistics on tax revenues across countries; the approach adopted by the *GFSM, SNA, ESA* could lead to fines and penalties relating to tax offences being included in the tax revenue figures for one country because they could not be separately identified and excluded for another where the statistical systems enabled identification;
- on the other hand, it is questionable whether the OECD should adopt an alternative approach to the other classification systems on what is essentially a very small component of total revenues.

On balance, it was decided to amend the text in paragraph 15 of the *Interpretative Guide* quoted above to achieve consistency with the *GFSM, SNA* and *ESA*.

2.5. The classification of profits from fiscal monopolies

The new *GFSM* now specifically includes new paragraphs confirming that the concept of fiscal monopoly also applies to state lotteries and other gambling to the extent that they are devices to raise revenue rather than further the interests of public economic or social policy. This is despite the fact that they may compete with privately organised lotteries and other gambling. State lotteries were specifically excluded from this category in *GFSM 2001* as they are in the current version of the *Interpretative Guide*.

WP2 discussed whether to retain the existing classification in the Interpretative Guide or to adopt the revised approach adopted by the *GFSM*. It was decided to acknowledge the previous approach that the traditional concept of fiscal monopoly is not generally extended to include state lotteries, the profits of which are usually accordingly regarded as non-tax revenues. However, it was also decided to add new text to say that they can be included as tax revenues if the prime reason for their operation is to raise revenues to finance government expenditure. Paragraph 63 of the new *Interpretative Guide* has been amended to reflect this addition and the revised entry on fiscal monopolies, contained in paragraphs 61 to 63, is set out in Annex A to this chapter.

2.6. An imputed tax resulting from the operation of multiple exchange rate systems

New text is also included in paragraphs 5.88 to 5.90 of the new *GFSM* (see Part b. of Annex B to this chapter) about the recording of imputed taxes and subsidies resulting from the operation of multiple exchange rate systems by a central bank or other official agency. The inclusion of this item is consistent with both *SNA 2008* and *SNA 1993* which also classify these transactions as taxes and subsidies, however, it was not previously included in the calculation of tax revenues in the *GFSM 2001*.

This item has historically been excluded from the OECD definition of tax revenues and is one of four items listed in paragraph 83 of the new *Interpretative Guide* as areas where the *OECD classification of taxes* has differed from *SNA* concepts. It was decided that the *Interpretative Guide* should continue to exclude this item from tax revenues for three main reasons:

- the OECD's definitions are intended to reflect the perspectives of tax policy makers and tax administrators; the general approach is to exclude implicit or imputed taxes and subsidies from the definition of taxes;
- no payments of tax are actually made in practice so these amounts are not likely to be perceived as tax payments either by the market participants or governments;
- central banks are not generally considered to be part of the general government sector.

2.7. An imputed tax resulting from the central bank paying a rate of interest that is below other market rates on required reserves

Imputed taxes and subsidies resulting from the central bank imposing a rate of interest other than the market rates are also included as tax revenues for the first time in paragraph 5.70 of the new *GFSM*. The relevant text is set out in Part a. of Annex B. It is consistent with the approach adopted in *SNA 2008* where the classification is explained in paragraphs 7.122 to 7.126.

This item is directly analogous to the position relating to imputed taxes and subsidies resulting from the operation of multiple exchange rate systems discussed in Section 2.6 of this chapter. It was decided that it should also be excluded from the OECD definition of tax revenues for the same reasons.

2.8. Taxes on financial capital transactions

Taxes on financial and capital transactions (OECD Category 4400) are described in paragraph 47 of the new *Interpretative Guide*. They include taxes on the issue, transfer, purchase and sale of securities, taxes on cheques, and taxes levied on specific legal transactions such as validation of contracts and the sale of immovable property.

Both *the Interpretative Guide* and the *GFSM 2001* classified these revenues under the heading of taxes on property. However, in the new editions of the *GFSM, SNA and ESA,* they are treated as general taxes on goods and services – i.e. a tax on the services of the unit selling the asset. This would be equivalent to being a sub-heading under the OECD category 5000. After discussion, WP2 decided to retain the original classification as a tax on property in order to align with the principle of maintaining consistency with historical data series as far as it is possible to do so.

2.9. Conclusion

On the basis of the above, the differences between the *OECD Interpretative Guide* and the new editions of the *GFSM, SNA* and *ESA* are as listed below:

- OECD includes compulsory social security contributions paid to general government in total tax revenues. Imputed and voluntary contributions plus those paid to private funds are not treated as taxes.
- OECD excludes imputed taxes or subsidies resulting from the operation of official multiple exchange rates and from the central banks imposing a rate of interest on required reserves that is different from other market rates.
- There are differences in the treatment of non-wastable tax or payable credits.
- OECD classifies taxes on financial and capital transactions under the heading of property taxes whereas the other classification systems classify them as general taxes on goods and services.
- There are different points of view on whether or not some levies and fees are classified as taxes.

ANNEX A

5122 – Profits of Fiscal Monopolies: New text for Interpretative Guide

61. This sub-heading covers that part of the profits of fiscal monopolies which is transferred to general government or which is used to finance any expenditures considered to be government expenditures (see §18). Amounts are shown when they are transferred to general government or used to make expenditures considered to be government expenditures.

62. Fiscal monopolies reflect the exercise of the taxing power of government by the use of monopoly powers. Fiscal monopolies are non-financial public enterprises exercising a monopoly in most cases over the production or distribution of tobacco, alcoholic beverages, salt, matches, playing cards and petroleum or agricultural products (i.e. on the kind of products which are likely to be, alternatively or additionally, subject to the excises of 5121), to raise the government revenues which in other countries are gathered through taxes on dealings in such commodities by private business units. The government monopoly may be at the production stage or, as in the case of government-owned and controlled liquor stores, at the distribution stage.

63. Fiscal monopolies are distinguished from public utilities such as rail transport, electricity, post offices, and other communications, which may enjoy a monopoly or quasi-monopoly position but where the primary purpose is normally to provide basic services rather than to raise revenue for government. Transfers from such other public enterprises to the government are considered as non-tax revenues. The traditional concept of fiscal monopoly is not generally extended to include state lotteries, the profits of which are usually accordingly regarded as non-tax revenues. However, they can be included as tax revenues if the prime reason for their operation is to raise revenues to finance government expenditure. Fiscal monopoly profits are distinguished from export and import monopoly profits (5127) transferred from marketing boards or other enterprises dealing with international trade.

ANNEX B

IMF text adding implicit taxes and subsidies to their list of taxes

a. An implicit tax resulting from central bank paying a rate of interest that is below other market rates on required reserves

5.70. This category also includes the implicit taxes resulting from the central bank imposing a rate of interest other than the market rates. The central bank's main responsibility is to formulate and carry out monetary policy as part of economic policy. It therefore often acts differently than other financial corporations and generally has received the authority from government to impose its policies. In cases where the central bank uses its special powers to set interest rates that are out of line with market rates, the difference gives rise to an implicit tax and subsidy (see paragraph 6.89 and Box 6.2 for an illustration of recording these implicit taxes and subsidies). This procedure is analogous to and consistent with the practice of treating the difference between the market exchange rate and an alternative exchange rate imposed by the central bank as an implicit tax or subsidy (see paragraph 5.89).

b. An implicit tax resulting from the operation of a multiple exchange rate regime by the central bank or other official agency

Exchange profits

5.88. ***Exchange profits*** include the profits generated when the monopoly powers of government or monetary authorities are exercised to extract a margin between the purchase and sale prices of foreign exchange, other than to cover administrative costs. The revenue derived constitutes a compulsory levy extracted from both purchaser and seller of foreign exchange. Similarly, an implicit tax results from the operation of a multiple exchange rate regime by the central bank or other official agency. It is the common equivalent of an import duty and export duty levied in a single exchange rate system or of a tax on the sale or purchase of foreign exchange. As in the case of the profits of export or import fiscal monopolies, the revenue represents the exercise of monopoly powers for tax purposes and is included in tax revenues when received by government.

5.89. Under a multiple exchange rate regime, two or more exchange rates are applicable to different categories of transactions; the rates favor some categories and discourage others. The multiple rates influence the values and the undertaking of transactions expressed in domestic currency. The net proceeds as a result of these transactions are calculated as implicit taxes or subsidies (see paragraph 6.89). The amount of the implicit tax or subsidy for each transaction can be calculated as the difference between the value of the transaction in domestic currency at the actual exchange rate applicable and the value of the transaction at a unitary rate that is calculated as a weighted average of all official rates used for external transactions.

5.90. Exchange profits are often included in a lump sum payment from the monetary authorities to government. Such a lump sum payment should be disaggregated according to the nature of the components, and each component classified according to their nature. These lump sum payments may include components of dividends, exchange profits, interest and/or equity withdrawals. This category for exchange profits should not include any payments to government of exchange profits realised other than as a result of maintenance of an exchange rate differential. Also excluded from this category are any transfers to government of unrealised revaluation profits, which are in the nature of a book entry resulting from revaluation of foreign exchange or gold holdings for the owner. As discussed in paragraph 5.115, such payments to government based on holding gains are classified as a withdrawal of equity rather than a tax. Any operational profits transferred to government should be classified as *dividends* (see paragraph 5.111).

Revenue Statistics 2016
Statistiques des recettes publiques 2016

Chapitre 2

Étude spéciale : Questions actuelles sur la comptabilisation des recettes fiscales

2.1. Introduction

La publication de la version définitive du *Manuel de statistiques de finances publiques 2014 (Manuel SFP 2014 du FMI)* achève le cycle de parution des versions révisées des trois systèmes de classification qui, historiquement, avaient beaucoup de points communs avec la *Classification des impôts et le guide d'interprétation de l'OCDE* dans le domaine des recettes publiques :

- le *Manuel SFP 2014 du FMI* ;
- le *Système de comptabilité nationale (SCN) 2008* ;
- le *Système européen des comptes économiques intégrés 2010 (SEC)*.

Le degré de chevauchement de ces référentiels est illustré par un tableau de « transition » inclus dans le *Guide d'interprétation de l'OCDE*, qui décrit les liens entre la nomenclature employée dans la *Classification des impôts de l'OCDE* et les nomenclatures utilisées dans les autres systèmes de classification. La version la plus récente de ce tableau figure à l'Annexe A du présent rapport.

Les éditions les plus récentes des trois systèmes de classification incorporent quelques modifications des définitions et de la classification des recettes publiques par rapport aux versions précédentes. C'est pourquoi il a été nécessaire de revoir certaines sections du *Guide d'interprétation* dans les domaines où soit la méthodologie de définition des recettes fiscales a été modifiée, soit des changements substantiels ont été apportés aux commentaires explicatifs des autres systèmes de classification.

Le présent Rapport aborde les thèmes ci-après, qui concernent la méthodologie du *Guide d'interprétation de l'OCDE* :

- les crédits d'impôt récupérables et non récupérables ;
- les ressources propres de l'UE fondées sur la TVA dans le SEC 2010 ;
- la classification des recettes provenant des amendes et pénalités ;
- les bénéfices des monopoles fiscaux ;
- les impôts et subventions imputés résultant de la mise en œuvre de régimes de taux de change multiples ;
- les impôts et subventions imputés résultant de l'application par les banques centrales d'un taux d'intérêt différent de celui du marché ;
- les impôts sur transactions mobilières et immobilières.

2.2. Crédits d'impôt récupérables et non récupérables

2.a. Deux sortes de crédits d'impôt

Il existe deux types de crédits d'impôt :

- Les crédits d'impôt non récupérables (ou non remboursables) ne peuvent être utilisés que pour réduire ou éliminer le montant de l'impôt à payer. Ils ne peuvent donner lieu à un versement sous forme d'avantage monétaire au profit des contribuables, qu'ils soient imposables ou non. Ils sont donc équivalents aux abattements ou déductions fiscales.

- Au contraire, il existe deux sortes de crédits d'impôt récupérables (ou remboursables). L'une sert à réduire, voire éliminer, le montant de l'impôt à payer de la même manière qu'un crédit d'impôt non remboursable. L'autre peut donner lieu à un paiement direct au récipiendaire sous forme monétaire dès lors que le montant de l'avantage fiscal dépasse celui de l'impôt à payer.

2.b. La méthode employée par l'OCDE pour constater les crédits d'impôt récupérables et deux alternatives

La méthode employée par l'OCDE pour le classement des crédits d'impôt récupérables est décrite dans les paragraphes 19 et 20 du *Guide d'interprétation*. Elle prévoit que seule la fraction du crédit d'impôt récupérable qui sert à réduire ou éliminer le montant de l'impôt dû par un contribuable doit être déduite dans la déclaration des recettes fiscales. Elle est appelée « composante fiscale » ou « élément de dépense fiscale » du crédit d'impôt. À l'inverse, la fraction du crédit d'impôt qui excède le montant de l'impôt dû par ce contribuable et qui lui est payée est considérée comme une dépense et n'est pas déduite dans la déclaration des recettes fiscales. Cette partie est appelée « composante transfert » ou « élément de transfert ». C'est aussi cette approche qui a été suivie dans les versions antérieures du *Manuel SFP du FMI*, le *SCN* et le *SEC*.

Le tableau 2.1 livre des informations sur les crédits d'impôt récupérables en 2014 pour les pays qui les déclarent dans les *Statistiques des recettes publiques 2016* (bien qu'il soit possible que certains pays accordant des crédits d'impôt récupérables n'apparaissent pas dans ce tableau). Ce tableau indique le montant des crédits d'impôt récupérables et de leurs deux composantes, ainsi que les résultats de l'utilisation des chiffres pour calculer le montant des recettes fiscales et les ratios recettes fiscales-PIB. Il est construit selon les mêmes modalités que celui qui figure dans la Partie I des *Statistiques des recettes publiques 2014* intitulée « Commentaires sur les tendances des recettes fiscales ». Comme le montrent les colonnes 5 et 8, le traitement conforme au *Guide d'interprétation* est appelé « répartition ». Deux alternatives à la procédure de répartition sont également présentées :

- la « comptabilisation en chiffres nets », qui assimile les crédits d'impôt récupérables à des dispositions fiscales, de telle sorte que la totalité du crédit d'impôt réduit le montant des recettes fiscales déclarées, comme le montrent les colonnes 4 et 7 ;
- la « comptabilisation en chiffres bruts » en est l'exact opposé ; elle considère la totalité des crédits d'impôts récupérables comme des dépenses directes, de sorte que, comme le montrent les colonnes 6 et 9, ni l'élément de transfert, ni l'élément de dépense fiscale ne sont déduits des recettes fiscales.

Historiquement, l'application des règles du *Guide d'interprétation* énoncées dans ces paragraphes s'est heurtée à des difficultés pratiques, ce qui a entraîné un certain manque d'homogénéité des déclarations. Au surplus, la distinction conceptuelle entre dispositions fiscales et dépenses directes peut se révéler épineuse, si bien que des arguments recevables plaident pour les méthodes de traitement alternatives. Cette question a été examinée dans des Études spéciales apparaissant dans les éditions 2000 et 2001 des *Statistiques des recettes publiques*. Il n'existe donc pas de solution idéale quant à la manière dont il convient de traiter ces crédits d'impôts. Cependant, toute comparaison avec les

Tableau 2.1. **Effets des différents traitements possibles des crédits d'impôts récupérables, 2014**

	Non-wastable tax credits in millions of national currency			Total tax revenues in millions of national currency			Total tax revenues as a percentage of GDP		
	Total value	Transfer component	Tax expenditure component	Net basis	Split basis (per current guidance)	Gross basis	Net basis	Split basis (per current guidance)	Gross basis
	(1)	(2)	(3)	(4) = (5) – (2)	(5)	(6) = (5) + (3)	(7)	(8)	(9)
Australie	8 280	4 936	3 344	441 891	**446 827**	450 171	27.5	**27.8**	28.1
Autriche	560	245	315	141 232	**141 477**	141 792	42.7	**42.8**	42.9
Belgique	1 052	317	735	179 863	**180 180**	180 915	44.9	**45.0**	45.2
Canada	11 519	10 489	1 030	607 728	**618 217**	619 247	30.7	**31.2**	31.3
Chili	..	..	..	**29 145 219**	..	..	**19.8**	..	..
République tchèque	28 969	8 258	20 711	1 419 016	**1 427 274**	1 447 984	32.9	**33.1**	33.6
Danemark	5 495	275	5 220	962 909	**963 184**	968 404	49.6	**49.6**	49.9
France	21 243	8 375	12 868	965 005	**973 380**	986 248	45.1	**45.5**	46.1
Allemagne	41 514	14 541	26 974	1 054 718	**1 069 259**	1 096 233	36.1	**36.6**	37.5
Islande	1 162	1 000	162	773 263	**774 263**	774 425	38.9	**38.9**	38.9
Irlande	..	..	667	..	**55 453**	56 120	..	**28.7**	29.1
Israël	625	587	38	341 127	**341 714**	341 752	31.2	**31.2**	31.2
Italie	12 611	7 585	5 027	696 633	**704 217**	709 244	43.2	**43.7**	44.0
Luxembourg	217	..	..	..	..	**18 761**	..	..	**38.4**
Mexique	43 716	2 423	41 293	2 605 273	**2 607 696**	2 648 989	15.1	**15.2**	15.4
Nouvelle-Zélande	2 555	1 686	869	76 225	**77 911**	78 780	31.8	**32.5**	32.9
Norvège	1 467	1 275	380	1 218 594	**1 219 869**	1 220 249	38.6	**38.7**	38.7
République slovaque	263	..	..	..	..	**23 612**	..	..	**31.2**
Espagne	582	..	..	..	..	**352 394**	..	..	**33.8**
Royaume-Uni	31 432	28 005	3 427	556 464	**584 469**	587 896	30.5	**32.1**	32.3
États-Unis	144 640	99 810	44 830	4 400 720	**4 500 530**	4 545 360	25.3	**25.9**	26.1

Notes : En Autriche, le crédit d'impôt pour enfant à charge n'est pas considéré comme un crédit d'impôt dans les Statistiques des recettes publiques et est traité entièrement comme une provision de dépense.

Pour le Danemark, la France et l'Espagne, le total des recettes fiscales a été diminué du montant de tout transfert en capital représentant les recettes non collectées.

Certains crédits d'impôts récupérables au Canada ne peuvent pas être ventilés entre l'élément de transfert et l'élément de dépense fiscale. Leur valeur totale a été ajoutée à l'élément de transfert.

« .. » signifie non disponible.

ratios recettes fiscales-PIB qui se fonde sur les deux méthodes alternatives de comptabilisation de ces crédits d'impôt doit prendre en compte leurs inconvénients.

- Si la méthode de constatation sur la base des « chiffres bruts » garantit que le traitement des dépenses publiques consacrées aux prestations sociales liées au revenu d'activité et celui des crédits d'impôt récupérables sont comparables, elle ne garantit pas qu'il en va de même pour les crédits d'impôt récupérables et non récupérables. Par exemple, la transformation d'un crédit d'impôt non récupérable en crédit d'impôt récupérable peut aboutir à une forte augmentation des recettes déclarées, même si son coût budgétaire ou son impact sur les contribuables sont des plus modestes. En effet, les sommes qui, auparavant, étaient déduites des recettes fiscales seraient assimilées à des dépenses directes et, par conséquent, non déductibles.
- L'inconvénient le plus grave de la « comptabilisation sur la base du solde net » tient au fait qu'elle n'assure pas la comparabilité entre les pays qui accordent des crédits d'impôt récupérables et ceux qui n'en accordent pas. Cela vient de ce qu'elle minore les recettes fiscales des pays qui accordent des crédits d'impôt récupérables de montants qui seraient considérés comme des dépenses dans les pays recourant à des programmes de

dépenses comparables pour assurer des transferts au profit de ceux qui ne paient pas d'impôts. Au demeurant, toutes choses par ailleurs, et même si l'on ne prend en considération que les pays accordant des crédits d'impôt récupérables, la comptabilisation en solde net ferait apparaître des recettes fiscales moindres dans ceux qui procurent aux contribuables non imposables une aide plus généreuse au moyen de ces crédits. On peut donc en conclure que ces disparités peuvent donner une impression trompeuse quant au champ du système fiscal.

Le tableau 2.1 montre cependant que, à quelques exceptions près, le choix de la méthode de comptabilisation des crédits d'impôt récupérables n'a qu'une faible incidence sur le ratio recettes fiscales-PIB. Dans les pays pour lesquels des données sont disponibles, l'écart entre les ratios calculés sur la base du solde net et du montant brut n'est supérieur ou égal à un point qu'en Allemagne, en France, en Nouvelle-Zélande et au Royaume-Uni et il est supérieur ou égal à un demi-point en Australie, au Canada, aux États-Unis, en Italie et en République tchèque.

2.c. Une nouvelle méthodologie adoptée par le Manuel SFP du FMI, le SCN et le SEC

Le SCN 2008 est la première des révisions des trois systèmes de classification « associés » à avoir été publié. Ce document incorporait un changement des règles de classification des impôts et des prestations associées aux crédits d'impôt récupérables. Dorénavant, la totalité des crédits d'impôt récupérables est enregistrée comme une « dépense fiscale » ou, en d'autres termes, une subvention ou une prestation sociale sans égard pour la part qui vient en déduction du montant de l'impôt à payer et celle qui est versée directement aux bénéficiaires. Aujourd'hui, les impôts et prestations sont portés pour leur « montant brut » dans les comptes nationaux, ce qui signifie que les recettes indiqueront le montant total de l'impôt dû avant imputation des crédits d'impôt récupérables et que l'intégralité des crédits relevant des crédits d'impôt récupérables est incluse dans les subventions ou les prestations sociales.

Le *Manuel SFP du FMI 2014* et le *SEC 2010* ont repris ces changements introduits par le *SCN 2008*.

La révision de la classification des crédits d'impôt récupérables dans le *SCN 2008* a été motivée par un rapport du Conseil des normes comptables internationales du secteur public (IPSASB). IPSAS 23 – Recettes provenant des transactions autres que des échanges (impôts et transferts), paru en décembre 2006, contenait l'extrait ci-après, intitulé « dépenses payées au moyen de dispositions fiscales et de dépenses directes ». L'avis clairement exprimé selon lequel le montant de ces crédits d'impôt doit être comptabilisé dans son intégralité sous forme de dépenses a été débattu par le Groupe de travail inter-secrétariats sur la comptabilité nationale et le Groupe consultatif d'experts lors de la rédaction de SCN 2008. En conséquence, une décision de principe sur la comptabilisation intégrale de ces crédits d'impôt dans les dépenses a été adoptée pour la nouvelle version.

Dépenses payées au moyen de dispositions fiscales et dépenses directes

Les recettes fiscales seront calculées en chiffres bruts. Elles ne seront pas diminuées des dépenses payées au moyen de dispositions fiscales.

Dans certains pays, l'État voit dans la fiscalité un moyen commode de payer aux contribuables des prestations qui autrement seraient servies au moyen d'une autre méthode de paiement telle que l'envoi d'un chèque, un virement direct sur le compte bancaire du bénéficiaire ou le règlement d'une autre dépense pour le compte de celui-ci. Par exemple, une partie des primes d'assurance santé des résidents peut être acquittée par l'État afin de les inciter à souscrire ce type d'assurance, soit en réduisant le montant de l'impôt à payer par les intéressés, soit en effectuant un paiement par chèque, soit en versant directement une somme à la compagnie d'assurance. Dans ce cas, le paiement de cette somme est indépendant du fait que l'intéressé paie des impôts. Cette somme est donc une dépense de l'État et doit être comptabilisée séparément dans les états financiers. Les recettes fiscales doivent être majorées du montant de toutes les dépenses qui sont ainsi payées via le système fiscal.

Les recettes fiscales ne doivent pas être majorées des dépenses directes.

Dans la plupart des pays, l'État se sert de la fiscalité pour encourager certains comportements financiers et en dissuader d'autres. À titre d'illustration, dans certains pays les propriétaires sont autorisés à déduire les intérêts hypothécaires et les taxes foncières de leur revenu brut pour calculer leur revenu imposable. Ces avantages ne sont offerts qu'aux seuls contribuables. Si une entité (y compris une personne physique) ne paie pas d'impôts, elle ne peut prétendre à l'avantage. Ces types de concessions sont appelés dépenses fiscales. Les dépenses fiscales sont des recettes auxquelles renonce l'État et non des dépenses et elles ne donnent pas naissance à des entrées ou sorties de fonds ; autrement dit, elles ne créent pas d'actifs, dettes, revenus ou dépenses pour l'État qui perçoit les impôts.

La distinction entre dépenses payées au moyen de dispositions fiscales et dépenses directes se résume au fait que, s'agissant des premières, une somme est mise à la disposition des bénéficiaires indépendamment du fait qu'ils paient des impôts ou qu'ils fassent usage d'un mécanisme particulier pour les acquitter. IPSAS 1 « Présentation des états financiers » interdit de compenser les postes de recettes et de dépenses, sauf si cela est autorisé par une autre Norme. « Il n'est pas permis de compenser recettes fiscales et dépenses payées au moyen de dispositions fiscales. »

2.d. La classification des crédits d'impôt récupérables demeure inchangée dans le Guide d'interprétation de l'OCDE

Le Groupe de travail n° 2 du Comité des affaires fiscales sur l'analyse des politiques et les statistiques fiscales a décidé de reconduire à l'identique les lignes directrices existantes sur la déclaration des crédits d'impôt récupérables plutôt que de les modifier de manière à les aligner sur les versions révisées des autres sources statistiques. Les paragraphes suivants reviennent sur plusieurs points pris en compte lors des débats.

Le parti de préserver la cohérence entre les lignes directrices sur la présentation de l'information provenant de sources statistiques différentes à la seule fin de s'épargner la confusion que peut engendrer la combinaison de plusieurs approches présente des avantages évidents. Toutes choses égales par ailleurs, une possibilité consistait donc à réviser le *Guide d'interprétation* de manière à le rendre compatible avec les révisions du *Manuel SFP du FMI*, du SCN et du SEC.

Cependant, il existe aussi d'excellentes raisons de conserver les lignes directrices existantes, à savoir :

- Ces questions avaient été débattues au cours des réunions du Groupe de travail n° 2 en 1999 et 2000. Les participants avaient conclu que, du point de vue des architectes de la politique fiscale et de ceux qui l'administrent, les lignes directrices actuelles décrivent la procédure la plus appropriée pour déclarer les crédits d'impôts récupérables. Cette question a été examinée dans des Études spéciales figurant dans les éditions 2000 et 2001 des *Statistiques des recettes publiques*.

- Il n'est pas rare que, quand il existe des crédits d'impôt récupérables, la partie à payer ne représente qu'une proportion assez faible (et parfois très faible) de la valeur totale du crédit d'impôt. La méthode de déclaration en « montants bruts » exige que les règles de déclaration de la valeur totale du crédit d'impôt soient conditionnées par l'existence de cet élément de faible montant. De plus, dans certains cas, le passage d'un crédit d'impôt non récupérable à un crédit récupérable pourrait être causé par un changement administratif mineur. Dans ce cas, la déclaration en « montant brut » pourrait donner naissance à des situations indésirables dans lesquelles une variation substantielle des recettes fiscales est causée par un changement administratif dont l'incidence sur les contribuables ou le coût budgétaire est minime. En effet, les sommes qui auparavant étaient déduites des recettes fiscales seraient assimilées à des dépenses directes, si bien qu'elles ne seraient plus déductibles.
- L'adoption du mode de déclaration en « montant brut » engendrerait des incohérences entre les chiffres déclarés dans les *Statistiques des recettes publiques* et certains indicateurs de la publication *Les impôts sur les salaires*. Dans cette dernière, le calcul tant du taux moyen de l'impôt sur le revenu des personnes physiques (défini comme le montant de l'impôt sur le revenu divisé par le revenu brut) que du taux d'imposition moyen des personnes physiques (défini comme le montant de l'impôt sur le revenu plus la part salariale des cotisations sociales divisé par le revenu brut) déduit la valeur totale de tout crédit d'impôt récupérable du montant dû au titre de l'impôt sur le revenu.
- L'application des nouvelles lignes directrices aux dépenses fiscales en général est incohérente parce que la manière dont elles traitent les crédits d'impôt récupérables diverge de la comptabilisation des autres dépenses fiscales.
- En outre, la déclaration en « montant brut » engendrerait des écarts entre les *Statistiques des recettes publiques* et la déclaration des Dépenses Fiscales. Normalement, l'intégralité de la valeur de tout crédit d'impôt récupérable devrait être incluse dans tout rapport sur les Dépenses Fiscales. Si le principe de déclaration en « montants bruts » était appliqué à ces dernières, un grand nombre de crédits d'impôt accordés tant aux personnes physiques, au titre de l'impôt sur le revenu, qu'aux personnes morales, au titre de l'impôt sur les bénéfices, ne devraient pas être pris en compte.
- D'autres dispositions fiscales donnent lieu à une déduction des recettes fiscales (à savoir les abattements fiscaux ou les crédits d'impôt non récupérables) dans laquelle on pourrait voir un substitut à des programmes de dépenses. La comptabilisation en « montant brut » ne garantit pas la comparabilité entre ces dispositions et les crédits d'impôt récupérables.
- Il est vraisemblable que ces questions prendront de plus en plus d'importance car le coût total des crédits d'impôt récupérables augmente avec le temps dans un certain nombre de pays membres de l'OCDE.

Ces sujets ont été abordés de nouveau lors des réunions du Groupe de travail n° 2 en 2015 et 2016. Au vu des arguments présentés dans la section 2.d de ce chapitre, il a été décidé que, du point de vue des responsables de la politique fiscale et des économistes spécialistes de la fiscalité, il serait opportun de conserver les principes directeurs actuels de l'OCDE sur la présentation des crédits d'impôt récupérables dans les *Statistiques des recettes publiques* et de ne pas basculer vers les nouveaux principes directeurs intégrés dans le *Manuel SFP 2014 du FMI*, le SCN 2008 et le SEC 2010.

2.3. Les ressources propres de l'UE fondées sur la TVA dans le SEC 2010

Le SEC 2010 incorpore un changement du mode de comptabilisation des ressources propres de l'UE assises sur la TVA. Ce sont les montants de TVA collectés par les États membres de l'UE et reversés aux Institutions de cette dernière. Le montant de la contribution de chaque État membre dépend du niveau de son assiette de TVA.

Dans le SEC 1995, ces recettes fiscales étaient comptabilisées comme des « taxes sur la production et les importations » (catégorie D 2) payées directement au reste du monde. Cependant, dans les *Statistiques des recettes publiques*, ces recettes ont toujours été considérées comme des recettes fiscales dans les États membres de l'UE et non comme des recettes de l'UE. C'est pourquoi elles ont été incluses dans le ratio recettes fiscales-PIB des États membres. Cette pratique est confirmée par le texte des paragraphes 102 à 105 du *Guide d'interprétation de l'OCDE* dans l'édition 2015 des *Statistiques des recette publiques* qui est cité plus bas en italiques.

Prélèvements effectués par les États membres de l'Union européenne (UE)

102. *Les prélèvements effectués par les États membres de l'Union européenne revêtent plusieurs formes :*

- les ressources propres fondées sur la TVA ;
- et les prélèvements spécifiques, qui comprennent :
  1. les droits de douane et les prélèvements agricoles (5123) ;
  2. les montants compensatoires monétaires bruts (5123 s'ils concernent les importations et 5124 s'ils concernent les exportations) ; et
  3. les prélèvements de la CECA, les cotisations sucre et les taxes de co-responsabilité sur le lait (5128).

103. *Les droits de douane collectés par les États membres pour le compte de l'UE sont comptabilisés :*

- sur une base qui ne tient pas compte des droits d'encaissement ;
- en utilisant des chiffres corrigés de manière à exprimer les droits sur la base de la « destination finale » et non du « pays de première entrée » lorsque de telles corrections sont possibles. Ces corrections concernent en particulier les droits prélevés dans des ports (maritimes) importants. Bien que les droits de l'UE soient prélevés par les autorités du pays de première entrée, ils doivent dans la mesure du possible être déduits des recettes du pays qui les recouvre et inclus dans celles du pays de destination finale.

104. *Ces droits de l'UE sont le plus clairement conformes au critère d'attribution décrit au §96 ci-dessus. En conséquence, à partir de 1998, ces montants apparaissent dans une note de bas de page à titre de rubrique « Pour mémoire » dans les tableaux des États membres de l'UE (chapitre 3) et ne figurent plus sous la rubrique 5123. Toutefois, ces montants sont inclus dans les grands tableaux de recettes fiscales à la ligne supérieure pour toutes les années indiquées dans les tableaux.*

105. *Les ressources de TVA qui sont déterminées par l'application d'un taux ne pouvant excéder 1 % d'une assiette précisée dans la 6*[e] *Directive des Communautés constituent un cas particulier. Elles ont en effet certaines caractéristiques d'une subvention (elles ne proviennent pas d'une source*

clairement identifiable de fonds effectivement collectés à cet effet) et certaines autres d'un impôt (le montant de la subvention est fixé par le sous-secteur d'administration bénéficiaire). Dans cette publication, ces ressources ne figurent pas comme un impôt de l'Union européenne (mais comme un impôt des États membres de l'Union) bien que les montants en question soient indiqués en note de bas de page dans le partie IV.

Dans le SEC 2010, les ressources propres de l'UE basées sur la TVA sont dorénavant comptabilisées comme un transfert courant payé par chaque État membre aux Institutions de l'UE. Cette contribution au budget des Institutions de l'UE est aujourd'hui enregistrée sous la rubrique « TVA et ressources propres de l'UE fondées sur le revenu national brut (RNB) » (catégorie D76). La troisième ressource propre de l'UE fondée sur la TVA (D761) et la quatrième ressource propre de l'UE fondée sur le revenu national brut (D762) représentent des contributions au budget de l'UE. Le niveau de la contribution de chaque État membre dépend respectivement du niveau de son assiette de TVA et de son RNB. La rubrique D76 englobe aussi diverses autres contributions des États aux Institutions de l'UE (D763).

Ce changement a pour conséquence que la constatation de la contribution au budget qui est fondée sur la TVA n'a plus aucune incidence sur celle des recettes fiscales dans les Comptes nationaux. La modification de la procédure de comptabilisation du transfert signifie que le montant des taxes sur la production et les importations (D2) dues au reste du monde diminuera.

L'incidence sur les recettes fiscales déclarées dans les *Statistiques des recettes publiques* est nulle parce que le montant du transfert était auparavant constaté en tant que recettes fiscales dans les États membres de l'UE. Cependant, ce changement ne veut pas dire que tout lien entre les ressources propres de l'UE fondées sur la TVA et la présentation des recettes de TVA dans l'édition 2016 des *Statistiques des recettes publiques* a disparu. De ce fait :

- les références aux ressources propres fondées sur la TVA ont été retirées du paragraphe 102 du *Guide d'interprétation* de l'édition 2015 des *Statistiques des recettes publiques* figurant plus haut ;
- le paragraphe 105 du *Guide d'interprétation* de l'édition 2015 des *Statistiques des recettes publiques* a été supprimé dans sa totalité ;
- et les chiffres sur les ressources propres de l'UE fondées sur la TVA ne seront plus indiqués dans les notes de bas de page sur les tableaux par pays du chapitre 5 « Recettes fiscales par sous-secteurs d'administration » dans la publication 2016 (c'est-à-dire, dans les Tables 5.13 to 5.47 qui concernent les pays membres de l'UE).

2.4. Le traitement des recettes provenant des amendes et pénalités

Dans les *Statistiques des recettes publiques*, les « amendes et pénalités » acquittées au titre de l'établissement et du recouvrement des impôts étaient traditionnellement incluses dans les recettes fiscales. Cette question est abordée comme suit dans le paragraphe 15 du *Guide d'interprétation* dans les *Statistiques des recettes publiques* 2015.

« 15. Les recettes provenant d'amendes et pénalités acquittées pour infraction aux réglementations relatives à un impôt particulier et les intérêts de retard afférents au dit impôt ont été enregistrées avec les recettes procurées par cet impôt. Mais les autres catégories d'amendes identifiables comme se rapportant à des infractions fiscales sont classées au poste résiduel 6000. Les amendes qui ne concernent pas des infractions fiscales (comme les infractions de stationnement), ou qui ne sont pas identifiables en tant que telles, ne sont pas considérées comme des impôts. »

Cette approche a été suivie dans les versions antérieures du *Manuel SFP du FMI*, le *SCN* et le *SEC*. Cependant, les versions révisées adoptent une autre démarche et posent le principe que les amendes et pénalités infligées au titre d'infractions fiscales ne doivent pas être assimilées à des impôts. Elles sont considérées comme des transferts courants obligatoires. Il est fait exception à cette règle dans le cas où il n'est pas possible de distinguer le paiement des amendes et autres pénalités des impôts auxquels elles se rapportent. Ces amendes et pénalités sont alors comptabilisées avec les recettes de ces impôts. Cette question est abordée comme suit dans le paragraphe 5.143 du nouveau *Manuel SFP*.

« 5.143. En principe, les amendes et pénalités infligées au titre des arriérés d'impôts ou de pénalités pour tentative d'évasion fiscale ne doivent pas être comptabilisées comme des impôts. Cependant, il peut être impossible de distinguer le paiement des amendes et autres pénalités des impôts auxquels elles se rapportent. Dans ce cas, les amendes et pénalités relatives à un impôt donné sont comptabilisées avec celui-ci et les amendes et pénalités relatives à des impôts non identifiables sont classées dans les « autres impôts (116) ».

Le Groupe de travail n° 2 s'est demandé, au cours d'une réunion tenue en 2016, s'il convient de conserver la classification actuelle du *Guide d'interprétation* ou de basculer vers l'approche révisée qui a été retenue pour les autres classifications. Les arguments ci-après ont été pris en considération durant cette réunion :

- on pourrait soutenir que la version actuelle du *Guide d'interprétation* donnerait de meilleures statistiques comparatives sur les recettes fiscales d'un pays à l'autre ; le raisonnement adopté par le *Manuel SFP*, le *SCN* et le *SEC* pourrait aboutir à ce que les amendes et pénalités se rapportant à des infractions fiscales soient incluses dans les recettes fiscales d'un pays parce qu'elles n'ont pu être identifiées séparément et exclues de celles d'un autre parce que son appareil statistique a permis de les identifier ;
- d'un autre côté, il n'est pas interdit de se demander si l'OCDE ne devrait pas adopter une approche alternative vis-à-vis des autres systèmes de classification pour cette composante des recettes qui, en tout état de cause, n'en représente qu'une fraction infime.

Après mûre réflexion, il a été décidé de modifier l'énoncé du paragraphe 15 du *Guide d'interprétation* mentionné ci-dessus de manière à le rendre homogène avec le *Manuel SFP*, le *SCN* et le *SEC*.

2.5. La classification des bénéfices des monopoles fiscaux

Le nouveau *Manuel SFP* s'est enrichi de paragraphes confirmant que la notion de monopole fiscal s'applique aussi aux loteries et autres paris parce que ce sont des outils destinés à procurer des recettes à la puissance publique plutôt qu'à mettre en œuvre la politique économique ou sociale. Cette position a été adoptée nonobstant le fait que ces monopoles peuvent être en concurrence avec des loteries et officines de paris privés. Les loteries d'État étaient expressément exclues de cette catégorie dans le *Manuel SFP 2001* et le sont aussi dans la version actuelle du *Guide d'interprétation*.

Le Groupe de travail n° 2 s'est demandé s'il convient de conserver la classification actuelle du *Guide d'interprétation* ou de basculer vers l'approche révisée qui a été retenue par le *Manuel SFP*. Il a été décidé de prendre acte du raisonnement suivi auparavant, à savoir que la notion traditionnelle de monopole fiscal ne s'étend généralement pas aux loteries nationales, dont les bénéfices sont par conséquent considérés comme des recettes non fiscales. Néanmoins, il a aussi été décidé d'insérer un passage précisant qu'ils peuvent être inclus dans les recettes fiscales si leur existence est motivée principalement par le souci de procurer des recettes à l'État. Le paragraphe 63 du nouveau *Guide d'interprétation* a été modifié de manière à incorporer cet ajout ; la nouvelle version des paragraphes 61 à 63 qui se rapportent aux monopoles fiscaux figure dans l'Annexe A du présent chapitre.

2.6. Les impôts imputés résultant de la mise en œuvre de régimes de taux de change multiples

De nouvelles mentions ont été insérées dans les paragraphes 5.88 à 5.90 du nouveau *Manuel SFP* (voir la Partie b. de l'Annexe B au présent chapitre) au sujet de la constatation des impôts et subventions implicites résultant de la mise en œuvre d'un régime de taux de change multiples par une banque centrale ou un autre organisme officiel. L'inclusion de ce passage concorde avec les *SCN* tant de *2008* que de *1993*, qui considéraient aussi ces transactions comme des impôts et subventions ; cependant, elles n'étaient pas incluses dans le calcul des recettes fiscales par le *Manuel SFP 2001*.

Cet élément, qui avait été traditionnellement exclu de la définition des recettes fiscales par l'OCDE, est, avec trois autres, signalé dans le paragraphe 83 du nouveau *Guide d'interprétation* comme un domaine dans lequel la *classification des impôts par l'OCDE* s'écarte de celle qui a été retenue dans le *SCN*. Il a été décidé que le *Guide d'interprétation* devait continuer à exclure cette composante des recettes fiscales pour trois raisons principales :

- les définitions de l'OCDE ont pour but de refléter le point de vue des architectes de la politique fiscale et de ceux qui l'administrent ; le principe général consiste à exclure les impôts et subventions implicites et imputés de la définition des impôts ;
- comme, en pratique, il n'y a aucun paiement d'impôt, il est peu probable que leur montant soit perçu sous forme d'impôts, que ce soit par les acteurs du marché ou par les États ;
- en général, les banques centrales ne sont pas considérées comme faisant partie des administrations publiques.

2.7. Impôt imputé résultant du fait que la banque centrale paie un taux d'intérêt inférieur aux taux de marché sur les réserves obligatoires

Les impôts et subventions imputés résultant du fait que la banque centrale applique un taux d'intérêt différent des taux de marché sont aussi inclus dans les recettes fiscales pour la première fois dans le paragraphe 5.70 du nouveau *Manuel SFP*. Cette mention figure dans la Partie a. de l'Annexe B. Elle s'accorde avec la démarche suivie dans le *SCN 2008*, dont la classification est expliquée dans les paragraphes 7.122 à 7.126.

Cet élément est directement calqué sur la logique des impôts et subventions imputés résultant de l'existence de régimes de change à taux multiples qui a été discutée dans la section 2.6 de la présente Étude spéciale. Il a été décidé pour les mêmes motifs qu'il devrait aussi être exclu de la définition des recettes fiscales de l'OCDE.

2.8. Impôts sur transactions mobilières et immobilières

Les impôts sur les transactions mobilières et immobilières (catégorie 4400 de l'OCDE) sont décrits dans le paragraphe 47 du nouveau *Guide d'interprétation*. Ils comprennent les taxes sur l'émission, la mutation, l'achat et la vente de titres, les taxes sur les chèques et les impôts frappant certaines opérations juridiques telles que l'homologation de contrats et la cession de biens immobiliers.

Le *Guide d'interprétation* comme le *Manuel SFP 2001* ont tous deux classé ces recettes dans la rubrique des impôts sur le patrimoine. Mais dans les nouvelles versions du *Manuel SFP*, du *SCN* et du *SEC*, elles sont assimilées aux impôts généraux sur les biens et services, c'est-à-dire à un impôt sur les services de l'unité qui vend un actif. Ce procédé est l'équivalent d'un sous-groupe de la catégorie 5000 de l'OCDE. Le Groupe de travail n° 2 a décidé à l'issue d'un débat de conserver la classification d'origine (impôt sur le patrimoine) par souci de préserver dans toute la mesure du possible la cohérence avec les séries statistiques historiques.

2.9. Conclusion

Au vu de ce qui précède, les différences entre Le *Guide d'interprétation de l'OCDE* et les nouvelles éditions du *Manuel SFP*, du *SCN* et du *SEC* sont recensées ci-dessous.

- L'OCDE inclut les cotisations de sécurité sociale payées aux administrations publiques dans le montant total des recettes fiscales. Les cotisations imputées et volontaires et celles qui sont payées à des fonds privés ne sont pas considérées comme des impôts.
- L'OCDE exclut les impôts et subventions imputés qui résultent de l'existence de taux de change officiels multiples et de l'application par la banque centrale d'un taux d'intérêt différent des taux de marché aux réserves obligatoires.
- Il existe des disparités dans le traitement des crédits d'impôt récupérables.
- L'OCDE classe les impôts sur les transactions mobilières et immobilières dans la rubrique des impôts sur le patrimoine, tandis que les autres systèmes de classification les incluent dans les impôts généraux sur les biens et services.
- Les points de vue divergent quant à l'inclusion ou non de certains prélèvements et redevances dans les impôts.

ANNEXE A

5122 – Bénéfices des monopoles fiscaux : Nouvelle formulation pour le *Guide d'interprétation*

61. Ce sous-groupe recouvre la partie des bénéfices des monopoles fiscaux qui est transférée aux administrations publiques ou qui sert à financer des dépenses considérées comme des dépenses publiques (voir §18). Les montants sont comptabilisés lorsqu'ils sont transférés aux administrations publiques ou utilisés pour effectuer des dépenses considérées comme des dépenses publiques.

62. Les monopoles fiscaux reflètent l'exercice du pouvoir d'imposition de l'État par l'intermédiaire du monopole. Les monopoles fiscaux sont des entreprises publiques non financières qui, dans la plupart des cas, exercent un monopole sur la production ou la distribution du tabac, des boissons alcoolisées, du sel, des allumettes, des cartes à jouer et des produits agricoles ou pétroliers (c'est-à-dire sur des types de produits qui peuvent être soumis, principalement ou accessoirement, aux droits d'accise visés au poste 5121) pour procurer à l'État des recettes publiques qui, dans d'autres pays, sont obtenues par le biais d'impôts frappant les transactions sur ces produits d'entreprises privées. Le monopole d'État peut être exercé au stade de la production, ou au stade de la distribution comme dans le cas des magasins de vente de boissons alcoolisées qui appartiennent à l'État ou sont contrôlés par lui.

63. Les monopoles fiscaux sont différents des services publics, comme les chemins de fer, l'électricité, les postes et autres moyens de communication, qui peuvent avoir une position de monopole ou de quasi-monopole, mais dont l'objet principal est, normalement, de fournir des services essentiels et non pas de procurer des recettes à l'État. Les transferts à l'administration de ces autres entreprises publiques sont considérés comme des recettes non fiscales. La notion traditionnelle de monopole fiscal n'a pas été élargie pour inclure les loteries nationales, dont les bénéfices sont donc considérés comme des recettes non fiscales. Néanmoins, ils peuvent être inclus dans les recettes fiscales si leur existence répond principalement à l'objectif de procurer à l'État des recettes destinées à financer des dépenses publiques. On distingue les bénéfices des monopoles fiscaux des bénéfices des monopoles d'exportation et d'importation (5127), qui sont transférés des offices de commercialisation ou d'autres entreprises s'occupant du commerce international.

ANNEXE B

Texte du FMI incorporant les impôts et subventions implicites à sa nomenclature des impôts

a. Impôt implicite résultant du fait que la banque centrale paie un taux d'intérêt inférieur aux taux de marché sur les réserves obligatoires

5.70. Cette catégorie comprend aussi les impôts implicites résultant de l'application par la banque centrale d'un taux d'intérêt différent de ceux du marché. La responsabilité principale d'une banque centrale est de définir et de mener une politique monétaire qui s'intègre dans la politique économique. C'est pourquoi elle se comporte souvent différemment des autres sociétés financières et que, en général, elle est investie par l'État de l'autorité nécessaire pour appliquer sa politique. Si une banque centrale fait usage de son pouvoir de fixer les taux d'intérêt à un niveau différent de ceux du marché, l'écart qui en résulte crée un impôt et une subvention implicites (voir le paragraphe 6.89 et l'encadré 6.2 pour une illustration de la comptabilisation de ces impôts et subventions implicites). Cette procédure est analogue et conforme à la pratique consistant à traiter la différence entre le taux de change du marché et un taux de change alternatif imposé par la banque centrale comme un impôt ou une subvention implicite (voir le paragraphe 5.89).

b. Impôt implicite résultant de la mise en œuvre d'un régime de change à taux multiples par la banque centrale ou un autre organisme officiel

Gains de change

5.88. ***Les gains de change*** désignent les bénéfices résultant de l'exercice par l'État ou les autorités monétaires de leur monopole afin de dégager une marge entre les prix d'achat et de vente de devises en sus de la marge nécessaire pour couvrir les frais administratifs. Les recettes qui en résultent constituent un prélèvement obligatoire imposé à l'acheteur comme au vendeur de devises. De même, l'application d'un régime de taux de change multiples par la banque centrale ou tout autre organisme officiel génère un impôt implicite. Il s'apparente à une taxe sur l'achat ou la vente de devises ou à un droit à l'importation et à l'exportation perçu dans un régime de taux de change unique. Comme les bénéfices des monopoles fiscaux sur les importations ou les exportations, ces recettes proviennent de l'exercice d'un pouvoir de monopole fiscal et sont comptabilisées comme recettes fiscales au moment où elles sont reçues par les administrations publiques.

5.89. Dans un régime de taux de change multiples, plusieurs taux de change sont appliqués à différentes catégories de transactions ; ils en favorisent certaines et en découragent d'autres. Les taux de change multiples influent sur la valeur des transactions exprimées en monnaie nationale et les dissuadent ou les encouragent. Le produit net issu de ces transactions est comptabilisé comme un impôt ou une subvention implicite (voir le paragraphe 6.89). Le montant de l'impôt ou de la subvention implicite est égal, pour chaque transaction, à la différence entre la valeur de cette transaction en monnaie nationale au taux de change effectif en vigueur et sa valeur déterminée à un taux unitaire correspondant à la moyenne pondérée de tous les taux de change officiels employés pour les transactions externes.

5.90. Les gains de change sont fréquemment inclus dans un paiement forfaitaire des autorités monétaires à l'État. Ce paiement forfaitaire doit être ventilé en fonction de la nature de ses composantes, dont chacune doit être classée selon sa nature. Le paiement forfaitaire peut comporter des dividendes, des gains de change, des intérêts et/ou des prélèvements en capital. Ce type de gains de change ne doit inclure aucun paiement à l'État au titre des gains de change imputables à des raisons autres que l'existence d'un différentiel de taux de change. Il exclut aussi tout transfert à l'État de plus-values de réévaluation non réalisées qui, par nature, sont des opérations comptables motivées par la réévaluation de réserves d'or ou de devises. Comme l'indique le paragraphe 5.115, ces versements à l'État en fonction de gains de détention sont considérés comme des prélèvements en capital plutôt que comme des impôts. Tout bénéfice opérationnel transféré à l'État doit être classé dans les *dividendes* (voir le paragraphe 5.111).

Revenue Statistics 2016
Statistiques des recettes publiques 2016

Chapter 3

Tax levels and tax structures, 1965-2015

Chapitre 3

Niveaux et structures des impôts, 1965-2015

3.1. Comparative tables, 1965-2014

In all of the following tables the symbol (..) indicates not available/or not applicable. The main series in this volume cover the years 1965 to 2014. Figures referring to 1966-1979, 1981-89, 1991-99, 2001-06 and 2010 have been omitted because of lack of space. A complete series is, however, available on line. Data for 1955 and 1960 (for nineteen OECD countries) are provided in Part V of the 1998 edition of this Report.

The Gross Domestic Product (GDP) figures are based on the 2008 System of National Accounts (SNA) for all OECD countries except Chile, Japan and Turkey.

3.1. Tableaux comparatifs, 1965-2014

Dans tous les tableaux suivants, le symbole (..) signifie que l'information n'est pas disponible ou qu'elle n'est pas significative. La principale série chronologique des statistiques de recettes fiscales couvre les années 1965 à 2014. Les chiffres de 1966-79, 1981-89, 1991-99, 2001-06 et 2010 ont été omis pour des raisons d'espace. Une série complète est cependant disponible en ligne. La Partie V dans l'édition 1998 de ce Rapport fournit des données pour les années 1955 et 1960 (pour dix-neuf pays de l'OCDE).

Les chiffres du Produit Intérieur Brut (PIB) se fondent sur le Système de comptabilité nationale de 2008 (SCN 2008) pour tous les pays membres de l'OCDE, à l'exception du Chili, du Japon et de la Turquie.

Treatment of capital transfers. Footnote 1 in Table 3.1 to 3.35 refers to the treatment of the capital transfers that some countries make to account for taxes that have been assessed but not collected. The capital transfer has been subtracted from the total tax revenue and this reduction has been allocated between tax headings in proportion to their tax revenues.

This applies to the following countries:

- Denmark from 1971.
- France from 1992.
- Greece for 1999 and 2000.
- Spain from 2000.

Traitements des transferts en capital. La note de bas de page n° 1 des Table 3.1 to 3.35 se réfère au traitement des transferts en capital que certains pays effectuent pour tenir compte des impôts qui ont été évalués mais non recouvrés. Le transfert en capital a été soustrait des recettes fiscales totales et cette réduction a été répartie entre les différentes rubriques en pourcentage de leurs recettes.

C'est le cas pour les pays suivants :

- Danemark à partir de 1971.
- France à partir de 1992.
- Grèce pour 1999 et 2000.
- Espagne à partir de 2000.

Table 3.1. **Total tax revenue as % of gross domestic product at market prices, 2014**
Tableau 3.1. **Total des recettes fiscales en % du produit intérieur brut aux prix du marché, 2014**

	Total Tax Revenue / Total des recettes fiscales	Excluding social security / Sécurité sociale non comprise
Australia / Australie	27.8	27.8
Austria / Autriche	42.8	28.2
Belgium / Belgique	45.0	30.8
Canada	31.2	26.5
Chile / Chili	19.8	18.3
Czech Republic / République tchèque	33.1	18.6
Denmark / Danemark[1]	49.6	49.5
Estonia / Estonie	32.4	21.5
Finland / Finlande	43.8	31.2
France[1]	45.5	28.5
Germany / Allemagne[2]	36.6	22.6
Greece / Grèce	35.8	25.5
Hungary / Hongrie	38.2	25.7
Iceland / Islande	38.9	35.2
Ireland / Irlande	28.7	23.7
Israel / Israël	31.2	26.1
Italy / Italie	43.7	30.7
Japan / Japon	32.0	19.3
Korea / Corée	24.6	18.0
Latvia / Lettonie	28.9	20.5
Luxembourg	38.4	27.3
Mexico / Mexique	15.2	12.0
Netherlands / Pays-Bas	37.5	22.7
New Zealand / Nouvelle-Zélande	32.5	32.5
Norway / Norvège	38.7	28.8
Poland / Pologne	32.1	19.9
Portugal	34.2	25.2
Slovak Republic / République slovaque	31.2	17.9
Slovenia / Slovénie	36.5	22.1
Spain / Espagne[1]	33.8	22.2
Sweden / Suède	42.8	32.9
Switzerland / Suisse	27.0	20.3
Turkey / Turquie	28.8	20.6
United Kingdom / Royaume-Uni	32.1	26.1
United States / États-Unis	25.9	19.7
Unweighted average / Moyenne non pondérée		
OECD Average / Moyenne OCDE	**34.2**	**25.1**

1. The total tax revenue has been reduced by the amount of any capital transfer that represents uncollected taxes. The capital transfer has been allocated between tax headings in proportion to the reported tax revenue.
2. From 1991, the figures relate to the united Germany.
1. Le total des recettes fiscales a été diminué du montant de tout transfert en capital représentant les impôts non perçus. Le transfert en capital a été réparti entre les différentes rubriques en proportion des recettes fiscales.
2. Depuis 1991, les chiffres se rapportent à l'Allemagne unifiée.

StatLink http://dx.doi.org/10.1787/888933416267

Table 3.2. **Total tax revenue as % of GDP, 1965-2014**
Tableau 3.2. **Total des recettes fiscales en % du PIB, 1965-2014**

	1965	1966	1967	1968	1969	1970	1971	1972	1973	1974
Australia / Australie	20.6	19.9	20.4	20.4	20.7	21.1	21.9	21.4	22.5	24.7
Austria / Autriche	33.6	34.3	34.2	34.2	34.7	33.7	34.3	34.8	34.9	35.9
Belgium / Belgique	30.6	32.7	33.4	34.2	34.4	33.2	34.4	34.2	35.3	36.2
Canada	25.2	26.3	27.3	28.1	30.3	30.3	29.8	30.3	29.8	32.2
Chile / Chili	..	..	..	..	..	..	..	..	..	..
Czech Republic / République tchèque	..	..	..	..	..	..	..	..	..	..
Denmark / Danemark[1]	29.1	29.9	30.4	33.2	32.9	37.3	40.0	39.5	38.9	40.7
Estonia / Estonie	..	..	..	..	..	..	..	..	..	..
Finland / Finlande	30.0	31.2	32.0	32.4	31.0	31.2	32.8	33.2	34.0	33.3
France[1]	33.6	33.4	33.7	33.8	34.4	33.6	33.1	33.5	33.5	33.6
Germany / Allemagne[2]	31.6	32.2	32.2	32.2	33.9	31.5	32.0	33.5	35.0	34.9
Greece / Grèce[1]	17.1	18.4	19.2	19.9	19.7	19.2	19.0	18.9	17.4	18.3
Hungary / Hongrie	..	..	..	..	..	..	..	..	..	..
Iceland / Islande	25.5	..	..	..	..	26.7	..	..	..	..
Ireland / Irlande	24.5	26.5	27.0	27.4	28.1	27.6	28.6	27.4	27.5	28.0
Israel / Israël	..	..	..	..	..	..	..	..	..	..
Italy / Italie	24.7	24.5	25.3	26.1	25.5	24.8	25.5	25.4	23.1	24.2
Japan / Japon	17.8	17.2	17.7	17.9	18.3	19.2	19.5	20.1	21.8	22.3
Korea / Corée	..	..	..	..	..	..	..	12.4	12.0	13.1
Latvia / Lettonie	..	..	..	..	..	..	..	..	..	..
Luxembourg	26.4	26.1	26.7	25.9	26.0	22.5	24.7	25.2	25.5	26.4
Mexico / Mexique	..	..	..	..	..	..	..	..	..	..
Netherlands / Pays-Bas	30.9	32.2	33.1	33.8	32.6	33.4	34.8	35.9	36.9	37.3
New Zealand / Nouvelle-Zélande	23.2	23.9	25.9	22.5	23.5	25.1	24.1	25.6	26.3	29.4
Norway / Norvège	29.4	30.6	32.4	33.3	34.6	34.3	36.7	38.6	39.0	38.6
Poland / Pologne	..	..	..	..	..	..	..	..	..	..
Portugal	15.7	16.1	16.7	16.8	17.4	17.6	17.3	17.1	16.7	17.1
Slovak Republic / République slovaque	..	..	..	..	..	..	..	..	..	..
Slovenia / Slovénie	..	..	..	..	..	..	..	..	..	..
Spain / Espagne[1]	14.3	13.3	16.5	15.6	16.0	15.5	15.8	16.6	17.2	16.6
Sweden / Suède	31.4	32.1	32.9	34.8	35.7	35.7	36.4	37.6	36.9	38.0
Switzerland / Suisse	16.6	17.2	17.2	18.0	18.9	18.2	17.9	18.3	20.2	20.9
Turkey / Turquie	10.6	10.7	11.4	11.3	12.2	9.3	10.7	10.8	11.3	10.5
United Kingdom / Royaume-Uni	29.3	30.0	31.8	33.0	34.7	35.0	33.1	31.6	29.7	32.8
United States / États-Unis	23.5	23.8	24.8	24.3	26.6	25.7	23.9	24.4	24.4	25.2
Unweighted average / Moyenne non pondérée										
OECD Average / Moyenne OCDE	**24.8**	**25.3**	**26.2**	**26.5**	**27.0**	**26.7**	**27.2**	**26.9**	**27.1**	**27.9**

StatLink http://dx.doi.org/10.1787/888933416270

Table 3.2. **Total tax revenue as % of GDP, 1965-2014** *(cont.)*
Tableau 3.2. **Total des recettes fiscales en % du PIB, 1965-2014** *(suite)*

	1975	1976	1977	1978	1979	1980	1981	1982	1983	1984
Australia / Australie	25.4	25.6	25.4	24.6	25.2	26.2	26.4	26.9	26.1	27.7
Austria / Autriche	36.4	36.3	36.6	38.8	38.2	38.7	39.7	38.5	38.2	39.9
Belgium / Belgique	38.7	38.9	40.8	41.4	42.2	40.5	40.8	42.0	42.7	43.4
Canada	31.4	30.9	30.1	29.8	29.6	30.4	32.7	32.5	31.8	31.8
Chile / Chili	..	..	..	..	..	..	..	..	..	..
Czech Republic / République tchèque	..	..	..	..	..	..	..	..	..	..
Denmark / Danemark[1]	37.0	37.9	38.3	39.5	40.5	41.3	41.0	39.9	41.5	42.6
Estonia / Estonie	..	..	..	..	..	..	..	..	..	..
Finland / Finlande	36.1	39.6	39.8	36.5	35.1	35.3	37.3	36.4	36.1	37.6
France[1]	34.9	36.7	36.7	36.7	38.1	39.4	39.5	40.3	40.7	41.8
Germany / Allemagne[2]	34.3	35.3	36.7	36.7	36.4	36.4	35.9	35.5	35.6	35.7
Greece / Grèce[1]	18.7	20.3	20.6	20.6	21.3	20.8	20.9	23.6	24.0	24.5
Hungary / Hongrie	..	..	..	..	..	..	..	..	..	..
Iceland / Islande	29.3	..	..	..	..	28.9	30.0	30.3	27.7	28.9
Ireland / Irlande	27.9	30.9	29.4	27.9	27.5	30.1	31.1	32.5	33.9	34.6
Israel / Israël	..	..	..	..	..	..	..	..	..	..
Italy / Italie	24.5	25.4	25.9	26.1	25.3	28.7	29.8	31.9	33.8	33.0
Japan / Japon	20.4	21.2	21.7	23.4	23.8	24.8	25.4	25.9	26.3	26.5
Korea / Corée	14.9	16.2	16.2	16.6	16.9	16.9	16.8	17.0	17.2	16.2
Latvia / Lettonie	..	..	..	..	..	..	..	..	..	..
Luxembourg	31.5	31.6	35.0	35.7	33.4	34.3	35.2	36.4	38.3	36.9
Mexico / Mexique	..	..	..	..	..	14.5	14.1	14.4	16.0	15.6
Netherlands / Pays-Bas	38.2	38.1	38.9	39.6	40.0	40.3	39.4	40.1	41.2	39.5
New Zealand / Nouvelle-Zélande	27.5	28.2	31.3	29.1	29.8	29.6	31.1	31.8	29.8	29.0
Norway / Norvège	38.8	40.2	41.0	40.4	40.3	41.9	43.4	42.6	41.3	40.5
Poland / Pologne	..	..	..	..	..	..	..	..	..	..
Portugal	18.9	20.5	20.9	20.2	19.9	21.9	23.1	23.7	25.1	24.6
Slovak Republic / République slovaque	..	..	..	..	..	..	..	..	..	..
Slovenia / Slovénie	..	..	..	..	..	..	..	..	..	..
Spain / Espagne[1]	18.0	17.9	19.7	20.9	21.4	22.0	23.2	23.5	25.4	25.7
Sweden / Suède	38.9	42.7	44.7	45.1	43.9	43.7	45.0	44.0	44.7	44.3
Switzerland / Suisse	22.5	23.8	24.0	23.9	23.5	23.3	23.4	23.7	24.2	24.4
Turkey / Turquie	11.9	12.1	12.7	12.4	11.7	13.3	14.1	13.7	12.8	10.7
United Kingdom / Royaume-Uni	34.2	34.0	33.4	31.6	30.7	33.4	34.5	36.7	35.1	35.2
United States / États-Unis	24.6	24.0	25.2	25.0	25.2	25.5	25.9	26.0	24.0	24.1
Unweighted average / Moyenne non pondérée										
OECD Average / Moyenne OCDE	**28.6**	**29.5**	**30.2**	**30.1**	**30.0**	**30.1**	**30.8**	**31.1**	**31.3**	**31.3**

StatLink http://dx.doi.org/10.1787/888933416270

Table 3.2. **Total tax revenue as % of GDP, 1965-2014** *(cont.)*
Tableau 3.2. **Total des recettes fiscales en % du PIB, 1965-2014** *(suite)*

	1985	1986	1987	1988	1989	1990	1991	1992	1993	1994
Australia / Australie	27.8	28.5	28.6	28.3	28.0	28.1	26.6	26.1	26.6	27.5
Austria / Autriche	40.5	40.4	40.1	40.1	39.0	39.4	39.8	41.4	41.8	41.5
Belgium / Belgique	43.5	43.2	43.9	42.5	40.7	41.2	41.4	41.0	42.4	42.7
Canada	31.7	32.5	33.5	33.1	34.2	35.2	35.6	35.2	34.5	34.4
Chile / Chili	..	..	..	..	..	17.0	17.9	18.5	18.7	18.5
Czech Republic / République tchèque	..	..	..	..	..	..	..	..	37.1	35.8
Denmark / Danemark[1]	43.9	46.0	46.6	47.1	46.0	44.4	43.9	44.2	45.5	46.5
Estonia / Estonie	..	..	..	..	..	..	..	..	..	..
Finland / Finlande	39.1	40.3	38.7	42.0	41.5	42.9	44.4	44.0	43.5	45.5
France[1]	41.9	41.5	42.1	41.2	41.0	41.0	41.3	40.9	42.1	42.2
Germany / Allemagne[2]	36.1	35.8	36.3	36.0	36.2	34.8	35.0	35.9	35.8	36.2
Greece / Grèce[1]	24.6	25.8	26.2	23.7	22.9	25.2	25.3	26.1	26.6	26.8
Hungary / Hongrie	..	..	..	..	..	..	44.8	44.6	45.4	42.9
Iceland / Islande	27.5	27.7	28.1	30.6	30.7	30.2	30.6	31.4	30.4	29.9
Ireland / Irlande	33.6	34.3	34.5	35.7	32.5	32.4	32.9	33.3	33.3	34.3
Israel / Israël	..	..	..	..	..	..	..	..	..	..
Italy / Italie	32.5	34.0	34.1	34.6	35.6	36.4	36.8	39.1	40.6	38.7
Japan / Japon	26.7	27.7	28.6	29.0	29.3	28.5	28.2	26.7	26.8	25.8
Korea / Corée	15.8	15.4	15.7	15.6	16.3	18.8	18.5	18.4	18.8	18.9
Latvia / Lettonie	..	..	..	..	..	..	..	..	..	..
Luxembourg	37.9	35.9	36.1	34.8	34.0	33.6	31.6	32.3	34.3	34.8
Mexico / Mexique	15.2	14.5	15.4	14.9	15.4	12.4	12.5	13.1	13.3	13.5
Netherlands / Pays-Bas	39.8	40.4	42.7	42.6	40.2	40.2	42.3	41.9	42.1	40.2
New Zealand / Nouvelle-Zélande	29.5	31.3	34.5	33.5	36.8	36.2	34.3	34.8	34.9	35.4
Norway / Norvège	41.9	43.6	41.9	41.4	39.7	40.2	40.4	39.5	38.7	40.0
Poland / Pologne	..	..	..	..	..	..	34.0	36.2	39.2	36.4
Portugal	24.1	25.5	24.0	25.6	26.3	26.5	27.5	29.5	28.0	28.8
Slovak Republic / République slovaque	..	..	..	..	..	..	..	..	..	..
Slovenia / Slovénie	..	..	..	..	..	..	..	..	..	..
Spain / Espagne[1]	26.8	28.2	30.0	30.1	31.8	31.6	31.9	32.9	32.0	32.0
Sweden / Suède	44.8	47.0	49.5	48.8	49.3	49.5	47.5	45.0	44.4	44.6
Switzerland / Suisse	23.9	24.8	24.6	24.8	24.1	23.6	23.5	23.9	24.4	24.8
Turkey / Turquie	11.5	13.0	14.0	13.2	13.9	14.9	15.6	16.7	16.9	16.5
United Kingdom / Royaume-Uni	35.1	35.5	34.0	33.8	33.0	32.9	31.7	30.9	29.9	30.6
United States / États-Unis	24.6	24.6	25.6	25.4	25.6	26.0	25.8	25.7	25.9	26.2
Unweighted average / Moyenne non pondérée										
OECD Average / Moyenne OCDE	**31.5**	**32.2**	**32.7**	**32.6**	**32.5**	**32.0**	**32.5**	**32.7**	**33.1**	**33.1**

StatLink http://dx.doi.org/10.1787/888933416270

Table 3.2. **Total tax revenue as % of GDP, 1965-2014** *(cont.)*
Tableau 3.2. **Total des recettes fiscales en % du PIB, 1965-2014** *(suite)*

	1995	1996	1997	1998	1999	2000	2001	2002	2003	2004
Australia / Australie	28.2	28.9	28.6	29.4	29.8	30.4	28.9	29.8	30.0	30.3
Austria / Autriche	41.1	42.4	43.2	43.3	42.9	42.1	43.7	42.5	42.3	41.8
Belgium / Belgique	42.6	43.0	43.5	44.1	43.9	43.5	43.5	43.6	43.1	43.2
Canada	34.8	35.0	35.8	35.9	35.6	34.8	34.1	32.6	32.5	32.3
Chile / Chili	18.4	19.6	19.1	18.8	18.1	18.8	19.0	19.0	18.7	19.1
Czech Republic / République tchèque	34.9	33.4	33.7	32.5	33.4	32.5	32.6	33.5	34.4	34.7
Denmark / Danemark[1]	46.5	46.7	46.7	47.3	47.9	46.9	45.9	45.4	45.6	46.4
Estonia / Estonie	36.0	34.1	34.1	34.0	32.5	31.1	30.4	31.2	30.9	31.2
Finland / Finlande	44.5	45.7	45.0	44.8	44.3	45.8	43.2	43.3	42.4	41.8
France[1]	41.9	43.0	43.3	43.1	43.9	43.1	42.7	42.1	42.0	42.2
Germany / Allemagne[2]	36.2	35.6	35.2	35.5	36.2	36.2	35.0	34.4	34.6	33.9
Greece / Grèce[1]	27.8	34.2	28.8	30.7	31.4	33.4	32.0	32.2	30.9	29.9
Hungary / Hongrie	41.0	39.6	37.9	37.6	38.3	38.6	37.7	37.5	37.4	37.2
Iceland / Islande	30.5	31.6	31.5	33.8	36.1	36.3	34.5	34.3	35.7	36.6
Ireland / Irlande	31.7	31.9	31.4	30.8	30.9	30.8	28.6	27.3	27.9	28.9
Israel / Israël	35.6	35.0	35.5	34.3	34.1	34.8	34.7	33.9	33.3	33.3
Italy / Italie	38.6	40.3	41.7	40.0	40.9	40.6	40.3	39.8	40.1	39.3
Japan / Japon	26.4	26.4	26.8	26.4	25.9	26.6	26.8	25.8	25.3	26.1
Korea / Corée	19.1	19.8	19.4	19.4	19.7	21.5	21.8	22.0	22.7	22.0
Latvia / Lettonie	29.7	29.2	30.3	31.2	30.3	29.1	28.2	27.8	27.4	27.6
Luxembourg	34.9	35.1	36.5	37.3	36.2	37.2	37.8	37.8	37.9	36.9
Mexico / Mexique	11.4	11.0	12.0	12.8	13.6	13.6	14.4	14.6	14.1	12.9
Netherlands / Pays-Bas	37.7	37.7	37.2	36.7	37.6	37.2	36.0	35.5	35.2	35.2
New Zealand / Nouvelle-Zélande	35.6	33.7	33.9	32.3	32.3	32.5	31.9	33.3	33.2	34.2
Norway / Norvège	40.0	40.0	40.7	41.6	41.9	41.9	42.1	42.4	41.7	42.4
Poland / Pologne	37.7	36.6	36.1	35.3	35.0	32.9	32.9	33.0	32.5	32.1
Portugal	29.3	30.0	29.9	30.2	31.0	31.1	30.8	31.2	31.3	30.2
Slovak Republic / République slovaque	39.6	38.6	36.5	36.1	34.8	33.6	32.7	32.8	32.4	31.4
Slovenia / Slovénie	38.4	37.2	36.1	36.9	37.3	36.6	36.8	37.2	37.3	37.4
Spain / Espagne[1]	31.3	31.0	32.0	32.4	33.3	33.4	33.0	33.4	33.3	34.3
Sweden / Suède	45.6	47.4	48.3	48.4	48.8	49.0	46.8	45.2	45.5	45.6
Switzerland / Suisse	25.4	25.9	25.5	26.2	26.4	27.4	26.8	27.5	26.8	26.5
Turkey / Turquie	16.8	18.9	20.7	21.1	23.1	24.2	26.1	24.6	25.9	24.1
United Kingdom / Royaume-Uni	29.8	29.7	30.3	31.8	32.5	32.8	32.9	31.7	31.5	32.1
United States / États-Unis	26.5	27.0	27.4	27.8	27.8	28.2	27.2	24.9	24.4	24.6
Unweighted average / Moyenne non pondérée										
OECD Average / Moyenne OCDE	**33.3**	**33.6**	**33.6**	**33.7**	**33.9**	**34.0**	**33.5**	**33.2**	**33.2**	**33.1**

StatLink http://dx.doi.org/10.1787/888933416270

Table 3.2. **Total tax revenue as % of GDP, 1965-2014** *(cont.)*
Tableau 3.2. **Total des recettes fiscales en % du PIB, 1965-2014** *(suite)*

	2005	2006	2007	2008	2009	2010	2011	2012	2013	2014
Australia / Australie	30.0	29.6	29.7	27.1	25.8	25.6	26.3	27.4	27.6	27.8
Austria / Autriche	40.9	40.4	40.5	41.4	41.0	40.8	41.0	41.7	42.5	42.8
Belgium / Belgique	43.2	43.0	42.7	43.3	42.4	42.6	43.1	44.2	45.0	45.0
Canada	32.2	32.4	32.1	31.7	32.0	30.6	30.5	31.0	31.0	31.2
Chile / Chili	20.7	22.0	22.8	21.4	17.4	19.7	21.2	21.5	20.0	19.8
Czech Republic / République tchèque	34.5	34.1	34.3	33.5	32.4	32.5	33.3	33.7	34.1	33.1
Denmark / Danemark[1]	48.0	46.4	46.4	44.9	45.2	45.1	45.1	45.8	46.8	49.6
Estonia / Estonie	30.0	30.5	31.3	31.4	34.9	33.2	31.5	31.5	31.5	32.4
Finland / Finlande	42.1	42.2	41.5	41.2	40.9	40.8	42.0	42.7	43.6	43.8
France[1]	42.8	43.1	42.4	42.2	41.3	42.0	43.2	44.3	45.2	45.5
Germany / Allemagne[2]	33.9	34.5	34.9	35.4	36.1	35.0	35.7	36.3	36.4	36.6
Greece / Grèce[1]	31.2	30.3	31.2	31.0	30.9	32.2	33.7	35.5	35.6	35.8
Hungary / Hongrie	36.7	36.7	39.6	39.7	39.2	37.5	36.5	38.6	38.2	38.2
Iceland / Islande	39.6	40.5	39.0	35.3	31.9	33.4	34.5	35.3	36.0	38.9
Ireland / Irlande	29.4	30.8	30.4	28.5	27.4	27.1	27.1	27.5	28.2	28.7
Israel / Israël	33.6	34.1	34.0	31.7	29.7	30.5	30.8	29.7	30.7	31.2
Italy / Italie	39.1	40.6	41.7	41.7	42.1	41.9	41.9	43.9	44.0	43.7
Japan / Japon	27.3	28.1	28.5	28.5	27.0	27.6	28.6	29.4	30.3	32.0
Korea / Corée	22.5	23.6	24.8	24.6	23.8	23.4	24.2	24.8	24.3	24.6
Latvia / Lettonie	27.9	28.7	28.2	27.7	27.9	28.1	27.8	28.5	28.5	28.9
Luxembourg	38.2	36.2	36.5	37.1	38.9	38.0	37.9	38.8	38.1	38.4
Mexico / Mexique	12.6	12.8	13.2	13.8	13.6	14.1	14.0	13.9	14.6	15.2
Netherlands / Pays-Bas	35.4	36.4	36.0	36.4	35.4	36.1	35.9	36.0	36.5	37.5
New Zealand / Nouvelle-Zélande	36.0	35.3	33.9	32.9	30.3	30.3	30.4	32.0	31.3	32.5
Norway / Norvège	42.6	42.8	42.1	41.4	41.2	41.9	42.1	41.5	39.9	38.7
Poland / Pologne	33.1	33.8	34.6	34.4	31.4	31.1	31.6	31.9	31.9	32.1
Portugal	30.8	31.3	31.8	31.7	29.9	30.4	32.3	31.8	34.1	34.2
Slovak Republic / République slovaque	31.3	29.3	29.2	29.0	28.9	28.1	28.6	28.4	30.3	31.2
Slovenia / Slovénie	38.0	37.6	37.1	36.4	36.2	36.9	36.5	36.9	36.8	36.5
Spain / Espagne[1]	35.3	36.1	36.5	32.3	30.0	31.5	31.4	32.4	33.3	33.8
Sweden / Suède	46.6	46.0	45.0	44.0	44.1	43.2	42.5	42.6	42.9	42.8
Switzerland / Suisse	26.5	26.4	26.1	26.4	27.0	26.5	27.0	26.8	26.9	27.0
Turkey / Turquie	24.3	24.5	24.1	24.2	24.6	26.2	27.8	27.6	29.3	28.8
United Kingdom / Royaume-Uni	32.5	33.2	33.0	33.0	31.5	32.5	33.4	32.7	32.5	32.1
United States / États-Unis	25.9	26.7	26.7	25.7	23.0	23.5	23.9	24.1	25.7	25.9
Unweighted average / Moyenne non pondérée										
OECD Average / Moyenne OCDE	**33.6**	**33.7**	**33.8**	**33.2**	**32.4**	**32.6**	**33.0**	**33.4**	**33.8**	**34.2**

1. The total tax revenue has been reduced by the amount of any capital transfer that represents uncollected taxes. The capital transfer has been allocated between tax headings in proportion to the reported tax revenue.
2. From 1991, the figures relate to the united Germany.

1. Le total des recettes fiscales a été diminué du montant de tout transfert en capital représentant les impôts non perçus. Le transfert en capital a été réparti entre les différentes rubriques en proportion des recettes fiscales.
2. Depuis 1991, les chiffres se rapportent à l'Allemagne unifiée.

StatLink http://dx.doi.org/10.1787/888933416270

Table 3.3. **Total tax revenue (excluding social security) as % of GDP**
Tableau 3.3. **Total des recettes fiscales (sécurité sociale non comprise) en % du PIB**

	1965	1980	1990	2000	2007	2009	2011	2012	2013	2014
Australia / Australie	20.6	26.2	28.1	30.4	29.7	25.8	26.3	27.4	27.6	27.8
Austria / Autriche	25.2	26.7	26.4	27.8	26.9	26.7	26.9	27.5	28.0	28.2
Belgium / Belgique	21.0	28.8	27.5	30.1	29.5	28.2	29.2	30.0	30.7	30.8
Canada	23.8	27.2	30.9	30.0	27.5	27.2	26.0	26.3	26.3	26.5
Chile / Chili	..	..	15.4	17.4	21.5	16.0	19.9	20.1	18.5	18.3
Czech Republic / République tchèque	..	..	..	18.1	19.3	18.1	18.7	19.0	19.4	18.6
Denmark / Danemark[1]	28.2	41.1	44.4	46.2	46.3	45.1	45.0	45.7	46.7	49.5
Estonia / Estonie	..	..	..	20.2	20.9	22.1	19.9	20.4	20.6	21.5
Finland / Finlande	28.0	27.1	31.9	34.3	30.0	28.8	30.0	30.0	31.0	31.2
France[1]	22.1	22.6	22.9	27.5	26.7	25.1	26.9	27.8	28.5	28.5
Germany / Allemagne[2]	23.1	23.9	21.8	22.1	22.1	22.2	21.9	22.4	22.6	22.6
Greece / Grèce[1]	11.7	13.9	17.6	23.2	20.5	20.6	22.9	24.5	24.8	25.5
Hungary / Hongrie	..	..	..	27.3	26.3	26.5	24.0	26.0	25.7	25.7
Iceland / Islande	23.4	28.3	29.3	33.5	36.1	29.0	30.5	31.6	32.3	35.2
Ireland / Irlande	22.9	25.8	27.8	27.1	26.3	22.2	21.9	22.6	23.2	23.7
Israel / Israël	..	..	..	29.7	28.9	24.6	25.6	24.6	25.6	26.1
Italy / Italie	16.2	17.8	24.4	29.0	29.2	28.9	29.0	30.8	30.9	30.7
Japan / Japon	13.9	17.5	21.0	17.3	18.1	15.9	16.7	17.2	18.0	19.3
Korea / Corée	..	16.8	16.9	17.9	19.6	18.2	18.4	18.7	17.9	18.0
Latvia / Lettonie	..	..	..	19.4	20.3	18.6	19.1	19.8	20.0	20.5
Luxembourg	17.8	24.4	24.3	27.5	26.4	27.3	26.8	27.5	27.1	27.3
Mexico / Mexique	..	12.4	10.3	10.9	10.5	10.7	11.2	11.0	11.6	12.0
Netherlands / Pays-Bas	21.4	24.9	25.2	22.8	23.5	22.6	22.1	21.3	21.6	22.7
New Zealand / Nouvelle-Zélande	23.2	29.6	36.2	32.5	33.9	30.3	30.4	32.0	31.3	32.5
Norway / Norvège	25.9	33.1	29.7	33.1	33.3	31.6	32.8	32.2	30.4	28.8
Poland / Pologne	..	..	..	20.0	22.8	20.3	20.5	19.9	19.7	19.9
Portugal	12.3	15.4	19.3	23.1	23.7	21.4	23.4	23.1	25.2	25.2
Slovak Republic / République slovaque	..	..	..	19.7	17.8	16.5	16.6	16.1	17.0	17.9
Slovenia / Slovénie	..	..	..	22.7	23.6	21.6	21.8	21.9	22.1	22.1
Spain / Espagne[1]	10.3	11.3	20.4	21.8	24.7	18.1	19.7	20.8	21.8	22.2
Sweden / Suède	27.6	31.2	36.0	36.1	33.2	33.2	32.6	32.4	32.9	32.9
Switzerland / Suisse	14.1	17.9	18.0	20.8	20.1	20.6	20.4	20.1	20.2	20.3
Turkey / Turquie	9.9	11.5	12.0	19.6	18.9	18.6	20.1	20.1	21.2	20.6
United Kingdom / Royaume-Uni	24.8	27.8	27.3	27.3	26.9	25.3	27.2	26.5	26.4	26.1
United States / États-Unis	20.4	19.9	19.3	21.6	20.4	16.8	18.4	18.6	19.5	19.7
Unweighted average / Moyenne non pondérée										
OECD Average / Moyenne OCDE	**20.3**	**23.2**	**24.6**	**25.4**	**25.3**	**23.6**	**24.1**	**24.5**	**24.7**	**25.1**

1. The total tax revenue has been reduced by the amount of any capital transfer that represents uncollected taxes. The capital transfer has been allocated between tax headings in proportion to the reported tax revenue.
2. From 1991, the figures relate to the united Germany.

1. Le total des recettes fiscales a été diminué du montant de tout transfert en capital représentant les impôts non perçus. Le transfert en capital a été réparti entre les différentes rubriques en proportion des recettes fiscales.
2. Depuis 1991, les chiffres se rapportent à l'Allemagne unifiée.

StatLink http://dx.doi.org/10.1787/888933416282

Table 3.4. **Total tax revenue as % of GDP – Three year moving average**
Tableau 3.4. **Total des recettes fiscales en % du PIB – Moyenne mobile sur trois ans**

	1966	1975	1985	1990	1995	2000	2003	2006	2009	2013
Australia / Australie	20.3	25.2	28.0	27.6	28.2	29.7	30.0	29.7	26.2	27.6
Austria / Autriche	34.0	36.2	40.3	39.4	41.7	42.9	42.2	40.6	41.1	42.3
Belgium / Belgique	32.2	38.0	43.4	41.1	42.8	43.6	43.3	42.9	42.7	44.7
Canada	26.3	31.5	32.0	35.0	34.7	34.8	32.5	32.3	31.4	31.1
Chile / Chili	..	..	..	..	18.8	18.6	18.9	21.8	19.5	20.4
Czech Republic / République tchèque	..	..	..	..	34.7	32.8	34.2	34.3	32.8	33.6
Denmark / Danemark[1]	29.8	38.5	44.2	44.8	46.6	46.9	45.8	47.0	45.0	47.4
Estonia / Estonie	..	..	..	..	..	31.3	31.1	30.6	33.2	31.8
Finland / Finlande	31.1	36.3	39.0	43.0	45.2	44.4	42.5	41.9	41.0	43.4
France[1]	33.6	35.1	41.7	41.1	42.4	43.2	42.1	42.8	41.8	45.0
Germany / Allemagne[2]	32.0	34.8	35.9	35.3	36.0	35.8	34.3	34.4	35.5	36.5
Greece / Grèce[1]	18.2	19.1	25.0	24.5	29.6	32.2	31.0	30.9	31.4	35.6
Hungary / Hongrie	..	..	..	..	41.2	38.2	37.3	37.7	38.8	38.3
Iceland / Islande	25.5	29.3	28.1	30.5	30.6	35.6	35.6	39.7	33.5	36.7
Ireland / Irlande	26.0	28.9	34.2	32.6	32.7	30.1	28.0	30.2	27.6	28.1
Israel / Israël	..	..	..	..	..	34.5	33.5	33.9	30.6	30.5
Italy / Italie	24.8	24.7	33.2	36.3	39.2	40.6	39.7	40.5	41.9	43.9
Japan / Japon	17.6	21.3	27.0	28.7	26.2	26.5	25.7	28.0	27.7	30.6
Korea / Corée	..	14.7	15.8	17.9	19.3	21.0	22.2	23.6	23.9	24.6
Latvia / Lettonie	..	..	..	..	..	29.2	27.6	28.2	27.9	28.6
Luxembourg	26.4	29.8	36.9	33.1	35.0	37.1	37.6	36.9	38.0	38.4
Mexico / Mexique	..	..	15.1	13.4	12.0	13.9	13.9	12.9	13.8	14.6
Netherlands / Pays-Bas	32.1	37.9	39.9	40.9	38.6	36.9	35.3	35.9	35.9	36.7
New Zealand / Nouvelle-Zélande	24.3	28.4	29.9	35.8	34.9	32.3	33.5	35.1	31.1	31.9
Norway / Norvège	30.8	39.2	42.0	40.1	40.0	41.9	42.1	42.5	41.5	40.0
Poland / Pologne	..	..	..	..	36.9	33.6	32.5	33.8	32.3	32.0
Portugal	16.2	18.8	24.7	26.8	29.3	30.9	30.9	31.3	30.7	33.3
Slovak Republic / République slovaque	..	..	..	..	..	33.7	32.2	29.9	28.7	30.0
Slovenia / Slovénie	..	..	..	..	..	36.9	37.3	37.6	36.5	36.7
Spain / Espagne[1]	14.7	17.5	26.9	31.8	31.4	33.3	33.7	36.0	31.3	33.2
Sweden / Suède	32.1	39.9	45.4	48.8	45.9	48.2	45.4	45.8	43.8	42.8
Switzerland / Suisse	17.0	22.4	24.4	23.7	25.4	26.9	26.9	26.3	26.6	26.9
Turkey / Turquie	10.9	11.5	11.7	14.8	17.4	24.5	24.9	24.3	25.0	28.6
United Kingdom / Royaume-Uni	30.4	33.6	35.3	32.5	30.0	32.8	31.8	32.9	32.4	32.4
United States / États-Unis	24.0	24.6	24.4	25.8	26.5	27.7	24.7	26.4	24.1	25.2
Unweighted average / Moyenne non pondérée										
OECD Average / Moyenne OCDE	**25.4**	**28.7**	**31.7**	**32.5**	**33.1**	**33.8**	**33.2**	**33.7**	**32.7**	**33.8**

1. The total tax revenue has been reduced by the amount of any capital transfer that represents uncollected taxes. The capital transfer has been allocated between tax headings in proportion to the reported tax revenue.
2. From 1991, the figures relate to the united Germany.

1. Le total des recettes fiscales a été diminué du montant de tout transfert en capital représentant les impôts non perçus. Le transfert en capital a été réparti entre les différentes rubriques en proportion des recettes fiscales.
2. Depuis 1991, les chiffres se rapportent à l'Allemagne unifiée.

StatLink http://dx.doi.org/10.1787/888933416294

Table 3.5. **Tax revenue of main headings as % of GDP, 2014**
Tableau 3.5. **Recettes fiscales sous les principales rubriques en % du PIB, 2014**

	1000 Income & profits / Revenu & bénéfices	2000 Social security / Sécurité sociale	3000 Payroll / Salaires	4000 Property / Patrimoine	5000 Goods and services / Biens & services	6000 Others / Autres	EU Custom Duties / UE droits de douane
Australia / Australie	16.1	0.0	1.4	2.8	7.5	0.0	..
Austria / Autriche	12.6	14.7	3.0	0.6	11.7	0.2	0.1
Belgium / Belgique	16.1	14.2	0.0	3.6	10.8	0.0	0.3
Canada	15.0	4.7	0.6	3.7	7.2	0.0	..
Chile / Chili	6.5	1.4	0.0	0.8	10.9	0.0	..
Czech Republic / République tchèque	7.1	14.5	0.0	0.4	10.9	0.0	0.2
Denmark / Danemark[1]	32.2	0.1	0.3	1.9	15.0	0.0	0.2
Estonia / Estonie	7.4	10.9	0.0	0.3	13.7	0.0	0.2
Finland / Finlande	15.3	12.7	0.0	1.3	14.4	0.0	0.1
France[1]	10.8	17.0	1.6	3.9	11.0	1.1	0.1
Germany / Allemagne[2]	11.4	13.9	0.0	1.0	10.1	0.0	0.2
Greece / Grèce	8.5	10.3	0.0	1.4	15.5	0.0	0.1
Hungary / Hongrie	6.8	12.5	0.6	1.3	16.8	0.2	0.1
Iceland / Islande	18.1	3.7	0.4	2.5	12.1	2.2	..
Ireland / Irlande	11.6	5.0	0.2	2.2	9.7	0.0	0.1
Israel / Israël	9.7	5.1	1.2	3.0	12.3	0.0	..
Italy / Italie	14.0	13.0	0.0	2.9	11.8	1.9	0.1
Japan / Japon	10.2	12.7	0.0	2.7	6.3	0.1	..
Korea / Corée	7.2	6.6	0.1	2.7	7.4	0.7	..
Latvia / Lettonie	7.5	8.4	0.0	1.0	11.8	0.0	0.2
Luxembourg	13.3	11.0	0.0	3.0	11.0	0.0	0.0
Mexico / Mexique	5.7	3.1	0.4	0.3	5.4	0.2	..
Netherlands / Pays-Bas	9.6	14.9	0.0	1.4	11.1	0.2	0.3
New Zealand / Nouvelle-Zélande	18.0	0.0	0.0	2.0	12.5	0.0	..
Norway / Norvège	16.4	9.9	0.0	1.2	11.1	0.0	..
Poland / Pologne	6.3	12.2	0.2	1.4	11.6	0.2	0.1
Portugal	10.5	9.0	0.0	1.2	13.0	0.3	0.1
Slovak Republic / République slovaque	6.5	13.4	0.0	0.4	10.7	0.0	0.2
Slovenia / Slovénie	6.5	14.4	0.1	0.6	14.7	0.0	0.1
Spain / Espagne[1]	9.7	11.6	0.0	2.4	9.6	0.3	0.1
Sweden / Suède	14.9	9.9	4.5	1.1	12.1	0.0	0.1
Switzerland / Suisse	12.3	6.7	0.0	1.8	6.1	0.1	..
Turkey / Turquie	6.1	8.2	0.0	1.4	12.7	0.4	..
United Kingdom / Royaume-Uni	11.2	6.0	0.0	4.1	10.7	0.0	0.2
United States / États-Unis	12.3	6.2	0.0	2.8	4.5	0.0	..
Unweighted average / Moyenne non pondérée							
OECD Average / Moyenne OCDE	**11.5**	**9.1**	**0.4**	**1.9**	**11.0**	**0.2**	**0.1**

1. The total tax revenue has been reduced by the amount of any capital transfer that represents uncollected taxes. The capital transfer has been allocated between tax headings in proportion to the reported tax revenue.
2. From 1991, the figures relate to the united Germany.
1. Le total des recettes fiscales a été diminué du montant de tout transfert en capital représentant les impôts non perçus. Le transfert en capital a été réparti entre les différentes rubriques en proportion des recettes fiscales.
2. Depuis 1991, les chiffres se rapportent à l'Allemagne unifiée.

StatLink http://dx.doi.org/10.1787/888933416308

Table 3.6. **Tax revenue of main headings as % of total taxation, 2014**
Tableau 3.6. **Recettes fiscales sous les principales rubriques en % du total des recettes fiscales, 2014**

	1000 Income & profits / Revenu & bénéfices	2000 Social security / Sécurité sociale	3000 Payroll / Salaires	4000 Property / Patrimoine	5000 Goods and services / Biens & services	6000 Others / Autres	EU Custom Duties / UE droits de douane
Australia / Australie	57.9	0.0	5.1	10.1	26.9	0.0	..
Austria / Autriche	29.5	34.2	6.9	1.4	27.3	0.4	0.3
Belgium / Belgique	35.8	31.6	0.0	7.9	23.9	0.0	0.7
Canada	48.0	15.1	2.0	11.7	23.0	0.1	..
Chile / Chili	33.0	7.2	0.0	4.2	55.3	0.2	..
Czech Republic / République tchèque	21.4	43.8	0.0	1.3	32.9	0.0	0.5
Denmark / Danemark[1]	64.9	0.1	0.7	3.7	30.2	0.0	0.3
Estonia / Estonie	22.8	33.6	0.0	0.9	42.1	0.0	0.5
Finland / Finlande	35.0	28.9	0.0	3.0	32.8	0.1	0.2
France[1]	23.8	37.4	3.5	8.5	24.1	2.4	0.2
Germany / Allemagne[2]	31.1	38.1	0.0	2.6	27.7	0.0	0.4
Greece / Grèce	23.7	28.7	0.0	4.0	43.4	0.0	0.2
Hungary / Hongrie	17.7	32.7	1.5	3.4	44.0	0.5	0.3
Iceland / Islande	46.6	9.5	0.9	6.4	31.0	5.7	..
Ireland / Irlande	40.3	17.3	0.6	7.7	33.6	0.0	0.5
Israel / Israël	30.9	16.4	3.8	9.5	39.4	0.0	..
Italy / Italie	32.0	29.8	0.0	6.6	27.0	4.3	0.3
Japan / Japon	31.8	39.7	0.0	8.5	19.8	0.3	..
Korea / Corée	29.1	26.9	0.3	11.0	30.0	2.8	..
Latvia / Lettonie	25.9	29.1	0.0	3.6	40.9	0.0	0.5
Luxembourg	34.6	28.7	0.0	7.8	28.8	0.1	0.1
Mexico / Mexique	37.6	20.6	2.5	2.1	35.8	1.4	..
Netherlands / Pays-Bas	25.6	39.6	0.0	3.9	29.6	0.5	0.8
New Zealand / Nouvelle-Zélande	55.4	0.0	0.0	6.2	38.4	0.0	..
Norway / Norvège	42.5	25.7	0.0	3.1	28.7	0.0	..
Poland / Pologne	19.7	38.1	0.7	4.4	36.1	0.8	0.3
Portugal	30.8	26.2	0.0	3.6	38.2	0.9	0.3
Slovak Republic / République slovaque	21.0	42.9	0.0	1.4	34.2	0.0	0.5
Slovenia / Slovénie	17.9	39.4	0.1	1.7	40.4	0.0	0.4
Spain / Espagne[1]	28.7	34.4	0.0	7.0	28.5	1.0	0.4
Sweden / Suède	34.9	23.2	10.6	2.5	28.4	0.1	0.3
Switzerland / Suisse	45.7	24.9	0.0	6.6	22.4	0.4	..
Turkey / Turquie	21.1	28.5	0.0	4.9	44.1	1.4	..
United Kingdom / Royaume-Uni	34.9	18.7	0.0	12.7	33.2	0.0	0.5
United States / États-Unis	47.7	24.1	0.0	10.8	17.4	0.0	..
Unweighted average / Moyenne non pondérée							
OECD Average / Moyenne OCDE	**33.7**	**26.2**	**1.1**	**5.6**	**32.6**	**0.7**	**0.4**

1. The total tax revenue has been reduced by the amount of any capital transfer that represents uncollected taxes. The capital transfer has been allocated between tax headings in proportion to the reported tax revenue.
2. From 1991, the figures relate to the united Germany.

1. Le total des recettes fiscales a été diminué du montant de tout transfert en capital représentant les impôts non perçus. Le transfert en capital a été réparti entre les différentes rubriques en proportion des recettes fiscales.
2. Depuis 1991, les chiffres se rapportent à l'Allemagne unifiée.

StatLink http://dx.doi.org/10.1787/888933416317

Table 3.7. **Taxes on income and profits (1000) as % of GDP**
Tableau 3.7. **Impôts sur le revenu et les bénéfices (1000) en % du PIB**

	1965	1980	1990	2000	2007	2009	2011	2012	2013	2014
Australia / Australie	10.5	14.7	16.0	17.7	17.7	14.4	15.5	15.9	15.7	16.1
Austria / Autriche	8.6	10.3	10.1	12.0	12.2	11.5	11.7	12.0	12.3	12.6
Belgium / Belgique	8.5	16.6	15.2	16.8	15.3	14.4	15.0	15.3	16.0	16.1
Canada	9.7	14.2	17.1	17.4	15.7	15.3	14.5	14.7	14.8	15.0
Chile / Chili	..	..	3.9	4.4	10.4	5.4	8.5	8.4	6.9	6.5
Czech Republic / République tchèque	..	..	..	7.4	8.5	6.9	6.8	6.9	7.1	7.1
Denmark / Danemark[1]	13.6	22.9	27.2	28.8	27.9	27.7	27.6	28.4	29.3	32.2
Estonia / Estonie	..	..	..	7.7	7.4	7.4	6.3	6.6	7.1	7.4
Finland / Finlande	12.4	13.8	16.8	19.7	16.3	14.6	14.9	14.6	15.1	15.3
France[1]	5.3	6.6	6.6	10.7	10.1	8.6	10.0	10.6	11.1	10.8
Germany / Allemagne[2]	10.7	12.8	11.3	10.9	10.9	10.4	10.5	11.0	11.3	11.4
Greece / Grèce[1]	1.6	4.0	5.0	9.0	7.3	7.5	7.2	8.5	7.8	8.5
Hungary / Hongrie	..	..	..	9.4	9.9	9.5	6.3	7.0	6.7	6.8
Iceland / Islande	5.5	7.4	9.0	14.5	17.7	15.1	15.7	16.0	16.8	18.1
Ireland / Irlande	6.3	11.0	12.3	13.4	12.4	10.6	10.6	11.2	11.4	11.6
Israel / Israël	..	..	..	13.8	12.4	8.9	9.2	9.1	9.6	9.7
Italy / Italie	4.4	8.9	13.3	13.5	14.1	13.7	13.4	14.3	14.5	14.0
Japan / Japon	7.8	11.4	14.3	9.3	10.4	8.0	8.6	9.1	9.9	10.2
Korea / Corée	..	4.3	6.2	6.2	7.9	6.8	7.3	7.4	7.1	7.2
Latvia / Lettonie	..	..	..	7.0	8.2	6.9	7.0	7.4	7.4	7.5
Luxembourg	9.5	14.8	13.5	13.6	12.7	13.8	13.5	13.7	13.5	13.3
Mexico / Mexique	..	4.3	4.2	4.5	4.9	4.9	5.3	5.1	6.0	5.7
Netherlands / Pays-Bas	11.0	13.2	13.0	9.7	10.2	10.0	9.6	9.1	9.1	9.6
New Zealand / Nouvelle-Zélande	14.1	20.7	21.6	19.5	21.3	17.2	16.3	17.8	17.3	18.0
Norway / Norvège	12.8	17.5	14.2	18.8	20.2	18.9	20.5	20.0	18.2	16.4
Poland / Pologne	..	..	..	6.7	7.9	6.8	6.4	6.5	6.3	6.3
Portugal	3.9	4.3	6.8	9.1	8.8	8.3	9.1	8.7	11.0	10.5
Slovak Republic / République slovaque	..	..	..	6.9	6.1	5.5	5.5	5.5	6.0	6.5
Slovenia / Slovénie	..	..	..	6.8	8.7	7.5	7.2	6.9	6.4	6.5
Spain / Espagne[1]	3.5	5.7	9.7	9.5	12.2	9.0	9.1	9.7	9.7	9.7
Sweden / Suède	17.2	19.0	20.6	20.0	17.4	15.5	14.8	14.5	14.8	14.9
Switzerland / Suisse	6.8	10.6	11.2	12.2	12.1	12.6	12.4	12.2	12.3	12.3
Turkey / Turquie	3.1	6.9	5.0	7.1	5.7	5.9	5.8	6.0	5.9	6.1
United Kingdom / Royaume-Uni	10.8	12.6	12.9	12.8	13.0	12.1	12.2	11.6	11.5	11.2
United States / États-Unis	11.3	12.7	11.7	14.1	12.9	9.3	11.0	11.3	12.1	12.3
Unweighted average / Moyenne non pondérée										
OECD Average / Moyenne OCDE	**8.7**	**11.6**	**12.2**	**12.0**	**12.2**	**10.9**	**11.0**	**11.2**	**11.4**	**11.5**

1. The total tax revenue has been reduced by the amount of any capital transfer that represents uncollected taxes. The capital transfer has been allocated between tax headings in proportion to the reported tax revenue.
2. From 1991, the figures relate to the united Germany.
1. Le total des recettes fiscales a été diminué du montant de tout transfert en capital représentant les impôts non perçus. Le transfert en capital a été réparti entre les différentes rubriques en proportion des recettes fiscales.
2. Depuis 1991, les chiffres se rapportent à l'Allemagne unifiée.

StatLink http://dx.doi.org/10.1787/888933416326

Table 3.8. **Taxes on income and profits (1000) as % of total taxation**
Tableau 3.8. **Impôts sur le revenu et les bénéfices (1000) en % du total des recettes fiscales**

	1965	1980	1990	2000	2007	2009	2011	2012	2013	2014
Australia / Australie	50.7	56.1	57.1	58.0	59.5	55.7	58.9	58.0	56.9	57.9
Austria / Autriche	25.5	26.7	25.5	28.5	30.0	28.0	28.5	28.8	29.0	29.5
Belgium / Belgique	27.6	41.1	36.9	38.6	35.9	33.9	34.7	34.7	35.5	35.8
Canada	38.6	46.6	48.6	50.1	49.0	47.8	47.3	47.5	47.7	48.0
Chile / Chili	..	..	23.2	23.3	45.7	30.8	40.1	39.0	34.8	33.0
Czech Republic / République tchèque	..	..	..	22.8	24.8	21.2	20.3	20.5	20.8	21.4
Denmark / Danemark[1]	46.6	55.5	61.2	61.4	60.1	61.3	61.2	61.9	62.6	64.9
Estonia / Estonie	..	..	..	24.8	23.5	21.2	19.9	20.8	22.7	22.8
Finland / Finlande	41.4	39.1	39.2	43.1	39.2	35.8	35.4	34.2	34.7	35.0
France[1]	15.9	16.8	16.1	24.9	23.9	20.7	23.3	24.0	24.5	23.8
Germany / Allemagne[2]	33.8	35.1	32.4	30.1	31.2	28.9	29.4	30.4	31.0	31.1
Greece / Grèce[1]	9.1	19.4	19.9	26.8	23.3	24.4	21.4	23.9	21.8	23.7
Hungary / Hongrie	..	..	..	24.3	25.1	24.4	17.2	18.0	17.7	17.7
Iceland / Islande	21.4	25.6	29.7	39.9	45.4	47.3	45.5	45.2	46.7	46.6
Ireland / Irlande	25.7	36.5	38.0	43.6	40.9	38.8	39.1	40.7	40.3	40.3
Israel / Israël	..	..	..	39.7	36.5	30.0	29.9	30.6	31.5	30.9
Italy / Italie	17.8	31.2	36.5	33.2	33.7	32.5	31.9	32.6	33.1	32.0
Japan / Japon	43.9	46.1	50.2	34.8	36.4	29.5	30.2	31.1	32.5	31.8
Korea / Corée	..	25.5	32.8	28.8	31.8	28.5	30.1	29.9	29.3	29.1
Latvia / Lettonie	..	..	..	24.1	29.2	24.8	25.3	25.9	26.0	25.9
Luxembourg	35.9	43.2	40.2	36.5	34.7	35.3	35.6	35.2	35.4	34.6
Mexico / Mexique	..	29.8	34.0	33.2	36.8	36.1	37.9	37.0	40.7	37.6
Netherlands / Pays-Bas	35.8	32.9	32.3	25.9	28.3	28.2	26.9	25.3	24.8	25.6
New Zealand / Nouvelle-Zélande	60.5	69.8	59.6	60.0	62.9	56.9	53.7	55.4	55.5	55.4
Norway / Norvège	43.4	41.8	35.2	45.0	47.8	46.0	48.8	48.3	45.5	42.5
Poland / Pologne	..	..	..	20.4	22.8	21.7	20.1	20.5	19.6	19.7
Portugal	24.6	19.7	25.7	29.3	27.7	27.7	28.1	27.4	32.2	30.8
Slovak Republic / République slovaque	..	..	..	20.5	20.9	19.1	19.1	19.5	19.9	21.0
Slovenia / Slovénie	..	..	..	18.5	23.3	20.8	19.8	18.8	17.3	17.9
Spain / Espagne[1]	24.5	26.0	30.6	28.3	33.5	30.0	29.0	29.9	29.2	28.7
Sweden / Suède	54.9	43.5	41.6	40.8	38.7	35.2	34.8	34.1	34.6	34.9
Switzerland / Suisse	41.1	45.3	47.4	44.3	46.2	46.4	46.0	45.4	45.6	45.7
Turkey / Turquie	29.6	51.8	33.5	29.5	23.7	24.1	21.0	21.8	20.2	21.1
United Kingdom / Royaume-Uni	37.0	37.8	39.3	39.0	39.4	38.5	36.7	35.6	35.4	34.9
United States / États-Unis	48.1	49.8	45.2	50.1	48.3	40.3	46.2	46.9	47.0	47.7
Unweighted average / Moyenne non pondérée										
OECD Average / Moyenne OCDE	**34.7**	**38.2**	**37.5**	**34.9**	**36.0**	**33.5**	**33.5**	**33.7**	**33.8**	**33.7**

1. The total tax revenue has been reduced by the amount of any capital transfer that represents uncollected taxes. The capital transfer has been allocated between tax headings in proportion to the reported tax revenue.
2. From 1991, the figures relate to the united Germany.
1. Le total des recettes fiscales a été diminué du montant de tout transfert en capital représentant les impôts non perçus. Le transfert en capital a été réparti entre les différentes rubriques en proportion des recettes fiscales.
2. Depuis 1991, les chiffres se rapportent à l'Allemagne unifiée.

StatLink http://dx.doi.org/10.1787/888933416339

Table 3.9. **Taxes on personal income (1100) as % of GDP**
Tableau 3.9. **Impôts sur le revenu des personnes physiques (1100) en % du PIB**

	1965	1980	1990	2000	2007	2009	2011	2012	2013	2014
Australia / Australie	7.1	11.5	12.1	11.5	10.9	9.6	10.3	10.7	10.7	11.4
Austria / Autriche	6.7	9.0	8.3	9.3	9.1	9.1	9.2	9.6	9.8	10.1
Belgium / Belgique	6.3	14.7	13.2	13.7	11.9	12.0	12.2	12.3	12.9	12.9
Canada	5.7	10.4	14.4	12.8	11.9	11.6	11.0	11.3	11.2	11.3
Chile / Chili	..	..	0.9	1.4	1.1	1.3	1.4	1.5	1.4	1.4
Czech Republic / République tchèque	..	..	..	4.2	4.0	3.5	3.5	3.6	3.7	3.6
Denmark / Danemark[1]	12.3	21.6	24.0	24.7	24.5	25.3	23.4	23.4	25.5	26.8
Estonia / Estonie	..	..	..	6.8	5.8	5.6	5.1	5.2	5.4	5.7
Finland / Finlande	10.0	12.6	14.9	14.0	12.5	12.7	12.3	12.5	12.8	13.4
France[1]	3.6	4.6	4.4	7.8	7.2	7.1	7.4	8.0	8.4	8.5
Germany / Allemagne[2]	8.2	10.8	9.6	9.2	8.7	9.1	8.8	9.3	9.5	9.6
Greece / Grèce[1]	1.2	3.1	3.6	4.8	4.7	4.5	4.8	7.0	6.0	5.9
Hungary / Hongrie	..	..	..	7.2	7.2	7.3	5.1	5.7	5.4	5.3
Iceland / Islande	5.0	6.7	8.1	12.6	13.2	12.1	13.0	13.2	13.8	13.6
Ireland / Irlande	4.1	9.6	10.7	9.8	9.2	8.3	8.4	8.9	9.0	9.2
Israel / Israël	..	..	..	10.1	7.6	5.8	5.5	5.3	5.5	5.8
Italy / Italie	2.7	6.6	9.6	10.1	10.7	11.2	11.0	11.6	11.6	11.3
Japan / Japon	3.9	6.0	7.9	5.6	5.6	5.4	5.3	5.5	5.8	6.1
Korea / Corée	..	1.9	3.8	3.1	4.1	3.4	3.5	3.7	3.7	4.0
Latvia / Lettonie	..	..	..	5.5	5.7	5.4	5.6	5.8	5.8	5.9
Luxembourg	6.6	9.2	8.1	6.9	7.3	8.0	8.4	8.5	8.7	8.9
Mexico / Mexique	..	..	..	..	2.1	2.3	2.4	2.5	2.6	3.0
Netherlands / Pays-Bas	8.6	10.6	9.9	5.6	6.8	7.8	7.4	7.0	6.9	7.0
New Zealand / Nouvelle-Zélande	9.1	18.3	17.4	14.0	14.3	12.4	11.3	12.1	11.9	12.6
Norway / Norvège	11.7	11.9	10.5	10.1	9.4	9.9	9.7	9.7	9.9	9.8
Poland / Pologne	..	..	..	4.3	5.2	4.6	4.3	4.5	4.5	4.6
Portugal	..	..	4.2	5.4	5.3	5.5	6.0	5.8	7.7	7.7
Slovak Republic / République slovaque	..	..	..	3.3	2.9	2.8	2.8	2.9	2.9	3.0
Slovenia / Slovénie	..	..	..	5.5	5.5	5.7	5.6	5.7	5.2	5.1
Spain / Espagne[1]	2.0	4.5	6.9	6.4	7.5	6.6	7.2	7.4	7.5	7.6
Sweden / Suède	15.3	18.0	19.1	16.3	13.9	12.7	11.7	11.9	12.2	12.2
Switzerland / Suisse	5.5	9.1	7.7	8.2	8.3	8.6	8.4	8.5	8.4	8.4
Turkey / Turquie	2.6	5.8	4.0	5.4	4.1	4.0	3.8	4.0	4.1	4.2
United Kingdom / Royaume-Uni	9.7	9.8	9.7	9.6	9.9	9.6	9.4	9.0	9.0	8.8
United States / États-Unis	7.4	10.0	9.8	11.9	10.2	7.9	9.3	9.3	9.9	10.2
Unweighted average / Moyenne non pondérée										
OECD Average / Moyenne OCDE	**6.7**	**9.8**	**9.7**	**8.7**	**8.2**	**8.0**	**7.8**	**8.1**	**8.3**	**8.4**

1. The total tax revenue has been reduced by the amount of any capital transfer that represents uncollected taxes. The capital transfer has been allocated between tax headings in proportion to the reported tax revenue.
2. From 1991, the figures relate to the united Germany.
1. Le total des recettes fiscales a été diminué du montant de tout transfert en capital représentant les impôts non perçus. Le transfert en capital a été réparti entre les différentes rubriques en proportion des recettes fiscales.
2. Depuis 1991, les chiffres se rapportent à l'Allemagne unifiée.

StatLink http://dx.doi.org/10.1787/888933416344

Table 3.10. **Taxes on personal income (1100) as % of total taxation**
Tableau 3.10. **Impôts sur le revenu des personnes physiques (1100) en % du total des recettes fiscales**

	1965	1980	1990	2000	2007	2009	2011	2012	2013	2014
Australia / Australie	34.4	44.0	43.0	37.8	36.6	37.3	39.3	39.1	39.0	41.0
Austria / Autriche	20.0	23.2	21.0	22.2	22.5	22.3	22.5	22.9	22.9	23.6
Belgium / Belgique	20.5	36.4	32.0	31.4	27.8	28.4	28.2	27.8	28.5	28.6
Canada	22.6	34.1	40.8	36.8	37.1	36.2	36.1	36.4	36.2	36.3
Chile / Chili	..	..	5.6	7.6	4.8	7.5	6.6	6.8	7.2	7.3
Czech Republic / République tchèque	..	..	..	12.9	11.7	10.7	10.6	10.6	10.7	10.8
Denmark / Danemark[1]	42.1	52.3	54.0	52.7	52.8	56.0	51.7	51.1	54.5	54.0
Estonia / Estonie	..	..	..	22.0	18.4	16.0	16.1	16.4	17.2	17.5
Finland / Finlande	33.3	35.7	34.7	30.6	30.2	31.1	29.2	29.3	29.3	30.6
France[1]	10.6	11.6	10.7	18.0	17.1	17.3	17.2	18.1	18.6	18.7
Germany / Allemagne[2]	26.0	29.6	27.6	25.3	25.0	25.2	24.7	25.7	26.1	26.3
Greece / Grèce[1]	6.8	14.9	14.1	14.5	14.9	14.5	14.1	19.6	16.8	16.4
Hungary / Hongrie	..	..	..	18.6	18.2	18.7	13.9	14.7	14.0	13.9
Iceland / Islande	19.5	23.1	26.9	34.8	33.9	37.9	37.6	37.4	38.3	34.9
Ireland / Irlande	16.7	32.0	33.1	31.9	30.3	30.4	31.1	32.4	31.9	32.0
Israel / Israël	..	..	..	29.1	22.5	19.6	18.0	18.0	17.8	18.6
Italy / Italie	10.9	23.1	26.3	24.8	25.6	26.5	26.3	26.4	26.4	25.9
Japan / Japon	21.7	24.3	27.8	21.1	19.6	20.0	18.4	18.6	19.2	18.9
Korea / Corée	..	11.5	20.0	14.6	16.7	14.1	14.7	15.0	15.3	16.3
Latvia / Lettonie	..	..	..	18.8	20.3	19.3	20.2	20.2	20.3	20.5
Luxembourg	24.9	27.0	24.1	18.5	20.0	20.6	22.2	21.9	22.9	23.2
Mexico / Mexique	..	..	..	..	15.9	17.1	17.3	18.3	18.1	19.7
Netherlands / Pays-Bas	27.7	26.3	24.7	15.1	18.7	22.1	20.8	19.4	18.8	18.7
New Zealand / Nouvelle-Zélande	39.4	61.6	48.0	43.1	42.1	41.1	37.0	37.7	38.0	38.6
Norway / Norvège	39.6	28.5	26.2	24.1	22.2	24.1	23.1	23.4	24.8	25.4
Poland / Pologne	..	..	..	13.2	15.0	14.5	13.7	14.0	14.1	14.3
Portugal	..	..	15.9	17.4	16.8	18.5	18.4	18.3	22.6	22.5
Slovak Republic / République slovaque	..	..	..	9.9	9.9	9.7	9.9	10.3	9.6	9.6
Slovenia / Slovénie	..	..	..	15.0	14.7	15.8	15.3	15.4	14.0	14.0
Spain / Espagne[1]	14.3	20.4	21.7	19.1	20.4	22.0	22.8	22.9	22.5	22.3
Sweden / Suède	48.7	41.0	38.5	33.2	30.9	28.8	27.5	28.0	28.4	28.6
Switzerland / Suisse	33.4	38.9	32.8	29.8	31.7	31.8	31.0	31.6	31.2	31.0
Turkey / Turquie	24.8	43.5	26.8	22.2	17.0	16.4	13.5	14.4	13.9	14.7
United Kingdom / Royaume-Uni	33.1	29.4	29.4	29.3	29.9	30.4	28.1	27.5	27.7	27.4
United States / États-Unis	31.7	39.1	37.7	42.2	38.3	34.3	38.8	38.5	38.7	39.3
Unweighted average / Moyenne non pondérée										
OECD Average / Moyenne OCDE	**26.2**	**31.3**	**28.6**	**24.6**	**23.7**	**23.9**	**23.3**	**23.7**	**23.9**	**24.0**

1. The total tax revenue has been reduced by the amount of any capital transfer that represents uncollected taxes. The capital transfer has been allocated between tax headings in proportion to the reported tax revenue.
2. From 1991, the figures relate to the united Germany.
1. Le total des recettes fiscales a été diminué du montant de tout transfert en capital représentant les impôts non perçus. Le transfert en capital a été réparti entre les différentes rubriques en proportion des recettes fiscales.
2. Depuis 1991, les chiffres se rapportent à l'Allemagne unifiée.

StatLink http://dx.doi.org/10.1787/888933416354

Table 3.11. **Taxes on corporate income (1200) as % of GDP**
Tableau 3.11. **Impôts sur les bénéfices des sociétés (1200) en % du PIB**

	1965	1980	1990	2000	2007	2009	2011	2012	2013	2014
Australia / Australie	3.4	3.2	4.0	6.2	6.8	4.8	5.2	5.2	4.9	4.7
Austria / Autriche	1.8	1.4	1.4	2.0	2.3	1.6	2.0	2.0	2.2	2.1
Belgium / Belgique	1.9	1.9	2.0	3.1	3.4	2.3	2.8	3.0	3.1	3.2
Canada	3.7	3.5	2.5	4.2	3.4	3.3	3.1	3.2	3.3	3.3
Chile / Chili	..	..	2.1	2.1	6.7	4.3	5.0	5.9	4.4	4.2
Czech Republic / République tchèque	..	..	..	3.2	4.5	3.4	3.2	3.3	3.4	3.5
Denmark / Danemark[1]	1.3	1.4	1.7	3.2	3.1	1.9	2.2	2.6	2.8	2.6
Estonia / Estonie	..	..	..	0.9	1.6	1.8	1.2	1.4	1.7	1.7
Finland / Finlande	2.4	1.2	1.9	5.7	3.7	1.9	2.6	2.1	2.4	1.9
France[1]	1.8	2.0	2.2	3.0	2.9	1.4	2.6	2.6	2.6	2.3
Germany / Allemagne[2]	2.5	2.0	1.7	1.8	2.2	1.3	1.7	1.7	1.8	1.7
Greece / Grèce[1]	0.3	0.8	1.4	4.0	2.5	2.5	2.1	1.1	1.1	1.9
Hungary / Hongrie	..	..	..	2.2	2.7	2.2	1.2	1.3	1.4	1.5
Iceland / Islande	0.5	0.7	0.8	1.2	2.4	1.7	1.7	1.9	2.2	3.4
Ireland / Irlande	2.2	1.4	1.6	3.6	3.2	2.3	2.2	2.3	2.4	2.4
Israel / Israël	..	..	..	3.3	4.1	2.5	3.0	2.7	3.5	3.2
Italy / Italie	1.7	2.2	3.7	2.8	3.1	2.4	2.2	2.4	2.6	2.2
Japan / Japon	3.9	5.4	6.4	3.7	4.8	2.6	3.4	3.7	4.0	4.1
Korea / Corée	..	1.9	2.4	3.0	3.7	3.4	3.7	3.7	3.4	3.2
Latvia / Lettonie	..	..	..	1.5	2.5	1.6	1.4	1.6	1.6	1.5
Luxembourg	2.9	5.6	5.4	6.7	5.4	5.7	5.1	5.2	4.8	4.4
Mexico / Mexique	..	..	..	..	1.9	1.6	2.1	1.8	2.4	2.6
Netherlands / Pays-Bas	2.5	2.7	3.0	4.0	3.4	2.2	2.2	2.1	2.2	2.6
New Zealand / Nouvelle-Zélande	4.8	2.3	2.3	4.0	4.8	3.3	3.9	4.5	4.4	4.3
Norway / Norvège	1.1	5.6	3.6	8.8	10.8	9.0	10.8	10.3	8.3	6.6
Poland / Pologne	..	..	..	2.4	2.7	2.3	2.0	2.1	1.8	1.7
Portugal	..	..	2.1	3.7	3.5	2.7	3.1	2.7	3.3	2.8
Slovak Republic / République slovaque	..	..	..	2.6	2.9	2.5	2.4	2.4	2.9	3.3
Slovenia / Slovénie	..	..	..	1.1	3.2	1.8	1.7	1.2	1.2	1.4
Spain / Espagne[1]	1.3	1.1	2.8	3.0	4.7	2.3	1.9	2.2	2.1	2.1
Sweden / Suède	1.9	1.1	1.5	3.7	3.5	2.8	3.1	2.6	2.7	2.7
Switzerland / Suisse	1.3	1.5	2.9	3.8	3.5	2.8	2.8	2.8	2.8	2.8
Turkey / Turquie	0.5	0.6	1.0	1.8	1.6	1.9	2.1	2.0	1.9	1.8
United Kingdom / Royaume-Uni	1.3	2.8	3.3	3.2	3.1	2.6	2.9	2.7	2.5	2.4
United States / États-Unis	3.9	2.7	2.0	2.2	2.7	1.4	1.8	2.0	2.1	2.2
Unweighted average / Moyenne non pondérée										
OECD Average / Moyenne OCDE	**2.1**	**2.3**	**2.5**	**3.3**	**3.6**	**2.7**	**2.9**	**2.9**	**2.9**	**2.8**

1. The total tax revenue has been reduced by the amount of any capital transfer that represents uncollected taxes. The capital transfer has been allocated between tax headings in proportion to the reported tax revenue.
2. From 1991, the figures relate to the united Germany.
1. Le total des recettes fiscales a été diminué du montant de tout transfert en capital représentant les impôts non perçus. Le transfert en capital a été réparti entre les différentes rubriques en proportion des recettes fiscales.
2. Depuis 1991, les chiffres se rapportent à l'Allemagne unifiée.

StatLink http://dx.doi.org/10.1787/888933416369

Table 3.12. **Taxes on corporate income (1200) as % of total taxation**
Tableau 3.12. **Impôts sur les bénéfices des sociétés (1200) en % du total des recettes fiscales**

	1965	1980	1990	2000	2007	2009	2011	2012	2013	2014
Australia / Australie	16.3	12.2	14.1	20.2	22.9	18.4	19.7	18.9	17.9	16.8
Austria / Autriche	5.4	3.5	3.6	4.6	5.8	4.0	4.9	4.8	5.1	5.0
Belgium / Belgique	6.2	4.7	4.8	7.2	8.0	5.5	6.5	6.8	6.9	7.2
Canada	14.9	11.6	7.0	12.2	10.6	10.4	10.3	10.2	10.6	10.5
Chile / Chili	..	..	12.4	11.2	29.4	24.5	23.4	27.3	22.1	21.3
Czech Republic / République tchèque	..	..	..	9.9	13.1	10.5	9.7	9.9	10.1	10.6
Denmark / Danemark[1]	4.6	3.3	3.8	6.8	6.8	4.2	4.8	5.7	5.9	5.3
Estonia / Estonie	..	..	..	2.8	5.1	5.2	3.8	4.4	5.5	5.3
Finland / Finlande	8.1	3.4	4.5	12.5	9.0	4.7	6.2	4.9	5.4	4.4
France[1]	5.3	5.1	5.3	6.9	6.8	3.5	6.1	5.8	5.8	5.1
Germany / Allemagne[2]	7.8	5.5	4.8	4.8	6.2	3.7	4.7	4.7	4.9	4.8
Greece / Grèce[1]	1.8	3.8	5.5	12.0	7.9	8.1	6.1	3.1	3.2	5.3
Hungary / Hongrie	..	..	..	5.7	6.9	5.6	3.3	3.3	3.6	3.8
Iceland / Islande	1.8	2.5	2.8	3.3	6.1	5.2	5.0	5.4	6.0	8.6
Ireland / Irlande	9.1	4.5	4.9	11.7	10.7	8.4	8.0	8.2	8.4	8.3
Israel / Israël	..	..	..	9.6	12.0	8.5	9.6	9.1	11.3	10.2
Italy / Italie	6.9	7.8	10.0	6.9	7.5	5.7	5.2	5.5	5.8	5.0
Japan / Japon	22.2	21.8	22.4	13.8	16.8	9.6	11.8	12.5	13.2	12.9
Korea / Corée	..	11.0	12.8	14.1	15.1	14.4	15.4	14.9	14.0	12.8
Latvia / Lettonie	..	..	..	5.3	9.0	5.6	5.1	5.7	5.7	5.3
Luxembourg	11.0	16.2	16.1	18.0	14.7	14.7	13.4	13.4	12.5	11.4
Mexico / Mexique	..	..	..	..	14.5	11.7	14.9	13.3	16.7	16.9
Netherlands / Pays-Bas	8.1	6.6	7.5	10.9	9.5	6.1	6.1	5.9	6.0	6.9
New Zealand / Nouvelle-Zélande	20.7	7.8	6.5	12.4	14.2	11.0	12.9	14.1	14.1	13.2
Norway / Norvège	3.8	13.3	9.0	20.9	25.6	21.9	25.7	24.9	20.7	17.1
Poland / Pologne	..	..	..	7.3	7.9	7.2	6.4	6.5	5.6	5.4
Portugal	..	..	8.0	11.9	10.9	9.2	9.7	8.6	9.6	8.3
Slovak Republic / République slovaque	..	..	..	7.7	10.0	8.6	8.4	8.3	9.5	10.6
Slovenia / Slovénie	..	..	..	3.1	8.6	5.0	4.5	3.4	3.3	3.9
Spain / Espagne[1]	9.2	5.1	8.8	9.1	12.9	7.8	5.9	6.8	6.5	6.1
Sweden / Suède	6.1	2.5	3.1	7.5	7.8	6.4	7.3	6.0	6.2	6.3
Switzerland / Suisse	7.7	6.4	12.2	13.8	13.6	10.4	10.4	10.4	10.4	10.4
Turkey / Turquie	4.8	4.1	6.7	7.3	6.8	7.7	7.5	7.4	6.3	6.4
United Kingdom / Royaume-Uni	4.4	8.4	9.9	9.7	9.5	8.1	8.6	8.1	7.7	7.5
United States / États-Unis	16.4	10.8	7.5	7.9	10.0	6.0	7.4	8.4	8.3	8.4
Unweighted average / Moyenne non pondérée										
OECD Average / Moyenne OCDE	**8.8**	**7.6**	**8.2**	**9.7**	**11.2**	**8.8**	**9.1**	**9.1**	**9.0**	**8.8**

1. The total tax revenue has been reduced by the amount of any capital transfer that represents uncollected taxes. The capital transfer has been allocated between tax headings in proportion to the reported tax revenue.
2. From 1991, the figures relate to the united Germany.

1. Le total des recettes fiscales a été diminué du montant de tout transfert en capital représentant les impôts non perçus. Le transfert en capital a été réparti entre les différentes rubriques en proportion des recettes fiscales.
2. Depuis 1991, les chiffres se rapportent à l'Allemagne unifiée.

StatLink http://dx.doi.org/10.1787/888933416372

Table 3.13. **Social security contributions (2000) as % of GDP**
Tableau 3.13. **Cotisations de sécurité sociale (2000) en % du PIB**

	1965	1980	1990	2000	2007	2009	2011	2012	2013	2014
Australia / Australie	0.0	0.0	0.0	0.0	0.0	0.0	0.0	0.0	0.0	0.0
Austria / Autriche	8.4	12.0	12.9	14.4	13.7	14.2	14.1	14.2	14.6	14.7
Belgium / Belgique	9.6	11.7	13.7	13.4	13.2	14.1	14.0	14.2	14.4	14.2
Canada	1.4	3.2	4.3	4.7	4.6	4.8	4.5	4.7	4.7	4.7
Chile / Chili	..	..	1.5	1.4	1.3	1.4	1.3	1.4	1.4	1.4
Czech Republic / République tchèque	..	..	..	14.4	15.0	14.2	14.6	14.7	14.7	14.5
Denmark / Danemark[1]	1.0	0.2	0.0	0.6	0.1	0.1	0.1	0.1	0.1	0.1
Estonia / Estonie	..	..	..	10.9	10.4	12.9	11.6	11.1	10.9	10.9
Finland / Finlande	2.1	8.2	11.0	11.6	11.5	12.2	12.1	12.6	12.6	12.7
France[1]	11.5	16.8	18.1	15.5	15.7	16.3	16.2	16.5	16.7	17.0
Germany / Allemagne[2]	8.5	12.5	13.0	14.1	12.8	13.9	13.8	13.9	13.9	13.9
Greece / Grèce[1]	5.4	6.8	7.6	10.1	10.7	10.3	10.8	11.0	10.8	10.3
Hungary / Hongrie	..	..	..	11.3	13.3	12.7	12.4	12.6	12.5	12.5
Iceland / Islande	2.1	0.6	0.9	2.8	2.9	2.9	3.9	3.7	3.7	3.7
Ireland / Irlande	1.6	4.3	4.6	3.6	4.1	5.2	5.2	4.8	5.0	5.0
Israel / Israël	..	..	..	5.1	5.1	5.0	5.2	5.0	5.1	5.1
Italy / Italie	8.4	10.9	12.0	11.6	12.5	13.2	12.9	13.1	13.1	13.0
Japan / Japon	3.9	7.2	7.5	9.4	10.4	11.0	11.9	12.2	12.4	12.7
Korea / Corée	..	0.2	1.9	3.6	5.1	5.6	5.8	6.1	6.4	6.6
Latvia / Lettonie	..	..	..	9.8	7.9	9.3	8.7	8.7	8.5	8.4
Luxembourg	8.5	9.8	9.3	9.7	10.1	11.7	11.1	11.3	11.0	11.0
Mexico / Mexique	..	2.0	2.1	2.7	2.7	2.9	2.8	2.9	3.1	3.1
Netherlands / Pays-Bas	9.5	15.3	15.0	14.4	12.6	12.8	13.8	14.7	14.9	14.9
New Zealand / Nouvelle-Zélande	0.0	0.0	0.0	0.0	0.0	0.0	0.0	0.0	0.0	0.0
Norway / Norvège	3.5	8.9	10.6	8.8	8.8	9.6	9.3	9.3	9.5	9.9
Poland / Pologne	..	..	..	12.9	11.8	11.2	11.1	12.0	12.2	12.2
Portugal	3.4	6.5	7.2	7.9	8.1	8.5	8.9	8.7	8.9	9.0
Slovak Republic / République slovaque	..	..	..	14.0	11.4	12.3	12.0	12.3	13.3	13.4
Slovenia / Slovénie	..	..	..	13.9	13.4	14.6	14.7	14.9	14.7	14.4
Spain / Espagne[1]	4.0	10.7	11.2	11.6	11.8	11.8	11.8	11.6	11.5	11.6
Sweden / Suède	3.8	12.6	13.5	12.9	11.8	10.9	9.9	10.2	10.0	9.9
Switzerland / Suisse	2.5	5.5	5.6	6.7	6.1	6.5	6.6	6.7	6.7	6.7
Turkey / Turquie	0.6	1.9	2.9	4.5	5.2	6.0	7.8	7.5	8.0	8.2
United Kingdom / Royaume-Uni	4.5	5.6	5.6	5.6	6.1	6.2	6.2	6.2	6.1	6.0
United States / États-Unis	3.1	5.6	6.6	6.6	6.3	6.3	5.5	5.5	6.2	6.2
Unweighted average / Moyenne non pondérée										
OECD Average / Moyenne OCDE	**4.5**	**6.9**	**7.4**	**8.6**	**8.5**	**8.9**	**8.9**	**9.0**	**9.1**	**9.1**

1. The total tax revenue has been reduced by the amount of any capital transfer that represents uncollected taxes. The capital transfer has been allocated between tax headings in proportion to the reported tax revenue.
2. From 1991, the figures relate to the united Germany.
1. Le total des recettes fiscales a été diminué du montant de tout transfert en capital représentant les impôts non perçus. Le transfert en capital a été réparti entre les différentes rubriques en proportion des recettes fiscales.
2. Depuis 1991, les chiffres se rapportent à l'Allemagne unifiée.

StatLink http://dx.doi.org/10.1787/888933416387

Table 3.14. **Social security contributions (2000) as % of total taxation**
Tableau 3.14. **Cotisations de sécurité sociale (2000) en % du total des recettes fiscales**

	1965	1980	1990	2000	2007	2009	2011	2012	2013	2014
Australia / Australie	0.0	0.0	0.0	0.0	0.0	0.0	0.0	0.0	0.0	0.0
Austria / Autriche	24.9	30.9	32.9	34.1	33.7	34.8	34.3	34.1	34.3	34.2
Belgium / Belgique	31.4	28.8	33.2	30.8	31.0	33.4	32.4	32.2	31.9	31.6
Canada	5.6	10.5	12.1	13.6	14.4	15.0	14.7	15.1	15.1	15.1
Chile / Chili	..	..	9.0	7.3	5.6	8.2	6.3	6.5	7.2	7.2
Czech Republic / République tchèque	..	..	..	44.3	43.6	44.0	43.9	43.7	43.2	43.8
Denmark / Danemark[1]	3.3	0.4	0.0	1.4	0.2	0.1	0.2	0.2	0.2	0.1
Estonia / Estonie	..	..	..	35.1	33.1	36.8	36.8	35.2	34.7	33.6
Finland / Finlande	6.8	23.3	25.6	25.2	27.6	29.8	28.7	29.6	28.9	28.9
France[1]	34.2	42.7	44.1	36.0	37.1	39.4	37.6	37.2	37.0	37.4
Germany / Allemagne[2]	26.8	34.3	37.5	39.0	36.6	38.6	38.6	38.3	38.1	38.1
Greece / Grèce[1]	31.6	32.9	30.2	30.3	34.4	33.3	32.1	30.9	30.4	28.7
Hungary / Hongrie	..	..	..	29.3	33.6	32.4	34.1	32.7	32.7	32.7
Iceland / Islande	8.1	2.2	3.1	7.7	7.4	9.0	11.4	10.4	10.3	9.5
Ireland / Irlande	6.5	14.3	14.1	11.8	13.5	18.9	19.3	17.6	17.8	17.3
Israel / Israël	..	..	..	14.7	15.1	17.0	16.9	16.9	16.5	16.4
Italy / Italie	34.2	38.0	32.9	28.5	29.9	31.4	30.8	29.8	29.8	29.8
Japan / Japon	21.8	29.1	26.4	35.2	36.5	41.0	41.5	41.6	40.8	39.7
Korea / Corée	..	1.1	10.1	16.7	20.7	23.4	24.0	24.7	26.4	26.9
Latvia / Lettonie	..	..	..	33.5	27.9	33.2	31.4	30.6	29.8	29.1
Luxembourg	32.3	28.7	27.5	26.1	27.6	30.0	29.2	29.1	28.9	28.7
Mexico / Mexique	..	14.1	16.8	20.1	20.4	21.1	20.2	20.9	20.9	20.6
Netherlands / Pays-Bas	30.8	38.1	37.4	38.7	34.9	36.1	38.4	40.8	40.8	39.6
New Zealand / Nouvelle-Zélande	0.0	0.0	0.0	0.0	0.0	0.0	0.0	0.0	0.0	0.0
Norway / Norvège	11.9	21.1	26.3	20.9	20.8	23.3	22.0	22.5	23.8	25.7
Poland / Pologne	..	..	..	39.2	34.1	35.5	35.2	37.5	38.4	38.1
Portugal	21.8	29.5	27.2	25.5	25.6	28.6	27.5	27.3	26.1	26.2
Slovak Republic / République slovaque	..	..	..	41.5	39.2	42.7	42.1	43.4	43.8	42.9
Slovenia / Slovénie	..	..	..	38.0	36.3	40.3	40.2	40.4	39.9	39.4
Spain / Espagne[1]	28.3	48.6	35.4	34.8	32.3	39.5	37.5	35.8	34.6	34.4
Sweden / Suède	12.1	28.8	27.2	26.3	26.2	24.6	23.3	24.0	23.3	23.2
Switzerland / Suisse	14.9	23.4	23.5	24.3	23.3	23.9	24.5	25.0	24.9	24.9
Turkey / Turquie	5.9	14.0	19.7	18.7	21.7	24.5	27.9	27.2	27.4	28.5
United Kingdom / Royaume-Uni	15.4	16.7	17.0	17.0	18.5	19.7	18.7	19.0	18.8	18.7
United States / États-Unis	13.3	21.9	25.6	23.6	23.5	27.2	22.9	22.7	24.1	24.1
Unweighted average / Moyenne non pondérée										
OECD Average / Moyenne OCDE	**17.6**	**22.1**	**22.0**	**24.8**	**24.7**	**26.8**	**26.4**	**26.4**	**26.3**	**26.2**

1. The total tax revenue has been reduced by the amount of any capital transfer that represents uncollected taxes. The capital transfer has been allocated between tax headings in proportion to the reported tax revenue.
2. From 1991, the figures relate to the united Germany.
1. Le total des recettes fiscales a été diminué du montant de tout transfert en capital représentant les impôts non perçus. Le transfert en capital a été réparti entre les différentes rubriques en proportion des recettes fiscales.
2. Depuis 1991, les chiffres se rapportent à l'Allemagne unifiée.

StatLink http://dx.doi.org/10.1787/888933416397

Table 3.15. Employees' social security contributions (2100) as % of GDP
Tableau 3.15. Cotisations de sécurité sociale à la charge des salariés (2100) en % du PIB

	1965	1980	1990	2000	2007	2009	2011	2012	2013	2014
Australia / Australie	0.0	0.0	0.0	0.0	0.0	0.0	0.0	0.0	0.0	0.0
Austria / Autriche	3.7	4.9	5.5	5.9	5.6	5.8	5.7	5.7	5.9	5.9
Belgium / Belgique	2.7	3.4	4.2	4.2	4.0	4.2	4.1	4.2	4.2	4.2
Canada	0.5	1.1	1.5	1.9	1.8	1.9	1.8	1.9	1.9	1.9
Chile / Chili	..	..	1.5	1.3	1.2	1.4	1.3	1.4	1.4	1.4
Czech Republic / République tchèque	..	..	..	3.3	3.3	2.9	3.0	3.0	3.0	2.9
Denmark / Danemark[1]	0.8	0.0	0.0	0.6	0.1	0.1	0.1	0.1	0.0	0.0
Estonia / Estonie	..	..	..	0.0	0.2	0.5	0.8	0.8	0.6	0.6
Finland / Finlande	0.0	1.2	1.3	2.1	2.2	2.3	2.6	2.9	2.9	3.0
France[1]	2.2	4.4	5.4	3.9	3.9	4.0	3.9	4.0	4.1	4.2
Germany / Allemagne[2]	3.7	5.6	5.6	6.2	5.6	6.1	6.1	6.2	6.2	6.2
Greece / Grèce[1]	2.2	3.0	3.8	4.0	4.1	4.1	4.3	4.4	4.4	4.2
Hungary / Hongrie	..	..	..	2.1	3.7	3.6	5.0	5.3	5.3	5.2
Iceland / Islande	0.0	0.0	0.1	..	..	..	..	..	..	..
Ireland / Irlande	0.8	1.4	1.5	0.9	1.0	1.9	1.9	1.8	1.8	1.7
Israel / Israël	..	..	..	3.3	3.5	3.5	3.5	3.4	3.3	3.3
Italy / Italie	..	2.0	2.3	2.2	2.2	2.4	2.3	2.3	2.4	2.4
Japan / Japon	1.3	2.5	3.0	3.9	4.3	4.7	5.2	5.3	5.4	5.5
Korea / Corée	..	0.0	0.7	1.4	2.1	2.2	2.4	2.6	2.7	2.8
Latvia / Lettonie	..	..	..	2.4	2.1	2.5	2.7	2.7	2.6	2.6
Luxembourg	3.1	3.9	3.6	4.3	4.6	5.3	5.1	5.2	5.0	5.0
Mexico / Mexique	..	..	..	..	..	..	..	..	..	..
Netherlands / Pays-Bas	4.7	6.3	9.3	7.9	6.7	6.5	7.1	7.6	7.6	7.3
New Zealand / Nouvelle-Zélande	0.0	0.0	0.0	0.0	0.0	0.0	0.0	0.0	0.0	0.0
Norway / Norvège	0.0	2.1	3.4	3.0	2.9	3.2	3.1	3.1	3.2	3.4
Poland / Pologne	..	..	..	5.4	4.7	4.2	4.4	4.7	4.9	4.6
Portugal	1.3	2.5	2.6	3.3	3.6	3.8	3.8	3.7	3.8	3.9
Slovak Republic / République slovaque	..	..	..	2.9	2.7	3.0	2.9	3.0	3.0	3.1
Slovenia / Slovénie	..	..	..	7.7	7.1	7.6	7.5	7.5	7.3	7.4
Spain / Espagne[1]	0.9	2.4	1.8	1.9	1.9	1.9	1.9	1.8	1.8	1.8
Sweden / Suède	0.6	0.0	0.1	2.7	2.5	2.6	2.6	2.6	2.7	2.7
Switzerland / Suisse	1.1	2.4	2.6	3.1	2.8	3.0	3.0	3.1	3.1	3.1
Turkey / Turquie	0.3	0.7	1.1	1.6	2.1	2.2	2.8	2.9	3.2	3.1
United Kingdom / Royaume-Uni	2.1	2.2	2.2	2.2	2.4	2.4	2.5	2.5	2.4	2.3
United States / États-Unis	1.2	2.3	2.9	3.0	2.8	2.8	2.0	2.0	2.7	2.8
Unweighted average / Moyenne non pondérée										
OECD Average / Moyenne OCDE	**1.4**	**2.2**	**2.5**	**3.0**	**3.0**	**3.1**	**3.2**	**3.3**	**3.3**	**3.3**

1. The total tax revenue has been reduced by the amount of any capital transfer that represents uncollected taxes. The capital transfer has been allocated between tax headings in proportion to the reported tax revenue.
2. From 1991, the figures relate to the united Germany.
1. Le total des recettes fiscales a été diminué du montant de tout transfert en capital représentant les impôts non perçus. Le transfert en capital a été réparti entre les différentes rubriques en proportion des recettes fiscales.
2. Depuis 1991, les chiffres se rapportent à l'Allemagne unifiée.

StatLink http://dx.doi.org/10.1787/888933416401

Table 3.16. **Employees' social security contributions (2100) as % of total taxation**
Tableau 3.16. **Cotisations de sécurité sociale à la charge des salariés (2100) en % du total des recettes fiscales**

	1965	1980	1990	2000	2007	2009	2011	2012	2013	2014
Australia / Australie	0.0	0.0	0.0	0.0	0.0	0.0	0.0	0.0	0.0	0.0
Austria / Autriche	11.1	12.7	13.9	13.9	13.7	14.1	13.9	13.7	13.8	13.8
Belgium / Belgique	8.9	8.4	10.2	9.7	9.4	9.9	9.6	9.5	9.3	9.3
Canada	2.1	3.7	4.4	5.5	5.7	6.0	5.8	6.0	6.0	6.0
Chile / Chili	..	..	8.7	7.0	5.3	7.8	6.1	6.3	7.0	7.0
Czech Republic / République tchèque	..	..	..	10.0	9.7	8.8	9.0	8.9	8.8	8.9
Denmark / Danemark[1]	2.7	0.0	0.0	1.3	0.1	0.1	0.1	0.1	0.1	0.1
Estonia / Estonie	..	..	..	0.0	0.5	1.5	2.4	2.4	1.8	1.8
Finland / Finlande	0.0	3.3	2.9	4.7	5.2	5.6	6.2	6.7	6.6	6.8
France[1]	6.6	11.1	13.2	9.0	9.3	9.6	9.0	9.0	9.1	9.3
Germany / Allemagne[2]	11.8	15.3	16.2	17.2	16.1	17.0	17.1	17.0	16.9	17.0
Greece / Grèce[1]	13.0	14.5	15.1	11.9	13.0	13.4	12.8	12.4	12.4	11.8
Hungary / Hongrie	..	..	..	5.4	9.3	9.1	13.6	13.8	13.9	13.5
Iceland / Islande	0.0	0.0	0.3	..	..	..	..	..	..	..
Ireland / Irlande	3.2	4.7	4.6	2.8	3.2	6.9	7.1	6.5	6.5	6.1
Israel / Israël	..	..	..	9.5	10.3	11.6	11.4	11.4	10.8	10.7
Italy / Italie	..	6.9	6.3	5.4	5.3	5.7	5.5	5.2	5.6	5.5
Japan / Japon	7.2	10.2	10.6	14.5	15.0	17.6	18.0	18.0	17.7	17.3
Korea / Corée	..	0.0	3.9	6.3	8.4	9.4	9.9	10.5	11.1	11.3
Latvia / Lettonie	..	..	..	8.3	7.5	9.0	9.8	9.5	9.3	8.9
Luxembourg	11.9	11.3	10.6	11.7	12.6	13.7	13.4	13.3	13.2	13.1
Mexico / Mexique	..	..	..	..	..	..	..	..	..	..
Netherlands / Pays-Bas	15.3	15.7	23.1	21.2	18.5	18.3	19.7	21.2	20.7	19.4
New Zealand / Nouvelle-Zélande	0.0	0.0	0.0	0.0	0.0	0.0	0.0	0.0	0.0	0.0
Norway / Norvège	0.0	5.0	8.4	7.2	6.9	7.8	7.5	7.6	8.0	8.8
Poland / Pologne	..	..	..	16.4	13.5	13.3	14.0	14.8	15.2	14.2
Portugal	8.5	11.3	9.9	10.7	11.4	12.8	11.7	11.6	11.0	11.5
Slovak Republic / République slovaque	..	..	..	8.5	9.3	10.2	10.0	10.4	10.0	9.8
Slovenia / Slovénie	..	..	..	20.9	19.1	20.9	20.6	20.3	20.0	20.4
Spain / Espagne[1]	6.5	10.8	5.8	5.6	5.2	6.2	5.9	5.6	5.4	5.4
Sweden / Suède	1.9	0.1	0.1	5.4	5.5	6.0	6.0	6.2	6.2	6.2
Switzerland / Suisse	6.4	10.4	11.0	11.4	10.9	11.0	11.3	11.6	11.5	11.5
Turkey / Turquie	2.6	5.1	7.4	6.7	8.8	9.0	10.0	10.4	10.9	10.8
United Kingdom / Royaume-Uni	7.0	6.4	6.6	6.8	7.2	7.8	7.5	7.5	7.4	7.3
United States / États-Unis	5.1	9.2	11.2	10.5	10.4	12.1	8.5	8.4	10.7	10.7
Unweighted average / Moyenne non pondérée										
OECD Average / Moyenne OCDE	**5.7**	**7.0**	**7.9**	**8.7**	**8.7**	**9.5**	**9.5**	**9.6**	**9.6**	**9.5**

1. The total tax revenue has been reduced by the amount of any capital transfer that represents uncollected taxes. The capital transfer has been allocated between tax headings in proportion to the reported tax revenue.
2. From 1991, the figures relate to the united Germany.

1. Le total des recettes fiscales a été diminué du montant de tout transfert en capital représentant les impôts non perçus. Le transfert en capital a été réparti entre les différentes rubriques en proportion des recettes fiscales.
2. Depuis 1991, les chiffres se rapportent à l'Allemagne unifiée.

StatLink http://dx.doi.org/10.1787/888933416416

Table 3.17. **Employers' social security contributions (2200) as % of GDP**
Tableau 3.17. **Cotisations de sécurité sociale à la charge des employeurs (2200) en % du PIB**

	1965	1980	1990	2000	2007	2009	2011	2012	2013	2014
Australia / Australie	0.0	0.0	0.0	0.0	0.0	0.0	0.0	0.0	0.0	0.0
Austria / Autriche	3.9	5.9	6.4	6.9	6.4	6.6	6.6	6.7	6.8	6.9
Belgium / Belgique	6.3	7.3	8.6	8.1	8.1	8.6	8.6	8.8	8.9	8.8
Canada	0.9	2.0	2.7	2.7	2.6	2.7	2.6	2.7	2.7	2.7
Chile / Chili	..	..	0.1	0.1	0.1	0.1	0.0	0.0	0.0	0.0
Czech Republic / République tchèque	..	..	..	9.3	9.4	8.8	9.2	9.3	9.3	9.2
Denmark / Danemark[1]	0.2	0.2	0.0	0.0	0.0	0.0	0.1	0.0	0.0	0.0
Estonia / Estonie	..	..	..	10.7	10.1	12.2	10.7	10.2	10.3	10.2
Finland / Finlande	2.0	6.6	8.9	8.5	8.4	9.0	8.6	8.8	8.8	8.7
France[1]	8.5	11.2	11.2	10.7	10.7	11.0	11.1	11.2	11.3	11.4
Germany / Allemagne[2]	4.6	6.7	6.6	7.0	6.1	6.5	6.4	6.5	6.5	6.5
Greece / Grèce[1]	2.1	3.0	3.8	4.7	4.9	4.6	4.8	4.8	4.7	4.5
Hungary / Hongrie	..	..	..	9.1	9.4	8.8	7.3	7.2	7.1	7.3
Iceland / Islande	2.1	0.6	0.9	..	..	..	..	..	..	..
Ireland / Irlande	0.8	2.8	2.9	2.6	2.9	3.1	3.1	2.9	3.0	3.0
Israel / Israël	..	..	..	1.5	1.4	1.3	1.4	1.3	1.4	1.5
Italy / Italie	..	8.2	8.6	8.1	8.6	9.1	8.9	8.9	8.8	8.7
Japan / Japon	1.7	3.7	3.6	4.4	4.7	5.0	5.4	5.6	5.6	5.8
Korea / Corée	..	0.2	0.9	1.5	2.3	2.5	2.6	2.7	2.9	3.0
Latvia / Lettonie	..	..	..	7.3	5.7	6.7	5.9	6.0	5.8	5.8
Luxembourg	4.9	5.4	4.5	4.2	4.3	5.0	4.8	4.8	4.7	4.7
Mexico / Mexique	..	..	..	..	..	..	..	..	..	..
Netherlands / Pays-Bas	3.9	7.2	3.0	4.2	4.2	4.6	4.7	5.1	4.8	5.3
New Zealand / Nouvelle-Zélande	0.0	0.0	0.0	0.0	0.0	0.0	0.0	0.0	0.0	0.0
Norway / Norvège	3.0	6.4	6.7	5.3	5.4	5.8	5.6	5.7	5.8	5.9
Poland / Pologne	..	..	..	5.7	4.8	4.6	4.6	4.8	5.2	5.0
Portugal	2.1	3.9	4.3	4.6	4.5	4.7	5.1	5.0	5.1	5.0
Slovak Republic / République slovaque	..	..	..	9.0	6.1	6.6	6.5	6.6	7.4	7.6
Slovenia / Slovénie	..	..	..	5.3	5.2	5.6	5.6	5.7	5.6	5.4
Spain / Espagne[1]	3.1	8.3	8.0	8.4	8.6	8.3	8.3	8.0	7.9	8.2
Sweden / Suède	2.8	12.1	12.9	10.0	9.1	8.1	7.2	7.4	7.2	7.1
Switzerland / Suisse	1.1	2.5	2.6	3.1	2.9	3.0	3.1	3.1	3.1	3.1
Turkey / Turquie	0.3	1.1	1.6	2.2	2.4	3.3	4.1	4.1	4.5	4.6
United Kingdom / Royaume-Uni	2.2	3.4	3.2	3.1	3.5	3.6	3.6	3.6	3.6	3.5
United States / États-Unis	1.8	3.0	3.4	3.3	3.2	3.1	3.1	3.1	3.1	3.1
Unweighted average / Moyenne non pondérée										
OECD Average / Moyenne OCDE	**2.5**	**4.5**	**4.4**	**5.2**	**5.0**	**5.2**	**5.1**	**5.2**	**5.2**	**5.2**

1. The total tax revenue has been reduced by the amount of any capital transfer that represents uncollected taxes. The capital transfer has been allocated between tax headings in proportion to the reported tax revenue.
2. From 1991, the figures relate to the united Germany.

1. Le total des recettes fiscales a été diminué du montant de tout transfert en capital représentant les impôts non perçus. Le transfert en capital a été réparti entre les différentes rubriques en proportion des recettes fiscales.
2. Depuis 1991, les chiffres se rapportent à l'Allemagne unifiée.

StatLink http://dx.doi.org/10.1787/888933416422

Table 3.18. **Employers' social security contributions (2200) as % of total taxation**

Tableau 3.18. **Cotisations de sécurité sociale à la charge des employeurs (2200) en % du total des recettes fiscales**

	1965	1980	1990	2000	2007	2009	2011	2012	2013	2014
Australia / Australie	0.0	0.0	0.0	0.0	0.0	0.0	0.0	0.0	0.0	0.0
Austria / Autriche	11.6	15.3	16.2	16.4	15.9	16.2	16.1	16.0	16.0	16.0
Belgium / Belgique	20.6	18.1	20.9	18.5	19.0	20.4	19.9	19.8	19.7	19.5
Canada	3.5	6.6	7.6	7.8	8.2	8.5	8.4	8.6	8.6	8.6
Chile / Chili	..	..	0.3	0.3	0.2	0.4	0.2	0.2	0.2	0.2
Czech Republic / République tchèque	..	..	..	28.5	27.4	27.2	27.8	27.6	27.4	27.7
Denmark / Danemark[1]	0.6	0.4	0.0	0.0	0.0	0.0	0.1	0.1	0.1	0.1
Estonia / Estonie	..	..	..	34.5	32.2	34.8	34.1	32.5	32.6	31.6
Finland / Finlande	6.8	18.7	20.8	18.5	20.3	21.9	20.5	20.7	20.2	19.9
France[1]	25.3	28.4	27.2	24.8	25.2	26.7	25.7	25.3	25.0	25.1
Germany / Allemagne[2]	14.4	18.4	19.1	19.2	17.4	18.1	18.0	17.9	17.9	17.9
Greece / Grèce[1]	12.2	14.4	15.1	14.1	15.9	15.1	14.2	13.7	13.2	12.5
Hungary / Hongrie	..	..	..	23.6	23.8	22.6	20.0	18.6	18.5	19.0
Iceland / Islande	8.1	2.2	2.9	..	..	..	..	..	..	..
Ireland / Irlande	3.3	9.4	8.9	8.4	9.7	11.4	11.4	10.4	10.5	10.5
Israel / Israël	..	..	..	4.4	4.0	4.2	4.4	4.5	4.6	4.7
Italy / Italie	..	28.4	23.6	19.9	20.5	21.6	21.2	20.2	20.1	20.0
Japan / Japon	9.5	14.8	12.7	16.4	16.6	18.5	19.0	18.9	18.5	18.1
Korea / Corée	..	1.1	4.5	6.9	9.1	10.6	10.7	10.8	12.0	12.3
Latvia / Lettonie	..	..	..	25.1	20.2	24.0	21.4	20.9	20.3	20.0
Luxembourg	18.6	15.8	13.5	11.3	11.8	12.8	12.5	12.4	12.2	12.2
Mexico / Mexique	..	..	..	..	..	..	..	..	..	..
Netherlands / Pays-Bas	12.6	17.8	7.5	11.2	11.7	12.9	13.1	14.0	13.3	14.1
New Zealand / Nouvelle-Zélande	0.0	0.0	0.0	0.0	0.0	0.0	0.0	0.0	0.0	0.0
Norway / Norvège	10.2	15.3	16.6	12.5	12.7	14.2	13.3	13.6	14.5	15.3
Poland / Pologne	..	..	..	17.4	13.8	14.7	14.5	15.2	16.2	15.7
Portugal	13.2	17.7	16.3	14.7	14.2	15.8	15.8	15.7	15.1	14.7
Slovak Republic / République slovaque	..	..	..	26.8	21.0	23.0	22.8	23.4	24.6	24.4
Slovenia / Slovénie	..	..	..	14.6	14.2	15.5	15.3	15.5	15.3	14.9
Spain / Espagne[1]	21.7	37.8	25.5	25.1	23.5	27.6	26.3	24.7	23.9	24.1
Sweden / Suède	8.9	27.6	26.0	20.4	20.2	18.3	16.9	17.4	16.8	16.7
Switzerland / Suisse	6.6	10.6	11.0	11.4	10.9	11.0	11.3	11.6	11.5	11.5
Turkey / Turquie	3.3	8.1	11.0	9.0	10.1	13.4	14.7	14.9	15.5	15.9
United Kingdom / Royaume-Uni	7.6	10.1	9.9	9.6	10.6	11.4	10.7	11.1	11.0	10.9
United States / États-Unis	7.6	11.9	13.1	11.8	11.8	13.6	13.1	13.0	12.1	12.0
Unweighted average / Moyenne non pondérée										
OECD Average / Moyenne OCDE	**9.8**	**14.0**	**12.7**	**14.6**	**14.3**	**15.3**	**15.0**	**14.8**	**14.8**	**14.7**

1. The total tax revenue has been reduced by the amount of any capital transfer that represents uncollected taxes. The capital transfer has been allocated between tax headings in proportion to the reported tax revenue.
2. From 1991, the figures relate to the united Germany.
1. Le total des recettes fiscales a été diminué du montant de tout transfert en capital représentant les impôts non perçus. Le transfert en capital a été réparti entre les différentes rubriques en proportion des recettes fiscales.
2. Depuis 1991, les chiffres se rapportent à l'Allemagne unifiée.

StatLink http://dx.doi.org/10.1787/888933416437

Table 3.19. **Taxes on payroll and workforce (3000) as % of GDP**
Tableau 3.19. **Impôts sur les salaires ou la main-d'œuvre (3000) en % du PIB**

	1965	1980	1990	2000	2007	2009	2011	2012	2013	2014
Australia / Australie	0.6	1.3	1.7	1.4	1.4	1.3	1.4	1.4	1.4	1.4
Austria / Autriche	2.6	2.7	2.4	2.7	2.6	2.8	2.8	2.9	2.9	3.0
Belgium / Belgique	0.0	0.0	0.0	0.0	0.0	0.0	0.0	0.0	0.0	0.0
Canada	0.0	0.0	0.8	0.7	0.6	0.7	0.6	0.6	0.6	0.6
Chile / Chili	..	..	0.0	0.0	0.0	0.0	0.0	0.0	0.0	0.0
Czech Republic / République tchèque	..	..	..	0.0	0.0	0.0	0.0	0.0	0.0	0.0
Denmark / Danemark[1]	0.0	0.0	0.3	0.2	0.2	0.2	0.3	0.3	0.3	0.3
Estonia / Estonie	..	..	..	0.0	0.0	0.0	0.0	0.0	0.0	0.0
Finland / Finlande	1.5	0.1	0.0	0.0	0.0	0.0	0.0	0.0	0.0	0.0
France[1]	1.6	0.9	0.8	1.0	1.2	1.3	1.3	1.4	1.6	1.6
Germany / Allemagne[2]	0.2	0.1	0.0	0.0	0.0	0.0	0.0	0.0	0.0	0.0
Greece / Grèce[1]	0.1	0.4	0.2	0.0	0.0	0.0	0.0	0.0	0.0	0.0
Hungary / Hongrie	..	..	..	1.4	0.3	0.3	0.5	0.5	0.6	0.6
Iceland / Islande	0.2	1.1	1.1	0.0	0.1	0.2	0.2	0.3	0.3	0.4
Ireland / Irlande	0.0	0.1	0.4	0.0	0.2	0.2	0.2	0.2	0.2	0.2
Israel / Israël	..	..	..	1.3	1.3	1.2	1.2	1.2	1.2	1.2
Italy / Italie	0.0	0.2	0.1	0.0	0.0	0.0	0.0	0.0	0.0	0.0
Japan / Japon	0.0	0.0	0.0	0.0	0.0	0.0	0.0	0.0	0.0	0.0
Korea / Corée	..	0.1	0.1	0.0	0.1	0.1	0.1	0.1	0.1	0.1
Latvia / Lettonie	..	..	..	0.0	0.0	0.0	0.0	0.0	0.0	0.0
Luxembourg	0.2	0.2	0.0	0.0	0.0	0.0	0.0	0.0	0.0	0.0
Mexico / Mexique	..	0.2	0.2	0.2	0.2	0.3	0.3	0.3	0.3	0.4
Netherlands / Pays-Bas	0.0	0.0	0.0	0.0	0.0	0.0	0.0	0.0	0.0	0.0
New Zealand / Nouvelle-Zélande	0.0	0.0	0.0	0.0	0.0	0.0	0.0	0.0	0.0	0.0
Norway / Norvège	0.0	0.0	0.0	0.0	0.0	0.0	0.0	0.0	0.0	0.0
Poland / Pologne	..	..	..	0.2	0.3	0.3	0.3	0.3	0.2	0.2
Portugal	0.1	0.6	0.0	0.0	0.0	0.0	0.0	0.0	0.0	0.0
Slovak Republic / République slovaque	..	..	..	0.0	0.0	0.0	0.0	0.0	0.0	0.0
Slovenia / Slovénie	..	..	..	1.5	1.2	0.1	0.1	0.1	0.1	0.1
Spain / Espagne[1]	0.0	0.0	0.0	0.0	0.0	0.0	0.0	0.0	0.0	0.0
Sweden / Suède	0.0	1.1	1.2	2.1	2.5	3.7	4.2	4.4	4.6	4.5
Switzerland / Suisse	0.0	0.0	0.0	0.0	0.0	0.0	0.0	0.0	0.0	0.0
Turkey / Turquie	0.0	0.0	0.0	0.0	0.0	0.0	0.0	0.0	0.0	0.0
United Kingdom / Royaume-Uni	0.0	1.4	0.0	0.0	0.0	0.0	0.0	0.0	0.0	0.0
United States / États-Unis	0.0	0.0	0.0	0.0	0.0	0.0	0.0	0.0	0.0	0.0
Unweighted average / Moyenne non pondérée										
OECD Average / Moyenne OCDE	**0.3**	**0.4**	**0.3**	**0.4**	**0.4**	**0.4**	**0.4**	**0.4**	**0.4**	**0.4**

1. The total tax revenue has been reduced by the amount of any capital transfer that represents uncollected taxes. The capital transfer has been allocated between tax headings in proportion to the reported tax revenue.
2. From 1991, the figures relate to the united Germany.
1. Le total des recettes fiscales a été diminué du montant de tout transfert en capital représentant les impôts non perçus. Le transfert en capital a été réparti entre les différentes rubriques en proportion des recettes fiscales.
2. Depuis 1991, les chiffres se rapportent à l'Allemagne unifiée.

StatLink http://dx.doi.org/10.1787/888933416445

Table 3.20. Taxes on payroll and workforce (3000) as % of total taxation
Tableau 3.20. Impôts sur les salaires ou la main-d'œuvre (3000) en % du total des recettes fiscales

	1965	1980	1990	2000	2007	2009	2011	2012	2013	2014
Australia / Australie	3.1	5.0	6.1	4.5	4.7	5.2	5.2	5.1	5.1	5.1
Austria / Autriche	7.6	7.0	6.0	6.4	6.3	6.9	6.9	6.9	6.9	6.9
Belgium / Belgique	0.0	0.0	0.0	0.0	0.0	0.0	0.0	0.0	0.0	0.0
Canada	0.0	0.0	2.3	2.1	2.0	2.1	2.1	2.1	2.1	2.0
Chile / Chili	..	..	0.0	0.0	0.0	0.0	0.0	0.0	0.0	0.0
Czech Republic / République tchèque	..	..	..	0.0	0.0	0.0	0.0	0.0	0.0	0.0
Denmark / Danemark[1]	0.0	0.0	0.7	0.4	0.5	0.5	0.6	0.6	0.7	0.7
Estonia / Estonie	..	..	..	0.0	0.0	0.0	0.0	0.0	0.0	0.0
Finland / Finlande	5.2	0.2	0.0	0.0	0.0	0.0	0.0	0.0	0.0	0.0
France[1]	4.6	2.2	1.9	2.3	2.8	3.2	3.1	3.2	3.5	3.5
Germany / Allemagne[2]	0.6	0.2	0.0	0.0	0.0	0.0	0.0	0.0	0.0	0.0
Greece / Grèce[1]	0.8	1.8	0.7	0.0	0.0	0.0	0.0	0.0	0.0	0.0
Hungary / Hongrie	..	..	..	3.6	0.8	0.9	1.3	1.4	1.5	1.5
Iceland / Islande	0.9	3.8	3.5	0.1	0.3	0.5	0.5	0.9	1.0	0.9
Ireland / Irlande	0.0	0.2	1.3	0.0	0.7	0.8	0.7	0.6	0.6	0.6
Israel / Israël	..	..	..	3.6	4.0	3.9	3.8	3.9	3.8	3.8
Italy / Italie	0.0	0.6	0.3	0.0	0.0	0.0	0.0	0.0	0.0	0.0
Japan / Japon	0.0	0.0	0.0	0.0	0.0	0.0	0.0	0.0	0.0	0.0
Korea / Corée	..	0.5	0.4	0.2	0.2	0.2	0.2	0.3	0.3	0.3
Latvia / Lettonie	..	..	..	0.0	0.1	0.1	0.1	0.0	0.0	0.0
Luxembourg	0.9	0.6	0.0	0.0	0.0	0.0	0.0	0.0	0.0	0.0
Mexico / Mexique	..	1.0	1.8	1.3	1.9	2.0	2.1	2.2	2.3	2.5
Netherlands / Pays-Bas	0.0	0.0	0.0	0.0	0.0	0.0	0.0	0.0	0.0	0.0
New Zealand / Nouvelle-Zélande	0.0	0.0	0.0	0.0	0.0	0.0	0.0	0.0	0.0	0.0
Norway / Norvège	0.0	0.0	0.0	0.0	0.0	0.0	0.0	0.0	0.0	0.0
Poland / Pologne	..	..	..	0.7	0.7	0.9	0.8	0.8	0.8	0.7
Portugal	0.9	2.6	0.0	0.0	0.0	0.0	0.0	0.0	0.0	0.0
Slovak Republic / République slovaque	..	..	..	0.0	0.0	0.0	0.0	0.0	0.0	0.0
Slovenia / Slovénie	..	..	..	4.2	3.2	0.2	0.2	0.2	0.2	0.1
Spain / Espagne[1]	0.0	0.0	0.0	0.0	0.0	0.0	0.0	0.0	0.0	0.0
Sweden / Suède	0.0	2.6	2.5	4.3	5.6	8.5	10.0	10.2	10.6	10.6
Switzerland / Suisse	0.0	0.0	0.0	0.0	0.0	0.0	0.0	0.0	0.0	0.0
Turkey / Turquie	0.0	0.0	0.0	0.0	0.0	0.0	0.0	0.0	0.0	0.0
United Kingdom / Royaume-Uni	0.0	4.3	0.0	0.0	0.0	0.0	0.0	0.0	0.0	0.0
United States / États-Unis	0.0	0.0	0.0	0.0	0.0	0.0	0.0	0.0	0.0	0.0
Unweighted average / Moyenne non pondérée										
OECD Average / Moyenne OCDE	**1.0**	**1.3**	**1.0**	**1.0**	**1.0**	**1.0**	**1.1**	**1.1**	**1.1**	**1.1**

1. The total tax revenue has been reduced by the amount of any capital transfer that represents uncollected taxes. The capital transfer has been allocated between tax headings in proportion to the reported tax revenue.
2. From 1991, the figures relate to the united Germany.

1. Le total des recettes fiscales a été diminué du montant de tout transfert en capital représentant les impôts non perçus. Le transfert en capital a été réparti entre les différentes rubriques en proportion des recettes fiscales.
2. Depuis 1991, les chiffres se rapportent à l'Allemagne unifiée.

StatLink http://dx.doi.org/10.1787/888933416455

Table 3.21. **Taxes on property (4000) as % of GDP**
Tableau 3.21. **Impôts sur le patrimoine (4000) en % du PIB**

	1965	1980	1990	2000	2007	2009	2011	2012	2013	2014
Australia / Australie	2.4	2.0	2.5	2.7	2.6	2.5	2.3	2.4	2.6	2.8
Austria / Autriche	1.3	1.1	1.1	0.6	0.6	0.5	0.5	0.6	0.7	0.6
Belgium / Belgique	1.1	1.3	1.6	2.0	3.1	2.9	3.1	3.3	3.5	3.6
Canada	3.6	2.8	3.5	3.3	3.4	3.9	3.7	3.7	3.7	3.7
Chile / Chili	..	..	1.0	1.3	1.1	0.9	0.8	0.9	0.8	0.8
Czech Republic / République tchèque	..	..	..	0.5	0.4	0.4	0.5	0.5	0.5	0.4
Denmark / Danemark[1]	2.4	2.4	1.9	1.6	1.8	1.8	1.9	1.8	1.8	1.9
Estonia / Estonie	..	..	..	0.4	0.2	0.3	0.3	0.3	0.3	0.3
Finland / Finlande	1.2	0.7	1.1	1.1	1.1	1.1	1.1	1.2	1.3	1.3
France[1]	1.4	1.9	2.6	2.9	3.3	3.3	3.6	3.8	3.8	3.9
Germany / Allemagne[2]	1.8	1.2	1.2	0.8	0.9	0.8	0.9	0.9	0.9	1.0
Greece / Grèce[1]	1.7	1.0	1.2	2.0	1.7	2.0	2.3	2.5	3.0	1.4
Hungary / Hongrie	..	..	..	0.7	0.8	0.8	1.1	1.2	1.3	1.3
Iceland / Islande	1.0	1.8	2.5	2.8	2.4	2.1	2.3	2.5	2.5	2.5
Ireland / Irlande	3.7	1.6	1.5	1.8	2.4	1.5	1.6	1.8	2.0	2.2
Israel / Israël	..	..	..	3.1	3.2	3.0	3.2	2.9	3.0	3.0
Italy / Italie	1.8	1.1	0.8	1.9	2.0	2.6	2.2	2.7	2.7	2.9
Japan / Japon	1.4	2.0	2.7	2.8	2.6	2.7	2.8	2.7	2.7	2.7
Korea / Corée	..	1.4	2.2	2.7	3.2	2.8	2.7	2.6	2.5	2.7
Latvia / Lettonie	..	..	..	1.1	0.9	0.7	1.0	1.0	1.0	1.0
Luxembourg	1.6	1.9	2.8	4.0	3.5	2.6	2.6	2.7	2.8	3.0
Mexico / Mexique	..	0.3	0.2	0.2	0.3	0.3	0.3	0.3	0.3	0.3
Netherlands / Pays-Bas	1.4	1.4	1.5	2.0	1.7	1.4	1.2	1.1	1.2	1.4
New Zealand / Nouvelle-Zélande	2.7	2.3	2.5	1.7	1.8	2.0	2.0	2.0	1.9	2.0
Norway / Norvège	0.9	0.7	1.2	1.0	1.2	1.2	1.2	1.2	1.2	1.2
Poland / Pologne	..	..	..	1.4	1.4	1.4	1.3	1.3	1.4	1.4
Portugal	0.8	0.3	0.7	1.1	1.3	1.1	1.1	1.1	1.1	1.2
Slovak Republic / République slovaque	..	..	..	0.6	0.4	0.4	0.4	0.4	0.4	0.4
Slovenia / Slovénie	..	..	..	0.6	0.6	0.6	0.6	0.6	0.6	0.6
Spain / Espagne[1]	0.9	1.0	1.7	2.1	2.9	2.0	1.9	2.0	2.2	2.4
Sweden / Suède	0.6	0.4	1.7	1.7	1.1	1.0	1.0	1.0	1.1	1.1
Switzerland / Suisse	1.6	1.9	1.9	2.5	2.1	1.9	1.8	1.7	1.7	1.8
Turkey / Turquie	1.1	0.7	0.3	0.8	0.9	0.9	1.1	1.2	1.4	1.4
United Kingdom / Royaume-Uni	4.3	4.0	2.7	3.8	4.1	3.8	3.9	3.9	4.0	4.1
United States / États-Unis	3.7	2.7	3.0	2.9	3.1	3.2	3.0	2.9	2.9	2.8
Unweighted average / Moyenne non pondérée										
OECD Average / Moyenne OCDE	**1.9**	**1.5**	**1.8**	**1.8**	**1.8**	**1.7**	**1.8**	**1.8**	**1.9**	**1.9**

1. The total tax revenue has been reduced by the amount of any capital transfer that represents uncollected taxes. The capital transfer has been allocated between tax headings in proportion to the reported tax revenue.
2. From 1991, the figures relate to the united Germany.
1. Le total des recettes fiscales a été diminué du montant de tout transfert en capital représentant les impôts non perçus. Le transfert en capital a été réparti entre les différentes rubriques en proportion des recettes fiscales.
2. Depuis 1991, les chiffres se rapportent à l'Allemagne unifiée.

StatLink http://dx.doi.org/10.1787/888933416468

Table 3.22. **Taxes on property (4000) as % of total taxation**
Tableau 3.22. **Impôts sur le patrimoine (4000) en % du total des recettes fiscales**

	1965	1980	1990	2000	2007	2009	2011	2012	2013	2014
Australia / Australie	11.5	7.8	9.0	8.8	8.9	9.5	8.6	8.6	9.4	10.1
Austria / Autriche	4.0	2.9	2.7	1.3	1.4	1.3	1.2	1.3	1.7	1.4
Belgium / Belgique	3.7	3.1	3.8	4.7	7.2	6.9	7.3	7.4	7.8	7.9
Canada	14.3	9.1	10.0	9.5	10.6	12.2	12.0	11.9	11.9	11.7
Chile / Chili	..	..	6.2	7.0	4.9	5.4	4.0	4.3	4.1	4.2
Czech Republic / République tchèque	..	..	..	1.4	1.2	1.1	1.5	1.5	1.4	1.3
Denmark / Danemark[1]	8.1	5.9	4.3	3.3	3.9	4.0	4.2	3.9	3.9	3.7
Estonia / Estonie	..	..	..	1.2	0.7	1.0	1.0	1.0	1.0	0.9
Finland / Finlande	4.0	1.9	2.4	2.4	2.6	2.6	2.6	2.8	2.9	3.0
France[1]	4.3	4.8	6.3	6.9	7.9	8.0	8.4	8.5	8.4	8.5
Germany / Allemagne[2]	5.8	3.3	3.4	2.3	2.5	2.3	2.4	2.5	2.5	2.6
Greece / Grèce[1]	9.7	4.6	4.6	6.1	5.3	6.4	6.9	7.1	8.4	4.0
Hungary / Hongrie	..	..	..	1.7	2.0	2.1	3.1	3.2	3.4	3.4
Iceland / Islande	4.0	6.3	8.4	7.9	6.1	6.5	6.7	7.1	6.9	6.4
Ireland / Irlande	15.1	5.3	4.6	5.7	8.0	5.3	6.1	6.4	7.2	7.7
Israel / Israël	..	..	..	8.8	9.5	10.1	10.4	9.8	9.6	9.5
Italy / Italie	7.2	3.7	2.3	4.6	4.9	6.2	5.3	6.2	6.2	6.6
Japan / Japon	8.1	8.2	9.4	10.5	9.0	10.1	9.7	9.1	8.8	8.5
Korea / Corée	..	8.0	11.8	12.4	12.8	11.6	11.4	10.6	10.3	11.0
Latvia / Lettonie	..	..	..	3.8	3.1	2.5	3.5	3.4	3.4	3.6
Luxembourg	6.2	5.7	8.4	10.7	9.6	6.6	6.9	7.0	7.3	7.8
Mexico / Mexique	..	1.9	1.9	1.7	2.2	2.2	2.0	2.1	2.0	2.1
Netherlands / Pays-Bas	4.4	3.6	3.7	5.3	4.7	4.0	3.4	3.0	3.4	3.9
New Zealand / Nouvelle-Zélande	11.5	7.9	6.8	5.3	5.3	6.5	6.6	6.3	6.1	6.2
Norway / Norvège	3.1	1.7	2.9	2.3	2.8	2.9	2.8	2.9	3.0	3.1
Poland / Pologne	..	..	..	4.3	4.2	4.3	4.1	4.2	4.4	4.4
Portugal	5.0	1.4	2.7	3.7	4.1	3.6	3.4	3.3	3.3	3.6
Slovak Republic / République slovaque	..	..	..	1.8	1.3	1.5	1.4	1.5	1.5	1.4
Slovenia / Slovénie	..	..	..	1.7	1.6	1.6	1.6	1.7	1.8	1.7
Spain / Espagne[1]	6.4	4.6	5.5	6.3	8.0	6.5	6.0	6.2	6.7	7.0
Sweden / Suède	1.8	0.9	3.5	3.4	2.4	2.4	2.4	2.4	2.5	2.5
Switzerland / Suisse	9.9	8.3	8.1	9.0	7.9	7.0	6.6	6.3	6.4	6.6
Turkey / Turquie	10.5	5.4	2.3	3.2	3.8	3.6	4.1	4.2	4.6	4.9
United Kingdom / Royaume-Uni	14.5	12.0	8.2	11.6	12.6	12.2	11.6	11.9	12.4	12.7
United States / États-Unis	15.9	10.7	11.6	10.2	11.4	14.1	12.4	12.0	11.3	10.8
Unweighted average / Moyenne non pondérée										
OECD Average / Moyenne OCDE	**7.9**	**5.3**	**5.7**	**5.5**	**5.6**	**5.5**	**5.5**	**5.5**	**5.6**	**5.6**

1. The total tax revenue has been reduced by the amount of any capital transfer that represents uncollected taxes. The capital transfer has been allocated between tax headings in proportion to the reported tax revenue.
2. From 1991, the figures relate to the united Germany.

1. Le total des recettes fiscales a été diminué du montant de tout transfert en capital représentant les impôts non perçus. Le transfert en capital a été réparti entre les différentes rubriques en proportion des recettes fiscales.
2. Depuis 1991, les chiffres se rapportent à l'Allemagne unifiée.

StatLink http://dx.doi.org/10.1787/888933416477

Table 3.23. **Taxes on goods and services (5000) as % of GDP**
Tableau 3.23. **Impôts sur les biens et services (5000) en % du PIB**

	1965	1980	1990	2000	2007	2009	2011	2012	2013	2014
Australia / Australie	7.2	8.2	7.8	8.7	8.0	7.6	7.2	7.7	7.9	7.5
Austria / Autriche	12.6	12.2	12.4	12.1	11.2	11.6	11.6	11.8	11.7	11.7
Belgium / Belgique	11.4	10.9	10.7	10.9	10.7	10.6	10.7	11.1	10.9	10.8
Canada	10.2	9.9	9.1	8.4	7.7	7.3	7.2	7.2	7.1	7.2
Chile / Chili	..	..	10.7	12.0	10.0	9.7	10.5	10.8	10.8	10.9
Czech Republic / République tchèque	..	..	..	10.2	10.3	10.8	11.2	11.4	11.7	10.9
Denmark / Danemark[1]	12.2	15.8	15.1	15.5	16.2	15.2	15.1	15.1	15.1	15.0
Estonia / Estonie	..	..	..	12.1	13.1	14.2	13.1	13.4	13.0	13.7
Finland / Finlande	12.7	12.5	14.0	13.3	12.6	12.9	13.8	14.1	14.5	14.4
France[1]	12.9	12.0	11.6	11.1	10.5	10.4	10.7	10.8	10.9	11.0
Germany / Allemagne[2]	10.4	9.9	9.3	10.2	10.2	10.8	10.4	10.3	10.2	10.1
Greece / Grèce[1]	8.4	8.6	11.2	12.1	11.4	11.0	13.2	13.4	13.9	15.5
Hungary / Hongrie	..	..	..	15.6	14.9	15.5	15.9	17.0	16.8	16.8
Iceland / Islande	16.0	17.3	15.5	16.0	15.8	11.3	11.9	12.3	12.1	12.1
Ireland / Irlande	12.9	13.2	13.6	11.7	11.1	9.8	9.3	9.4	9.5	9.7
Israel / Israël	..	..	..	11.6	11.9	11.6	12.0	11.5	11.9	12.3
Italy / Italie	9.7	7.6	10.2	11.3	10.5	10.4	11.3	11.6	11.5	11.8
Japan / Japon	4.7	4.0	3.9	5.1	5.1	5.1	5.3	5.3	5.3	6.3
Korea / Corée	..	10.6	8.3	8.2	7.8	7.6	7.5	7.7	7.5	7.4
Latvia / Lettonie	..	..	..	11.2	11.0	10.9	10.9	11.3	11.5	11.8
Luxembourg	6.5	7.5	7.9	9.8	10.1	10.8	10.6	11.0	10.7	11.0
Mexico / Mexique	..	7.4	5.4	5.8	5.0	5.0	5.1	5.0	4.7	5.4
Netherlands / Pays-Bas	8.8	10.2	10.6	10.7	11.2	10.8	10.8	10.7	10.9	11.1
New Zealand / Nouvelle-Zélande	6.5	6.6	12.1	11.3	10.7	11.1	12.1	12.3	12.0	12.5
Norway / Norvège	12.1	14.8	14.3	13.3	12.0	11.5	11.1	10.9	11.0	11.1
Poland / Pologne	..	..	..	11.6	13.1	11.7	12.5	11.7	11.5	11.6
Portugal	7.5	10.2	11.7	12.5	13.2	11.6	12.9	12.9	12.7	13.0
Slovak Republic / République slovaque	..	..	..	12.2	11.0	10.4	10.5	9.9	10.4	10.7
Slovenia / Slovénie	..	..	..	13.8	13.0	13.3	13.7	14.2	14.9	14.7
Spain / Espagne[1]	5.8	4.6	9.0	9.8	9.2	6.8	8.2	8.6	9.4	9.6
Sweden / Suède	9.8	10.5	12.4	12.1	12.0	12.7	12.4	12.3	12.3	12.1
Switzerland / Suisse	5.7	5.4	4.9	6.1	5.9	6.0	6.1	6.2	6.1	6.1
Turkey / Turquie	5.7	3.4	4.2	10.1	11.5	11.2	12.6	12.4	13.5	12.7
United Kingdom / Royaume-Uni	9.7	9.7	10.2	10.5	9.6	9.2	10.9	10.8	10.7	10.7
United States / États-Unis	5.3	4.5	4.6	4.6	4.5	4.2	4.4	4.4	4.5	4.5
Unweighted average / Moyenne non pondérée										
OECD Average / Moyenne OCDE	**9.4**	**9.5**	**10.0**	**10.9**	**10.6**	**10.3**	**10.6**	**10.8**	**10.8**	**11.0**

1. The total tax revenue has been reduced by the amount of any capital transfer that represents uncollected taxes. The capital transfer has been allocated between tax headings in proportion to the reported tax revenue.
2. From 1991, the figures relate to the united Germany.
1. Le total des recettes fiscales a été diminué du montant de tout transfert en capital représentant les impôts non perçus. Le transfert en capital a été réparti entre les différentes rubriques en proportion des recettes fiscales.
2. Depuis 1991, les chiffres se rapportent à l'Allemagne unifiée.

StatLink http://dx.doi.org/10.1787/888933416484

Table 3.24. Taxes on goods and services (5000) as % of total taxation
Tableau 3.24. Impôts sur les biens et services (5000) en % du total des recettes fiscales

	1965	1980	1990	2000	2007	2009	2011	2012	2013	2014
Australia / Australie	34.7	31.1	27.8	28.7	26.9	29.6	27.3	28.3	28.6	26.9
Austria / Autriche	37.4	31.5	31.5	28.7	27.7	28.2	28.3	28.2	27.5	27.3
Belgium / Belgique	37.2	27.0	26.1	25.0	25.0	24.9	24.8	25.0	24.2	23.9
Canada	40.5	32.6	25.8	24.2	24.0	22.9	23.7	23.4	23.0	23.0
Chile / Chili	..	..	62.9	63.8	43.8	55.6	49.3	50.1	54.0	55.3
Czech Republic / République tchèque	..	..	..	31.5	29.9	33.3	33.7	33.9	34.3	32.9
Denmark / Danemark[1]	41.9	38.1	33.9	33.1	34.9	33.6	33.4	33.0	32.3	30.2
Estonia / Estonie	..	..	..	38.8	41.9	40.6	41.7	42.4	41.2	42.1
Finland / Finlande	42.5	35.3	32.5	29.0	30.2	31.6	32.9	33.1	33.2	32.8
France[1]	38.4	30.4	28.4	25.9	24.9	25.2	24.7	24.4	24.0	24.1
Germany / Allemagne[2]	33.0	27.1	26.7	28.1	29.3	29.8	29.1	28.5	28.0	27.7
Greece / Grèce[1]	48.8	41.2	44.5	36.3	36.6	35.5	39.3	37.8	39.1	43.4
Hungary / Hongrie	..	..	..	40.5	37.6	39.5	43.6	44.0	43.9	44.0
Iceland / Islande	62.7	59.9	51.3	44.1	40.4	35.5	34.6	34.9	33.5	31.0
Ireland / Irlande	52.6	43.7	41.9	38.2	36.4	35.7	34.3	34.3	33.6	33.6
Israel / Israël	..	..	..	33.2	34.9	39.0	39.0	38.9	38.6	39.4
Italy / Italie	39.5	26.5	28.0	27.9	25.3	24.8	26.9	26.5	26.1	27.0
Japan / Japon	26.2	16.3	13.7	19.3	18.0	19.1	18.4	18.0	17.6	19.8
Korea / Corée	..	62.7	44.3	38.4	31.3	31.8	31.2	31.2	30.7	30.0
Latvia / Lettonie	..	..	..	38.6	39.1	39.0	39.3	39.5	40.4	40.9
Luxembourg	24.7	21.8	23.6	26.3	27.8	27.9	28.0	28.3	28.2	28.8
Mexico / Mexique	..	51.2	44.0	42.8	37.6	37.0	36.2	36.1	32.4	35.8
Netherlands / Pays-Bas	28.6	25.3	26.4	28.9	31.0	30.6	30.1	29.8	29.8	29.6
New Zealand / Nouvelle-Zélande	27.9	22.3	33.6	34.7	31.7	36.6	39.7	38.3	38.4	38.4
Norway / Norvège	41.1	35.3	35.5	31.8	28.5	27.9	26.4	26.3	27.6	28.7
Poland / Pologne	..	..	..	35.3	37.8	37.1	39.4	36.6	36.1	36.1
Portugal	47.6	46.5	44.2	40.3	41.6	38.7	39.8	40.7	37.3	38.2
Slovak Republic / République slovaque	..	..	..	36.2	37.8	36.1	36.7	35.0	34.4	34.2
Slovenia / Slovénie	..	..	..	37.6	35.0	36.7	37.7	38.4	40.4	40.4
Spain / Espagne[1]	40.8	20.7	28.4	29.5	25.2	22.7	26.0	26.6	28.1	28.5
Sweden / Suède	31.2	24.0	25.0	24.8	26.6	28.9	29.1	28.9	28.6	28.4
Switzerland / Suisse	34.2	23.0	20.8	22.1	22.5	22.3	22.6	23.0	22.7	22.4
Turkey / Turquie	54.0	25.6	27.9	42.0	47.7	45.7	45.2	45.0	46.1	44.1
United Kingdom / Royaume-Uni	33.1	29.2	31.0	31.9	29.2	29.1	32.5	32.9	32.9	33.2
United States / États-Unis	22.8	17.6	17.6	16.1	16.8	18.4	18.5	18.4	17.6	17.4
Unweighted average / Moyenne non pondérée										
OECD Average / Moyenne OCDE	**38.4**	**32.5**	**32.5**	**33.0**	**31.9**	**32.3**	**32.7**	**32.6**	**32.4**	**32.6**

1. The total tax revenue has been reduced by the amount of any capital transfer that represents uncollected taxes. The capital transfer has been allocated between tax headings in proportion to the reported tax revenue.
2. From 1991, the figures relate to the united Germany.

1. Le total des recettes fiscales a été diminué du montant de tout transfert en capital représentant les impôts non perçus. Le transfert en capital a été réparti entre les différentes rubriques en proportion des recettes fiscales.
2. Depuis 1991, les chiffres se rapportent à l'Allemagne unifiée.

StatLink http://dx.doi.org/10.1787/888933416491

Table 3.25. **Consumption taxes (5100) as % of GDP**
Tableau 3.25. **Impôts sur la consommation (5100) en % du PIB**

	1965	1980	1990	2000	2007	2009	2011	2012	2013	2014
Australia / Australie	6.2	7.3	6.6	8.0	7.2	6.8	6.3	6.4	6.5	6.5
Austria / Autriche	12.3	11.7	11.8	11.4	10.6	10.9	10.9	11.1	11.0	10.9
Belgium / Belgique	10.4	10.4	10.2	10.1	10.0	9.9	10.0	10.4	10.3	10.1
Canada	8.7	7.5	8.6	7.9	7.2	6.9	6.8	6.8	6.7	6.7
Chile / Chili	..	..	10.2	11.4	9.5	9.1	9.9	10.1	10.1	10.3
Czech Republic / République tchèque	..	..	..	9.5	9.6	10.1	10.6	10.8	11.1	10.3
Denmark / Danemark[1]	11.5	15.0	14.4	14.7	15.1	14.1	14.0	14.0	13.9	13.8
Estonia / Estonie	..	..	..	11.7	12.7	13.8	12.8	13.0	12.6	13.0
Finland / Finlande	12.6	12.3	13.8	13.0	12.2	12.5	13.4	13.7	14.0	13.9
France[1]	12.6	11.6	11.3	10.8	10.2	10.1	10.4	10.5	10.5	10.7
Germany / Allemagne[2]	9.8	9.4	9.0	9.8	9.9	10.4	10.0	9.9	9.8	9.8
Greece / Grèce[1]	7.5	7.9	10.7	11.0	10.5	9.7	12.0	12.1	12.7	14.3
Hungary / Hongrie	..	..	..	15.4	14.6	15.1	15.5	16.6	16.3	16.4
Iceland / Islande	15.7	17.0	14.9	14.3	14.1	10.6	11.3	11.8	11.5	11.5
Ireland / Irlande	12.0	12.9	13.0	11.2	10.5	9.0	8.5	8.6	8.6	8.8
Israel / Israël	..	..	..	10.7	11.0	10.7	11.1	10.7	11.0	11.5
Italy / Italie	9.1	7.2	9.2	10.1	9.5	9.3	10.1	10.4	10.1	10.4
Japan / Japon	4.4	3.5	3.4	4.5	4.5	4.5	4.7	4.8	4.8	5.8
Korea / Corée	..	10.4	8.1	7.9	7.5	7.3	7.1	7.2	7.0	6.9
Latvia / Lettonie	..	..	..	10.8	10.8	9.9	10.4	10.6	10.8	11.1
Luxembourg	6.2	7.3	7.7	9.7	9.9	10.6	10.4	10.8	10.6	10.9
Mexico / Mexique	..	7.3	5.4	5.1	4.3	4.4	4.5	4.6	4.3	5.0
Netherlands / Pays-Bas	8.4	9.3	9.7	9.7	10.1	9.7	9.6	9.5	9.7	9.8
New Zealand / Nouvelle-Zélande	6.1	6.3	11.4	10.5	10.0	10.3	11.3	11.5	11.2	11.7
Norway / Norvège	11.7	14.4	13.7	12.3	11.3	10.9	10.6	10.4	10.5	10.5
Poland / Pologne	..	..	..	11.4	12.7	11.3	12.1	11.3	11.2	11.2
Portugal	6.9	9.9	11.5	12.2	12.9	11.1	12.4	12.4	12.0	12.4
Slovak Republic / République slovaque	..	..	..	11.5	10.2	9.6	9.7	9.1	9.6	9.7
Slovenia / Slovénie	..	..	..	13.1	12.3	12.7	13.1	13.5	13.9	13.8
Spain / Espagne[1]	5.8	4.6	8.4	9.1	8.6	6.3	7.6	8.1	8.8	9.1
Sweden / Suède	9.3	9.9	11.9	11.8	11.6	12.2	11.9	11.9	11.8	11.7
Switzerland / Suisse	5.3	5.0	4.5	5.5	5.2	5.3	5.3	5.3	5.3	5.3
Turkey / Turquie	5.6	3.4	4.1	9.8	11.0	10.7	12.1	11.9	13.0	12.2
United Kingdom / Royaume-Uni	9.1	9.3	9.7	10.0	9.2	8.7	10.4	10.4	10.3	10.3
United States / États-Unis	4.7	3.9	3.9	3.9	3.7	3.6	3.7	3.7	3.8	3.8
Unweighted average / Moyenne non pondérée										
OECD Average / Moyenne OCDE	**8.8**	**9.0**	**9.5**	**10.3**	**10.0**	**9.7**	**10.0**	**10.1**	**10.2**	**10.3**

1. The total tax revenue has been reduced by the amount of any capital transfer that represents uncollected taxes. The capital transfer has been allocated between tax headings in proportion to the reported tax revenue.
2. From 1991, the figures relate to the united Germany.
1. Le total des recettes fiscales a été diminué du montant de tout transfert en capital représentant les impôts non perçus. Le transfert en capital a été réparti entre les différentes rubriques en proportion des recettes fiscales.
2. Depuis 1991, les chiffres se rapportent à l'Allemagne unifiée.

StatLink http://dx.doi.org/10.1787/888933416509

Table 3.26. **Consumption taxes (5100) as % of total taxation**
Tableau 3.26. **Impôts sur la consommation (5100) en % du total des recettes fiscales**

	1965	1980	1990	2000	2007	2009	2011	2012	2013	2014
Australia / Australie	30.0	27.8	23.4	26.2	24.3	26.4	24.1	23.3	23.7	23.3
Austria / Autriche	36.6	30.3	29.9	27.1	26.1	26.6	26.7	26.5	25.8	25.4
Belgium / Belgique	34.1	25.7	24.7	23.1	23.4	23.4	23.2	23.6	22.8	22.5
Canada	34.7	24.6	24.4	22.8	22.4	21.5	22.3	22.0	21.6	21.6
Chile / Chili	..	..	60.4	60.6	41.6	52.2	46.4	47.1	50.7	51.9
Czech Republic / République tchèque	..	..	..	29.3	27.9	31.2	31.8	32.0	32.5	31.2
Denmark / Danemark[1]	39.6	36.4	32.3	31.4	32.6	31.1	31.0	30.6	29.8	27.8
Estonia / Estonie	..	..	..	37.7	40.6	39.4	40.6	41.4	40.1	40.2
Finland / Finlande	41.9	35.0	32.1	28.3	29.4	30.6	31.9	32.1	32.1	31.7
France[1]	37.5	29.5	27.5	25.2	24.2	24.4	24.0	23.7	23.3	23.4
Germany / Allemagne[2]	31.1	25.9	25.8	27.1	28.2	28.7	28.1	27.4	27.0	26.7
Greece / Grèce[1]	44.1	38.2	42.5	33.0	33.5	31.3	35.7	34.2	35.7	39.9
Hungary / Hongrie	..	..	..	39.9	36.8	38.4	42.6	42.9	42.9	42.9
Iceland / Islande	61.7	58.7	49.2	39.5	36.1	33.3	32.9	33.3	31.8	29.5
Ireland / Irlande	49.1	43.0	40.3	36.5	34.6	33.0	31.4	31.4	30.6	30.7
Israel / Israël	..	..	..	30.8	32.3	36.2	36.2	36.1	35.9	36.7
Italy / Italie	37.0	25.2	25.3	25.0	22.8	22.2	24.0	23.6	23.1	23.9
Japan / Japon	25.0	14.1	12.0	17.0	15.9	16.9	16.5	16.2	15.9	18.2
Korea / Corée	..	61.5	43.0	36.7	30.3	30.7	29.2	29.2	28.8	28.1
Latvia / Lettonie	..	..	..	37.0	38.2	35.5	37.3	37.4	38.0	38.4
Luxembourg	23.5	21.2	23.0	26.0	27.2	27.3	27.5	27.9	27.7	28.3
Mexico / Mexique	..	50.3	43.3	37.2	32.7	32.3	32.3	33.2	29.6	32.8
Netherlands / Pays-Bas	27.1	23.2	24.0	26.1	28.1	27.3	26.7	26.5	26.5	26.2
New Zealand / Nouvelle-Zélande	26.2	21.4	31.6	32.4	29.4	34.1	37.3	35.9	35.9	36.0
Norway / Norvège	39.9	34.4	34.1	29.4	26.8	26.4	25.1	25.1	26.2	27.2
Poland / Pologne	..	..	..	34.5	36.6	35.9	38.2	35.4	35.3	35.0
Portugal	44.0	45.0	43.4	39.2	40.4	37.2	38.3	39.1	35.3	36.3
Slovak Republic / République slovaque	..	..	..	34.1	35.0	33.2	33.9	32.2	31.5	31.2
Slovenia / Slovénie	..	..	..	35.8	33.3	35.1	36.0	36.6	37.9	37.8
Spain / Espagne[1]	40.6	20.7	26.5	27.2	23.5	20.9	24.2	24.9	26.4	26.8
Sweden / Suède	29.5	22.6	24.0	24.1	25.7	27.7	28.1	27.9	27.5	27.4
Switzerland / Suisse	31.9	21.3	18.9	20.1	19.8	19.4	19.6	19.9	19.8	19.4
Turkey / Turquie	53.5	25.2	27.5	40.6	45.6	43.6	43.5	43.2	44.3	42.4
United Kingdom / Royaume-Uni	31.1	27.9	29.4	30.5	28.0	27.7	31.3	31.7	31.7	32.0
United States / États-Unis	19.9	15.3	15.2	13.9	14.0	15.5	15.5	15.4	14.8	14.7
Unweighted average / Moyenne non pondérée										
OECD Average / Moyenne OCDE	**36.2**	**30.9**	**30.9**	**31.0**	**29.9**	**30.2**	**30.7**	**30.5**	**30.4**	**30.5**

1. The total tax revenue has been reduced by the amount of any capital transfer that represents uncollected taxes. The capital transfer has been allocated between tax headings in proportion to the reported tax revenue.
2. From 1991, the figures relate to the united Germany.
1. Le total des recettes fiscales a été diminué du montant de tout transfert en capital représentant les impôts non perçus. Le transfert en capital a été réparti entre les différentes rubriques en proportion des recettes fiscales.
2. Depuis 1991, les chiffres se rapportent à l'Allemagne unifiée.

StatLink http://dx.doi.org/10.1787/888933416515

Table 3.27. **Taxes on general consumption (5110) as % of GDP**
Tableau 3.27. **Impôts généraux sur la consommation (5110) en % du PIB**

	1965	1980	1990	2000	2007	2009	2011	2012	2013	2014
Australia / Australie	1.5	1.4	2.3	3.7	3.9	3.7	3.4	3.4	3.6	3.6
Austria / Autriche	6.3	7.8	8.2	7.9	7.4	7.8	7.6	7.8	7.7	7.7
Belgium / Belgique	6.5	6.8	6.8	7.1	7.0	6.8	6.9	7.0	7.0	6.9
Canada	4.5	3.5	5.0	4.9	4.5	4.2	4.3	4.3	4.3	4.3
Chile / Chili	..	..	6.3	7.9	7.5	7.3	7.9	8.1	8.1	8.2
Czech Republic / République tchèque	..	..	..	6.0	6.1	6.6	6.9	7.0	7.4	7.4
Denmark / Danemark[1]	3.0	9.4	9.4	9.2	10.0	9.7	9.6	9.6	9.4	9.5
Estonia / Estonie	..	..	..	8.4	8.8	8.7	8.3	8.4	8.2	8.6
Finland / Finlande	5.5	6.1	8.3	8.0	8.2	8.4	8.8	9.0	9.3	9.2
France[1]	7.8	8.3	7.7	7.4	7.3	7.0	7.1	7.1	7.1	7.2
Germany / Allemagne[2]	5.2	6.1	5.8	6.7	6.8	7.2	7.0	7.0	7.0	7.0
Greece / Grèce[1]	1.8	2.7	6.7	7.2	7.4	6.6	7.6	7.5	7.4	7.5
Hungary / Hongrie	..	..	..	10.1	10.3	10.9	10.9	11.7	11.4	11.6
Iceland / Islande	4.3	8.4	9.8	10.4	10.1	7.6	7.7	8.0	8.0	8.1
Ireland / Irlande	1.4	4.4	6.6	7.1	7.3	6.1	5.6	5.8	5.8	6.0
Israel / Israël	..	..	..	9.2	9.2	8.8	9.1	8.8	9.2	9.7
Italy / Italie	3.2	4.5	5.3	6.3	5.9	5.5	6.0	6.0	5.9	6.0
Japan / Japon	0.0	0.0	1.3	2.4	2.5	2.6	2.7	2.7	2.8	3.9
Korea / Corée	..	3.7	3.5	3.7	3.9	4.1	4.1	4.3	4.1	4.2
Latvia / Lettonie	..	..	..	7.0	7.7	5.9	6.8	7.2	7.4	7.7
Luxembourg	3.3	4.0	4.1	5.0	6.0	6.6	6.7	7.2	7.2	7.5
Mexico / Mexique	..	2.3	3.2	3.1	3.6	3.4	3.7	3.7	3.5	3.9
Netherlands / Pays-Bas	3.8	6.4	6.6	6.4	7.0	6.5	6.5	6.5	6.5	6.4
New Zealand / Nouvelle-Zélande	1.8	3.0	8.1	8.1	8.0	8.4	9.4	9.6	9.4	9.7
Norway / Norvège	6.3	7.7	7.6	8.3	8.1	7.7	7.6	7.6	7.7	7.8
Poland / Pologne	..	..	..	6.9	8.2	7.3	7.8	7.1	7.0	7.1
Portugal	0.0	3.5	5.2	7.6	8.2	6.8	8.1	8.3	8.1	8.5
Slovak Republic / République slovaque	..	..	..	6.9	6.6	6.6	6.7	6.0	6.4	6.6
Slovenia / Slovénie	..	..	..	8.7	8.3	7.9	8.1	8.0	8.5	8.5
Spain / Espagne[1]	3.2	2.2	5.1	5.9	5.8	3.8	5.2	5.4	5.9	6.1
Sweden / Suède	3.3	5.8	7.4	8.4	8.7	9.2	9.2	9.0	9.1	9.1
Switzerland / Suisse	1.8	2.4	2.8	3.7	3.5	3.4	3.5	3.6	3.6	3.5
Turkey / Turquie	0.0	0.0	3.0	5.8	5.1	4.9	6.1	5.8	6.4	5.9
United Kingdom / Royaume-Uni	1.7	4.9	5.5	5.9	6.0	5.3	6.8	6.8	6.8	6.8
United States / États-Unis	1.1	1.8	2.1	2.2	2.1	2.0	2.0	2.0	2.0	2.0
Unweighted average / Moyenne non pondérée										
OECD Average / Moyenne OCDE	**3.2**	**4.5**	**5.7**	**6.7**	**6.8**	**6.4**	**6.7**	**6.8**	**6.8**	**7.0**

1. The total tax revenue has been reduced by the amount of any capital transfer that represents uncollected taxes. The capital transfer has been allocated between tax headings in proportion to the reported tax revenue.
2. From 1991, the figures relate to the united Germany.
1. Le total des recettes fiscales a été diminué du montant de tout transfert en capital représentant les impôts non perçus. Le transfert en capital a été réparti entre les différentes rubriques en proportion des recettes fiscales.
2. Depuis 1991, les chiffres se rapportent à l'Allemagne unifiée.

StatLink http://dx.doi.org/10.1787/888933416529

Table 3.28. **Taxes on general consumption (5110) as % of total taxation**
Tableau 3.28. **Impôts généraux sur la consommation (5110) en % du total des recettes fiscales**

	1965	1980	1990	2000	2007	2009	2011	2012	2013	2014
Australia / Australie	7.4	5.3	8.0	12.0	13.0	14.3	12.8	12.3	13.0	12.9
Austria / Autriche	18.7	20.1	20.8	18.8	18.3	19.0	18.6	18.6	18.2	18.0
Belgium / Belgique	21.1	16.9	16.4	16.2	16.4	16.1	16.1	15.8	15.5	15.4
Canada	17.8	11.5	14.1	14.2	13.9	13.2	14.0	13.9	13.7	13.8
Chile / Chili	..	..	37.4	41.8	32.9	42.1	37.0	37.7	40.8	41.6
Czech Republic / République tchèque	..	..	..	18.3	17.7	20.4	20.6	20.9	21.8	22.4
Denmark / Danemark[1]	10.3	22.7	21.1	19.5	21.6	21.6	21.2	21.0	20.2	19.2
Estonia / Estonie	..	..	..	27.1	28.0	24.8	26.3	26.6	26.0	26.4
Finland / Finlande	18.5	17.3	19.3	17.4	19.6	20.5	20.9	21.1	21.3	21.0
France[1]	23.3	21.1	18.8	17.1	17.1	16.9	16.4	16.0	15.7	15.8
Germany / Allemagne[2]	16.5	16.6	16.6	18.4	19.4	20.1	19.7	19.4	19.2	19.0
Greece / Grèce[1]	10.3	13.2	26.5	21.5	23.8	21.4	22.7	21.2	20.7	21.0
Hungary / Hongrie	..	..	..	26.1	25.9	27.8	30.0	30.4	29.8	30.5
Iceland / Islande	16.7	28.9	32.3	28.5	25.9	23.7	22.4	22.8	22.2	20.8
Ireland / Irlande	5.7	14.8	20.4	22.9	24.0	22.2	20.8	21.2	20.4	20.8
Israel / Israël	..	..	..	26.5	26.9	29.7	29.7	29.7	30.1	30.9
Italy / Italie	12.9	15.6	14.7	15.4	14.2	13.1	14.4	13.6	13.3	13.8
Japan / Japon	0.0	0.0	4.4	9.1	8.8	9.6	9.4	9.2	9.2	12.2
Korea / Corée	..	22.0	18.7	17.0	15.8	17.2	17.0	17.2	17.0	17.2
Latvia / Lettonie	..	..	..	23.9	27.2	21.2	24.4	25.3	26.0	26.7
Luxembourg	12.4	11.6	12.1	13.4	16.4	17.1	17.7	18.4	19.0	19.6
Mexico / Mexique	..	15.7	26.1	22.8	27.2	24.9	26.4	26.7	23.7	25.6
Netherlands / Pays-Bas	12.4	15.8	16.5	17.3	19.4	18.4	18.1	18.0	17.8	17.2
New Zealand / Nouvelle-Zélande	7.7	10.2	22.4	24.9	23.5	27.6	31.0	30.0	30.0	29.9
Norway / Norvège	21.5	18.2	18.8	19.8	19.1	18.6	18.0	18.2	19.2	20.1
Poland / Pologne	..	..	..	21.0	23.8	23.3	24.8	22.4	22.1	22.2
Portugal	0.0	16.2	19.6	24.4	25.7	22.8	25.0	26.2	23.6	24.8
Slovak Republic / République slovaque	..	..	..	20.4	22.6	22.9	23.4	21.1	21.0	21.3
Slovenia / Slovénie	..	..	..	23.7	22.4	21.9	22.3	21.8	23.1	23.2
Spain / Espagne[1]	22.2	10.2	16.0	17.6	16.0	12.6	16.4	16.6	17.8	18.1
Sweden / Suède	10.4	13.4	14.9	17.1	19.3	20.9	21.5	21.3	21.1	21.3
Switzerland / Suisse	10.6	10.3	11.7	13.4	13.2	12.6	13.1	13.3	13.3	13.1
Turkey / Turquie	0.0	0.0	20.1	24.2	21.3	20.0	21.8	20.8	22.0	20.4
United Kingdom / Royaume-Uni	5.9	14.7	16.9	18.1	18.2	16.7	20.5	20.8	20.9	21.3
United States / États-Unis	4.8	7.0	8.1	7.6	7.9	8.5	8.3	8.2	7.9	7.9
Unweighted average / Moyenne non pondérée										
OECD Average / Moyenne OCDE	**11.9**	**14.2**	**18.2**	**19.9**	**20.2**	**20.1**	**20.6**	**20.5**	**20.5**	**20.7**

1. The total tax revenue has been reduced by the amount of any capital transfer that represents uncollected taxes. The capital transfer has been allocated between tax headings in proportion to the reported tax revenue.
2. From 1991, the figures relate to the united Germany.
1. Le total des recettes fiscales a été diminué du montant de tout transfert en capital représentant les impôts non perçus. Le transfert en capital a été réparti entre les différentes rubriques en proportion des recettes fiscales.
2. Depuis 1991, les chiffres se rapportent à l'Allemagne unifiée.

StatLink http://dx.doi.org/10.1787/888933416539

Table 3.29. **Taxes on specific goods and services (5120) as % of GDP**
Tableau 3.29. **Impôts sur les biens et services déterminés (5120) en % du PIB**

	1965	1980	1990	2000	2007	2009	2011	2012	2013	2014
Australia / Australie	4.7	5.9	4.3	4.3	3.4	3.1	3.0	3.0	3.0	2.9
Austria / Autriche	6.0	3.9	3.6	3.5	3.1	3.1	3.3	3.3	3.2	3.2
Belgium / Belgique	4.0	3.6	3.4	3.0	3.0	3.1	3.1	3.4	3.3	3.2
Canada	4.2	4.0	3.6	3.0	2.7	2.7	2.5	2.5	2.4	2.4
Chile / Chili	..	..	3.9	3.5	2.0	1.8	2.0	2.0	2.0	2.0
Czech Republic / République tchèque	..	..	..	3.6	3.5	3.5	3.7	3.7	3.7	2.9
Denmark / Danemark[1]	8.5	5.7	5.0	5.5	5.1	4.3	4.4	4.4	4.5	4.3
Estonia / Estonie	..	..	..	3.3	3.9	5.1	4.5	4.6	4.4	4.5
Finland / Finlande	7.0	6.2	5.5	5.0	4.0	4.2	4.6	4.7	4.7	4.7
France[1]	4.8	3.3	3.6	3.5	3.0	3.1	3.3	3.4	3.5	3.5
Germany / Allemagne[2]	4.6	3.4	3.2	3.2	3.1	3.1	3.0	2.9	2.8	2.8
Greece / Grèce[1]	5.8	5.2	3.9	3.8	3.0	3.0	4.2	4.1	4.4	4.5
Hungary / Hongrie	..	..	..	5.3	4.3	4.2	4.6	4.8	5.0	4.8
Iceland / Islande	11.5	8.6	5.1	4.0	4.0	3.1	3.6	3.7	3.5	3.4
Ireland / Irlande	10.6	8.5	6.4	4.2	3.2	3.0	2.9	2.8	2.9	2.9
Israel / Israël	..	..	..	1.5	1.8	1.9	2.0	1.9	1.8	1.8
Italy / Italie	5.9	2.8	3.9	3.9	3.6	3.8	4.0	4.4	4.3	4.4
Japan / Japon	4.4	3.5	2.2	2.1	2.0	2.0	2.0	2.0	2.0	1.9
Korea / Corée	..	6.7	4.6	4.2	3.6	3.2	2.9	3.0	2.9	2.7
Latvia / Lettonie	..	..	..	3.8	3.1	4.0	3.6	3.4	3.4	3.4
Luxembourg	2.9	3.3	3.7	4.7	4.0	4.0	3.7	3.7	3.3	3.3
Mexico / Mexique	..	5.0	2.1	2.0	0.7	1.0	0.8	0.9	0.9	1.1
Netherlands / Pays-Bas	4.5	2.9	3.0	3.3	3.1	3.2	3.1	3.1	3.2	3.4
New Zealand / Nouvelle-Zélande	4.3	3.3	3.3	2.5	2.0	1.9	1.9	1.9	1.8	2.0
Norway / Norvège	5.4	6.8	6.2	4.0	3.2	3.2	3.0	2.8	2.8	2.8
Poland / Pologne	..	..	..	4.5	4.4	4.0	4.2	4.2	4.2	4.1
Portugal	6.9	6.3	6.3	4.6	4.7	4.3	4.3	4.1	4.0	3.9
Slovak Republic / République slovaque	..	..	..	4.6	3.6	3.0	3.0	3.2	3.2	3.1
Slovenia / Slovénie	..	..	..	4.4	4.1	4.8	5.0	5.5	5.4	5.3
Spain / Espagne[1]	2.6	2.3	3.3	3.2	2.7	2.5	2.5	2.7	2.9	2.9
Sweden / Suède	6.0	4.0	4.5	3.4	2.9	3.0	2.8	2.8	2.7	2.6
Switzerland / Suisse	3.5	2.6	1.7	1.8	1.7	1.8	1.8	1.8	1.7	1.7
Turkey / Turquie	5.6	3.4	1.1	4.0	5.8	5.8	6.0	6.2	6.5	6.3
United Kingdom / Royaume-Uni	7.4	4.4	4.1	4.1	3.2	3.5	3.6	3.6	3.5	3.4
United States / États-Unis	3.6	2.1	1.8	1.8	1.6	1.6	1.7	1.7	1.8	1.8
Unweighted average / Moyenne non pondérée										
OECD Average / Moyenne OCDE	**5.6**	**4.5**	**3.8**	**3.6**	**3.2**	**3.2**	**3.3**	**3.3**	**3.3**	**3.3**

1. The total tax revenue has been reduced by the amount of any capital transfer that represents uncollected taxes. The capital transfer has been allocated between tax headings in proportion to the reported tax revenue.
2. From 1991, the figures relate to the united Germany.
1. Le total des recettes fiscales a été diminué du montant de tout transfert en capital représentant les impôts non perçus. Le transfert en capital a été réparti entre les différentes rubriques en proportion des recettes fiscales.
2. Depuis 1991, les chiffres se rapportent à l'Allemagne unifiée.

StatLink http://dx.doi.org/10.1787/888933416547

Table 3.30. Taxes on specific goods and services (5120) as % of total taxation

Tableau 3.30. Impôts sur les biens et services déterminés (5120) en % du total des recettes fiscales

	1965	1980	1990	2000	2007	2009	2011	2012	2013	2014
Australia / Australie	22.7	22.6	15.3	14.1	11.3	12.2	11.3	10.9	10.7	10.4
Austria / Autriche	18.0	10.1	9.0	8.2	7.7	7.6	8.1	7.9	7.6	7.4
Belgium / Belgique	13.0	8.8	8.3	6.9	7.0	7.3	7.2	7.8	7.2	7.1
Canada	16.8	13.0	10.3	8.6	8.5	8.3	8.3	8.0	7.9	7.8
Chile / Chili	..	..	23.0	18.8	8.7	10.1	9.4	9.4	9.9	10.3
Czech Republic / République tchèque	..	..	..	11.0	10.2	10.8	11.2	11.1	10.7	8.8
Denmark / Danemark[1]	29.3	13.7	11.2	11.8	11.0	9.6	9.7	9.6	9.6	8.7
Estonia / Estonie	..	..	..	10.6	12.6	14.6	14.3	14.7	14.1	13.8
Finland / Finlande	23.4	17.6	12.9	10.9	9.7	10.2	11.0	11.0	10.8	10.6
France[1]	14.3	8.4	8.7	8.0	7.0	7.5	7.6	7.7	7.7	7.7
Germany / Allemagne[2]	14.6	9.3	9.2	8.8	8.8	8.6	8.4	7.9	7.8	7.6
Greece / Grèce[1]	33.8	25.1	15.6	11.5	9.6	9.8	12.4	11.6	12.4	12.5
Hungary / Hongrie	..	..	..	13.8	10.9	10.7	12.6	12.6	13.1	12.5
Iceland / Islande	45.0	29.8	16.9	11.0	10.2	9.6	10.5	10.5	9.7	8.8
Ireland / Irlande	43.4	28.3	19.9	13.6	10.6	10.8	10.6	10.3	10.2	9.9
Israel / Israël	..	..	..	4.3	5.4	6.5	6.5	6.4	5.9	5.8
Italy / Italie	24.1	9.7	10.6	9.6	8.5	9.1	9.7	10.0	9.8	10.1
Japan / Japon	25.0	14.1	7.5	8.0	7.1	7.3	7.1	6.9	6.7	6.0
Korea / Corée	..	39.5	24.3	19.7	14.5	13.6	12.2	12.0	11.8	10.8
Latvia / Lettonie	..	..	..	13.1	11.0	14.2	12.9	12.1	12.0	11.7
Luxembourg	11.1	9.6	11.0	12.6	10.8	10.2	9.8	9.5	8.8	8.7
Mexico / Mexique	..	34.4	17.2	14.5	5.5	7.4	6.0	6.5	5.9	7.2
Netherlands / Pays-Bas	14.7	7.3	7.5	8.8	8.7	8.9	8.7	8.5	8.7	9.0
New Zealand / Nouvelle-Zélande	18.5	11.2	9.2	7.5	5.9	6.4	6.3	6.0	5.8	6.0
Norway / Norvège	18.4	16.1	15.3	9.6	7.7	7.8	7.1	6.9	7.0	7.1
Poland / Pologne	..	..	..	13.5	12.8	12.6	13.4	13.1	13.2	12.7
Portugal	44.0	28.9	23.8	14.8	14.7	14.4	13.3	12.9	11.7	11.6
Slovak Republic / République slovaque	..	..	..	13.7	12.4	10.3	10.5	11.1	10.5	9.9
Slovenia / Slovénie	..	..	..	12.1	10.9	13.2	13.8	14.8	14.8	14.6
Spain / Espagne[1]	18.4	10.5	10.5	9.6	7.5	8.3	7.8	8.3	8.7	8.7
Sweden / Suède	19.2	9.2	9.2	7.0	6.4	6.8	6.6	6.7	6.4	6.1
Switzerland / Suisse	21.3	11.0	7.2	6.6	6.5	6.8	6.5	6.6	6.4	6.3
Turkey / Turquie	53.5	25.2	7.3	16.4	24.3	23.6	21.7	22.4	22.4	22.0
United Kingdom / Royaume-Uni	25.2	13.3	12.5	12.4	9.8	11.0	10.8	10.9	10.8	10.7
United States / États-Unis	15.1	8.3	7.1	6.3	6.1	7.0	7.2	7.1	6.9	6.8
Unweighted average / Moyenne non pondérée										
OECD Average / Moyenne OCDE	**24.3**	**16.7**	**12.6**	**11.1**	**9.7**	**10.1**	**10.0**	**10.0**	**9.8**	**9.6**

1. The total tax revenue has been reduced by the amount of any capital transfer that represents uncollected taxes. The capital transfer has been allocated between tax headings in proportion to the reported tax revenue.
2. From 1991, the figures relate to the united Germany.
1. Le total des recettes fiscales a été diminué du montant de tout transfert en capital représentant les impôts non perçus. Le transfert en capital a été réparti entre les différentes rubriques en proportion des recettes fiscales.
2. Depuis 1991, les chiffres se rapportent à l'Allemagne unifiée.

StatLink http://dx.doi.org/10.1787/888933416552

Table 3.31. **Total tax revenue in millions of US dollars at market exchange rates**
Tableau 3.31. **Total des recettes fiscales en millions de dollars des É-U au taux de change du marché**

	1965	1980	1990	2000	2007	2009	2011	2012	2013	2014
Australia / Australie	5 625	45 465	90 886	124 326	292 892	261 231	404 172	431 749	421 366	402 749
Austria / Autriche	..	41 355	68 606	82 751	156 698	162 879	176 048	169 848	182 114	187 711
Belgium / Belgique	..	52 031	89 387	103 607	201 600	205 303	227 421	219 965	234 781	239 062
Canada	14 208	86 383	209 202	262 765	477 199	445 313	552 470	570 109	574 082	559 628
Chile / Chili	..	..	5 829	14 650	39 444	29 984	53 292	57 028	55 285	51 075
Czech Republic / République tchèque	..	..	..	19 971	64 752	66 605	75 914	69 979	71 396	68 759
Denmark / Danemark[1]	3 011	29 274	61 400	76 903	148 319	144 481	154 429	148 956	158 540	171 424
Estonia / Estonie	..	..	..	1 768	6 957	6 862	7 303	7 300	7 949	8 589
Finland / Finlande	..	16 529	49 576	57 539	106 021	102 949	115 065	109 599	117 733	119 448
France[1]	..	248 154	550 698	589 281	1 128 960	1 113 178	1 235 880	1 188 867	1 270 165	1 291 477
Germany / Allemagne[2]	..	399 174	577 350	706 891	1 200 351	1 233 156	1 341 915	1 288 509	1 367 263	1 418 689
Greece / Grèce[1]	..	2 050	14 564	43 422	99 338	101 902	97 008	87 170	85 204	84 270
Hungary / Hongrie	..	..	..	18 211	55 090	50 931	51 071	49 119	51 303	52 885
Iceland / Islande	139	989	1 969	3 229	8 299	4 104	5 049	5 007	5 535	6 635
Ireland / Irlande	..	5 623	15 565	30 723	82 029	64 547	65 168	62 010	67 390	73 575
Israel / Israël	..	..	..	46 105	61 041	61 783	80 642	77 133	89 744	95 528
Italy / Italie	..	83 964	336 581	463 642	918 826	919 318	954 168	910 232	936 592	934 353
Japan / Japon	17 074	275 448	903 503	1 262 348	1 241 928	1 365 456	1 702 089	1 748 801	1 500 043	1 482 009
Korea / Corée	..	11 008	52 630	120 547	278 198	214 634	290 720	303 158	317 220	347 014
Latvia / Lettonie	..	..	..	1 839	8 693	7 284	7 817	7 987	8 621	9 032
Luxembourg	..	2 144	4 660	7 853	18 366	19 624	22 233	21 727	23 543	24 892
Mexico / Mexique	..	33 627	35 908	88 149	137 840	121 387	163 946	165 122	184 024	195 987
Netherlands / Pays-Bas	..	97 249	132 567	153 741	302 470	303 294	320 523	298 676	316 592	330 092
New Zealand / Nouvelle-Zélande	1 386	7 393	16 372	18 037	47 059	37 192	51 777	56 783	60 188	64 612
Norway / Norvège	2 355	27 041	48 226	71 798	168 972	159 212	209 646	211 652	208 652	193 572
Poland / Pologne	..	..	..	56 617	148 692	137 255	167 295	159 786	167 105	174 857
Portugal	..	2 498	18 821	36 760	76 427	72 914	79 194	68 784	77 015	78 625
Slovak Republic / République slovaque	..	..	..	9 793	25 141	25 588	28 024	26 406	29 685	31 328
Slovenia / Slovénie	..	..	..	6 381	17 837	18 194	18 713	17 050	17 521	18 061
Spain / Espagne[1]	..	30 574	131 605	198 962	540 493	449 063	468 082	434 819	455 189	467 555
Sweden / Suède	7 755	61 292	127 730	127 285	219 400	189 440	239 523	231 683	248 395	244 374
Switzerland / Suisse	2 596	27 674	60 770	74 597	124 805	146 193	188 233	178 208	184 095	189 701
Turkey / Turquie	1 265	12 343	30 200	64 490	156 208	151 706	216 045	218 560	240 846	229 588
United Kingdom / Royaume-Uni	30 605	188 624	359 508	537 335	1 010 535	747 478	871 864	867 961	882 793	962 304
United States / États-Unis	167 022	730 672	1 552 413	2 900 519	3 867 405	3 318 696	3 708 707	3 888 470	4 283 029	4 500 530
Unweighted average / Moyenne non pondérée										
OECD Average / Moyenne OCDE	..	**96 868**	**205 427**	**239 509**	**383 951**	**355 975**	**410 041**	**410 235**	**425 743**	**437 428**

1. The total tax revenue has been reduced by the amount of any capital transfer that represents uncollected taxes. The capital transfer has been allocated between tax headings in proportion to the reported tax revenue.
2. From 1991, the figures relate to the united Germany.
1. Le total des recettes fiscales a été diminué du montant de tout transfert en capital représentant les impôts non perçus. Le transfert en capital a été réparti entre les différentes rubriques en proportion des recettes fiscales.
2. Depuis 1991, les chiffres se rapportent à l'Allemagne unifiée.

StatLink http://dx.doi.org/10.1787/888933416567

Table 3.32. **Tax revenue of individual countries as % of total OECD tax revenue**
Tableau 3.32. **Recettes fiscales de chaque pays en % du total des recettes des pays membres de l'OCDE**

	1965	1980	1990	2000	2007	2009	2011	2012	2013	2014
Australia / Australie	..	1.8	1.6	1.5	2.2	2.1	2.8	3.0	2.8	2.6
Austria / Autriche	..	1.6	1.2	1.0	1.2	1.3	1.2	1.2	1.2	1.2
Belgium / Belgique	..	2.1	1.6	1.2	1.5	1.6	1.6	1.5	1.6	1.6
Canada	..	3.4	3.8	3.1	3.6	3.6	3.9	4.0	3.9	3.7
Chile / Chili	..	..	0.1	0.2	0.3	0.2	0.4	0.4	0.4	0.3
Czech Republic / République tchèque	..	..	..	0.2	0.5	0.5	0.5	0.5	0.5	0.4
Denmark / Danemark[1]	..	1.2	1.1	0.9	1.1	1.2	1.1	1.0	1.1	1.1
Estonia / Estonie	..	..	..	0.0	0.1	0.1	0.1	0.1	0.1	0.1
Finland / Finlande	..	0.7	0.9	0.7	0.8	0.8	0.8	0.8	0.8	0.8
France[1]	..	9.9	9.9	7.0	8.4	8.9	8.6	8.3	8.5	8.4
Germany / Allemagne[2]	..	15.8	10.4	8.4	8.9	9.9	9.4	9.0	9.2	9.3
Greece / Grèce[1]	..	0.1	0.3	0.5	0.7	0.8	0.7	0.6	0.6	0.6
Hungary / Hongrie	..	..	..	0.2	0.4	0.4	0.4	0.3	0.3	0.3
Iceland / Islande	..	0.0	0.0	0.0	0.1	0.0	0.0	0.0	0.0	0.0
Ireland / Irlande	..	0.2	0.3	0.4	0.6	0.5	0.5	0.4	0.5	0.5
Israel / Israël	..	..	..	0.6	0.5	0.5	0.6	0.5	0.6	0.6
Italy / Italie	..	3.3	6.1	5.5	6.8	7.4	6.6	6.3	6.3	6.1
Japan / Japon	..	10.9	16.3	15.1	9.2	11.0	11.9	12.2	10.1	9.7
Korea / Corée	..	0.4	0.9	1.4	2.1	1.7	2.0	2.1	2.1	2.3
Latvia / Lettonie	..	..	..	0.0	0.1	0.1	0.1	0.1	0.1	0.1
Luxembourg	..	0.1	0.1	0.1	0.1	0.2	0.2	0.2	0.2	0.2
Mexico / Mexique	..	1.3	0.6	1.1	1.0	1.0	1.1	1.2	1.2	1.3
Netherlands / Pays-Bas	..	3.9	2.4	1.8	2.3	2.4	2.2	2.1	2.1	2.2
New Zealand / Nouvelle-Zélande	..	0.3	0.3	0.2	0.4	0.3	0.4	0.4	0.4	0.4
Norway / Norvège	..	1.1	0.9	0.9	1.3	1.3	1.5	1.5	1.4	1.3
Poland / Pologne	..	..	..	0.7	1.1	1.1	1.2	1.1	1.1	1.1
Portugal	..	0.1	0.3	0.4	0.6	0.6	0.6	0.5	0.5	0.5
Slovak Republic / République slovaque	..	..	..	0.1	0.2	0.2	0.2	0.2	0.2	0.2
Slovenia / Slovénie	..	..	..	0.1	0.1	0.1	0.1	0.1	0.1	0.1
Spain / Espagne[1]	..	1.2	2.4	2.4	4.0	3.6	3.3	3.0	3.1	3.1
Sweden / Suède	..	2.4	2.3	1.5	1.6	1.5	1.7	1.6	1.7	1.6
Switzerland / Suisse	..	1.1	1.1	0.9	0.9	1.2	1.3	1.2	1.2	1.2
Turkey / Turquie	..	0.5	0.5	0.8	1.2	1.2	1.5	1.5	1.6	1.5
United Kingdom / Royaume-Uni	..	7.5	6.5	6.4	7.5	6.0	6.1	6.0	5.9	6.3
United States / États-Unis	..	29.0	28.0	34.6	28.8	26.6	25.8	27.1	28.7	29.4
Cumulative sum / Somme cumulative										
OECD Total / Total OCDE	..	**100.0**	**100.0**	**100.0**	**100.0**	**100.0**	**100.0**	**100.0**	**100.0**	**100.0**

1. The total tax revenue has been reduced by the amount of any capital transfer that represents uncollected taxes. The capital transfer has been allocated between tax headings in proportion to the reported tax revenue.
2. From 1991, the figures relate to the united Germany.
1. Le total des recettes fiscales a été diminué du montant de tout transfert en capital représentant les impôts non perçus. Le transfert en capital a été réparti entre les différentes rubriques en proportion des recettes fiscales.
2. Depuis 1991, les chiffres se rapportent à l'Allemagne unifiée.

StatLink http://dx.doi.org/10.1787/888933416573

Table 3.33. **Tax revenue in US dollars per capita at market exchange rates**
Tableau 3.33. **Recettes fiscales en dollars des É-U par habitant, au taux de change du marché**

	1965	1980	1990	2000	2007	2009	2011	2012	2013	2014
Australia / Australie	496	3 094	5 326	6 534	14 062	12 044	18 092	18 995	18 222	17 146
Austria / Autriche	..	5 478	8 936	10 329	18 890	19 526	20 987	20 157	21 505	22 076
Belgium / Belgique	..	5 277	8 968	10 107	18 973	19 016	20 585	19 766	20 970	21 187
Canada	711	3 523	7 555	8 563	14 492	13 203	16 021	16 345	16 255	15 671
Chile / Chili	..	..	442	951	2 376	1 771	3 090	3 277	3 149	2 884
Czech Republic / République tchèque	..	..	..	1 944	6 273	6 348	7 232	6 659	6 793	6 533
Denmark / Danemark[1]	633	5 714	11 943	14 402	27 157	26 159	27 722	26 639	28 236	30 630
Estonia / Estonie	..	..	..	1 282	5 183	5 127	5 471	5 492	6 021	6 528
Finland / Finlande	..	3 458	9 941	11 119	20 042	19 286	21 364	20 247	21 642	21 857
France[1]	..	4 606	9 711	9 977	18 219	17 778	19 548	18 718	19 913	20 067
Germany / Allemagne[2]	..	5 099	7 268	8 598	14 591	15 056	16 559	16 021	16 954	17 533
Greece / Grèce[1]	..	213	1 434	3 977	8 899	9 111	8 721	7 860	7 500	7 405
Hungary / Hongrie	..	..	..	1 783	5 478	5 082	5 128	4 951	5 189	5 373
Iceland / Islande	721	4 334	7 727	11 483	26 652	12 855	15 826	15 668	17 184	20 418
Ireland / Irlande	..	1 653	4 440	8 107	18 746	14 238	14 245	13 524	14 672	15 960
Israel / Israël	..	..	..	7 331	8 501	8 254	10 384	9 751	11 132	11 669
Italy / Italie	..	1 438	5 934	8 142	15 475	15 273	15 738	14 942	15 309	15 213
Japan / Japon	174	2 353	7 309	9 945	9 720	10 709	13 318	13 714	11 784	11 674
Korea / Corée	..	289	1 228	2 564	5 725	4 364	5 840	6 063	6 317	6 882
Latvia / Lettonie	..	..	..	777	3 951	3 401	3 795	3 926	4 205	4 425
Luxembourg	..	5 888	12 204	17 998	38 263	39 423	42 893	40 921	47 830	50 131
Mexico / Mexique	..	504	412	874	1 256	1 076	1 417	1 411	1 554	1 637
Netherlands / Pays-Bas	..	6 873	8 866	9 654	18 464	18 348	19 201	17 826	18 840	19 511
New Zealand / Nouvelle-Zélande	525	2 332	4 829	4 675	11 141	8 644	11 811	12 882	13 550	14 327
Norway / Norvège	633	6 619	11 370	15 987	35 882	32 972	42 336	42 179	41 073	37 682
Poland / Pologne	..	..	..	1 480	3 901	3 597	4 342	4 147	4 391	4 597
Portugal	..	256	1 885	3 572	7 249	6 899	7 501	6 542	7 365	7 547
Slovak Republic / République slovaque	..	..	..	1 817	4 678	4 750	5 191	4 883	5 481	5 784
Slovenia / Slovénie	..	..	..	3 206	8 833	8 909	9 117	8 292	8 509	8 760
Spain / Espagne[1]	..	817	3 387	4 906	11 948	9 685	10 015	9 298	9 769	10 063
Sweden / Suède	1 003	7 375	14 924	14 347	23 983	20 373	25 348	24 338	25 848	25 198
Switzerland / Suisse	443	4 379	9 054	10 383	16 528	18 879	23 790	22 401	22 960	23 493
Turkey / Turquie	41	278	548	1 003	2 227	2 106	2 911	2 907	3 167	2 985
United Kingdom / Royaume-Uni	563	3 348	6 281	9 125	16 708	12 169	13 964	13 808	13 960	15 119
United States / États-Unis	860	3 216	6 219	10 280	12 839	10 818	11 897	12 379	13 533	14 115
Unweighted average / Moyenne non pondérée										
OECD Average / Moyenne OCDE	..	**3 402**	**6 598**	**7 064**	**13 637**	**12 493**	**14 326**	**13 912**	**14 594**	**14 916**

1. The total tax revenue has been reduced by the amount of any capital transfer that represents uncollected taxes. The capital transfer has been allocated between tax headings in proportion to the reported tax revenue.
2. From 1991, the figures relate to the united Germany.
1. Le total des recettes fiscales a été diminué du montant de tout transfert en capital représentant les impôts non perçus. Le transfert en capital a été réparti entre les différentes rubriques en proportion des recettes fiscales.
2. Depuis 1991, les chiffres se rapportent à l'Allemagne unifiée.

StatLink http://dx.doi.org/10.1787/888933416583

Table 3.34. **Annual % change in total tax revenue**
Tableau 3.34. **Variation annuelle en % des recettes fiscales totales**

	1966	1980	1990	2000	2007	2009	2011	2012	2013	2014
Australia / Australie	7.3	18.0	3.0	8.9	9.0	-1.7	8.5	6.5	4.7	2.3
Austria / Autriche	11.2	8.8	8.4	2.9	6.4	-3.0	5.2	4.4	3.8	3.1
Belgium / Belgique	14.7	4.5	7.2	4.9	4.9	-3.5	5.1	4.6	3.3	1.9
Canada	15.5	15.9	5.2	6.6	4.7	-1.8	5.8	4.2	3.8	4.5
Chile / Chili	..	..	..	14.3	14.2	-16.6	17.9	7.6	-1.2	6.4
Czech Republic / République tchèque	..	..	..	3.4	9.9	-5.7	4.3	1.9	2.1	2.2
Denmark / Danemark[1]	17.5	10.2	1.0	4.6	3.3	-4.0	2.1	4.3	3.3	8.1
Estonia / Estonie	..	..	..	9.6	23.0	-4.9	7.3	8.1	5.4	8.1
Finland / Finlande	11.3	16.2	9.4	11.1	6.4	-7.2	8.4	3.0	4.0	1.5
France[1]	7.6	17.4	5.7	3.5	3.3	-4.8	6.0	4.1	3.4	1.7
Germany / Allemagne[2]	8.3	7.1	4.5	2.7	6.2	-2.1	6.8	3.9	2.7	3.8
Greece / Grèce[1]	19.8	16.8	32.5	12.2	9.8	-2.1	-4.3	-2.8	-5.4	-1.0
Hungary / Hongrie	..	..	..	15.4	14.1	-4.1	1.1	7.6	3.9	7.3
Iceland / Islande	..	..	14.8	9.1	9.7	-6.6	8.5	6.9	7.9	14.5
Ireland / Irlande	13.8	29.2	7.3	16.5	5.1	-13.0	3.5	2.9	5.2	9.2
Israel / Israël	..	..	..	13.5	6.9	-1.7	7.7	3.0	9.1	5.5
Italy / Italie	7.4	42.0	13.6	4.9	6.8	-2.8	2.2	3.2	-0.4	-0.2
Japan / Japon	14.1	13.4	5.8	3.6	2.3	-8.5	2.4	2.9	4.9	7.1
Korea / Corée	..	23.0	39.5	19.8	13.6	0.5	8.8	6.0	1.8	5.2
Latvia / Lettonie	..	..	..	5.2	29.7	-22.2	11.6	10.5	4.5	4.8
Luxembourg	4.1	11.5	6.6	12.8	11.1	1.1	6.4	5.7	4.9	5.8
Mexico / Mexique	..	..	8.1	19.2	11.6	-3.0	8.9	6.5	8.2	11.0
Netherlands / Pays-Bas	13.6	8.4	5.8	7.0	4.9	-6.2	1.1	0.8	2.6	4.3
New Zealand / Nouvelle-Zélande	7.6	17.2	-0.7	7.3	3.4	-4.6	5.2	6.9	4.8	6.1
Norway / Norvège	12.2	23.1	7.2	19.2	4.3	-7.3	8.1	4.7	-0.4	-0.5
Poland / Pologne	..	..	..	4.3	14.4	-2.4	10.1	4.9	1.6	4.4
Portugal	12.4	39.3	18.5	7.7	7.2	-7.5	4.1	-6.0	8.4	2.1
Slovak Republic / République slovaque	..	..	..	6.9	11.7	-7.1	6.6	1.9	8.8	5.6
Slovenia / Slovénie	..	..	..	7.9	9.7	-5.2	0.6	-1.4	-0.5	3.1
Spain / Espagne[1]	7.6	18.9	10.7	9.0	8.5	-10.4	-1.2	0.5	1.4	2.8
Sweden / Suède	11.2	13.2	10.6	6.8	4.1	-2.8	2.2	0.9	3.2	3.6
Switzerland / Suisse	11.4	6.4	6.1	9.7	5.5	0.6	4.1	0.0	2.2	1.7
Turkey / Turquie	20.0	109.1	85.4	66.3	9.2	1.9	25.5	8.4	17.1	9.6
United Kingdom / Royaume-Uni	9.1	27.6	8.2	6.8	4.4	-7.2	6.3	0.7	3.1	3.5
United States / États-Unis	11.4	10.3	7.2	7.8	4.7	-12.2	5.5	4.8	10.1	5.1
Unweighted average / Moyenne non pondérée										
OECD Average / Moyenne OCDE	**11.7**	**21.1**	**12.8**	**10.6**	**8.7**	**-5.4**	**6.1**	**3.8**	**4.1**	**4.7**

1. The total tax revenue has been reduced by the amount of any capital transfer that represents uncollected taxes. The capital transfer has been allocated between tax headings in proportion to the reported tax revenue.
2. From 1991, the figures relate to the united Germany.
1. Le total des recettes fiscales a été diminué du montant de tout transfert en capital représentant les impôts non perçus. Le transfert en capital a été réparti entre les différentes rubriques en proportion des recettes fiscales.
2. Depuis 1991, les chiffres se rapportent à l'Allemagne unifiée.

StatLink http://dx.doi.org/10.1787/888933416591

Table 3.35. **Gross domestic product for tax reporting years at market prices, in billions of national currency units**

Tableau 3.35. **Produit intérieur brut pour les années de déclaration fiscale au prix du marché, en milliards de monnaie nationale**

	1965	1980	1990	2000	2007	2009	2011	2012	2013	2014
Australia / Australie[1]	24	152	415	705	1 178	1 297	1 491	1 524	1 585	1 605
Austria / Autriche	18	77	137	213	282	286	309	317	323	330
Belgium / Belgique	21	92	171	258	345	349	379	387	393	400
Canada[1]	61	332	694	1 122	1 596	1 589	1 789	1 838	1 910	1 980
Chile / Chili	..	.	10 482	42 095	90 429	96 444	121 319	129 028	137 230	147 568
Czech Republic / République tchèque	..	.	..	2 373	3 832	3 922	4 034	4 060	4 098	4 314
Denmark / Danemark	71	399	855	1 327	1 739	1 714	1 833	1 883	1 904	1 943
Estonia / Estonie	..	..	..	6	16	14	17	18	19	20
Finland / Finlande	5	34	91	136	187	181	197	200	203	205
France	77	453	1 059	1 485	1 946	1 939	2 059	2 087	2 115	2 140
Germany / Allemagne	235	789	1 307	2 116	2 513	2 460	2 703	2 758	2 826	2 924
Greece / Grèce	1	7	46	141	233	238	207	191	180	178
Hungary / Hongrie	..	..	..	13 310	25 539	26 259	28 134	28 628	30 065	32 180
Iceland / Islande	0	16	380	702	1 364	1 589	1 701	1 775	1 879	1 989
Ireland / Irlande	1	13	38	108	197	170	173	176	180	193
Israel / Israël	..	..	..	540	738	818	937	1 001	1 056	1 094
Italy / Italie	22	210	729	1 239	1 610	1 573	1 637	1 613	1 604	1 612
Japan / Japon[1]	34 708	252 254	458 413	510 835	513 023	473 996	474 171	474 404	482 401	489 558
Korea / Corée	..	39 471	197 712	635 185	1 043 258	1 151 708	1 332 681	1 377 457	1 429 445	1 486 079
Latvia / Lettonie	..	..	..	7	23	19	20	22	23	24
Luxembourg	1	5	11	23	37	36	42	44	47	49
Mexico / Mexique	..	5	825	6 132	11 399	12 073	14 527	15 599	16 077	17 210
Netherlands / Pays-Bas	35	174	260	448	613	618	643	645	653	663
New Zealand / Nouvelle-Zélande[1]	4	26	76	122	189	197	215	219	235	240
Norway / Norvège	57	318	750	1 508	2 350	2 430	2 792	2 965	3 071	3 154
Poland / Pologne	..	..	..	747	1 187	1 362	1 567	1 629	1 656	1 719
Portugal	1	8	56	128	175	175	176	168	170	173
Slovak Republic / République slovaque	..	..	..	32	63	64	70	72	74	76
Slovenia / Slovénie	..	..	..	19	35	36	37	36	36	37
Spain / Espagne	9	100	328	646	1 081	1 079	1 070	1 043	1 031	1 041
Sweden / Suède	128	593	1 528	2 380	3 297	3 289	3 657	3 685	3 770	3 918
Switzerland / Suisse	68	199	358	459	573	587	618	624	635	642
Turkey / Turquie	0	0	1	167	843	953	1 298	1 417	1 567	1 747
United Kingdom / Royaume-Uni	37	243	616	1 081	1 531	1 519	1 628	1 675	1 740	1 822
United States / États-Unis	711	2 863	5 980	10 285	14 478	14 419	15 518	16 155	16 692	17 393

1. GDP is fiscal year. The year Y is calculated (at annual rate) as the average of: Q2(Y) to Q1(Y + 1) for Canada and Japan; and Q3(Y) to Q2(Y + 1) for Australia and New Zealand.

Source: OECD National Accounts.

1. PIB se référant á l'année fiscale. L'année A est calculée (taux annuel) comme la moyenne de: T2(A) à T1(A + 1) pour le Canada et le Japon ; et T3(A) à T2(A + 1) pour l'Australie et la Nouvelle-Zélande.

Source : Comptes nationaux de l'OCDE.

StatLink http://dx.doi.org/10.1787/888933416608

Table 3.36. **Exchange rates used, national currency per US dollar at market exchange rates**
Tableau 3.36. **Taux de change utilisés, unités de monnaie nationale par dollar des É-U au taux de change du marché**

	1965	1980	1990	2000	2007	2009	2011	2012	2013	2014
Australia / Australie	0.893	0.877	1.282	1.727	1.195	1.282	0.969	0.966	1.036	1.109
Austria / Autriche	..	0.720	0.788	1.085	0.730	0.720	0.719	0.778	0.753	0.754
Belgium / Belgique	..	0.720	0.788	1.085	0.730	0.720	0.719	0.778	0.753	0.754
Canada	1.078	1.169	1.167	1.485	1.074	1.141	0.989	0.999	1.030	1.105
Chile / Chili	..	..	304.903	539.388	522.228	558.942	483.421	485.984	495.282	570.636
Czech Republic / République tchèque	..	..	..	38.637	20.289	19.050	17.672	19.538	19.560	20.758
Denmark / Danemark	6.915	5.636	6.186	8.088	5.443	5.359	5.357	5.790	5.618	5.619
Estonia / Estonie	..	..	..	1.085	0.730	0.720	0.719	0.778	0.753	0.754
Finland / Finlande	..	0.720	0.788	1.085	0.730	0.720	0.719	0.778	0.753	0.754
France	..	0.720	0.788	1.085	0.730	0.720	0.719	0.778	0.753	0.754
Germany / Allemagne	..	0.720	0.788	1.085	0.730	0.720	0.719	0.778	0.753	0.754
Greece / Grèce	..	0.720	0.788	1.085	0.730	0.720	0.719	0.778	0.753	0.754
Hungary / Hongrie	..	..	..	282.286	183.595	202.062	200.907	224.823	223.582	232.619
Iceland / Islande	0.431	4.785	58.378	78.845	64.075	123.665	116.058	125.118	122.167	116.688
Ireland / Irlande	..	0.720	0.788	1.085	0.730	0.720	0.719	0.778	0.753	0.754
Israel / Israël	..	..	..	4.077	4.109	3.927	3.574	3.850	3.609	3.577
Italy / Italie	..	0.720	0.788	1.085	0.730	0.720	0.719	0.778	0.753	0.754
Japan / Japon	361.491	226.696	144.796	107.835	117.755	93.572	79.707	79.814	97.598	105.848
Korea / Corée	..	607.446	707.995	1 130.640	929.450	1 274.947	1 107.302	1 125.935	1 094.926	1 053.064
Latvia / Lettonie	..	..	..	1.085	0.730	0.720	0.719	0.778	0.753	0.754
Luxembourg	..	0.720	0.788	1.085	0.730	0.720	0.719	0.778	0.753	0.754
Mexico / Mexique	..	0.023	2.841	9.453	10.929	13.504	12.434	13.150	12.770	13.305
Netherlands / Pays-Bas	..	0.720	0.788	1.085	0.730	0.720	0.719	0.778	0.753	0.754
New Zealand / Nouvelle-Zélande	0.722	1.027	1.678	2.205	1.361	1.600	1.266	1.235	1.220	1.206
Norway / Norvège	7.151	4.937	6.258	8.797	5.858	6.290	5.605	5.815	5.877	6.302
Poland / Pologne	..	..	..	4.346	2.765	3.119	2.962	3.252	3.160	3.154
Portugal	..	0.720	0.788	1.085	0.730	0.720	0.719	0.778	0.753	0.754
Slovak Republic / République slovaque	..	..	..	1.085	0.730	0.720	0.719	0.778	0.753	0.754
Slovenia / Slovénie	..	..	..	1.085	0.730	0.720	0.719	0.778	0.753	0.754
Spain / Espagne	..	0.720	0.788	1.085	0.730	0.720	0.719	0.778	0.753	0.754
Sweden / Suède	5.158	4.229	5.918	9.161	6.758	7.653	6.489	6.769	6.513	6.860
Switzerland / Suisse	4.328	1.676	1.389	1.688	1.200	1.086	0.887	0.937	0.927	0.915
Turkey / Turquie	0.000	0.000	0.003	0.624	1.300	1.547	1.672	1.792	1.905	2.189
United Kingdom / Royaume-Uni	0.358	0.430	0.563	0.661	0.500	0.641	0.624	0.631	0.640	0.607
United States / États-Unis	1.000	1.000	1.000	1.000	1.000	1.000	1.000	1.000	1.000	1.000

Source : OECD Financial indicators data/Indicateurs financiers de l'OCDE.

StatLink http://dx.doi.org/10.1787/888933416619

3.2. Comparative figures, 1965-2014/Graphiques comparatifs, 1965-2014

Figure 3.1. **Total tax revenue as % of GDP, 2014**
Graphique 3.1. **Total des recettes fiscales en % du PIB, 2014**

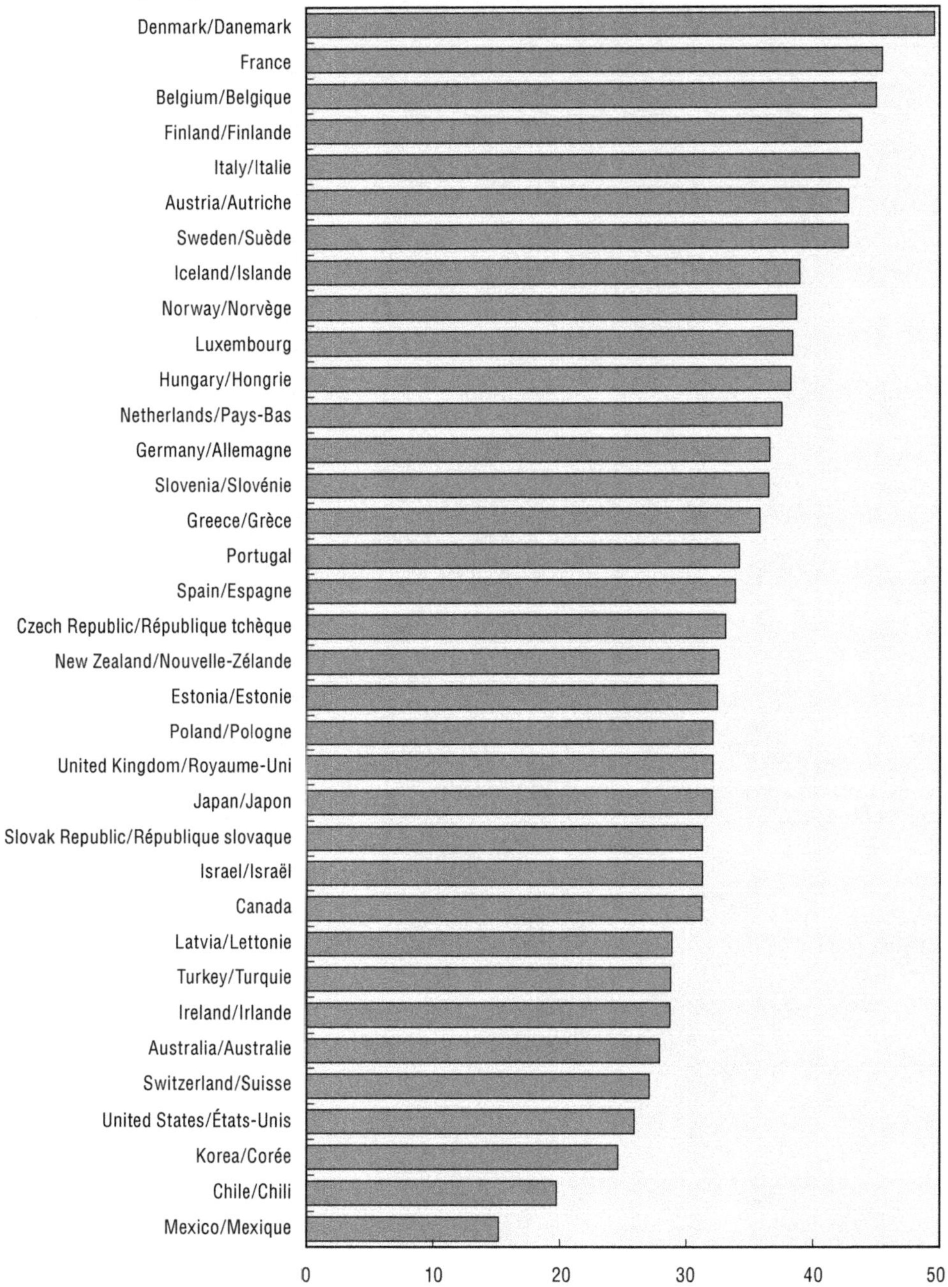

Note : Countries have been ranked by their total tax revenue to GDP ratios./Le classement des pays a été fait en fonction du total des recettes par rapport au PIB.
Source : Table 3.1./Tableau 3.1.

StatLink http://dx.doi.org/10.1787/888933416108

Figure 3.2. **Tax revenue of main headings as % of total revenue, 2014**

Graphique 3.2. **Recettes fiscales sous les principales rubriques en % du total des recettes fiscales, 2014**

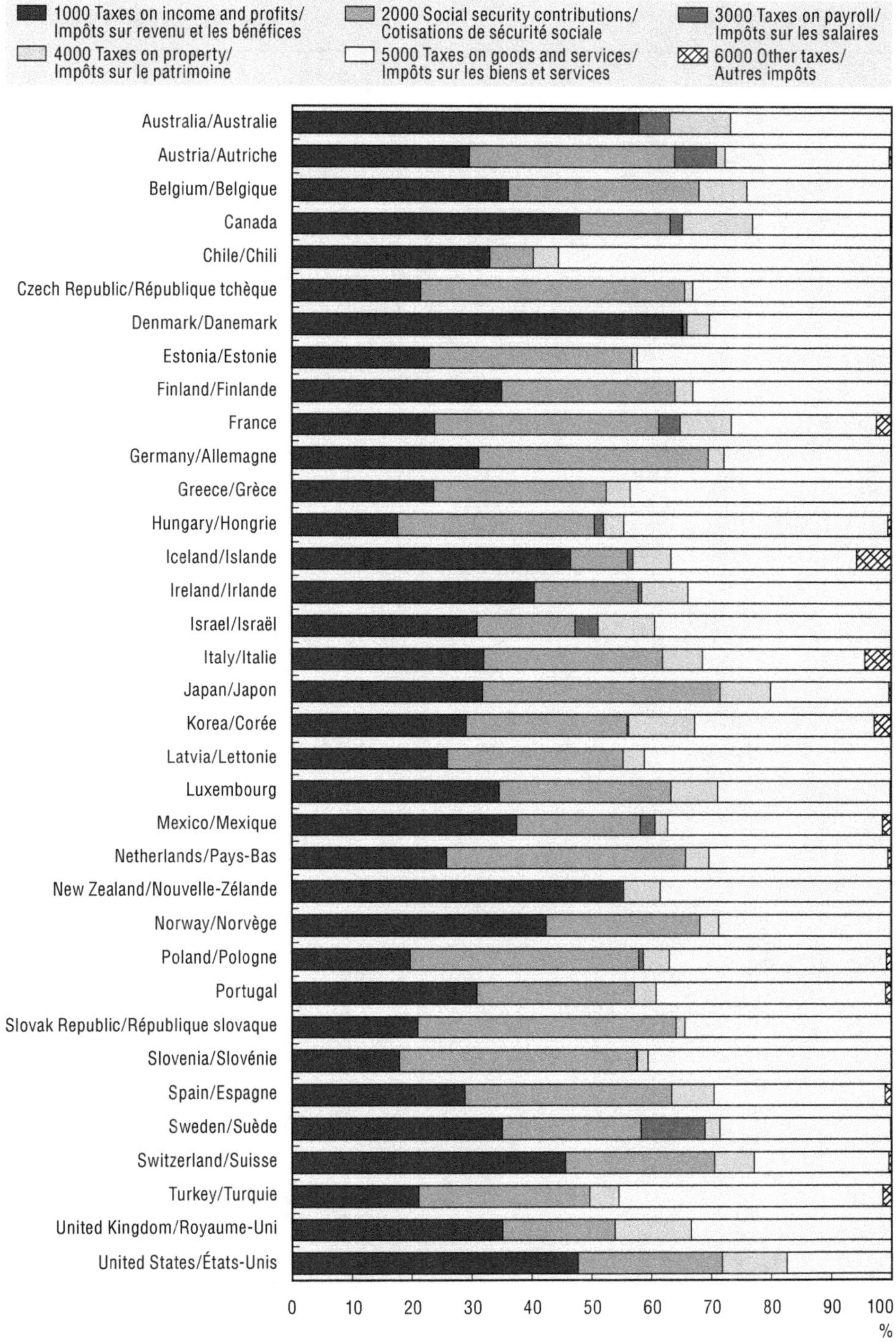

Source : Table 3.6./Tableau 3.6.

StatLink http://dx.doi.org/10.1787/888933416116

Figure 3.3. **Total tax revenue as % of GDP, 1965-2014**
Graphique 3.3. **Total des recettes fiscales en % du PIB, 1965-2014**

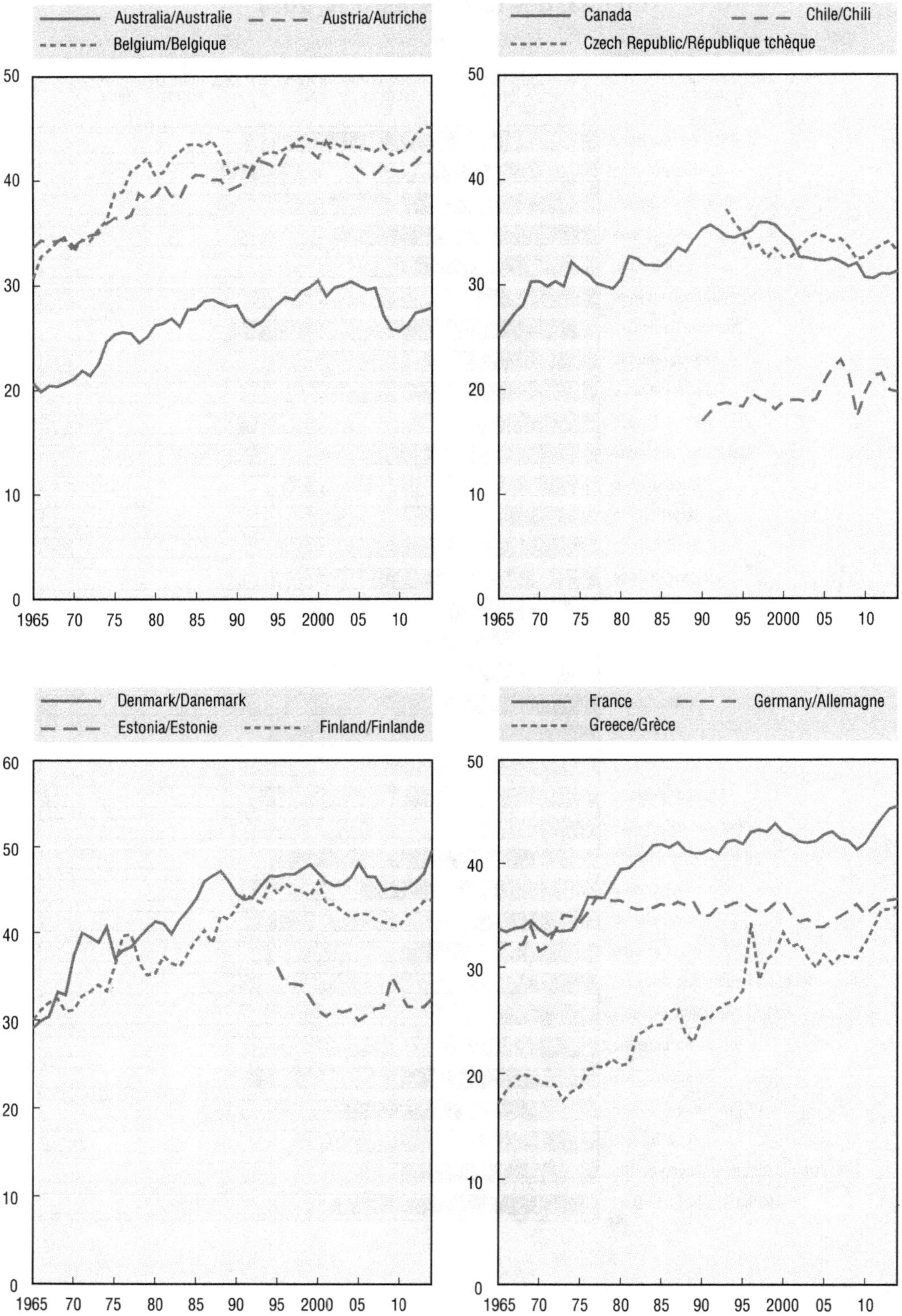

Source : Table 3.2./Tableau 3.2.

StatLink http://dx.doi.org/10.1787/888933416126

Figure 3.3. **Total tax revenue as % of GDP, 1965-2014** *(cont.)*

Graphique 3.3. **Total des recettes fiscales en % du PIB, 1965-2014** *(suite)*

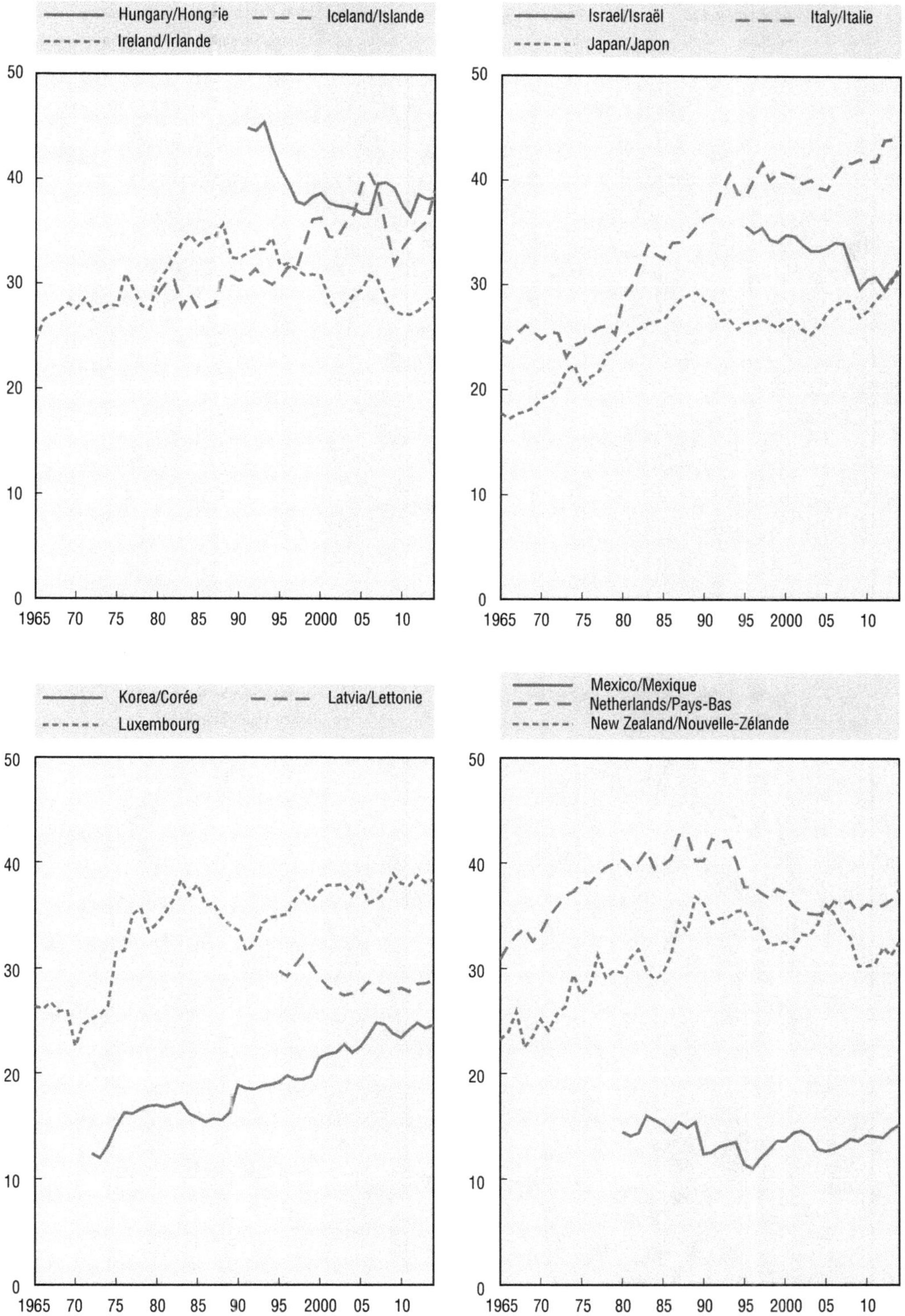

Source : Table 3.2./Tableau 3.2.

StatLink http://dx.doi.org/10.1787/888933416126

Figure 3.3. **Total tax revenue as % of GDP, 1965-2014** *(cont.)*
Graphique 3.3. **Total des recettes fiscales en % du PIB, 1965-2014** *(suite)*

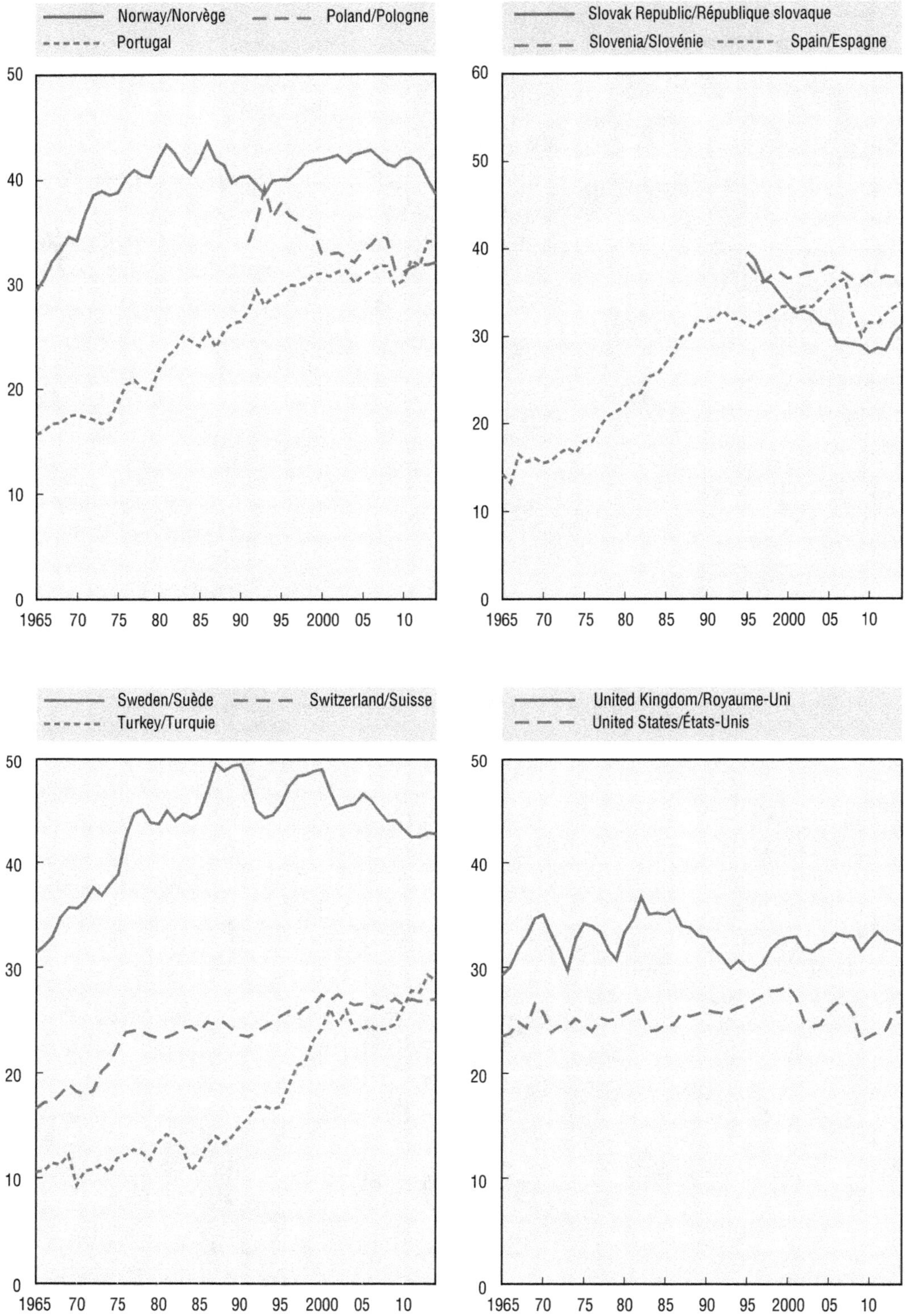

Source : Table 3.2./Tableau 3.2.

StatLink http://dx.doi.org/10.1787/888933416126

Figure 3.4. **Tax structures in OECD member countries, 1965-2014**
Graphique 3.4. **Structure de la fiscalité dans les pays membres de l'OCDE, 1965-2014**

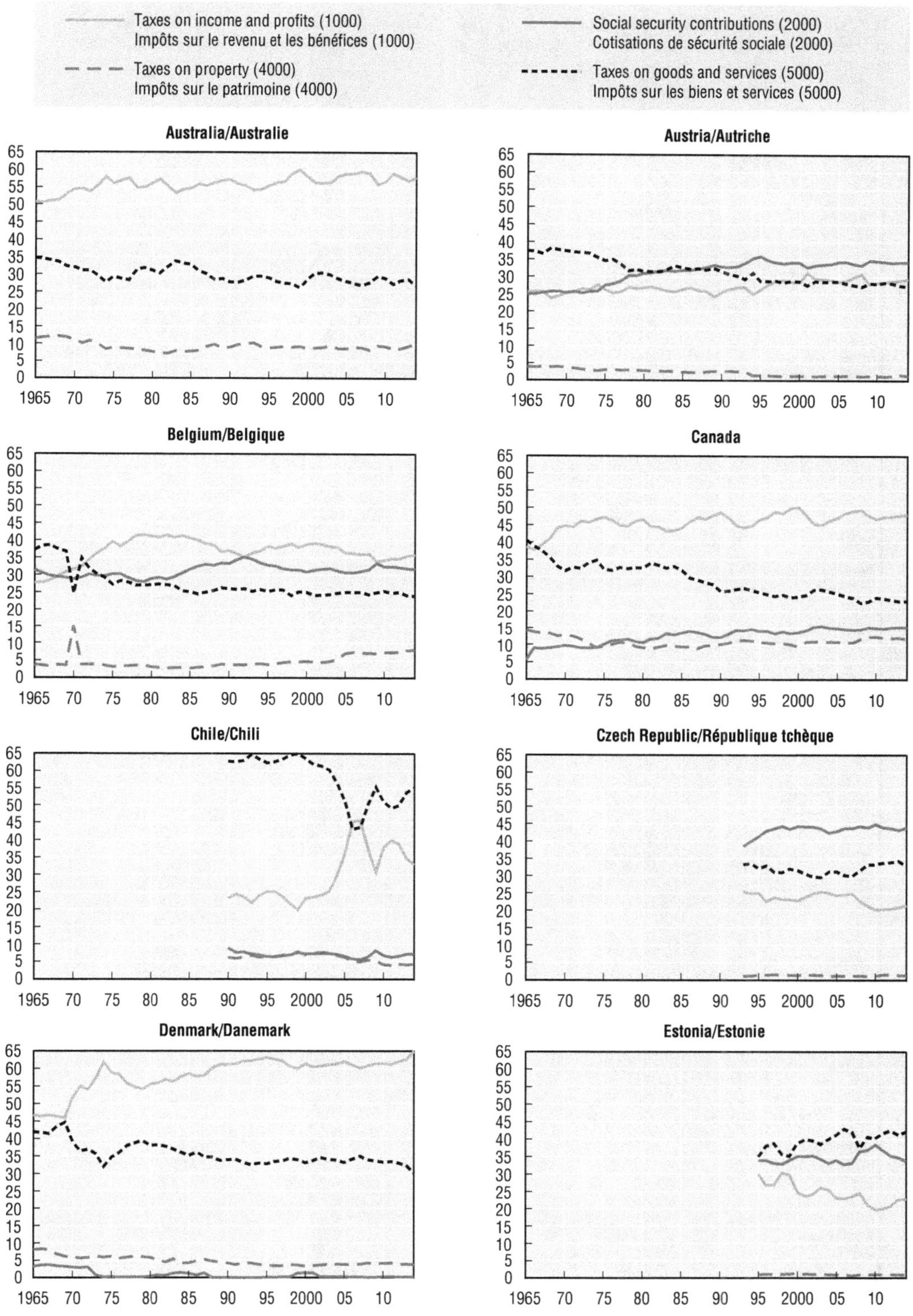

Source : Table 3.2./Tableau 3.2.

StatLink http://dx.doi.org/10.1787/888933416136

Figure 3.4. **Tax structures in OECD member countries, 1965-2014** *(cont.)*

Graphique 3.4. **Structure de la fiscalité dans les pays membres de l'OCDE, 1965-2014** *(suite)*

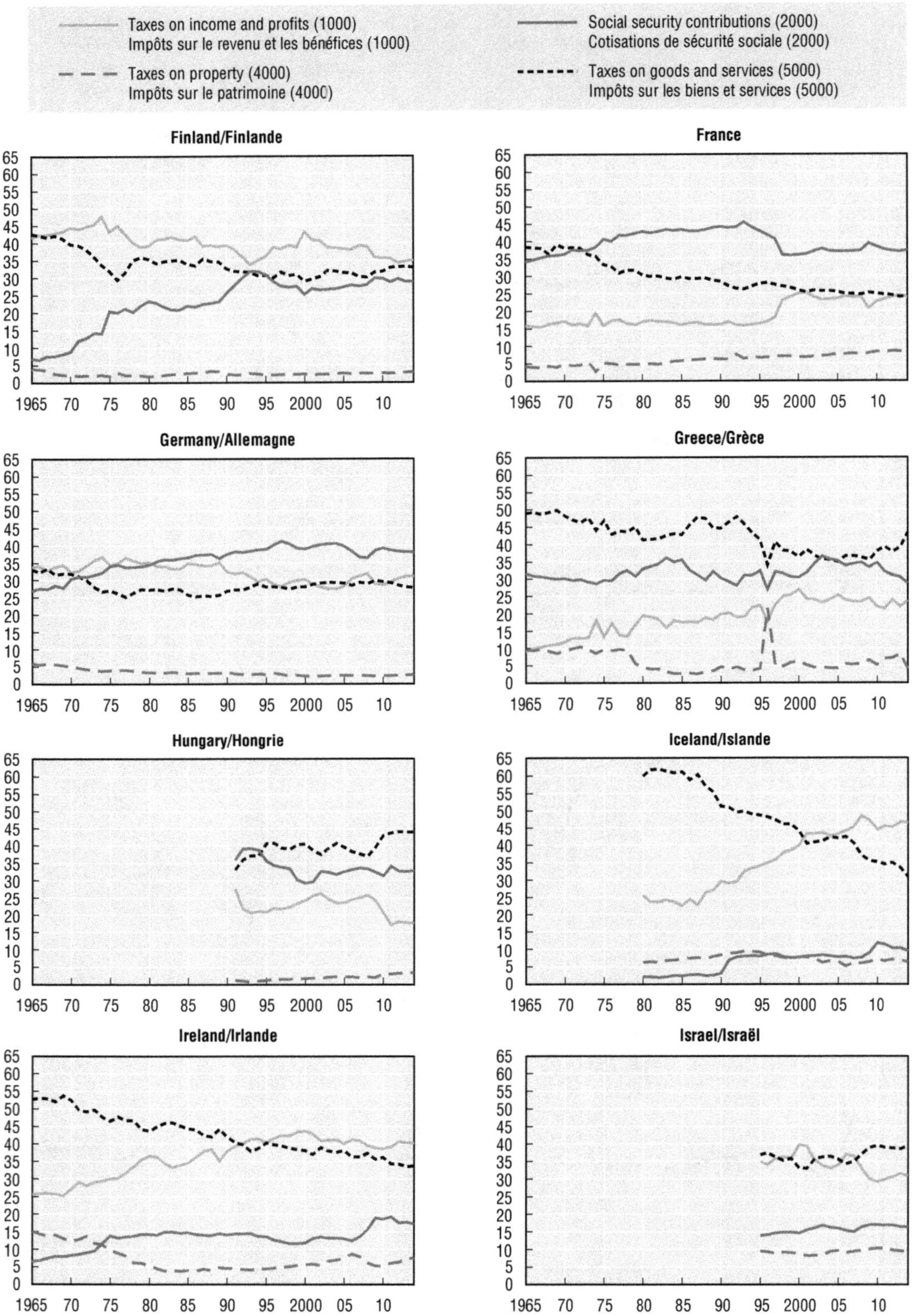

Source : Table 3.2./Tableau 3.2.

StatLink http://dx.doi.org/10.1787/888933416136

Figure 3.4. **Tax structures in OECD member countries, 1965-2014** *(cont.)*
Graphique 3.4. **Structure de la fiscalité dans les pays membres de l'OCDE, 1965-2014** *(suite)*

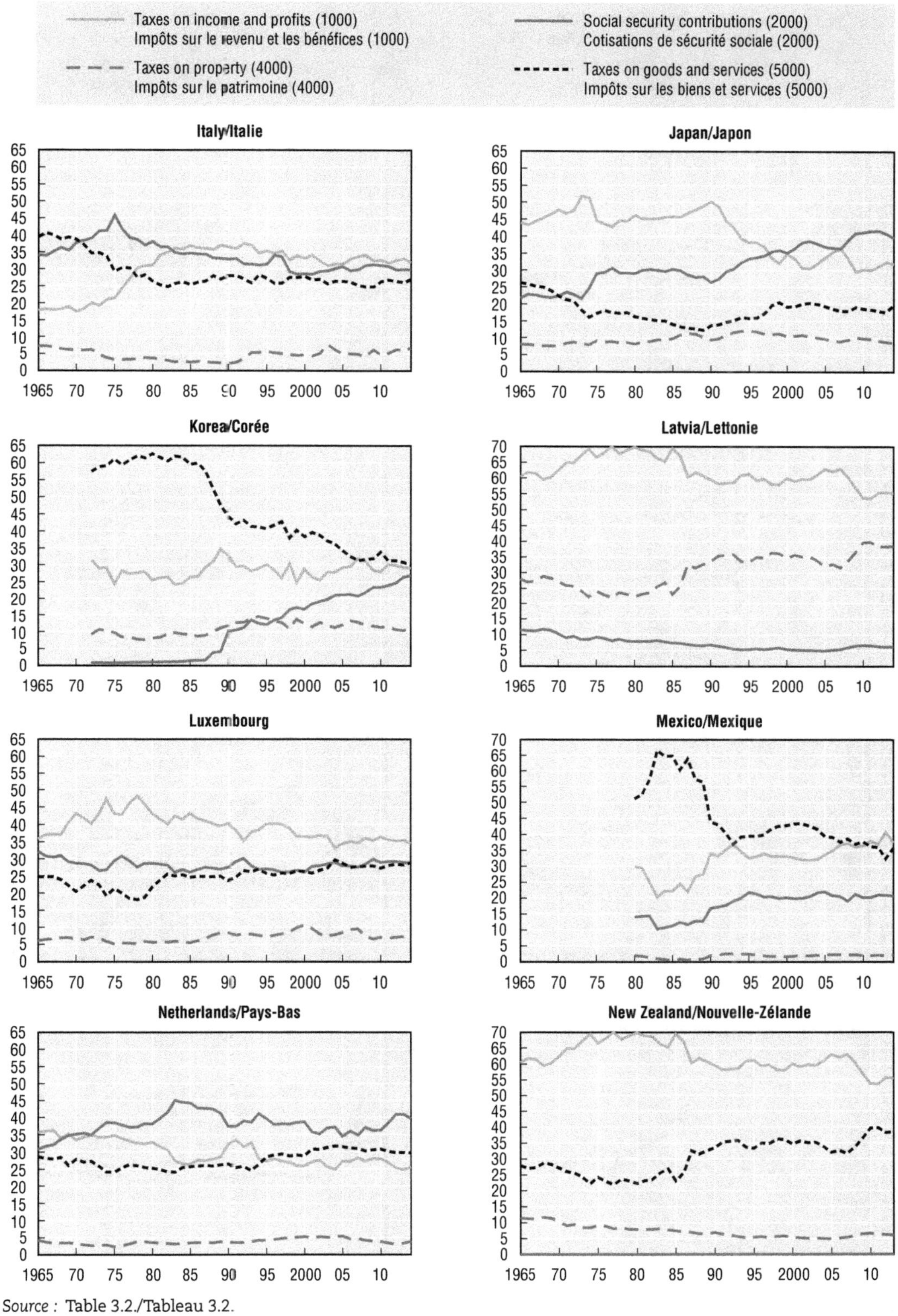

Source : Table 3.2./Tableau 3.2.

StatLink http://dx.doi.org/10.1787/888933416136

Figure 3.4. **Tax structures in OECD member countries, 1965-2014** *(cont.)*
Graphique 3.4. **Structure de la fiscalité dans les pays membres de l'OCDE, 1965-2014** *(suite)*

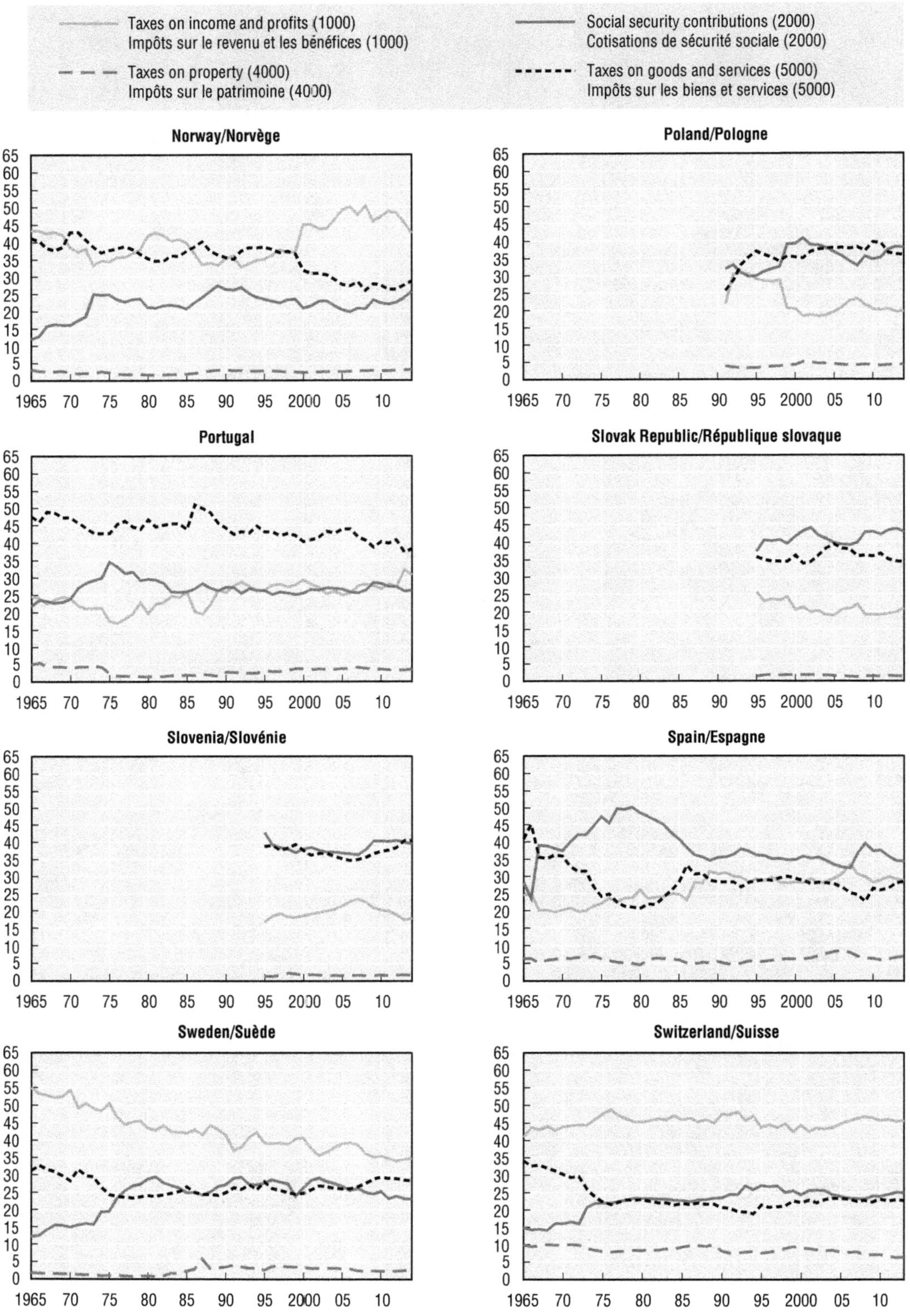

Source : Table 3.2./Tableau 3.2.

StatLink http://dx.doi.org/10.1787/888933416136

Figure 3.4. **Tax structures in OECD member countries, 1965-2014** *(cont.)*
Graphique 3.4. **Structure de la fiscalité dans les pays membres de l'OCDE, 1965-2014** *(suite)*

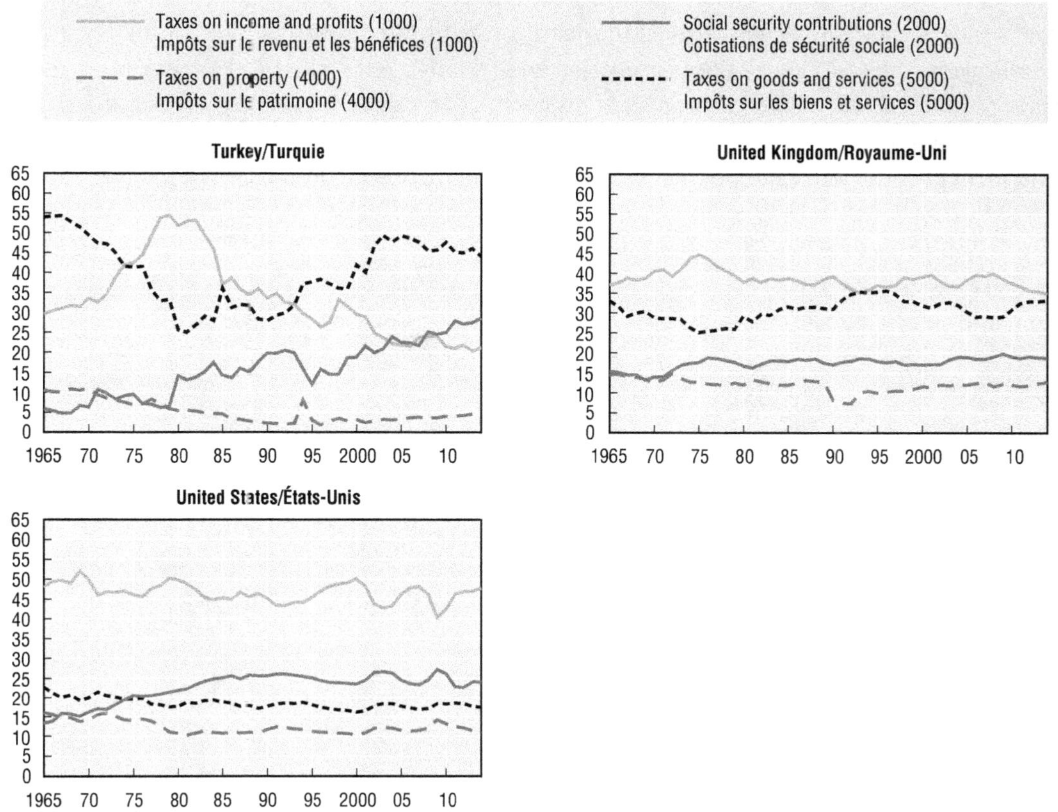

Source : Table 3.2./Tableau 3.2.

StatLink http://dx.doi.org/10.1787/888933416136

3.3. Estimates of Tax Revenues, 2015

Data provided in the preceding Sections 3.1 (Tables) and 3.2 (Figures) cover the years 1965 to 2014, because most countries are unable to provide definitive figures for the most recent year. However, provisional estimates of tax revenues in 2015 for the main headings in the OECD list of tax categories were available for most OECD countries at the time of publication. Two countries exclude revenues for specific levels of government and so their revenues cannot be compared with earlier years. Mexico excludes those for state and local government and Japan excludes social security contributions.

3.3. Estimations des recettes fiscales pour 2015

Les données rassemblées dans les Sections 3.1 (Tableaux) et 3.2 (Graphiques) concernent les années 1965 à 2014, car la plupart des pays ne sont pas en mesure de fournir des chiffres définitifs pour la période la plus récente. Cependant, des estimations provisoires des recettes fiscales en 2015 concernant les principales rubriques de la liste de l'OCDE de catégories fiscales étaient disponibles pour la plupart des pays de l'OCDE au moment de la publication. Deux pays ne fournissent pas d'estimations des recettes fiscales pour des niveaux d'administration spécifiques ; par conséquent, leurs recettes fiscales ne sont pas comparables aux chiffres des années précédentes. Le Mexique ne donne pas d'estimations pour les administrations d'États et les administrations locales et le Japon ne donne pas d'estimations pour les cotisations de sécurité sociale.

Table 3.37. Estimates of tax revenues in billions of national currency units, 2015
Tableau 3.37. Estimations des recettes fiscales en milliards de monnaie nationale, 2015

	Australia	Austria	Belgium	Canada	Chile	Czech Republic	Denmark[1]	Estonia	Finland
1000 Taxes on income, profits and capital gains	..	**44.8**	**65.5**	**302.3**	**11 836.5**	**326.6**	**579.1**	**1.6**	**32.4**
1100 Of individuals	..	35.9	51.6	233.9	2 313.4	164.5	504.3	1.2	27.8
1200 Corporate	..	7.7	13.9	62.3	7 721.6	162.1	52.5	0.4	4.5
1300 Unallocable between 1100 and 1200	..	1.3	0.1	6.2	1 801.5	0.0	22.3	0.0	0.0
2000 Social security contributions	..	**50.3**	**58.5**	**97.2**	**2 252.5**	**659.7**	**1.4**	**2.3**	**26.6**
2100 Employees	..	20.3	16.9	39.0	2 188.6	133.9	0.8	0.1	6.4
2200 Employers	..	23.4	36.1	54.9	63.9	417.8	0.5	2.2	18.2
2300 Self-employed or non-employed	..	6.6	5.4	3.3	0.0	108.1	0.0	0.0	2.0
2400 Unallocable between 2100, 2200 and 2300	..	0.0	0.0	0.0	0.0	0.0	0.0	0.0	0.0
3000 Taxes on payroll and workforce	..	**10.0**	**0.0**	**12.7**	**0.0**	**0.0**	**5.8**	**0.0**	**0.0**
4000 Taxes on property	..	**2.0**	**14.4**	**75.0**	**1 418.5**	**17.0**	**38.8**	**0.1**	**3.0**
4100 Recurrent taxes on immovable property	..	0.8	5.4	58.1	1 054.2	9.9	27.8	0.1	1.6
4200 Recurrent taxes on net wealth	..	0.0	0.7	0.3	0.0	0.0	0.0	0.0	0.0
4300 Estate, inheritance and gift taxes	..	0.0	3.0	0.3	92.2	-4.4	5.1	0.0	0.6
4400 Taxes on financial and capital transactions	..	1.1	4.4	4.5	272.1	11.6	5.8	0.0	0.8
4500 Non-recurrent taxes	..	0.1	0.6	11.8	0.0	0.0	0.0	0.0	0.0
4600 Other recurrent taxes on property	..	0.0	0.3	0.0	0.0	0.0	0.0	0.0	0.0
5000 Taxes on goods and services	..	**39.7**	**43.6**	**147.5**	**17 562.1**	**512.8**	**297.0**	**2.9**	**29.7**
5100 Taxes on production, sale, transfer, etc	..	36.9	41.1	138.7	16 480.6	487.4	273.4	2.8	28.7
5110 General taxes	..	26.3	27.8	88.3	13 274.0	333.3	187.9	1.9	19.0
5120 Taxes on specific goods and services	..	10.6	13.3	50.4	3 206.7	154.1	85.5	0.9	9.7
5130 Unallocable between 5110 and 5120	..	0.0	0.0	0.0	0.0	0.0	0.0	0.0	0.0
5200 Taxes on use of goods and perform activities	..	2.7	2.5	8.8	1 081.5	25.5	16.5	0.1	1.1
5300 Unallocable between 5100 and 5200	..	0.0	0.0	0.0	0.0	0.0	7.1	0.0	0.0
6000 Other taxes	..	**0.5**	**0.0**	**0.8**	**-544.7**	**0.4**	**0.3**	**0.0**	**0.1**
Customs duties collected for the EU	..	**0.4**	**1.4**	..	..	**7.9**	**3.3**	**0.0**	**0.2**
Total tax revenue	..	**147.7**	**183.4**	**635.5**	**32 524.9**	**1 524.4**	**925.6**	**6.9**	**92.0**

	France[1]	Germany[2]	Greece	Hungary[3]	Iceland	Ireland	Israel	Italy	Japan[4]
1000 Taxes on income, profits and capital gains	**233.2**	**352.5**	**15.3**	**2 313.8**	**383.0**	**26.1**	**113.8**	**227.0**	**51 870.1**
1100 Of individuals	187.1	299.6	..	1 688.6	291.9	19.2	70.7	185.5	30 540.7
1200 Corporate	46.1	52.9	..	625.2	63.7	6.9	34.7	33.7	21 329.4
1300 Unallocable between 1100 and 1200	0.0	0.0	..	0.0	27.4	0.0	8.4	7.8	0.0
2000 Social security contributions	**368.1**	**424.7**	**18.8**	**4 428.9**	**78.9**	**10.0**	**59.5**	**213.9**	..
2100 Employees	93.2	188.9	..	1 836.1	..	3.4	38.7	39.7	..
2200 Employers	246.4	199.2	..	2 592.9	..	6.2	17.2	142.6	..
2300 Self-employed or non-employed	28.5	36.5	..	0.0	..	0.5	3.6	31.6	..
2400 Unallocable between 2100, 2200 and 2300	0.0	0.0	..	0.0	78.9	0.0	0.0	0.0	..
3000 Taxes on payroll and workforce	**34.4**	**0.0**	**0.0**	**195.8**	**7.6**	**0.4**	**13.7**	**0.0**	**0.0**
4000 Taxes on property	**88.7**	**32.7**	**3.4**	**437.1**	**43.5**	**3.9**	**35.6**	**45.7**	**13 049.7**
4100 Recurrent taxes on immovable property	57.0	13.2	..	200.4	34.3	1.8	23.1	25.5	9 900.2
4200 Recurrent taxes on net wealth	5.2	1.9	..	136.0	1.5	0.2	0.0	0.1	0.0
4300 Estate, inheritance and gift taxes	12.2	6.3	..	7.4	2.9	0.4	0.0	0.7	1 761.0
4400 Taxes on financial and capital transactions	14.3	11.2	..	93.4	4.2	1.5	5.1	17.3	1 388.5
4500 Non-recurrent taxes	0.0	0.0	..	0.0	0.3	0.0	7.5	0.3	0.0
4600 Other recurrent taxes on property	0.0	0.0	..	0.0	0.3	0.0	0.0	1.9	0.0
5000 Taxes on goods and services	**241.7**	**305.0**	**27.2**	**5 809.6**	**259.1**	**19.7**	**138.2**	**192.1**	**33 819.2**
5100 Taxes on production, sale, transfer, etc	234.8	294.0	..	5 664.1	247.2	17.8	128.3	169.9	31 417.1
5110 General taxes	155.8	211.7	..	4 082.9	179.5	12.0	107.8	101.2	21 984.3
5120 Taxes on specific goods and services	79.0	82.0	..	1 581.2	67.6	5.9	20.5	68.7	9 432.8
5130 Unallocable between 5110 and 5120	0.0	0.3	..	0.0	0.0	0.0	0.0	0.0	0.0
5200 Taxes on use of goods and perform activities	6.9	11.0	..	145.5	11.9	1.9	10.0	10.9	2 402.1
5300 Unallocable between 5100 and 5200	0.0	0.0	..	0.0	0.0	0.0	0.0	11.3	0.0
6000 Other taxes	**24.4**	**0.2**	**0.0**	**56.7**	**40.6**	**0.0**	**0.0**	**28.1**	**405.8**
Customs duties collected for the EU	**1.9**	**5.2**	..	**39.0**	..	**0.3**	..	**2.2**	..
Total tax revenue	**992.5**	**1 120.2**	**64.7**	**13 280.9**	**812.7**	**60.4**	**360.9**	**709.1**	..

StatLink http://dx.doi.org/10.1787/888933416624

Table 3.37. **Estimates of tax revenues in billions of national currency units, 2015** *(cont.)*
Tableau 3.37. **Estimations des recettes fiscales en milliards de monnaie nationale, 2015** *(suite)*

	Korea	Latvia	Luxembourg	Mexico[5]	Netherlands	New Zealand	Norway	Poland	Portugal
1000 Taxes on income, profits and capital gains	**119 150.0**	**1.8**	**7.0**	**1 230.6**	**70.9**	**45.2**	**468.3**	**..**	**18.8**
1100 Of individuals	68 625.0	1.4	4.7	609.4	52.4	31.1	326.6	..	13.1
1200 Corporate	50 525.0	0.4	2.3	592.4	18.4	11.0	141.7	..	5.7
1300 Unallocable between 1100 and 1200	0.0	0.0	0.0	28.7	0.0	3.0	0.0	..	0.0
2000 Social security contributions	**104 693.0**	**2.0**	**5.6**	**588.3**	**96.4**	**0.0**	**326.3**	**..**	**16.2**
2100 Employees	44 281.0	0.6	2.6	..	46.8	0.0	113.4	..	7.0
2200 Employers	47 846.0	1.4	2.4	..	34.8	0.0	191.4	..	9.1
2300 Self-employed or non-employed	12 566.0	0.0	0.6	..	14.8	0.0	21.5	..	0.0
2400 Unallocable between 2100, 2200 and 2300	0.0	0.0	0.0	588.3	0.0	0.0	0.0	..	0.0
3000 Taxes on payroll and workforce	**1 122.0**	**0.0**	**0.0**	**..**	**0.0**	**0.0**	**0.0**	**..**	**0.0**
4000 Taxes on property	**48 625.0**	**0.2**	**1.7**	**..**	**9.7**	**5.1**	**34.9**	**..**	**2.4**
4100 Recurrent taxes on immovable property	12 486.0	0.2	0.0	..	6.3	5.0	12.7	..	1.6
4200 Recurrent taxes on net wealth	0.0	0.0	1.3	..	0.0	0.0	13.5	..	..
4300 Estate, inheritance and gift taxes	5 044.0	0.0	0.1	..	1.6	0.0	0.3	..	0.0
4400 Taxes on financial and capital transactions	31 095.0	0.0	0.3	..	1.8	0.1	8.4	..	0.8
4500 Non-recurrent taxes	0.0	0.0	0.0	..	0.0	0.0	0.0	..	0.0
4600 Other recurrent taxes on property	0.0	0.0	0.0	..	0.0	0.0	0.0	..	0.0
5000 Taxes on goods and services	**110 326.0**	**2.9**	**4.9**	**..**	**75.6**	**31.4**	**362.4**	**..**	**23.8**
5100 Taxes on production, sale, transfer, etc	103 254.0	2.8	4.9	..	67.0	29.4	343.4	..	22.7
5110 General taxes	60 162.0	1.9	3.4	707.2	44.9	24.5	256.3	..	15.4
5120 Taxes on specific goods and services	43 092.0	0.8	1.4	..	22.1	4.8	87.2	..	7.3
5130 Unallocable between 5110 and 5120	0.0	0.0	0.0	..	0.0	0.0	0.0	..	0.0
5200 Taxes on use of goods and perform activities	7 072.0	0.2	0.1	..	8.5	2.1	19.0	..	1.1
5300 Unallocable between 5100 and 5200	0.0	0.0	0.0	..	0.0	0.0	0.0	..	0.0
6000 Other taxes	**9 642.0**	**0.0**	**0.0**	**..**	**0.4**	**0.0**	**0.0**	**..**	**0.5**
Customs duties collected for the EU	**..**	**0.0**	**0.0**	**..**	**2.4**	**..**	**..**	**..**	**0.2**
Total tax revenue	**393 558.0**	**7.1**	**19.3**	**..**	**255.4**	**81.6**	**1 192.0**	**..**	**61.9**

	Slovak Republic	Slovenia	Spain[1]	Sweden	Switzerland	Turkey	United Kingdom	United States	
1000 Taxes on income, profits and capital gains	**5.4**	**2.6**	**105.1**	**642.4**	**82.9**	**119.1**	**215.3**	**2 334.0**	**..**
1100 Of individuals	2.5	2.0	78.0	518.0	55.5	85.8	169.4	1 938.1	..
1200 Corporate	2.8	0.6	26.1	124.4	19.5	33.4	45.9	395.9	..
1300 Unallocable between 1100 and 1200	0.2	0.0	1.0	0.0	8.0	0.0	0.0	0.0	..
2000 Social security contributions	**10.8**	**5.6**	**123.2**	**405.2**	**43.9**	**170.3**	**113.3**	**1 125.9**	**..**
2100 Employees	2.4	2.9	19.6	108.1	20.5	64.2	44.4	499.7	..
2200 Employers	6.2	2.1	87.4	291.7	20.3	95.1	66.0	561.2	..
2300 Self-employed or non-employed	2.2	0.6	16.1	5.6	3.1	11.0	2.8	65.0	..
2400 Unallocable between 2100, 2200 and 2300	0.0	0.0	0.0	-0.3	0.0	0.0	0.0	0.0	..
3000 Taxes on payroll and workforce	**0.0**	**0.0**	**0.0**	**192.0**	**0.0**	**0.0**	**0.0**	**0.0**	**..**
4000 Taxes on property	**0.3**	**0.2**	**25.9**	**43.9**	**11.9**	**28.6**	**76.0**	**494.9**	**..**
4100 Recurrent taxes on immovable property	0.3	0.2	12.3	32.5	1.1	5.9	57.5	462.2	..
4200 Recurrent taxes on net wealth	0.0	0.0	1.2	0.0	7.9	0.0	0.0	0.0	..
4300 Estate, inheritance and gift taxes	0.0	0.0	2.7	0.0	1.2	0.4	4.4	24.8	..
4400 Taxes on financial and capital transactions	0.0	0.0	7.2	11.4	1.7	22.3	13.8	0.0	..
4500 Non-recurrent taxes	0.0	0.0	2.5	0.0	0.0	0.0	0.2	0.0	..
4600 Other recurrent taxes on property	0.0	0.0	0.0	0.0	0.0	0.0	0.0	7.9	..
5000 Taxes on goods and services	**8.6**	**5.6**	**106.7**	**509.5**	**38.9**	**259.6**	**200.3**	**799.3**	**..**
5100 Taxes on production, sale, transfer, etc	7.9	5.3	100.7	490.8	33.6	249.9	193.2	683.2	..
5110 General taxes	5.4	3.2	68.7	383.1	22.6	120.8	128.9	366.0	..
5120 Taxes on specific goods and services	2.5	2.0	32.0	107.7	10.9	129.1	64.3	317.2	..
5130 Unallocable between 5110 and 5120	0.0	0.0	0.0	0.0	0.1	0.0	0.0	0.0	..
5200 Taxes on use of goods and perform activities	0.5	0.4	5.3	18.8	5.3	9.7	7.1	116.1	..
5300 Unallocable between 5100 and 5200	0.2	0.0	0.7	0.0	0.0	0.0	0.0	0.0	..
6000 Other taxes	**0.0**	**0.0**	**3.3**	**1.4**	**0.7**	**8.7**	**0.0**	**0.0**	**..**
Customs duties collected for the EU	**0.1**	**0.1**	**1.8**	**6.2**	**..**	**..**	**3.1**	**..**	**..**
Total tax revenue	**25.2**	**14.1**	**366.0**	**1 800.7**	**178.4**	**586.4**	**607.9**	**4 754.1**	**..**

1. The total tax revenues have been reduced by the amount of any capital transfer that represents uncollected taxes./Le total des recettes fiscales a été diminué du montant de tout transfert en capital représentant les impôts non perçus.
2. From 1991, the figures relate to the united Germany./Depuis 1991, les chiffres se rapportent à l'Allemagne unifiée.
3. The figures are on a cash basis./Les données sont sur la base de la trésorerie.
4. The tax revenue figures exclude revenue from Social security funds, figures are not available./Les données excluent les chiffres de l'administration de sécurité sociale, les données n'étant pas disponibles.
5. Central government and Social security funds only./Administration centrale et administrations de sécurité sociale seulement.

StatLink http://dx.doi.org/10.1787/888933416624

Table 3.38. **Estimates of tax revenues as % of GDP, 2015**
Tableau 3.38. **Estimations des recettes fiscales en % du PIB, 2015**

	Total tax revenue / Total des recettes fiscales	1000 Income & profits / Revenu & bénéfices	2000 Social security / Sécurité sociale	3000 Payroll / Salaires	4000 Property / Patrimoine	5000 Goods & services / Biens & services	6000 Other / Autres	EU Custom Duties / UE droits de douane
Australia / Australie	..	..	..	..	..	..	..	..
Austria / Autriche	43.5	13.2	14.8	3.0	0.6	11.7	0.2	0.1
Belgium / Belgique	44.8	16.0	14.3	0.0	3.5	10.7	0.0	0.3
Canada	31.9	15.2	4.9	0.6	3.8	7.4	0.0	..
Chile / Chili	20.7	7.5	1.4	0.0	0.9	11.2	-0.3	..
Czech Republic / République tchèque	33.5	7.2	14.5	0.0	0.4	11.3	0.0	0.2
Denmark / Danemark[1]	46.6	29.2	0.1	0.3	2.0	15.0	0.0	0.2
Estonia / Estonie	33.6	7.9	11.2	0.0	0.3	14.1	0.0	0.2
Finland / Finlande	44.0	15.5	12.7	0.0	1.4	14.2	0.0	0.1
France[1]	45.5	10.7	16.9	1.6	4.1	11.1	1.1	0.1
Germany / Allemagne[2]	36.9	11.6	14.0	0.0	1.1	10.1	0.0	0.2
Greece / Grèce	36.8	8.7	10.7	0.0	2.0	15.5	0.0	0.0
Hungary / Hongrie[3]	39.4	6.9	13.1	0.6	1.3	17.2	0.2	0.1
Iceland / Islande	37.1	17.5	3.6	0.3	2.0	11.8	1.9	..
Ireland / Irlande	23.6	10.2	3.9	0.1	1.5	7.7	0.0	0.1
Israel / Israël	31.4	9.9	5.2	1.2	3.1	12.0	0.0	..
Italy / Italie	43.3	13.9	13.1	0.0	2.8	11.7	1.7	0.1
Japan / Japon[4]	..	10.4	..	0.0	2.6	6.8	0.1	..
Korea / Corée	25.3	7.6	6.7	0.1	3.1	7.1	0.6	..
Latvia / Lettonie	29.0	7.5	8.3	0.0	1.0	12.0	0.0	0.2
Luxembourg	37.0	13.4	10.7	0.0	3.3	9.5	0.0	0.0
Mexico / Mexique[5]	17.4	6.8	3.3	..	..	..	..	..
Netherlands / Pays-Bas	37.8	10.5	14.2	0.0	1.4	11.2	0.1	0.4
New Zealand / Nouvelle-Zélande	32.8	18.1	0.0	0.0	2.0	12.6	0.0	..
Norway / Norvège	38.1	15.0	10.4	0.0	1.1	11.6	0.0	..
Poland / Pologne	..	..	..	..	..	..	..	..
Portugal	34.5	10.5	9.0	0.0	1.3	13.3	0.3	0.1
Slovak Republic / République slovaque	32.3	6.9	13.8	0.0	0.4	11.0	0.0	0.2
Slovenia / Slovénie	36.6	6.6	14.5	0.1	0.6	14.6	0.0	0.1
Spain / Espagne[1]	33.8	9.7	11.4	0.0	2.4	9.9	0.3	0.2
Sweden / Suède	43.3	15.5	9.8	4.6	1.1	12.3	0.0	0.2
Switzerland / Suisse	27.9	13.0	6.9	0.0	1.9	6.1	0.1	..
Turkey / Turquie	30.0	6.1	8.7	0.0	1.5	13.3	0.4	..
United Kingdom / Royaume-Uni	32.5	11.5	6.1	0.0	4.1	10.7	0.0	0.2
United States / États-Unis	26.4	12.9	6.2	0.0	2.7	4.4	0.0	..

1. The total tax revenue has been reduced by the amount of any capital transfer that represents uncollected taxes. The capital transfer has been allocated between tax headings in proportion to the reported tax revenue.
2. From 1991, the figures relate to the united Germany.
3. The tax revenue figures are on a cash basis.
4. The tax revenue figures exclude revenue for Social Security funds, figures are not available.
5. Central government and Social security funds only.

1. Le total des recettes fiscales a été diminué du montant de tout transfert en capital représentant les impôts non perçus. Le transfert en capital a été réparti entre les différentes rubriques en proportion des recettes fiscales.
2. Depuis 1991, les chiffres se rapportent à l'Allemagne unifiée.
3. Les chiffres relatifs aux recettes fiscales sont sur la base de la trésorerie.
4. Les données excluent les chiffres de l'administration de sécurité sociale, les données n'étant pas disponibles.
5. Administration centrale et administrations de sécurité sociale seulement.

StatLink http://dx.doi.org/10.1787/888933416633

Table 3.39. **Tax revenue of main headings as % of total taxation, 2015**
Tableau 3.39. **Recettes fiscales sous les principales rubriques en % du total des recettes fiscales, 2015**

	Total tax revenue / Total des recettes fiscales	1000 Income & profits / Revenu & bénéfices	2000 Social security / Sécurité sociale	3000 Payroll / Salaires	4000 Property / Patrimoine	5000 Goods & services / Biens & services	6000 Other / Autres	EU Custom Duties / UE droits de douane
Australia / Australie	..	..	..	..	..	..	..	..
Austria / Autriche	100.0	30.3	34.0	6.8	1.3	26.9	0.4	0.3
Belgium / Belgique	100.0	35.7	31.9	0.0	7.8	23.8	0.0	0.7
Canada	100.0	47.6	15.3	2.0	11.8	23.2	0.1	..
Chile / Chili	100.0	36.4	6.9	0.0	4.4	54.0	-1.7	..
Czech Republic / République tchèque	100.0	21.4	43.3	0.0	1.1	33.6	0.0	0.5
Denmark / Danemark[1]	100.0	62.6	0.1	0.6	4.2	32.1	0.0	0.4
Estonia / Estonie	100.0	23.4	33.3	0.0	0.8	42.0	0.0	0.5
Finland / Finlande	100.0	35.2	29.0	0.0	3.3	32.3	0.1	0.2
France[1]	100.0	23.5	37.1	3.5	8.9	24.4	2.5	0.2
Germany / Allemagne[2]	100.0	31.5	37.9	0.0	2.9	27.2	0.0	0.5
Greece / Grèce	100.0	23.6	29.0	0.0	5.3	42.0	0.0	0.0
Hungary / Hongrie[3]	100.0	17.4	33.3	1.5	3.3	43.7	0.4	0.3
Iceland / Islande	100.0	47.1	9.7	0.9	5.4	31.9	5.0	..
Ireland / Irlande	100.0	43.2	16.6	0.6	6.4	32.7	0.0	0.5
Israel / Israël	100.0	31.5	16.5	3.8	9.9	38.3	0.0	..
Italy / Italie	100.0	32.0	30.2	0.0	6.4	27.1	4.0	0.3
Japan / Japon	..	..	..	..	..	..	..	..
Korea / Corée	100.0	30.3	26.6	0.3	12.4	28.0	2.5	..
Latvia / Lettonie	100.0	25.9	28.7	0.0	3.4	41.3	0.0	0.6
Luxembourg	100.0	36.3	28.9	0.0	8.9	25.6	0.1	0.1
Mexico / Mexique	..	..	..	..	..	..	..	..
Netherlands / Pays-Bas	100.0	27.7	37.7	0.0	3.8	29.6	0.2	1.0
New Zealand / Nouvelle-Zélande	100.0	55.3	0.0	0.0	6.2	38.5	0.0	..
Norway / Norvège	100.0	39.3	27.4	0.0	2.9	30.4	0.0	..
Poland / Pologne	..	..	..	..	..	..	..	..
Portugal	100.0	30.4	26.1	0.0	3.8	38.5	0.9	0.3
Slovak Republic / République slovaque	100.0	21.4	42.8	0.0	1.3	34.0	0.0	0.5
Slovenia / Slovénie	100.0	18.1	39.7	0.1	1.7	39.9	0.0	0.4
Spain / Espagne[1]	100.0	28.7	33.7	0.0	7.1	29.2	0.9	0.5
Sweden / Suède	100.0	35.7	22.5	10.7	2.4	28.3	0.1	0.3
Switzerland / Suisse	100.0	46.5	24.6	0.0	6.7	21.8	0.4	..
Turkey / Turquie	100.0	20.3	29.0	0.0	4.9	44.3	1.5	..
United Kingdom / Royaume-Uni	100.0	35.4	18.6	0.0	12.5	32.9	0.0	0.5
United States / États-Unis	100.0	49.1	23.7	0.0	10.4	16.8	0.0	..

1. The total tax revenue has been reduced by the amount of any capital transfer that represents uncollected taxes. The capital transfer has been allocated between tax headings in proportion to the reported tax revenue.
2. From 1991, the figures relate to the united Germany.
3. The tax revenue figures are on a cash basis.

1. Le total des recettes fiscales a été diminué du montant de tout transfert en capital représentant les impôts non perçus. Le transfert en capital a été réparti entre les différentes rubriques en proportion des recettes fiscales.
2. Depuis 1991, les chiffres se rapportent à l'Allemagne unifiée.
3. Les chiffres relatifs aux recettes fiscales sont sur la base de la trésorerie.

StatLink http://dx.doi.org/10.1787/888933416646

Table 3.40. **Gross domestic product at market prices, in billions of national currency units**
Tableau 3.40. **Produit intérieur brut au prix du marché, en milliards de monnaie nationale**

	2015
Australia / Australie[1]	1 657
Austria / Autriche	340
Belgium / Belgique	409
Canada[1]	1 990
Chile / Chili	157 131
Czech Republic / République tchèque	4 555
Denmark / Danemark	1 985
Estonia / Estonie	20
Finland / Finlande	209
France	2 181
Germany / Allemagne	3 033
Greece / Grèce	176
Hungary / Hongrie	33 712
Iceland / Islande	2 190
Ireland / Irlande	256
Israel / Israël	1 150
Italy / Italie	1 636
Japan / Japon[1]	500 535
Korea / Corée	1 558 592
Latvia / Lettonie	24
Luxembourg	52
Mexico / Mexique	18 079
Netherlands / Pays-Bas	677
New Zealand / Nouvelle-Zélande[1]	249
Norway / Norvège	3 131
Poland / Pologne	1 790
Portugal	179
Slovak Republic / République slovaque	78
Slovenia / Slovénie	39
Spain / Espagne	1 081
Sweden / Suède	4 155
Switzerland / Suisse	640
Turkey / Turquie	1 953
United Kingdom / Royaume-Uni	1 870
United States / États-Unis	18 037

1. GDP is fiscal year. The year Y is calculated (at annual rate) as the average of: Q2(Y) to Q1(Y + 1) for Canada and Japan; and Q3(Y) to Q2(Y + 1) for Australia and New Zealand.

Source: OECD National Accounts.

1. PIB se référant á l'année fiscale. L'année A est calculée (taux annuel) comme la moyenne de : T2(A) à T1(A + 1) pour le Canada et le Japon ; et T3(A) à T2(A + 1) pour l'Australie et la Nouvelle-Zélande.

Source : Comptes nationaux de l'OCDE.

StatLink http://dx.doi.org/10.1787/888933416651

Revenue Statistics 2016
Statistiques des recettes publiques 2016

Chapter 4

Country tables, 1965-2014

Chapitre 4

Tableaux par pays, 1965-2014

4.1. Tax revenues/Recettes fiscales

Table 4.1. **Australia/Australie**

Details of tax revenue/Recettes fiscales détaillées

Million AUD

	1965	1980	1990	2000	2007	2009	2011	2012	2013	2014
Total tax revenue	**5 024**	**39 878**	**116 500**	**214 651**	**350 059**	**334 940**	**391 719**	**417 054**	**436 706**	**446 827**
1000 Taxes on income, profits and capital gains	**2 547**	**22 383**	**66 542**	**124 602**	**208 234**	**186 659**	**230 870**	**241 728**	**248 448**	**258 605**
1100 Of individuals	1 729	17 532	50 062	81 166	127 993	124 941	153 760	162 993	170 313	183 383
1110 On income and profits	1 729	17 532	49 888	81 166	127 993	124 941	153 760	162 993	170 313	183 383
1120 On capital gains	0	0	174	0	0	0	0	0	0	0
1200 Corporate	818	4 851	16 480	43 436	80 241	61 718	77 110	78 735	78 135	75 222
1210 On profits	818	4 851	16 315	43 436	80 241	61 718	77 110	78 735	78 135	75 222
Income tax on companies	791	4 574	15 220	42 221	78 577	60 654	75 856	77 691	76 682	73 573
Dividend and interest taxes	17	161	899	846	1 664	1 064	1 254	1 044	1 453	1 649
Other withholding taxes	0	116	196	369	0	0	0	0	0	0
1220 On capital gains	0	0	165	0	0	0	0	0	0	0
1300 Unallocable between 1100 and 1200	0	0	0	0	0	0	0	0	0	0
2000 Social security contributions	**0**	**0**	**0**	**0**	**0**	**0**	**0**	**0**	**0**	**0**
2100 Employees	0	0	0	0	0	0	0	0	0	0
2110 On a payroll basis	..	..	..	..	..	..	..	..	..	..
2120 On an income tax basis	..	..	..	..	..	..	..	..	..	..
2200 Employers	0	0	0	0	0	0	0	0	0	0
2210 On a payroll basis	..	..	..	..	..	..	..	..	..	..
2220 On an income tax basis	..	..	..	..	..	..	..	..	..	..
2300 Self-employed or non-employed	0	0	0	0	0	0	0	0	0	0
2310 On a payroll basis	..	..	..	..	..	..	..	..	..	..
2320 On an income tax basis	..	..	..	..	..	..	..	..	..	..
2400 Unallocable between 2100, 2200 and 2300	0	0	0	0	0	0	0	0	0	0
2410 On a payroll basis	..	..	..	..	..	..	..	..	..	..
2420 On an income tax basis	..	..	..	..	..	..	..	..	..	..
3000 Taxes on payroll and workforce	**157**	**1 988**	**7 115**	**9 624**	**16 407**	**17 304**	**20 307**	**21 443**	**22 221**	**22 985**
4000 Taxes on property	**576**	**3 105**	**10 427**	**18 818**	**31 130**	**31 897**	**33 583**	**36 006**	**40 929**	**45 260**
4100 Recurrent taxes on immovable property	341	1 886	6 148	9 067	15 615	18 685	20 759	21 806	23 603	25 062
4110 Households	..	..	..	..	..	..	..	..	..	..
4120 Others	..	..	..	..	..	..	..	..	..	..
4200 Recurrent taxes on net wealth	0	0	0	0	0	0	0	0	0	0
4210 Individual	..	..	..	..	..	..	..	..	..	..
4220 Corporate	..	..	..	..	..	..	..	..	..	..
4300 Estate, inheritance and gift taxes	137	175	0	0	0	0	0	0	0	0
4310 Estate and inheritance taxes	131	174	..	..	..	..	..	..	..	..
Estate duty central government	36	17	..	..	..	..	..	..	..	..
St. and loc. estate probate and succession	95	157	..	..	..	..	..	..	..	..
4320 Gift taxes	7	1	..	..	..	..	..	..	..	..
4400 Taxes on financial and capital transactions	98	1 044	4 279	9 751	15 515	13 212	12 824	14 200	17 326	20 198
4500 Non-recurrent taxes	0	0	0	0	0	0	0	0	0	0
4510 On net wealth	..	..	..	..	..	..	..	..	..	..
4520 Other non-recurrent taxes	..	..	..	..	..	..	..	..	..	..
4600 Other recurrent taxes on property	0	0	0	0	0	0	0	0	0	0
5000 Taxes on goods and services	**1 744**	**12 402**	**32 416**	**61 607**	**94 288**	**99 080**	**106 959**	**117 877**	**125 108**	**119 977**
5100 Taxes on production, sale, transfer, etc	1 508	11 097	27 213	56 180	85 022	88 585	94 210	97 072	103 678	104 225
5110 General taxes	370	2 102	9 365	25 830	45 486	47 800	50 004	51 462	56 819	57 830
5111 Value added taxes	0	0	0	23 854	44 381	46 553	48 849	50 313	55 517	56 462
5112 Sales tax	370	2 102	9 365	1 976	1 105	1 247	1 155	1 149	1 302	1 368
5113 Other	0	0	0	0	0	0	0	0	0	0
5120 Taxes on specific goods and services	1 138	8 995	17 848	30 350	39 536	40 785	44 206	45 610	46 859	46 395
5121 Excises	781	6 183	11 975	19 768	24 357	25 372	26 325	26 425	26 472	24 506
Excises central government	752	5 834	10 359	19 019	23 526	24 547	25 480	25 710	25 648	23 687
Statutory corporate payments	0	83	378	295	231	444	436	248	343	321
Primary production charges	29	266	1 238	454	600	381	409	467	481	498
5122 Profits of fiscal monopolies	0	0	0	0	0	0	0	0	0	0
5123 Customs and import duties	271	1 799	3 319	4 606	6 070	5 748	7 105	8 172	9 280	10 884
Customs duties central government	271	1 799	3 319	4 606	6 070	5 748	7 105	8 172	9 280	10 884
5124 Taxes on exports	1	117	57	0	10	14	12	9	10	12
Customs duties on coal exports	0	85	54	..	0	0	0	0	0	0
Other	1	32	3	..	10	14	12	9	10	12

StatLink http://dx.doi.org/10.1787/888933416660

Table 4.1. **Australia/Australie** *(cont./suite)*

Details of tax revenue/Recettes fiscales détaillées

Million AUD

	1965	1980	1990	2000	2007	2009	2011	2012	2013	2014
5125 Taxes on investment goods	0	0	0	0	0	0	0	0	0	0
5126 Taxes on specific services	85	896	2 497	5 976	9 099	9 651	10 764	11 004	11 097	10 993
Taxes race meetings	31	240	651	300	358	376	359	325	318	290
Poker machines	16	140	295	2 064	2 985	2 976	3 161	3 195	3 220	3 457
Lotteries	7	122	325	890	1 118	1 230	1 256	1 354	1 257	1 270
Levies on fire insurance companies	16	157	363	574	937	1 109	1 395	1 279	740	739
Other	15	237	863	2 148	3 701	3 960	4 593	4 851	5 562	5 237
5127 Other taxes on internat. trade and transactions	0	0	0	0	0	0	0	0	0	0
5128 Other taxes	0	0	0	0	0	0	0	0	0	0
5130 Unallocable between 5110 and 5120	0	0	0	0	0	0	0	0	0	0
5200 Taxes on use of goods and perform activities	236	1 305	5 203	5 427	9 266	10 495	12 749	20 805	21 430	15 752
5210 Recurrent taxes	197	1 260	5 109	5 427	9 266	10 495	12 749	20 805	21 430	15 752
5211 Paid by households: motor vehicles	65	448	1 373	3 908	6 196	6 787	7 631	8 246	8 591	9 155
5212 Paid by others: motor vehicles	65	351	937	125	189	205	254	285	301	308
Fees on motor vehicle registry	46	312	794	0	0	0	0	0	0	0
Drivers licences	12	30	111	0	0	0	0	0	0	0
Stamp duty on vehicle registry	6	9	32	125	189	205	254	285	301	308
5213 Paid in respect of other goods	67	461	2 799	1 394	2 880	3 503	4 865	12 273	12 538	6 289
Broadcasting tv licences	37	21	125	210	288	241	231	167	157	185
Business franchise lic. tobac. fuel	0	221	2 016	227	0	3	1	1	2	0
Other taxes	2	12	33	860	2 589	3 257	4 609	12 080	12 355	6 080
Liquor taxes	28	206	603	97	2	1	24	24	24	23
Dog licenses	0	1	22	0	0	0	0	0	0	0
5220 Non-recurrent taxes	39	45	94	0	0	0	0	0	0	0
5300 Unallocable between 5100 and 5200	0	0	0	0	0	0	0	0	0	0
6000 Other taxes	**0**	**0**	**0**	**0**	**0**	**0**	**0**	**0**	**0**	**0**
6100 Paid solely by business	..	..	..	..	..	..	..	..	..	..
6200 Other	..	..	..	..	..	..	..	..	..	..
Non-wastable tax credits										
Non-wastable tax credits against 1110	..	..	..	195	2 585	840	973	326	323	366
Tax expenditure component	..	..	..	175	178	67	581	232	215	253
Transfer component	..	..	..	20	2 407	773	392	94	108	113
Non-wastable tax credits against 1210	..	..	..	0	4 534	5 793	6 406	7 218	7 914	7 914
Tax expenditure component	..	..	..	..	1 922	2 227	2 426	2 736	3 091	3 091
Transfer component	..	..	..	..	2 642	3 566	3 980	4 482	4 823	4 823
Total tax revenue on cash basis	**5 024**	**39 878**	**116 500**	..	..	..	..	..	..	..
Total tax revenue on accrual basis	..	..	..	**214 651**	**350 059**	**334 940**	**391 719**	**417 054**	**436 706**	**446 827**
Conciliation with National Accounts										
Additional taxes included in National Accounts	..	..	..	..	..	..	..	..	..	..
Taxes excluded from National Accounts	..	..	..	..	..	..	..	..	..	..
Difference in treatment of tax credits	..	..	..	..	..	..	..	..	..	..
Capital transfer for uncollected revenue	..	..	..	..	..	..	..	..	..	..
Voluntary social security contributions	..	..	..	..	..	..	..	..	..	..
Miscellaneous differences	..	..	..	..	..	..	..	..	..	..
National Accounts: Taxes and actual social contributions	..	..	..	..	..	..	..	..	..	..
Imputed social contributions	..	..	..	..	..	..	..	..	..	..
National Accounts: Taxes and all social contributions	..	..	..	..	..	..	..	..	..	..

Notes : Data are on a fiscal year basis beginning 1st July.

From 1998, taxes are recorded on an accrual basis; prior to that they were on a cash basis.

Direct taxes paid by public trading enterprises are excluded from receipts.

The figures for total tax revenue do not match the published totals in Taxation Revenue Australia. The latter is based on an accrual IMF GFS methodology and there are some differences between that and the OECD equivalent.

Heading 5213 includes radio and television licenses fees, though these are usually not regarded as a tax revenue in the OECD list.

Headings for non-wastable tax credits 1110 and 1210 include the private health insurance tax offset, family benefit, baby bonus tax offsets (paid during the 2003-04 budget year), film tax offset, and research and development tax offsets. The estimation of non-wastable credits into the expenditure and transfer components is in accordance with the OECD guidelines on the treatment and the data for this memorandum item has been provided by the Australian Taxation Office.

Source : Australian Bureau of Statistics.

StatLink http://dx.doi.org/10.1787/888933416660

Table 4.2. **Austria/Autriche**

Details of tax revenue/Recettes fiscales détaillées

Million EUR

	1965	1980	1990	2000	2007	2009	2011	2012	2013	2014
Total tax revenue	**6 210**	**29 759**	**54 040**	**89 793**	**114 465**	**117 240**	**126 607**	**132 143**	**137 186**	**141 477**
Total tax revenue exclusive of custom duties	..	..	..	**89 436**	**114 068**	**116 920**	**126 229**	**131 799**	**136 858**	**141 107**
1000 Taxes on income, profits and capital gains	**1 584**	**7 959**	**13 797**	**25 553**	**34 319**	**32 780**	**36 074**	**38 067**	**39 792**	**41 733**
1100 Of individuals	1 240	6 899	11 326	19 890	25 741	26 152	28 546	30 289	31 474	33 428
1110 On income and profits	1 240	6 899	11 326	19 890	25 741	26 152	28 546	30 289	31 474	33 428
Income tax	415	1 576	2 501	3 202	3 253	3 314	3 374	3 537	3 737	4 020
Special income tax	0	0	0	0	0	0	0	0	0	0
Wage tax	417	4 626	7 823	15 630	20 607	20 997	23 031	24 759	25 669	27 088
Tax on industry and trade	196	402	454	7	0	0	0	1	0	0
Tax on capital yields	2	14	46	354	970	858	1 087	884	981	1 183
Contribution to chambers	60	279	501	697	910	983	1 054	1 107	1 087	1 137
Water supply fund	151	0	0	0	0	0	0	0	0	0
Contribution emergency fund	0	0	0	0	0	0	0	0	0	0
1120 On capital gains	0	0	0	0	0	0	0	0	0	0
1200 Corporate	334	1 049	1 930	4 157	6 622	4 683	6 180	6 379	6 963	7 011
1210 On profits	334	1 049	1 930	4 157	6 622	4 683	6 180	6 379	6 963	7 011
Corporation tax	195	698	998	3 865	6 094	4 177	5 582	5 835	6 377	6 359
Tax on industry and trade	83	254	624	10	0	1	0	1	0	0
Special tax on income	0	0	0	0	0	0	0	0	0	0
Tax on capital yields	5	33	108	118	346	323	388	328	370	430
Water supply fund	35	0	0	0	0	0	0	0	0	0
Contribution emergency fund	0	0	0	0	0	0	0	0	0	0
Contribution to chambers	14	58	200	164	182	182	210	216	216	222
Directors tax	2	6	0	0	0	0	0	0	0	0
1220 On capital gains	0	0	0	0	0	0	0	0	0	0
1300 Unallocable between 1100 and 1200	10	12	540	1 506	1 956	1 946	1 348	1 398	1 354	1 294
Fines related to tax offences	10	12	18	33	77	75	84	66	73	102
Tax on interest	0	0	522	1 473	1 879	1 871	1 263	1 332	1 282	1 192
2000 Social security contributions	**1 548**	**9 200**	**17 763**	**30 613**	**38 583**	**40 771**	**43 486**	**45 058**	**46 988**	**48 454**
2100 Employees	686	3 792	7 512	12 524	15 671	16 534	17 596	18 169	18 997	19 512
2110 On a payroll basis	..	..	..	12 524	15 671	16 534	17 596	18 169	18 997	19 512
Health insurance contributions	..	..	..	2 606	3 326	3 599	3 824	3 940	4 082	4 208
Pension insurance contributions	..	..	..	6 410	8 274	8 771	9 406	9 777	10 183	10 517
Pension contributions, civil servants	..	..	..	1 536	1 638	1 693	1 674	1 627	1 738	1 669
Unemployment insurance contributions	..	..	..	1 854	2 284	2 308	2 510	2 637	2 803	2 921
Health insurance contributions, local government employees	..	..	..	100	130	144	161	167	169	174
Special unemployment insurance contributions	..	..	..	17	19	19	20	21	22	22
2120 On an income tax basis	..	..	..	0	0	0	0	0	0	0
2200 Employers	721	4 563	8 768	14 707	18 162	19 023	20 377	21 158	21 998	22 683
2210 On a payroll basis	..	..	..	14 707	18 162	19 023	20 377	21 158	21 998	22 683
Health insurance contributions	..	..	..	2 667	3 395	3 593	3 818	3 934	4 075	4 201
Pension insurance contributions	..	..	..	7 888	10 214	10 859	11 684	12 154	12 642	13 065
Pension contributions, civil servants	..	..	..	494	446	445	424	417	374	371
Accident insurance contributions	..	..	..	952	1 157	1 223	1 307	1 355	1 409	1 400
Unemployment insurance contributions	..	..	..	1 854	2 284	2 308	2 510	2 637	2 803	2 921
Health insurance contributions, local government employees	..	..	..	101	141	155	161	167	170	175
Contributions to sickness benefit fund	..	..	..	341	0	0	0	0	0	0
Special pension contributions, nightshift workers	..	..	..	11	18	16	15	18	31	36
Contributions to insolvency fund	..	..	..	381	488	406	437	455	473	492
Special unemployment insurance contributions construction workers	..	..	..	17	19	19	20	21	22	22
2220 On an income tax basis	..	..	..	0	0	0	0	0	0	0
2300 Self-employed or non-employed	141	845	1 482	3 382	4 750	5 214	5 514	5 732	5 993	6 259
2310 On a payroll basis	..	..	..	3 382	4 750	5 214	5 514	5 732	5 993	6 259
Health insurance contributions	..	..	..	1 971	2 724	3 020	3 186	3 315	3 441	3 573
Pension insurance contributions	..	..	..	1 117	1 527	1 661	1 778	1 830	1 973	2 091
Pension contributions, civil servants (retired)	..	..	..	116	274	291	300	329	315	324
Accident insurance contributions	..	..	..	77	85	87	88	91	95	97
Health insurance contributions, local government employees	..	..	..	101	140	154	161	167	169	174
2320 On an income tax basis	..	..	..	0	0	0	0	0	0	0
2400 Unallocable between 2100, 2200 and 2300	0	0	0	0	0	0	0	0	0	0
2410 On a payroll basis	..	..	..	..	..	..	..	..	..	..
2420 On an income tax basis	..	..	..	..	..	..	..	..	..	..

StatLink http://dx.doi.org/10.1787/888933416678

Table 4.2. **Austria/Autriche** *(cont./suite)*

Details of tax revenue/Recettes fiscales détaillées

Million EUR

	1965	1980	1990	2000	2007	2009	2011	2012	2013	2014
3000 Taxes on payroll and workforce	**472**	**2 097**	**3 259**	**5 788**	**7 266**	**8 143**	**8 756**	**9 156**	**9 489**	**9 779**
Emplr. contr. equaliz. of family.burdens	318	1 397	2 147	3 140	3 915	4 624	4 977	5 157	5 319	5 493
Tax on sum of wages	82	375	669	1 735	2 238	2 342	2 533	2 650	2 742	2 826
Promotion residential buildings	44	217	389	595	754	796	844	876	915	936
Tax on employment (Vienna undergr.)	0	20	21	21	22	24	22	42	67	66
Special levy for households allowances	26	80	0	0	0	0	0	0	0	0
Disabled persons equalization levy	2	8	34	54	83	93	92	131	138	142
Contributions to chambers	0	0	0	242	253	265	288	300	308	316
4000 Taxes on property	**246**	**858**	**1 473**	**1 206**	**1 572**	**1 511**	**1 576**	**1 765**	**2 341**	**1 990**
4100 Recurrent taxes on immovable property	92	231	355	526	626	667	693	709	736	749
4110 Households	47	66	84	87	92	94	93	96	105	110
Duty on farms	9	15	20	20	20	20	20	20	29	32
Farm contr. equaliz. of family burdens	5	6	6	6	6	6	6	6	6	7
Farm contribution to chambers	14	23	32	32	39	41	40	44	43	45
Contr. residential buildings reconstruction	4	0	0	0	0	0	0	0	0	0
Land tax A	16	22	25	28	26	27	26	26	26	26
4120 Others	45	165	271	440	534	573	601	613	631	639
Tax on vacant plots	1	4	5	5	5	5	6	6	6	6
Land tax B	44	161	266	435	529	568	595	607	625	632
4200 Recurrent taxes on net wealth	103	401	642	1	0	0	0	0	0	0
4210 Individual	37	140	189	1	..	..	..	..	..	..
Capital tax	25	109	189	1	..	..	..	..	..	..
Contribution emergency fund	0	0	0	0	..	..	..	..	..	..
Tax on industry and trade	10	26	0	0	..	..	..	..	..	..
Contribution to chambers	2	6	0	0	..	..	..	..	..	..
4220 Corporate	66	260	453	0	..	..	..	..	..	..
Capital tax	24	139	322	0	..	..	..	..	..	..
Capital death duty	20	53	131	0	..	..	..	..	..	..
Contribution emergency fund	0	0	0	0	..	..	..	..	..	..
Tax on industry and trade	19	56	0	0	..	..	..	..	..	..
Contribution to chambers	3	13	0	0	..	..	..	..	..	..
4300 Estate, inheritance and gift taxes	16	50	77	111	155	116	33	21	19	4
4310 Estate and inheritance taxes	..	..	..	..	..	..	..	..	..	..
4320 Gift taxes	..	..	..	..	..	..	..	..	..	..
4400 Taxes on financial and capital transactions	35	176	399	568	791	714	831	1 025	858	945
Land transfer tax	30	150	251	452	644	623	754	935	790	867
Capital transfer tax	5	27	148	115	147	91	77	89	67	79
4500 Non-recurrent taxes	0	0	0	0	0	14	18	11	728	292
4510 On net wealth	..	..	..	..	..	0	0	0	717	264
Withholding tax	..	..	..	..	..	0	0	0	717	264
4520 Other non-recurrent taxes	..	..	..	..	..	14	18	11	11	28
Foundation tax	..	..	..	..	..	14	18	11	11	28
4600 Other recurrent taxes on property	0	0	0	0	0	0	0	0	0	0
5000 Taxes on goods and services	**2 321**	**9 379**	**17 034**	**25 727**	**31 688**	**33 088**	**35 881**	**37 263**	**37 755**	**38 650**
5100 Taxes on production, sale, transfer, etc	2 275	9 006	16 169	24 297	29 830	31 141	33 771	35 056	35 452	35 960
5110 General taxes	1 160	5 984	11 229	16 894	20 988	22 231	23 498	24 601	24 978	25 467
5111 Value added taxes	0	5 984	11 229	16 894	20 988	22 231	23 498	24 601	24 978	25 467
5112 Sales tax	0	0	0	0	0	0	0	0	0	0
5113 Other	1 160	0	0	0	0	0	0	0	0	0
Turnover tax	664	..	..	..	..	..	..	..	..	..
Additional federal levy-turnover	332	..	..	..	..	..	..	..	..	..
Additional lieu invoice stp.	164	..	..	..	..	..	..	..	..	..
5120 Taxes on specific goods and services	1 115	2 996	4 873	7 365	8 839	8 907	10 270	10 453	10 472	10 493

StatLink http://dx.doi.org/10.1787/888933416678

Table 4.2. **Austria/Autriche** (*cont./suite*)

Details of tax revenue/Recettes fiscales détaillées

Million EUR

	1965	1980	1990	2000	2007	2009	2011	2012	2013	2014
5121 Excises	610	2 219	3 290	5 484	6 760	6 714	7 472	7 562	7 598	7 539
Tax on beer	39	44	56	161	200	193	189	191	193	195
Tax on wine	7	0	0	0	0	0	0	0	0	0
Tax on sparkling wine	1	7	25	25	1	1	1	1	1	6
Tax on tobacco	188	519	820	1 197	1 446	1 458	1 568	1 621	1 664	1 701
Tax on mineral oils	50	136	1 426	2 726	3 689	3 800	4 213	4 181	4 173	4 135
Additional federal levy mineral oils	202	876	0	0	0	0	0	0	0	0
Special duty alcoholic drinks	0	142	193	0	0	0	0	0	0	0
Special duty vehicles	0	0	0	0	0	0	0	0	0	0
Duty on starch products	0	4	13	0	0	0	0	0	0	0
Beverage tax	46	216	364	178	3	-21	-2	0	-1	-1
Other receipts-Market Organisation Act	26	35	9	0	1	0	0	0	0	0
Transport equality levy	0	5	1	0	0	0	0	0	0	0
Market Organisation Act - milk	35	177	192	0	0	0	0	0	0	0
Market Organisation Act - livestock	0	0	0	0	0	0	0	0	0	0
Market Organisation Act - grain	16	23	142	0	0	0	0	0	0	0
Duty promotion milk distrib.	0	34	13	0	0	0	0	0	0	0
Special tax on mineral oils	0	0	37	0	0	0	0	0	0	0
Duty on vehicles (fuel consumption)	0	0	0	433	457	450	484	505	455	424
Agricultural fund	0	0	0	23	16	17	18	18	18	18
Tax on energy	0	0	0	562	764	655	792	831	886	850
Social contributions to the artists' fund	0	0	0	0	11	6	7	8	7	4
Duty on exceeding milk-quota	0	0	0	36	24	0	33	29	26	33
Car registration taxes	0	0	0	143	148	153	168	177	175	173
5122 Profits of fiscal monopolies	37	57	52	130	122	130	318	332	324	369
Duty on spirits	5	14	17	130	122	130	132	128	130	172
Federal monopolies salt	1	0	0	0	0	0	0	0	0	0
Federal monopolies spirits	30	43	35	0	0	0	0	0	0	0
Federal monopolies gambling	0	0	0	0	0	0	186	204	194	198
5123 Customs and import duties	332	354	677	-5	-8	0	0	0	0	0
Customs duties	310	237	418	-5	-8	0	0	0	..	0
Other import duties	0	21	61	0	0	0	0	0	..	0
Contribution promote foreign trade	10	63	171	0	0	0	0	0	..	0
Import equalization duties	12	33	27	0	0	0	0	0	..	0
5124 Taxes on exports	8	36	1	0	0	0	0	0	0	0
Contribution to promote foreign trade	8	36	1	..	..	..	..	..	..	..
5125 Taxes on investment goods	0	33	0	0	0	0	0	0	0	0
5126 Taxes on specific services	129	297	854	1 720	1 967	2 059	2 475	2 551	2 545	2 589
Insurance tax	25	135	384	745	993	1 033	1 071	1 053	1 056	1 101
Transport tax	63	0	0	0	0	0	0	0	0	0
Duty on casinos	2	28	64	105	71	67	47	47	45	44
Fire protection tax	5	24	50	45	54	57	57	57	57	60
Advertisement tax	7	31	65	62	0	0	0	0	0	0
Entertainment tax	2	2	2	5	8	9	12	18	21	20
Tax on tourism	8	43	71	103	142	153	166	180	182	190
Amusement tax	13	17	51	73	94	101	98	86	84	79
Announcement tax	3	18	40	81	0	0	0	0	0	0
Tax on interest yields	0	0	0	0	0	0	0	0	0	0
Tax on gambling stakes - licenses	0	0	116	197	202	232	268	257	251	247
Tax on advertisement	0	0	0	33	108	105	111	110	110	107
Levy on dangerous waste	0	0	10	71	72	57	53	53	53	54
Duty for airways security	0	0	0	28	56	62	5	0	0	0
Tax on gambling stakes - gains	0	0	0	171	166	183	16	0	0	0
Flight Charge	0	0	0	0	0	0	59	107	98	100
Financial Institutions Stability Fee	0	0	0	0	0	0	510	583	588	586
5127 Other taxes on internat. trade and transactions	0	0	0	0	0	0	0	0	0	0
5128 Other taxes	0	0	0	34	-3	4	4	8	4	-4
Levy on sugar	..	..	..	34	-3	4	4	8	4	-4
5130 Unallocable between 5110 and 5120	0	26	66	38	3	2	3	3	2	0
Fines related to tax offenses	..	26	66	38	3	2	3	3	2	0
5200 Taxes on use of goods and perform activities	46	373	865	1 430	1 858	1 948	2 110	2 207	2 303	2 690
5210 Recurrent taxes	38	335	757	1 283	1 683	1 742	1 881	1 952	2 017	2 368
5211 Paid by households: motor vehicles	22	156	366	811	1 173	1 265	1 382	1 437	1 482	1 768
5212 Paid by others: motor vehicles	13	41	97	298	370	327	342	340	352	413
5213 Paid in respect of other goods	3	138	294	174	140	149	157	175	183	187
Hunting and fishing duties	1	4	7	10	10	10	10	17	19	20
Dog tax	1	4	6	8	10	11	12	15	17	18
Contribution to promotion of arts	1	3	8	11	16	17	17	18	18	18
Tax on radio and tv - licenses	0	15	46	61	104	112	117	125	129	131
Road transport duty	0	112	226	84	0	0	0	0	0	0

StatLink http://dx.doi.org/10.1787/888933416678

Table 4.2. **Austria/Autriche** *(cont./suite)*

Details of tax revenue/Recettes fiscales détaillées

Million EUR

	1965	1980	1990	2000	2007	2009	2011	2012	2013	2014
5220 Non-recurrent taxes	8	38	108	147	175	206	229	255	286	322
Certain user fees	8	38	108	147	175	206	229	255	286	322
5300 Unallocable between 5100 and 5200	0	0	0	0	0	0	0	0	0	0
6000 Other taxes	**38**	**266**	**714**	**548**	**641**	**626**	**457**	**489**	**493**	**501**
Tax on financial institutions	0	0	123	-3	0	0	0	0	0	0
Administration duties	4	17	32	57	79	75	74	82	79	80
Stamp fees	7	46	76	135	92	79	78	88	27	30
Contributions of interested persons	0	0	130	0	0	0	0	0	0	0
Parking duty	0	0	6	0	0	0	0	0	0	0
Contrbutions to students' associations	0	0	0	4	8	9	11	11	12	13
Duty on contribution to political parties	0	0	0	0	-1	1	1	1	0	0
Other fees, taxes on production n.e.c.	0	0	0	272	346	336	160	161	227	228
Embossing fee	0	0	0	0	1	1	1	1	1	1
Other taxes	28	202	347	83	115	125	133	145	146	149
6100 Paid solely by business	..	..	..	..	..	..	..	..	..	..
6200 Other	..	..	..	..	..	..	..	..	..	..
Custom duties collected for the EU	..	..	..	**356**	**397**	**320**	**378**	**344**	**328**	**369**
Non-wastable tax credits										
Non-wastable tax credits against 1110	..	..	..	650	650	650	570	560	570	560
Tax expenditure component	..	..	..	590	450	447	344	330	341	315
Transfer component	..	..	..	60	200	203	226	230	229	245
Non-wastable tax credits against 1210	..	..	..	0	0	0	0	0	0	0
Tax expenditure component	..	..	..	..	..	..	..	..	..	..
Transfer component	..	..	..	..	..	..	..	..	..	..
Total tax revenue on cash basis	**6 210**	**29 759**	**54 040**	**89 768**	**114 364**	**116 701**	**126 408**	**131 912**	..	..
Total tax revenue on accrual basis	..	..	..	**89 793**	**114 465**	**117 240**	**126 607**	**132 143**	**137 186**	**141 477**
Conciliation with National Accounts										
Additional taxes included in National Accounts	..	..	..	0	0	0	0	0	0	0
Taxes excluded from National Accounts	..	..	..	0	0	0	0	0	0	0
Difference in treatment of tax credits	..	..	..	590	450	447	344	330	341	315
Capital transfer for uncollected revenue	..	..	..	0	0	0	0	0	0	0
Voluntary social security contributions	..	..	..	206	256	300	343	310	299	311
Miscellaneous differences	..	..	..	0	0	0	0	0	0	0
National Accounts: Taxes and actual social contributions	..	..	..	90 589	115 172	117 987	127 293	132 782	137 825	142 103
Imputed social contributions	..	..	..	2 420	2 133	2 084	2 026	1 964	1 893	1 828
National Accounts: Taxes and all social contributions	..	..	..	93 009	117 305	120 071	129 319	134 746	139 718	143 931

Notes : Year ending 31st December.

From 1995, data are on accrual basis.

Following national practice, one-third of the revenues from stamp fees (heading 6000) and fifty percent of the revenues from administration duties (heading 6000) are treated as tax revenues, the remainder being treated as non-tax revenue.

From 1988 onwards, promoting residential building is being mainly financed by capital transfers from the Federal Government to the Länder. For the years 1985 to 1987, legally fixed shares of some taxes have been transmitted automatically from Federal Government to the Länder for this purpose and these funds have been classified as tax receipts of the Länder in those years. From 1988, they are classified as Federal Government tax revenues. This break in the time series (1987/88) affects only the shares of the different subsectors and not total tax revenues.

From 1998, contributions of interested persons and parking duties are classified as non-tax revenues (sales) and no longer reported under heading 6000.

Source : Statistics Austria.

StatLink http://dx.doi.org/10.1787/888933416678

Table 4.3. **Belgium/Belgique**

Details of tax revenue/Recettes fiscales détaillées

Million EUR

	1965	1980	1990	2000	2007	2009	2011	2012	2013	2014
Recettes fiscales totales	**6 421**	**37 443**	**70 408**	**112 423**	**147 266**	**147 778**	**163 552**	**171 135**	**176 860**	**180 180**
Recettes fiscales totales excluant les droits de douane	..	..	..	**111 463**	**145 878**	**146 631**	**162 267**	**169 888**	**175 675**	**178 923**
1000 Impôts sur revenu, bénéfices et gains en capital	**1 774**	**15 379**	**25 983**	**43 421**	**52 805**	**50 135**	**56 776**	**59 301**	**62 729**	**64 522**
1100 Des personnes physiques	1 317	13 626	22 538	35 260	40 971	41 997	46 072	47 647	50 470	51 576
1110 Sur le revenu et les bénéfices	1 317	13 626	22 538	35 260	40 971	41 997	46 072	47 647	50 470	51 576
Précompte immobilier	148	532	1 053	1 857	0	0	0	0	0	0
Précompte mobilier	119	1 062	3 014	1 737	2 351	2 295	2 691	3 377	4 298	4 315
Précompte professionnel	740	9 119	15 422	27 738	35 969	39 062	42 144	43 353	44 635	45 535
Impôt versé par non-salariés	125	1 776	2 144	1 959	1 747	1 539	1 513	1 412	1 508	1 496
Impôt des non-résidents	0	-2	4	585	796	791	783	830	860	975
Impôt sur revenu global	183	1 128	878	774	-915	-2 830	-2 153	-2 448	-1 988	-1 893
Cotisation spéciale séc. sociale	0	0	19	602	957	1 048	1 069	1 094	1 117	1 116
Autres (personnes physiques)	0	12	2	8	65	93	25	30	41	33
1120 Sur les gains en capital	0	0	0	0	0	0	0	0	0	0
1200 Des sociétés	397	1 744	3 405	8 083	11 749	8 108	10 673	11 626	12 210	12 891
1210 Sur les bénéfices	397	1 744	3 405	8 083	11 749	8 108	10 673	11 626	12 210	12 891
Précompte immobilier	33	0	0	0	0	0	0	0	0	0
Précompte mobilier	41	367	1 206	544	686	295	391	362	494	660
Versements anticipés (sociétés)	262	1 273	2 735	7 112	9 733	6 841	7 858	7 921	7 931	8 466
Impôt sur revenu global	60	79	-553	404	1 270	870	2 379	3 211	3 662	3 750
Impôt des non-résidents (sociétés)	0	-6	18	17	41	62	36	120	113	9
Autres (sociétés)	0	32	-2	5	19	39	10	12	10	7
1220 Sur les gains en capital	0	0	0	0	0	0	0	0	0	0
1300 Non-ventilables entre 1100 et 1200	61	9	40	78	85	30	31	27	49	55
Anciens impôts sur revenu	51	0	0	0	0	0	0	0	0	0
Amendes	3	0	0	0	0	0	0	0	0	0
Autres	7	9	40	78	85	30	31	27	49	55
2000 Cotisations de sécurité sociale	**2 018**	**10 798**	**23 386**	**34 636**	**45 659**	**49 315**	**52 971**	**55 066**	**56 362**	**57 026**
2100 A la charge des salariés	569	3 130	7 152	10 936	13 851	14 647	15 699	16 244	16 481	16 687
2110 Sur la base du salaire	..	3 130	7 152	10 936	13 851	14 647	15 699	16 244	16 481	16 687
Sur les salaires et traitements bruts	..	3 130	7 062	10 936	13 851	14 647	15 699	16 244	16 481	16 687
Sur les prestations sociales	..	0	89	0	0	0	0	0	0	0
2120 Sur la base de l'impôt sur les revenus	..	0	0	0	0	0	0	0	0	0
2200 A la charge des employeurs	1 320	6 791	14 689	20 794	27 943	30 097	32 563	33 959	34 814	35 187
2210 Sur la base du salaire	..	6 791	14 689	20 794	27 943	30 097	32 563	33 959	34 814	35 187
A la charge des administrations publiques	..	1 059	1 769	3 105	4 493	5 032	5 571	6 115	6 533	6 815
A la charge des autres secteurs	..	5 732	12 920	17 689	23 450	25 065	26 993	27 844	28 281	28 372
2220 Sur la base de l'impôt sur les revenus	..	0	0	0	0	0	0	0	0	0
2300 A charge des travailleurs indép. ou sans emploi	129	877	1 546	2 906	3 866	4 572	4 709	4 863	5 066	5 152
Travailleurs indépendants	..	803	1 230	2 053	2 678	3 234	3 400	3 539	3 703	3 726
Sans emploi	..	0	0	0	0	0	0	0	0	0
Pensionnés, retraités	..	29	198	709	1 012	1 156	1 201	1 218	1 285	1 349
Autres	..	45	118	144	176	182	108	106	78	78
2310 Sur la base du salaire	..	877	1 546	2 906	3 866	4 572	4 709	4 863	5 066	5 152
2320 Sur la base de l'impôt sur les revenus	..	0	0	0	0	0	0	0	0	0
2400 Non-ventilables entre 2100, 2200 et 2300	0	0	0	0	0	0	0	0	0	0
2410 Sur la base du salaire	..	..	..	..	..	..	..	..	..	..
2420 Sur la base de l'impôt sur les revenus	..	..	..	..	..	..	..	..	..	..
3000 Sur salaires ou main d'oeuvre	**0**	**0**	**0**	**0**	**6**	**6**	**9**	**8**	**8**	**8**
Cotisation mandats publics	..	..	..	..	6	6	9	8	8	8
4000 Impôts sur le patrimoine	**240**	**1 161**	**2 679**	**5 282**	**10 550**	**10 247**	**11 938**	**12 645**	**13 805**	**14 257**
4100 Impôts périodiques sur la propriété immobilière	2	210	599	1 164	4 146	4 439	4 854	4 899	5 187	5 343
4110 Ménages	0	26	63	102	2 779	2 981	3 252	3 289	3 478	3 590
4120 Autres agents	2	184	536	1 063	1 367	1 458	1 602	1 610	1 710	1 753
Taxes sur associations sans but lucratif	2	7	17	41	32	28	35	36	38	39
Précompte immobilier (soc.)	0	177	519	929	1 269	1 358	1 485	1 499	1 584	1 626
Taxe régionale (Br.)	0	0	0	94	66	72	81	76	88	88
4200 Impôts périodiques sur l'actif net	0	0	0	92	253	209	254	328	451	625
4210 Personnes physiques	..	..	..	0	0	0	0	0	0	0
4220 Sociétés	..	..	..	92	253	209	254	328	451	625
4300 Impôts sur mut. par décès, succ. et donations	75	309	504	1 101	2 053	2 050	2 434	2 728	3 096	2 809
4310 Impôts sur mut. par décès et successions	69	281	475	1 042	1 702	1 780	2 064	2 332	2 634	2 313
4320 Impôts sur les donations	6	29	29	59	351	270	370	397	463	495

StatLink http://dx.doi.org/10.1787/888933416680

Table 4.3. **Belgium/Belgique** *(cont./suite)*

Details of tax revenue/Recettes fiscales détaillées

Million EUR

	1965	1980	1990	2000	2007	2009	2011	2012	2013	2014
4400 Impôts sur transact. mobilières et immob.	163	633	1 478	2 669	3 704	3 096	3 771	3 782	3 886	4 081
Droits d'enregistrement	153	527	1 213	1 967	3 325	2 820	3 496	3 467	3 542	3 724
Droits d'hypothèque	2	10	29	37	76	74	75	74	72	78
Droits de greffe	2	8	29	38	31	34	34	35	37	36
Fonds d'expansion économique	0	0	0	0	0	0	0	0	0	0
Taxe sur opérations de bourse	4	31	92	386	234	129	128	164	193	201
Taxe sur titres cotés en bourse	2	4	21	0	0	0	0	0	0	0
Taxe sur les titres au porteur	0	0	0	79	3	0	0	4	6	2
Droits de timbre, droits d'écriture	0	53	94	161	35	39	39	39	36	40
4500 Impôts non-périodiques	0	0	0	74	163	185	337	590	877	1 091
4510 Sur l'actif net	..	..	..	0	0	0	0	0	0	0
4520 Autres non-périodiques	..	..	..	74	163	185	337	590	877	1 091
Taxe sur l'épargne à long terme	..	..	..	74	163	185	203	400	207	211
Déclaration libératoire unique (DLU)	..	..	..	0	0	0	0	0	0	0
Déclaration libératoire unique (Diamant)	..	..	..	0	0	0	0	0	0	0
Régularisation fiscale (DLU bis)	..	..	..	0	0	0	134	74	614	575
Régularisation fiscale (DLU ter)	..	..	..	0	0	0	0	0	54	305
Contr. spéciale associations de crédit	..	..	..	0	0	0	0	116	2	0
4600 Autres impôts périodiques sur patrimoine	0	8	99	182	232	269	287	318	309	309
5000 Impôts sur les biens et services	**2 386**	**10 105**	**18 360**	**28 125**	**36 798**	**36 870**	**40 531**	**42 824**	**42 725**	**43 067**
5100 Impôts sur production, vente, transfert, etc.	2 187	9 606	17 387	26 021	34 427	34 546	37 984	40 385	40 295	40 604
5110 Impôts généraux	1 355	6 321	11 570	18 240	24 135	23 808	26 257	27 070	27 491	27 743
5111 Taxes sur la valeur ajoutée	0	6 321	11 547	18 114	23 864	23 576	25 979	26 844	27 250	27 518
T V A	..	6 293	11 491	18 114	23 864	23 576	25 979	26 844	27 250	27 518
Droits de timbre	..	0	0	0	0	0	0	0	0	0
Taxe d'immatriculation	..	28	56	0	0	0	0	0	0	0
5112 Impôts sur les ventes	0	0	23	126	271	232	278	226	241	225
5113 Autres impôts	1 355	0	0	0	0	0	0	0	0	0
Taxes assimilées au timbre	1 355	..	..	..	..	..	..	..	..	..
5120 Impôts sur biens et services déterminés	832	3 285	5 818	7 781	10 292	10 738	11 727	13 315	12 804	12 861
5121 Accises	531	1 997	3 478	5 690	7 367	7 286	7 850	7 947	8 036	8 209
Huiles minérales	278	1 109	2 017	3 392	3 891	3 929	4 330	4 209	4 072	4 306
Gaz de pétrole, hydroc. liquéfiés, benzoles	0	4	0	0	0	0	0	0	0	0
Sur le tabac	132	501	868	1 342	1 821	1 811	1 696	1 909	2 197	2 184
Eaux de vie	23	123	191	206	225	229	239	249	272	292
Taxe consommation alcools, eaux de vie	26	54	0	0	0	0	0	0	0	0
Boissons fermentées mousseuses	1	7	11	24	39	50	61	66	77	85
Boissons fermentées de fruits	18	57	88	101	115	115	116	115	132	140
Bières	38	93	170	208	191	183	184	181	183	197
Eaux de boisson et limonades	10	44	113	148	49	53	56	54	58	57
Sucres et sirops de raffinage + café	5	5	22	13	12	13	14	14	15	15
Cotisation sur l'énergie	0	0	0	193	341	335	341	328	337	325
Produits intermédiaires alcoolisés	0	0	0	32	28	26	24	24	26	26
Redevance de contrôle fuel domestique	0	0	0	29	43	44	40	39	41	32
Ecotaxes	0	0	0	2	1	0	2	2	1	0
Cotisation d'emballage	0	0	0	0	296	310	320	318	332	331
Cotisation fédérale sur l'électricité et le gaz naturel	0	0	0	0	311	175	414	426	281	208
Cotisation environnementale	0	0	0	0	5	12	12	14	14	13
5122 Bénéfices des monopoles fiscaux	0	0	0	0	0	0	0	0	0	0
5123 Droits de douane et droits à l'importation	272	627	809	0	0	0	0	0	0	0
Droits d'entrée	206	0	0	..	..	..	..	..	..	..
Prélèvements agricoles	63	0	0	..	..	..	..	..	..	..
Prélèvements CECA	2	0	0	..	..	..	..	..	..	..
Prélèvements UE, droit d'entrée	0	383	716	..	..	..	..	..	..	..
Prélèvements agricoles UE	0	244	93	..	..	..	..	..	..	..
5124 Taxes à l'exportation	0	1	0	0	0	0	0	0	0	0
5125 Impôts sur biens d'équipement	0	0	0	0	0	0	0	0	0	0
5126 Impôts sur services déterminés	29	452	937	1 365	2 044	2 241	2 951	3 528	3 137	2 914
Taxes jeux et paris	9	47	51	45	64	74	58	63	73	76
Taxe annuelle contrats assurances	19	404	885	1 282	1 930	2 019	2 109	2 223	2 285	2 263
Taxe d'affichage	0	0	1	1	3	3	3	3	3	3
Protection des dépôts	0	0	0	36	48	145	780	1 000	609	438
Fonds de résolution	0	0	0	0	0	0	0	238	167	135
5127 Autres impôts sur commerce et transact. internat.	0	0	0	0	0	0	0	0	0	0
5128 Autres impôts	0	208	593	726	881	1 211	927	1 840	1 631	1 738
5130 Non-ventilables entre 5110 et 5120	0	0	0	0	0	0	0	0	0	0
5200 Impôts sur utilisation des biens et exerc. activités	199	496	966	2 096	2 363	2 315	2 540	2 431	2 420	2 456
5210 Impôts périodiques	199	496	966	1 887	2 032	1 972	2 161	2 061	2 023	1 973
Taxe de circulation	100	368	712	1 413	1 693	1 705	1 898	1 791	1 830	1 814
5211 A la charge des ménages : véhicules à moteur	0	204	458	889	1 051	1 037	1 178	1 121	1 148	1 127

StatLink http://dx.doi.org/10.1787/888933416680

Table 4.3. **Belgium/Belgique** *(cont./suite)*

Details of tax revenue/Recettes fiscales détaillées

Million EUR

	1965	1980	1990	2000	2007	2009	2011	2012	2013	2014
5212 A la charge autres agents : véhicules à moteur	0	164	254	525	642	667	720	670	683	687
5213 Autres impôts périodiques	99	127	254	474	338	267	263	270	193	159
Taxe appareils de divertissement	6	20	20	71	56	49	53	47	74	55
Taxe débits de boissons	1	5	24	18	0	0	0	0	0	0
Taxe sur la chasse	2	0	0	0	0	0	0	0	0	0
Collectivités locales	90	15	19	38	99	107	113	113	10	13
Radio, TV	0	87	191	347	184	111	97	111	108	91
5220 Impôts non-périodiques	0	0	0	209	332	343	379	371	397	483
Taxe de mise en circulation	..	..	..	209	332	343	379	371	360	326
Ménages	..	..	..	139	221	229	252	247	240	217
Autres agents	..	..	..	70	111	114	126	124	120	109
Droits d'émission	..	..	..	0	0	0	0	0	36	157
5300 Non-ventilables entre 5100 et 5200	0	3	7	7	7	9	7	7	10	7
6000 Autres impôts	**2**	**0**	**0**	**0**	**61**	**59**	**43**	**45**	**46**	**43**
6100 A la charge exclusive des entreprises	0	..	..	..	0	0	0	0	0	0
6200 A la charge d'autres agents	2	..	..	..	61	59	43	45	46	43
Amendes et intérets	2	..	..	..	0	0	0	0	0	0
Droits de douane perçus pour l'UE	**..**	**..**	**..**	**960**	**1 388**	**1 147**	**1 285**	**1 247**	**1 185**	**1 257**
Crédits d'impôts récupérables										
Crédits d'impôts récupérables contre 1110	..	..	..	..	348	1 022	1 469	1 761	1 492	1 052
Composante fiscale	..	..	..	..	78	205	1 019	1 293	1 077	735
Composante transfert	..	..	..	..	270	817	449	468	415	317
Crédits d'impôts récupérables contre 1210	..	..	..	..	0	0	0	0	0	0
Composante fiscale	..	..	..	..	..	..	..	..	..	..
Composante transfert	..	..	..	..	..	..	..	..	..	..
Recettes fiscales totales sur la base d'encaissements	**6 421**	**37 438**	**70 268**	**..**	**..**	**..**	**..**	**..**	**..**	**..**
Recettes fiscales totales sur la base des droits constatés	**..**	**37 443**	**70 408**	**112 423**	**147 266**	**147 778**	**163 552**	**171 135**	**176 860**	**180 180**
Conciliation avec les Comptes nationaux										
Impôts additionnels inclus dans les comptes nationaux	..	107	447	1 300	1 387	1 505	1 612	1 618	1 597	1 634
Bénéfices de la loterie nationale	..	107	262	279	225	240	231	242	215	206
Taxes sur les eaux (RF, RW et RB-C)	..	0	66	378	119	122	117	122	122	112
Cot. producteurs produits animaux (Sanitel)	..	0	0	14	13	11	13	14	14	14
Taxe sur les déchets industriels	..	0	27	74	68	56	59	53	46	51
Taxe sur le lisier (RF)	..	0	0	11	11	4	5	5	5	3
Taxe sur les déchets ménagers (RW)	..	0	0	20	0	0	0	0	0	0
Retenue à la source sur salaires (UE)	..	0	93	174	270	311	330	335	339	355
Cotisations de sécurité sociale (UE)	..	0	0	136	250	275	327	331	335	350
Cotisations sociales imputées (UE)	..	0	0	213	431	485	530	517	522	542
Impôt exclus des comptes nationaux	..	0	0	0	0	0	0	0	0	0
Protection des dépots	..	..	..	..	..	..	..	..	..	..
Différence dans les traitements des crédits d'impôts	..	0	0	0	78	205	1 019	1 293	1 077	735
Transfert en capital des recettes non collectées	..	0	0	0	0	0	0	0	0	0
Cotisations de sécurité sociale volontaires	..	41	52	54	55	62	67	71	75	74
Différences diverses	..	0	0	0	0	0	0	0	0	0
Ré-allocation niveaux d'administration nationaux	..	..	..	..	..	..	..	..	..	..
Ré-allocation UE	..	..	..	..	..	..	..	..	..	..
Comptes nationaux: impôts et cotisations sociales effectives	..	37 590	70 907	113 564	148 354	149 064	165 720	173 599	179 087	182 080
Cotisations sociales imputées	..	1 497	2 886	5 377	7 568	8 428	9 269	9 667	10 082	10 163
Comptes nationaux: impôts et toutes les cotisations sociales	..	39 087	73 793	118 940	155 922	157 492	174 988	183 266	189 169	192 243

Notes : Données établies sur la base de l'année civile se terminant le 31 décembre.

À partir de 1970, les données sont sur la base des droits constatés.

La rubrique 5100 comprend des taxes sur la fourniture d'eau, de gaz et d'éléctricité, sur le téléphone et les transports, taxes qui seraient classées dans d'autres postes de la rubrique 5100 si elles ne faisaient pas partie de la taxe de transmission (impôt sur le chiffre d'affaires) qui a été remplacée au 1er janvier 1971 par une taxe sur la valeur ajoutée.

Source : Ministère des Finances, service d'Étude et de Documentation.

StatLink http://dx.doi.org/10.1787/888933416680

Table 4.4. **Canada**

Details of tax revenue/Recettes fiscales détaillées

Million CAD

	1965	1980	1990	2000	2007	2009	2011	2012	2013	2014
Total tax revenue	**15 318**	**101 015**	**244 152**	**390 234**	**512 663**	**508 270**	**546 463**	**569 675**	**591 377**	**618 217**
1000 Taxes on income, profits and capital gains	**5 910**	**47 064**	**118 566**	**195 320**	**251 198**	**242 843**	**258 637**	**270 359**	**282 254**	**296 647**
1100 Of individuals	3 464	34 451	99 722	143 652	190 025	184 090	197 077	207 452	214 126	224 676
1110 On income and profits	3 464	34 451	99 722	143 652	190 025	184 090	197 077	207 452	214 126	224 676
Taxes federal government	2 635	21 231	60 252	90 694	116 395	110 504	120 632	124 064	127 655	133 114
Taxes on individuals - province	829	13 220	39 470	52 958	73 630	73 586	76 445	83 388	86 471	91 562
1120 On capital gains	0	0	0	0	0	0	0	0	0	0
1200 Corporate	2 276	11 741	17 190	47 643	54 272	52 885	56 052	57 907	62 754	65 151
1210 On profits	2 276	11 741	17 190	47 643	54 272	52 885	56 052	57 907	62 754	65 151
Taxes federal government	1 752	8 110	11 726	31 570	37 093	32 739	35 200	35 599	38 451	40 451
Taxes on corporations - province	524	3 631	5 464	16 073	17 179	20 146	20 852	22 308	24 303	24 700
1220 On capital gains	0	0	0	0	0	0	0	0	0	0
1300 Unallocable between 1100 and 1200	170	872	1 654	4 025	6 901	5 868	5 508	5 000	5 374	6 820
Non-resident withhold taxes - federal	170	872	1 654	4 025	6 901	5 868	5 508	5 000	5 374	6 820
2000 Social security contributions	**854**	**10 649**	**29 653**	**53 109**	**73 722**	**76 386**	**80 513**	**85 866**	**89 589**	**93 576**
2100 Employees	318	3 756	10 634	21 361	29 361	30 434	31 894	34 027	35 680	37 369
Canada pension plan	47	1 265	3 745	9 401	16 194	17 607	17 940	19 105	19 677	20 748
Quebec pension plan	15	431	1 108	2 897	4 124	4 865	5 300	5 690	5 815	6 095
Employment insurance	164	1 393	5 284	7 782	7 084	7 100	7 702	8 271	9 158	9 478
Hospital insurance premiums	92	667	496	1 281	1 959	863	952	960	1 029	1 048
2110 On a payroll basis	..	..	10 634	20 976	28 654	29 571	30 942	33 067	34 651	36 321
2120 On an income tax basis	..	..	0	385	707	863	952	960	1 029	1 048
2200 Employers	536	6 697	18 449	30 307	41 922	43 267	45 855	48 892	50 878	53 013
Canada pension plan	48	1 266	3 745	9 401	16 194	17 607	17 940	19 105	19 677	20 748
Quebec pension plan	15	432	1 108	2 897	4 124	4 865	5 300	5 690	5 815	6 095
Employment insurance	164	2 006	7 398	10 894	9 917	9 939	10 783	11 580	12 822	13 270
Hospital insurance premiums	92	1 270	496	897	1 252	0	0	0	0	0
Social insurance levies	217	1 723	5 702	6 218	10 434	10 856	11 833	12 517	12 563	12 900
2210 On a payroll basis	..	..	18 449	30 307	41 922	43 267	45 855	48 892	50 878	53 013
2220 On an income tax basis	..	..	0	0	0	0	0	0	0	0
2300 Self-employed or non-employed	0	196	570	1 442	2 440	2 685	2 764	2 947	3 032	3 194
Canada pension plan	..	153	478	1 200	2 096	2 278	2 321	2 472	2 546	2 685
Quebec pension plan	..	43	92	242	344	406	442	475	486	509
2310 On a payroll basis	..	196	570	1 442	2 440	2 685	2 764	2 947	3 032	3 194
2320 On an income tax basis	..	0	0	0	0	0	0	0	0	0
2400 Unallocable between 2100, 2200 and 2300	0	0	0	0	0	0	0	0	0	0
2410 On a payroll basis	..	..	..	..	..	..	..	..	..	..
2420 On an income tax basis	..	..	..	..	..	..	..	..	..	..
3000 Taxes on payroll and workforce	**0**	**0**	**5 499**	**8 013**	**10 038**	**10 442**	**11 560**	**11 903**	**12 353**	**12 595**
4000 Taxes on property	**2 186**	**9 195**	**24 467**	**37 157**	**54 507**	**61 764**	**65 415**	**67 694**	**70 604**	**72 592**
4100 Recurrent taxes on immovable property	1 830	8 315	20 189	30 242	44 567	49 874	53 555	55 719	57 720	59 833
On property provincial government	11	133	1 645	3 078	3 164	4 426	4 551	4 728	4 935	5 556
Personal property local government	17	0	18 544	27 165	41 403	45 448	49 004	50 991	52 785	54 277
Real property local government	1 802	8 182	0	0	0	0	0	0	0	0
4110 Households	..	..	..	..	..	..	..	..	..	..
4120 Others	..	..	..	..	..	..	..	..	..	..
4200 Recurrent taxes on net wealth	25	512	1 911	4 171	2 970	1 960	945	632	373	375
4210 Individual	0	0	0	0	0	0	0	0	0	0
4220 Corporate	25	512	1 911	4 171	2 970	1 960	945	632	373	375
4300 Estate, inheritance and gift taxes	223	75	3	2	0	181	205	197	218	220
4310 Estate and inheritance taxes	216	75	3	2	..	181	205	197	218	220
On inheritances federal government	108	0	0	0	..	0	0	0	0	0
Succession duties provincial government	108	75	3	2	..	181	205	197	218	220
4320 Gift taxes	7	0	0	0	..	0	0	0	0	0
On gifts federal government	7	..	..	..	..	..	..	..	..	..
4400 Taxes on financial and capital transactions	0	0	0	0	2 868	2 682	3 419	3 387	3 646	4 029
4500 Non-recurrent taxes	108	293	2 365	2 742	4 102	7 067	7 291	7 759	8 646	8 134
4510 On net wealth	0	0	0	0	0	0	0	0	0	0
4520 Other non-recurrent taxes	108	293	2 365	2 742	4 102	7 067	7 291	7 759	8 646	8 134
Special assessments and charges local govt.	108	293	2 365	2 742	4 102	7 067	7 291	7 759	8 646	8 134
4600 Other recurrent taxes on property	0	0	0	0	0	0	0	0	0	0
5000 Taxes on goods and services	**6 202**	**32 909**	**63 092**	**94 468**	**122 855**	**116 245**	**129 698**	**133 170**	**135 890**	**142 074**
5100 Taxes on production, sale, transfer, etc	5 310	24 808	59 627	88 879	114 701	109 436	121 713	125 239	128 019	133 529
5110 General taxes	2 730	11 658	34 475	55 313	71 242	67 293	76 542	79 393	81 244	85 179
5111 Value added taxes	0	0	0	35 884	46 072	64 305	74 869	77 936	79 099	83 623
5112 Sales tax	2 730	11 658	34 475	19 429	25 170	2 988	1 673	1 457	2 145	1 556
Sales taxes federal government	813	5 429	16 866	0	0	0	0	0	0	0
Sales taxes provincial, local govt.	1 917	6 229	17 609	19 429	25 170	2 988	1 673	1 457	2 145	1 556
5113 Other	0	0	0	0	0	0	0	0	0	0
5120 Taxes on specific goods and services	2 580	13 150	25 153	33 565	43 459	42 143	45 171	45 846	46 775	48 350

StatLink http://dx.doi.org/10.1787/888933416695

Table 4.4. **Canada** *(cont./suite)*

Details of tax revenue/Recettes fiscales détaillées

Million CAD

	1965	1980	1990	2000	2007	2009	2011	2012	2013	2014
5121 Excises	1 499	6 805	14 473	18 417	22 759	21 693	23 672	23 660	24 338	25 397
Excises federal government	740	3 850	6 405	8 377	9 249	9 705	10 190	10 003	10 127	10 866
Liquor	..	..	926	1 103	1 224	1 487	1 598	1 595	1 498	1 665
Tobacco	..	..	2 247	2 176	2 466	2 629	2 986	2 821	2 905	3 334
Gasoline and motive fuel	..	..	2 472	4 807	5 272	5 321	5 341	5 355	5 430	5 574
Remitted gaming profits	..	..	45	0	0	0	0	0	0	0
Miscellaneous consumption taxes	..	..	715	291	287	269	265	232	294	293
Excises provincial government	759	2 955	8 067	10 039	13 510	11 988	13 483	13 657	14 211	14 530
Motor fuel	680	1 863	4 674	7 031	8 065	7 918	8 590	8 827	9 110	9 151
Tobacco	53	772	2 776	2 279	4 181	4 215	4 677	4 648	4 916	5 063
Other	26	320	617	730	1 264	-145	216	182	185	316
5122 Profits of fiscal monopolies	294	1 406	3 758	8 756	11 565	11 196	11 615	11 903	11 877	12 172
Own enterprises contributions	294	1 406	3 758	8 756	11 565	11 196	11 615	11 903	11 877	12 172
5123 Customs and import duties	686	3 199	4 021	2 824	3 829	3 704	3 851	4 016	4 143	4 506
Customs and import duties federal govt.	686	3 199	4 021	2 824	3 829	3 704	3 851	4 016	4 143	4 506
5124 Taxes on exports	0	842	0	0	0	0	0	0	0	0
5125 Taxes on investment goods	0	0	0	0	0	0	0	0	0	0
5126 Taxes on specific services	84	575	2 385	2 524	4 088	4 200	4 596	4 882	5 062	4 984
Tax on insurance premiums, provincial govt.	45	261	1 141	1 740	2 796	3 158	3 440	3 722	3 891	3 772
Tax on insurance premiums, federal govt.	0	1	1	1	11	18	13	10	13	10
Amusement and admission taxes	4	25	126	538	537	318	300	289	276	267
Air transportation taxes	0	166	488	0	403	375	631	636	662	696
Racetrack betting	35	122	155	55	36	42	35	34	32	33
Tax on meals and hotels	0	0	473	191	305	289	177	191	188	206
5127 Other taxes on internat. trade and transactions	0	0	0	0	0	0	0	0	0	0
5128 Other taxes	17	323	517	1 045	1 217	1 350	1 436	1 384	1 355	1 292
Other taxes federal government	0	98	272	758	762	525	578	512	439	398
Other taxes provincial government	17	225	245	287	455	825	858	872	916	894
5130 Unallocable between 5110 and 5120	0	0	0	0	0	0	0	0	0	0
5200 Taxes on use of goods and perform activities	892	8 101	3 465	5 589	8 154	6 809	7 985	7 931	7 871	8 545
5210 Recurrent taxes	306	1 500	2 393	3 644	4 368	4 246	4 492	4 725	5 041	5 301
5211 Paid by households: motor vehicles	103	666	1 056	1 696	2 241	1 937	2 022	2 139	2 252	2 374
5212 Paid by others: motor vehicles	141	509	697	1 039	1 242	1 120	1 160	1 224	1 352	1 428
5213 Paid in respect of other goods	62	325	640	909	885	1 189	1 310	1 362	1 437	1 499
5220 Non-recurrent taxes	586	6 601	1 072	1 945	3 786	2 563	3 493	3 206	2 830	3 244
Licences and permits local govt.	36	132	317	499	889	683	840	944	952	999
Licences and permits provincial govt.	550	6 469	755	1 446	2 897	1 880	2 653	2 262	1 878	2 245
5300 Unallocable between 5100 and 5200	0	0	0	0	0	0	0	0	0	0
6000 Other taxes	**166**	**1 198**	**2 875**	**2 167**	**342**	**590**	**641**	**683**	**687**	**734**
6100 Paid solely by business	139	943	2 386	1 280	0	0	0	0	0	0
6200 Other	27	255	489	887	342	590	641	683	687	734
Poll tax local government	5	0	0	0	0	0	0	0	0	0
Miscellaneous local government	11	358	489	887	342	590	641	683	687	734
Other federal government	11	-103	0	0	0	0	0	0	0	0
Non-wastable tax credits										
Non-wastable tax credits against 1110	..	..	..	1 633	5 550	6 937	6 866	6 950	7 326	7 696
Tax expenditure component	..	..	..	276	824	928	938	921	965	1 013
Transfer component	..	..	..	1 357	4 726	6 009	5 928	6 029	6 361	6 683
Non-wastable tax credits against 1210	..	..	..	1 758	3 445	4 189	4 858	3 589	3 963	3 823
Tax expenditure component	..	..	..	20	12	17	18	14	17	17
Transfer component	..	..	..	1 738	3 433	4 172	4 840	3 575	3 946	3 806
Total tax revenue on cash basis	**15 318**	**101 015**	**244 152**	**388 833**	**527 734**	..	..	..	..	..
Total tax revenue on accrual basis	..	..	..	**390 234**	**512 663**	**508 270**	**546 463**	**569 675**	**591 377**	**618 217**
Conciliation with National Accounts										
Additional taxes included in National Accounts	..	..	..	0	0	0	0	0	0	0
Taxes excluded from National Accounts	..	..	..	0	0	0	0	0	0	0
Difference in treatment of tax credits	..	..	..	0	0	0	0	0	0	0
Capital transfer for uncollected revenue	..	..	..	0	0	0	0	0	0	0
Voluntary social security contributions	..	..	..	0	0	0	0	0	0	0
Miscellaneous differences	..	..	..	0	0	0	0	0	0	0
National Accounts: Taxes and actual social contributions	..	..	..	390 234	512 663	508 270	546 463	569 675	591 377	618 217
Imputed social contributions	..	..	..	0	0	0	0	0	0	0
National Accounts: Taxes and all social contributions	..	..	..	390 234	512 663	508 270	546 463	569 675	591 377	618 217

StatLink http://dx.doi.org/10.1787/888933416695

Table 4.4. **Canada** *(cont./suite)*

Details of tax revenue/Recettes fiscales détaillées

Notes : From 2001, all data are for the year ending 31st December. For 2005 and earlier years, data for the Federal, Provincial and Territorial governments are on a fiscal year basis commencing 1st April. Data for local government are on a fiscal year basis commencing 1st January.
From 1999, data are on accrual basis, except that personal income taxes are on a modified cash basis.
There are some minor differences between the data for the years 1965 to 1978 and those for subsequent years. These mostly relate to the inclusion of fines and penalities or late payment of taxes and deductions for the child tax credits in the data for the years 1979 to 1983.
Heading 1210 – Taxes federal government: Federal corporate taxes include capital taxes.
Heading 2000: Includes receipts from the Canadian Pension Plan, Quebec Pension Plan, Unemployement Insurance Fund and Provincial Health Insurance. Premiums, Medicare Premiums and Social Insurance levies but excludes that part of the taxes on income and sales taxes earmarked for old age security. The practice of earmarking these taxes was discontinued in June 1975.
Heading 4400: From 2002 onward, includes land transfer taxes of the provincial, territorial and local governments. Prior to 2002, land transfer taxes of the local government were included in line 6000 and those provincial and territorial governments were included in line 4520.
Heading 5121: The large increase in this heading between 1980 and 1981 is due to the introduction of a «special petroleum compensation charge», a «Canadian ownership special charge» and to an increase in the natural gas tax of C$ 2 399 millions.
Heading 5122: From 1988, profits on fiscal monopolies include lottery profits.
Heading 5128: From 1988, other taxes of Federal Government include the annual fees for managing the spectrum (airwaves) allocation to the cellular industry.
Heading 5211: Some Québec motor vehicle licence administrative fees are included in sales of goods and services for the period 1988-89 to 1997-98. From 1998-99 onward, these fees are included under other taxes – motor vehicle licences.
Source : Statistics Canada.

StatLink http://dx.doi.org/10.1787/888933416695

Table 4.5. **Chile/Chili**

Details of tax revenue/Recettes fiscales détaillées

Million CLP

	1965	1980	1990	2000	2007	2009	2011	2012	2013	2014
Total tax revenue	..	..	**1 777 218**	**7 901 998**	**20 598 963**	**16 759 274**	**25 762 449**	**27 714 772**	**27 381 686**	**29 145 219**
1000 Taxes on income, profits and capital gains	..	..	**412 974**	**1 841 630**	**9 412 056**	**5 162 043**	**10 322 824**	**10 803 031**	**9 520 709**	**9 628 037**
1100 Of individuals	..	..	99 154	604 100	989 348	1 252 672	1 690 230	1 893 620	1 964 172	2 114 296
Second category tax	..	..	65 552	490 980	993 129	1 239 815	1 663 293	1 917 675	1 981 699	2 140 345
Global complementary tax	..	..	33 603	113 120	-3 781	12 857	26 936	-24 055	-17 527	-26 050
1110 On income and profits	..	..	..	..	..	..	..	..	..	..
1120 On capital gains	..	..	..	..	..	..	..	..	..	..
1200 Corporate	..	..	219 586	882 896	6 054 487	4 110 485	6 021 408	7 560 906	6 041 089	6 196 077
First category tax	..	..	200 891	815 747	5 084 996	3 729 488	5 254 907	6 770 329	5 473 355	5 182 214
Surtax on state owned enterprises	..	..	16 074	47 634	113 334	44 974	116 725	80 084	124 220	100 851
Mining tax	..	..	0	0	835 452	312 473	598 790	619 150	324 577	801 647
Other	..	..	2 621	19 516	20 705	23 550	50 987	91 343	118 937	111 365
1210 On profits	..	..	..	..	..	..	..	..	..	..
1220 On capital gains	..	..	..	..	..	..	..	..	..	..
1300 Unallocable between 1100 and 1200	..	..	94 233	354 634	2 368 221	-201 113	2 611 186	1 348 506	1 515 449	1 317 664
Adicionel tax	..	..	59 082	350 301	1 462 715	1 023 497	1 187 866	1 178 917	1 337 721	1 454 847
Other	..	..	35 151	4 332	905 507	-1 224 610	1 423 320	169 589	177 727	-137 183
2000 Social security contributions	..	..	**159 559**	**576 758**	**1 148 647**	**1 371 750**	**1 623 818**	**1 802 468**	**1 968 973**	**2 110 087**
2100 Employees	..	..	154 021	553 937	1 098 620	1 312 793	1 565 828	1 742 526	1 906 340	2 044 356
2110 On a payroll basis	..	..	154 021	553 937	1 098 620	1 312 793	1 565 828	1 742 526	1 906 340	2 044 356
2120 On an income tax basis	..	..	0	0	0	0	0	0	0	0
2200 Employers	..	..	5 538	22 821	50 027	58 957	57 990	59 942	62 633	65 731
2210 On a payroll basis	..	..	5 538	22 821	50 027	58 957	57 990	59 942	62 633	65 731
2220 On an income tax basis	..	..	0	0	0	0	0	0	0	0
2300 Self-employed or non-employed	..	..	0	0	0	0	0	0	0	0
2310 On a payroll basis	..	..	..	..	..	..	..	..	..	..
2320 On an income tax basis	..	..	..	..	..	..	..	..	..	..
2400 Unallocable between 2100, 2200 and 2300	..	..	0	0	0	0	0	0	0	0
2410 On a payroll basis	..	..	..	..	..	..	..	..	..	..
2420 On an income tax basis	..	..	..	..	..	..	..	..	..	..
3000 Taxes on payroll and workforce	..	..	**0**	**0**	**0**	**0**	**0**	**0**	**0**	**0**
4000 Taxes on property	..	..	**109 319**	**554 037**	**1 013 571**	**909 121**	**1 027 627**	**1 180 307**	**1 133 765**	**1 228 961**
4100 Recurrent taxes on immovable property	..	..	59 968	302 244	496 311	646 316	731 191	788 919	840 842	924 062
4110 Households	..	..	..	..	..	..	..	..	..	..
4120 Others	..	..	..	..	..	..	..	..	..	..
4200 Recurrent taxes on net wealth	..	..	0	0	0	0	0	0	0	0
4210 Individual	..	..	..	..	..	..	..	..	..	..
4220 Corporate	..	..	..	..	..	..	..	..	..	..
4300 Estate, inheritance and gift taxes	..	..	3 444	10 906	28 501	200 203	30 876	66 719	45 550	31 340
4310 Estate and inheritance taxes	..	..	..	..	..	..	..	..	..	..
4320 Gift taxes	..	..	..	..	..	..	..	..	..	..
4400 Taxes on financial and capital transactions	..	..	45 907	240 886	488 759	62 602	265 560	324 669	247 373	273 559
4500 Non-recurrent taxes	..	..	0	0	0	0	0	0	0	0
4510 On net wealth	..	..	..	..	..	..	..	..	..	..
4520 Other non-recurrent taxes	..	..	..	..	..	..	..	..	..	..
4600 Other recurrent taxes on property	..	..	0	0	0	0	0	0	0	0
5000 Taxes on goods and services	..	..	**1 118 722**	**5 041 769**	**9 023 666**	**9 321 798**	**12 700 180**	**13 873 611**	**14 779 915**	**16 127 841**
5100 Taxes on production, sale, transfer, etc	..	..	1 074 009	4 789 827	8 578 636	8 741 074	11 963 914	13 052 989	13 869 529	15 131 661
5110 General taxes	..	..	664 421	3 306 350	6 781 501	7 051 079	9 536 786	10 447 374	11 170 794	12 133 710
5111 Value added taxes	..	..	664 421	3 306 350	6 781 501	7 051 079	9 536 786	10 447 374	11 170 794	12 133 710
5112 Sales tax	..	..	0	0	0	0	0	0	0	0
5113 Other	..	..	0	0	0	0	0	0	0	0
5120 Taxes on specific goods and services	..	..	409 588	1 483 477	1 797 135	1 689 995	2 427 128	2 605 615	2 698 735	2 997 951
5121 Excises	..	..	166 050	816 160	1 299 844	1 248 243	1 750 916	1 892 713	1 987 475	2 224 209
Cigarettes and tobacco	..	..	60 604	283 275	455 595	556 651	744 302	783 995	815 991	856 595
Gasolene and diesel	..	..	105 445	532 885	844 249	684 698	1 006 614	1 108 718	1 171 483	1 361 724
Oil stabilisation fund	..	..	0	0	0	6 894	0	0	0	0
Fisheries Law Extraction Rights	..	..	0	0	0	0	0	0	0	5 890
5122 Profits of fiscal monopolies	..	..	0	0	0	0	0	0	0	0
5123 Customs and import duties	..	..	222 486	548 571	300 416	162 987	301 828	314 441	303 393	337 839
5124 Taxes on exports	..	..	0	0	0	0	0	0	0	0
5125 Taxes on investment goods	..	..	0	0	0	0	0	0	0	0
5126 Taxes on specific services	..	..	21 052	118 746	196 875	278 765	374 384	398 461	407 867	435 903
5127 Other taxes on internat. trade and transactions	..	..	0	0	0	0	0	0	0	0
5128 Other taxes	..	..	0	0	0	0	0	0	0	0
5130 Unallocable between 5110 and 5120	..	..	0	0	0	0	0	0	0	0
5200 Taxes on use of goods and perform activities	..	..	44 714	251 942	445 030	580 724	736 266	820 622	910 386	996 180
5210 Recurrent taxes	..	..	44 714	251 942	445 030	580 724	736 266	820 622	910 386	996 180
Motor vehicles	..	..	24 469	93 880	155 158	187 569	267 116	301 895	330 754	365 316
5211 Paid by households: motor vehicles	..	..	0	0	0	0	0	0	0	0

StatLink http://dx.doi.org/10.1787/888933416704

Table 4.5. **Chile/Chili** *(cont./suite)*

Details of tax revenue/Recettes fiscales détaillées

Million CLP

	1965	1980	1990	2000	2007	2009	2011	2012	2013	2014
5212 Paid by others: motor vehicles	..	..	0	0	0	0	0	0	0	0
5213 Paid in respect of other goods	..	..	20 245	158 062	289 872	393 155	469 150	518 727	579 632	630 864
Municipal permits	..	..	18 401	136 138	263 996	359 730	425 138	468 938	527 955	578 671
Mining patents	..	..	3 374	34 730	25 184	32 690	42 944	47 899	50 094	50 448
Other	..	..	-1 530	-12 806	692	735	1 068	1 890	1 583	1 745
5220 Non-recurrent taxes	..	..	0	0	0	0	0	0	0	0
5300 Unallocable between 5100 and 5200	..	..	0	0	0	0	0	0	0	0
6000 Other taxes	..	..	**-23 356**	**-112 195**	**1 023**	**-5 438**	**88 000**	**55 355**	**-21 676**	**50 293**
6100 Paid solely by business	..	..	0	0	0	0	0	0	0	0
6200 Other	..	..	-23 356	-112 195	1 023	-5 438	88 000	55 355	-21 676	50 293
Non-wastable tax credits										
Non-wastable tax credits against 1110	..	..	..	..	..	..	..	..	..	..
Tax expenditure component	..	..	..	..	..	..	..	..	..	..
Transfer component	..	..	..	..	..	..	..	..	..	..
Non-wastable tax credits against 1210	..	..	..	..	..	..	..	..	..	..
Tax expenditure component	..	..	..	..	..	..	..	..	..	..
Transfer component	..	..	..	..	..	..	..	..	..	..
Total tax revenue on cash basis	..	..	**1 777 218**	**7 901 998**	**20 598 963**	**16 759 274**	**25 762 449**	**27 714 772**	**27 381 686**	**29 145 219**
Total tax revenue on accrual basis	..	..	..	..	..	..	..	..	..	..
Conciliation with National Accounts										
Additional taxes included in National Accounts	..	..	..	..	..	..	..	..	..	..
Taxes excluded from National Accounts	..	..	..	..	..	..	..	..	..	..
Difference in treatment of tax credits	..	..	..	..	..	..	..	..	..	..
Capital transfer for uncollected revenue	..	..	..	..	..	..	..	..	..	..
Voluntary social security contributions	..	..	..	..	..	..	..	..	..	..
Miscellaneous differences	..	..	..	..	..	..	..	..	..	..
National Accounts: Taxes and actual social contributions	..	..	..	..	..	..	..	..	..	..
Imputed social contributions	..	..	..	..	..	..	..	..	..	..
National Accounts: Taxes and all social contributions	..	..	..	..	..	..	..	..	..	..

Notes : Year ending 31st December.
The data are on a cash basis.
Source : Servicio de Impuestos internos (Chile's Tax Service).

StatLink http://dx.doi.org/10.1787/888933416704

Table 4.6. **Czech Republic/République tchèque**

Details of tax revenue/Recettes fiscales détaillées

Million CZK

	1965	1980	1990	2000	2007	2009	2011	2012	2013	2014
Total tax revenue	..	..	..	**771 596**	**1 313 753**	**1 268 851**	**1 341 575**	**1 367 270**	**1 396 543**	**1 427 274**
Total tax revenue exclusive of custom duties	..	..	..	..	**1 307 310**	**1 263 303**	**1 334 614**	**1 361 098**	**1 390 999**	**1 420 306**
1000 Taxes on income, profits and capital gains	..	..	..	**175 846**	**325 328**	**269 343**	**272 467**	**280 058**	**290 263**	**305 712**
1100 Of individuals	..	..	..	99 668	153 374	136 023	142 752	144 831	149 831	153 763
1110 On income and profits	..	..	..	99 668	153 374	136 023	142 752	144 831	149 831	153 763
Wages and salaries withholding	..	..	..	73 474	126 736	113 119	122 569	124 005	129 793	135 717
Of unincorporated individuals	..	..	..	17 254	17 825	12 750	7 866	7 767	7 437	3 712
Withheld on interest and dividends paid to individuals	..	..	..	8 940	8 813	10 154	12 317	13 059	12 602	14 334
1120 On capital gains	..	..	..	0	0	0	0	0	0	0
1200 Corporate	..	..	..	76 178	171 954	133 319	129 715	135 227	140 432	151 950
1210 On profits	..	..	..	76 178	171 954	133 319	129 715	135 227	140 432	151 950
Profit tax	..	..	..	68 945	164 016	123 301	120 320	119 978	124 820	135 158
Withheld on interest and dividends paid to corporations	..	..	..	7 233	7 162	9 027	8 710	7 503	7 736	9 249
Levy on lottery revenue	..	..	..	0	776	992	685	7 747	7 876	7 543
1220 On capital gains	..	..	..	0	0	0	0	0	0	0
1300 Unallocable between 1100 and 1200	..	..	..	0	0	0	0	0	0	0
2000 Social security contributions	..	..	..	**341 544**	**573 417**	**557 702**	**588 996**	**596 841**	**603 072**	**625 508**
2100 Employees	..	..	..	77 272	127 662	112 156	120 070	121 892	123 353	126 894
2110 On a payroll basis	..	..	..	77 272	127 662	112 156	120 070	121 892	123 353	126 894
Retirement	..	..	..	40 489	66 644	66 042	70 999	71 647	71 871	74 040
State employment policy	..	..	..	2 492	4 101	0	0	0	0	0
Sick leave	..	..	..	6 852	11 279	0	0	0	0	0
Health insurance	..	..	..	27 439	45 638	46 114	49 071	50 245	51 482	52 854
2120 On an income tax basis	..	..	..	0	0	0	0	0	0	0
2200 Employers	..	..	..	220 207	359 493	345 361	372 760	377 834	382 498	395 998
2210 On a payroll basis	..	..	..	220 207	359 493	345 361	372 760	377 834	382 498	395 998
Retirement	..	..	..	121 547	220 591	218 310	235 129	237 277	239 248	248 198
State employment policy	..	..	..	19 933	12 303	11 836	13 054	13 236	13 345	13 856
Sick leave	..	..	..	20 555	33 834	21 500	24 904	25 234	25 454	26 396
Health insurance	..	..	..	54 879	91 275	92 229	98 141	100 491	102 964	105 709
Penalties	..	..	..	3 293	1 490	1 486	1 532	1 596	1 487	1 839
2220 On an income tax basis	..	..	..	0	0	0	0	0	0	0
2300 Self-employed or non-employed	..	..	..	44 065	86 262	100 185	96 166	97 114	97 221	102 616
2310 On a payroll basis	..	..	..	44 065	86 262	100 185	96 166	97 114	97 221	102 616
Retirement	..	..	..	7 819	19 508	25 320	22 225	22 334	21 262	21 006
State employment policy	..	..	..	1 082	1 114	1 446	976	957	911	900
Sick leave	..	..	..	0	0	0	0	0	0	0
Health insurance	..	..	..	34 992	65 483	73 241	72 815	73 671	74 908	80 537
Self-employed	..	..	..	7 328	15 921	20 572	17 632	18 352	18 732	18 148
Non-employed	..	..	..	200	2 103	3 996	2 466	2 451	2 500	2 522
Government	..	..	..	27 464	47 459	48 673	52 717	52 867	53 676	59 867
Penalties	..	..	..	172	157	178	150	153	140	174
2320 On an income tax basis	..	..	..	0	0	0	0	0	0	0
2400 Unallocable between 2100, 2200 and 2300	..	..	..	0	0	0	0	0	0	0
2410 On a payroll basis	..	..	..	..	..	..	..	..	..	..
2420 On an income tax basis	..	..	..	..	..	..	..	..	..	..
3000 Taxes on payroll and workforce	..	..	..	**0**	**0**	**0**	**0**	**0**	**0**	**0**
4000 Taxes on property	..	..	..	**10 890**	**15 495**	**14 085**	**20 439**	**20 554**	**19 210**	**19 168**
4100 Recurrent taxes on immovable property	..	..	..	4 469	5 126	6 366	8 484	9 546	9 852	9 561
4110 Households	..	..	..	1 452	2 228	2 912	4 344	4 837	4 993	4 837
Real property tax	..	..	..	1 452	2 228	2 912	4 344	4 837	4 993	4 837
4120 Others	..	..	..	3 017	2 898	3 454	4 140	4 708	4 859	4 724
Levy collected by Winery Fund	..	..	..	0	2	5	5	5	5	21
Real property tax	..	..	..	3 017	2 895	3 448	4 135	4 703	4 855	4 703
4200 Recurrent taxes on net wealth	..	..	..	0	0	0	0	0	0	0
4210 Individual	..	..	..	..	..	..	..	..	..	..
4220 Corporate	..	..	..	..	..	..	..	..	..	..
4300 Estate, inheritance and gift taxes	..	..	..	587	460	225	4 401	3 392	215	0
4310 Estate and inheritance taxes	..	..	..	112	115	87	71	76	76	0
Inheritance tax	..	..	..	112	115	87	71	76	76	0
4320 Gift taxes	..	..	..	475	345	138	4 330	3 316	139	0
Gift tax	..	..	..	475	345	138	4 330	3 316	139	0
4400 Taxes on financial and capital transactions	..	..	..	5 834	9 909	7 495	7 554	7 617	9 143	9 606
Real property transfer tax	..	..	..	5 834	9 909	7 495	7 554	7 617	9 143	9 606
4500 Non-recurrent taxes	..	..	..	0	0	0	0	0	0	0
4510 On net wealth	..	..	..	..	..	..	..	..	..	..
4520 Other non-recurrent taxes	..	..	..	..	..	..	..	..	..	..
4600 Other recurrent taxes on property	..	..	..	0	0	0	0	0	0	0
5000 Taxes on goods and services	..	..	..	**242 960**	**393 041**	**421 958**	**452 578**	**463 459**	**478 386**	**469 826**
5100 Taxes on production, sale, transfer, etc	..	..	..	226 354	365 998	396 042	426 528	438 090	453 863	444 660

StatLink http://dx.doi.org/10.1787/888933416715

Table 4.6. **Czech Republic/République tchèque** *(cont./suite)*

Details of tax revenue/Recettes fiscales détaillées

Million CZK

	1965	1980	1990	2000	2007	2009	2011	2012	2013	2014
5110 General taxes	..	..	..	141 235	232 288	258 627	276 533	286 116	303 822	319 485
5111 Value added taxes	..	..	..	141 235	232 288	258 627	276 533	286 116	303 822	319 485
5112 Sales tax	..	..	..	0	0	0	0	0	0	0
5113 Other	..	..	..	0	0	0	0	0	0	0
Previous turnover tax	..	..	..	..	..	..	..	..	..	..
5120 Taxes on specific goods and services	..	..	..	85 119	133 710	137 414	149 995	151 975	150 041	125 175
5121 Excises	..	..	..	71 404	133 492	137 203	149 757	151 719	149 760	124 870
On mineral oils	..	..	..	46 998	81 661	80 867	80 561	77 991	77 160	80 245
On alcohol and liquor	..	..	..	5 629	7 201	7 689	6 870	5 998	6 658	6 794
On beer	..	..	..	3 410	3 564	3 478	4 553	4 611	4 545	4 605
On wine	..	..	..	350	342	366	296	308	288	302
On tobacco products	..	..	..	14 984	40 713	41 581	48 203	53 334	52 193	28 091
Duty on CFC	..	..	..	33	0	0	0	0	0	0
Levy collected by Winery Fund	..	..	..	0	11	26	19	29	21	0
On electricity	..	..	..	0	0	1 391	1 368	1 342	1 305	1 146
On natural gas	..	..	..	0	0	1 299	1 299	1 261	1 256	1 192
On solid fuels	..	..	..	0	0	507	476	447	469	623
Fee on electricity from solar radiation	..	..	..	0	0	0	6 111	6 397	5 866	1 873
5122 Profits of fiscal monopolies	..	..	..	0	0	0	0	0	0	0
5123 Customs and import duties	..	..	..	13 572	0	0	0	0	0	0
Customs duties	..	..	..	13 572	..	..	..	..	..	..
Previous import surcharge	..	..	..	0	..	..	..	..	..	..
5124 Taxes on exports	..	..	..	0	0	0	0	0	0	0
5125 Taxes on investment goods	..	..	..	0	0	0	0	0	0	0
5126 Taxes on specific services	..	..	..	143	218	211	238	256	281	305
Fees on entry tickets	..	..	..	65	61	63	60	58	56	55
Fees on recreational units (based on capacity)	..	..	..	69	144	135	166	188	213	224
Fees on advertising facilities	..	..	..	0	0	0	0	0	0	0
Restaurant sale alcoh. beverages and tobac. products	..	..	..	0	0	0	0	0	0	0
Fees collected by the cinematography EBF	..	..	..	9	13	13	11	11	12	26
5127 Other taxes on internat. trade and transactions	..	..	..	0	0	0	0	0	0	0
5128 Other taxes	..	..	..	0	0	0	0	0	0	0
5130 Unallocable between 5110 and 5120	..	..	..	0	0	0	0	0	0	0
5200 Taxes on use of goods and perform activities	..	..	..	16 606	27 043	25 916	26 049	25 368	24 523	25 167
5210 Recurrent taxes	..	..	..	10 788	18 100	18 132	19 002	18 342	18 176	18 724
Highway fee	..	..	..	1 753	2 429	2 845	3 186	3 872	3 803	4 138
5211 Paid by households: motor vehicles	..	..	..	0	0	0	0	0	0	0
5212 Paid by others: motor vehicles	..	..	..	5 456	5 882	4 944	5 256	5 224	5 323	5 598
Road tax (commercial)	..	..	..	5 456	5 882	4 944	5 256	5 224	5 323	5 598
5213 Paid in respect of other goods	..	..	..	3 579	9 790	10 343	10 560	9 246	9 050	8 988
Resort and recreation fees on visitors	..	..	..	232	312	282	302	304	301	304
Dog fees	..	..	..	191	277	287	287	286	281	277
Motor vehicle entry fees	..	..	..	32	25	22	11	13	14	11
Water pollution fee	..	..	..	520	404	192	224	215	208	212
Air pollution fee	..	..	..	685	525	376	439	408	268	322
Waste deposit fee	..	..	..	454	5 728	6 002	5 172	5 864	6 162	6 318
Levy on temp. withdrawal of land from agriculture	..	..	..	94	40	40	32	51	52	39
Radioactive waste fee	..	..	..	642	1 310	1 375	1 479	1 543	1 563	1 462
Fees on operated gambling machines	..	..	..	722	1 145	1 055	1 305	188	131	0
Fees on registration and recording of packaging	..	..	..	0	17	17	17	17	16	17
Levy on temp. withdrawal of land from forestry	..	..	..	7	6	7	7	5	6	6
Other environmental fees	..	..	..	0	0	688	1 284	353	47	19
5220 Non-recurrent taxes	..	..	..	5 818	8 943	7 784	7 048	7 027	6 348	6 442
Levy on withdrawal of land from agriculture	..	..	..	532	361	361	290	457	469	294
Levy on withdrawal of land from forestry	..	..	..	40	57	63	59	49	55	57
Tax on use of public space	..	..	..	645	639	632	682	655	629	640
Misc. licence and permit fees	..	..	..	4 601	7 881	6 715	6 000	5 855	5 187	5 441
Land betterment fee	..	..	..	0	4	11	16	10	7	10
Licence for lorry transport	..	..	..	0	1	2	1	1	0	1
5300 Unallocable between 5100 and 5200	..	..	..	0	0	0	0	0	0	0
6000 Other taxes	..	..	..	**356**	**29**	**216**	**135**	**187**	**67**	**92**
Unallocated previous taxes and levies	..	..	..	0	0	0	0	0	0	0
6100 Paid solely by business	..	..	..	0	0	0	0	0	0	0
6200 Other	..	..	..	356	29	216	135	187	67	92
Other taxes, fees and related payments	..	..	..	356	29	216	135	187	67	92
Custom duties collected for the EU	..	..	..	..	**6 443**	**5 548**	**6 961**	**6 172**	**5 544**	**6 968**
Non-wastable tax credits										
Non-wastable tax credits against 1110	..	..	..	0	16 022	26 074	28 277	28 379	29 493	28 969
Tax expenditure component	..	..	..	..	13 416	19 110	21 032	19 862	21 000	20 711
Transfer component	..	..	..	..	2 606	6 964	7 245	8 517	8 493	8 258

StatLink http://dx.doi.org/10.1787/888933416715

Table 4.6. **Czech Republic/République tchèque** *(cont./suite)*

Details of tax revenue/Recettes fiscales détaillées

Million CZK

	1965	1980	1990	2000	2007	2009	2011	2012	2013	2014
Total tax revenue on cash basis	..	..	..	**772 272**	**1 310 618**	**1 242 426**	**1 316 448**	**1 342 342**	**1 353 469**	**1 408 574**
Total tax revenue on accrual basis	..	..	..	**771 596**	**1 313 753**	**1 268 851**	**1 341 575**	**1 367 270**	**1 396 543**	**1 427 274**
Conciliation with National Accounts										
Additional taxes included in National Accounts	..	..	..	2 837	5 757	6 140	6 286	6 408	6 424	6 482
Compulsory injury insurance	..	..	..	2 837	5 757	6 140	6 286	6 408	6 424	6 482
Driving licence fees	..	..	..	0	0	0	0	0	0	0
Taxes excluded from National Accounts	..	..	..	-9 488	-17 797	-20 129	-18 714	-19 143	-18 893	-19 829
Tax on use of public space	..	..	..	-645	-639	-710	-682	-655	-629	-640
Waste deposit fee	..	..	..	-454	-5 728	-6 002	-5 172	-5 864	-6 162	-6 318
Misc. licence and permit fees	..	..	..	-2 301	-3 940	-3 357	-3 000	-2 928	-2 593	-2 721
Radioactive waste fee	..	..	..	-642	-1 310	-1 375	-1 479	-1 543	-1 563	-1 462
Health insurance: non-employed	..	..	..	-200	-2 103	-3 996	-2 466	-2 451	-2 500	-2 522
Health insurance: government	..	..	..	0	0	0	0	0	0	0
Soc. Security contr. employers: Penalties	..	..	..	-3 293	-1 490	-1 486	-1 532	-1 596	-1 487	-1 839
Soc. Security contr. Self-employed or non-employed: Penalties	..	..	..	-200	-157	-178	-150	-153	-140	-174
Licence for lorry transport	..	..	..	0	-1	-2	-1	-1	0	-1
Highway fee	..	..	..	-1 753	-2 429	-2 845	-3 186	-3 872	-3 803	-4 138
Other environmental fees	..	..	..	0	0	-18	-829	-19	-14	-15
Levy on loterry revenue	..	..	..	0	0	-158	-218	-63	0	0
Value added taxes	..	..	..	0	0	0	0	0	0	0
Difference in treatment of tax credits	..	..	..	0	0	0	0	0	0	0
Capital transfer for uncollected revenue	..	..	..	0	0	0	0	0	0	0
Voluntary social security contributions	..	..	..	1 099	974	635	423	313	326	345
Miscellaneous differences	..	..	..	2 162	0	0	0	0	0	0
National Accounts: Taxes and actual social contributions	..	..	..	768 206	1 302 688	1 255 498	1 329 570	1 354 848	1 384 400	1 414 272
Imputed social contributions	..	..	..	423	299	828	739	632	654	492
National Accounts: Taxes and all social contributions	..	..	..	768 629	1 302 987	1 256 326	1 330 309	1 355 480	1 385 054	1 414 764

Notes : Year ending 31st December.
From 1995, data are on accrual basis.
Source : Ministry of Finance, Economic Department.

StatLink http://dx.doi.org/10.1787/888933416715

Table 4.7. **Denmark/Danemark**

Details of tax revenue/Recettes fiscales détaillées

Million DKK

	1965	1980	1990	2000	2007	2009	2011	2012	2013	2014
Total tax revenue	**20 821**	**166 358**	**382 232**	**623 911**	**809 988**	**777 375**	**831 172**	**866 284**	**899 379**	**971 772**
Total tax revenue exclusive of custom duties	..	..	..	**621 586**	**806 707**	**774 728**	**827 994**	**863 322**	**896 556**	**968 771**
1000 Taxes on income, profits and capital gains	**9 712**	**92 404**	**233 739**	**383 244**	**486 845**	**476 879**	**508 455**	**536 098**	**563 312**	**631 165**
1100 Of individuals	8 758	86 958	206 478	328 532	427 412	435 208	430 120	443 072	490 233	524 883
1110 On income and profits	8 758	86 909	206 335	328 305	427 070	434 874	429 816	442 771	489 973	524 634
Central government income tax	5 020	33 351	91 638	77 491	155 540	136 756	129 538	133 588	140 780	140 409
County income tax	0	10 742	31 361	56 135	0	0	0	0	0	0
Municipality income tax	2 948	33 555	77 571	121 975	173 114	176 284	196 751	203 629	209 277	214 095
Seaman's income tax	66	457	0	0	0	0	0	0	0	0
Old-age pension fund contributions	592	2 163	0	0	0	0	0	0	0	0
Social pension fund contributions	0	3 340	0	0	0	0	0	0	0	0
Sickness benefit fund contributions	0	1 804	0	0	0	0	0	0	0	0
Pension schemes and annuity insurance	22	355	2 627	6 923	8 948	28 294	9 269	9 269	42 974	71 086
Special income tax	101	1 054	2 810	0	0	0	0	0	0	0
Duty on canceled pension schemes	9	82	0	0	0	0	0	0	0	0
Duty on feed rent increases	0	8	5	0	0	0	0	0	0	0
Duty on employees' remuneration compens. fund releases	0	0	325	654	1 144	1 552	1 089	1 224	1 129	1 014
Duty on interest on consumer loans	0	0	0	0	0	0	0	0	0	0
Labour market contributions	0	0	0	56 729	76 609	79 626	80 357	82 048	82 590	84 638
Imputed income from owner-occupied dwelling	0	0	0	8 399	11 716	12 361	12 814	13 014	13 223	13 393
1120 On capital gains	0	49	144	226	343	335	305	301	260	248
Tax on winnings from lotteries, pools, etc.	0	49	144	226	343	335	305	301	260	248
1200 Corporate	954	5 446	14 660	42 279	54 871	32 886	40 286	49 474	53 095	51 892
1210 On profits	954	5 446	14 660	42 279	54 871	32 886	40 286	49 474	53 095	51 892
1220 On capital gains	0	0	0	0	0	0	0	0	0	0
1300 Unallocable between 1100 and 1200	0	0	12 601	12 434	4 562	8 784	38 048	43 552	19 984	54 391
2000 Social security contributions	**690**	**710**	**101**	**8 453**	**1 286**	**1 018**	**2 040**	**1 824**	**1 618**	**1 451**
2100 Employees	567	1	98	8 209	1 057	877	1 049	1 078	879	714
Sickness benefit fund contributions	30	0	0	0	0	0	0	0	0	0
Sickday benefit contributions, ordinary	534	0	0	0	0	0	0	0	0	0
Sickday benefit contributions, special	3	0	0	0	0	0	0	0	0	0
Contribution to merchant marine's welf. board	0	1	1	0	0	0	0	0	0	0
Special pension scheme savings	0	0	0	6 846	0	0	0	0	0	0
Contr. to pension funds from officials in companies	0	0	0	879	555	463	448	644	476	440
Contr. to pension funds from officials in non-profit institutions	0	0	96	485	502	414	601	434	403	274
2110 On a payroll basis	..	..	..	..	..	..	..	..	..	..
2120 On an income tax basis	..	..	..	..	..	..	..	..	..	..
2200 Employers	123	709	3	244	229	141	991	746	739	737
Unemployment insurance contributions	41	598	0	0	0	0	0	0	0	0
Disablement insurance contributions	21	58	0	0	0	0	0	0	0	0
Sickness benefit fund contributions	61	0	0	0	0	0	0	0	0	0
Contribution to employee's wage guarantee fund	0	50	0	241	227	135	982	733	731	724
Contribution to merchant marine's welf. board	0	1	1	0	0	0	0	0	0	0
Shipping owners contr. sickness assist. seamen	0	1	2	3	2	6	9	13	8	13
2210 On a payroll basis	..	..	..	..	..	..	..	..	..	..
2220 On an income tax basis	..	..	..	..	..	..	..	..	..	..
2300 Self-employed or non-employed	0	0	0	0	0	0	0	0	0	0
2310 On a payroll basis	..	..	..	..	..	..	..	..	..	..
2320 On an income tax basis	..	..	..	..	..	..	..	..	..	..
2400 Unallocable between 2100, 2200 and 2300	0	0	0	0	0	0	0	0	0	0
2410 On a payroll basis	..	..	..	..	..	..	..	..	..	..
2420 On an income tax basis	..	..	..	..	..	..	..	..	..	..
3000 Taxes on payroll and workforce	**0**	**0**	**2 494**	**2 258**	**3 975**	**4 153**	**4 635**	**5 547**	**6 130**	**6 343**
4000 Taxes on property	**1 691**	**9 806**	**16 269**	**20 738**	**31 556**	**31 472**	**34 910**	**33 772**	**34 995**	**36 291**
4100 Recurrent taxes on immovable property	1 029	5 676	8 891	13 565	18 996	22 562	25 018	24 821	26 370	27 156
Central government land tax	130	264	0	0	0	0	0	0	0	0
County land tax	169	2 315	2 915	4 070	0	0	0	0	0	0
Municipal land tax	408	2 257	4 123	7 049	15 601	18 102	20 547	20 947	22 580	23 671
Centr. Govt. fixed tax on real property	32	11	0	0	0	0	0	0	0	0
County fixed tax on real property	45	0	0	0	0	0	0	0	0	0
Municipal fixed tax on real property	190	91	0	0	0	0	0	0	0	0
County duty on land (public property)	4	22	22	25	0	0	0	0	0	0
County duty on buildings (public property)	0	53	88	97	0	0	0	0	0	0
Municipal duty on land (public property)	26	103	244	383	393	601	420	360	359	359
Municipal duty on buildings (residential)	0	195	335	381	757	916	768	664	641	594
Municipal duty on buildings (business)	25	366	1 165	1 560	2 244	2 943	3 284	2 851	2 789	2 532
4110 Households	..	..	..	..	..	..	..	..	..	..
4120 Others	..	..	..	..	..	..	..	..	..	..

StatLink http://dx.doi.org/10.1787/888933416727

Table 4.7. **Denmark/Danemark** *(cont./suite)*

Details of tax revenue/Recettes fiscales détaillées

Million DKK

	1965	1980	1990	2000	2007	2009	2011	2012	2013	2014
4200 Recurrent taxes on net wealth	306	963	934	0	0	0	0	0	0	0
4210 Individual	306	963	934	..	..	..	..	..	..	..
4220 Corporate	0	0	0	..	..	..	..	..	..	..
4300 Estate, inheritance and gift taxes	137	738	2 197	2 863	3 896	3 669	4 792	4 042	3 940	3 848
4310 Estate and inheritance taxes	..	..	..	..	..	..	..	..	..	..
4320 Gift taxes	..	..	..	..	..	..	..	..	..	..
4400 Taxes on financial and capital transactions	219	2 313	4 166	4 171	8 659	5 232	5 100	4 910	4 685	5 253
Stamp duties	214	2 243	2 829	4 125	8 574	5 181	5 069	4 883	4 664	5 228
Duty on share capital creation	0	32	500	0	0	0	0	0	0	0
Duty to land registry office	5	38	28	46	85	51	31	27	21	25
Duty on transfers of shares	0	0	809	0	0	0	0	0	0	0
4500 Non-recurrent taxes	0	116	81	140	6	9	0	0	0	34
4510 On net wealth	..	0	0	0	0	0	0	0	..	0
4520 Other non-recurrent taxes	..	116	81	140	6	9	0	0	..	34
4600 Other recurrent taxes on property	0	0	0	0	0	0	0	0	0	0
5000 Taxes on goods and services	**8 727**	**63 437**	**129 630**	**206 502**	**282 855**	**261 019**	**277 780**	**285 889**	**290 350**	**293 301**
5100 Taxes on production, sale, transfer, etc	8 239	60 545	123 645	195 666	264 043	242 044	257 292	265 047	267 674	270 474
5110 General taxes	2 139	37 727	80 650	121 955	174 639	167 530	176 448	181 618	181 381	186 261
5111 Value added taxes	2 139	37 727	72 120	121 955	174 639	167 530	176 448	181 618	181 381	186 261
5112 Sales tax	0	0	0	0	0	0	0	0	0	0
5113 Other	0	0	8 530	0	0	0	0	0	0	0
Labour market contrib. concerning imports	..	..	4 903	..	..	..	..	..	..	..
Labour market contrib. concerning value added	..	..	3 627	..	..	..	..	..	..	..
5120 Taxes on specific goods and services	6 100	22 817	42 995	73 711	89 405	74 514	80 844	83 429	86 292	84 213

StatLink http://dx.doi.org/10.1787/888933416727

Table 4.7. **Denmark/Danemark** *(cont./suite)*

Details of tax revenue/Recettes fiscales détaillées

Million DKK

	1965	1980	1990	2000	2007	2009	2011	2012	2013	2014
5121 Excises	5 466	20 473	38 339	68 977	82 861	68 727	75 392	78 796	81 894	79 845
Duty on petrol	1 016	3 713	5 637	10 005	9 154	8 700	7 731	7 392	7 286	7 315
Motor vehicle registration duty	818	2 989	7 917	13 858	24 289	11 864	13 613	13 075	15 218	15 967
Cigarettes and tobacco duties	1 469	4 472	6 516	7 489	7 201	7 119	7 448	8 163	8 417	7 090
Duties on cigars, cheroots and cigarillos	234	220	128	80	40	33	32	52	47	54
Sale of revenue labels	0	3	10	13	13	8	3	3	4	4
Sales duties on chocolate and sugar	254	331	801	1 205	1 289	1 196	1 530	1 735	2 020	1 992
Raw material duty on chocolate and sugar	11	14	54	60	93	125	159	193	180	204
Special tax on chocolate and sugar	0	2	13	76	46	31	58	91	68	87
Duty on ice-cream	33	58	135	168	180	175	217	265	297	301
Duty on coffee	5	249	224	266	250	253	248	259	271	259
Duty on mineral water	68	195	466	505	418	413	397	505	374	0
Duty on beer	622	1 983	3 100	1 510	1 080	949	885	1 037	977	937
Duty on wine	122	611	1 448	1 166	1 032	1 054	1 133	1 519	1 674	1 688
Duty on spirits	412	1 432	1 982	1 756	1 213	1 065	1 062	1 074	1 127	1 155
Duty on restaurant sales of alcoholic bev.	150	0	0	0	0	0	0	0	0	0
Duty on wireless sets	55	67	0	0	0	0	0	0	0	0
Duty on television sets	0	93	-18	0	0	0	0	0	0	0
Duty on video recorders	0	17	-15	0	0	0	0	0	0	0
Duty on major household appliances	0	199	-10	0	0	0	0	0	0	0
Duty on grammophone records	10	46	84	0	0	0	0	0	0	0
Duty on playing cards	1	2	0	0	0	0	0	0	0	0
Duty on matches	5	3	-1	0	0	0	0	0	0	0
Duty on lighters	1	8	-4	0	0	0	0	0	0	0
Duty on electric bulbs	36	67	152	176	211	144	117	103	95	98
Duty on perfumery and toilet articles	91	214	506	0	0	0	0	0	0	0
Duty on almanacs	3	0	0	0	0	0	0	0	0	0
Duty on salmon	0	1	0	0	0	0	0	0	0	0
Duty on paper and cardboard	45	0	0	0	0	0	0	0	0	0
Duty on sugar	0	174	-8	0	0	0	0	0	0	0
Duty on tea	0	12	10	8	8	8	7	8	8	8
Duty on electricity	0	1 222	4 317	7 430	8 665	8 600	11 944	11 167	10 013	11 951
Duty on certain oil products	0	1 719	2 938	6 757	8 549	8 970	9 557	9 231	9 306	9 281
Duty on certain retail containers	0	100	397	594	727	693	640	690	715	311
Duty on gas	0	56	47	0	0	0	0	0	0	0
Duty on extraction and import of raw materials	0	16	129	172	220	121	149	133	132	136
Duty on disposable tableware	0	0	72	65	126	124	121	121	121	127
Duty on insecticides, herbicides, etc.	0	0	13	366	449	436	480	553	656	446
Duty on videotapes	0	0	0	0	0	0	0	0	0	0
Duty on coal, etc.	0	0	849	1 217	1 450	1 583	2 357	2 583	2 991	2 739
Other duties on goods and services	5	186	20	53	147	149	152	51	-13	180
Duty on waste	0	0	404	1 025	1 225	961	178	164	167	166
Duty on CFC	0	0	27	0	53	55	70	72	82	73
Duty on CO2	0	0	0	4 883	5 108	5 006	5 882	5 709	5 762	3 524
Duty on cigarette paper	0	0	0	68	32	28	29	35	36	38
Duty on rechargeable Ni-Cd batteries	0	0	0	21	17	6	3	1	3	2
Duty on piped water	0	0	0	1 357	1 371	1 371	1 333	1 516	1 584	1 603
Duty on carrier bags made of paper, plastic, etc.	0	0	0	178	210	202	197	194	186	184
Duty on tires	0	0	0	29	45	44	57	49	50	50
Duty on sulpher	0	0	0	165	108	68	48	44	51	41
Duty on chlorinated solvents	0	0	0	2	0	0	0	0	0	0
Duty on natural gas	0	0	0	2 532	3 375	3 515	4 324	4 033	5 255	4 090
Duty on nitrogen	0	0	0	30	27	22	17	13	21	16
Duty on specific growth stimulants	0	0	0	0	0	0	0	0	0	0
Duty on PVC-film	0	0	0	7	12	11	11	10	10	10
Duty on PVC and phathalates	0	0	0	31	42	26	21	21	18	19
Duty on lead accumulators	0	0	0	14	0	0	0	0	0	0
Duty on mineral phosphorus	0	0	0	0	51	40	51	47	49	52
Surcharge on alcoholic soft drinks	0	0	0	0	17	12	49	37	33	34
Duty on nitrogen oxides	0	0	0	0	0	0	197	505	870	743
Duty on saturated fat	0	0	0	0	0	0	283	1 223	0	0
Duty on PSO (Public Service Obligations)	0	0	0	3 641	4 319	3 549	2 601	5 121	5 734	6 874
5122 Profits of fiscal monopolies	16	183	404	1 402	1 648	1 429	1 576	1 413	1 339	1 221
5123 Customs and import duties	556	1 113	1 849	0	0	0	0	0	0	0
Customs duties	0	1 032	1 779	..	..	..	..	..	..	..
Temporary import surcharge	556	0	0	..	..	..	..	..	..	..
Import duties on agricultural produce	0	81	70	..	..	..	..	..	..	..
5124 Taxes on exports	0	0	0	0	0	0	0	0	0	0
5125 Taxes on investment goods	0	0	0	0	0	0	0	0	0	0

StatLink http://dx.doi.org/10.1787/888933416727

Table 4.7. **Denmark/Danemark** *(cont./suite)*

Details of tax revenue/Recettes fiscales détaillées

Million DKK

	1965	1980	1990	2000	2007	2009	2011	2012	2013	2014
5126 Taxes on specific services	62	771	1 567	3 019	4 525	4 011	3 843	3 187	3 008	3 114
Sales tax on gambling stakes races	17	28	20	12	18	16	16	16	15	14
Tax on football pools	31	152	284	942	1 143	1 039	1 102	39	0	0
Tax on cinema tickets	14	0	0	0	0	0	0	0	0	0
Duty on motor vehicle compl. insurance	0	470	923	1 327	2 104	1 898	1 746	1 732	1 598	1 578
Duty on insurance on pleasure boats	0	13	57	66	100	115	112	102	127	130
Duty on charter flight	0	109	283	0	0	0	0	0	0	0
Turnover tax on 6-win horse race betting	0	0	0	0	0	0	0	0	0	0
Duty on casinos	0	0	0	180	261	185	186	197	192	187
Passenger duty	0	0	0	477	6	0	0	0	0	0
Duty on the Danish State Lottery	0	0	0	16	35	40	42	42	42	45
Duty on slot machines	0	0	0	0	858	718	638	651	545	590
Duty on gambling	0	0	0	0	0	0	0	235	288	355
Duty on online casinos	0	0	0	0	0	0	0	173	202	215
5127 Other taxes on internat. trade and transactions	0	0	0	0	0	0	0	0	0	0
5128 Other taxes	0	277	837	312	370	348	33	33	51	33
Duty paid to ECSC	..	4	5	0	0	0	0	0	0	0
Sugar storing duty	..	83	113	62	0	0	0	0	0	0
Duty on the production of sugar	..	81	145	249	-26	33	33	33	51	33
Duty on milk co-reponsibility levy	..	109	255	0	0	0	0	0	0	0
Grain co-reponsibility levy	..	0	319	0	0	0	0	0	0	0
Restructuring scheme for EU sugar system	..	0	0	0	397	314	0	0	0	0
5130 Unallocable between 5110 and 5120	0	0	0	0	0	0	0	0	0	0
5200 Taxes on use of goods and perform activities	488	2 893	4 410	7 468	14 088	14 510	14 719	15 010	16 180	15 972
5210 Recurrent taxes	488	2 893	4 410	7 468	14 088	14 510	14 719	15 010	15 966	15 771
5211 Paid by households: motor vehicles	199	1 874	2 922	5 485	7 105	7 384	7 538	7 568	7 867	8 021
Weight duty automobiles	199	1 874	2 922	5 318	6 954	7 224	7 385	7 424	7 709	7 787
Recycling fee on cars	0	0	0	167	151	160	153	144	158	234
5212 Paid by others: motor vehicles	287	1 014	1 441	1 919	3 125	3 080	2 919	3 028	3 563	3 220
Weight duty automobiles	287	1 014	1 441	1 612	2 652	2 650	2 547	2 651	3 180	2 839
Road charges	0	0	0	307	473	430	372	378	383	381
5213 Paid in respect of other goods	2	5	47	64	3 858	4 046	4 262	4 414	4 537	4 530
5220 Non-recurrent taxes	0	0	0	0	0	0	0	0	214	201
5300 Unallocable between 5100 and 5200	0	0	1 575	3 368	4 724	4 465	5 769	5 831	6 497	6 855
6000 Other taxes	**0**	**0**	**0**	**391**	**190**	**187**	**174**	**193**	**152**	**220**
6100 Paid solely by business	..	..	..	391	190	187	174	193	152	220
6200 Other	..	..	..	0	0	0	0	0	0	0
Custom duties collected for the EU	..	..	..	**2 325**	**3 282**	**2 647**	**3 177**	**2 962**	**2 824**	**3 001**
Non-wastable tax credits										
Non-wastable tax credits against 1110	..	..	..	..	..	..	4 908	4 875	5 515	5 495
Tax expenditure component	..	..	..	..	..	..	4 663	4 631	5 239	5 220
Transfer component	..	..	..	..	..	..	245	244	276	275
Non-wastable tax credits against 1210	..	..	..	..	..	..	0	0	0	0
Tax expenditure component	..	..	..	..	..	..	..	..	..	..
Transfer component	..	..	..	..	..	..	..	..	..	..
Total tax revenue on cash basis	..	..	..	..	..	..	..	..	..	..
Total tax revenue on accrual basis	**20 821**	**166 358**	**382 232**	**623 911**	**809 988**	**777 375**	**831 172**	**866 284**	**899 379**	**971 772**
Conciliation with National Accounts										
Additional taxes included in National Accounts	0	0	0	0	0	0	0	0	0	0
Taxes excluded from National Accounts	0	0	0	0	0	0	0	0	0	0
Difference in treatment of tax credits	0	0	0	0	0	0	4 663	4 632	5 240	5 221
Capital transfer for uncollected revenue	0	-1 374	-2 387	-1 917	-2 726	-3 043	-3 905	-3 837	-8 738	-8 588
Voluntary social security contributions	0	1 673	8 087	16 633	17 061	16 816	17 610	16 320	14 655	14 718
Miscellaneous differences	0	0	0	0	0	0	0	0	0	0
National Accounts: Taxes and actual social contributions	20 821	166 657	387 932	638 626	824 324	791 148	849 539	883 399	910 536	983 122
Imputed social contributions	0	5 958	4 592	6 223	5 693	5 453	5 100	4 842	4 520	4 256
National Accounts: Taxes and all social contributions	20 821	172 615	392 525	644 849	830 017	796 601	854 639	888 242	915 056	987 378

Notes : Year ending 31st December.

The figures are on an accrual basis.

Heading 2300 includes a small amount of voluntary contributions which cannot be isolated.

Source : Danmarks Statistik.

StatLink http://dx.doi.org/10.1787/888933416727

Table 4.8. **Estonia/Estonie**

Details of tax revenue/Recettes fiscales détaillées

Million EUR

	1965	1980	1990	2000	2007	2009	2011	2012	2013	2014
Total tax revenue	..	..	..	**1 919**	**5 082**	**4 939**	**5 252**	**5 680**	**5 988**	**6 473**
Total tax revenue exclusive of customs duties	..	..	..	..	**5 047**	**4 920**	**5 223**	**5 650**	**5 960**	**6 443**
1000 Taxes on income, profits and capital gains	..	..	..	**476**	**1 197**	**1 045**	**1 047**	**1 184**	**1 357**	**1 479**
1100 Of individuals	..	..	..	421	936	789	846	931	1 031	1 134
1110 On income and profits	..	..	..	421	936	789	846	931	1 031	1 134
1120 On capital gains	..	..	..	0	0	0	0	0	0	0
1200 Corporate	..	..	..	55	261	256	201	252	327	345
1210 On profits	..	..	..	55	65	39	37	56	62	69
1220 On capital gains	..	..	..	0	196	218	164	197	265	276
1300 Unallocable between 1100 and 1200	..	..	..	0	0	0	0	0	0	0
2000 Social security contributions	..	..	..	**674**	**1 683**	**1 819**	**1 935**	**2 000**	**2 077**	**2 178**
2100 Employees	..	..	..	0	28	75	127	137	109	114
2110 On a payroll basis	..	..	..	..	28	75	127	137	109	114
2120 On an income tax basis	..	..	..	..	0	0	0	0	0	0
2200 Employers	..	..	..	662	1 635	1 720	1 789	1 845	1 949	2 045
2210 On a payroll basis	..	..	..	662	1 635	1 720	1 789	1 845	1 949	2 045
2220 On an income tax basis	..	..	..	0	0	0	0	0	0	0
2300 Self-employed or non-employed	..	..	..	12	21	25	19	18	19	20
2310 On a payroll basis	..	..	..	12	21	25	19	18	19	20
2320 On an income tax basis	..	..	..	0	0	0	0	0	0	0
2400 Unallocable between 2100, 2200 and 2300	..	..	..	0	0	0	0	0	0	0
2410 On a payroll basis	..	..	..	..	..	..	..	..	..	..
2420 On an income tax basis	..	..	..	..	..	..	..	..	..	..
3000 Taxes on payroll and workforce	..	..	..	**0**	**0**	**0**	**0**	**0**	**0**	**0**
4000 Taxes on property	..	..	..	**24**	**35**	**48**	**51**	**59**	**57**	**59**
4100 Recurrent taxes on immovable property	..	..	..	24	35	48	51	59	57	59
Land tax	..	..	..	24	35	48	51	59	57	59
4110 Households	..	..	..	..	..	..	..	..	..	..
4120 Others	..	..	..	..	..	..	..	..	..	..
4200 Recurrent taxes on net wealth	..	..	..	0	0	0	0	0	0	0
4210 Individual	..	..	..	..	..	..	..	..	..	..
4220 Corporate	..	..	..	..	..	..	..	..	..	..
4300 Estate, inheritance and gift taxes	..	..	..	0	0	0	0	0	0	0
4310 Estate and inheritance taxes	..	..	..	..	..	..	..	..	..	..
4320 Gift taxes	..	..	..	..	..	..	..	..	..	..
4400 Taxes on financial and capital transactions	..	..	..	0	0	0	0	0	0	0
4500 Non-recurrent taxes	..	..	..	0	0	0	0	0	0	0
4510 On net wealth	..	..	..	..	..	..	..	..	..	..
4520 Other non-recurrent taxes	..	..	..	..	..	..	..	..	..	..
4600 Other recurrent taxes on property	..	..	..	0	0	0	0	0	0	0
5000 Taxes on goods and services	..	..	..	**745**	**2 131**	**2 007**	**2 190**	**2 408**	**2 468**	**2 727**
5100 Taxes on production, sale, transfer, etc	..	..	..	723	2 064	1 946	2 130	2 349	2 402	2 602
5110 General taxes	..	..	..	521	1 423	1 224	1 380	1 513	1 558	1 711
5111 Value added taxes	..	..	..	520	1 423	1 224	1 363	1 508	1 558	1 711
5112 Sales tax	..	..	..	0	0	0	17	5	0	0
5113 Other	..	..	..	0	0	0	0	0	0	0
5120 Taxes on specific goods and services	..	..	..	202	640	721	751	836	844	891
5121 Excises	..	..	..	183	577	697	711	791	796	844
Alcohol	..	..	..	62	153	174	181	204	212	233
Tobacco	..	..	..	36	134	171	139	160	169	171
Fuel	..	..	..	76	290	331	359	394	383	406
Motor vehicle	..	..	..	9	0	0	0	0	0	0
Package	..	..	..	0	0	0	0	0	0	0
Fur	..	..	..	0	0	0	0	0	0	0
Electricity	..	..	..	0	0	22	32	33	33	33
5122 Profits of fiscal monopolies	..	..	..	0	0	0	0	0	0	0
5123 Customs and import duties	..	..	..	2	0	0	0	0	0	0
5124 Taxes on exports	..	..	..	0	0	0	0	0	0	0
5125 Taxes on investment goods	..	..	..	0	0	0	0	0	0	0
5126 Taxes on specific services	..	..	..	17	64	24	39	45	48	47
Gambling tax	..	..	..	7	30	18	19	21	22	23
Advertising tax	..	..	..	1	3	2	3	3	4	4
Postal service payment	..	..	..	0	0	0	0	0	0	0
Liquid fuel stockpiling fee	..	..	..	0	2	3	5	5	6	6
Contributions to the Guarantee Fund	..	..	..	9	29	1	12	16	17	13
5127 Other taxes on internat. trade and transactions	..	..	..	0	0	0	0	0	0	0
5128 Other taxes	..	..	..	0	0	0	0	0	0	0
5130 Unallocable between 5110 and 5120	..	..	..	0	0	0	0	0	0	0
5200 Taxes on use of goods and perform activities	..	..	..	22	68	62	60	59	65	125

StatLink http://dx.doi.org/10.1787/888933416735

Table 4.8. **Estonia/Estonie** *(cont./suite)*

Details of tax revenue/Recettes fiscales détaillées

Million EUR

	1965	1980	1990	2000	2007	2009	2011	2012	2013	2014
5210 Recurrent taxes	..	..	..	22	68	62	60	59	65	107
Car registration fee	..	..	..	2	5	3	6	7	7	7
Heavy vehicle tax	..	..	..	0	4	4	4	4	4	4
5211 Paid by households: motor vehicles	..	..	..	..	..	..	..	..	..	..
5212 Paid by others: motor vehicles	..	..	..	..	..	..	..	..	..	..
5213 Paid in respect of other goods	..	..	..	20	58	55	50	48	55	96
Business and professional licenses	..	..	..	3	2	1	1	1	1	1
Pollution fee	..	..	..	10	44	41	34	31	37	44
Specific use of water	..	..	..	4	9	11	13	13	14	12
Fees for closure of roads, streets and squares	..	..	..	0	1	1	1	1	1	1
Fishing fees	..	..	..	1	1	1	1	2	2	2
Tax on motor vehicle	..	..	..	2	0	0	0	0	0	0
Boat tax	..	..	..	0	0	0	0	0	0	0
Animal tax	..	..	..	0	0	0	0	0	0	0
5220 Non-recurrent taxes	..	..	..	0	0	0	0	0	0	18
Revenue from the sale of emission permits	..	..	..	..	..	..	..	..	..	18
5300 Unallocable between 5100 and 5200	..	..	..	0	0	0	0	0	0	0
6000 Other taxes	**..**	**..**	**..**	**0**	**0**	**0**	**0**	**0**	**0**	**0**
6100 Paid solely by business	..	..	..	..	..	..	..	..	..	..
6200 Other	..	..	..	..	..	..	..	..	..	..
Other taxes	..	..	..	..	..	..	..	..	..	..
Custom duties collected for the EU	**..**	**..**	**..**	**..**	**35**	**20**	**29**	**29**	**29**	**30**
Total tax revenue on cash basis	**..**	**..**	**..**	**1 907**	**5 003**	**4 862**	**5 229**	**5 640**	**5 964**	**6 402**
Total tax revenue on accrual basis	**..**	**..**	**..**	**1 919**	**5 082**	**4 939**	**5 252**	**5 680**	**5 988**	**6 473**
Conciliation with National Accounts										
Additional taxes included in National Accounts	..	..	..	0	0	0	0	0	0	0
Taxes excluded from National Accounts	..	..	..	0	0	0	0	0	0	0
Difference in treatment of tax credits	..	..	..	0	0	0	0	0	0	0
Capital transfer for uncollected revenue	..	..	..	0	0	0	0	0	0	0
Voluntary social security contributions	..	..	..	0	0	0	0	0	0	0
Miscellaneous differences	..	..	..	0	0	0	0	0	0	0
National Accounts: Taxes and actual social contributions	..	..	..	1 919	5 082	4 939	5 252	5 680	5 988	6 473
Imputed social contributions	.	..	..	4	20	32	33	35	38	44
National Accounts: Taxes and all social contributions	..	..	..	1 922	5 102	4 972	5 285	5 715	6 026	6 517

Notes : Year ending 31st December.
Data on an accrual basis.
Source : Statistics Estonia.

StatLink http://dx.doi.org/10.1787/888933416735

Table 4.9. Finland/Finlande

Details of tax revenue/Recettes fiscales détaillées

Million EUR

	1965	1980	1990	2000	2007	2009	2011	2012	2013	2014
Total tax revenue	**1 362**	**11 895**	**39 050**	**62 435**	**77 447**	**74 103**	**82 750**	**85 269**	**88 688**	**90 027**
Total tax revenue exclusive of custom duties	..	..	..	**62 306**	**77 248**	**73 951**	**82 561**	**85 085**	**88 522**	**89 857**
1000 Taxes on income, profits and capital gains	**564**	**4 654**	**15 323**	**26 911**	**30 358**	**26 505**	**29 334**	**29 202**	**30 797**	**31 479**
1100 Of individuals	453	4 248	13 562	19 118	23 396	23 011	24 181	24 989	25 998	27 523
1110 On income and profits	453	4 234	13 521	19 118	23 396	23 011	24 181	24 989	25 998	27 523
Tax on income	125	1 827	5 918	9 036	9 086	7 103	7 682	7 890	7 903	9 148
The final withdrawal tax on interest income	0	0	0	92	254	493	198	237	207	142
Communal tax	279	2 376	7 603	9 990	14 056	15 415	16 301	16 862	17 888	18 233
Seaman's tax	3	31	0	0	0	0	0	0	0	0
National pension contributions	32	0	0	0	0	0	0	0	0	0
National health insurance contributions	15	0	0	0	0	0	0	0	0	0
1120 On capital gains	0	14	42	0	0	0	0	0	0	0
Tax on lottery prizes	..	14	42	..	..	..	..	..	..	..
1200 Corporate	111	405	1 761	7 792	6 962	3 494	5 153	4 213	4 799	3 956
1210 On profits	111	405	1 761	7 792	6 962	3 494	5 153	4 213	4 799	3 956
Tax on income	72	202	1 001	4 758	5 298	2 222	3 375	2 906	3 227	2 433
Communal tax	36	187	699	2 900	1 541	1 184	1 647	1 208	1 456	1 412
Church tax	3	16	61	134	123	88	131	99	116	111
1220 On capital gains	0	0	0	0	0	0	0	0	0	0
1300 Unallocable between 1100 and 1200	0	0	0	0	0	0	0	0	0	0
2000 Social security contributions	**93**	**2 776**	**10 012**	**15 756**	**21 384**	**22 055**	**23 776**	**25 261**	**25 632**	**26 011**
2100 Employees	1	394	1 152	2 926	4 050	4 141	5 124	5 724	5 811	6 101
For employment pension schemes	1	10	23	2 120	2 950	3 093	3 692	4 190	4 235	4 545
For unemployment schemes	0	0	0	435	369	188	427	459	457	378
2110 On a payroll basis	..	10	23	2 565	3 319	3 281	4 119	4 649	4 692	4 923
2120 On an income tax basis	..	384	1 129	361	731	860	1 005	1 075	1 119	1 178
National pension contributions	..	251	502	2	0	0	0	0	0	0
National health insurance contributions	..	133	627	359	731	860	1 005	1 075	1 119	1 178
2200 Employers	93	2 230	8 127	11 571	15 715	16 261	16 937	17 674	17 888	17 885
For national pension schemes	29	685	1 502	1 566	1 331	632	0	0	0	0
For national health insurance	10	244	792	839	1 142	1 418	1 592	1 658	1 612	1 696
For unemployment schemes	3	106	206	1 143	1 346	1 296	1 610	1 736	1 775	1 579
For employment pension schemes	50	1 195	5 627	8 023	11 896	12 915	13 735	14 280	14 501	14 610
For accident and group life insurance premiums	0	0	0	0	0	0	0	0	0	0
2210 On a payroll basis	..	2 230	8 127	11 571	15 715	16 261	16 937	17 674	17 888	17 885
2220 On an income tax basis	..	0	0	0	0	0	0	0	0	0
2300 Self-employed or non-employed	0	152	733	1 259	1 619	1 653	1 715	1 863	1 933	2 025
For employment pension schemes	..	84	394	576	817	888	1 045	1 147	1 187	1 240
2310 On a payroll basis	..	84	394	576	817	888	1 045	1 147	1 187	1 240
2320 On an income tax basis	..	68	339	683	802	765	670	716	746	785
National pension contributions	..	43	151	5	0	0	0	0	0	0
National health insurance contributions	..	25	188	678	802	765	670	716	746	785
2400 Unallocable between 2100, 2200 and 2300	0	0	0	0	0	0	0	0	0	0
2410 On a payroll basis	..	..	..	..	..	..	..	..	..	..
2420 On an income tax basis	..	..	..	..	..	..	..	..	..	..
3000 Taxes on payroll and workforce	**70**	**22**	**0**	**0**	**0**	**0**	**0**	**0**	**0**	**0**
Soc. Sec. contr. for children allowance	70	22	..	..	..	..	..	..	..	..
4000 Taxes on property	**54**	**221**	**956**	**1 518**	**2 012**	**1 903**	**2 138**	**2 361**	**2 599**	**2 719**
4100 Recurrent taxes on immovable property	0	0	76	569	855	974	1 199	1 270	1 363	1 512
4110 Households	..	..	46	273	405	462	592	628	623	691
4120 Others	..	..	30	296	450	512	607	642	740	821
4200 Recurrent taxes on net wealth	24	24	26	179	0	0	0	0	0	0
4210 Individual	11	23	25	175	..	..	..	..	..	..
4220 Corporate	13	2	1	4	..	..	..	..	..	..
4300 Estate, inheritance and gift taxes	3	26	146	368	459	440	395	509	646	499
4310 Estate and inheritance taxes	3	21	121	307	384	368	330	426	541	418
4320 Gift taxes	1	5	25	61	75	72	65	83	105	81
4400 Taxes on financial and capital transactions	27	170	707	401	698	489	544	582	590	708
Stamp duty excluded entertainment	27	170	688	-20	0	0	0	0	0	0
Credit tax	0	0	19	0	0	0	0	0	0	0
Transfer tax	0	0	0	421	698	489	544	582	590	708
4500 Non-recurrent taxes	0	0	0	0	0	0	0	0	0	0
4510 On net wealth	..	..	..	..	..	..	..	..	..	..
4520 Other non-recurrent taxes	..	..	..	..	..	..	..	..	..	..
4600 Other recurrent taxes on property	0	0	0	0	0	0	0	0	0	0
5000 Taxes on goods and services	**578**	**4 202**	**12 710**	**18 091**	**23 425**	**23 419**	**27 240**	**28 186**	**29 430**	**29 572**
5100 Taxes on production, sale, transfer, etc	570	4 158	12 553	17 651	22 754	22 700	26 407	27 355	28 496	28 522
5110 General taxes	251	2 062	7 519	10 869	15 207	15 176	17 315	17 987	18 888	18 948

StatLink http://dx.doi.org/10.1787/888933416746

Table 4.9. **Finland/Finlande** *(cont./suite)*

Details of tax revenue/Recettes fiscales détaillées

Million EUR

	1965	1980	1990	2000	2007	2009	2011	2012	2013	2014
5111 Value added taxes	251	2 062	7 519	10 869	15 207	15 176	17 315	17 987	18 888	18 948
Value added taxes	251	2 062	7 519	9 616	13 657	13 434	15 281	15 814	16 561	16 638
VAT repayments of local government	0	0	0	849	1 550	1 742	2 034	2 173	2 327	2 310
Social Insur. Institutions' part of VAT revenue	0	0	0	404	0	0	0	0	0	0
5112 Sales tax	0	0	0	0	0	0	0	0	0	0
5113 Other	0	0	0	0	0	0	0	0	0	0
Suppl. sales tax on consumer durables	..	..	..	..	..	..	..	..	..	..
5120 Taxes on specific goods and services	319	2 096	5 034	6 782	7 547	7 524	9 092	9 368	9 608	9 574
5121 Excises	183	1 615	3 811	5 613	6 013	5 888	7 319	7 514	7 511	7 431
Excise on tobacco products	52	206	473	561	622	693	718	749	852	788
Excise on sweetments	6	23	26	0	0	0	0	0	0	0
Excise on medium, strong beer	3	109	419	0	0	0	0	0	0	0
Excise on non-alcoholic beverages	2	17	22	32	35	35	134	197	204	257
Excise on certain foodstuffs	3	218	36	0	0	0	0	0	0	0
Excise on liquid fuels	58	504	983	2 582	2 907	3 052	3 875	3 956	3 925	3 846
Excise on motor cars	28	238	697	1 059	1 217	687	1 068	1 006	931	916
Tax on alcoholic beverages	29	353	813	1 239	1 016	1 223	1 291	1 374	1 355	1 381
Levies on pharmacy	2	16	46	86	113	129	144	145	153	158
Levies for price reduction on butter	0	3	0	0	0	0	0	0	0	0
Levies for marketing of milk	0	12	58	0	0	0	0	0	0	0
Excise on margarines	0	18	55	0	0	0	0	0	0	0
Stock-building levies on liquid fuels	0	15	44	46	50	45	46	44	45	43
Excise on sugar products	0	18	34	0	0	0	0	0	0	0
Excise on feeding stuffs	0	0	0	0	0	0	0	0	0	0
Excise on fertilizers	0	21	21	0	0	0	0	0	0	0
Excise on oil-based concentrated feed	0	1	0	0	0	0	0	0	0	0
Excise on protein feed	0	0	0	0	0	0	0	0	0	0
Equalization fee agricultural products	0	8	29	0	0	0	0	0	0	0
Excise on albumen	0	0	30	0	0	0	0	0	0	0
Tax on electricity	0	65	0	0	0	0	0	0	0	0
Oil damage levy	0	0	7	5	8	8	24	24	27	25
Oil waste levy	0	0	4	3	4	4	4	4	4	3
Price difference compensations	0	-231	0	0	0	0	0	0	0	0
The milk quota charge	0	0	6	0	0	0	0	0	0	0
Levies for marketing of special agric. prod.	0	0	0	0	0	0	0	0	0	0
Excise on phosphorous fertilizers	0	0	7	0	0	0	0	0	0	0
Excise on certain beverage packages	0	0	0	0	41	12	15	15	15	14
5122 Profits of fiscal monopolies	38	86	202	0	0	0	0	0	0	0
Excess profits on alcohol	38	86	202	..	..	..	..	..	..	..
5123 Customs and import duties	88	235	423	0	0	0	0	0	0	0
Import duties	62	126	232	..	..	..	..	..	..	..
Import levies on agricultural products	26	6	12	..	..	..	..	..	..	..
Local import duties (Town dues)	1	0	0	..	..	..	..	..	..	..
Import levies price stabilisation fund	0	3	0	..	..	..	..	..	..	..
Custom duties and levies on agricultural goods	0	0	0	..	..	..	..	..	..	..
Equalization tax	0	100	179	..	..	..	..	..	..	..
5124 Taxes on exports	0	0	0	0	0	0	0	0	0	0
Export duties	..	..	..	..	..	..	..	..	..	..
Levies on export	..	..	..	..	..	..	..	..	..	..
Counter-cyclical tax exports	..	..	..	..	..	..	..	..	..	..
5125 Taxes on investment goods	0	0	0	0	0	0	0	0	0	0
Investment tax on buildings	..	..	..	..	..	..	..	..	..	..
5126 Taxes on specific services	9	161	599	1 160	1 533	1 635	1 772	1 853	2 096	2 142
Net revenue of betting	8	94	329	703	807	868	883	901	948	963
Tax on motion pictures	0	0	0	0	0	0	0	0	0	0
Stamp duties on entertainment	2	5	0	0	0	0	0	0	0	0
Fire protection levy	0	3	7	6	8	9	9	10	10	11
Tax on waste	0	0	0	33	56	45	64	56	56	44
Rail tax	0	0	0	0	18	17	18	16	19	18
Tax on insurance premiums	0	58	263	337	509	557	626	660	712	750
Tax on lottery prizes	0	0	0	80	135	139	172	210	217	218
Tax on telecommunications	0	0	0	0	0	0	0	0	0	0
Bank tax	0	0	0	0	0	0	0	0	134	138
Contributions to the Resolution Fund	0	0	0	0	0	0	0	0	0	0
5127 Other taxes on internat. trade and transactions	0	0	0	0	0	0	0	0	0	0
Tax on charter flights	..	..	..	..	..	..	..	..	..	..
5128 Other taxes	0	0	0	9	1	1	1	1	1	1
Sugar levy	..	..	..	9	1	1	1	1	1	1
Steel and coal levy	..	..	..	0	0	0	0	0	0	0
5130 Unallocable between 5110 and 5120	0	0	0	0	0	0	0	0	0	0

StatLink http://dx.doi.org/10.1787/888933416746

Table 4.9. **Finland/Finlande** *(cont./suite)*

Details of tax revenue/Recettes fiscales détaillées

Million EUR

	1965	1980	1990	2000	2007	2009	2011	2012	2013	2014
5200 Taxes on use of goods and perform activities	8	44	157	440	671	719	833	831	934	1 050
5210 Recurrent taxes	8	44	157	423	637	686	792	791	897	910
5211 Paid by households: motor vehicles	0	2	5	165	486	511	585	615	696	706
5212 Paid by others: motor vehicles	7	32	135	235	126	144	174	143	170	171
5213 Paid in respect of other goods	1	10	17	22	25	31	33	33	31	33
Dog licenses	1	2	4	5	3	2	1	2	2	1
Hunting and fishing licenses	1	7	13	17	17	23	24	23	23	23
Seamens welfare and rescue levy	0	0	0	1	1	1	1	1	1	1
Nuclear energy research levy	0	0	0	0	4	5	7	7	5	8
5220 Non-recurrent taxes	0	0	0	17	34	33	41	40	37	140
Vehicle registration tax	..	..	..	17	34	33	41	40	37	36
Income from auction of emission allowances	..	..	..	0	0	0	0	0	0	104
5300 Unallocable between 5100 and 5200	0	0	0	0	0	0	0	0	0	0
6000 Other taxes	**2**	**21**	**50**	**30**	**69**	**69**	**73**	**75**	**64**	**76**
6100 Paid solely by business	0	0	0	0	0	0	0	0	0	0
6200 Other	2	21	50	30	69	69	73	75	64	76
Custom duties collected for the EU	..	..	..	**129**	**199**	**152**	**189**	**184**	**166**	**170**
Total tax revenue on cash basis	**1 362**	**11 895**	**39 398**	**61 639**	**77 110**	**74 057**	**82 474**	**85 244**	**88 416**	**89 907**
Total tax revenue on accrual basis	..	..	**39 050**	**62 435**	**77 447**	**74 103**	**82 750**	**85 269**	**88 688**	**90 027**
Conciliation with National Accounts										
Additional taxes included in National Accounts	..	0	0	0	0	0	0	0	0	0
Taxes excluded from National Accounts	..	0	0	0	0	0	0	0	0	0
Difference in treatment of tax credits	..	0	0	0	0	0	0	0	0	0
Capital transfer for uncollected revenue	..	0	0	0	0	0	0	0	0	0
Voluntary social security contributions	..	262	632	235	228	220	261	267	270	277
Miscellaneous differences	..	0	0	0	0	0	0	0	0	0
National Accounts: Taxes and actual social contributions	..	12 157	39 682	62 671	77 675	74 323	83 011	85 536	88 958	90 304
Imputed social contributions	..	513	688	30	0	0	0	0	0	0
National Accounts: Taxes and all social contributions	..	12 670	40 370	62 701	77 675	74 323	83 011	85 536	88 958	90 304

Notes : Year ending 31st December.

From 1988, data are on accrual basis.

Finland has an imputation system where the full credit is taken into account in shareholders taxation. According to estimates made by the National Board of Taxation, the credit given to shareholders was 193 millions euros in 1991; the effects on personal income taxation are estimated.

Headings 2120 and 2320: The breakdown of contributions paid by employees and self-employed or non-employed is estimated.

Heading 4200: All figures in this subheading are estimated.

Heading 4400: Stamp duties include payment for some government services where the levy can be regarded as requited (the levy is linked to the cost of providing the service). However, they are classified as taxes and recorded under this subheading as taxes on financial and capital transactions because the amounts involved cannot be identified.

Heading 5121: The negative item under the title «Price difference compensations» refers to the subsidies paid out on agricultural products under the price compensation scheme which can be offset against any positive tax liability which arising under the same scheme. From 1983, this item has been offset against revenues from excises on certain foodstuffs, on medium and stronger beer and on non-alcoholic beverages.

Heading 5126: Prior to 1979, no figures are available for amounts paid under the Fire protection levy.

Heading 5212: Prior to 1990, a part of the tax is paid by «households».

Source : Bulletin of Statistics; Central Statistical Office (for Central Government revenues); the Annual report of the National Pension Institute and Official Statistics of Finland Series XXIIA published by the Ministry and Social Affairs (for the Social Security and private pension respectively); supplementary information from unpublished sources.

StatLink http://dx.doi.org/10.1787/888933416746

Table 4.10. **France**

Details of tax revenue/Recettes fiscales détaillées

Million EUR

	1965	1980	1990	2000	2007	2009	2011	2012	2013	2014
Recettes fiscales totales	**25 776**	**178 576**	**433 771**	**643 309**	**828 971**	**806 916**	**895 101**	**929 943**	**963 951**	**979 844**
Recettes fiscales totales excluant les droits de douane	..	..	..	**641 796**	**827 314**	**805 455**	**893 235**	**928 060**	**962 109**	**978 017**
1000 Impôts sur revenu, bénéfices et gains en capital	**4 095**	**30 019**	**69 649**	**160 363**	**197 939**	**167 118**	**208 366**	**223 128**	**235 964**	**233 613**
1100 Des personnes physiques	2 736	20 734	46 272	115 885	141 405	139 193	153 911	168 780	179 715	183 614
1110 Sur le revenu et les bénéfices	2 723	20 674	46 252	115 884	141 405	139 193	153 911	168 780	179 715	183 614
Impôt sur revenu personnes physiques	..	18 207	39 237	49 548	48 597	46 113	53 245	61 308	70 098	72 116
Retenue source sur B.N.C.	..	51	189	293	559	416	530	621	598	646
Retenue sur capitaux mobiliers	..	2 333	3 971	0	0	0	0	0	0	0
CSG, FSV, CRDS	..	0	0	65 953	92 204	92 564	99 877	106 123	108 247	109 044
Taxe forfaitaire sur métaux précieux,	..	70	58	47	37	39	88	100	69	67
Ressources sur cumuls rémunérations	..	7	20	38	0	0	0	0	0	0
Contribution sociale de solidarité	..	0	2 207	5	0	30	109	386	381	0
Autres	..	6	571	0	8	31	62	242	322	1 741
1120 Sur les gains en capital	14	59	20	1	0	0	0	0	0	0
Sur les gains en capital	..	0	0	0	..	..	..	..	..	0
Prélèv. sur bénéf. construction immobilière	..	59	20	1	..	..	..	..	..	0
1200 Des sociétés	1 358	9 158	23 117	44 478	56 534	27 925	54 455	54 348	56 249	49 999
1210 Sur les bénéfices	1 358	9 158	23 117	44 478	56 534	27 925	54 455	54 348	56 249	49 999
Impôts sur les sociétés (émission de rôles)	..	8 524	20 804	39 755	51 063	20 286	46 075	44 554	46 474	42 080
3% dividendes	..	0	0	0	0	0	0	193	1 943	1 927
Retenue sur capitaux mobiliers	..	487	1 333	1 460	3 492	5 480	6 916	8 057	5 894	4 956
Précomptes sur bénéfices distribués (devenu prélèvement exceptionnel de 25% en 2005)	..	36	247	1 135	88	63	13	1	-6	60
Prélèv. except. entrep. travail temporaire	..	0	0	0	0	0	0	0	0	0
Contribution sociale sur bénéfices des sociétés	..	0	0	589	158	601	776	769	1 160	887
Imposition annuelle forfaitaire	..	111	658	1 484	1 656	1 399	592	662	680	15
Prélèvement except. assurances	..	0	61	55	64	96	83	112	104	74
Autres (prélèv. except. entrep. pétrol.)	..	0	14	0	13	0	0	0	0	0
1220 Sur les gains en capital	0	0	0	0	0	0	0	0	0	0
1300 Non-ventilables entre 1100 et 1200	0	127	260	0	0	0	0	0	0	0
2000 Cotisations de sécurité sociale	**8 804**	**76 235**	**191 141**	**231 875**	**307 663**	**317 560**	**336 595**	**346 137**	**356 934**	**366 338**
2100 A la charge des salariés	1 701	19 851	57 347	57 686	76 815	77 172	80 987	83 669	88 097	91 057
Cotisations effectives	..	19 851	57 347	57 686	76 815	77 172	80 987	83 669	88 097	91 057
2110 Sur la base du salaire	..	..	..	57 686	76 815	77 172	80 987	83 669	88 097	91 057
2120 Sur la base de l'impôt sur les revenus	..	..	..	0	0	0	0	0	0	0
2200 A la charge des employeurs	6 525	50 742	118 079	159 476	208 688	215 326	229 873	235 530	240 672	246 351
Cotisations effectives	..	50 742	118 079	159 476	208 688	215 326	229 873	235 530	240 672	246 351
2210 Sur la base du salaire	..	..	..	159 476	208 688	215 326	229 873	235 530	240 672	246 351
2220 Sur la base de l'impôt sur les revenus	..	..	..	0	0	0	0	0	0	0
2300 A charge des travailleurs indép. ou sans emploi	578	5 642	15 714	14 713	22 160	25 062	25 735	26 938	28 165	28 930
Cotisations effectives	..	5 642	15 714	14 713	22 160	25 062	25 735	26 938	28 165	28 930
2310 Sur la base du salaire	..	..	..	14 713	22 160	25 062	25 735	26 938	28 165	28 930
2320 Sur la base de l'impôt sur les revenus	..	..	..	0	0	0	0	0	0	0
2400 Non-ventilables entre 2100, 2200 et 2300	0	0	0	0	0	0	0	0	0	0
2410 Sur la base du salaire	..	..	..	..	..	..	..	..	..	..
2420 Sur la base de l'impôt sur les revenus	..	..	..	..	..	..	..	..	..	..
3000 Sur salaires ou main d'oeuvre	**1 189**	**3 935**	**8 254**	**14 916**	**22 874**	**25 676**	**27 807**	**29 707**	**33 595**	**34 434**
Taxe sur les salaires	..	2 413	5 208	7 583	10 272	11 201	11 675	12 094	13 127	13 108
Forfait social	..	0	0	0	0	314	1 150	2 716	4 654	4 925
Taxe d'apprentissage	..	172	101	102	964	474	459	515	554	601
Divers contributions directes	..	263	379	551	736	1 111	1 498	1 418	1 435	1 461
Taxe de formation professionnelle	..	236	30	97	19	16	14	17	17	20
Fonds national d'aide au logement	..	120	754	1 506	2 412	2 438	2 570	2 663	3 123	3 008
Taxe au profit des syndicats de transports	..	731	1 600	3 786	5 738	6 793	7 358	7 780	8 089	8 487
Versement au profit de l'UNEDIC	..	0	23	24	0	0	0	0	0	0
Taxe sur salaires retraités réemployés	..	0	0	0	0	0	0	0	0	0
Cotisation de prévoyance	..	0	0	415	773	1 427	1 081	470	496	395
Autres	..	0	159	851	100	6	30	20	49	34
Caisse nationale de solidarité pour l'autonomie (CNSA)	..	0	0	0	1 860	1 896	1 972	2 014	2 051	2 085
Contribution employeurs pour le FCAATA	..	0	0	0	0	0	0	0	0	0
Taxe exceptionnelle de solidarité sur les hautes rémunérations	..	0	0	0	0	0	0	0	0	310
4000 Impôts sur le patrimoine	**1 105**	**8 591**	**27 434**	**44 070**	**65 318**	**64 429**	**75 043**	**78 882**	**81 343**	**83 593**
4100 Impôts périodiques sur la propriété immobilière	506	5 358	14 808	27 340	39 875	45 099	49 782	52 184	54 545	55 493

StatLink http://dx.doi.org/10.1787/888933416757

Table 4.10. **France** *(cont./suite)*

Details of tax revenue/Recettes fiscales détaillées

Million EUR

	1965	1980	1990	2000	2007	2009	2011	2012	2013	2014
4110 Ménages	198	4 454	11 493	20 186	30 584	34 562	38 110	39 964	41 818	42 412
Taxe d'habitation	..	2 306	5 100	8 366	12 433	14 407	15 894	16 780	17 470	17 790
Contributions foncieres (bâti)	..	1 034	4 040	8 460	11 983	13 647	15 145	15 868	16 539	17 003
Taxe d'enlèvement ordures ménagères	..	534	1 219	3 103	5 117	5 411	5 910	6 101	6 552	6 369
Imposition foncier non-bâti	..	506	979	172	851	895	917	933	955	961
Taxe au profit chambre d'agriculture	..	0	0	53	59	61	62	62	62	63
Taxe de balayage	..	0	0	68	74	71	75	109	109	109
Autres	..	74	156	-36	67	70	107	111	131	117
4120 Autres agents	308	904	3 315	7 154	9 291	10 537	11 672	12 220	12 727	13 081
Contribution foncière propriété bâtie	..	759	3 032	6 256	9 054	10 295	11 425	11 971	12 477	12 827
Impositions foncier non-bâti	..	127	245	688	0	0	0	0	0	0
Taxe au profit chambre d'agriculture	..	18	39	210	237	242	247	249	250	254
Autres	..	0	0	0	0	0	0	0	0	0
4200 Impôts périodiques sur l'actif net	0	0	2 615	2 440	4 390	3 580	4 305	5 030	4 372	5 182
4210 Personnes physiques	..	..	938	2 440	4 390	3 580	4 305	5 030	4 372	5 182
4220 Sociétés	..	..	1 677	0	0	0	0	0	0	0
4300 Impôts sur mut. par décès, succ. et donations	145	1 010	4 124	6 907	8 910	7 462	8 668	9 616	10 456	10 273
4310 Impôts sur mut. par décès et successions	140	875	3 490	5 508	7 853	6 887	7 075	8 225	9 368	8 837
Mutations à titre gratuit	..	861	3 453	5 428	7 794	6 782	6 881	7 596	8 433	8 762
Recettes diverses et pénalités	..	14	37	80	59	105	194	629	935	75
4320 Impôts sur les donations	5	135	634	1 399	1 057	575	1 593	1 391	1 088	1 436
Donations	..	113	568	1 399	1 057	575	1 593	1 391	1 088	1 436
Recettes diverses et pénalités	..	0	0	0	0	0	0	0	0	0
Autres	..	22	66	0	0	0	0	0	0	0
4400 Impôts sur transact. mobilières et immob.	447	2 224	5 886	7 383	12 143	8 288	12 288	12 052	11 970	12 645
Créances rentes offices	..	30	209	279	443	224	358	384	359	304
Fonds de commerce	..	253	518	199	268	135	161	159	135	133
Meubles corporels	..	14	18	0	0	1	1	1	0	0
Immeubles et droits immobiliers	..	63	4	2	2	2	0	0	1	1
Sociétés	..	95	218	4	5	7	7	7	6	7
Recettes diverses et pénalités	..	35	60	367	179	183	260	54	4	3
Actes judiciaires et extra-judiciaires	..	6	10	0	0	0	0	0	0	0
Taxe de publicité foncière	..	781	38	68	130	135	122	161	703	710
Droits et timbres divers	..	94	242	0	0	0	0	0	0	0
Impôts sur opérations de bourse	..	168	525	407	271	0	0	0	0	0
Taxe sur les transactions financières	..	0	0	0	0	0	0	245	697	770
Taxe additionnelle droits d'enregistrement	..	679	4 002	5 339	10 396	7 188	10 909	10 489	9 538	10 142
Autres droits et recettes	..	5	44	718	449	413	470	552	527	575
4500 Impôts non-périodiques	8	0	0	0	0	0	0	0	0	0
4510 Sur l'actif net	8	..	..	..	..	..	..	..	..	..
4520 Autres non-périodiques	0	..	..	..	..	..	..	..	..	..
4600 Autres impôts périodiques sur patrimoine	0	0	0	0	0	0	0	0	0	0
5000 Impôts sur les biens et services	**9 902**	**54 317**	**123 235**	**166 608**	**206 293**	**203 264**	**221 478**	**227 362**	**231 413**	**236 300**
5100 Impôts sur production, vente, transfert, etc.	9 676	52 719	119 201	162 007	200 452	197 004	214 729	220 156	224 764	229 446
5110 Impôts généraux	5 994	37 760	81 341	110 296	142 033	136 313	146 489	148 768	150 935	154 485
5111 Taxes sur la valeur ajoutée	5 173	37 282	79 972	107 511	137 137	130 861	141 160	143 168	145 264	149 033
TVA (budget général)	..	36 895	78 902	103 054	136 927	130 303	140 552	142 527	144 490	148 208
TVA (BAPSA)	..	62	101	4 111	0	0	0	0	0	0
Autres TVA	..	325	969	0	0	0	0	0	0	0
Sous-compensation TVA agriculture	..	0	0	346	138	330	376	406	462	360
TVA sur subventions	..	0	0	0	72	228	232	235	312	465
5112 Impôts sur les ventes	822	0	0	0	0	0	0	0	0	0
5113 Autres impôts	0	477	1 369	2 784	4 896	5 452	5 329	5 600	5 671	5 452
Contribution sociale de solidarité	..	477	1 369	2 784	4 896	5 452	5 329	5 600	5 671	5 452
5120 Impôts sur biens et services déterminés	3 682	14 960	37 860	51 712	58 419	60 691	68 240	71 388	73 829	74 961

StatLink http://dx.doi.org/10.1787/888933416757

Table 4.10. **France** *(cont./suite)*

Details of tax revenue/Recettes fiscales détaillées

Million EUR

	1965	1980	1990	2000	2007	2009	2011	2012	2013	2014
5121 Accises	2 775	11 013	26 834	39 850	44 013	44 636	48 513	49 656	52 343	53 067
Taxe sur les produits pétroliers	..	7 136	17 476	23 493	24 318	23 547	23 923	23 564	23 693	23 794
Prélèv. except. sur entrep. produits pétroliers	..	0	0	0	0	0	0	0	0	0
Droits sur vins, cidres et hydromels	..	97	174	0	121	117	122	281	486	489
Droits sur alcools	..	1 238	1 593	3 025	484	2 564	2 987	2 625	2 950	2 954
Droits sur bière et eaux minérales	..	58	91	20	409	397	395	413	803	971
Autres droits et recettes	..	136	38	19	2 169	136	97	103	90	101
Impôts et taxes sur tabacs et allumettes	..	1 188	2 989	7 965	9 659	10 295	11 768	12 149	12 227	12 099
Amendes et confiscations	..	2	1	0	0	0	0	0	0	0
Garantie matières or et argent	..	6	19	29	2	0	0	0	0	0
Taxes au profit de l'ANDA	..	84	147	89	0	0	0	0	0	0
Taxe sanitaire et d'org. marché des viandes	..	0	0	48	46	46	42	40	41	41
Taxe sur les céréales	..	147	275	19	19	18	18	17	18	18
Redevances débits de tabac	..	0	0	0	0	0	0	0	0	0
Redevances sur sel de potasse	..	0	0	0	0	0	0	0	0	0
Taxe sur les farines	..	0	0	38	0	0	0	0	0	0
Redevances incluses dans prix carburants	..	36	32	453	485	489	492	482	499	487
Taxe au profit du Fonds National du Livre	..	7	17	0	0	0	0	0	0	0
Taxe sur produit exploitations forestières	..	11	0	0	0	0	0	0	0	0
Redevances des mines	..	16	59	43	23	25	24	23	22	20
Taxe sur électricité et chauffage	..	426	1 340	1 061	2 990	3 390	4 778	5 573	7 253	7 682
Surtaxe sur les apéritifs	..	12	17	0	0	0	0	0	0	0
Vignettes pharmaceutiques	..	4	559	0	0	0	0	0	0	0
Taxe sur betterave, sucre et alcool	..	22	400	0	0	0	0	0	0	0
Taxe solidarité sur graines oléagineuses	..	8	41	0	0	0	0	0	0	0
Taxe sur corps gras alimentaires	..	32	89	99	0	0	0	0	0	0
Taxe au profit Caisse Nationale des Lettres	..	23	0	0	0	0	0	0	0	0
Taxe sur consommation eau au profit FNAE	..	34	51	74	5	4	7	1	1	2
Taxe sur les viandes	..	25	36	0	19	18	157	278	1	0
Taxe au profit agences financières de bassin	..	217	609	1 624	1 821	1 905	2 051	2 212	2 175	2 302
Taxe au profit du FIRS (marché du sucre)	..	0	0	0	0	0	0	0	0	0
Contrib. except. pharmacies et laboratoires	..	16	0	522	0	0	0	0	0	0
Taxe locale	..	5	8	241	247	303	352	138	127	128
Contrib. distributeurs énergie élec. au profit du FACE	..	0	0	183	322	346	354	349	374	376
Taxe au profit de l'ADEME	..	0	0	80	212	387	479	491	499	449
Octroi de mer	..	0	0	449	544	589	376	378	386	415
Taxe générale sur les activités polluantes	..	0	0	6	16	3	36	123	205	186
Stocks sur les produits pétroliers	..	0	0	0	0	0	0	354	367	393
Autres	..	30	772	78	102	57	55	62	126	160
Institut français du pétrole (IFP)	..	0	0	193	0	0	0	0	0	0
5122 Bénéfices des monopoles fiscaux	0	0	0	0	0	0	0	0	0	0
5123 Droits de douane et droits à l'importation	471	966	1 669	297	386	378	771	655	763	726
Droits à l'importation (Etat)	..	0	0	0	0	0	0	0	0	0
Droits à l'importation (UE)	..	873	1 623	0	0	0	0	0	0	0
Octroi de mer	..	0	0	267	327	299	614	607	627	668
Autres	..	94	46	30	59	79	157	48	136	58
5124 Taxes à l'exportation	0	75	15	0	0	0	0	0	0	0
Prélèv. agricoles (part de l'Etat)	..	0	0	..	..	..	..	..	..	0
Prélèv. agricoles (part UE)	..	75	15	..	..	..	..	..	..	0
5125 Impôts sur biens d'équipement	0	0	0	0	0	0	0	0	0	0

StatLink http://dx.doi.org/10.1787/888933416757

Table 4.10. **France** *(cont./suite)*

Details of tax revenue/Recettes fiscales détaillées

Million EUR

	1965	1980	1990	2000	2007	2009	2011	2012	2013	2014
5126 Impôts sur services déterminés	431	2 690	8 373	11 204	14 007	15 623	18 902	21 019	20 656	21 104
Prélèvements sur le PMU	..	446	545	502	719	688	449	429	434	452
Prélèv. produit jeux et casinos	..	0	0	727	1 022	793	760	742	708	689
Prélèv. sur loterie nationale et loto	..	200	702	1 305	1 982	1 721	2 143	2 050	1 941	2 111
Prélèv. except. sur banque et établ. crédit	..	0	0	0	0	0	0	0	0	0
Taxe sur convention d'assurance	..	1 292	4 782	5 097	6 571	6 846	8 429	9 826	9 973	10 220
Baux enregistrement	..	264	633	573	29	-3	-4	0	-1	0
Taxes funéraires	..	11	32	14	11	12	11	11	12	12
Droits de timbre contrat transport	..	9	77	10	0	0	0	0	0	0
Expertises et vérifications techniques	..	0	0	0	0	0	0	0	0	0
Taxe au profit de l'ANAEM	..	0	0	33	58	108	141	149	145	143
Taxe sur l'utilisation des voies navigables	..	0	0	104	157	171	175	187	192	187
Autres taxes diverses	..	98	272	273	449	983	947	905	547	425
Taxes sur les jeux et spectacles	..	75	195	274	372	309	788	808	799	754
Taxe sur fonds de garantie automobile (FGAC)	..	32	135	223	274	321	384	372	387	440
Taxes assurance auto. (Etat + Séc. Soc.)	..	0	0	55	0	0	0	0	0	0
Taxe Fonds National Calamités Agricoles	..	0	0	261	96	97	106	114	120	123
Prélèv. 5% Fonds Nat. Amélioration Habitat	..	114	258	678	604	595	619	663	726	725
Cotisat. des entrep. au Centre Nat. du Cinéma	..	52	207	397	144	612	818	733	735	707
Taxe alimentation au Fonds Assurances Agricoles	..	0	0	0	0	0	0	0	0	0
Taxe au profit du Fonds National Sportif	..	3	0	0	0	0	0	0	0	0
Taxe Fonds de Revalorisation Rentes et Pensions	..	15	0	0	0	0	0	0	0	0
Taxe annuelle sur encours de crédits	..	0	0	0	0	0	0	0	0	0
Taxe sur la publicité	..	0	26	52	38	152	190	205	219	225
Prélèv. sur salaires des conserv. hypothèques	..	67	188	0	0	0	0	0	0	0
Taxe de sécurité et sûreté	..	0	0	220	353	450	477	521	521	560
Taxe de risque systémique	..	0	0	0	0	0	495	1 026	899	979
Taxe sur les mutuelles au profit de la CMU	..	0	0	247	560	1 566	1 735	1 862	1 851	1 916
Taxe au profit du FPRNM (Fonds de prévention des risques naturels majeurs)	..	0	0	0	0	0	0	193	197	201
Autres	..	10	320	159	568	202	239	223	251	235
5127 Autres impôts sur commerce et transact. internat.	0	0	0	0	0	0	0	0	0	0
5128 Autres impôts	5	215	970	360	13	54	54	58	67	64
Taxe de co-responsabilité sur le lait	..	48	119	0	0	0	0	0	0	0
Taxe de co-responsabilité sur les céréales	..	0	520	0	0	0	0	0	0	0
Prélèvement pour la CECA	..	14	0	0	0	0	0	0	0	0
Receveur des douanes	..	9	24	0	0	0	0	0	0	0
Divers (collect. locales)	..	0	0	0	0	0	0	0	0	0
Cotisations sur les sucres	..	68	185	270	0	41	41	45	54	51
Taxe au profit du FIRS (marché du sucre)	..	76	120	76	0	0	0	0	0	0
Autres	..	0	2	14	13	13	13	13	13	13
5130 Non-ventilables entre 5110 et 5120	0	0	0	0	0	0	0	0	0	0
5200 Impôts sur utilisation des biens et exerc. activités	226	1 598	4 034	4 601	5 841	6 260	6 749	7 206	6 649	6 854
5210 Impôts périodiques	178	1 226	3 024	2 810	3 009	2 821	2 888	3 139	2 849	2 887
5211 A la charge des ménages : véhicules à moteur	27	545	1 236	126	0	0	0	0	0	0
Taxe différentielle (budget gén. et collect. loc.)	..	545	1 236	126	0	0	0	0	0	0
5212 A la charge autres agents : véhicules à moteur	79	545	1 086	1 280	1 559	1 376	1 215	1 255	1 181	1 112
Taxe sur les véhicules des sociétés	..	197	345	644	891	1 098	927	983	876	827
Taxe sur les véhicules (budg. gén. et coll. loc.)	..	348	741	636	668	278	288	272	305	285
5213 Autres impôts périodiques	72	136	702	1 404	1 450	1 445	1 673	1 884	1 668	1 775
Taxe spéciale usage des routes	..	0	0	420	526	528	612	570	573	590
Droit de pesage	..	17	14	0	0	0	0	0	0	0
Divers taxes (collectivités locales)	..	7	33	0	0	0	0	0	0	0
Taxe magnétoscopes	..	0	0	0	0	0	0	0	0	0
Redev. pour surveillance centrales nucléaires	..	8	41	0	0	0	0	0	0	0
Taxe d'usage des abattoirs	..	19	13	0	0	0	0	0	0	0
Contrib. des entrepr. à la prépa. médicaments	..	0	20	238	0	284	362	318	213	298
Taxe sur les pylones électriques	..	1	66	128	183	190	223	233	244	214
Licence débit de boisson	..	8	22	23	0	0	0	0	0	0
Droit annuel de francisation et de navigation	..	0	0	0	0	37	39	37	37	37
Redevances d'usage des fréquences radioélectriques	..	0	0	191	280	244	177	325	262	294
Autres	..	75	493	404	461	162	260	401	339	342

StatLink http://dx.doi.org/10.1787/888933416757

Table 4.10. **France** *(cont./suite)*

Details of tax revenue/Recettes fiscales détaillées

Million EUR

	1965	1980	1990	2000	2007	2009	2011	2012	2013	2014
5220 Impôts non-périodiques	47	372	1 010	1 791	2 832	3 439	3 861	4 067	3 800	3 967
Récépissés de mise en circulation	..	75	0	0	0	0	0	0	0	0
Taxes et licences débits de boissons	..	0	0	3	0	0	0	0	0	0
Redevance pour droit de construire	..	79	53	72	0	1	18	18	18	18
Taxe locale d'équipement	..	146	263	305	848	1 239	1 483	1 614	1 381	1 455
Taxe sur les certificats d'immatriculation des véhicules	..	0	0	1 373	1 939	1 917	2 080	2 117	2 042	2 077
Dépassement plafond légal de densité	..	38	270	38	45	82	82	82	82	82
Taxe additionnelle sur certif. d'immatric. des véhicules	..	0	0	0	0	200	198	236	277	335
Autres	..	35	423	0	0	0	0	0	0	0
5300 Non-ventilables entre 5100 et 5200	0	0	0	0	0	0	0	0	0	0
6000 Autres impôts	**681**	**5 480**	**14 060**	**23 964**	**27 227**	**27 408**	**23 946**	**22 844**	**22 860**	**23 739**
6100 A la charge exclusive des entreprises	678	5 480	14 060	22 278	27 219	27 383	23 940	22 838	22 854	23 733
Taxes au profit de l'INPI	..	43	67	115	156	160	170	171	180	189
Taxe sur les frais généraux	..	0	0	0	0	0	0	0	0	0
Taxe professionnelle	..	5 152	13 381	19 641	22 035	21 885	0	0	0	0
Taxe des prestations des syndicats (collect. loc.)	..	36	197	293	0	0	0	0	0	0
Taxes diverses (budget gén. et org. div. adm. cent.)	..	0	0	61	236	219	232	293	478	647
Taxe annuelle sur les encours de crédits	..	110	0	0	0	0	0	0	0	0
Prélèv. except. sur entreprises d'assurances	..	0	0	0	0	0	0	0	0	0
Produit de l'imposition (Chambre des Métiers)	..	36	125	155	203	217	187	205	233	237
Contribution au FNE	..	4	240	204	33	12	4	4	3	1
Autres	..	98	50	1 007	3 721	3 824	2 212	1 182	775	964
Taxe ANDA - ADAR	..	0	0	32	0	0	0	0	0	0
Cotisation foncière des entreprises	..	0	0	0	0	0	5 160	5 465	5 908	6 162
Cotisation sur la valeur ajoutée des entreprises	..	0	0	0	0	0	11 703	12 584	12 168	12 841
Imposition forfaitaire sur les entreprises de réseaux	..	0	0	0	0	0	1 085	1 142	1 206	1 272
Exit taxe sur les assurances	..	0	0	0	0	0	1 670	0	0	0
Produit imposition Chambre de Commerce	..	0	0	770	835	937	1 180	1 328	1 323	1 014
Contribution patronale sur stock-options	..	0	0	0	0	129	262	309	380	406
Taxe sur le résultat des entreprises ferroviaires	..	0	0	0	0	0	75	155	200	0
6200 A la charge d'autres agents	3	0	0	1 686	8	25	6	6	6	6
Autres	..	..	..	1 686	8	25	6	6	6	6
Ecart aux comptes de secteurs	..	..	..	0	0	0	0	0	0	0
Droits de douane perçus pour l'UE	..	..	..	**1 513**	**1 657**	**1 461**	**1 866**	**1 883**	**1 842**	**1 827**
Crédits d'impôts récupérables										
Crédits d'impôts récupérables contre 1110	..	..	..	0	7 663	10 966	9 750	9 030	8 214	7 875
Composante fiscale	..	..	..	..	..	..	7 270	7 236	6 755	5 767
Composante transfert	..	..	..	..	..	..	2 480	1 794	1 459	2 108
Crédits d'impôts récupérables contre 1210	..	..	..	457	1 860	7 633	5 180	5 563	5 466	13 368
Composante fiscale	.	..	..	..	..	..	1 529	3 319	3 572	7 101
Composante transfert	..	..	..	..	..	..	3 651	2 244	1 894	6 267
Recettes fiscales totales sur la base d'encaissements	**25 776**	**178 576**	**433 771**	**639 427**	**824 688**	**801 266**	**888 794**	**924 946**	**956 812**	**973 380**
Recettes fiscales totales sur la base des droits constatés	..	..	..	**643 309**	**828 971**	**806 916**	**895 101**	**929 943**	**963 951**	**979 844**
Conciliation avec les comptes nationaux										
Impôts additionnels inclus dans les comptes nationaux	..	..	..	0	0	0	0	0	0	0
Impôt exclus des comptes nationaux	..	..	..	-3 171	-5 191	-5 482	-5 985	-6 210	-6 661	-6 478
Taxe d'enlèvement des ordures ménagères	..	..	..	-3 103	-5 117	-5 411	-5 910	-6 101	-6 552	-6 369
Taxe sur les pylônes	..	..	..	0	0	0	0	0	0	0
Taxe de balayage	..	..	..	-68	-74	-71	-75	-109	-109	-109
Différence dans les traitements des crédits d'impôts	..	..	..	0	0	0	0	0	0	0
Transfert en capital des recettes non collectées	..	..	..	-3 882	-4 283	-5 650	-6 307	-4 997	-7 139	-6 464
Cotisations de sécurité sociale volontaires	.	..	..	0	0	0	0	0	0	0
Différences diverses	..	..	..	0	0	0	0	0	0	0
Comptes nationaux: impôts et cotisations sociales effectives	..	..	..	636 256	819 497	795 784	882 809	918 736	950 151	966 902
Cotisations sociales imputées	..	..	..	25 875	33 510	36 723	39 560	40 980	41 947	42 466
Comptes nationaux: impôts et toutes les cotisations sociales	..	..	..	662 131	853 007	832 507	922 369	959 716	992 098	1 009 368

Notes : Année civile se terminant le 31 décembre.

À partir de 1992, les données sont sur la base des droits constatés.

À partir de 1970, les chiffres ont été calculés selon le nouveau Système de Comptes Nationaux et ne sont pas, de ce fait, comparables à ceux des années précédentes.

La rubrique 2000 comprend certaines contributions volontaires.

La rubrique 4220 correspond à la rémunération de la garantie de l'État accordée aux caisses d'épargne.

Source : Compte général de l'Administration des finances pour les chiffres de recettes fiscales. OSCE pour les chiffres de sécurité sociale de 1965 à 1969, et SEC pourles années suivantes.

StatLink http://dx.doi.org/10.1787/888933416757

Table 4.11. **Germany/Allemagne**

Details of tax revenue/Recettes fiscales détaillées

Million EUR

	1965	1980	1990	2000	2007	2009	2011	2012	2013	2014
Total tax revenue	**74 190**	**287 252**	**454 764**	**767 045**	**876 839**	**887 626**	**965 050**	**1 002 468**	**1 029 956**	**1 069 259**
Total tax revenue exclusive of customs duties	..	..	..	**763 651**	**872 867**	**883 848**	**960 494**	**998 051**	**1 025 705**	**1 064 651**
1000 Taxes on income, profits and capital gains	**25 059**	**100 821**	**147 257**	**231 249**	**273 596**	**256 140**	**284 069**	**304 597**	**319 051**	**332 549**
1100 Of individuals	19 254	85 134	125 296	194 173	218 848	223 610	238 671	257 147	268 543	281 585
1110 On income and profits	19 254	85 134	125 296	194 173	218 848	223 610	238 671	257 147	268 543	281 585
Taxes on wages and salaries	8 558	57 039	90 801	135 733	146 365	150 086	155 518	165 122	173 668	183 051
Assessed income tax	7 567	18 813	18 672	12 225	25 341	30 675	32 478	37 777	42 557	46 062
Withholding tax on dividends	691	2 135	5 538	13 515	13 572	11 850	18 136	20 060	17 258	17 424
Supplementary tax	0	0	0	10 347	10 907	11 245	11 660	12 479	13 083	13 704
Enterprise tax	2 438	7 147	10 285	16 486	14 630	12 446	15 646	16 281	16 544	16 824
Stabilisation tax	0	0	0	0	0	0	0	0	0	0
Withholding tax on interest	0	0	0	5 867	8 033	7 308	5 233	5 428	5 433	4 520
1120 On capital gains	0	0	0	0	0	0	0	0	0	0
1200 Corporate	5 806	15 686	21 961	37 076	54 748	32 530	45 398	47 450	50 508	50 964
1210 On profits	5 806	15 686	21 961	37 076	54 748	32 530	45 398	47 450	50 508	50 964
Corporation tax	4 177	10 902	15 385	23 575	23 386	7 864	16 348	17 250	19 762	20 246
Supplementary tax	0	20	1	1 494	1 550	758	1 170	1 215	1 337	1 352
Sacrifice for Berlin	3	0	0	0	0	0	0	0	0	0
Enterprise tax	1 625	4 765	6 576	10 540	25 486	19 974	25 062	26 063	26 483	26 932
Stabilisation tax	0	0	0	0	0	0	0	0	0	0
Withholding tax on interest	0	0	0	1 467	4 326	3 934	2 818	2 922	2 926	2 434
1220 On capital gains	0	0	0	0	0	0	0	0	0	0
1300 Unallocable between 1100 and 1200	0	0	0	0	0	0	0	0	0	0
2000 Social security contributions	**19 875**	**98 659**	**170 449**	**299 440**	**320 594**	**342 658**	**372 025**	**383 489**	**392 290**	**407 726**
2100 Employees	8 723	43 833	73 580	131 610	141 079	150 578	164 960	170 564	174 333	181 608
Payments by employees total	8 723	43 833	73 580	131 610	141 079	150 578	164 960	170 564	174 333	181 608
2110 On a payroll basis	..	..	..	131 610	141 079	150 578	164 960	170 564	174 333	181 608
2120 On an income tax basis	..	..	..	0	0	0	0	0	0	0
2200 Employers	10 693	52 985	86 659	147 410	152 198	160 936	173 782	179 852	184 215	191 409
Payments by employers total	10 693	52 985	86 659	147 410	152 198	160 936	173 782	179 852	184 215	191 409
2210 On a payroll basis	..	..	..	147 410	152 198	160 936	173 782	179 852	184 215	191 409
2220 On an income tax basis	..	..	..	0	0	0	0	0	0	0
2300 Self-employed or non-employed	460	1 841	10 210	20 420	27 317	31 144	33 283	33 073	33 742	34 709
Payments total	460	1 841	10 210	20 420	27 317	31 144	33 283	33 073	33 742	34 709
2310 On a payroll basis	..	..	..	20 420	27 317	31 144	33 283	33 073	33 742	34 709
2320 On an income tax basis	..	..	..	0	0	0	0	0	0	0
2400 Unallocable between 2100, 2200 and 2300	0	0	0	0	0	0	0	0	0	0
2410 On a payroll basis	..	..	..	..	..	..	..	..	..	..
2420 On an income tax basis	..	..	..	..	..	..	..	..	..	..
3000 Taxes on payroll and workforce	**477**	**445**	**0**	**0**	**0**	**0**	**0**	**0**	**0**	**0**
Payroll tax	477	445	..	..	..	..	..	..	..	..
4000 Taxes on property	**4 313**	**9 414**	**15 321**	**17 505**	**21 873**	**20 350**	**23 030**	**24 580**	**26 105**	**28 163**
4100 Recurrent taxes on immovable property	1 079	2 968	4 461	8 849	10 713	10 936	11 674	12 017	12 377	12 690
4110 Households	644	1 187	1 784	3 540	4 285	4 374	4 670	4 807	4 951	5 076
4120 Others	435	1 780	2 676	5 309	6 428	6 562	7 004	7 210	7 426	7 614
4200 Recurrent taxes on net wealth	2 530	4 362	6 213	433	5	7	744	869	701	682
4210 Individual	973	977	1 425	191	2	3	-2	0	0	-1
General wealth tax	471	954	1 425	191	2	3	-2	0	0	-1
Equalization of war burden	502	23	0	0	0	0	0	0	0	0
4220 Corporate	1 557	3 385	4 788	242	3	4	746	869	701	683
General wealth tax	490	1 431	1 813	242	3	4	-2	-1	0	-1
Equalization of war burden	350	15	0	0	0	0	0	0	0	0
Enterprise tax	717	1 939	2 975	0	0	0	0	0	0	0
Bank levy	0	0	0	0	0	0	592	694	521	516
Contribution to Deposit Protection Fund	0	0	0	0	0	0	156	176	180	168
4300 Estate, inheritance and gift taxes	162	520	1 545	2 982	4 203	4 550	4 246	4 305	4 633	5 452
4310 Estate and inheritance taxes	134	416	1 359	2 624	3 699	4 004	3 736	3 788	4 077	4 798
4320 Gift taxes	28	104	186	358	504	546	510	517	556	654
4400 Taxes on financial and capital transactions	542	1 564	3 103	5 241	6 952	4 857	6 366	7 389	8 394	9 339
Real property transfer tax	150	521	1 999	5 081	6 952	4 857	6 366	7 389	8 394	9 339
Additional real property transfer	198	680	148	160	0	0	0	0	0	0
Capital transfer tax	111	200	807	0	0	0	0	0	0	0
Bill of exchange tax	83	163	149	0	0	0	0	0	0	0
4500 Non-recurrent taxes	0	0	0	0	0	0	0	0	0	0
4510 On net wealth	..	..	..	..	..	..	..	..	..	..
4520 Other non-recurrent taxes	..	..	..	..	..	..	..	..	..	..
4600 Other recurrent taxes on property	0	0	0	0	0	0	0	0	0	0
5000 Taxes on goods and services	**24 462**	**77 863**	**121 577**	**215 292**	**256 708**	**264 602**	**281 256**	**285 266**	**288 131**	**296 041**
5100 Taxes on production, sale, transfer, etc	23 079	74 406	117 209	208 050	247 547	255 051	271 122	274 263	277 725	285 387
5110 General taxes	12 235	47 779	75 459	140 871	170 387	178 020	190 229	194 353	197 326	203 401

StatLink http://dx.doi.org/10.1787/888933416767

Table 4.11. **Germany/Allemagne** *(cont./suite)*

Details of tax revenue/Recettes fiscales détaillées

Million EUR

	1965	1980	1990	2000	2007	2009	2011	2012	2013	2014
5111 Value added taxes	0	47 779	75 459	140 871	170 387	178 020	190 229	194 353	197 326	203 401
5112 Sales tax	0	0	0	0	0	0	0	0	0	0
5113 Other	12 235	0	0	0	0	0	0	0	0	0
Turnover tax old	11 028	..	..	..	..	..	..	..	..	..
Old turnover tax on import	1 208	..	..	..	..	..	..	..	..	..
5120 Taxes on specific goods and services	10 844	26 627	41 750	67 179	76 808	76 667	80 577	79 626	80 111	81 702
5121 Excises	8 213	20 566	31 158	57 224	63 811	63 684	66 343	64 868	64 624	65 103
Duty on mineral oils	3 798	10 917	17 701	37 826	38 877	39 693	40 279	39 351	39 260	39 829
Duty on power	0	0	0	3 356	6 439	6 251	7 278	6 970	6 987	6 741
Duty on tobacco	2 402	5 771	8 898	11 443	14 108	13 503	14 455	14 249	14 131	14 332
Duty on alcohol	771	1 986	2 162	2 151	2 169	2 042	2 144	2 097	2 098	2 070
Duty on beer	501	645	693	843	750	730	702	690	675	684
Duty on coffee	488	756	986	1 087	1 016	1 007	1 021	1 046	1 033	1 019
Duty on sugar	59	72	79	0	0	0	0	0	0	0
Duty on tea	16	32	31	0	0	0	0	0	0	0
Duty on salt	20	20	23	0	0	0	0	0	0	0
Duty on electric lamps	34	63	83	0	0	0	0	0	0	0
Duty on playing cards	2	4	0	0	0	0	0	0	0	0
Duty on beverages	46	22	8	6	1	0	0	0	0	0
Duty on acetic acid	3	2	0	0	0	0	0	0	0	0
Duty on champagne	69	274	494	512	451	458	464	465	440	428
Duty on matches	5	2	0	0	0	0	0	0	0	0
Duty on ice cream	1	0	0	0	0	0	0	0	0	0
5122 Profits of fiscal monopolies	8	2	0	0	0	0	0	0	0	0
5123 Customs and import duties	1 658	3 125	3 847	0	0	0	0	0	0	0
Monetary compensation accounts	0	368	1	..	..	..	..	..	..	..
Customs (mainly EU)	1 294	2 353	3 662	..	..	..	..	..	..	..
Agricultural levies EU	364	404	184	..	..	..	..	..	..	..
5124 Taxes on exports	0	0	0	0	0	0	0	0	0	0
5125 Taxes on investment goods	0	0	0	0	0	0	0	0	0	0
5126 Taxes on specific services	942	2 689	6 443	9 599	13 025	12 944	14 196	14 707	15 421	16 648
Duty transport goods on residents	0	0	0	0	0	0	0	0	0	0
Transport tax	452	0	0	0	0	0	0	0	0	0
Insurance tax	198	910	2 266	7 243	10 410	10 555	10 767	11 165	11 588	12 663
Fire insurance tax	33	124	200	288	319	323	365	380	392	409
Entertainment tax	55	44	140	267	210	302	480	617	708	784
Taxes on betting and gambling	204	655	1 046	1 801	1 702	1 511	1 420	1 432	1 635	1 673
Tax on electricity bills	0	956	2 792	0	0	0	0	0	0	0
Aviation tax	0	0	0	0	0	0	959	954	955	988
Gaming casinos levy	0	0	0	0	384	253	205	159	143	131
5127 Other taxes on internat. trade and transactions	0	0	4	5	1	3	2	2	2	2
5128 Other taxes	24	244	298	351	-29	36	36	49	64	-51
Levies CECA	24	56	36	0	0	0	0	0	0	0
Cotisation sugar EU	0	112	224	351	-29	36	36	49	64	-51
Levy on milk	0	75	38	0	0	0	0	0	0	0
5130 Unallocable between 5110 and 5120	0	0	0	0	352	364	316	284	288	284
Contributions to the German National Petroleum Stockpiling Agency	..	..	..	..	352	364	316	284	288	284
5200 Taxes on use of goods and perform activities	1 383	3 457	4 368	7 242	9 161	9 551	10 134	11 003	10 406	10 654
5210 Recurrent taxes	1 369	3 454	4 368	7 239	9 161	8 470	9 481	10 475	10 084	9 880
5211 Paid by households: motor vehicles	614	1 892	2 950	5 177	6 823	6 288	6 404	6 405	6 393	6 316
5212 Paid by others: motor vehicles	728	1 475	1 300	1 838	2 075	1 913	2 018	2 038	2 097	2 185
5213 Paid in respect of other goods	27	87	118	224	263	269	1 059	2 032	1 594	1 379
Dog taxes	24	75	101	198	240	247	275	288	299	309
Hunting and fishing taxes	4	13	17	26	23	22	16	13	10	10
Nuclear fuel tax	0	0	0	0	0	0	768	1 731	1 285	1 060
5220 Non-recurrent taxes	14	3	1	3	0	1 081	653	528	322	774
Non-recurrent taxes	..	..	..	..	..	0	0	0	0	0
CO2 emission certificates	..	..	..	..	..	1 081	653	528	322	774
5300 Unallocable between 5100 and 5200	0	0	0	0	0	0	0	0	0	0
6000 Other taxes	**4**	**51**	**160**	**165**	**96**	**98**	**114**	**119**	**128**	**172**
6100 Paid solely by business	0	0	0	0	0	0	0	0	0	0
6200 Other	4	51	160	165	96	98	114	119	128	172
Custom duties collected for the EU	**..**	**..**	**..**	**3 394**	**3 972**	**3 778**	**4 556**	**4 417**	**4 251**	**4 608**

StatLink http://dx.doi.org/10.1787/888933416767

Table 4.11. **Germany/Allemagne** *(cont./suite)*

Details of tax revenue/Recettes fiscales détaillées

Million EUR

	1965	1980	1990	2000	2007	2009	2011	2012	2013	2014
Non-wastable tax credits										
Non-wastable tax credits against 1110	..	..	..	38 356	43 602	45 035	43 647	42 802	41 890	41 162
Tax expenditure component	..	..	..	..	29 499	28 802	27 939	27 548	27 120	26 824
Transfer component	..	..	..	..	14 104	16 231	15 708	15 254	14 772	14 339
Non-wastable tax credits against 1210	..	..	..	962	804	1 106	594	540	426	352
Tax expenditure component	..	..	..	..	348	414	238	224	172	150
Transfer component	..	..	..	..	456	690	356	316	254	202
Total tax revenue on cash basis	**74 190**	**287 252**	**454 764**	**767 045**	**874 109**	**888 454**	**964 286**	**1 001 217**	**1 028 658**	**1 068 040**
Total tax revenue on accrual basis	..	..	..	..	**876 839**	**887 626**	**965 050**	**1 002 468**	**1 029 956**	**1 069 259**
Conciliation with National Accounts										
Additional taxes included in National Accounts	..	..	..	..	2 348	2 096	2 243	2 265	2 334	2 391
Several duties, administrative fees and other revenues	..	..	..	..	2 348	2 096	2 243	2 265	2 334	2 391
Taxes excluded from National Accounts	..	..	..	..	0	0	0	0	0	0
Difference in treatment of tax credits	..	..	..	..	12 623	11 355	8 092	7 113	6 391	5 638
Capital transfer for uncollected revenue	..	..	..	..	0	0	0	0	0	0
Voluntary social security contributions	..	..	..	..	20 930	7 763	6 237	6 913	7 353	7 744
Miscellaneous differences	..	..	..	..	33 538	34 066	31 148	31 058	31 869	32 494
National Accounts: Taxes and actual social contributions	..	..	..	..	946 278	942 906	1 012 770	1 049 817	1 077 903	1 117 526
Imputed social contributions	..	..	..	..	29 424	31 400	32 871	32 820	33 355	33 956
National Accounts: Taxes and all social contributions	..	..	..	..	975 702	974 306	1 045 641	1 082 637	1 111 258	1 151 482

Notes : Year ending 31st December.

From 2002, data are on accrual basis.

The tax revenues for Germany refer to the old Länder until 1990 and to all Germany beginning in 1991.

Heading 1000: In the years up to 2000, the revenues shown take into account the whole amount of non-wastable tax credits including that part paid out by the tax authorities which should, under the OECD criteria, be treated as expenditure. From 2001, the data necessary to make the adjustment have become available and the revenue figures comply with the OECD criteria from that year. The impact of this change is shown in Table 5 in Chapter 1 of this Report.

Heading for non-wastable tax credits against 1110 comprise child tax credits (paid out of wage tax revenue), tax credits for owner occupied housing (paid out of assessed income tax revenue) and investment tax credits for unincorporated businesses (for investment in former East Germany; paid out of assessed income tax revenue).

Heading for non-wastable tax credits against 1210 are investment tax credits for incorporated businesses (for investment in former East Germany; paid out of corporate income tax revenue).

Source : Finanzbericht, Bonn; Tax Statistics; Unpublished estimates by the Ministry of Finance.

StatLink http://dx.doi.org/10.1787/888933416767

Table 4.12. **Greece/Grèce**

Details of tax revenue/Recettes fiscales détaillées

Million EUR

	1965	1980	1990	2000	2007	2009	2011	2012	2013	2014
Total tax revenue	**116**	**1 475**	**11 472**	**47 178**	**72 565**	**73 349**	**69 764**	**67 819**	**64 184**	**63 514**
Total tax revenue exclusive of custom duties	..	..	..	**46 968**	**72 258**	**73 097**	**69 578**	**67 657**	**64 036**	**63 366**
1000 Taxes on income, profits and capital gains	**11**	**286**	**2 283**	**12 664**	**16 890**	**17 868**	**14 913**	**16 208**	**14 005**	**15 023**
1100 Of individuals	8	220	1 619	6 827	10 821	10 622	9 849	13 293	10 770	10 438
1110 On income and profits	8	220	1 619	6 802	10 767	10 563	9 784	13 221	10 688	10 360
Personal income tax	..	..	1 414	6 802	..	..	..	..	..	..
Receipts from previous years	..	..	62	0	..	..	..	..	..	..
Agricultural social security fund	..	..	143	0	..	..	..	..	..	..
1120 On capital gains	0	0	0	25	54	59	65	72	82	78
1200 Corporate	2	56	631	5 642	5 704	5 961	4 283	2 088	2 071	3 344
1210 On profits	2	56	631	5 642	5 704	5 961	4 283	2 088	2 071	3 344
Corporation income tax	2	39	553	5 642	..	..	..	..	..	..
Receipts from previous years	0	8	33	0	..	..	..	..	..	..
Agricultural social security fund	0	9	46	0	..	..	..	..	..	..
1220 On capital gains	0	0	0	0	0	0	0	0	0	0
1300 Unallocable between 1100 and 1200	1	10	32	195	365	1 285	781	827	1 164	1 241
Extraordinary taxes	0	10	32	0	..	..	..	..	..	..
Other taxes on income and profits	1	0	0	195	..	..	..	..	..	..
2000 Social security contributions	**37**	**485**	**3 466**	**14 299**	**24 941**	**24 453**	**22 410**	**20 988**	**19 537**	**18 234**
2100 Employees	15	214	1 735	5 608	9 428	9 797	8 918	8 402	7 937	7 489
2110 On a payroll basis	..	..	..	..	..	..	..	..	..	..
2120 On an income tax basis	..	..	..	..	..	..	..	..	..	..
2200 Employers	14	213	1 728	6 664	11 516	11 044	9 928	9 270	8 473	7 956
2210 On a payroll basis	..	..	..	..	..	..	..	..	..	..
2220 On an income tax basis	..	..	..	..	..	..	..	..	..	..
2300 Self-employed or non-employed	0	0	3	2 027	3 997	3 612	3 564	3 316	3 127	2 789
2310 On a payroll basis	..	..	..	..	..	..	..	..	..	..
2320 On an income tax basis	..	..	..	..	..	..	..	..	..	..
2400 Unallocable between 2100, 2200 and 2300	7	58	0	0	0	0	0	0	0	0
2410 On a payroll basis	..	..	..	..	..	..	..	..	..	..
2420 On an income tax basis	..	..	..	..	..	..	..	..	..	..
3000 Taxes on payroll and workforce	**1**	**27**	**79**	**0**	**0**	**0**	**0**	**0**	**0**	**0**
4000 Taxes on property	**11**	**68**	**532**	**2 875**	**3 861**	**4 725**	**4 832**	**4 837**	**5 393**	**2 552**
4100 Recurrent taxes on immovable property	0	4	22	236	367	793	2 226	2 476	2 314	755
4110 Households	0	3	22	..	..	..	..	..	..	..
4120 Others	0	1	0	..	..	..	..	..	..	..
Taxes on immovable property	0	0	..	..	..	..	..	..	..	..
4200 Recurrent taxes on net wealth	0	0	0	65	488	1 294	1 255	1 224	1 084	1 017
4210 Individual	..	..	..	..	..	..	..	..	..	..
4220 Corporate	..	..	..	..	..	..	..	..	..	..
4300 Estate, inheritance and gift taxes	1	18	141	372	224	160	123	92	99	111
4310 Estate and inheritance taxes	1	13	85	..	..	..	..	..	..	..
4320 Gift taxes	0	4	55	..	..	..	..	..	..	..
4400 Taxes on financial and capital transactions	10	44	368	2 049	2 550	1 939	859	733	615	539
Stamp and transaction taxes	10	41	368	2 049	2 550	1 939	859	733	615	539
Receipts from previous years	0	3	0	0	0	0	0	0	0	0
4500 Non-recurrent taxes	0	2	1	0	0	0	0	0	0	0
4510 On net wealth	0	0	0	..	..	..	..	..	..	..
4520 Other non-recurrent taxes	0	2	1	..	..	..	..	..	..	..
4600 Other recurrent taxes on property	0	0	0	153	232	539	369	312	1 281	130
5000 Taxes on goods and services	**57**	**608**	**5 109**	**17 130**	**26 566**	**26 051**	**27 423**	**25 624**	**25 101**	**27 557**
5100 Taxes on production, sale, transfer, etc	51	564	4 881	15 576	24 332	22 978	24 877	23 215	22 894	25 324
5110 General taxes	12	194	3 040	10 128	17 253	15 700	15 835	14 357	13 277	13 338
5111 Value added taxes	0	0	2 821	9 824	16 611	14 879	15 021	13 713	12 593	12 676
5112 Sales tax	9	185	123	36	147	347	284	155	177	104
5113 Other	2	9	96	268	495	474	530	489	507	558
Other taxes on goods and services	1	9	34	268	495	474	530	489	507	558
Receipts from previous years	1	0	62	0	0	0	0	0	0	0
5120 Taxes on specific goods and services	39	370	1 789	5 405	6 972	7 168	8 685	7 883	7 983	7 914
5121 Excises	20	165	1 372	4 178	5 748	5 957	7 739	7 020	6 820	6 756
Duty on tobacco products	8	45	357	1 764	2 650	2 798	3 053	2 444	2 500	2 399
Duty on alcohol and spirits	1	7	50	252	353	369	466	418	417	399
Duty on mineral oil	7	75	637	2 151	2 739	2 784	4 027	3 974	3 725	3 782
Duty on sugar	3	6	0	0	0	0	0	0	0	0
Duty on coton and other products	0	30	328	11	6	6	193	184	178	176
5122 Profits of fiscal monopolies	2	6	0	0	0	0	0	0	0	0
5123 Customs and import duties	12	94	112	-7	7	2	4	0	5	5
Import duties	11	90	111	-7	7	2	4	0	5	5
Agricultural social security fund	1	5	1	0	0	0	0	0	0	0
5124 Taxes on exports	0	1	1	5	0	0	0	0	0	0

StatLink http://dx.doi.org/10.1787/888933416772

Table 4.12. **Greece/Grèce** *(cont./suite)*

Details of tax revenue/Recettes fiscales détaillées

Million EUR

	1965	1980	1990	2000	2007	2009	2011	2012	2013	2014
5125 Taxes on investment goods	0	0	0	0	0	0	0	0	0	0
5126 Taxes on specific services	2	47	293	1 229	1 217	1 209	942	863	1 158	1 153
5127 Other taxes on internat. trade and transactions	0	0	0	0	0	0	0	0	0	0
5128 Other taxes	4	58	10	0	0	0	0	0	0	0
Agricultural social security fund	2	..	..	..	..	..	..	..	..	..
Other taxes	2	..	..	..	..	..	..	..	..	..
5130 Unallocable between 5110 and 5120	0	0	52	43	107	110	357	975	1 634	4 072
5200 Taxes on use of goods and perform activities	6	44	228	1 254	2 146	2 046	1 674	1 728	1 711	1 763
5210 Recurrent taxes	5	24	219	1 254	2 146	2 046	1 674	1 728	1 711	1 763
Motor vehicle tax	5	0	..	..	..	..	..	..	..	..
5211 Paid by households: motor vehicles	..	23	210	227	606	866	872	978	783	772
5212 Paid by others: motor vehicles	..	0	8	750	1 190	696	155	106	120	178
5213 Paid in respect of other goods	0	1	1	277	350	484	647	644	808	813
Taxes on boats/ships	0	0	1	0	..	..	..	..	..	..
5220 Non-recurrent taxes	1	20	9	0	0	0	0	0	0	0
Exceptional tax on construction of buildings	0	..	9	..	..	..	..	..	..	..
Building permits	0	..	0	..	..	..	..	..	..	..
5300 Unallocable between 5100 and 5200	0	0	0	300	88	1 027	872	681	496	470
6000 Other taxes	**1**	**1**	**3**	**0**	**0**	**0**	**0**	**0**	**0**	**0**
6100 Paid solely by business	–	0	0	..	..	..	..	..	..	..
6200 Other	–	1	3	..	..	..	..	..	..	..
Custom duties collected for the EU	..	..	..	**210**	**307**	**252**	**186**	**162**	**148**	**148**
Total tax revenue on cash basis	**116**	**1 475**	**11 472**	**46 548**	**72 311**	**71 833**	**68 202**	**67 187**	**62 632**	**62 814**
Total tax revenue on accrual basis	..	..	..	**47 178**	**72 565**	**73 349**	**69 764**	**67 819**	**64 184**	**63 514**
Conciliation with National Accounts										
Additional taxes included in National Accounts	–	..	..	0	0	0	0	0	0	0
Taxes excluded from National Accounts	–	..	..	0	0	0	0	0	0	0
Difference in treatment of tax credits	–	..	..	0	0	0	0	0	0	0
Capital transfer for uncollected revenue	–	..	..	-61	0	0	0	0	0	0
Tax (Employer's actual social contributions)	–	..	..	-30	..	..	..	..	..	..
Tax (Employee's actual social contributions)	–	..	..	-31	..	..	..	..	..	..
Voluntary social security contributions	–	..	..	0	0	0	0	0	0	0
Miscellaneous differences	–	..	..	0	0	0	0	0	0	0
National Accounts: Taxes and actual social contributions	–	..	..	47 117	72 565	73 349	69 764	67 819	64 184	63 514
Imputed social contributions	–	..	..	2 690	4 021	5 194	5 134	5 486	4 972	5 340
National Accounts: Taxes and all social contributions	–	..	..	49 807	76 586	78 543	74 898	73 305	69 156	68 854

Notes : Year ending 31st December.

From 1998, data are on accrual basis.

Source : Ministry of Finance, General accounting Office, 20th Directorate of Budget, except the heading 2000, provided by the National Statistics Bureau.

StatLink http://dx.doi.org/10.1787/888933416772

Table 4.13. **Hungary/Hongrie**

Details of tax revenue/Recettes fiscales détaillées

Million HUF

	1965	1980	1990	2000	2007	2009	2011	2012	2013	2014
Total tax revenue	..	..	..	**5 140 592**	**10 114 322**	**10 291 289**	**10 260 605**	**11 043 097**	**11 470 387**	**12 302 136**
Total tax revenue exclusive of custom duties	..	..	..	..	**10 086 341**	**10 265 631**	**10 233 143**	**11 015 891**	**11 444 049**	**12 270 209**
1000 Taxes on income, profits and capital gains	..	..	..	**1 247 420**	**2 539 389**	**2 507 179**	**1 760 627**	**1 990 265**	**2 026 518**	**2 177 039**
1100 Of individuals	..	..	..	954 698	1 838 563	1 928 107	1 422 112	1 622 030	1 610 329	1 705 112
1110 On income and profits	..	..	..	954 698	1 838 563	1 928 107	1 422 112	1 622 030	1 610 329	1 705 112
1120 On capital gains	..	..	..	0	0	0	0	0	0	0
1200 Corporate	..	..	..	292 722	700 826	579 072	338 515	368 235	416 189	471 927
Corporate income tax	..	..	..	292 722	510 781	385 543	316 620	342 305	322 467	394 813
Research and development fund levy	..	..	..	0	0	0	0	0	0	0
Credit institutions' special tax	..	..	..	0	10 890	12 255	20 921	19 783	27 686	29 703
Separate tax for companies	..	..	..	0	178 598	156 859	-16 100	0	0	0
Medicine tax	..	..	..	0	558	245	188	537	111	1
Energy corporations' special tax	..	..	..	0	0	24 170	16 886	5 610	54 060	34 959
Small business tax	..	..	..	0	0	0	0	0	11 865	12 451
1210 On profits	..	..	..	..	..	..	..	..	..	..
1220 On capital gains	..	..	..	..	..	..	..	..	..	..
1300 Unallocable between 1100 and 1200	..	..	..	0	0	0	0	0	0	0
Interest withholding	..	..	..	..	..	..	..	..	..	..
2000 Social security contributions	..	..	..	**1 506 755**	**3 402 194**	**3 334 455**	**3 495 557**	**3 607 882**	**3 745 638**	**4 025 298**
2100 Employees	..	..	..	275 323	941 682	936 961	1 393 288	1 521 230	1 593 836	1 660 500
Pensions	..	..	..	150 585	336 855	402 509	823 476	852 117	875 707	909 607
Health	..	..	..	81 874	513 633	438 314	457 163	551 446	591 729	615 272
Unemployment	..	..	..	42 864	91 194	96 138	112 649	117 667	126 400	135 621
2110 On a payroll basis	..	..	..	..	..	..	..	..	..	..
2120 On an income tax basis	..	..	..	..	..	..	..	..	..	..
2200 Employers	..	..	..	1 213 190	2 402 941	2 323 354	2 056 887	2 057 218	2 126 488	2 337 141
Pensions	..	..	..	734 456	1 508 490	1 792 977	1 824 097	1 798 618	2 101 798	2 203 428
Health	..	..	..	385 019	693 705	366 530	157 690	187 561	24 690	113 725
Unemployment	..	..	..	93 715	200 746	163 847	75 100	71 039	0	19 988
2210 On a payroll basis	..	..	..	..	..	..	..	..	..	..
2220 On an income tax basis	..	..	..	..	..	..	..	..	..	..
2300 Self-employed or non-employed	..	..	..	873	2 534	17 310	22 882	0	0	0
Pensions: of which	..	..	..	0	0	0	0	..	..	..
Self-employed	..	..	..	..	..	..	..	..	..	..
Unemployed	..	..	..	..	..	..	..	..	..	..
Retired	..	..	..	..	..	..	..	..	..	..
Other	..	..	..	..	..	..	..	..	..	..
Health: of which	..	..	..	873	2 534	17 310	22 882	..	..	..
Self-employed	..	..	..	873	2 534	17 310	22 882	..	..	..
Unemployed	..	..	..	0	0	0	0	..	..	..
Retired	..	..	..	0	0	0	0	..	..	..
Other	..	..	..	0	0	0	0	..	..	..
2310 On a payroll basis	..	..	..	..	..	..	..	..	..	..
2320 On an income tax basis	..	..	..	..	..	..	..	..	..	..
2400 Unallocable between 2100, 2200 and 2300	..	..	..	17 368	55 037	56 830	22 500	29 434	25 314	27 657
2410 On a payroll basis	..	..	..	..	..	..	..	..	..	..
2420 On an income tax basis	..	..	..	..	..	..	..	..	..	..
3000 Taxes on payroll and workforce	..	..	..	**183 430**	**82 068**	**89 019**	**128 417**	**156 392**	**168 749**	**180 464**
Rehabilitation contribution	..	..	..	2 184	13 559	14 951	66 427	63 409	64 400	66 166
Training levy	..	..	..	13 186	36 612	43 516	49 647	80 157	63 536	61 416
Wage guarantee contribution	..	..	..	0	0	0	0	0	0	0
Communal tax on enterprises	..	..	..	1 192	1 261	1 291	102	16	2	0
Health contribution	..	..	..	166 869	20 427	21 042	4	0	0	0
Medicine tax	..	..	..	0	10 209	8 219	12 232	12 799	9 547	9 749
Tax on home-workers	..	..	..	0	0	0	5	11	23	26
Lump sum tax for small taxpayers	..	..	..	0	0	0	0	0	31 241	43 107
4000 Taxes on property	..	..	..	**89 024**	**202 711**	**215 068**	**317 081**	**351 136**	**388 824**	**417 379**
4100 Recurrent taxes on immovable property	..	..	..	30 810	72 071	87 328	102 454	127 032	190 249	191 180
Land tax	..	..	..	0	0	0	0	0	0	0
Building tax	..	..	..	22 262	54 556	66 683	80 987	96 318	102 719	105 022
Development land tax	..	..	..	3 099	6 900	9 114	10 310	17 523	19 395	17 937
Communal tax on recreational howes	..	..	..	893	1 412	1 450	58	30	21	198
Communal tax on households	..	..	..	4 557	9 069	10 077	11 099	13 161	13 175	13 002
Luxury tax	..	..	..	0	134	3	0	0	0	0
Public utility tax	..	..	..	0	0	0	0	0	54 939	55 021
4110 Households	..	..	..	..	..	..	..	..	..	..
4120 Others	..	..	..	..	..	..	..	..	..	..
4200 Recurrent taxes on net wealth	..	..	..	0	0	0	139 222	138 581	128 560	138 141
Surtax payable by financial institutions	..	..	..	..	..	..	139 222	138 581	128 560	138 141
4210 Individual	..	..	..	..	..	..	..	..	..	..

StatLink http://dx.doi.org/10.1787/888933416789

Table 4.13. **Hungary/Hongrie** *(cont./suite)*

Details of tax revenue/Recettes fiscales détaillées

Million HUF

	1965	1980	1990	2000	2007	2009	2011	2012	2013	2014
4220 Corporate	..	..	..	..	..	..	..	..	..	..
4300 Estate, inheritance and gift taxes	..	..	..	5 460	13 175	9 259	6 500	5 654	5 307	6 179
4310 Estate and inheritance taxes	..	..	..	4 020	10 775	5 871	5 201	4 591	4 097	4 983
Inheritance tax-local	..	..	..	2 010	4 658	2 561	2 244	616	0	0
Inheritance tax-central	..	..	..	2 010	6 117	3 310	2 957	3 975	4 097	4 983
4320 Gift taxes	..	..	..	1 440	2 400	3 387	1 298	1 063	1 210	1 196
Gift tax-local	..	..	..	720	1 038	1 478	560	143	0	0
Gift tax-central	..	..	..	720	1 363	1 910	738	920	1 210	1 196
4400 Taxes on financial and capital transactions	..	..	..	52 754	117 465	118 482	68 905	79 869	64 708	81 879
Property transfer tax-local	..	..	..	26 349	50 783	51 689	29 733	10 720	0	0
Property transfer tax-central	..	..	..	26 405	66 682	66 792	39 172	69 149	64 708	81 879
4500 Non-recurrent taxes	..	..	..	0	0	0	0	0	0	0
4510 On net wealth	..	..	..	..	..	..	..	..	..	..
4520 Other non-recurrent taxes	..	..	..	..	..	..	..	..	..	..
4600 Other recurrent taxes on property	..	..	..	0	0	0	0	0	0	0
5000 Taxes on goods and services	..	..	..	**2 081 107**	**3 803 630**	**4 061 730**	**4 476 168**	**4 858 734**	**5 038 155**	**5 409 188**
5100 Taxes on production, sale, transfer, etc	..	..	..	2 052 380	3 722 487	3 954 201	4 365 926	4 741 036	4 915 359	5 282 174
5110 General taxes	..	..	..	1 340 572	2 622 027	2 857 504	3 077 927	3 353 969	3 414 342	3 748 164
5111 Value added taxes	..	..	..	1 153 750	2 013 271	2 192 234	2 379 253	2 627 571	2 693 555	3 011 162
5112 Sales tax	..	..	..	0	0	0	43 598	55 040	47 927	48 145
Public health product tax	..	..	..	..	..	..	4 643	19 208	19 090	20 390
Hydrocarbons stockholding fee	..	..	..	..	..	..	38 955	35 832	28 837	27 755
5113 Other	..	..	..	186 823	608 756	665 270	655 076	671 358	672 860	688 857
Local tax on company sales	..	..	..	186 823	427 134	472 155	457 308	471 031	500 868	523 125
Simplified business tax	..	..	..	0	152 812	169 704	172 273	146 531	110 021	96 829
Research and development contribution	..	..	..	0	28 810	23 411	25 495	53 796	61 971	68 903
5120 Taxes on specific goods and services	..	..	..	711 808	1 100 461	1 096 698	1 287 999	1 387 067	1 501 017	1 534 010
5121 Excises	..	..	..	533 502	969 730	971 431	959 962	1 022 624	992 270	1 027 609
Road fund petrol tax	..	..	..	0	0	0	0	0	0	0
Alcohol production duty	..	..	..	3 848	5 621	8 272	180	183	196	444
Water fund tax	..	..	..	6 017	13 171	14 708	14 282	13 640	13 164	12 482
Forestry fund tax	..	..	..	2 858	3 353	108	36	319	0	331
Environment petrol tax	..	..	..	14 837	19 447	27 704	18 368	55 031	46 711	48 094
Budget excises (central budget)	..	..	..	505 942	916 869	906 910	909 775	937 288	915 547	951 458
Coffee	..	..	..	3 200	0	0	0	0	0	0
Alcohol	..	..	..	53 500	88 600	83 300	85 779	85 974	85 487	98 409
Tobacco	..	..	..	107 000	252 400	307 200	285 346	339 845	312 509	292 647
Petrol	..	..	..	156 000	218 200	215 400	203 997	189 984	189 755	197 747
Diesel	..	..	..	157 000	256 600	264 900	297 242	302 561	308 736	340 165
Other oil	..	..	..	6 000	2 200	2 600	2 932	5 253	3 451	3 679
Other budget excises	..	..	..	30 343	93 442	33 552	34 479	13 671	15 608	18 810
Energy tax	..	..	..	0	11 269	13 729	17 321	16 163	16 652	14 801
5122 Profits of fiscal monopolies	..	..	..	0	0	0	0	0	0	0
5123 Customs and import duties	..	..	..	137 730	9 193	7 995	9 380	8 999	8 970	10 986
Customs duties	..	..	..	137 730	9 193	7 995	9 380	8 999	8 970	10 986
5124 Taxes on exports	..	..	..	0	0	0	0	0	0	0
5125 Taxes on investment goods	..	..	..	0	0	0	0	0	0	0
5126 Taxes on specific services	..	..	..	40 576	105 879	109 627	317 613	354 640	498 897	494 590
Gambling tax	..	..	..	27 935	71 804	65 050	64 088	61 452	41 316	45 830
Tourism tax	..	..	..	4 379	0	0	0	0	0	0
Communal tourism tax	..	..	..	2 943	4 935	5 481	6 761	7 682	8 411	9 126
Cultural contribution	..	..	..	4 387	8 432	7 433	136	207	105	146
Pork slaughterhouse tax	..	..	..	32	0	0	0	0	0	0
Breeding contribution	..	..	..	899	919	0	0	0	0	0
Medicine tax	..	..	..	0	19 789	31 663	40 055	41 441	40 496	42 263
Surtax payable by financial institutions	..	..	..	0	0	0	34 630	33 964	1 217	1 293
Specific sectors' surtax	..	..	..	0	0	0	171 943	165 645	9 815	-970
Telecommunication services tax	..	..	..	0	0	0	0	18 322	50 176	55 841
Accident tax	..	..	..	0	0	0	0	25 927	23 313	23 902
Insurance tax	..	..	..	0	0	0	0	0	28 088	28 746
Financial transaction levy	..	..	..	0	0	0	0	0	289 321	274 535
Waste dumping contribution	..	..	..	0	0	0	0	0	6 639	9 796
Advertising tax	..	..	..	0	0	0	0	0	0	4 082
5127 Other taxes on internat. trade and transactions	..	..	..	0	0	0	0	0	0	0
Previous differential producer's turnover tax	..	..	..	..	..	..	..	..	..	..
5128 Other taxes	..	..	..	0	15 659	7 645	1 044	804	881	825
Sugar duty	..	..	..	..	15 659	7 645	1 044	804	881	825
5130 Unallocable between 5110 and 5120	..	..	..	0	0	0	0	0	0	0
5200 Taxes on use of goods and perform activities	..	..	..	28 727	81 143	107 529	110 242	117 698	122 796	127 014

StatLink http://dx.doi.org/10.1787/888933416789

Table 4.13. **Hungary/Hongrie** *(cont./suite)*

Details of tax revenue/Recettes fiscales détaillées

Million HUF

	1965	1980	1990	2000	2007	2009	2011	2012	2013	2014
5210 Recurrent taxes	..	..	..	25 454	74 268	100 861	106 512	113 675	119 226	121 450
Tax on domestically registered vehicles-local	..	..	..	12 622	62 432	63 754	72 073	70 660	69 248	70 786
Tax on domestically registered vehicles-extra budget	..	..	..	0	0	0	0	0	0	0
Tax on domestically registered vehicles-central	..	..	..	8 250	0	0	37	0	0	0
Tax on foreign registered vehicles extra budget fund	..	..	..	0	0	0	0	0	0	0
Tax on foreign registered vehicles-central	..	..	..	3 078	1 655	1 630	1 422	0	0	0
Company car tax	..	..	..	0	0	23 060	25 239	34 293	32 935	31 539
5211 Paid by households: motor vehicles	..	..	..	0	0	0	0	0	0	0
5212 Paid by others: motor vehicles	..	..	..	0	0	0	0	0	0	0
5213 Paid in respect of other goods	..	..	..	1 504	10 181	12 417	7 741	8 722	17 043	19 125
Environmental protection fee	..	..	..	5	13	20	0	0	0	0
Fishing development contribution	..	..	..	40	104	0	0	0	0	0
Environmental protection charge	..	..	..	0	8 785	11 787	7 292	8 272	7 861	6 735
Air pollution levy	..	..	..	751	610	38	0	0	0	0
Water pollution levy	..	..	..	225	186	1	0	0	0	0
Toxic waste levy	..	..	..	65	42	18	0	0	0	0
Noise abatement levy	..	..	..	13	8	12	0	0	0	0
Unidentified environmental protection levies paid to local governments	..	..	..	404	433	541	449	450	521	361
Sale of emission allowances	..	..	..	0	0	0	0	0	8 661	12 029
5220 Non-recurrent taxes	..	..	..	3 273	6 875	6 667	3 730	4 023	3 570	5 564
Land protection levy	..	..	..	1 640	3 777	4 408	962	1 856	1 881	3 367
Vehicle weight fee	..	..	..	805	1 288	676	1 037	1 161	624	1 000
Game protection contribution	..	..	..	178	176	0	0	-1	0	0
Casino license fee	..	..	..	650	1 635	1 583	1 731	1 007	1 065	1 197
5300 Unallocable between 5100 and 5200	..	..	..	0	0	0	0	0	0	0
6000 Other taxes	..	..	..	**32 857**	**56 348**	**58 181**	**55 293**	**51 482**	**76 165**	**60 840**
Unallocable tax penalties	..	..	..	23 546	33 321	35 354	32 165	32 153	56 836	39 546
6100 Paid solely by business	..	..	..	..	..	..	..	..	..	..
Nuclear contribution	..	..	..	..	..	..	..	..	..	..
Medicine tax	..	..	..	..	..	..	..	..	..	..
6200 Other	..	..	..	..	..	..	..	..	..	..
Custom duties collected for the EU	..	..	..	..	**27 981**	**25 657**	**27 462**	**27 206**	**26 337**	**31 927**
Total tax revenue on cash basis	..	..	..	**5 140 592**	**10 020 734**	**10 158 013**	**10 033 880**	**11 017 202**	**11 451 047**	**12 262 390**
Total tax revenue on accrual basis	..	..	..	..	**10 114 322**	**10 291 289**	**10 260 605**	**11 043 097**	**11 470 387**	**12 302 136**
Conciliation with National Accounts										
Additional taxes included in National Accounts	..	..	..	..	45 120	41 214	145 119	36 337	67 094	80 092
Social security contributions	.	..	..	..	0	0	111 510	40	29 592	45 896
Duty for state procedures	..	..	..	..	45 084	41 176	33 545	36 234	37 417	34 172
Other taxes	..	..	..	..	36	38	64	63	85	24
Taxes excluded from National Accounts	..	..	..	..	-49 439	-52 322	-49 360	-47 415	-71 167	-52 444
Water fund tax	..	..	..	..	-13 171	-14 708	-14 282	-13 640	-13 164	-12 482
Tax on foreign registered vehicles	..	..	..	..	-1 655	-1 630	-1 422	0	0	0
Environmental protection fee	..	..	..	..	-446	-561	-449	-450	-520	-361
Air pollution levy	..	..	..	..	-610	-38	0	0	0	0
Water pollution levy	..	..	..	..	-186	-1	0	0	0	0
Toxic waste levy	..	..	..	..	-42	-18	0	0	0	0
Noise abatement levy	..	..	..	..	-8	-12	0	0	0	0
Vehicle weight fee	..	..	..	..	0	0	-1 037	-1 161	-624	-1 000
Unallocable tax penalties	..	..	..	..	-33 320	-35 354	-32 165	-32 153	-56 836	-39 546
Waste dumping contribution	..	..	..	..	0	0	0	0	-23	-26
Tax on home-workers	..	..	..	..	0	0	-5	-11	0	970
Difference in treatment of tax credits	..	..	..	..	0	0	0	0	0	0
Capital transfer for uncollected revenue	..	..	..	..	0	0	0	0	0	0
Voluntary social security contributions	..	..	..	..	1 762	1 626	1 676	1 590	1 503	1 335
Miscellaneous differences	..	..	..	..	-2 687	307	0	1	-2	0
Inheritance tax	..	..	..	..	0	0	..	0	0	..
Gift tax	..	..	..	..	0	0	..	0	0	..
Property transfer tax	..	..	..	..	0	0	..	0	0	..
Rounding	..	..	..	..	4	-2	..	1	-2	..
Taxes on income and profits	..	..	..	..	-2 087	0	..	0	0	..
Corporate income tax	..	..	..	..	0	0	..	0	0	..
Customs duties	..	..	..	..	-603	-56	..	0	0	..
Vehicle weight fee	..	..	..	..	0	0	..	0	0	..
Environment petrol tax	..	..	..	..	0	0	..	0	0	..
Social security contributions	..	..	..	..	0	0	..	0	0	..
Credit institutions' special tax	..	..	..	..	0	364	..	0	0	..
National Accounts: Taxes and actual social contributions	..	..	..	..	10 109 078	10 282 113	10 358 040	11 033 610	11 467 815	12 331 118
Imputed social contributions	..	..	..	..	21 113	23 835	23 039	20 664	21 669	24 486
National Accounts: Taxes and all social contributions	..	..	..	..	10 130 191	10 305 948	10 381 079	11 054 274	11 489 484	12 355 604

StatLink http://dx.doi.org/10.1787/888933416789

Table 4.13. **Hungary/Hongrie** *(cont./suite)*

Details of tax revenue/Recettes fiscales détaillées

Notes : Year ending 31st December.
From 2002, data are on accrual basis.
Heading 5121: The aggregate figure for excise tax revenues is on a cash basis. Revenue from specific excises is in several cases reported on an accrual basis.
Tax base for «Environment petrol tax» is broader than petrol only.
Heading 5123: Part of environmentally related payments is attributable to Local government. It is not possible to present a more detailed breakdown of these figures.
Source : Ministry of Finance, Economic Department.

StatLink http://dx.doi.org/10.1787/888933416789

Table 4.14. **Iceland/Islande**

Details of tax revenue/Recettes fiscales détaillées

Million ISK

	1965	1980	1990	2000	2007	2009	2011	2012	2013	2014
Total tax revenue	**60**	**4 731**	**114 932**	**254 556**	**531 760**	**507 481**	**585 936**	**626 450**	**676 142**	**774 263**
1000 Taxes on income, profits and capital gains	**13**	**1 211**	**34 106**	**101 473**	**241 378**	**239 890**	**266 823**	**283 238**	**315 577**	**360 474**
1100 Of individuals	12	1 092	30 908	88 492	180 070	192 275	220 571	234 475	258 623	270 583
1110 On income and profits	..	..	..	88 492	180 070	192 275	220 571	234 475	258 623	270 583
1120 On capital gains	..	..	..	0	0	0	0	0	0	0
1200 Corporate	1	119	3 198	8 356	32 555	26 499	29 480	33 980	40 479	66 803
1210 On profits	..	..	..	8 356	32 555	26 499	29 480	33 980	40 479	66 803
1220 On capital gains	..	..	..	0	0	0	0	0	0	0
1300 Unallocable between 1100 and 1200	0	0	0	4 625	28 754	21 116	16 772	14 784	16 475	23 088
2000 Social security contributions	**5**	**102**	**3 607**	**19 680**	**39 594**	**45 912**	**66 820**	**64 882**	**69 899**	**73 432**
2100 Employees	0	0	315	..	..	..	..	..	..	..
2110 On a payroll basis	..	..	..	..	..	..	..	..	..	..
2120 On an income tax basis	..	..	..	..	..	..	..	..	..	..
2200 Employers	5	102	3 292	..	..	..	..	..	..	..
2210 On a payroll basis	..	..	..	..	..	..	..	..	..	..
2220 On an income tax basis	..	..	..	..	..	..	..	..	..	..
2300 Self-employed or non-employed	0	0	0	..	..	..	..	..	..	..
2310 On a payroll basis	..	..	..	..	..	..	..	..	..	..
2320 On an income tax basis	..	..	..	..	..	..	..	..	..	..
2400 Unallocable between 2100, 2200 and 2300	0	0	0	19 680	39 594	45 912	66 820	64 882	69 899	73 432
2410 On a payroll basis	..	..	..	19 680	39 594	45 912	66 820	64 882	69 899	73 432
2420 On an income tax basis	..	..	..	0	0	0	0	0	0	0
3000 Taxes on payroll and workforce	**1**	**180**	**4 071**	**184**	**1 519**	**2 470**	**2 900**	**5 402**	**6 534**	**6 994**
4000 Taxes on property	**2**	**297**	**9 689**	**19 983**	**32 523**	**32 806**	**39 282**	**44 304**	**46 493**	**49 634**
4100 Recurrent taxes on immovable property	1	138	4 131	10 107	20 567	27 647	28 348	29 129	30 664	32 344
4110 Households	0	50	1 862	..	..	..	..	..	..	..
4120 Others	1	88	2 269	..	..	..	..	..	..	..
4200 Recurrent taxes on net wealth	0	69	2 402	5 173	-8	12	6 312	9 396	8 886	10 751
4210 Individual	..	29	1 476	..	..	..	..	..	..	..
4220 Corporate	..	40	926	..	..	..	..	..	..	..
4300 Estate, inheritance and gift taxes	0	6	235	765	1 663	1 643	1 292	1 916	2 437	2 507
4310 Estate and inheritance taxes	0	6	235	765	1 663	1 643	1 292	1 916	2 437	2 507
4320 Gift taxes	0	0	0	0	0	0	0	0	0	0
4400 Taxes on financial and capital transactions	1	84	2 921	3 143	9 484	2 934	2 890	3 352	3 973	3 485
4500 Non-recurrent taxes	0	0	0	113	460	311	177	227	233	237
4510 On net wealth	..	..	..	0	0	0	0	0	0	0
4520 Other non-recurrent taxes	..	..	..	113	460	311	177	227	233	237
4600 Other recurrent taxes on property	0	0	0	681	356	260	263	284	299	311
5000 Taxes on goods and services	**37**	**2 834**	**58 943**	**112 245**	**214 988**	**180 199**	**202 441**	**218 630**	**226 619**	**239 915**
5100 Taxes on production, sale, transfer, etc	37	2 778	56 564	100 669	191 957	168 932	192 602	208 704	215 271	228 715
5110 General taxes	10	1 368	37 084	72 667	137 593	120 241	131 057	142 814	149 828	160 871
5111 Value added taxes	0	0	32 698	72 667	137 593	120 241	131 057	142 814	149 828	160 871
5112 Sales tax	10	1 368	4 386	0	0	0	0	0	0	0
5113 Other	0	0	0	0	0	0	0	0	0	0
5120 Taxes on specific goods and services	27	1 410	19 480	28 002	54 364	48 692	61 544	65 890	65 444	67 844
5121 Excises	1	311	2 346	23 585	45 891	39 935	50 239	53 930	55 171	57 521
5122 Profits of fiscal monopolies	5	263	5 986	0	0	0	0	0	0	0
5123 Customs and import duties	20	715	9 181	2 702	5 446	5 303	7 288	7 682	5 815	6 058
5124 Taxes on exports	1	2	0	1	0	5	0	0	0	0
5125 Taxes on investment goods	0	0	0	0	0	0	0	0	0	0
5126 Taxes on specific services	1	69	1 404	1 715	3 026	3 448	4 018	4 278	4 457	4 265
5127 Other taxes on internat. trade and transactions	0	50	563	0	0	0	0	0	0	0
5128 Other taxes	0	0	0	0	0	0	0	0	0	0
5130 Unallocable between 5110 and 5120	0	0	0	0	0	0	0	0	0	0
5200 Taxes on use of goods and perform activities	1	56	2 379	11 576	23 032	11 267	9 839	9 926	11 347	11 199
5210 Recurrent taxes	1	56	2 379	..	..	..	..	..	..	..
5211 Paid by households: motor vehicles	0	10	970	..	..	..	..	..	..	..
5212 Paid by others: motor vehicles	0	41	1 331	..	..	..	..	..	..	..
5213 Paid in respect of other goods	0	5	78	..	..	..	..	..	..	..
5220 Non-recurrent taxes	0	0	0	..	..	..	..	..	..	..
5300 Unallocable between 5100 and 5200	0	0	0	0	0	0	0	0	0	0
6000 Other taxes	**2**	**107**	**4 516**	**991**	**1 758**	**6 203**	**7 670**	**9 993**	**11 020**	**43 814**
6100 Paid solely by business	2	107	4 145	418	628	1 049	2 474	4 383	5 255	37 762
6200 Other	0	0	371	573	1 130	5 154	5 196	5 610	5 766	6 052

StatLink http://dx.doi.org/10.1787/888933416799

Table 4.14. **Iceland/Islande** *(cont./suite)*

Details of tax revenue/Recettes fiscales détaillées

Million ISK

	1965	1980	1990	2000	2007	2009	2011	2012	2013	2014
Non-wastable tax credits										
Non-wastable tax credits against 1110	..	..	..	..	..	..	0	0	0	0
Tax expenditure component	..	..	..	..	..	..	..	..	..	..
Transfer component	..	..	..	..	..	..	..	..	..	..
Non-wastable tax credits against 1210	..	..	..	..	..	..	486	834	1 025	1 162
Tax expenditure component	..	..	..	..	..	..	45	71	127	162
Transfer component	..	..	..	..	..	..	441	764	898	1 000
Total tax revenue on cash basis	**60**	**4 731**	**114 932**	..	..	..	..	..	..	..
Total tax revenue on accrual basis	..	..	..	**254 556**	**531 760**	**507 481**	**585 936**	**626 450**	**676 142**	**774 263**
Conciliation with National Accounts										
Additional taxes included in National Accounts	..	..	..	0	0	0	0	0	0	0
Taxes excluded from National Accounts	..	..	..	-765	-1 663	-1 643	-1 292	-1 916	-2 437	-2 507
Estate and inheritance taxes (4310)	..	..	..	-765	-1 663	-1 643	-1 292	-1 916	-2 437	-2 507
Difference in treatment of tax credits	..	..	..	0	0	0	0	0	0	0
Capital transfer for uncollected revenue	..	..	..	0	0	0	0	0	0	0
Voluntary social security contributions	..	..	..	0	0	0	0	0	0	0
Miscellaneous differences	..	..	..	0	0	0	0	0	0	0
National Accounts: Taxes and actual social contributions	..	..	..	253 791	530 097	505 837	584 644	624 534	673 704	771 756
Imputed social contributions	..	..	..	0	0	0	0	0	0	0
National Accounts: Taxes and all social contributions	..	..	..	253 791	530 097	505 837	584 644	624 534	673 704	771 756

Notes : Year ending 31st December.
From 1998, data are on accrual basis.
Source : Ministry of Finance, Economic Department.

StatLink http://dx.doi.org/10.1787/888933416799

Table 4.15. **Ireland/Irlande**

Details of tax revenue/Recettes fiscales détaillées

Million EUR

	1965	1980	1990	2000	2007	2009	2011	2012	2013	2014
Total tax revenue	**317**	**4 046**	**12 260**	**33 337**	**59 921**	**46 461**	**46 866**	**48 245**	**50 765**	**55 453**
Total tax revenue exclusive of custom duties	..	..	..	**33 130**	**59 648**	**46 253**	**46 626**	**48 002**	**50 518**	**55 178**
1000 Taxes on income, profits and capital gains	**82**	**1 478**	**4 662**	**14 551**	**24 521**	**18 043**	**18 339**	**19 613**	**20 482**	**22 349**
1100 Of individuals	53	1 294	4 059	10 650	18 127	14 147	14 582	15 643	16 204	17 727
1110 On income and profits	53	1 286	4 023	9 876	15 029	13 602	14 166	15 230	15 836	17 187
Income tax	66	1 286	4 023	9 876	15 029	13 602	14 166	15 230	15 836	17 187
Surtax	3	0	0	0	0	0	0	0	0	0
Income tax paid by corporations	-17	0	0	0	0	0	0	0	0	0
1120 On capital gains	0	8	36	774	3 097	545	416	413	369	539
1200 Corporate	29	184	603	3 900	6 395	3 892	3 753	3 965	4 273	4 618
1210 On profits	29	184	603	3 900	6 395	3 892	3 753	3 965	4 273	4 618
Corporation profits tax	12	2	0	0	0	0	0	0	0	0
Corporation tax	0	176	603	3 885	6 393	3 889	3 751	3 964	4 272	4 617
Income tax paid by corporation	17	0	0	0	0	0	0	0	0	0
Agricultural produce duty	0	6	0	14	1	2	1	1	1	1
1220 On capital gains	0	0	0	0	0	0	0	0	0	0
1300 Unallocable between 1100 and 1200	0	0	0	2	0	4	4	4	4	4
2000 Social security contributions	**21**	**578**	**1 729**	**3 941**	**8 118**	**8 795**	**9 039**	**8 482**	**9 020**	**9 581**
2100 Employees	10	190	570	937	1 901	3 183	3 326	3 150	3 290	3 357
2110 On a payroll basis	..	..	570	937	1 901	3 183	3 326	3 150	3 290	3 357
2120 On an income tax basis	..	..	0	0	0	0	0	0	0	0
2200 Employers	10	380	1 092	2 814	5 796	5 297	5 365	5 008	5 326	5 817
2210 On a payroll basis	..	..	1 092	2 814	5 796	5 297	5 365	5 008	5 326	5 817
2220 On an income tax basis	..	..	0	0	0	0	0	0	0	0
2300 Self-employed or non-employed	0	8	67	190	421	315	348	324	403	406
2310 On a payroll basis	..	..	67	190	421	315	348	324	403	406
2320 On an income tax basis	..	..	0	0	0	0	0	0	0	0
2400 Unallocable between 2100, 2200 and 2300	0	0	0	0	0	0	0	0	0	0
2410 On a payroll basis	..	..	..	..	..	..	..	..	..	..
2420 On an income tax basis	..	..	..	..	..	..	..	..	..	..
3000 Taxes on payroll and workforce	**0**	**9**	**159**	**15**	**411**	**368**	**318**	**295**	**314**	**338**
4000 Taxes on property	**48**	**213**	**569**	**1 902**	**4 789**	**2 461**	**2 845**	**3 075**	**3 633**	**4 242**
4100 Recurrent taxes on immovable property	39	139	312	587	1 233	1 322	1 342	1 478	1 724	1 895
4110 Households	..	..	..	..	..	..	..	..	..	..
4120 Others	..	..	..	..	..	..	..	..	..	..
4200 Recurrent taxes on net wealth	0	1	0	0	0	0	460	483	536	743
4210 Individual	..	..	..	..	..	..	0	0	0	0
4220 Corporate	..	..	..	..	..	..	460	483	536	743
4300 Estate, inheritance and gift taxes	6	14	48	225	405	258	242	282	278	359
4310 Estate and inheritance taxes	6	14	45	210	337	210	215	256	259	334
Estate duty	5	..	..	..	..	..	..	..	..	..
Legacy duty	1	..	..	..	..	..	..	..	..	..
Succession duty	0	..	..	..	..	..	..	..	..	..
4320 Gift taxes	0	0	3	15	68	48	27	26	20	24
4400 Taxes on financial and capital transactions	3	59	209	1 090	3 151	882	801	832	1 094	1 245
Stamp duty	3	59	209	1 090	3 151	882	801	832	1 094	1 245
4500 Non-recurrent taxes	0	0	0	0	0	0	0	0	0	0
4510 On net wealth	..	..	..	..	..	..	..	..	..	..
4520 Other non-recurrent taxes	..	..	..	..	..	..	..	..	..	..
4600 Other recurrent taxes on property	0	0	0	0	0	0	0	0	0	0
5000 Taxes on goods and services	**167**	**1 769**	**5 141**	**12 721**	**21 809**	**16 582**	**16 075**	**16 528**	**17 046**	**18 645**
5100 Taxes on production, sale, transfer, etc	155	1 741	4 940	12 166	20 710	15 354	14 719	15 169	15 546	17 028
5110 General taxes	18	597	2 500	7 643	14 355	10 324	9 755	10 219	10 372	11 521
5111 Value added taxes	0	597	2 500	7 643	14 355	10 324	9 755	10 219	10 372	11 521
Value added tax	..	597	2 500	7 643	14 355	10 324	9 755	10 219	10 372	11 521
5112 Sales tax	18	0	0	0	0	0	0	0	0	0
Turnover tax	18	..	..	..	..	..	..	..	..	..
Wholesale tax	0	..	..	..	..	..	..	..	..	..
5113 Other	0	0	0	0	0	0	0	0	0	0
5120 Taxes on specific goods and services	137	1 143	2 440	4 523	6 354	5 029	4 963	4 949	5 174	5 507
5121 Excises	124	1 045	2 084	4 402	6 103	4 870	4 855	4 774	5 013	5 178
Beer	19	192	356	475	459	397	309	309	363	428
Oils	31	330	745	1 491	2 204	2 170	2 119	2 035	2 035	2 043
Spirits	16	148	153	241	363	267	251	263	282	296
Table waters	0	11	23	0	0	0	0	0	0	0
Tobacco	50	187	419	1 035	1 192	1 217	1 127	1 072	1 064	990
Wine, cider, perry	1	18	46	154	297	297	270	280	354	416
Motor vehicle (incl. tyres)	7	148	331	985	1 554	373	394	384	459	572
Others	1	11	11	20	34	149	385	431	457	432
5122 Profits of fiscal monopolies	0	0	0	0	0	0	0	0	0	0

StatLink http://dx.doi.org/10.1787/888933416802

Table 4.15. **Ireland/Irlande** *(cont./suite)*

Details of tax revenue/Recettes fiscales détaillées

Million EUR

	1965	1980	1990	2000	2007	2009	2011	2012	2013	2014
5123 Customs and import duties	10	62	147	0	0	0	0	0	0	0
5124 Taxes on exports	0	0	0	0	0	0	0	0	0	0
UE agriculture levies	..	..	..	..	..	..	..	..	..	..
5125 Taxes on investment goods	0	0	0	0	0	0	0	0	0	0
5126 Taxes on specific services	3	21	171	122	252	160	109	176	161	329
Duty on betting	2	19	37	59	36	31	28	27	26	27
Sweepstakes duty	1	1	0	0	0	0	0	0	0	0
Bank levy	0	0	46	61	66	-1	-103	-32	-23	128
Other	0	1	88	2	150	130	184	181	159	174
5127 Other taxes on internat. trade and transactions	0	0	0	0	0	0	0	0	0	0
5128 Other taxes	0	14	37	0	0	0	0	0	0	0
5130 Unallocable between 5110 and 5120	0	0	0	0	0	0	0	0	0	0
5200 Taxes on use of goods and perform activities	11	28	201	555	1 100	1 228	1 357	1 359	1 500	1 618
5210 Recurrent taxes	11	28	201	555	1 100	1 228	1 357	1 359	1 500	1 618
5211 Paid by households: motor vehicles	6	14	100	373	723	793	758	791	885	904
5212 Paid by others: motor vehicles	5	11	82	124	239	264	253	264	284	290
5213 Paid in respect of other goods	0	3	20	58	138	170	347	304	331	424
5220 Non-recurrent taxes	0	0	0	0	0	0	0	0	0	0
5300 Unallocable between 5100 and 5200	0	0	0	0	0	0	0	0	0	0
6000 Other taxes	**0**	**0**	**0**	**0**	**0**	**4**	**10**	**10**	**23**	**23**
6100 Paid solely by business	..	..	..	..	..	0	0	0	0	0
6200 Other	..	..	..	..	..	4	10	10	23	23
Custom duties collected for the EU	..	..	..	**208**	**273**	**208**	**240**	**242**	**247**	**275**
Non-wastable tax credits										
Non-wastable tax credits against 1110	..	..	..	..	..	..	..	..	..	..
Tax expenditure component	..	..	..	..	843	1 076	1 096	1 224	816	667
Transfer component	..	..	..	..	..	..	..	..	..	..
Total tax revenue on cash basis	**317**	**4 046**	**12 260**	**33 055**	**60 810**	**47 905**	**47 441**	**49 548**	**51 435**	**55 587**
Total tax revenue on accrual basis	..	..	..	**33 337**	**59 921**	**46 461**	**46 866**	**48 245**	**50 765**	**55 453**
Conciliation with National Accounts										
Additional taxes included in National Accounts	..	..	..	0	0	196	183	185	184	184
Taxes excluded from National Accounts	..	..	..	0	0	0	0	0	0	0
Difference in treatment of tax credits	..	..	..	0	843	1 076	1 096	1 224	816	667
Capital transfer for uncollected revenue	..	..	..	0	0	0	0	0	0	0
Voluntary social security contributions	..	..	..	0	0	0	0	0	0	0
Miscellaneous differences	..	..	..	0	0	0	0	0	0	0
National Accounts: Taxes and actual social contributions	..	..	..	33 337	60 764	47 732	48 145	49 653	51 765	56 304
Imputed social contributions	..	..	..	1 366	2 579	1 448	1 330	1 393	1 390	1 403
National Accounts: Taxes and all social contributions	..	..	..	34 704	63 343	49 180	49 474	51 046	53 155	57 707

Notes : The data for personal income tax revenues differs from the ESA2010 presentation as payable tax credits are excluded, in accordance with the presentation in earlier editions of the publication.

The data for years 1965 to 1973 are on fiscal year basis (commencing on 1st April) and are therefore not strictly comparable with the data for later years, which are on a calendar year basis.

From 1998, data are on accrual basis.

Heading 1200: Capital gains taxes paid by corporations are included in heading 1210.

Heading 2100: Includes contributions by self-employed and certain voluntary contributions.

Heading 2200: Since 1976, income tax paid by corporations and corporation profits tax have been replaced by corporation tax.

Heading 5111: Includes arrears of the wholesale and turnover taxes.

Tax receipts in 1988 were inflated by the success of the new arrangements for assessment and collection of tax. These arrangements included an amnesty for tax arrears paid by 30th September. This amnesty waived penalities and interest charge tax. It resulted in payments of 631 millons of euros spread across the main tax headings.

Source : Annual Report of The Revenue Commissioners, Financial Accounts and National Income and Expenditure Accounts.

StatLink http://dx.doi.org/10.1787/888933416802

Table 4.16. **Israel/Israël**

Details of tax revenue/Recettes fiscales détaillées

Million ILS

	1965	1980	1990	2000	2007	2009	2011	2012	2013	2014
Total tax revenue	..	..	..	**187 949**	**250 813**	**242 607**	**288 226**	**296 965**	**323 895**	**341 714**
1000 Taxes on income, profits and capital gains	..	..	..	**74 551**	**91 522**	**72 815**	**86 190**	**90 739**	**101 879**	**105 628**
1100 Of individuals	..	..	..	54 753	56 426	47 572	51 866	53 530	57 709	63 402
1110 On income and profits	..	..	..	53 698	55 205	46 964	50 980	52 791	56 279	61 152
On wages – deduction at source	..	..	..	45 278	45 507	39 141	42 817	43 415	46 856	50 746
On self employement income – deduction at source	..	..	..	2 655	3 676	2 699	3 149	3 372	3 891	3 786
On self employement income – other	..	..	..	5 764	6 022	5 125	5 015	6 004	5 532	6 620
1120 On capital gains	..	..	..	1 055	1 221	608	886	739	1 430	2 250
1200 Corporate	..	..	..	18 001	30 210	20 663	27 636	27 054	36 639	34 957
1210 On profits	..	..	..	16 109	27 582	20 049	26 860	26 083	33 939	31 957
deduction at source	..	..	..	1 991	2 550	2 090	2 308	2 423	2 611	2 586
In lieu of VAT on the profits of Financial Institutions	..	..	..	1 287	2 198	1 757	1 431	2 149	2 236	2 133
Other	..	..	..	12 831	22 834	16 202	23 121	21 511	29 092	27 237
1220 On capital gains	..	..	..	1 892	2 628	614	776	971	2 700	3 000
1300 Unallocable between 1100 and 1200	..	..	..	1 797	4 886	4 580	6 688	10 155	7 531	7 269
Tax deducted at the source on the capital market	..	..	..	1 797	4 886	4 580	6 688	10 155	7 531	7 269
2000 Social security contributions	..	..	..	**27 565**	**37 909**	**41 227**	**48 759**	**50 296**	**53 364**	**56 130**
2100 Employees	..	..	..	17 895	25 729	28 236	32 922	33 936	35 134	36 546
2110 On a payroll basis	..	..	..	17 895	25 729	28 236	32 922	33 936	35 134	36 546
2120 On an income tax basis	..	..	..	0	0	0	0	0	0	0
2200 Employers	..	..	..	8 182	9 960	10 278	12 805	13 313	15 026	16 163
2210 On a payroll basis	..	..	..	8 182	9 960	10 278	12 805	13 313	15 026	16 163
2220 On an income tax basis	..	..	..	0	0	0	0	0	0	0
2300 Self-employed or non-employed	..	..	..	1 488	2 220	2 712	3 033	3 047	3 204	3 421
2310 On a payroll basis	..	..	..	1 488	2 220	2 712	3 033	3 047	3 204	3 421
2320 On an income tax basis	..	..	..	0	0	0	0	0	0	0
2400 Unallocable between 2100, 2200 and 2300	..	..	..	0	0	0	0	0	0	0
2410 On a payroll basis	..	..	..	..	..	..	..	..	..	..
2420 On an income tax basis	..	..	..	..	..	..	..	..	..	..
3000 Taxes on payroll and workforce	..	..	..	**6 850**	**9 920**	**9 570**	**10 850**	**11 530**	**12 274**	**12 967**
Employers tax on the the non-profit sector other than govt	..	..	..	1 250	1 500	300	350	400	392	381
In lieu of VAT on the wage-bill in the non-profit sector	..	..	..	4 260	6 580	7 250	8 050	8 550	9 012	9 980
In lieu VAT on the wage-bill in Financial Institutions	..	..	..	1 340	1 840	2 020	2 450	2 580	2 870	2 606
4000 Taxes on property	..	..	..	**16 595**	**23 814**	**24 444**	**30 021**	**29 024**	**31 241**	**32 416**
4100 Recurrent taxes on immovable property	..	..	..	11 311	16 156	17 973	19 954	20 752	21 541	22 476
Land tax	..	..	..	442	52	45	82	57	59	95
4110 Households	..	..	..	0	0	0	0	0	0	0
4120 Others	..	..	..	10 869	16 104	17 928	19 872	20 695	21 483	22 381
4200 Recurrent taxes on net wealth	..	..	..	0	0	0	0	0	0	0
4210 Individual	..	..	..	..	..	..	..	..	..	..
4220 Corporate	..	..	..	..	..	..	..	..	..	..
4300 Estate, inheritance and gift taxes	..	..	..	0	0	0	0	0	0	0
4310 Estate and inheritance taxes	..	..	..	..	..	..	..	..	..	..
4320 Gift taxes	..	..	..	..	..	..	..	..	..	..
4400 Taxes on financial and capital transactions	..	..	..	2 841	3 087	2 229	3 113	2 788	3 398	3 727
Transaction tax on the buyer of real estate	..	..	..	1 632	2 616	2 166	3 086	2 786	3 398	3 727
Transaction tax on the seller of real estate	..	..	..	206	404	43	21	1	0	0
Stamp tax	..	..	..	1 003	67	20	7	1	0	0
4500 Non-recurrent taxes	..	..	..	2 443	4 571	4 242	6 954	5 484	6 302	6 213
4510 On net wealth	..	..	..	0	0	0	0	0	0	0
4520 Other non-recurrent taxes	..	..	..	2 443	4 571	4 242	6 954	5 484	6 302	6 213
Capital gains tax on real estate	..	..	..	2 443	4 571	4 242	6 954	5 484	6 302	6 213
4600 Other recurrent taxes on property	..	..	..	0	0	0	0	0	0	0
5000 Taxes on goods and services	..	..	..	**62 388**	**87 648**	**94 551**	**112 405**	**115 376**	**125 137**	**134 573**
5100 Taxes on production, sale, transfer, etc	..	..	..	57 887	81 109	87 834	104 407	107 155	116 335	125 577
5110 General taxes	..	..	..	49 876	67 571	71 954	85 586	88 167	97 357	105 700
5111 Value added taxes	..	..	..	39 805	53 984	59 223	70 197	72 777	81 524	87 812
5112 Sales tax	..	..	..	10 071	13 587	12 731	15 389	15 390	15 833	17 888
On domestic production	..	..	..	662	287	229	307	305	457	394
On imports	..	..	..	9 409	13 300	12 502	15 082	15 085	15 376	17 494
5113 Other	..	..	..	0	0	0	0	0	0	0
5120 Taxes on specific goods and services	..	..	..	8 011	13 538	15 880	18 821	18 988	18 978	19 877
5121 Excises	..	..	..	6 595	11 323	13 478	15 910	16 445	16 680	17 101
On domestically refined fuel	..	..	..	5 666	10 590	12 714	15 118	15 628	15 876	16 362
On domestically processed tobacco products	..	..	..	929	733	764	792	817	804	739
5122 Profits of fiscal monopolies	..	..	..	0	0	0	0	0	0	0
5123 Customs and import duties	..	..	..	1 417	2 215	2 402	2 911	2 543	2 298	2 776
5124 Taxes on exports	..	..	..	0	0	0	0	0	0	0
5125 Taxes on investment goods	..	..	..	0	0	0	0	0	0	0

StatLink http://dx.doi.org/10.1787/888933416813

Table 4.16. **Israel/Israël** *(cont./suite)*

Details of tax revenue/Recettes fiscales détaillées

Million ILS

	1965	1980	1990	2000	2007	2009	2011	2012	2013	2014
5126 Taxes on specific services	..	..	..	0	0	0	0	0	0	0
5127 Other taxes on internat. trade and transactions	..	..	..	0	0	0	0	0	0	0
5128 Other taxes	..	..	..	0	0	0	0	0	0	0
5130 Unallocable between 5110 and 5120	..	..	..	0	0	0	0	0	0	0
5200 Taxes on use of goods and perform activities	..	..	..	4 501	6 540	6 717	7 998	8 221	8 803	8 996
5210 Recurrent taxes	..	..	..	4 501	6 540	6 717	7 998	8 221	8 803	8 996
5211 Paid by households: motor vehicles	..	..	..	1 436	1 895	2 047	2 424	2 533	2 872	3 041
5212 Paid by others: motor vehicles	..	..	..	479	632	682	808	844	957	1 014
5213 Paid in respect of other goods	..	..	..	2 587	4 014	3 988	4 766	4 843	4 973	4 942
Licences collected by the Ministry of Transportation	..	..	..	257	535	357	287	345	132	132
Licences collected by the Ministry of Communication	..	..	..	151	332	282	148	269	299	247
Licences collected by other ministries	..	..	..	1 600	2 262	2 346	3 134	2 971	3 227	3 194
Business and professional licences paid locally	..	..	..	528	799	900	1 094	1 148	1 190	1 240
Other local authority fees	..	..	..	51	86	102	102	110	125	129
5220 Non-recurrent taxes	..	..	..	0	0	0	0	0	0	0
5300 Unallocable between 5100 and 5200	..	..	..	0	0	0	0	0	0	0
6000 Other taxes	**..**	**..**	**..**	**0**	**0**	**0**	**0**	**0**	**0**	**0**
6100 Paid solely by business	..	..	..	..	..	..	..	..	..	..
6200 Other	..	..	..	..	..	..	..	..	..	..
Non-wastable tax credits										
Non-wastable tax credits against 1110	..	..	..	..	..	87	141	196	911	625
Tax expenditure component	..	..	..	..	..	2	5	8	32	38
Transfer component	..	..	..	..	..	85	136	188	879	587
Non-wastable tax credits against 1210	..	..	..	..	..	0	0	0	0	0
Tax expenditure component	..	..	..	..	..	..	..	..	..	..
Transfer component	..	..	..	..	..	..	..	..	..	..
Total tax revenue on cash basis	**..**	**..**	**..**	**187 949**	**250 813**	**242 607**	**288 226**	**296 965**	**323 895**	**341 714**
Total tax revenue on accrual basis	**..**	**..**	**..**	**..**	**..**	**..**	**..**	**..**	**..**	**..**
Conciliation with National Accounts										
Additional taxes included in National Accounts	..	..	..	0	0	0	0	0	0	0
Taxes excluded from National Accounts	..	..	..	0	0	0	0	0	0	0
Difference in treatment of tax credits	..	..	..	0	0	0	0	0	0	0
Capital transfer for uncollected revenue	..	..	..	0	0	0	0	0	0	0
Voluntary social security contributions	..	..	..	0	0	0	0	0	0	0
Miscellaneous differences	..	..	..	0	0	0	0	0	0	0
National Accounts: Taxes and actual social contributions	..	..	..	187 949	250 813	242 607	288 226	296 965	323 895	341 714
Imputed social contributions	..	..	..	6 076	6 926	7 570	8 253	8 476	8 730	8 515
National Accounts: Taxes and all social contributions	..	..	..	194 026	257 739	250 176	296 478	305 441	332 626	350 229

Notes : Year ending 31st December.

Data are on a cash basis.

The statistical data for Israel are supplied by and under the responsibility of the relevant Israeli authorities. The use of such data by the OECD is without prejudice to the status of the Golan Heights, East Jerusalem and Israeli settlements in the West Bank under the terms of International law.

Source : Israel Central Bureau of Statistics and Israel Ministry of Finance.

StatLink http://dx.doi.org/10.1787/888933416813

Table 4.17. **Italy/Italie**

Details of tax revenue/Recettes fiscales détaillées

Million EUR

	1965	1980	1990	2000	2007	2009	2011	2012	2013	2014
Total tax revenue	**5 505**	**60 422**	**265 116**	**503 096**	**671 189**	**661 725**	**686 198**	**708 166**	**705 533**	**704 217**
Total tax revenue exclusive of custom duties	..	..	..	**501 560**	**668 928**	**659 717**	**683 879**	**706 089**	**703 643**	**702 195**
1000 Taxes on income, profits and capital gains	**982**	**18 821**	**96 707**	**166 912**	**226 498**	**215 238**	**218 920**	**230 829**	**233 294**	**225 175**
1100 Of individuals	603	13 940	69 654	124 918	172 136	175 462	180 499	187 298	185 996	182 276
1110 On income and profits	603	13 796	68 786	124 233	172 122	175 452	180 492	187 293	185 991	182 271
Personal income tax	0	11 538	57 318	121 211	162 644	166 131	173 605	178 265	175 921	171 920
Local income tax paid by households	0	829	4 492	67	0	0	0	0	0	0
Tax on income from investiments (60%)	319	55	15	0	0	0	0	8	11	22
10% Surcharge on income	94	37	5	0	0	0	0	0	0	0
10% proportional surcharge	1	0	0	0	0	0	0	0	0	0
Withholding tax on company dividends paid by households	23	51	496	110	542	428	445	644	564	976
Law 1177 proportional surcharge (60%)	39	0	1	0	0	0	0	0	0	0
Direct taxes 5% proportional surcharge (60%)	0	8	72	0	0	0	0	0	0	0
Additional Treasury increase (60%)	23	6	1	0	0	0	0	0	0	0
Decree 1132 revenues (60%)	0	0	0	0	0	0	0	0	0	0
Tax on households	65	7	0	0	0	0	0	0	0	0
Rental value tax	2	0	0	0	0	0	0	0	0	0
Driving licence tax	1	0	0	0	0	0	0	0	0	0
Municipal surcharge on buildings (40%)	37	5	0	22	0	0	0	0	0	0
Withholding tax on income from deposits paid by households	0	1 206	6 223	2 823	8 402	8 191	5 824	7 865	8 994	8 869
Direct taxes refund (60%)	0	0	41	0	0	0	0	0	0	0
Other	0	53	123	0	534	702	618	511	501	484
1120 On capital gains	0	144	867	685	14	10	7	5	5	5
Tax on capital gains on land	..	0	0	0	0	0	0	0	0	0
Municipal capital gains tax on buildings paid by households (60%)	..	144	867	685	14	10	7	5	5	5
1200 Corporate	379	4 710	26 605	34 699	50 529	37 444	35 798	38 611	41 194	35 246
1210 On profits	379	4 494	26 027	34 242	50 520	37 438	35 794	38 608	41 190	35 243
Corporation tax	0	1 245	9 042	28 877	47 192	33 674	35 072	36 537	39 160	31 150
Municipal surcharge on buildings (60%)	37	8	0	32	0	0	0	0	0	0
Tax on income from investments (40%)	213	37	10	0	0	0	0	5	8	15
Company franchise and liabilities tax	88	12	2	0	0	0	0	0	0	0
Law 1177 proportional surcharge (40%)	26	0	0	0	0	0	0	0	0	0
Direct taxes 5% proportional surcharge (40%)	0	20	48	0	0	0	0	0	0	0
Decree 1132 revenues (40%)	0	0	0	0	0	0	0	0	0	0
Additional Treasury increase (40%)	15	4	0	0	0	0	0	0	0	0
Withholding tax on company dividends paid by firms	0	77	745	166	0	0	0	0	0	0
Withholding tax on income from deposits paid by firms	0	1 810	9 334	4 235	2 370	3 030	372	1 280	1 464	1 097
Local income tax paid by firms	0	1 245	6 738	100	15	22	10	15	12	16
Direct taxes refund (40%)	0	0	27	0	0	0	0	0	0	0
Other	0	36	82	832	943	712	340	771	546	2 965
1220 On capital gains	0	216	578	457	9	6	4	3	4	3
Municipal capital gains tax on buildings paid by firms (40%)	..	216	578	457	9	6	4	3	4	3
1300 Unallocable between 1100 and 1200	0	171	448	7 295	3 833	2 332	2 623	4 920	6 104	7 653
Refunds tax on income	..	-240	-1 768	-5 175	0	0	0	0	0	0
Other	..	412	2 216	12 470	3 833	2 332	2 623	4 920	6 104	7 653
2000 Social security contributions	**1 881**	**22 976**	**87 256**	**143 629**	**200 772**	**207 635**	**211 637**	**210 897**	**210 462**	**209 653**
2100 Employees	..	4 171	16 753	27 333	35 715	37 866	37 607	36 689	39 284	38 616
2110 On a payroll basis	..	..	..	27 333	35 715	37 866	37 607	36 689	39 284	38 616
2120 On an income tax basis	..	..	..	0	0	0	0	0	0	0
2200 Employers	..	17 152	62 540	99 904	137 924	142 787	145 554	143 324	141 629	140 608
2210 On a payroll basis	..	..	..	99 904	137 924	142 787	145 554	143 324	141 629	140 608
2220 On an income tax basis	..	..	..	0	0	0	0	0	0	0
2300 Self-employed or non-employed	..	1 654	7 962	16 392	27 133	26 982	28 476	30 884	29 549	30 429
2310 On a payroll basis	..	..	..	16 392	27 133	26 982	28 476	30 884	29 549	30 429
2320 On an income tax basis	..	..	..	0	0	0	0	0	0	0
2400 Unallocable between 2100, 2200 and 2300	1 881	0	0	0	0	0	0	0	0	0
2410 On a payroll basis	..	..	..	..	..	..	..	..	..	..
2420 On an income tax basis	..	..	..	..	..	..	..	..	..	..
3000 Taxes on payroll and workforce	**0**	**387**	**890**	**0**	**0**	**0**	**0**	**0**	**0**	**0**
Contributions to GESCAL	..	387	890	..	..	..	..	..	..	..
4000 Taxes on property	**397**	**2 248**	**5 983**	**23 360**	**32 646**	**40 985**	**36 098**	**43 643**	**43 883**	**46 762**

StatLink http://dx.doi.org/10.1787/888933416825

Table 4.17. **Italy/Italie** *(cont./suite)*

Details of tax revenue/Recettes fiscales détaillées

Million EUR

	1965	1980	1990	2000	2007	2009	2011	2012	2013	2014
4100 Recurrent taxes on immovable property	96	7	1	9 354	12 778	9 461	9 848	23 942	20 748	25 199
Income tax on landowners	2	0	0	0	0	0	0	0	0	0
Income tax on buildings	12	2	1	0	0	0	0	0	0	0
Income tax on luxury buildings	1	0	0	0	0	0	0	0	0	0
Surcharge on land (provincial)	16	0	0	0	0	0	0	0	0	0
Surcharge on land (municipal)	18	0	0	0	0	0	0	0	0	0
Surcharge on buildings (provincial)	26	2	0	0	0	0	0	0	0	0
Surcharge on buildings (municipal)	21	3	0	0	0	0	0	0	0	0
Municipal real estate tax	0	0	0	9 354	12 778	9 461	9 848	23 942	20 748	20 553
Tax on indivisible services (TASI)	0	0	0	0	0	0	0	0	0	4 646
4110 Households	..	..	..	..	..	..	..	..	..	..
4120 Others	..	..	..	..	..	..	..	..	..	..
4200 Recurrent taxes on net wealth	0	0	0	14	1	6 575	5 117	778	2 547	829
4210 Individuals	..	..	..	5	0	0	0	0	0	0
4220 Corporate	..	..	..	9	1	6 575	5 117	778	2 547	829
4300 Estate, inheritance and gift taxes	47	128	376	1 005	149	462	510	592	622	621
Inheritance and gift duty	33	119	376	1 005	149	462	510	592	622	621
Estate duty	11	9	0	0	0	0	0	0	0	0
Proportional surcharge and premium	3	0	0	0	0	0	0	0	0	0
4310 Estate and inheritance taxes	..	..	..	..	..	..	..	..	..	..
4320 Gift taxes	..	..	..	..	..	..	..	..	..	..
4400 Taxes on financial and capital transactions	255	2 113	5 606	12 320	18 256	17 349	16 798	15 317	17 092	17 990
Registration tax	120	1 048	2 421	6 794	9 410	8 833	8 411	7 557	7 353	7 646
Mortgage taxes and land registry duties	22	190	469	1 067	2 525	2 076	2 112	1 854	1 841	1 513
5% proportional surcharge	6	0	0	0	0	0	0	0	0	0
Additional surcharge	4	0	0	0	0	0	0	0	0	0
Stamp duties and surcharges accruing on cadastral acts	104	751	2 185	4 459	6 321	6 440	6 275	5 906	7 898	8 423
Other	0	123	530	0	0	0	0	0	0	408
4500 Non-recurrent taxes	0	0	0	98	151	5 219	1 354	154	985	131
4510 On net wealth	..	..	..	0	0	0	0	0	0	0
4520 Other non-recurrent taxes	..	..	..	98	151	5 219	1 354	154	985	131
4600 Other recurrent taxes on property	0	0	0	569	1 311	1 919	2 471	2 860	1 889	1 992
5000 Taxes on goods and services	**2 173**	**15 990**	**74 280**	**140 316**	**169 608**	**164 207**	**184 275**	**187 524**	**184 024**	**190 220**
5100 Taxes on production, sale, transfer, etc.	2 037	15 251	67 083	125 745	152 930	146 855	164 900	167 312	162 707	168 151
Direct taxes refund	0	-73	-86	0	0	0	0	0	0	0
5110 General taxes	710	9 438	38 940	77 473	95 623	86 544	98 650	96 170	93 921	97 041
5111 Value added taxes	0	9 438	38 940	77 473	95 623	86 544	98 650	96 170	93 921	97 041
VAT	..	9 438	38 940	77 473	95 623	86 544	98 650	96 170	93 921	97 041
5112 Sales tax	0	0	0	0	0	0	0	0	0	0
5113 Other	710	0	0	0	0	0	0	0	0	0
General tax on receipts	662	..	..	..	..	..	..	..	..	..
Compensation tax on imported products	48	..	..	..	..	..	..	..	..	..
5120 Taxes on specific goods and services	1 327	5 886	28 048	48 272	57 307	60 311	66 250	71 142	68 786	71 110
5121 Excises	816	4 088	20 304	31 479	32 904	35 639	41 088	46 796	45 720	48 661
Duty on mineral oils	465	3 462	15 928	22 172	23 252	23 157	23 771	27 680	26 332	25 659
Duty on spirits	27	87	206	486	595	569	552	545	571	674
Duty on beer	12	54	172	242	489	463	528	494	532	642
Duty on sugars	22	25	68	120	0	6	5	7	10	-2
Duty on electricity	20	51	2 018	3 079	3 034	5 960	10 361	13 099	13 542	16 266
Duty on bananas	9	53	97	0	0	0	0	0	0	0
Duty on coffee	31	60	74	0	0	0	0	0	0	0
Duty on cocoa	3	4	7	0	0	0	0	0	0	0
Duty on olive oil	0	0	0	0	0	0	0	0	0	0
Other duty	44	190	1 037	5 201	5 385	5 425	5 816	4 910	4 659	5 357
Alcohol, spirits, liquor	5	0	0	0	0	0	0	0	0	0
On matches and flints	13	22	47	0	0	0	0	0	0	0
Meat	26	0	0	0	0	0	0	0	0	0
In-bond surcharge	0	81	650	174	143	59	48	54	67	59
Combustible materials	39	0	0	0	0	0	0	0	0	0
Construction materials	30	0	0	0	0	0	0	0	0	0
Excise duty on sound and video	3	0	0	0	0	0	0	0	0	0
Tax on phonograph records	1	0	0	0	0	0	0	0	0	0
Stamp duty on playing cards	1	0	0	0	0	0	0	0	0	0
Other	66	0	0	5	6	0	7	7	7	6
5122 Profits of fiscal monopolies	303	1 033	3 248	7 718	10 440	10 945	11 247	11 362	10 683	10 426
Duty on tobacco	292	1 033	3 248	7 712	10 436	10 941	11 243	11 358	10 679	10 423
On salt	10	0	0	0	0	0	0	0	0	0
Duty on products of Monopoli di Stato	1	0	0	6	4	4	4	4	4	3

StatLink http://dx.doi.org/10.1787/888933416825

Table 4.17. **Italy/Italie** *(cont./suite)*

Details of tax revenue/Recettes fiscales détaillées

Million EUR

	1965	1980	1990	2000	2007	2009	2011	2012	2013	2014
5123 Customs and import duties	142	261	1 164	0	0	0	0	0	0	0
Common Customs tariff (CEE)	0	0	836	..	..	..	..	..	..	..
Customs and shipping duties	115	14	0	..	..	..	..	..	..	..
Administrative services duties	11	0	0	..	..	..	..	..	..	..
Tax on agriculture	15	228	207	..	..	..	..	..	..	..
Other duties	0	9	68	..	..	..	..	..	..	..
Compensatory amounts	0	9	53	..	..	..	..	..	..	..
5124 Taxes on exports	0	0	0	0	0	0	0	0	0	0
5125 Taxes on investment goods	0	0	0	0	0	0	0	0	0	0
5126 Taxes on specific services	67	483	3 141	9 029	13 932	13 727	13 915	12 984	12 383	12 023
Entertainment tax	20	59	167	118	68	56	52	44	42	44
Stamp duty	6	0	0	0	0	0	0	0	0	0
Tax on advertisements	6	56	168	389	392	393	440	424	424	392
Tax on lotto, lotteries, betting and Totocalcio game	3	123	617	4 164	7 144	7 980	8 090	7 477	7 088	7 427
Casino takings, special duties, etc.	0	0	0	158	152	151	192	191	130	134
Single tax on games of skill and betting-levied indirectly	9	74	476	487	405	237	186	144	85	95
Aerotaxi passengers tax	0	0	0	0	0	0	0	5	7	8
Local tax (including insurance)	23	171	1 714	3 713	5 771	4 910	4 955	4 699	4 607	3 923
5127 Other taxes on internat. trade and transactions	0	0	0	0	0	0	0	0	0	0
Special Duty on foreign payments and currency selling	..	..	..	..	..	..	..	..	..	..
5128 Other taxes	0	21	192	46	31	0	0	0	0	0
ECSC taxes and contributions on sugar and other levies	..	21	121	0	0	..	..	..	..	..
Other	..	0	70	46	31	..	..	..	..	..
5130 Unallocable between 5110 and 5120	0	0	180	0	0	0	0	0	0	0
5200 Taxes on use of goods and perform activities	136	456	4 474	8 479	10 550	10 407	10 907	11 185	10 930	11 341
5210 Recurrent taxes	136	456	4 474	8 479	10 550	10 407	10 907	11 185	10 930	11 341
Public motor vehicle register tax	64	152	967	1 034	1 326	1 192	1 242	1 368	1 359	1 420
Tax on vehicles 5% proportional surcharge	3	13	450	0	0	0	0	0	0	0
Surcharge on diesel cars	0	66	683	0	0	0	0	0	0	0
Surcharge on gas cars	0	0	171	0	0	0	0	0	0	0
5211 Paid by households: motor vehicles	..	..	..	3 433	4 652	4 497	4 658	4 803	4 487	4 758
5212 Paid by others: motor vehicles	..	..	..	1 006	1 332	1 293	1 392	1 382	1 395	1 390
Motor vehicle duty paid by firms	3	..	..	1 006	1 332	1 293	1 392	1 382	1 395	1 390
5213 Paid in respect of other goods	67	225	2 203	3 006	3 240	3 425	3 615	3 632	3 689	3 773
Law 1177 proportional surcharge	22	0	0	0	0	0	0	0	0	0
Taxes on signs	2	4	0	0	0	0	0	0	0	0
Tax on dog tags	0	7	12	0	0	0	0	0	0	0
Tax on hunting and fishing	0	0	0	0	0	0	0	0	0	0
Duty on official franchises	43	215	2 191	3 006	3 240	3 425	3 615	3 632	3 689	3 773
5220 Non-recurrent taxes	0	0	0	0	0	0	0	0	0	0
Motor vehicles, airplanes	..	..	..	..	..	..	..	..	..	..
Pro-Friuli tax on vehicles	..	..	..	..	..	..	..	..	..	..
5300 Unallocable between 5100 and 5200	0	283	2 724	6 092	6 128	6 945	8 468	9 027	10 387	10 728
Indirect taxes refund	..	0	160	288	616	523	684	769	477	575
Other	..	283	2 564	5 804	5 512	6 422	7 784	8 258	9 910	10 153
6000 Other taxes	**72**	**0**	**0**	**27 343**	**39 404**	**31 652**	**32 949**	**33 196**	**31 980**	**30 385**
6100 Paid solely by business	0	..	..	27 343	39 404	31 652	32 949	33 196	31 980	30 385
6200 Other	72	..	..	0	0	0	0	0	0	0
Capital levies	2	..	..	..	..	..	..	..	..	..
Other taxes	71	..	..	..	..	..	..	..	..	..
Custom duties collected for the EU	**..**	**..**	**..**	**1 536**	**2 261**	**2 008**	**2 319**	**2 077**	**1 890**	**2 022**
Non-wastable tax credits										
Non-wastable tax credits against 1110	..	..	..	..	0	253	302	337	357	6 292
Tax expenditure component	..	..	..	..	..	158	187	206	206	5 027
Transfer component	..	..	..	..	..	96	115	132	151	1 266
Non-wastable tax credits against 1210	..	..	..	..	0	0	0	4 240	2 401	6 319
Tax expenditure component	..	..	..	..	..	..	..	0	0	0
Transfer component	..	..	..	..	..	..	..	4 240	2 401	6 319
Total tax revenue on cash basis	**5 505**	**60 422**	**265 116**	**488 738**	**653 836**	**660 267**	**675 057**	**694 770**	**687 732**	**693 240**
Total tax revenue on accrual basis	**..**	**..**	**..**	**503 096**	**671 189**	**661 725**	**686 198**	**708 166**	**705 533**	**704 217**

StatLink http://dx.doi.org/10.1787/888933416825

Table 4.17. **Italy/Italie** *(cont./suite)*

Details of tax revenue/Recettes fiscales détaillées

Million EUR

	1965	1980	1990	2000	2007	2009	2011	2012	2013	2014
Conciliation with National Accounts										
Additional taxes included in National Accounts	..	..	..	0	0	0	0	0	0	0
Taxes excluded from National Accounts	..	..	..	-5 416	-5 470	-6 137	-7 517	-7 997	-9 628	-9 852
The tax for the urban solid waste disposal (TARSU)	..	..	..	-4 387	-4 443	-5 133	-6 404	-6 802	-8 363	-8 541
Other	..	..	..	-1 029	-1 027	-1 004	-1 113	-1 195	-1 265	-1 311
Difference in treatment of tax credits	..	..	..	0	0	0	0	0	0	0
Capital transfer for uncollected revenue	..	..	..	0	0	0	0	0	0	0
Voluntary social security contributions	..	..	..	464	567	531	579	836	738	739
Miscellaneous differences	..	..	..	0	0	0	0	0	0	0
National Accounts: Taxes and actual social contributions	..	..	..	498 144	666 286	656 119	679 260	701 005	696 643	695 104
Imputed social contributions	..	..	..	3 884	3 980	3 959	4 108	4 089	4 093	3 931
National Accounts: Taxes and all social contributions	..	..	..	502 028	670 266	660 078	683 368	705 094	700 736	699 035

Notes : The tax year ends on 31st December

As from 2000, revenues data are computed on accrual basis.

As from 1997, revenues data are based on data provided to the European Union, as for the Treaty of Maastricht excessive deficit procedure.

Section 6000: Regional Tax on Productive Activities (IRAP); it is a tax on the value of production, therefore its taxable base is different from other groups tax bases.

Regarding the section «Taxes excluded National Accounts» the item «Others» includes: tax on the public areas utilisation and tax on the collection and disposal of waste water.

Source : Ministero dell'economia e delle finanze; Istituto nazionale di statistica.

StatLink http://dx.doi.org/10.1787/888933416825

Table 4.18. **Japan/Japon**

Details of tax revenue/Recettes fiscales détaillées

Billion JPY

	1965	1980	1990	2000	2007	2009	2011	2012	2013	2014
Total tax revenue	**6 172**	**62 443**	**130 823**	**136 125**	**146 243**	**127 768**	**135 668**	**139 578**	**146 401**	**156 867**
1000 Taxes on income, profits and capital gains	**2 708**	**28 800**	**65 682**	**47 398**	**53 174**	**37 739**	**40 910**	**43 352**	**47 534**	**49 939**
1100 Of individuals	1 338	15 180	36 394	28 677	28 600	25 518	24 951	25 946	28 150	29 655
1110 On income and profits	1 338	15 180	36 394	28 677	28 600	25 518	24 951	25 946	28 150	29 655
Income tax	970	10 800	25 996	18 789	16 080	12 914	13 476	14 044	15 865	17 139
Prefectural inhabitants tax	123	1 415	3 675	3 621	5 008	5 052	4 608	4 783	5 090	5 215
Municipal inhabitants tax	220	2 890	6 475	6 044	7 294	7 349	6 688	6 942	7 015	7 114
Enterprise tax	25	75	249	223	218	204	179	178	181	186
1120 On capital gains	0	0	0	0	0	0	0	0	0	0
1200 Corporate	1 370	13 620	29 288	18 721	24 573	12 221	15 959	17 406	19 384	20 284
1210 On profits	1 370	13 620	29 288	18 721	24 573	12 221	15 959	17 406	19 384	20 284
Corporation tax	927	8 923	18 384	11 747	14 744	6 356	9 351	10 408	11 698	11 464
Prefectural inhabitants tax	53	557	1 414	879	1 206	715	800	846	854	963
Municipal inhabitants tax	85	1 297	3 198	2 176	3 015	1 775	2 011	2 129	2 157	2 445
Enterprise tax	305	2 843	6 293	3 918	5 608	2 701	2 240	2 354	2 674	3 017
Local special corporate tax	0	0	0	0	0	674	1 556	1 670	2 001	2 395
Local corporate tax	0	0	0	0	0	0	0	0	0	1
1220 On capital gains	0	0	0	0	0	0	0	0	0	0
1300 Unallocable between 1100 and 1200	0	0	0	0	0	0	0	0	0	0
2000 Social security contributions	**1 344**	**18 178**	**34 593**	**47 857**	**53 321**	**52 342**	**56 321**	**58 068**	**59 800**	**62 232**
2100 Employees	446	6 393	13 883	19 786	21 972	22 484	24 431	25 182	25 982	27 146
2110 On a payroll basis	..	..	13 883	19 786	21 972	22 484	24 431	25 182	25 982	27 146
2120 On an income tax basis	..	..	0	0	0	0	0	0	0	0
2200 Employers	588	9 267	16 642	22 388	24 240	23 575	25 735	26 333	27 141	28 394
2210 On a payroll basis	..	..	16 642	22 388	24 240	23 575	25 735	26 333	27 141	28 394
2220 On an income tax basis	..	..	0	0	0	0	0	0	0	0
2300 Self-employed or non-employed	107	2 518	4 069	5 683	7 108	6 282	6 156	6 553	6 676	6 693
2310 On a payroll basis	..	..	4 069	5 683	7 108	6 282	6 156	6 553	6 676	6 693
2320 On an income tax basis	..	..	0	0	0	0	0	0	0	0
2400 Unallocable between 2100, 2200 and 2300	203	0	0	0	0	0	0	0	0	0
2410 On a payroll basis	..	..	..	..	..	..	..	..	..	..
2420 On an income tax basis	..	..	..	..	..	..	..	..	..	..
3000 Taxes on payroll and workforce	**0**	**0**	**0**	**0**	**0**	**0**	**0**	**0**	**0**	**0**
4000 Taxes on property	**498**	**5 114**	**12 296**	**14 294**	**13 138**	**12 949**	**13 100**	**12 716**	**12 940**	**13 306**
4100 Recurrent taxes on immovable property	319	3 326	7 099	10 414	9 949	10 128	10 237	9 799	9 882	10 016
Prefectural property tax	4	8	15	11	14	19	3	2	2	2
Municipal property tax	296	2 784	6 023	9 041	8 729	8 874	8 966	8 580	8 653	8 769
City planning tax	19	469	942	1 318	1 202	1 233	1 268	1 216	1 227	1 244
Special landholding tax	0	65	118	43	4	2	1	1	1	2
Water and land utilization tax	0	0	0	0	0	0	0	0	0	0
Land value tax	0	0	0	1	0	0	0	0	0	0
4110 Households	..	..	..	..	..	..	..	..	..	..
4120 Others	..	..	..	..	..	..	..	..	..	..
4200 Recurrent taxes on net wealth	0	0	0	0	0	0	0	0	0	0
4210 Individual	..	..	..	..	..	..	..	..	..	..
4220 Corporate	..	..	..	..	..	..	..	..	..	..
4300 Estate, inheritance and gift taxes	44	441	1 918	1 782	1 503	1 350	1 474	1 504	1 574	1 883
4310 Estate and inheritance taxes	34	375	..	..	..	..	..	..	..	..
Inheritance tax	34	375	..	..	..	..	..	..	..	..
4320 Gift taxes	10	65	..	..	..	..	..	..	..	..
Tax on gifts	10	65	..	..	..	..	..	..	..	..
4400 Taxes on financial and capital transactions	135	1 347	3 280	2 099	1 686	1 472	1 388	1 413	1 483	1 407
Bourse tax	3	15	41	0	0	0	0	0	0	0
Securities transaction	8	209	748	0	0	0	0	0	0	0
Bank of Japan note issue tax	0	0	0	0	0	0	0	0	0	0
Stamp revenues	83	841	1 894	1 532	1 202	1 068	1 047	1 078	1 126	1 035
Real property acquisition tax	41	282	596	567	485	404	342	336	357	372
4500 Non-recurrent taxes	0	0	0	0	0	0	0	0	0	0
4510 On net wealth	..	..	..	..	..	..	..	..	..	..
4520 Other non-recurrent taxes	..	..	..	..	..	..	..	..	..	..
4600 Other recurrent taxes on property	0	0	0	0	0	0	0	0	0	0
5000 Taxes on goods and services	**1 620**	**10 200**	**17 917**	**26 227**	**26 256**	**24 364**	**24 966**	**25 056**	**25 744**	**30 991**
5100 Taxes on production, sale, transfer, etc	1 544	8 822	15 647	23 180	23 241	21 561	22 410	22 592	23 313	28 587
5110 General taxes	0	0	5 778	12 350	12 841	12 221	12 745	12 902	13 479	19 135
5111 Value added taxes	..	..	5 778	12 350	12 841	12 221	12 745	12 902	13 479	19 135
5112 Sales tax	..	..	0	0	0	0	0	0	0	0
5113 Other	..	..	0	0	0	0	0	0	0	0
5120 Taxes on specific goods and services	1 544	8 822	9 868	10 830	10 400	9 340	9 665	9 690	9 834	9 452

StatLink http://dx.doi.org/10.1787/888933416836

Table 4.18. **Japan/Japon** *(cont./suite)*

Details of tax revenue/Recettes fiscales détaillées

Billion JPY

	1965	1980	1990	2000	2007	2009	2011	2012	2013	2014
5121 Excises	1 062	6 674	8 637	9 837	9 374	8 527	8 719	8 721	8 728	8 308
Liquor tax	353	1 424	1 935	1 816	1 524	1 417	1 369	1 350	1 371	1 328
Sugar excises	29	43	0	0	0	0	0	0	0	0
Local gasoline tax	46	278	361	296	302	291	283	281	275	266
Gasoline tax	254	1 547	2 007	2 769	2 820	2 715	2 648	2 622	2 574	2 486
Liquefied petroleum gas tax	0	30	31	28	27	25	23	21	21	19
Aviation fuel tax	0	58	76	104	104	94	60	64	67	67
Commodity tax	138	1 038	5	0	0	0	0	0	0	0
Playing-card tax	1	1	0	0	0	0	0	0	0	0
Prefectural tobacco tax	44	229	361	282	278	250	293	289	173	155
Municipal tobacco tax	73	402	636	865	853	767	900	887	983	950
Timber delivery tax	3	3	0	0	0	0	0	0	0	0
Mineral product tax	2	5	3	2	2	2	2	2	2	2
Electricity and gas tax	54	386	0	0	0	0	0	0	0	0
Diesel oil tax	65	447	834	1 208	1 034	908	932	925	943	936
Vehicle acquisition tax	0	270	613	464	425	231	168	210	193	86
Promotion of power resources development tax	0	109	295	375	352	329	331	328	328	321
Petroleum and coal tax	0	404	487	489	513	487	519	567	600	631
Tobacco tax	0	0	996	876	925	822	1 032	1 018	1 038	919
Special tobacco tax	0	0	0	264	214	190	160	158	161	142
5122 Profits of fiscal monopolies	179	808	0	0	0	0	0	0	0	0
Monopoly profits	179	808	..	..	..	..	..	..	..	..
5123 Customs and import duties	222	786	928	877	941	732	874	897	1 034	1 073
Customs duty	222	786	928	877	941	732	874	897	1 034	1 073
5124 Taxes on exports	0	0	0	0	0	0	0	0	0	0
5125 Taxes on investment goods	0	0	0	0	0	0	0	0	0	0
5126 Taxes on specific services	81	554	303	116	85	81	72	73	71	70
Travel tax	4	64	0	0	0	0	0	0	0	0
Admission tax	10	5	0	0	0	0	0	0	0	0
Local entertainment tax	10	74	0	0	0	0	0	0	0	0
Golf course utilization tax	0	0	90	81	60	58	51	51	49	48
Meal and lodging tax	56	398	0	0	0	0	0	0	0	0
Special local consumption tax	0	0	195	12	0	0	0	0	0	0
Bathing tax	1	13	18	23	25	23	21	22	22	22
5127 Other taxes on internat. trade and transactions	0	0	0	0	0	0	0	0	0	0
5128 Other taxes	0	0	0	0	0	0	0	0	0	0
5130 Unallocable between 5110 and 5120	0	0	0	0	0	0	0	0	0	0
5200 Taxes on use of goods and perform activities	76	1 378	2 270	3 047	3 015	2 803	2 557	2 464	2 431	2 404
5210 Recurrent taxes	69	1 358	2 250	3 027	2 993	2 783	2 535	2 442	2 409	2 382
Automobile tax	55	781	1 276	1 765	1 717	1 654	1 597	1 586	1 574	1 556
Light vehicle tax	13	43	88	125	164	174	180	184	189	195
Motor vehicle tonnage tax	0	527	881	1 134	1 110	953	755	669	643	629
Hunter licence tax	0	3	2	2	0	0	0	0	0	0
Hunting tax	0	3	2	1	2	2	2	2	2	2
Mine lot tax	1	1	1	1	0	0	0	0	0	0
5211 Paid by households: motor vehicles	..	..	..	..	..	..	..	..	..	..
5212 Paid by others: motor vehicles	..	..	..	..	..	..	..	..	..	..
5213 Paid in respect of other goods	..	..	..	..	..	..	..	..	..	..
5220 Non-recurrent taxes	7	20	20	20	22	20	22	22	22	23
5300 Unallocable between 5100 and 5200	0	0	0	0	0	0	0	0	0	0
6000 Other taxes	**2**	**151**	**335**	**348**	**356**	**374**	**371**	**386**	**384**	**399**
6100 Paid solely by business	0	139	288	324	313	328	339	350	348	356
Business office tax	..	139	288	324	313	328	339	350	348	356
6200 Other	2	12	47	24	43	46	32	36	36	43
Taxes not in local tax law	2	12	47	24	43	46	32	36	36	43
Other	0	0	0	0	0	0	0	0	0	0
Total tax revenue on cash basis	**6 172**	**62 443**	**..**	**..**	**..**	**..**	**..**	**..**	**..**	**..**
Total tax revenue on accrual basis	**..**	**..**	**130 823**	**136 125**	**146 243**	**127 768**	**135 668**	**139 578**	**146 401**	**156 867**
Conciliation with National Accounts										
Additional taxes included in National Accounts	..	..	..	..	..	..	..	..	..	..
Taxes excluded from National Accounts	..	..	..	..	..	..	..	..	..	..
Difference in treatment of tax credits	..	..	..	..	..	..	..	..	..	..
Capital transfer for uncollected revenue	..	..	..	..	..	..	..	..	..	..
Voluntary social security contributions	..	..	..	..	..	..	..	..	..	..
Miscellaneous differences	..	..	..	..	..	..	..	..	..	..
National Accounts: Taxes and actual social contributions	..	..	..	..	..	..	..	..	..	..
Imputed social contributions	..	..	..	..	..	..	..	..	..	..
National Accounts: Taxes and all social contributions	..	..	..	..	..	..	..	..	..	..

StatLink http://dx.doi.org/10.1787/888933416836

Table 4.18. **Japan/Japon** *(cont./suite)*

Details of tax revenue/Recettes fiscales détaillées

Notes : Data are on a fiscal year basis beginning 1st April.

From 1990, data are on accrual basis.

The figures for different groups of taxes are reported on different reporting bases, namely: Social security contributions (heading 2000): in principle, accrual basis; Central government taxes: accrual basis (revenues accrued during the fiscal year plus cash receipts collected before the end of May (the end of April until 1977); Local government taxes: accrual basis (due to be paid during the fiscal year and cash receipts collected before the end of May).

The Japanese authorities take the view that the Enterprise tax (classified in 1100 and 1200) and the Mineral product tax (classified in 5121) should be classified in heading 6000, since under articles 72 and 519 of the Local Tax Law these taxes are regarded as levies on the business or mining activity itself.

Heading 2000 includes some unidentifiable voluntary contributions.

Heading 2300: Includes contibutions to the National pension, National Health Insurance and the Farmer's pension fund. Contributions to the Farmer's pension fund are not available for the years before 1999.

Heading 4100: Municipal property tax, includes Prefectural property tax from 1990 to 1994, because data is not available to provide a breakdown.

Heading 5121: Municipal tobacco tax, includes Prefectural tobacco tax from 1990 to 1994, because data is not available to provide a breakdown.

Heading 5121: In sub-item Petroleum and coal tax, the data before 2003 refer to petroleum tax.

Source : Tax Bureau, Ministry of Finance.

StatLink http://dx.doi.org/10.1787/888933416836

Table 4.19. **Korea/Corée**

Details of tax revenue/Recettes fiscales détaillées

Billion KRW

	1965	1980	1990	2000	2007	2009	2011	2012	2013	2014
Total tax revenue	..	**6 687**	**37 262**	**136 295**	**258 571**	**273 647**	**321 915**	**341 336**	**347 332**	**365 428**
1000 Taxes on income, profits and capital gains	..	**1 704**	**12 203**	**39 254**	**82 239**	**77 897**	**96 845**	**101 944**	**101 792**	**106 353**
1100 Of individuals	..	766	7 440	19 950	43 276	38 618	47 299	51 185	53 311	59 457
Income tax	..	0	0	0	0	0	0	0	0	0
Dividends and interest income tax	..	0	0	0	4 682	4 762	4 896	5 152	4 889	4 628
Wages and salaries income tax	..	0	0	0	14 124	13 407	18 337	19 627	21 931	25 359
Other income tax	..	0	0	0	2 607	2 829	3 365	3 595	3 432	3 805
Global income tax	..	661	4 723	16 128	6 151	6 117	8 300	9 938	10 901	11 486
Defence tax on income tax	..	105	938	0	0	0	0	0	0	0
Education tax on income tax	..	0	325	0	0	0	0	0	0	0
Rural development tax on interest, bus. Inc. & cap.gains relief	..	0	0	156	160	199	156	125	124	115
Inhabitant tax on income tax (local)	..	0	341	2 285	4 260	3 996	4 856	5 293	5 377	6 017
1110 On income and profits	..	766	6 327	18 569	31 984	31 310	39 910	43 730	46 654	51 410
1120 On capital gains	..	0	1 113	1 381	11 292	7 308	7 389	7 455	6 657	8 047
Capital gains tax	..	..	1 113	1 381	11 292	7 308	7 389	7 455	6 657	8 047
1200 Corporate	..	738	4 757	19 271	38 963	39 279	49 546	50 759	48 481	46 896
Corporation tax - withholding	..	..	677	8 577	8 360	4 681	10 534	11 516	12 176	12 172
Corporation tax - final returns	..	..	2 549	9 302	27 057	30 570	34 339	34 416	31 679	30 478
Defence tax on corporation tax	..	..	1 323	0	0	0	0	0	0	0
Inhabitant tax on corporation tax (local)	..	..	207	1 142	3 152	3 556	3 953	4 258	4 118	3 882
Rural development tax corporate income	..	..	0	251	394	472	720	569	508	364
1210 On profits	..	738	4 757	19 271	38 963	39 279	49 546	50 759	48 481	46 896
Excess profit tax	..	0	0	0	0	0	0	0	0	0
1220 On capital gains	..	0	0	0	0	0	0	0	0	0
Capital gains tax	..	..	..	..	..	..	..	..	..	..
1300 Unallocable between 1100 and 1200	..	199	6	33	0	0	0	0	0	0
Business income tax	..	0	0	0	..	..	..	..	..	..
Real estate income tax	..	0	0	0	..	..	..	..	..	..
Defence tax on real estate & business income	..	0	0	0	..	..	..	..	..	..
Rural dev. tax on bus. inc. & cap. gains relief	..	0	0	30	..	..	..	..	..	..
Inhabitant tax before 1990 (local)	..	117	0	0	..	..	..	..	..	..
Farm land tax (local)	..	83	6	3	..	..	..	..	..	..
Inhabitant tax on farm land tax (local)	..	0	0	0	..	..	..	..	..	..
2000 Social security contributions	..	**73**	**3 760**	**22 759**	**53 588**	**63 939**	**77 234**	**84 380**	**91 596**	**98 184**
2100 Employees	..	0	1 464	8 578	21 773	25 638	31 875	35 670	38 396	41 355
Veterans' relief fund	..	0	0	0	0	0	0	0	0	0
Soldiers' annuity fund	..	0	0	0	0	0	0	0	0	0
Unemployment assurance	..	0	0	598	1 164	1 346	1 698	2 138	2 418	2 866
National welfare pension fund	..	0	429	4 325	9 338	10 358	11 832	12 867	13 890	14 823
Social benefit fund	..	0	0	0	0	0	0	0	0	0
Health Insurance	..	0	483	2 066	8 180	10 581	13 954	15 718	17 128	18 492
Teachers' pensions	..	0	86	279	581	621	940	1 229	1 077	1 081
Government employees pensions	..	0	406	1 144	2 202	2 308	3 106	3 345	3 435	3 593
Military personal pensions	..	0	60	166	308	313	345	373	448	500
2110 On a payroll basis	..	..	..	8 578	21 773	25 638	31 875	35 670	38 396	41 355
2120 On an income tax basis	..	..	..	0	0	0	0	0	0	0
2200 Employers	..	73	1 694	9 409	23 557	28 981	34 366	36 911	41 518	44 806
Ind. works' insurance fund	..	73	550	1 876	4 431	4 732	4 632	5 508	5 436	5 797
Soldiers' annuity fund	..	0	0	0	0	0	0	0	0	0
Pneumoconiosis fund	..	0	0	0	0	0	0	0	0	0
Unemployment insurance	..	0	0	1 449	2 474	2 843	3 347	4 166	4 545	5 150
Veterans' relief fund	..	0	0	0	0	0	0	0	0	0
National welfare pension fund	..	0	430	4 340	9 383	10 393	11 833	12 930	13 958	14 909
Social benefit fund	..	0	0	0	0	0	0	0	0	0
Health Insurance	..	0	658	1 547	6 844	8 980	13 889	13 576	16 826	18 133
Teachers' pensions	..	0	56	197	425	456	665	731	753	0
Government employees pensions	..	0	0	0	0	0	0	0	0	817
2210 On a payroll basis	..	..	..	9 409	23 557	28 981	34 366	36 911	41 518	44 806
2220 On an income tax basis	..	..	..	0	0	0	0	0	0	0
2300 Self-employed or non-employed	..	0	602	4 772	8 258	9 320	10 993	11 799	11 682	12 023
2310 On a payroll basis	..	..	0	0	0	0	0	0	0	0
2320 On an income tax basis	..	..	602	4 772	8 258	9 234	10 993	11 799	11 682	12 023
2400 Unallocable between 2100, 2200 and 2300	..	0	0	0	0	0	0	0	0	0
2410 On a payroll basis	..	..	..	..	..	..	..	..	..	..
2420 On an income tax basis	..	..	..	..	..	..	..	..	..	..
3000 Taxes on payroll and workforce	..	**34**	**153**	**258**	**619**	**681**	**803**	**868**	**981**	**1 042**
Workshop tax on workforce (local)	..	31	124	258	619	681	803	868	981	1 042
Vocational training promotion fund	..	3	29	0	0	0	0	0	0	0
4000 Taxes on property	..	**537**	**4 389**	**16 846**	**33 109**	**31 803**	**36 555**	**36 213**	**35 847**	**40 305**

StatLink http://dx.doi.org/10.1787/888933416846

Table 4.19. **Korea/Corée** *(cont./suite)*

Details of tax revenue/Recettes fiscales détaillées

Billion KRW

	1965	1980	1990	2000	2007	2009	2011	2012	2013	2014
4100 Recurrent taxes on immovable property	..	183	980	3 385	9 196	8 859	9 779	10 315	10 809	11 654
Property tax (local)	..	119	227	728	3 755	4 423	7 617	8 049	8 267	8 780
City planning tax on urban real estate (local)	..	51	244	815	1 883	2 269	5	3	0	0
Community facilities tax (local)	..	13	86	341	543	591	705	766	912	1 138
Tax on excessive land holdings (local)	..	0	1	0	0	0	0	0	0	0
Tax on aggregate land holdings (local)	..	0	400	1 282	5	0	0	0	0	0
Rural dev. tax on local agg. land holdings tax	..	0	0	81	1	0	0	0	0	0
Tax on excessively increased land value	..	0	0	0	0	0	0	0	0	0
Comprehensive real estate tax	..	0	0	0	2 414	1 207	1 102	1 131	1 224	1 307
Rural dev. tax on comprehensive real estate tax	..	0	0	0	483	242	223	228	250	265
4110 Households	..	..	0	0	0	0	0	0	0	0
4120 Others	..	..	22	138	112	127	127	138	156	164
Workshop tax on property (local)	..	..	22	138	112	127	127	138	156	164
4200 Recurrent taxes on net wealth	..	0	0	0	0	0	0	0	0	0
4210 Individual	..	..	..	..	..	..	..	..	..	..
4220 Corporate	..	..	..	..	..	..	..	..	..	..
4300 Estate, inheritance and gift taxes	..	12	354	989	2 842	2 431	3 333	4 021	4 290	4 625
4310 Estate and inheritance taxes	..	5	85	449	1 059	1 221	1 259	1 719	1 587	1 696
Inheritance tax	..	3	71	449	1 059	1 221	1 259	1 719	1 587	1 696
Defence tax on inheritance tax	..	2	14	0	0	0	0	0	0	0
4320 Gift taxes	..	7	269	540	1 783	1 210	2 074	2 302	2 703	2 929
Gift tax	..	7	225	540	1 783	1 210	2 074	2 302	2 703	2 929
Defence tax on gift tax	..	0	44	0	0	0	0	0	0	0
4400 Taxes on financial and capital transactions	..	319	2 960	11 935	21 071	20 513	23 443	21 877	20 748	24 026
Registration tax (local)	..	122	1 378	4 528	7 254	7 131	7 680	7 645	1 312	1 485
Registration tax	..	0	0	0	0	0	0	0	0	0
Defence tax on registration tax	..	0	0	0	0	0	0	0	0	0
Rural dev. tax on local acquisition tax	..	0	0	246	627	621	982	853	874	843
Rural dev. tax on local registration tax	..	0	0	66	143	169	2	2	1	1
Securities transactions tax	..	0	224	2 736	3 469	3 534	4 279	3 681	3 077	3 121
Rural dev. tax on securities transaction tax	..	0	0	823	1 729	1 870	2 515	1 769	1 529	1 459
Acquisition tax (local)	..	163	1 165	3 148	7 261	6 644	7 361	7 326	13 318	16 391
Stamp tax	..	34	193	388	588	544	624	601	637	726
4500 Non-recurrent taxes	..	22	95	537	0	0	0	0	0	0
Asset revaluation tax	..	22	95	537	..	..	..	..	..	..
4510 On net wealth	..	..	..	..	..	..	..	..	..	..
4520 Other non-recurrent taxes	..	..	..	..	..	..	..	..	..	..
4600 Other recurrent taxes on property	..	0	0	0	0	0	0	0	0	0
5000 Taxes on goods and services	..	**4 190**	**16 497**	**52 271**	**80 861**	**87 043**	**100 551**	**106 402**	**106 717**	**109 451**
5100 Taxes on production, sale, transfer, etc	..	4 114	16 024	50 023	78 414	84 135	93 983	99 731	99 970	102 531
5110 General taxes	..	1 471	6 964	23 212	40 942	46 992	54 868	58 702	59 105	62 975
5111 Value added taxes	..	1 471	6 964	23 212	40 942	46 992	54 868	58 702	59 105	62 975
Value added tax	..	1 471	6 964	23 212	40 942	46 992	54 868	58 702	59 105	62 975
5112 Sales tax	..	0	0	0	0	0	0	0	0	0
Business tax	..	..	..	..	..	..	..	..	..	..
5113 Other	..	0	0	0	0	0	0	0	0	0
5120 Taxes on specific goods and services	..	2 643	9 059	26 811	37 472	37 143	39 115	41 029	40 865	39 556
5121 Excises	..	1 029	4 924	18 155	27 880	25 341	25 401	28 410	27 661	28 226
Commodity tax	..	0	0	0	0	0	0	0	0	0
Defence tax on commodity tax	..	0	0	0	0	0	0	0	0	0
Liquor tax	..	298	1 022	1 963	2 268	2 771	2 529	2 999	2 947	2 852
Defence tax on liquor tax	..	78	0	0	0	0	0	0	0	0
Education tax on liquor tax	..	0	81	516	580	713	644	774	764	728
Textile tax	..	0	0	0	0	0	0	0	0	0
Petroleum tax	..	0	0	0	0	0	0	0	0	0
Transport tax on petrol products	..	0	0	8 404	11 464	10 092	11 546	13 809	13 248	13 440
Education tax on transport tax	..	0	0	1 247	1 715	1 483	1 726	2 030	1 895	2 074
Electricity and gas tax	..	0	0	0	0	0	0	0	0	0
Special excise tax	..	583	1 912	2 985	5 161	3 642	5 537	5 336	5 484	5 624
Defence tax on special excise tax	..	70	337	0	0	0	0	0	0	0
Education tax on special excise tax	..	0	0	498	607	322	589	525	485	495
Rural development on special excise tax	..	0	0	37	54	20	45	56	56	60
Tobacco sales tax (local)	..	0	0	0	0	0	0	0	0	0
Tobacco consumption tax (local)	..	0	1 572	2 251	2 761	3 011	2 785	2 881	2 782	2 953
Motor fuel tax (local)	..	0	0	254	3 270	3 287	0	0	0	0
5122 Profits of fiscal monopolies	..	510	0	0	0	0	0	0	0	0
Monopoly profit	..	510	..	..	..	..	..	..	..	..

StatLink http://dx.doi.org/10.1787/888933416846

Table 4.19. **Korea/Corée** *(cont./suite)*

Details of tax revenue/Recettes fiscales détaillées

Billion KRW

	1965	1980	1990	2000	2007	2009	2011	2012	2013	2014
5123 Customs and import duties	..	1 014	3 692	5 936	7 690	9 486	11 350	10 220	11 012	9 132
Customs duties	..	762	2 765	5 800	7 411	9 169	10 990	9 816	10 562	8 721
Defence tax on customs duties	..	248	919	0	0	0	0	0	0	0
Special customs duties	..	0	0	0	0	0	0	0	0	0
Tonnage tax	..	0	0	0	0	0	0	0	0	0
Education tax on imports	..	0	7	99	234	273	322	375	429	390
Rural dev. tax on customs exemptions	..	0	0	37	45	44	38	29	21	21
Previous year receipts	..	4	0	0	0	0	0	0	0	0
5124 Taxes on exports	..	0	0	0	0	0	0	0	0	0
5125 Taxes on investment goods	..	0	0	0	0	0	0	0	0	0
5126 Taxes on specific services	..	90	444	2 720	1 902	2 316	2 364	2 399	2 192	2 198
Telephone tax	..	50	262	1 457	0	0	0	0	0	0
Defence tax on telephone tax	..	33	0	0	0	0	0	0	0	0
Entertainment tax	..	0	0	0	0	0	0	0	0	0
Defence tax on entertainment tax	..	0	0	0	0	0	0	0	0	0
Entertainment tax (local)	..	0	0	0	0	0	0	0	0	0
Travel tax	..	0	0	0	0	0	0	0	0	0
Admission tax	..	0	0	0	0	0	0	0	0	0
Defence tax on admission tax	..	0	0	0	0	0	0	0	0	0
Education tax on banking & insurance	..	0	108	473	721	964	966	932	938	920
Horse race tax (local)	..	3	56	566	864	1 002	1 072	1 129	1 042	1 073
Rural dev. tax on horse race tax	..	0	0	84	165	203	214	221	212	205
Butchery tax (local)	..	5	18	51	52	56	5	0	0	0
Regional development tax (local)	..	0	0	89	100	91	107	117	0	0
5127 Other taxes on internat. trade and transactions	..	0	0	0	0	0	0	0	0	0
5128 Other taxes	..	0	0	0	0	0	0	0	0	0
5130 Unallocable between 5110 and 5120	..	0	0	0	0	0	0	0	0	0
5200 Taxes on use of goods and perform activities	..	75	474	2 248	2 447	2 908	6 568	6 671	6 747	6 920
5210 Recurrent taxes	..	75	474	2 248	2 447	2 908	6 568	6 671	6 747	6 920
License tax (local)	..	18	48	241	77	74	78	78	0	0
Automobile tax (local)	..	57	426	2 007	2 370	2 834	6 490	6 593	6 747	6 920
5211 Paid by households: motor vehicles	..	..	..	..	..	..	..	..	..	..
5212 Paid by others: motor vehicles	..	..	..	..	..	..	..	..	..	..
5213 Paid in respect of other goods	..	..	..	..	..	..	..	..	..	..
5220 Non-recurrent taxes	..	0	0	0	0	0	0	0	0	0
5300 Unallocable between 5100 and 5200	..	0	0	0	0	0	0	0	0	0
6000 Other taxes	..	**150**	**259**	**4 907**	**8 155**	**12 284**	**9 927**	**11 529**	**10 399**	**10 093**
6100 Paid solely by business	..	0	0	0	0	0	0	0	0	0
6200 Other	..	150	259	4 907	8 155	12 284	9 927	11 529	10 399	10 093
Unallocable tax revenue	..	143	0	0	0	0	0	0	0	0
Previous year tax	..	0	213	1 474	2 965	6 890	4 232	5 768	4 774	4 049
Previous year tax (local)	..	6	47	474	672	600	728	680	601	589
Unallocable defence tax	..	0	0	-3	0	0	0	0	0	0
Education tax on local taxes	..	0	0	2 962	4 518	4 794	4 967	5 081	5 024	5 455
Total tax revenue on cash basis	..	**6 687**	**37 262**	**136 295**	**258 571**	**273 647**	**321 915**	**341 336**	**347 332**	**365 428**
Total tax revenue on accrual basis	..	..	..	..	..	..	..	..	..	..
Conciliation with National Accounts										
Additional taxes included in National Accounts	..	..	..	..	..	..	..	..	..	..
Taxes excluded from National Accounts	..	..	..	..	..	..	..	..	..	..
Difference in treatment of tax credits	..	..	..	..	..	..	..	..	..	..
Capital transfer for uncollected revenue	..	..	..	..	..	..	..	..	..	..
Voluntary social security contributions	..	..	..	..	..	..	..	..	..	..
Miscellaneous differences	..	..	..	..	..	..	..	..	..	..
National Accounts: Taxes and actual social contributions	..	..	..	..	..	..	..	..	..	..
Imputed social contributions	..	..	..	..	..	..	..	..	..	..
National Accounts: Taxes and all social contributions	..	..	..	..	..	..	..	..	..	..

Notes : Year ending 31st December.

Data are on cash basis.

Heading 2000: From 1997, the contributions to the three funds (civil servant pension fund, private school teachers pension fund and medical insurance fund) are classified as security social contributions. The reasons for the change are that the contributions either became mandatory or the fund started to be managed by public authorities in that year, thereby meeting the OECD definition of social security contributions.

Heading 2200: From 2007, this includes long-term care insurance.

Source : Ministry of Finance and Economy, Ministry of Home Affairs.

StatLink http://dx.doi.org/10.1787/888933416846

Table 4.20. **Latvia/Lettonie**

Details of tax revenue/Recettes fiscales détaillées

Million EUR

	1965	1980	1990	2000	2007	2009	2011	2012	2013	2014
Total tax revenue	..	..	..	**1 995**	**6 350**	**5 243**	**5 622**	**6 214**	**6 494**	**6 808**
Total tax revenue exclusive of customs duties	..	..	..	1 995	6 314	5 222	5 591	6 182	6 466	6 772
1000 Taxes on income, profits and capital gains	..	..	..	**480**	**1 857**	**1 302**	**1 421**	**1 612**	**1 690**	**1 761**
1100 Of individuals	..	..	..	376	1 287	1 010	1 137	1 258	1 320	1 397
1110 On income and profits	..	..	..	376	1 287	1 010	1 137	1 258	1 320	1 397
1120 On capital gains	..	..	..	0	0	0	0	0	0	0
1200 Corporate	..	..	..	105	570	292	285	354	370	364
1210 On profits	..	..	..	105	570	292	285	354	370	364
1220 On capital gains	..	..	..	0	0	0	0	0	0	0
1300 Unallocable between 1100 and 1200	..	..	..	0	0	0	0	0	0	0
2000 Social security contributions	..	..	..	**669**	**1 774**	**1 742**	**1 763**	**1 903**	**1 933**	**1 982**
2100 Employees	..	..	..	167	479	471	549	593	603	607
2110 On a payroll basis	..	..	..	167	479	471	549	593	603	607
2120 On an income tax basis	..	..	..	0	0	0	0	0	0	0
2200 Employers	..	..	..	501	1 283	1 260	1 203	1 299	1 319	1 364
2210 On a payroll basis	..	..	..	501	1 283	1 260	1 203	1 299	1 319	1 364
2220 On an income tax basis	..	..	..	0	0	0	0	0	0	0
2300 Self-employed or non-employed	..	..	..	1	12	11	11	11	11	12
2310 On a payroll basis	..	..	..	1	12	11	11	11	11	12
2320 On an income tax basis	..	..	..	0	0	0	0	0	0	0
2400 Unallocable between 2100, 2200 and 2300	..	..	..	0	0	0	0	0	0	0
2410 On a payroll basis	..	..	..	..	..	..	..	..	..	..
2420 On an income tax basis	..	..	..	..	..	..	..	..	..	..
3000 Taxes on payroll and workforce	..	..	..	**0**	**4**	**3**	**3**	**3**	**3**	**3**
Risk duty of business	..	..	..	..	4	3	3	3	3	3
4000 Taxes on property	..	..	..	**76**	**195**	**132**	**196**	**209**	**218**	**243**
4100 Recurrent taxes on immovable property	..	..	..	63	106	104	157	167	173	191
4110 Households	..	..	..	0	0	0	18	21	22	23
4120 Others	..	..	..	63	106	104	139	146	151	168
Tax on property	..	..	..	63	106	104	139	146	151	168
Tax on land	..	..	..	0	0	0	0	0	0	0
4200 Recurrent taxes on net wealth	..	..	..	0	0	0	0	0	0	0
4210 Individual	..	..	..	..	..	..	..	..	..	..
4220 Corporate	..	..	..	..	..	..	..	..	..	..
4300 Estate, inheritance and gift taxes	..	..	..	0	3	3	2	2	2	2
4310 Estate and inheritance taxes	..	..	..	..	3	3	2	2	2	2
Duty for legacies and donations	..	..	..	..	0	0	0	0	0	0
Stamp duty for transactions made in Land Register in relation to legacies and donations	..	..	..	..	1	0	0	0	0	0
Duty for consolidation of ownership and legal cliens in Land Register anent legacies and donations	..	..	..	..	2	3	2	2	2	2
4320 Gift taxes	..	..	..	..	0	0	0	0	0	0
4400 Taxes on financial and capital transactions	..	..	..	13	86	25	37	40	43	49
Duties on transactions with privatization vouchers	..	..	..	0	0	0	0	0	0	0
Stamp duty for transactions made in Land Register, which have been collected from juridical persons, except legacies and donations	..	..	..	0	1	1	1	1	1	1
Duty for consolidation of ownership and legal liens in Land Register, which have been collected from juridical persons, except legacies and donations	..	..	..	4	27	11	18	19	17	21
Stamp duty for transactions made in Land Register, which have been collected from physical persons, except legacies and donations	..	..	..	1	8	1	2	2	2	2
Duty for consolidation of ownership and legal liens in Land Register, which have been collected from physical persons, except legacies and donations	..	..	..	7	51	12	16	18	23	25
4500 Non-recurrent taxes	..	..	..	0	0	0	0	0	0	0
4510 On net wealth	..	..	..	..	..	..	..	..	..	..
4520 Other non-recurrent taxes	..	..	..	..	..	..	..	..	..	..
4600 Other recurrent taxes on property	..	..	..	0	0	0	0	0	0	0
5000 Taxes on goods and services	..	..	..	**770**	**2 484**	**2 043**	**2 208**	**2 455**	**2 623**	**2 783**
5100 Taxes on production, sale, transfer, etc	..	..	..	739	2 428	1 861	2 099	2 321	2 469	2 616
5110 General taxes	..	..	..	476	1 727	1 114	1 374	1 570	1 690	1 818
5111 Value added taxes	..	..	..	476	1 727	1 114	1 374	1 570	1 690	1 787
5112 Sales tax	..	..	..	0	0	0	0	0	0	30
Subsidised electricity tax	..	..	..	..	..	..	..	..	..	30
5113 Other	..	..	..	0	0	0	0	0	0	0
5120 Taxes on specific goods and services	..	..	..	262	701	747	724	751	779	798

StatLink http://dx.doi.org/10.1787/888933416857

Table 4.20. **Latvia/Lettonie** *(cont./suite)*

Details of tax revenue/Recettes fiscales détaillées

Million EUR

	1965	1980	1990	2000	2007	2009	2011	2012	2013	2014
5121 Excises	..	..	..	232	626	691	697	717	742	762
Excise duty on alcoholic beverages	..	..	..	63	127	119	115	120	124	127
Excise duty on beer	..	..	..	4	15	20	26	24	24	25
Excise duty on oil products	..	..	..	124	359	381	376	379	388	403
Excise duty on tobacco	..	..	..	27	92	155	149	150	160	160
Excise duty on other products	..	..	..	14	32	15	22	22	24	25
Excise duty on coffee and non alcoholic beverages	..	..	..	6	8	11	14	13	14	14
Excise duty / Tax on cars and motorcycles	..	..	..	8	24	4	8	9	10	11
Excise duty on natural gas	..	..	..	0	0	0	10	21	22	20
Tax on electricity	..	..	..	0	1	1	1	1	1	2
5122 Profits of fiscal monopolies	..	..	..	0	0	0	0	0	0	0
5123 Customs and import duties	..	..	..	21	33	27	1	1	2	2
Customs duties	..	..	..	21	3	0	-1	0	0	0
Levies on imported agricultural products	..	..	..	0	2	1	0	0	0	0
Excise duty of imported goods for omission for free turnover	..	..	..	0	28	26	2	1	2	2
5124 Taxes on exports	..	..	..	0	0	0	0	0	0	0
5125 Taxes on investment goods	..	..	..	0	0	0	0	0	0	0
5126 Taxes on specific services	..	..	..	10	42	29	26	33	35	34
Taxes on lotteries and gambling	..	..	..	7	42	29	23	28	29	30
Financial stability fee	..	..	..	0	0	0	3	5	5	4
Passenger departure duty	..	..	..	3	0	0	0	0	0	0
5127 Other taxes on internat. trade and transactions	..	..	..	0	0	0	0	0	0	0
5128 Other taxes	..	..	..	0	0	0	0	0	0	0
5130 Unallocable between 5110 and 5120	..	..	..	0	0	0	0	0	0	0
5200 Taxes on use of goods and perform activities	..	..	..	32	57	182	109	134	154	167
5210 Recurrent taxes	..	..	..	32	57	52	109	126	140	140
5211 Paid by households: motor vehicles	..	..	..	12	16	19	42	44	48	50
Vehicle tax for vehicles which have been registered on physical persons	..	..	..	0	0	0	40	44	48	50
Annual vehicle duty for vehicles which have been registered on physical persons	..	..	..	12	16	19	2	0	0	0
5212 Paid by others: motor vehicles	..	..	..	0	20	18	41	40	45	43
Tax on cars belonging to enterprises	..	..	..	..	0	0	17	17	21	19
Vehicle tax for vehicles which have been registered on judical persons	..	..	..	..	0	0	23	23	24	24
Annual vehicle duty for vehicles which have been registered on judical persons	..	..	..	..	20	18	1	0	0	0
5213 Paid in respect of other goods	..	..	..	20	21	15	25	42	47	47
Duty for keeping animals	..	..	..	0	0	0	0	0	0	0
Income from lease of reservoirs and fishing rights and non-production use of fishing rights (fishing cards)	..	..	..	0	0	0	0	0	1	1
Business and professional licences	..	..	..	5	6	4	10	24	27	26
State duties and payments for issue of special permits (licences) and registration of documents that commensurate correspondence of professional qualification	..	..	..	1	0	0	0	0	0	0
Lottery and gambling state duty	..	..	..	1	4	2	2	2	2	3
Gambling equipment marking duty	..	..	..	0	1	1	0	0	0	0
Payment for rental of commercial fishing rights	..	..	..	0	0	0	0	0	0	0
Lottery of goods and services organization duty	..	..	..	2	0	0	0	0	0	0
State duty for using numerative rights	..	..	..	0	0	0	0	0	0	0
State duty for keeping oil products` security reserves	..	..	..	0	0	0	6	20	24	22
Tax on natural resources	..	..	..	15	15	10	15	17	19	20
5220 Non-recurrent taxes	..	..	..	0	0	130	0	8	14	27
Revenue from state-owned greenhouse gas emission unit trade	..	..	..	..	..	130	0	8	14	0
Payment for emission quota trading	..	..	..	..	..	0	0	0	0	17
The fee for the appeal of procurement	..	..	..	..	..	0	0	0	0	0
Toll for the use of motorways	..	..	..	..	..	0	0	0	0	10
5300 Unallocable between 5100 and 5200	..	..	..	0	0	0	0	0	0	0
6000 Other taxes	..	..	..	**0**	**0**	**0**	**0**	**0**	**0**	**0**
6100 Paid solely by business	..	..	..	..	..	..	..	..	..	..
6200 Other	..	..	..	..	..	..	..	..	..	..
Custom duties collected for the EU	..	..	..	..	**37**	**21**	**31**	**32**	**28**	**36**
Total tax revenue on cash basis	..	..	..	..	..	..	..	..	..	..
Total tax revenue on accrual basis	..	..	..	**1 995**	**6 350**	**5 243**	**5 622**	**6 214**	**6 494**	**6 808**

StatLink http://dx.doi.org/10.1787/888933416857

Table 4.20. **Latvia/Lettonie** *(cont./suite)*

Details of tax revenue/Recettes fiscales détaillées

Million EUR

	1965	1980	1990	2000	2007	2009	2011	2012	2013	2014
Conciliation with National Accounts										
Additional taxes included in National Accounts	..	..	..	14	1	0	0	0	0	0
Taxes excluded from National Accounts	..	..	..	0	0	0	0	0	0	0
Difference in treatment of tax credits	..	..	..	0	0	0	0	0	0	0
Capital transfer for uncollected revenue	..	..	..	0	0	0	0	0	0	0
Voluntary social security contributions	..	..	..	0	0	0	0	0	0	0
Miscellaneous differences	..	..	..	0	0	0	0	0	0	0
National Accounts: Taxes and actual social contributions	..	..	..	2 009	6 351	5 244	5 622	6 214	6 494	6 808
Imputed social contributions	..	..	..	12	51	64	31	45	59	71
National Accounts: Taxes and all social contributions	..	..	..	2 022	6 402	5 308	5 653	6 259	6 553	6 879

Notes : Year ending 31st December.
Data on accrual basis.
Source : Ministry of Finance.

StatLink http://dx.doi.org/10.1787/888933416857

Table 4.21. **Luxembourg**

Details of tax revenue/Recettes fiscales détaillées

Million EUR

	1965	1980	1990	2000	2007	2009	2011	2012	2013	2014
Recettes fiscales totales	**266**	**1 543**	**3 671**	**8 521**	**13 416**	**14 125**	**15 989**	**16 904**	**17 735**	**18 761**
Recettes fiscales totales excluant les droits de douane	..	..	..	**8 494**	**13 393**	**14 112**	**15 972**	**16 889**	**17 720**	**18 742**
1000 Impôts sur revenu, bénéfices et gains en capital	**95**	**667**	**1 476**	**3 107**	**4 655**	**4 992**	**5 695**	**5 956**	**6 275**	**6 484**
1100 Des personnes physiques	66	417	884	1 573	2 678	2 917	3 546	3 699	4 062	4 344
1110 Sur le revenu et les bénéfices	66	417	884	1 573	2 678	2 917	3 546	3 699	4 062	4 344
Impôt sur le revenu des personnes physiques	27	106	184	258	389	480	597	609	666	660
Impôt solidarité majoration personnes physiques	0	10	41	37	59	64	128	148	268	287
Impôt sur traitements et salaires	36	287	601	1 178	1 910	1 996	2 327	2 504	2 797	3 033
Impôt sur le revenu des capitaux	2	11	52	88	188	271	271	315	223	251
Impôt sur les tantièmes	1	2	5	11	20	23	32	38	38	48
Impôt sur le revenu de certains non-résidents	0	1	1	2	1	1	1	1	1	1
Impôt retenu sur revenus épargne (non résidents)	0	0	0	0	51	41	43	47	40	40
Retenu libératoire nationale sur les intérêts	0	0	0	0	60	42	37	37	28	24
Contribution à la crise	0	0	0	0	0	0	111	0	0	0
1120 Sur les gains en capital	0	0	0	0	0	0	0	0	0	0
Prélèvement sur gains des paris	..	..	..	..	..	..	..	..	..	..
1200 Des sociétés	29	250	592	1 533	1 977	2 075	2 148	2 257	2 213	2 140
1210 Sur les bénéfices	29	250	592	1 533	1 977	2 075	2 148	2 257	2 213	2 140
Impôt sur le revenu des collectivites	18	168	376	1 031	1 381	1 431	1 378	1 557	1 530	1 483
Impôt de solidarité sur le revenu des collectivités	0	2	8	43	58	59	83	83	113	111
Impôt commercial communal	0	80	209	460	538	585	687	617	569	546
1220 Sur les gains en capital	0	0	0	0	0	0	0	0	0	0
1300 Non-ventilables entre 1100 et 1200	0	0	0	0	0	0	0	0	0	0
2000 Cotisations de sécurité sociale	**86**	**443**	**1 011**	**2 223**	**3 704**	**4 231**	**4 669**	**4 926**	**5 128**	**5 388**
2100 A la charge des salariés	32	175	388	993	1 690	1 932	2 138	2 256	2 350	2 461
2110 Sur la base du salaire	..	175	388	993	1 690	1 932	2 138	2 256	2 350	2 461
2120 Sur la base de l'impôt sur les revenus	..	0	0	0	0	0	0	0	0	0
2200 A la charge des employeurs	49	243	494	963	1 577	1 806	2 006	2 094	2 171	2 280
2210 Sur la base du salaire	..	243	494	963	1 577	1 806	2 006	2 094	2 171	2 280
2220 Sur la base de l'impôt sur les revenus	..	0	0	0	0	0	0	0	0	0
2300 A charge des travailleurs indép. ou sans emploi	5	25	129	266	437	493	525	576	608	647
2310 Sur la base du salaire	..	25	129	266	437	493	525	576	608	647
2320 Sur la base de l'impôt sur les revenus	..	0	0	0	0	0	0	0	0	0
2400 Non-ventilables entre 2100, 2200 et 2300	0	0	0	0	0	0	0	0	0	0
2410 Sur la base du salaire	..	..	..	..	..	..	..	..	..	..
2420 Sur la base de l'impôt sur les revenus	..	..	..	..	..	..	..	..	..	..
3000 Sur salaires ou main d'oeuvre	**2**	**10**	**0**	**0**	**0**	**0**	**0**	**0**	**0**	**0**
Impôt sur la somme des salaires	2	10	..	..	..	..	..	..	..	..
4000 Impôts sur le patrimoine	**16**	**87**	**309**	**910**	**1 294**	**936**	**1 111**	**1 191**	**1 296**	**1 455**
4100 Impôts périodiques sur la propriété immobilière	4	9	14	21	27	29	31	33	33	34
Impôt foncier	4	9	14	21	27	29	31	33	33	34
4110 Ménages	..	..	..	..	..	..	..	..	..	..
4120 Autres agents	..	..	..	..	..	..	..	..	..	..
4200 Impôts périodiques sur l'actif net	7	44	172	633	878	716	858	898	980	1 077
4210 Personnes physiques	2	15	58	152	172	211	256	267	269	274
Impôt sur la fortune	2	15	58	152	172	211	256	267	269	274
4220 Sociétés	5	29	114	481	706	505	602	630	710	803
Impôt sur la fortune	3	29	114	481	706	505	602	630	710	803
Taxe d'abonnement	3	0	0	0	0	0	0	0	0	0
4300 Impôts sur mut. par décès, succ. et donations	1	5	11	23	47	52	43	71	72	74
4310 Impôts sur mut. par décès et successions	1	5	11	23	47	52	43	71	72	74
4320 Impôts sur les donations	0	0	0	0	0	0	0	0	0	0
4400 Impôts sur transact. mobilières et immob.	4	30	112	232	343	139	179	189	212	270
Droits d'enregistrement	4	26	94	208	288	103	137	145	164	208
Droits d'hypothèque	1	3	9	12	29	19	24	26	28	34
Droits de timbre	0	2	2	5	7	4	4	5	7	5
Taxe pour construction dans secteurs centraux	0	0	0	0	1	1	1	2	1	2
Surtaxe sur les mutations immobilières	0	0	6	7	17	11	11	10	10	19
Hypothèques salaires	0	0	1	1	1	1	1	1	1	1
Autorisations à bâtir	0	0	0	0	0	0	0	0	0	0
Taxe d'infrastructure	0	0	0	0	0	0	0	0	0	0
Taxes d'autorisation sur les réservoirs de mazout	0	0	0	0	0	0	0	0	0	0
Taxe sur les résidences secondaires	0	0	0	0	0	0	0	1	0	1
4500 Impôts non-périodiques	0	0	0	0	0	0	0	0	0	0
4510 Sur l'actif net	..	..	..	..	..	..	..	..	..	..
4520 Autres non-périodiques	..	..	..	..	..	..	..	..	..	..
4600 Autres impôts périodiques sur patrimoine	0	0	0	0	0	0	0	0	0	0
5000 Impôts sur les biens et services	**66**	**336**	**866**	**2 243**	**3 726**	**3 934**	**4 478**	**4 790**	**4 998**	**5 396**
5100 Impôts sur production, vente, transfert, etc.	62	327	846	2 213	3 651	3 852	4 404	4 719	4 920	5 316
5110 Impôts généraux	33	179	443	1 138	2 196	2 411	2 836	3 118	3 366	3 684

StatLink http://dx.doi.org/10.1787/888933416866

Table 4.21. **Luxembourg** *(cont./suite)*

Details of tax revenue/Recettes fiscales détaillées

Million EUR

	1965	1980	1990	2000	2007	2009	2011	2012	2013	2014
5111 Taxes sur la valeur ajoutée	0	179	443	1 138	2 196	2 411	2 836	3 118	3 366	3 684
TVA ressources propres UE	..	18	75	92	50	35	43	44	49	41
5112 Impôts sur les ventes	0	0	0	0	0	0	0	0	0	0
5113 Autres impôts	33	0	0	0	0	0	0	0	0	0
Impôt sur chiffre d'affaires	33	..	..	..	..	..	..	..	..	..
5120 Impôts sur biens et services déterminés	30	148	403	1 075	1 455	1 441	1 568	1 601	1 554	1 632
5121 Accises	26	134	365	1 036	1 394	1 371	1 499	1 530	1 484	1 563
Droits d'accises autonomes huiles minérales	1	1	10	100	135	126	174	200	197	192
Droits d'accises autonomes tabac	..	0	8	24	66	67	76	83	85	108
Droits d'accises sur les huiles minérales (R203)	..	76	173	414	559	526	562	558	530	515
Taxe sur la consommation d'alcool	1	5	19	20	21	21	23	22	25	27
Droits d'accises sur le tabac	..	40	141	407	418	423	447	454	445	523
Produit de la contrib.sociale prélevée sur les carburants	..	0	0	59	145	133	137	134	126	122
Redevance de contrôle sur le fuel domestique	..	0	0	2	3	3	2	2	2	2
Droits d'accises sur gaz liquéfiés (R203)	..	0	0	0	0	0	0	0	0	0
Droits d'accises sur benzols (R203)	..	0	0	1	1	1	1	1	1	1
Droits d'accises sur alcools étrangers (R203)	..	3	5	5	6	6	6	6	7	7
Droits d'accises sur bières indigènes	..	4	2	3	4	4	4	4	4	4
Droits d'accises sur boissons fermentées fruits (R203)	..	2	3	0	0	0	0	0	0	0
Droits d'accises boissons fermentées mousseuses (R203)	..	0	1	0	0	0	0	0	0	0
Droits d'accises sur sucres et sirops raffinés (R203)	..	0	1	0	0	0	0	0	0	0
Ajustement accises U.E.B.L.	..	0	0	0	0	0	0	0	0	0
Droits d'accises sur alcools indigènes	..	1	1	0	0	0	0	0	0	0
Accise "Kyoto"	..	0	0	0	37	61	65	65	62	60
Surtaxe sur les boissons confectionnées (alcopops)	..	0	0	0	0	0	0	0	0	0
5122 Bénéfices des monopoles fiscaux	0	0	0	0	0	0	0	0	0	0
5123 Droits de douane et droits à l'importation	1	5	11	0	1	1	1	1	0	0
Prélèvements agricoles UE	1	0	0	0	1	1	1	1	0	0
Droits de douane	0	0	0	0	0	0	0	0	0	0
Droits de douane + mobiles + C.E.C.A.	0	4	11	0	0	0	0	0	0	0
Montants compensatoires agricoles communautaires	0	0	0	0	0	0	0	0	0	0
5124 Taxes à l'exportation	0	0	0	0	0	0	0	0	0	0
5125 Impôts sur biens d'équipement	0	0	0	0	0	0	0	0	0	0
5126 Impôts sur services déterminés	2	6	22	39	60	69	69	71	70	68
Prélèv. sommes engagées dans les paris	0	0	0	0	0	0	0	0	0	0
Taxe sur les assurances	1	5	15	23	32	39	38	42	45	45
Taxe sur les transports	1	0	0	0	0	0	0	0	0	0
Taxe de séjour	0	0	1	1	2	2	2	2	2	2
Taxe sur le loto	0	0	3	4	3	3	3	3	0	0
Prélèvement sur les jeux du casino	0	0	3	9	21	24	23	22	21	19
Impôts sur les billets de banque	0	0	0	0	0	0	0	0	0	0
Taxe sur amusements publics (nuits blanches)	0	1	1	2	2	1	2	2	2	2
5127 Autres impôts sur commerce et transact. internat.	0	0	0	0	0	0	0	0	0	0
5128 Autres impôts	0	4	4	0	0	0	0	0	0	0
C.E.C.A.	..	3	4	..	..	..	..	..	..	..
Taxe de coresponsabilité sur le lait	..	1	0	..	..	..	..	..	..	..
Taxe de coresponsabilité sur les céréales	..	0	0	..	..	..	..	..	..	..
5130 Non-ventilables entre 5110 et 5120	0	0	0	0	0	0	0	0	0	0
5200 Impôts sur utilisation des biens et exerc. activités	3	9	20	30	75	82	74	72	78	80
5210 Impôts périodiques	3	8	17	26	65	72	63	61	68	68
5211 A la charge des ménages : véhicules à moteur	2	4	9	16	39	43	38	36	40	41
5212 A la charge autres agents : véhicules à moteur	1	4	7	11	26	29	26	25	27	28
5213 Autres impôts périodiques	0	0	1	2	2	3	3	3	4	3
Taxe sur les cabarets	0	0	0	0	1	1	1	1	1	1
Taxes d'immatriculation (Com. aux affaires maritimes)	0	0	0	1	1	1	1	1	2	1
Taxe sur les chiens	0	0	1	1	1	1	1	1	1	1
Taxe de colportage	0	0	0	0	0	0	0	0	0	0
Taxe sur les navires	0	0	0	0	0	0	0	0	0	0
5220 Impôts non-périodiques	0	0	2	2	7	7	8	8	6	9
5300 Non-ventilables entre 5100 et 5200	0	0	0	0	0	0	0	0	0	0
6000 Autres impôts	**0**	**0**	**8**	**12**	**14**	**19**	**20**	**25**	**22**	**19**

StatLink http://dx.doi.org/10.1787/888933416866

Table 4.21. **Luxembourg** *(cont./suite)*

Details of tax revenue/Recettes fiscales détaillées

Million EUR

	1965	1980	1990	2000	2007	2009	2011	2012	2013	2014
6100 A la charge exclusive des entreprises	..	0	6	11	13	18	19	24	21	18
Taxe supplémentaire sur l'électricité	..	0	0	2	2	2	2	2	2	2
Taxe sur la distribution d'électricité	..	0	3	4	1	1	1	1	1	1
Taxe sur la production d'électricité	..	0	2	2	1	1	1	1	1	0
Taxe sur la consommation de gaz naturel	..	0	0	0	3	4	8	13	11	10
Registre aux firmes: taxes	..	0	1	1	0	0	0	0	0	0
Recettes conc. les dép. des affaires étrangères	..	0	0	0	2	7	4	5	5	4
Timbres de chancellerie	..	0	1	2	4	3	3	3	2	1
TVA reclassée et autres impôts sur la production	..	0	0	1	1	1	1	1	1	1
Sous-compensation TVA	..	0	2	0	0	0	0	0	0	0
6200 A la charge d'autres agents	..	0	0	0	0	0	0	0	0	0
Droits de douane perçus pour l'UE	**..**	**..**	**..**	**27**	**23**	**13**	**17**	**15**	**15**	**19**
Crédits d'impôts récupérables										
Crédits d'impôts récupérables contre 1110	..	..	..	..	..	..	..	..	..	217
Composante fiscale	..	..	..	..	..	..	..	..	..	..
Composante transfert	..	..	..	..	..	..	..	..	..	..
Recettes fiscales totales sur la base d'encaissements	**266**	**1 543**	**3 722**	**8 624**	**13 393**	**14 118**	**16 180**	**16 815**	**17 834**	**18 745**
Recettes fiscales totales sur la base des droits constatés	**..**	**..**	**3 671**	**8 521**	**13 416**	**14 125**	**15 989**	**16 904**	**17 735**	**18 761**
Conciliation avec les comptes nationaux										
Impôts additionnels inclus dans les comptes nationaux	..	..	0	0	0	0	0	0	0	0
Impôt exclus des comptes nationaux	..	..	0	0	0	0	0	0	0	0
Différence dans les traitements des crédits d'impôts	..	..	0	0	0	0	0	0	0	0
Transfert en capital des recettes non collectées	..	..	0	0	0	0	0	0	0	0
Cotisations de sécurité sociale volontaires	..	..	4	18	18	25	30	33	34	36
Différences diverses	..	..	0	0	0	0	0	0	0	0
Comptes nationaux: impôts et cotisations sociales effectives	..	..	3 674	8 539	13 434	14 151	16 020	16 937	17 769	18 797
Cotisations sociales imputées	..	..	267	287	429	485	535	572	574	601
Comptes nationaux: impôts et toutes les cotisations sociales	..	..	3 941	8 826	13 863	14 635	16 554	17 509	18 342	19 398

Notes : Année civile se terminant le 31 décembre.

À partir de 1990, les données sont sur la base des droits constatés.

À la rubrique 2000, la différence entre le total des cotisations de sécurité sociale et celles recueillies par les parastataux de la sécurité sociale correspond au prélèvement pour la péréquation des pensions opéré sur les rémunérations et les pensions des salariés et anciens agents de P&T de la Caisse d'épargne de l'État; ces établissements ressortissant l'un au secteur «sociétés et quasi-sociétés non financières» et l'autre à celui des institutions de crédit.

Source : Compte Général de l'État.

StatLink http://dx.doi.org/10.1787/888933416866

Table 4.22. **Mexico/Mexique**

Details of tax revenue/Recettes fiscales détaillées

Million MXN

	1965	1980	1990	2000	2007	2009	2011	2012	2013	2014
Total tax revenue	..	**771**	**102 005**	**833 275**	**1 506 399**	**1 639 243**	**2 038 462**	**2 171 389**	**2 349 963**	**2 607 696**
1000 Taxes on income, profits and capital gains	..	**230**	**34 673**	**276 548**	**554 099**	**591 942**	**772 704**	**803 071**	**957 213**	**979 251**
1100 Of individuals	..	..	..	..	238 938	280 230	352 386	397 701	425 621	514 208
Tax on income of individuals	..	..	..	..	238 938	280 230	352 386	397 701	425 621	514 208
1110 On income and profits	..	..	..	..	..	..	..	..	..	..
1120 On capital gains	..	..	..	..	..	..	..	..	..	..
1200 Corporate	..	..	..	..	217 790	191 685	303 176	288 360	392 199	441 317
Tax on income of corporations	..	..	..	..	217 790	191 685	303 176	288 360	392 199	441 317
1210 On profits	..	..	..	..	..	..	..	..	..	..
1220 On capital gains	..	..	..	..	..	..	..	..	..	..
1300 Unallocable between 1100 and 1200	..	230	34 673	276 548	97 370	120 027	117 143	117 010	139 393	23 726
Tax on income of other individuals and corporations	..	..	..	244 841	54 785	64 816	66 004	74 042	89 028	31 076
Tax on asset	..	..	..	13 913	15 670	-2 540	-1 120	-1 192	-1 325	-735
Credit on salary	..	..	..	17 794	23 177	12 113	2 076	1 387	1 274	2 423
Oil yields tax	..	..	..	0	3 738	921	3 019	573	3 210	4 669
IETU	..	..	..	0	0	44 718	47 165	42 199	47 205	-13 707
Imposed by Activity Exploration and extraction of hydrocarbon	..	..	..	0	0	0	0	0	0	0
2000 Social security contributions	..	**109**	**17 165**	**167 292**	**307 026**	**346 031**	**411 289**	**454 778**	**490 918**	**538 213**
2100 Employees	..	..	..	..	..	..	..	..	..	..
2110 On a payroll basis	..	..	..	..	..	..	..	..	..	..
2120 On an income tax basis	..	..	..	..	..	..	..	..	..	..
2200 Employers	..	..	..	..	..	..	..	..	..	..
2210 On a payroll basis	..	..	..	..	..	..	..	..	..	..
2220 On an income tax basis	..	..	..	..	..	..	..	..	..	..
2300 Self-employed or non-employed	..	..	..	..	..	..	..	..	..	..
2310 On a payroll basis	..	..	..	..	..	..	..	..	..	..
2320 On an income tax basis	..	..	..	..	..	..	..	..	..	..
2400 Unallocable between 2100, 2200 and 2300	..	109	17 165	167 292	307 026	346 031	411 289	454 778	490 918	538 213
2410 On a payroll basis	..	..	..	167 292	307 026	346 031	411 289	454 778	490 918	538 213
2420 On an income tax basis	..	..	..	0	0	0	0	0	0	0
3000 Taxes on payroll and workforce	..	**8**	**1 797**	**11 217**	**28 071**	**31 965**	**41 980**	**48 033**	**53 042**	**64 713**
Substitute tax on salary	..	..	..	0	0	0	0	0	0	0
Payroll tax	..	..	..	11 101	20 277	23 530	31 817	35 480	41 184	64 581
Tax on remuneration to the personal work	..	..	..	65	7 578	8 180	9 990	12 333	11 645	0
Tax on professions and fees	..	..	..	36	68	70	58	48	50	51
Tax on operations by contract	..	..	..	15	148	186	116	173	163	81
4000 Taxes on property	..	**15**	**1 914**	**13 964**	**33 161**	**35 484**	**41 186**	**45 186**	**46 238**	**54 920**
4100 Recurrent taxes on immovable property	..	10	1 036	9 948	19 425	22 862	28 728	31 544	31 338	37 693
4110 Households	..	0	0	0	0	0	0	0	0	0
4120 Others	..	10	1 036	9 948	19 425	22 862	28 728	31 544	31 338	37 693
Property tax	..	..	..	9 948	19 425	22 862	28 728	31 544	31 338	37 693
4200 Recurrent taxes on net wealth	..	0	0	0	0	0	0	0	0	0
4210 Individual	..	..	..	..	..	..	..	..	..	..
4220 Corporate	..	..	..	..	..	..	..	..	..	..
4300 Estate, inheritance and gift taxes	..	0	8	0	0	0	0	0	0	0
4310 Estate and inheritance taxes	..	..	8	..	..	..	..	..	..	..
4320 Gift taxes	..	..	0	..	..	..	..	..	..	..
4400 Taxes on financial and capital transactions	..	5	870	4 017	13 736	12 622	12 458	13 642	14 900	17 227
Alienation of immovable property	..	..	..	1 763	1 076	1 163	1 379	1 341	1 271	1 308
Transfer of ownership of real estate	..	..	..	2 236	8 147	5 005	3 923	4 575	4 518	5 008
Purchasing property	..	..	..	18	4 513	6 454	7 157	7 725	9 110	10 911
4500 Non-recurrent taxes	..	0	0	0	0	0	0	0	0	0
4510 On net wealth	..	..	..	..	..	..	..	..	..	..
4520 Other non-recurrent taxes	..	..	..	..	..	..	..	..	..	..
4600 Other recurrent taxes on property	..	0	0	0	0	0	0	0	0	0
5000 Taxes on goods and services	..	**395**	**44 837**	**356 603**	**567 137**	**606 742**	**738 891**	**783 241**	**761 349**	**933 832**
5100 Taxes on production, sale, transfer, etc	..	388	44 171	310 325	491 928	529 540	658 962	720 052	695 675	854 189
5110 General taxes	..	121	26 635	189 606	409 013	407 795	537 143	579 988	556 794	667 085
5111 Value added taxes	..	120	26 635	189 606	409 013	407 795	537 143	579 988	556 794	667 085
5112 Sales tax	..	0	0	0	0	0	0	0	0	0
5113 Other	..	1	0	0	0	0	0	0	0	0
5120 Taxes on specific goods and services	..	265	17 519	120 720	82 915	121 745	121 819	140 064	138 881	187 104
5121 Excises	..	45	10 072	86 163	47 008	69 770	94 623	98 490	104 111	155 764
Special tax on production and services	..	..	..	81 544	41 532	65 708	89 544	92 620	97 860	149 337
Tax on new automobiles	..	..	..	4 619	5 476	4 063	5 079	5 870	6 252	6 427
Tax on luxury goods and services	..	..	..	0	0	0	0	0	0	0
5122 Profits of fiscal monopolies	..	0	0	0	0	0	0	0	0	0

StatLink http://dx.doi.org/10.1787/888933416871

Table 4.22. **Mexico/Mexique** *(cont./suite)*

Details of tax revenue/Recettes fiscales détaillées

Million MXN

	1965	1980	1990	2000	2007	2009	2011	2012	2013	2014
5123 Customs and import duties	..	45	6 998	33 285	33 344	31 732	29 946	31 161	32 324	36 841
Step customs officer	..	..	..	423	1 156	1 535	3 065	3 255	3 065	2 913
Import taxes	..	..	..	32 861	32 188	30 196	26 881	27 906	29 260	33 928
5124 Taxes on exports	..	2	75	4	3	1	2	1	1	1
Tax on exports	..	..	..	4	3	1	2	1	1	1
5125 Taxes on investment goods	..	0	0	0	0	0	0	0	0	0
5126 Taxes on specific services	..	8	132	1 042	2 146	18 461	-5 610	7 169	-1 441	-7 541
IDE	..	8	..	0	0	15 888	-8 442	2 786	-5 988	-12 322
Tax on lodging	..	0	..	504	1 059	1 147	1 375	1 702	1 890	2 067
Public entertainment tax	..	0	..	240	365	486	360	625	566	543
Tax on lotteries, raffles and gambling	..	0	..	267	705	789	952	1 329	1 213	1 218
Tax on commercials	..	0	..	4	17	150	145	16	203	216
Various indirect taxes	..	0	..	28	0	0	0	711	674	738
5127 Other taxes on internat. trade and transactions	..	0	0	0	0	0	0	0	0	0
5128 Other taxes	..	165	242	226	414	1 782	2 858	3 243	3 886	2 040
Mining fees	..	..	..	226	414	1 782	2 858	3 243	3 886	2 040
5130 Unallocable between 5110 and 5120	..	2	17	0	0	0	0	0	0	0
5200 Taxes on use of goods and perform activities	..	7	666	46 278	75 209	77 202	79 930	63 189	65 674	79 643
5210 Recurrent taxes	..	7	666	46 278	75 209	77 202	79 930	63 189	65 674	79 643
5211 Paid by households: motor vehicles	..	3	567	8 878	20 692	21 301	22 186	16 464	19 174	20 370
Tax on motor vehicules	..	..	..	8 878	20 692	21 301	22 186	16 464	19 174	20 370
5212 Paid by others: motor vehicles	..	0	0	301	275	270	296	370	357	367
Tax on federal auto transport	..	..	..	301	275	270	296	370	357	367
5213 Paid in respect of other goods	..	4	99	37 099	54 242	55 631	57 447	46 355	46 143	58 906
Sport fishing	..	..	..	40	98	68	50	55	50	65
Sport hunting	..	..	..	3	0	0	0	0	0	0
Tax on commercial activities	..	..	..	63	147	42	66	42	26	33
Trade in books and magazines	..	..	..	0	0	0	0	0	3	1
Tax on industrial activities	..	..	..	2	0	35	38	145	49	13
Mining	..	..	..	0	0	1	0	0	1	2
Fee on use of public assets	..	..	..	36 991	53 997	55 485	57 292	46 113	46 013	58 792
5220 Non-recurrent taxes	..	0	0	0	0	0	0	0	0	0
5300 Unallocable between 5100 and 5200	..	0	0	0	0	0	0	0	0	0
6000 Other taxes	**..**	**14**	**1 619**	**7 651**	**16 905**	**27 078**	**32 412**	**37 080**	**41 204**	**36 767**
6100 Paid solely by business	..	0	0	0	0	0	0	0	0	0
6200 Other	..	14	1 619	7 651	16 905	27 078	32 412	37 080	41 204	36 767
Accessories	..	..	..	5 504	12 403	21 710	24 059	24 077	25 301	23 717
Unallocable between 1000 and 5000 caused in exercices fiscal previous liquidation slopes or of payment	..	..	..	374	222	7	-118	2 260	1 618	504
Additional state and local taxes	..	..	..	1 773	4 280	5 361	8 471	10 743	14 285	12 546
Non-wastable tax credits										
Non-wastable tax credits against 1000	..	..	..	..	59 065	44 601	32 737	30 981	41 800	43 716
Tax expenditure component	..	..	..	..	35 888	32 488	30 661	29 594	40 526	41 293
Transfer component	..	..	..	..	23 177	12 113	2 076	1 387	1 274	2 423
Total tax revenue on cash basis	**..**	**771**	**102 005**	**833 275**	**1 506 399**	**1 639 243**	**2 038 462**	**2 171 389**	**2 349 963**	**2 607 696**
Total tax revenue on accrual basis	..	..	..	..	..	..	..	..	..	..
Conciliation with National Accounts										
Additional taxes included in National Accounts	..	..	..	..	..	..	..	..	..	..
Taxes excluded from National Accounts	..	..	..	..	..	..	..	..	..	..
Difference in treatment of tax credits	..	..	..	..	..	..	..	..	..	..
Capital transfer for uncollected revenue	..	..	..	..	..	..	..	..	..	..
Voluntary social security contributions	..	..	..	..	..	..	..	..	..	..
Miscellaneous differences	..	..	..	..	..	..	..	..	..	..
National Accounts: Taxes and actual social contributions	..	..	..	..	..	..	..	..	..	..
Imputed social contributions	..	..	..	..	..	..	..	..	..	..
National Accounts: Taxes and all social contributions	..	..	..	..	..	..	..	..	..	..

Notes : Year ending 31st December.
Data are on cash basis.
Source : Ministry of Finance, Economic Department.

StatLink http://dx.doi.org/10.1787/888933416871

Table 4.23. **Netherlands/Pays-Bas**

Details of tax revenue/Recettes fiscales détaillées

Million EUR

	1965	1980	1990	2000	2007	2009	2011	2012	2013	2014
Total tax revenue	**10 860**	**69 982**	**104 419**	**166 824**	**220 950**	**218 311**	**230 507**	**232 372**	**238 488**	**248 789**
Total tax revenue exclusive of custom duties	..	..	..	**165 514**	**219 271**	**216 793**	**228 618**	**230 592**	**236 732**	**246 743**
1000 Taxes on income, profits and capital gains	**3 884**	**22 998**	**33 689**	**43 256**	**62 463**	**61 489**	**61 929**	**58 869**	**59 085**	**63 671**
1100 Of individuals	3 008	18 383	25 806	25 116	41 414	48 196	47 883	45 172	44 830	46 581
1110 On income and profits	3 007	18 364	25 757	25 057	41 276	47 974	47 646	44 943	44 592	46 361
Income tax	1 359	2 895	2 455	-880	2 294	535	-533	-902	-1 337	-190
Wage tax	1 466	14 984	22 258	24 433	37 729	47 044	47 226	45 207	45 546	45 656
Dividend tax	123	486	1 044	1 504	1 253	395	953	638	383	895
Directors tax	14	0	0	0	0	0	0	0	0	0
Inhabited house tax	45	0	0	0	0	0	0	0	0	0
1120 On capital gains	1	18	50	59	138	222	237	229	238	220
Tax on games of chance	1	18	50	59	138	222	237	229	238	220
1200 Corporate	876	4 615	7 882	18 140	21 049	13 293	14 046	13 697	14 255	17 090
1210 On profits	876	4 615	7 882	18 140	21 049	13 293	14 046	13 697	14 255	17 090
Corporation tax	876	4 615	7 882	18 140	21 049	13 293	14 046	13 697	14 255	17 090
1220 On capital gains	0	0	0	0	0	0	0	0	0	0
1300 Unallocable between 1100 and 1200	0	0	0	0	0	0	0	0	0	0
2000 Social security contributions	**3 342**	**26 641**	**39 075**	**64 522**	**77 072**	**78 839**	**88 470**	**94 844**	**97 372**	**98 616**
2100 Employees	1 659	11 018	24 109	35 305	40 918	39 988	45 419	49 155	49 327	48 351
2110 On a payroll basis	..	..	..	35 305	40 918	39 988	45 419	49 155	49 327	48 351
2120 On an income tax basis	..	..	..	0	0	0	0	0	0	0
2200 Employers	1 371	12 465	7 837	18 671	25 925	28 221	30 241	32 623	31 603	34 996
2210 On a payroll basis	..	..	..	18 671	25 925	28 221	30 241	32 623	31 603	34 996
2220 On an income tax basis	..	..	..	0	0	0	0	0	0	0
2300 Self-employed or non-employed	311	3 158	7 129	10 546	10 229	10 630	12 810	13 066	16 442	15 269
2310 On a payroll basis	..	..	..	0	0	0	0	0	0	0
2320 On an income tax basis	..	..	..	10 546	10 229	10 630	12 810	13 066	16 442	15 269
2400 Unallocable between 2100, 2200 and 2300	0	0	0	0	0	0	0	0	0	0
2410 On a payroll basis	..	..	..	..	..	..	..	..	..	..
2420 On an income tax basis	..	..	..	..	..	..	..	..	..	..
3000 Taxes on payroll and workforce	**0**	**0**	**0**	**0**	**0**	**0**	**0**	**0**	**0**	**0**
4000 Taxes on property	**476**	**2 509**	**3 816**	**8 797**	**10 363**	**8 667**	**7 910**	**7 061**	**8 084**	**9 606**
4100 Recurrent taxes on immovable property	111	1 021	1 711	3 094	3 488	4 078	4 433	4 549	5 249	6 515
Municipal immovable property tax	-59	821	1 398	..	..	..	..	..	..	..
Tax on land	59	0	0	..	..	..	..	..	..	..
Other municipal taxes	66	5	18	..	..	..	..	..	..	..
Contributions polder boards	44	195	295	..	..	..	..	..	..	..
4110 Households	..	..	..	1 806	1 642	1 972	2 173	2 192	2 802	4 016
Municipal immovable property tax	..	..	..	1 651	1 368	1 496	1 617	1 701	1 754	1 820
Contributions polder boards	..	..	..	155	274	403	450	466	492	517
Levies on social housing corporations	..	..	..	0	0	73	106	25	556	1 679
4120 Others	..	..	..	1 288	1 846	2 106	2 260	2 357	2 447	2 499
Municipal immovable property tax	..	..	..	893	1 319	1 440	1 555	1 636	1 686	1 721
Contributions polder boards	..	..	..	395	527	666	705	721	761	778
4200 Recurrent taxes on net wealth	86	517	554	824	30	25	11	2	1	0
4210 Individual	86	517	554	824	30	25	11	2	1	..
Property tax of individuals	86	517	554	824	30	25	11	2	1	..
4220 Corporate	0	0	0	0	0	0	0	0	0	..
4300 Estate, inheritance and gift taxes	117	336	522	1 483	1 877	1 813	1 536	1 382	1 730	1 525
4310 Estate and inheritance taxes	..	304	472	1 303	1 877	1 813	1 536	1 382	1 730	1 525
Estate tax	..	0	0	0	0	0	0	0	0	0
Inheritance tax	..	304	472	1 303	1 877	1 813	1 536	1 382	1 730	1 525
4320 Gift taxes	..	32	50	180	0	0	0	0	0	0
4400 Taxes on financial and capital transactions	162	635	1 030	3 396	4 968	2 751	1 930	1 128	1 104	1 566
Stamp duties	44	0	0	0	0	0	0	0	0	0
Registration duties	118	0	0	0	0	0	0	0	0	0
Tax on legal transactions	0	635	1 030	0	0	0	0	0	0	0
Tax on the sale of immovable property	0	0	0	2 804	4 925	2 745	1 935	1 128	1 104	1 566
Tax on capital formation	0	0	0	592	43	6	-5	0	0	0
4500 Non-recurrent taxes	0	0	0	0	0	0	0	0	0	0
4510 On net wealth	..	..	..	..	..	..	..	..	..	..
4520 Other non-recurrent taxes	..	..	..	..	..	..	..	..	..	..
4600 Other recurrent taxes on property	0	0	0	0	0	0	0	0	0	0
5000 Taxes on goods and services	**3 110**	**17 675**	**27 585**	**48 162**	**68 405**	**66 807**	**69 332**	**69 211**	**71 068**	**73 617**
5100 Taxes on production, sale, transfer, etc	2 943	16 204	25 067	43 597	62 049	59 627	61 579	61 463	63 313	65 241
5110 General taxes	1 344	11 081	17 216	28 857	42 884	40 102	41 636	41 733	42 459	42 741
5111 Value added taxes	0	11 081	17 216	28 849	42 873	40 086	41 610	41 699	42 424	42 708
5112 Sales tax	0	0	0	0	0	0	0	0	0	0
5113 Other	1 344	0	0	8	11	16	26	34	35	33
Turnover tax	1 344	..	..	..	..	..	..	..	..	..

StatLink http://dx.doi.org/10.1787/888933416883

Table 4.23. **Netherlands/Pays-Bas** *(cont./suite)*

Details of tax revenue/Recettes fiscales détaillées

Million EUR

	1965	1980	1990	2000	2007	2009	2011	2012	2013	2014
5120 Taxes on specific goods and services	1 600	5 123	7 850	14 740	19 165	19 525	19 943	19 730	20 854	22 500
5121 Excises	880	3 789	5 985	13 791	17 779	17 913	18 240	17 393	17 348	17 911
Excise on spirits	129	463	422	397	335	306	314	348	306	311
Excise on beer	34	123	259	263	310	390	383	387	413	423
Excise on sugar	45	9	27	0	0	0	0	0	0	0
Excise on tobacco	307	839	948	1 590	2 136	2 318	2 527	2 653	2 228	2 632
Excise on wine	14	82	91	173	257	285	299	316	348	357
Registration tax on motor vehicles	0	613	1 189	2 875	3 647	2 145	1 978	1 500	1 159	1 121
Excise on soft drinks	0	59	186	216	155	158	159	158	154	213
Levies for nuclear reactor	0	0	0	0	0	0	0	0	0	0
Excise on petrol	310	1 280	1 684	3 151	4 010	4 028	4 054	4 007	3 960	4 042
Excise on other mineral oils	41	295	808	2 139	2 965	3 369	3 691	3 578	3 630	3 833
Noise nuisance tax civil aviation	0	0	0	36	55	49	35	49	39	39
Levies on air pollution	0	27	304	0	0	0	0	0	0	0
Levies on petroleum products	0	0	68	462	456	331	320	86	141	107
Levies on petroleum product stocks	0	0	0	68	85	94	89	117	101	292
Levies on energy	0	0	0	2 387	3 333	4 148	4 088	3 896	4 856	4 518
Other excise duties and consumption taxes	0	0	0	0	0	0	0	0	0	0
Other environmental taxes	0	0	0	34	35	292	303	298	13	23
5122 Profits of fiscal monopolies	0	0	0	0	0	0	0	0	0	0
5123 Customs and import duties	702	971	1 375	0	0	0	0	0	0	0
Agriculture levy	338	295	168	..	..	..	..	..	..	..
MCA levy	0	9	0	..	..	..	..	..	..	..
Remaining import duties	364	667	1 207	..	..	..	..	..	..	..
5124 Taxes on exports	0	0	0	0	0	0	0	0	0	0
5125 Taxes on investment goods	0	77	0	0	0	0	0	0	0	0
Selective investment regulation levy	..	77	..	..	..	..	..	..	..	..
5126 Taxes on specific services	16	222	372	662	1 041	1 310	1 406	2 070	3 253	4 219
Tax on fire insurance	2	0	0	0	0	0	0	0	0	0
Entertainment tax	14	0	0	0	0	0	0	0	0	0
Tax on insurances	0	209	340	512	807	849	1 020	1 145	2 343	2 366
Tourist tax	0	14	32	83	125	121	148	159	164	180
Tax on games of chance	0	0	0	67	109	222	238	230	239	220
Flight tax	0	0	0	0	0	118	0	0	0	0
Bank levies	0	0	0	0	0	0	0	536	507	1 453
5127 Other taxes on internat. trade and transactions	0	0	0	0	0	0	0	0	0	0
5128 Other taxes	1	64	118	287	345	302	297	267	253	370
ESCC levy	1	5	0	0	0	0	0	0	0	0
Sugar contribution	0	23	36	0	0	0	0	0	0	0
Milk levy	0	36	82	0	0	0	0	0	0	0
EU levies on food products	0	0	0	273	345	302	297	267	253	370
Sugar storage duty	0	0	0	14	0	0	0	0	0	0
5130 Unallocable between 5110 and 5120	0	0	0	0	0	0	0	0	0	0
5200 Taxes on use of goods and perform activities	167	1 470	2 518	4 565	6 356	7 180	7 753	7 748	7 755	8 376
5210 Recurrent taxes	165	1 470	2 518	4 565	6 356	7 180	7 661	7 692	7 712	8 228
5211 Paid by households: motor vehicles	27	463	799	2 288	3 211	3 841	4 078	4 047	4 008	4 386
Motor vehicle tax	27	427	744	2 288	3 211	3 841	4 078	4 047	4 008	4 386
Motor vehicle licence	0	36	54	0	0	0	0	0	0	0
5212 Paid by others: motor vehicles	132	604	1 044	554	760	918	976	968	959	1 048
Motor vehicle tax	132	590	1 026	554	760	918	976	968	959	1 048
Motor vehicle licence	0	14	18	0	0	0	0	0	0	0
Heavy motor vehicle tax	0	0	0	0	0	0	0	0	0	0
5213 Paid in respect of other goods	6	404	676	1 723	2 385	2 421	2 607	2 677	2 745	2 794
Dog licences	3	23	27	40	54	58	61	65	67	67
Commuter tax	0	5	5	12	21	24	26	28	29	28
Levies on water pollution	1	372	644	1 003	1 220	1 088	1 150	1 161	1 182	1 198
Permission to sell spirits	2	5	0	0	0	0	0	0	0	0
Sewerage charges	0	0	0	650	1 094	1 249	1 368	1 419	1 463	1 497
Levies on manure surplus	0	0	0	18	-4	2	2	4	4	4
5220 Non-recurrent taxes	2	0	0	0	0	0	92	56	43	148
Emission permits	..	..	..	..	..	..	92	56	43	148
5300 Unallocable between 5100 and 5200	0	0	0	0	0	0	0	0	0	0
6000 Other taxes	**48**	**159**	**254**	**777**	**968**	**991**	**977**	**607**	**1 123**	**1 233**
6100 Paid solely by business	48	159	254	410	322	328	335	316	139	33
Administrative levies	48	159	254	410	322	328	335	316	139	33
6200 Other	0	0	0	367	646	663	642	291	984	1 200
Wage Tax reductions	..	..	..	331	497	616	541	165	804	951
Other taxes	..	..	..	36	149	47	101	126	180	249
Custom duties collected for the EU	**..**	**..**	**..**	**1 310**	**1 679**	**1 518**	**1 889**	**1 780**	**1 756**	**2 046**
Total tax revenue on cash basis	**10 860**	**69 982**	**104 419**	**165 503**	**219 982**	**..**	**..**	**..**	**..**	**..**

StatLink http://dx.doi.org/10.1787/888933416883

Table 4.23. **Netherlands/Pays-Bas** *(cont./suite)*

Details of tax revenue/Recettes fiscales détaillées

Million EUR

	1965	1980	1990	2000	2007	2009	2011	2012	2013	2014
Total tax revenue on accrual basis	..	..	..	**166 824**	**220 950**	**218 311**	**230 507**	**232 372**	**238 488**	**248 789**
Conciliation with National Accounts										
Additional taxes included in National Accounts	..	..	..	1 400	0	0	0	0	0	0
Wage Tax reductions	..	..	..	1 400	..	..	..	..	..	..
Taxes excluded from National Accounts	..	..	..	0	0	0	0	0	0	0
Difference in treatment of tax credits	..	..	..	0	0	0	0	0	0	0
Capital transfer for uncollected revenue	..	..	..	0	0	0	0	0	0	0
Voluntary social security contributions	..	..	..	0	0	0	0	0	0	0
Miscellaneous differences	..	..	..	-70	0	0	0	0	0	0
National Accounts: Taxes and actual social contributions	..	..	..	168 154	220 950	218 311	230 507	232 372	238 488	248 789
Imputed social contributions	..	..	..	3 808	3 509	3 624	3 556	3 369	3 414	3 315
National Accounts: Taxes and all social contributions	..	..	..	171 962	224 459	221 935	234 063	235 741	241 902	252 104

Notes : Year ending 31st December.

From 1999, data are on accrual basis.

Heading 2000: From 1998, the figures include some voluntary contributions and the breakdown between premiums paid by employees (2100) and by self-employed/non-employed has been estimated. This is also the case for the breakdown between premiums paid on a payroll or on an income tax basis for those years where both apply.

Heading 4100: From 1992, there was a structural break in the data for the «municipal immovable property tax». The tax ceased to be collected by the central government at that time and the figures are presented on a different type of statistical registration (no longer cash basis).

Heading 5110: Includes 358 millions of euros (1969) and 186 millions of euros (1970) in respect of deduction of turnover tax on stocks existing at 1st January 1969.

Heading 5213: Small amounts (less than 2.3 millions euros) of hunting and fishing licence receipts which should be classified here have been omitted.

Source : Social security contributions and local taxes: Central Bureau of Statistics; other taxes: Ministry of Finance.

StatLink http://dx.doi.org/10.1787/888933416883

Table 4.24. **New Zealand/Nouvelle-Zélande**

Details of tax revenue/Recettes fiscales détaillées

Million NZD

	1965	1980	1990	2000	2007	2009	2011	2012	2013	2014
Total tax revenue	**1 001**	**7 594**	**27 471**	**39 765**	**64 046**	**59 508**	**65 573**	**70 121**	**73 453**	**77 911**
1000 Taxes on income, profits and capital gains	**606**	**5 299**	**16 370**	**23 861**	**40 308**	**33 860**	**35 208**	**38 876**	**40 764**	**43 161**
1100 Of individuals	394	4 679	13 177	17 126	26 965	24 475	24 259	26 426	27 904	30 069
1110 On income and profits	394	4 679	13 177	17 126	26 965	24 475	24 259	26 426	27 904	30 069
1120 On capital gains	0	0	0	0	0	0	0	0	0	0
1200 Corporate	207	589	1 780	4 914	9 069	6 568	8 484	9 889	10 344	10 250
1210 On profits	207	589	1 780	4 914	9 069	6 568	8 484	9 889	10 344	10 250
1220 On capital gains	0	0	0	0	0	0	0	0	0	0
1300 Unallocable between 1100 and 1200	5	31	1 413	1 821	4 274	2 817	2 465	2 561	2 516	2 842
NRWT	5	24	277	760	1 506	884	497	417	427	470
Property speculation	0	0	0	0	0	0	0	0	0	0
Absentee income tax	0	7	0	0	0	0	0	0	0	0
Interest	0	0	1 028	990	2 699	1 803	1 676	1 628	1 643	1 829
Dividends	0	0	83	71	69	130	292	516	446	543
Other	0	0	25	0	0	0	0	0	0	0
2000 Social security contributions	**0**	**0**	**0**	**0**	**0**	**0**	**0**	**0**	**0**	**0**
2100 Employees	0	0	0	0	0	0	0	0	0	0
2110 On a payroll basis	..	..	..	..	..	..	..	..	..	..
2120 On an income tax basis	..	..	..	..	..	..	..	..	..	..
2200 Employers	0	0	0	0	0	0	0	0	0	0
2210 On a payroll basis	..	..	..	..	..	..	..	..	..	..
2220 On an income tax basis	..	..	..	..	..	..	..	..	..	..
2300 Self-employed or non-employed	0	0	0	0	0	0	0	0	0	0
2310 On a payroll basis	..	..	..	..	..	..	..	..	..	..
2320 On an income tax basis	..	..	..	..	..	..	..	..	..	..
2400 Unallocable between 2100, 2200 and 2300	0	0	0	0	0	0	0	0	0	0
2410 On a payroll basis	..	..	..	..	..	..	..	..	..	..
2420 On an income tax basis	..	..	..	..	..	..	..	..	..	..
3000 Taxes on payroll and workforce	**0**	**0**	**0**	**0**	**0**	**0**	**0**	**0**	**0**	**0**
4000 Taxes on property	**116**	**602**	**1 880**	**2 112**	**3 417**	**3 858**	**4 297**	**4 386**	**4 516**	**4 804**
4100 Recurrent taxes on immovable property	84	515	1 722	2 049	3 322	3 774	4 208	4 302	4 423	4 704
Local govt rates and services	81	503	1 550	2 049	3 322	3 774	4 208	4 302	4 423	4 704
Land tax	3	12	172	0	0	0	0	0	0	0
4110 Households	..	..	0	..	..	..	..	..	..	..
4120 Others	..	..	172	..	..	..	..	..	..	..
4200 Recurrent taxes on net wealth	0	0	0	0	0	0	0	0	0	0
4210 Individual	..	..	..	..	..	..	..	..	..	..
4220 Corporate	..	..	..	..	..	..	..	..	..	..
4300 Estate, inheritance and gift taxes	23	39	80	2	3	2	0	0	0	0
4310 Estate and inheritance taxes	21	37	74	0	0	0	..	..	..	..
4320 Gift taxes	2	2	6	2	3	2	..	..	..	..
4400 Taxes on financial and capital transactions	9	48	78	61	92	82	89	84	93	100
Instrument duty	7	40	62	51	85	77	85	82	91	100
Cheque duty	2	8	16	10	7	5	4	3	2	0
4500 Non-recurrent taxes	0	0	0	0	0	0	0	0	0	0
4510 On net wealth	..	..	..	..	..	..	..	..	..	..
4520 Other non-recurrent taxes	..	..	..	..	..	..	..	..	..	..
4600 Other recurrent taxes on property	0	0	0	0	0	0	0	0	0	0
5000 Taxes on goods and services	**280**	**1 693**	**9 220**	**13 792**	**20 290**	**21 781**	**26 063**	**26 856**	**28 170**	**29 944**
5100 Taxes on production, sale, transfer, etc	262	1 624	8 680	12 887	18 832	20 278	24 437	25 193	26 346	28 009
5110 General taxes	77	776	6 163	9 885	15 046	16 449	20 314	21 004	22 063	23 306
5111 Value added taxes	0	0	6 163	9 885	15 046	16 449	20 314	21 004	22 063	23 306
5112 Sales tax	77	776	0	0	0	0	0	0	0	0
Motor vehicles	..	231	..	..	..	..	..	..	..	..
Other sales tax	..	544	..	..	..	..	..	..	..	..
5113 Other	0	0	0	0	0	0	0	0	0	0
5120 Taxes on specific goods and services	186	849	2 517	3 002	3 786	3 829	4 123	4 189	4 283	4 703

StatLink http://dx.doi.org/10.1787/888933416893

Table 4.24. **New Zealand/Nouvelle-Zélande** *(cont./suite)*

Details of tax revenue/Recettes fiscales détaillées

Million NZD

	1965	1980	1990	2000	2007	2009	2011	2012	2013	2014
5121 Excises	124	548	1 929	2 148	1 627	1 691	1 814	1 866	1 856	2 048
On alcoholic beverages	37	84	411	436	573	600	656	664	650	651
Beer	33	64	0	201	290	304	252	251	250	253
Wine	0	0	0	100	163	171	213	220	204	216
Spirits	4	20	0	135	120	125	191	193	196	182
Tobacco	33	99	568	764	159	217	244	281	273	310
Motor vehicles	0	0	7	0	0	0	0	0	0	0
Refined sugar	2	0	0	0	0	0	0	0	0	0
CA petroleum fuels	0	140	835	810	819	805	847	855	865	1 018
NRF fuel excise	49	121	0	0	0	0	0	0	0	0
Local petroleum fuels	0	18	21	27	30	30	31	32	33	33
CA mileage tax	0	0	0	0	0	0	0	0	0	0
NRF mileage tax	3	0	0	0	0	0	0	0	0	0
Road user charges	0	68	0	0	0	0	0	0	0	0
Energy resources levy	0	20	87	111	46	39	36	34	35	36
5122 Profits of fiscal monopolies	0	0	0	0	0	0	0	0	0	0
5123 Customs and import duties	49	231	505	648	1 857	1 873	2 038	2 056	2 160	2 391
5124 Taxes on exports	0	0	0	0	0	0	0	0	0	0
5125 Taxes on investment goods	0	0	0	0	0	0	0	0	0	0
5126 Taxes on specific services	13	57	83	206	302	265	271	267	267	264
Lottery (national)	1	6	26	167	290	252	258	253	254	249
Lottery (overseas)	0	0	0	0	0	0	0	0	0	0
Racing	12	46	57	39	12	13	13	14	13	15
Film hire tax	0	1	0	0	0	0	0	0	0	0
Domestic air travel tax	0	3	0	0	0	0	0	0	0	0
5127 Other taxes on internat. trade and transactions	0	12	0	0	0	0	0	0	0	0
Foreign fishing vessels tax	..	0	..	..	..	..	..	..	..	..
Foreign travel tax	..	0	..	..	..	..	..	..	..	..
International departure tax	..	12	..	..	..	..	..	..	..	..
5128 Other taxes	0	0	0	0	0	0	0	0	0	0
5130 Unallocable between 5110 and 5120	0	0	0	0	0	0	0	0	0	0
5200 Taxes on use of goods and perform activities	18	69	539	905	1 458	1 503	1 626	1 663	1 824	1 935
5210 Recurrent taxes	18	69	539	905	1 458	1 503	1 626	1 663	1 824	1 935
Motor vehicle registration	7	47	154	181	226	171	175	174	187	181
Heavy traffic fees	8	0	285	532	851	910	1 045	1 066	1 205	1 283
Accident compensation levies	0	0	0	0	0	0	0	0	0	0
5211 Paid by households: motor vehicles	0	0	0	0	0	0	0	0	0	0
5212 Paid by others: motor vehicles	0	0	0	0	0	0	0	0	0	0
5213 Paid in respect of other goods	3	23	100	192	381	422	406	423	432	471
Local authority fees and charges	3	23	100	192	381	422	406	423	432	471
5220 Non-recurrent taxes	0	0	0	0	0	0	0	0	0	0
5300 Unallocable between 5100 and 5200	0	0	0	0	0	0	0	0	0	0
6000 Other taxes	**0**	**0**	**1**	**0**	**31**	**9**	**5**	**3**	**3**	**2**
6100 Paid solely by business	..	..	0	..	0	0	0	0	0	0
6200 Other	..	..	1	..	31	9	5	3	3	2
Non-wastable tax credits										
Non-wastable tax credits against 1110	..	..	..	1 057	2 568	2 835	2 707	2 636	2 582	2 555
Tax expenditure component	..	..	..	311	873	964	920	896	878	869
Transfer component	..	..	..	746	1 695	1 871	1 787	1 740	1 704	1 686
Non-wastable tax credits against 1210	..	..	..	0	0	0	0	0	0	0
Tax expenditure component	..	..	..	..	..	..	..	..	..	..
Transfer component	..	..	..	..	..	..	..	..	..	..
Total tax revenue on cash basis	**1 001**	**7 594**	**27 471**	**39 276**	**64 273**	**60 029**	**65 153**	**69 162**	**73 089**	**78 548**
Total tax revenue on accrual basis	**..**	**..**	**..**	**39 765**	**64 046**	**59 508**	**65 573**	**70 121**	**73 453**	**77 911**
Conciliation with National Accounts										
Additional taxes included in National Accounts	..	..	..	..	0	0	0	0	0	0
Taxes excluded from National Accounts	..	..	..	..	0	0	0	0	0	0
Difference in treatment of tax credits	..	..	..	..	0	0	0	0	0	0
Capital transfer for uncollected revenue	..	..	..	..	0	0	0	0	0	0
Voluntary social security contributions	..	..	..	..	0	0	0	0	0	0
Miscellaneous differences	..	..	..	..	0	0	0	0	0	0
National Accounts: Taxes and actual social contributions	..	..	..	..	64 046	59 508	65 573	70 121	73 453	77 911
Imputed social contributions	..	..	..	..	0	0	0	0	0	0
National Accounts: Taxes and all social contributions	..	..	..	..	64 046	59 508	65 573	70 121	73 453	77 911

StatLink http://dx.doi.org/10.1787/888933416893

Table 4.24. **New Zealand/Nouvelle-Zélande** *(cont./suite)*

Details of tax revenue/Recettes fiscales détaillées

Notes : For the years before 1989, data are on a fiscal year basis ending 31st March. The figures provided for 1989 and onwards relate to the financial year ending 30th June of the following year.

From 1993, data are on accrual basis.

Heading 1000: Tax credits to exporters under the export incentives schemes are non-wastable, but that part of the excess of tax liability paid out to taxpayers is not identifiable.

Heading 1100: The figures up to 1969 include revenues collected by a social security income tax. The base of this tax was the same as the ordinary income tax base and the two have now been incorporated into a single income tax.

Heading 5121: From October 1986, incorporates that portion of the selective impost on wine, spirits, tobacco and motor vehicles which was formerly collected and reported as sales tax. The revenue collected on those imported goods which are subject to the equivalent of the domestic excise has been classified as excise duty. In this respect, there is a discontinuity between the excises recorded before and after October 1986.

Heading 5210: The other local authority licence fees include some small items which could be regarded as non-tax revenues.

Heading for non-wastable tax credits 1110 comprises four Family assistance tax credits. The total in item 1100 is net of the tax expenditure component, but not net of the transfer component.

Source : Local Authorities Statistics, Department of Statistics, Wellington.

StatLink http://dx.doi.org/10.1787/888933416893

Table 4.25. **Norway/Norvège**

Details of tax revenue/Recettes fiscales détaillées

Million NOK

	1965	1980	1990	2000	2007	2009	2011	2012	2013	2014
Total tax revenue	**16 842**	**133 499**	**301 812**	**631 581**	**989 915**	**1 001 461**	**1 174 978**	**1 230 742**	**1 226 148**	**1 219 869**
1000 Taxes on income, profits and capital gains	**7 316**	**55 837**	**106 290**	**284 189**	**473 563**	**460 265**	**573 259**	**594 360**	**558 116**	**518 251**
1100 Of individuals	6 671	38 018	79 068	152 013	219 726	241 108	271 322	288 119	304 409	309 618
1110 On income and profits	6 671	38 018	79 068	152 013	219 726	241 108	271 322	288 119	304 409	309 618
Employee social security contributions	1 305	0	0	0	0	0	0	0	0	0
Income taxes	5 366	38 018	79 068	152 013	219 726	241 108	271 322	288 119	304 409	309 618
1120 On capital gains	0	0	0	0	0	0	0	0	0	0
1200 Corporate	645	17 819	27 222	132 176	253 837	219 157	301 937	306 241	253 707	208 633
1210 On profits	..	..	..	132 176	253 837	219 157	301 937	306 241	253 707	208 633
1220 On capital gains	..	..	..	0	0	0	0	0	0	0
1300 Unallocable between 1100 and 1200	0	0	0	0	0	0	0	0	0	0
2000 Social security contributions	**2 009**	**28 205**	**79 362**	**132 170**	**206 314**	**233 083**	**258 760**	**276 790**	**292 278**	**312 942**
2100 Employees	0	6 639	25 345	45 162	68 707	77 766	87 838	93 196	98 124	107 875
2110 On a payroll basis	..	..	..	45 162	68 707	77 766	87 838	93 196	98 124	107 875
2120 On an income tax basis	..	..	..	0	0	0	0	0	0	0
2200 Employers	1 716	20 454	50 116	79 242	125 902	141 949	155 813	167 553	177 275	186 469
2210 On a payroll basis	..	..	..	79 242	125 902	141 949	155 813	167 553	177 275	186 469
2220 On an income tax basis	..	..	..	0	0	0	0	0	0	0
2300 Self-employed or non-employed	293	1 112	3 901	7 766	11 705	13 368	15 109	16 041	16 879	18 598
2310 On a payroll basis	..	..	..	7 766	11 705	13 368	15 109	16 041	16 879	18 598
2320 On an income tax basis	..	..	..	0	0	0	0	0	0	0
2400 Unallocable between 2100, 2200 and 2300	0	0	0	0	0	0	0	0	0	0
2410 On a payroll basis	..	..	..	..	..	..	..	..	..	..
2420 On an income tax basis	..	..	..	..	..	..	..	..	..	..
3000 Taxes on payroll and workforce	**0**	**0**	**0**	**0**	**0**	**0**	**0**	**0**	**0**	**0**
4000 Taxes on property	**523**	**2 295**	**8 887**	**14 546**	**27 709**	**29 112**	**32 798**	**35 306**	**37 268**	**38 288**
4100 Recurrent taxes on immovable property	100	431	2 216	2 848	6 335	7 970	9 083	9 803	10 579	11 162
4110 Households	..	431	2 216	2 724	5 571	6 500	7 566	8 022	3 693	4 167
4120 Others	..	0	0	124	764	1 470	1 517	1 781	6 886	6 995
4200 Recurrent taxes on net wealth	341	1 450	5 118	7 703	13 244	13 635	15 250	16 417	17 134	17 602
4210 Individual	235	907	3 692	6 869	10 746	11 913	12 742	13 329	14 039	13 485
4220 Corporate	106	543	1 426	834	2 498	1 722	2 508	3 088	3 095	4 117
4300 Estate, inheritance and gift taxes	45	122	446	1 273	2 576	2 431	1 754	1 887	2 246	1 880
4310 Estate and inheritance taxes	0	122	446	1 273	2 576	2 431	1 754	1 887	2 246	1 880
4320 Gift taxes	0	0	0	0	0	0	0	0	0	0
4400 Taxes on financial and capital transactions	37	292	1 107	2 722	5 554	5 076	6 711	7 199	7 309	7 644
4500 Non-recurrent taxes	0	0	0	0	0	0	0	0	0	0
4510 On net wealth	..	..	..	..	..	..	..	..	..	..
4520 Other non-recurrent taxes	..	..	..	..	..	..	..	..	..	..
4600 Other recurrent taxes on property	0	0	0	0	0	0	0	0	0	0
5000 Taxes on goods and services	**6 928**	**47 154**	**107 262**	**200 676**	**282 329**	**279 001**	**310 161**	**324 286**	**338 486**	**350 388**
5100 Taxes on production, sale, transfer, etc	6 720	45 882	102 901	185 926	265 669	264 495	295 394	308 450	321 605	331 701
5110 General taxes	3 622	24 350	56 656	124 985	189 424	186 759	211 689	224 062	235 771	244 767
5111 Value added taxes	0	24 350	56 656	124 166	188 705	186 211	211 037	223 425	234 941	243 798
Value added tax	..	24 350	56 656	124 166	188 705	186 211	211 037	223 425	234 941	243 798
5112 Sales tax	3 622	0	0	819	719	548	652	637	830	969
Turnover tax	3 622	..	..	819	719	548	652	637	830	969
5113 Other	0	0	0	0	0	0	0	0	0	0
5120 Taxes on specific goods and services	3 098	21 532	46 245	60 941	76 245	77 736	83 705	84 388	85 834	86 934
5121 Excises	2 338	14 914	37 453	54 876	71 047	71 764	76 966	77 303	78 514	79 039
Stamp duty on tobacco	392	1 076	3 750	6 806	6 815	8 061	7 488	7 403	6 375	7 891
Taxes on spirits and wines	449	2 013	3 454	5 217	0	0	0	0	0	0
Excise on beer	162	605	2 195	3 650	0	0	0	0	0	0
Excise on petrol	480	2 310	7 057	14 558	14 556	15 492	16 034	15 774	16 923	16 624
Vehicles transfer tax	395	2 761	4 554	10 956	22 898	18 672	22 564	23 409	22 229	20 556
Chocolate and sweets	123	247	551	789	1 078	1 123	1 155	1 223	1 261	1 319
Sugar	0	0	217	230	192	197	183	193	201	197
Non-alcoholic beverages	38	120	487	1 113	1 024	1 696	1 742	1 866	1 803	2 089
Electric energy	89	1 515	3 414	5 091	7 079	7 579	8 116	7 913	8 656	8 187
Oil and gas products	0	3 703	8 729	88	92	88	100	102	108	99
Sales of radio and tv sets	0	163	220	920	0	0	0	0	0	0
Mineral oil	0	113	1 098	4 015	5 154	5 718	6 058	5 650	6 296	6 971
Cosmetics	0	0	0	159	0	0	0	0	0	0
Recording equipment	0	0	92	35	0	0	0	0	0	0
Others	210	288	1 635	1 249	1 821	1 850	1 918	1 923	2 060	2 291
Taxes on alcoholic beverages	0	0	0	0	10 338	11 288	11 608	11 847	12 602	12 815
5122 Profits of fiscal monopolies	31	395	751	2 534	2 115	3 070	3 651	3 780	3 800	4 261
Profits state wine monopoly	31	30	67	41	32	51	36	27	36	0
Norsk tipping	0	365	684	2 493	2 083	3 019	3 615	3 753	3 764	4 261

StatLink http://dx.doi.org/10.1787/888933416908

Table 4.25. **Norway/Norvège** *(cont./suite)*

Details of tax revenue/Recettes fiscales détaillées

Million NOK

	1965	1980	1990	2000	2007	2009	2011	2012	2013	2014
5123 Customs and import duties	634	697	1 360	1 944	2 132	2 120	2 649	2 921	3 111	3 192
Customs revenue	615	689	1 305	1 944	2 132	2 120	2 649	2 921	3 111	3 192
Loading and lighthouse dues	11	0	0	0	0	0	0	0	0	0
Other import duties	8	8	55	0	0	0	0	0	0	0
5124 Taxes on exports	7	105	227	0	112	128	174	184	177	206
5125 Taxes on investment goods	0	4 274	4 454	0	0	0	0	0	0	0
5126 Taxes on specific services	88	195	1 233	1 386	131	135	140	144	140	135
Excise on race tracks	9	25	15	88	119	135	140	144	140	135
Taxes on specific services	34	49	150	1 298	0	0	0	0	0	0
Pengelotteriet (national lotteries)	45	121	462	0	0	0	0	0	0	0
Excise on lotto games	0	0	606	0	12	0	0	0	0	0
5127 Other taxes on internat. trade and transactions	0	0	0	0	0	0	0	0	0	0
5128 Other taxes	0	952	767	201	708	519	125	56	92	101
5130 Unallocable between 5110 and 5120	0	0	0	0	0	0	0	0	0	0
5200 Taxes on use of goods and perform activities	208	1 272	4 361	14 750	16 660	14 506	14 767	15 836	16 881	18 687
5210 Recurrent taxes	208	1 272	4 361	14 750	16 660	14 506	14 767	15 165	16 593	18 228
5211 Paid by households: motor vehicles	88	458	1 789	4 435	6 699	6 872	7 462	7 734	8 007	8 239
5212 Paid by others: motor vehicles	108	696	2 072	1 346	712	520	520	496	494	408
5213 Paid in respect of other goods	12	118	500	8 969	9 249	7 114	6 785	6 935	8 092	9 581
CO2 tax	0	0	0	3 047	3 385	2 215	2 189	2 251	3 293	4 576
Excise on pharmacies	6	32	59	105	153	97	67	81	78	76
Others	6	86	441	5 817	4 504	4 677	4 395	4 485	4 656	4 809
Tax on emissions of NOX	0	0	0	0	1 207	125	134	118	65	120
5220 Non-recurrent taxes	0	0	0	0	0	0	0	671	288	459
5300 Unallocable between 5100 and 5200	0	0	0	0	0	0	0	0	0	0
6000 Other taxes	**66**	**8**	**11**	**0**	**0**	**0**	**0**	**0**	**0**	**0**
6100 Paid solely by business	0	3	2	..	..	..	..	..	..	..
6200 Other	66	5	9	..	..	..	..	..	..	..
Non-wastable tax credits										
Non-wastable tax credits against 1210	..	..	..	..	952	1 184	1 311	1 397	1 398	1 467
Tax expenditure component	..	..	..	..	253	75	277	306	362	380
Transfer component	..	..	..	..	741	1 109	1 034	1 091	1 214	1 275
Total tax revenue on cash basis	**16 842**	**133 499**	**301 812**	**575 989**	**967 171**	**1 015 366**	**1 156 926**	**1 220 956**	**1 248 965**	**1 241 543**
Total tax revenue on accrual basis	**..**	**..**	**..**	**631 581**	**989 915**	**1 001 461**	**1 174 978**	**1 230 742**	**1 226 148**	**1 219 869**
Conciliation with National Accounts										
Additional taxes included in National Accounts	..	..	..	0	0	0	0	0	0	0
Taxes excluded from National Accounts	..	..	..	0	0	0	0	0	0	0
Difference in treatment of tax credits	..	..	..	0	0	0	0	0	0	0
Capital transfer for uncollected revenue	..	..	..	0	0	0	0	0	0	0
Voluntary social security contributions	..	..	..	0	0	0	0	0	0	0
Miscellaneous differences	..	..	..	0	0	0	0	0	0	0
National Accounts: Taxes and actual social contributions	..	..	..	631 581	989 915	1 001 461	1 174 978	1 230 742	1 226 148	1 219 869
Imputed social contributions	..	..	..	400	656	350	253	225	243	255
National Accounts: Taxes and all social contributions	..	..	..	631 981	990 571	1 001 811	1 175 231	1 230 967	1 226 391	1 220 124

Notes : Year ending 31st December.

From 2000, data are on accrual basis.

Heading 5211: Up to 1971, this item contains motor vehicle licences paid by both households and enterprises.

Heading 5121: From 2005, taxes on alcoholic beverages include both «taxes on spirits and wines» and «excise on beer».

Heading 5125: From 1998, revenue from taxes on investments goods is included in item 5121 «Others».

Source : Statistics Norway; National Accounts.

StatLink http://dx.doi.org/10.1787/888933416908

Table 4.26. **Poland/Pologne**

Details of tax revenue/Recettes fiscales détaillées

Million PLN

	1965	1980	1990	2000	2007	2009	2011	2012	2013	2014
Total tax revenue	..	..	..	**246 039**	**411 175**	**428 116**	**495 546**	**519 598**	**528 100**	**551 544**
Total tax revenue exclusive of custom duties	..	..	..	..	**409 892**	**426 808**	**494 099**	**517 987**	**526 487**	**549 753**
1000 Taxes on income, profits and capital gains	..	..	..	**50 268**	**93 795**	**92 877**	**99 510**	**106 480**	**103 567**	**108 759**
1100 Of individuals	..	..	..	32 415	61 471	62 161	67 861	72 617	74 216	78 719
Individual income tax	..	..	..	32 415	61 403	62 078	67 768	72 516	74 124	78 617
Tax on winnings from lottery or gambling	..	..	..	0	68	83	93	101	92	102
Tax on salaries	..	..	..	0	0	0	0	0	0	0
Tax on salaries-local	..	..	..	0	0	0	0	0	0	0
Presumptive income tax-local	..	..	..	0	0	0	0	0	0	0
Income equalization tax	..	..	..	0	0	0	0	0	0	0
Income equalization tax-local	..	..	..	0	0	0	0	0	0	0
Health contribution	..	..	..	0	0	0	0	0	0	0
1110 On income and profits	..	..	..	..	..	..	..	..	..	..
1120 On capital gains	..	..	..	..	..	..	..	..	..	..
1200 Corporate	..	..	..	17 853	32 324	30 716	31 649	33 863	29 351	30 040
Income from legal entities	..	..	..	..	..	..	..	..	..	..
Income from legal entities-local	..	..	..	..	..	..	..	..	..	..
1210 On profits	..	..	..	..	..	..	..	..	..	..
1220 On capital gains	..	..	..	..	..	..	..	..	..	..
1300 Unallocable between 1100 and 1200	..	..	..	0	0	0	0	0	0	0
2000 Social security contributions	..	..	..	**96 386**	**140 086**	**152 032**	**174 212**	**194 720**	**202 629**	**209 902**
2100 Employees	..	..	..	40 410	55 644	56 763	69 152	76 834	80 326	78 494
2110 On a payroll basis	..	..	..	..	..	..	..	..	..	..
2120 On an income tax basis	..	..	..	..	..	..	..	..	..	..
2200 Employers	..	..	..	42 796	56 607	63 085	71 613	78 819	85 458	86 474
2210 On a payroll basis	..	..	..	..	..	..	..	..	..	..
2220 On an income tax basis	..	..	..	..	..	..	..	..	..	..
2300 Self-employed or non-employed	..	..	..	13 180	27 835	32 184	33 447	39 067	36 845	44 934
2310 On a payroll basis	..	..	..	..	..	..	..	..	..	..
2320 On an income tax basis	..	..	..	..	..	..	..	..	..	..
2400 Unallocable between 2100, 2200 and 2300	..	..	..	0	0	0	0	0	0	0
2410 On a payroll basis	..	..	..	..	..	..	..	..	..	..
2420 On an income tax basis	..	..	..	..	..	..	..	..	..	..
3000 Taxes on payroll and workforce	..	..	..	**1 628**	**3 081**	**3 787**	**4 182**	**4 290**	**3 998**	**4 042**
Tax on wages	..	..	..	0	0	0	0	0	0	0
Tax on wages-local	..	..	..	0	0	0	0	0	0	0
Penalties for excessive payroll increases	..	..	..	0	0	0	0	0	0	0
Excessive wage tax	..	..	..	0	0	0	0	0	0	0
Rehabilitation fund contribution	..	..	..	1 508	2 860	3 429	3 819	3 915	3 633	3 652
Wage guarantee fund contribution	..	..	..	120	221	358	363	375	365	390
4000 Taxes on property	..	..	..	**10 584**	**17 116**	**18 434**	**20 089**	**21 744**	**23 120**	**23 991**
4100 Recurrent taxes on immovable property	..	..	..	8 404	13 515	15 908	17 492	19 468	20 747	21 423
Agricultural tax-local	..	..	..	720	906	1 227	1 055	1 573	1 666	1 651
Forest tax-local	..	..	..	96	157	183	188	227	228	209
Real estate tax-local	..	..	..	7 588	12 452	14 498	16 249	17 668	18 853	19 563
4110 Households	..	..	..	2 348	3 613	4 553	4 925	5 878	6 289	6 444
4120 Others	..	..	..	6 056	9 902	11 355	12 567	13 590	14 458	14 979
4200 Recurrent taxes on net wealth	..	..	..	0	0	0	0	0	0	0
4210 Individual	..	..	..	..	..	..	..	..	..	..
4220 Corporate	..	..	..	..	..	..	..	..	..	..
4300 Estate, inheritance and gift taxes	..	..	..	172	328	313	279	293	252	263
Inheritance and gift tax-local	..	..	..	172	328	313	279	293	252	263
4310 Estate and inheritance taxes	..	..	..	..	..	..	..	..	..	..
4320 Gift taxes	..	..	..	..	..	..	..	..	..	..
4400 Taxes on financial and capital transactions	..	..	..	2 008	3 273	2 213	2 318	1 983	2 121	2 305
Tax on public sale of shares	..	..	..	2 008	3 273	2 213	2 318	1 983	2 121	2 305
4500 Non-recurrent taxes	..	..	..	0	0	0	0	0	0	0
4510 On net wealth	..	..	..	..	..	..	..	..	..	..
4520 Other non-recurrent taxes	..	..	..	..	..	..	..	..	..	..
4600 Other recurrent taxes on property	..	..	..	0	0	0	0	0	0	0
5000 Taxes on goods and services	..	..	..	**86 880**	**155 290**	**159 029**	**195 460**	**190 024**	**190 777**	**198 912**
5100 Taxes on production, sale, transfer, etc	..	..	..	84 885	150 570	153 543	189 215	184 109	186 195	192 900
5110 General taxes	..	..	..	51 615	97 848	99 562	122 647	116 265	116 607	122 671
5111 Value added taxes	..	..	..	51 615	97 848	99 562	122 647	116 265	116 607	122 671
Taxes on goods and services (VAT)	..	..	..	..	..	..	..	..	..	..
VAT on imported goods	..	..	..	..	..	..	..	..	..	..

StatLink http://dx.doi.org/10.1787/888933416915

Table 4.26. **Poland/Pologne** *(cont./suite)*

Details of tax revenue/Recettes fiscales détaillées

Million PLN

	1965	1980	1990	2000	2007	2009	2011	2012	2013	2014
5112 Sales tax	..	..	..	0	0	0	0	0	0	0
Turnover tax, of which:	..	..	..	..	..	..	..	..	..	..
On spirits	..	..	..	..	..	..	..	..	..	..
On fuels	..	..	..	..	..	..	..	..	..	..
On tobacco	..	..	..	..	..	..	..	..	..	..
5113 Other	..	..	..	0	0	0	0	0	0	0
5120 Taxes on specific goods and services	..	..	..	33 270	52 722	53 981	66 568	67 844	69 588	70 229
5121 Excises	..	..	..	27 170	49 376	50 962	63 019	64 438	65 764	66 131
On domestic excise products, of which:	..	..	..	24 213	45 752	48 001	59 724	60 075	60 228	59 165
On spirits	..	..	..	..	..	..	..	..	..	..
On fuels	..	..	..	..	..	..	..	..	..	..
On tobacco	..	..	..	..	..	..	..	..	..	..
On beer	..	..	..	..	..	..	..	..	..	..
On wine	..	..	..	..	..	..	..	..	..	..
On other products	..	..	..	..	..	..	..	..	..	..
On imported excise products, of which:	..	..	..	2 957	3 624	2 961	3 295	4 363	5 536	6 966
On spirits	..	..	..	..	..	..	..	..	..	..
On fuels	..	..	..	..	..	..	..	..	..	..
On tobacco	..	..	..	..	..	..	..	..	..	..
On beer	..	..	..	..	..	..	..	..	..	..
On wine	..	..	..	..	..	..	..	..	..	..
On other products	..	..	..	..	..	..	..	..	..	..
5122 Profits of fiscal monopolies	..	..	..	0	0	0	0	0	0	0
5123 Customs and import duties	..	..	..	5 038	477	281	508	339	428	690
Customs duties	..	..	..	5 038	..	..	..	..	..	..
Import tax	..	..	..	0	..	..	..	..	..	..
Compensatory fees on agricultural imports	..	..	..	0	..	..	..	..	..	..
5124 Taxes on exports	..	..	..	0	0	0	0	0	0	0
5125 Taxes on investment goods	..	..	..	0	0	0	0	0	0	0
5126 Taxes on specific services	..	..	..	1 062	1 297	1 895	2 251	2 145	2 493	2 568
Lump sum tax occasional passenger transp. serv.	..	..	..	443	189	319	747	844	1 036	1 328
Gambling tax	..	..	..	619	1 108	1 576	1 504	1 301	1 457	1 240
5127 Other taxes on internat. trade and transactions	..	..	..	0	0	0	0	0	0	0
5128 Other taxes	..	..	..	0	1 572	843	790	922	903	840
5130 Unallocable between 5110 and 5120	..	..	..	0	0	0	0	0	0	0
5200 Taxes on use of goods and perform activities	..	..	..	1 995	4 720	5 486	6 245	5 915	4 582	6 012
Local fees	..	..	..	..	..	..	..	..	..	..
Tax on means of transportation-local	..	..	..	..	..	..	..	..	..	..
5210 Recurrent taxes	..	..	..	433	2 224	2 817	3 441	3 222	2 788	3 650
5211 Paid by households: motor vehicles	..	..	..	0	0	0	0	0	0	0
5212 Paid by others: motor vehicles	..	..	..	0	0	0	0	0	0	0
5213 Paid in respect of other goods	..	..	..	433	2 224	2 817	3 441	3 222	2 788	3 650
5220 Non-recurrent taxes	..	..	..	1 562	2 496	2 669	2 804	2 693	1 794	2 362
5300 Unallocable between 5100 and 5200	..	..	..	0	0	0	0	0	0	0
6000 Other taxes	**..**	**..**	**..**	**293**	**524**	**649**	**646**	**729**	**2 396**	**4 147**
Abolished taxes	..	..	..	..	..	..	..	..	..	..
Abolished taxes-local	..	..	..	..	..	..	..	..	..	..
6100 Paid solely by business	..	..	..	0	0	0	0	0	0	0
6200 Other	..	..	..	293	524	649	646	729	2 396	4 147
Custom duties collected for the EU	**..**	**..**	**..**	**..**	**1 283**	**1 308**	**1 447**	**1 611**	**1 613**	**1 791**
Total tax revenue on cash basis	**..**	**..**	**..**	**..**	**..**	**..**	**..**	**..**	**..**	**..**
Total tax revenue on accrual basis	**..**	**..**	**..**	**246 039**	**411 175**	**428 116**	**495 546**	**519 598**	**528 100**	**551 544**
Conciliation with National Accounts										
Additional taxes included in National Accounts	..	..	..	..	..	..	..	..	..	..
Taxes excluded from National Accounts	..	..	..	..	..	..	..	..	..	..
Difference in treatment of tax credits	..	..	..	..	..	..	..	..	..	..
Capital transfer for uncollected revenue	..	..	..	..	..	..	..	..	..	..
Voluntary social security contributions	..	..	..	..	..	..	..	..	..	..
Miscellaneous differences	..	..	..	..	..	..	..	..	..	..
National Accounts: Taxes and actual social contributions	..	..	..	..	..	..	..	..	..	..
Imputed social contributions	..	..	..	..	..	..	..	..	..	..
National Accounts: Taxes and all social contributions	..	..	..	..	..	..	..	..	..	..

Notes : Year ending 31st December.
From 2002, data are on accrual basis.
Source : Ministry of Finance, Economic Department.

StatLink http://dx.doi.org/10.1787/888933416915

Table 4.27. **Portugal**

Details of tax revenue/Recettes fiscales détaillées

Million EUR

	1965	1980	1990	2000	2007	2009	2011	2012	2013	2014
Total tax revenue	**99**	**1 798**	**14 825**	**39 888**	**55 829**	**52 484**	**56 953**	**53 515**	**58 015**	**59 259**
Total tax revenue exclusive of customs duties	..	..	..	**39 684**	**55 644**	**52 330**	**56 785**	**53 359**	**57 872**	**59 110**
1000 Taxes on income, profits and capital gains	**24**	**355**	**3 805**	**11 691**	**15 443**	**14 521**	**16 028**	**14 672**	**18 664**	**18 247**
1100 Of individuals	..	..	2 350	6 947	9 369	9 702	10 507	9 791	13 120	13 318
Individual income tax	..	..	2 350	6 947	9 369	9 702	10 507	9 791	13 120	13 318
1110 On income and profits	..	..	..	..	..	..	..	..	..	..
1120 On capital gains	..	..	..	..	..	..	..	..	..	..
1200 Corporate	..	..	1 182	4 744	6 073	4 819	5 521	4 623	5 545	4 929
Corporate income tax>	..	..	1 088	4 457	5 760	4 507	5 273	4 362	5 327	4 717
Local corporate income tax ('Derrama')	..	..	84	287	313	312	248	261	217	212
Other	..	..	11	0	0	0	0	0	0	0
1210 On profits	..	..	..	..	..	..	..	..	..	..
1220 On capital gains	..	..	..	..	..	..	..	..	..	..
1300 Unallocable between 1100 and 1200	24	355	273	0	0	0	0	258	0	0
Tax on wages and professional income	2	93	9	..	..	..	..	0	..	..
Industrial tax	7	108	129	..	..	..	..	0	..	..
Tax on income from movable capital	2	71	1	..	..	..	..	0	..	..
Property income tax	3	23	17	..	..	..	..	0	..	..
Agricultural income tax	0	0	1	..	..	..	..	0	..	..
Complementary income ax	4	43	58	..	..	..	..	0	..	..
Tax on capital gains	0	3	1	..	..	..	..	258	..	..
Taxes abolished by DL 442-A/88 and DL 442-B/88	0	0	0	..	..	..	..	0	..	..
Other	6	15	58	..	..	..	..	0	..	..
2000 Social security contributions	**22**	**531**	**4 026**	**10 168**	**14 274**	**14 998**	**15 671**	**14 621**	**15 139**	**15 544**
2100 Employees	8	203	1 470	4 286	6 344	6 718	6 666	6 194	6 403	6 810
2110 On a payroll basis	8	203	1 470	4 286	6 344	6 718	6 666	6 194	6 403	6 810
Compulsory employee's social contributions	8	203	1 470	4 286	6 344	6 718	6 666	6 194	6 403	6 810
2120 On an income tax basis	0	0	0	0	0	0	0	0	0	0
2200 Employers	13	318	2 413	5 882	7 930	8 281	9 005	8 428	8 736	8 734
2210 On a payroll basis	13	318	2 413	5 882	7 930	8 281	9 005	8 428	8 736	8 734
Employers' social contributions	13	318	2 413	5 882	7 930	8 281	9 005	8 428	8 736	8 734
2220 On an income tax basis	0	0	0	0	0	0	0	0	0	0
2300 Self-employed or non-employed	0	10	143	0	0	0	0	0	0	0
Compulsory social contributions by self-employed	0	10	143	..	..	..	..	..	..	..
2310 On a payroll basis	..	..	..	..	..	..	..	..	..	..
2320 On an income tax basis	..	..	..	..	..	..	..	..	..	..
2400 Unallocable between 2100, 2200 and 2300	0	0	0	0	0	0	0	0	0	0
2410 On a payroll basis	..	..	..	..	..	..	..	..	..	..
2420 On an income tax basis	..	..	..	..	..	..	..	..	..	..
3000 Taxes on payroll and workforce	**1**	**47**	**0**	**0**	**0**	**0**	**0**	**0**	**0**	**0**
Contributions for Unemployment Fund	1	47	..	..	..	..	..	..	..	..
Stamp duty on wages and salaries	0	0	..	..	..	..	..	..	..	..
4000 Taxes on property	**5**	**26**	**402**	**1 468**	**2 284**	**1 905**	**1 946**	**1 768**	**1 914**	**2 158**
4100 Recurrent taxes on immovable property	0	0	133	508	1 008	1 055	1 205	1 140	1 345	1 465
Real estate tax	..	..	133	508	1 008	1 055	1 205	1 140	1 337	1 445
4110 Households	..	..	..	..	..	..	..	..	..	..
4120 Others	..	..	..	..	..	..	..	..	8	20
4200 Recurrent taxes on net wealth	0	0	0	0	0	0	0	0	0	0
4210 Individual	..	..	..	..	..	..	..	..	..	..
4220 Corporate	..	..	..	..	..	..	..	..	..	..
4300 Estate, inheritance and gift taxes	2	4	74	103	10	0	0	0	2	0
Inheritance and gift taxes	2	4	74	103	10	0	0	..	2	0
4310 Estate and inheritance taxes	..	..	..	..	..	..	..	..	..	..
4320 Gift taxes	..	..	..	..	..	..	..	..	..	..
4400 Taxes on financial and capital transactions	2	21	195	857	1 266	850	741	628	567	693
Real estate transfer tax	2	21	195	674	973	635	513	417	356	483
Stamp duty on registrations and mortgages	0	0	0	34	35	19	33	32	32	31
Stamp duty on the raising of capital	0	0	0	0	10	14	0	0	0	0
Stamp duty on real estate transactions	0	0	0	150	249	182	195	179	180	179
4500 Non-recurrent taxes	0	0	0	0	0	0	0	0	0	0
4510 On net wealth	..	..	..	..	..	..	..	..	..	..
4520 Other non-recurrent taxes	..	..	..	..	..	..	..	..	..	..
4600 Other recurrent taxes on property	0	0	0	0	0	0	0	0	0	0
5000 Taxes on goods and services	**47**	**837**	**6 555**	**16 069**	**23 225**	**20 304**	**22 675**	**21 775**	**21 638**	**22 622**
5100 Taxes on production, sale, transfer, etc	44	810	6 440	15 634	22 550	19 539	21 834	20 921	20 482	21 517
5110 General taxes	0	290	2 906	9 734	14 333	11 971	14 265	13 995	13 710	14 672
5111 Value added taxes	0	0	2 899	9 734	14 333	11 971	14 265	13 995	13 710	14 672
VAT	..	..	2 899	9 734	14 333	11 971	14 265	13 995	13 710	14 672
5112 Sales tax	0	290	7	0	0	0	0	0	0	0
General sales tax	..	290	7	..	..	..	..	..	..	..

StatLink http://dx.doi.org/10.1787/888933416923

Table 4.27. **Portugal** *(cont./suite)*

Details of tax revenue/Recettes fiscales détaillées

Million EUR

	1965	1980	1990	2000	2007	2009	2011	2012	2013	2014
5113 Other	0	0	0	0	0	0	0	0	0	0
5120 Taxes on specific goods and services	44	519	3 534	5 901	8 217	7 568	7 569	6 926	6 772	6 845
5121 Excises	15	295	2 052	4 501	5 940	5 316	5 367	4 775	4 697	4 832
Excise duties on tobacco	3	62	362	1 077	1 165	1 232	1 530	1 432	1 387	1 372
Excise duties on beer	1	0	55	90	100	84	79	75	76	90
Tax on motor vehicle sales	1	59	304	1 239	1 221	714	644	370	360	476
Tax on oil products	6	166	1 251	1 969	3 325	3 177	3 002	2 790	2 740	2 780
Excise duties on alcoholic beverages	0	0	23	126	128	108	111	107	109	98
Excise duties on alcohol	0	0	0	1	1	1	1	0	1	1
Other	4	7	59	0	0	0	0	0	23	16
5122 Profits of fiscal monopolies	0	0	0	261	521	467	470	522	419	422
5123 Customs and import duties	21	96	511	1	1	1	1	1	0	0
Import levies	14	36	392	0	1	1	1	1	0	0
Import surtax	0	26	1	0	0	0	0	0	0	0
Other	6	34	119	0	0	0	0	0	0	0
5124 Taxes on exports	0	0	0	0	0	0	0	0	0	0
Taxes on Oporto wine exports	0	0	..	..	..	..	..	..	..	..
Other	0	0	..	..	..	..	..	..	..	..
5125 Taxes on investment goods	0	0	0	0	0	0	0	0	0	0
5126 Taxes on specific services	1	38	547	1 102	1 712	1 726	1 624	1 529	1 557	1 492
Tax on insurance premiums	0	6	47	131	170	209	214	208	200	200
Stamp duty on bank transactions	1	24	405	330	734	796	580	534	536	534
Stamp duty on debt related operations, interest and leasing of buildings	0	0	22	258	384	259	298	275	276	208
Stamp duty on insurance premiums	0	0	0	248	347	378	314	288	289	289
Bank levies	0	0	0	100	48	55	200	206	237	244
Other	2	8	73	34	29	29	18	17	19	15
5127 Other taxes on internat. trade and transactions	0	0	0	0	0	0	0	0	0	0
5128 Other taxes	6	91	424	36	43	58	107	99	99	99
Stamp taxes (miscellaneous)	6	91	424	36	43	58	107	99	99	99
Other	0	0	0	0	0	0	0	0	0	0
5130 Unallocable between 5110 and 5120	0	0	0	0	0	0	0	0	0	0
5200 Taxes on use of goods and perform activities	4	27	115	382	615	724	815	822	937	1 081
5210 Recurrent taxes	4	27	115	382	615	724	815	822	937	1 081
5211 Paid by households: motor vehicles	0	4	15	55	94	133	130	138	185	178
Local tax on vehicles	..	4	15	55	94	133	130	138	185	178
5212 Paid by others: motor vehicles	2	10	20	67	132	188	234	262	342	361
Local tax on vehicles	0	2	6	0	0	0	0	0	0	0
Road taxes	2	8	14	67	132	188	234	262	342	361
5213 Paid in respect of other goods	2	13	80	260	390	403	451	423	409	542
Gambling tax	0	3	72	110	140	148	141	113	107	119
Tax on the use, carrying and possession of weapons	0	0	1	3	6	7	4	7	7	7
Tax on motor vehicles - compensation	2	8	0	0	0	0	0	0	0	0
Hunting and fishery licenses	0	1	4	1	1	1	1	0	5	2
Fee for the use of water resources	0	0	0	0	2	8	18	29	13	14
Other	0	1	2	146	241	240	287	273	278	402
5220 Non-recurrent taxes	0	0	0	0	0	0	0	0	0	0
Special tax on motor vehicles	..	..	0	..	..	..	..	..	..	..
5300 Unallocable between 5100 and 5200	0	0	0	53	60	40	26	31	219	24
Miscellneous taxes on production	..	..	..	53	60	40	26	31	219	24
6000 Other taxes	**0**	**3**	**37**	**288**	**417**	**602**	**465**	**522**	**516**	**540**
6100 Paid solely by business	0	2	17	105	217	244	224	216	271	258
General services and licenses granted to corporations	0	2	17	105	217	244	224	216	271	258
6200 Other	0	0	20	183	200	359	242	306	245	282
Fees collected by courts of justice	0	0	0	177	189	355	233	232	219	237
Miscellaneous taxes	0	0	20	6	11	4	8	74	25	44
Custom duties collected for the EU	..	..	..	**204**	**185**	**154**	**168**	**155**	**144**	**149**
Import duties	..	..	..	170	156	135	155	120	119	140
Agricultural levies	..	..	..	30	29	19	13	35	25	9
Levy on sugar and isoglucose	..	..	..	4	0	0	0	0	0	0
Total tax revenue on cash basis	**99**	**1 798**	**14 825**	..	..	..	..	..	..	..
Total tax revenue on accrual basis	..	..	..	**39 888**	**55 829**	**52 484**	**56 953**	**53 515**	**58 015**	**59 259**

StatLink http://dx.doi.org/10.1787/888933416923

Table 4.27. **Portugal** *(cont./suite)*

Details of tax revenue/Recettes fiscales détaillées

Million EUR

	1965	1980	1990	2000	2007	2009	2011	2012	2013	2014
Conciliation with National Accounts										
Additional taxes included in National Accounts	..	..	..	0	0	0	0	0	0	0
Taxes excluded from National Accounts	..	..	..	0	0	0	0	0	0	0
Difference in treatment of tax credits	..	..	..	0	0	0	0	0	0	0
Capital transfer for uncollected revenue	..	..	..	0	0	0	0	0	0	0
Voluntary social security contributions	..	..	..	0	0	0	0	0	0	0
Miscellaneous differences	..	..	..	0	0	0	0	0	0	0
National Accounts: Taxes and actual social contributions	..	..	..	39 888	55 829	52 484	56 953	53 515	58 015	59 259
Imputed social contributions	..	..	..	3 292	5 592	6 192	5 530	4 521	5 310	4 827
National Accounts: Taxes and all social contributions	..	..	..	43 181	61 421	58 676	62 483	58 036	63 326	64 086

Notes : Fiscal year ending 31 December.
From 1995, data are on accrual basis.
Source : Instituto Nacionale de Estatistica; Conta do Estado, *Contas de Gerência dos Fundos e Serviços Autonomos da Administraçao Central*; Estatisticas das Financas publicas; Relatorio do Instituto de Gestao Financeira da Seguranta Social, *Contas de Gerência das Regioes Autonomas da Madeira e dos Atores.*

StatLink http://dx.doi.org/10.1787/888933416923

Table 4.28. Slovak Republic/République slovaque

Details of tax revenue/Recettes fiscales détaillées

Million EUR

	1965	1980	1990	2000	2007	2009	2011	2012	2013	2014
Total tax revenue	..	..	..	**10 626**	**18 365**	**18 418**	**20 153**	**20 544**	**22 361**	**23 612**
Total tax revenue exclusive of custom duties	..	..	..	..	**18 229**	**18 307**	**19 997**	**20 415**	**22 247**	**23 485**
1000 Taxes on income, profits and capital gains	..	..	..	**2 181**	**3 844**	**3 526**	**3 842**	**4 005**	**4 440**	**4 949**
1100 Of individuals	..	..	..	1 055	1 820	1 794	2 000	2 123	2 144	2 275
1110 On income and profits	..	..	..	1 055	1 820	1 794	2 000	2 123	2 144	2 275
Wages and salaries withholding	..	..	..	..	..	..	..	..	..	..
Of unincorporated individuals	..	..	..	..	..	..	..	..	..	..
1120 On capital gains	..	..	..	0	0	0	0	0	0	0
1200 Corporate	..	..	..	813	1 835	1 577	1 699	1 715	2 118	2 498
1210 On profits	..	..	..	..	..	..	..	..	..	..
1220 On capital gains	..	..	..	..	..	..	..	..	..	..
1300 Unallocable between 1100 and 1200	..	..	..	314	189	156	143	167	178	175
2000 Social security contributions	..	..	..	**4 409**	**7 192**	**7 858**	**8 479**	**8 907**	**9 783**	**10 125**
2100 Employees	..	..	..	901	1 700	1 886	2 016	2 138	2 238	2 304
Retirement	..	..	..	..	..	..	..	..	..	..
State employment policy	..	..	..	..	..	..	..	..	..	..
Health insurance	..	..	..	..	..	..	..	..	..	..
Sick leave	..	..	..	..	..	..	..	..	..	..
2110 On a payroll basis	..	..	..	901	1 700	1 886	2 016	2 138	2 238	2 304
2120 On an income tax basis	..	..	..	0	0	0	0	0	0	0
2200 Employers	..	..	..	2 850	3 861	4 243	4 591	4 810	5 492	5 763
Retirement	..	..	..	..	..	..	..	..	..	..
State employment policy	..	..	..	..	..	..	..	..	..	..
Health insurance	..	..	..	..	..	..	..	..	..	..
Sick leave	..	..	..	..	..	..	..	..	..	..
2210 On a payroll basis	..	..	..	2 850	3 861	4 243	4 591	4 810	5 492	5 763
2220 On an income tax basis	..	..	..	0	0	0	0	0	0	0
2300 Self-employed or non-employed	..	..	..	658	1 631	1 729	1 872	1 960	2 054	2 057
Retirement	..	..	..	..	..	..	..	..	..	..
State employment policy	..	..	..	..	..	..	..	..	..	..
Health insurance	..	..	..	..	..	..	..	..	..	..
Sick leave	..	..	..	..	..	..	..	..	..	..
2310 On a payroll basis	..	..	..	658	1 631	1 729	1 872	1 960	2 054	2 057
2320 On an income tax basis	..	..	..	0	0	0	0	0	0	0
2400 Unallocable between 2100, 2200 and 2300	..	..	..	0	0	0	0	0	0	0
2410 On a payroll basis	..	..	..	..	..	..	..	..	..	..
2420 On an income tax basis	..	..	..	..	..	..	..	..	..	..
3000 Taxes on payroll and workforce	..	..	..	**0**	**0**	**0**	**0**	**0**	**0**	**0**
4000 Taxes on property	..	..	..	**194**	**245**	**267**	**286**	**316**	**327**	**331**
4100 Recurrent taxes on immovable property	..	..	..	143	243	267	286	316	327	331
4110 Households	..	..	..	55	76	84	91	101	105	106
4120 Others	..	..	..	88	168	182	195	215	223	225
4200 Recurrent taxes on net wealth	..	..	..	0	0	0	0	0	0	0
4210 Individual	..	..	..	..	..	..	..	..	..	..
4220 Corporate	..	..	..	..	..	..	..	..	..	..
4300 Estate, inheritance and gift taxes	..	..	..	8	0	0	0	0	0	0
4310 Estate and inheritance taxes	..	..	..	3	0	0	0	0	0	0
4320 Gift taxes	..	..	..	5	0	0	0	0	0	0
4400 Taxes on financial and capital transactions	..	..	..	43	1	0	0	0	0	0
Real property transfer tax	..	..	..	30	1	0	0	0	0	0
4500 Non-recurrent taxes	..	..	..	0	0	0	0	0	0	0
4510 On net wealth	..	..	..	..	..	..	..	..	..	..
4520 Other non-recurrent taxes	..	..	..	..	..	..	..	..	..	..
4600 Other recurrent taxes on property	..	..	..	0	0	0	0	0	0	0
5000 Taxes on goods and services	..	..	..	**3 842**	**6 948**	**6 656**	**7 389**	**7 187**	**7 697**	**8 081**
5100 Taxes on production, sale, transfer, etc	..	..	..	3 621	6 419	6 115	6 835	6 612	7 051	7 365
5110 General taxes	..	..	..	2 168	4 147	4 221	4 711	4 328	4 696	5 021
5111 Value added taxes	..	..	..	2 168	4 147	4 221	4 711	4 328	4 696	5 021
5112 Sales tax	..	..	..	0	0	0	0	0	0	0
5113 Other	..	..	..	0	0	0	0	0	0	0
5120 Taxes on specific goods and services	..	..	..	1 453	2 271	1 894	2 124	2 284	2 355	2 344
5121 Excises	..	..	..	971	2 171	1 762	1 999	1 973	1 985	2 015
On hydrocarbon fuels and lubricants	..	..	..	617	1 118	1 047	1 071	1 036	1 045	1 077
On alcohol and liquers	..	..	..	143	201	197	205	195	201	202
On beer	..	..	..	43	66	58	58	56	56	55
On wine	..	..	..	12	4	4	4	4	4	4
On tobacco products	..	..	..	156	783	436	623	640	636	640
On electricity	..	..	..	0	0	8	16	17	17	14
On coal	..	..	..	0	0	1	1	1	1	0
On natural gas	..	..	..	0	0	11	21	23	25	22

StatLink http://dx.doi.org/10.1787/888933416934

Table 4.28. **Slovak Republic/République slovaque** *(cont./suite)*

Details of tax revenue/Recettes fiscales détaillées

Million EUR

	1965	1980	1990	2000	2007	2009	2011	2012	2013	2014
5122 Profits of fiscal monopolies	..	..	..	0	0	0	0	0	0	0
5123 Customs and import duties	..	..	..	437	1	0	0	0	0	0
Customs duties	..	..	..	122	0	0	0	0	0	0
Import surcharges	..	..	..	315	0	0	0	0	0	0
Other customs revenues	..	..	..	0	0	0	0	0	0	0
5124 Taxes on exports	..	..	..	0	0	0	0	0	0	0
5125 Taxes on investment goods	..	..	..	0	0	0	0	0	6	3
5126 Taxes on specific services	..	..	..	45	99	132	125	311	364	327
5127 Other taxes on internat. trade and transactions	..	..	..	0	0	0	0	0	0	0
5128 Other taxes	..	..	..	0	0	0	0	0	0	0
5130 Unallocable between 5110 and 5120	..	..	..	0	0	0	0	0	0	0
5200 Taxes on use of goods and perform activities	..	..	..	219	424	412	416	430	495	566
5210 Recurrent taxes	..	..	..	219	372	384	392	400	466	492
5211 Paid by households: motor vehicles	..	..	..	0	0	0	0	0	0	0
5212 Paid by others: motor vehicles	..	..	..	76	124	124	140	138	153	157
5213 Paid in respect of other goods	..	..	..	143	248	260	253	261	313	335
5220 Non-recurrent taxes	..	..	..	0	53	27	24	30	29	74
5300 Unallocable between 5100 and 5200	..	..	..	2	105	129	138	145	151	150
6000 Other taxes	**..**	**..**	**..**	**0**	**0**	**0**	**0**	**0**	**0**	**0**
6100 Paid solely by business	..	..	..	..	..	..	..	..	..	..
6200 Other	..	..	..	..	..	..	..	..	..	..
Custom duties collected for the EU	**..**	**..**	**..**	**..**	**136**	**111**	**157**	**129**	**115**	**127**
Non-wastable tax credits										
Non-wastable tax credits against 1110	..	..	..	..	..	..	..	..	..	..
Tax expenditure component	..	..	..	..	252	270	269	264	265	263
Transfer component	..	..	..	..	..	..	..	..	..	..
Non-wastable tax credits against 1210	..	..	..	..	..	..	..	..	..	..
Tax expenditure component	..	..	..	..	0	0	0	0	0	0
Transfer component	..	..	..	..	..	..	..	..	..	..
Total tax revenue on cash basis	**..**	**..**	**..**	**10 821**	**17 941**	**18 386**	**19 617**	**20 068**	**21 870**	**22 601**
Total tax revenue on accrual basis	**..**	**..**	**..**	**10 626**	**18 365**	**18 418**	**20 153**	**20 544**	**22 361**	**23 612**
Conciliation with National Accounts										
Additional taxes included in National Accounts	..	..	..	53	33	46	48	25	0	32
Taxes excluded from National Accounts	..	..	..	0	-103	-126	-135	-142	-148	-146
Difference in treatment of tax credits	..	..	..	0	0	0	0	0	0	0
Capital transfer for uncollected revenue	..	..	..	0	0	0	0	0	0	0
Voluntary social security contributions	..	..	..	0	22	26	34	22	17	13
Miscellaneous differences	..	..	..	0	0	0	0	0	0	0
National Accounts: Taxes and actual social contributions	..	..	..	10 679	18 317	18 364	20 101	20 449	22 231	23 511
Imputed social contributions	..	..	..	19	78	94	147	118	140	153
National Accounts: Taxes and all social contributions	..	..	..	10 699	18 395	18 458	20 248	20 567	22 371	23 665

Notes : Year ending 31st December.
Data are on accrual basis.
Source : Ministry of Finance.

StatLink http://dx.doi.org/10.1787/888933416934

Table 4.29. **Slovenia/Slovénie**

Details of tax revenue/Recettes fiscales détaillées

Million EUR

	1965	1980	1990	2000	2007	2009	2011	2012	2013	2014
Total tax revenue	..	..	..	**6 924**	**13 030**	**13 096**	**13 458**	**13 265**	**13 198**	**13 612**
Total tax revenue exclusive of customs duties	..	..	..	..	**12 945**	**13 039**	**13 396**	**13 211**	**13 146**	**13 560**
1000 Taxes on income, profits and capital gains	..	..	..	**1 280**	**3 041**	**2 722**	**2 670**	**2 494**	**2 285**	**2 437**
1100 Of individuals	..	..	..	1 041	1 919	2 066	2 056	2 045	1 849	1 907
1110 On income and profits	..	..	..	1 039	1 916	2 063	2 053	2 040	1 847	1 896
Personal income tax	..	..	..	1 039	1 916	2 063	2 053	2 040	1 847	1 896
Special contribution for the reconstruction of the Posocje region	..	..	..	0	0	0	0	0	0	0
1120 On capital gains	..	..	..	2	3	4	3	4	3	0
Taxes on winnings from lottery and gambling	..	..	..	2	3	4	3	4	3	11
1200 Corporate	..	..	..	216	1 116	652	611	446	433	529
1210 On profits	..	..	..	216	1 116	652	611	446	433	529
1220 On capital gains	..	..	..	0	0	0	0	0	0	0
1300 Unallocable between 1100 and 1200	..	..	..	24	5	4	3	4	3	2
Tax on income - copy rights, patents and trademarks	..	..	..	24	5	4	3	3	2	2
Tax on profits due to changes in land use	..	..	..	0	0	0	0	0	0	0
2000 Social security contributions	..	..	..	**2 631**	**4 724**	**5 276**	**5 407**	**5 365**	**5 269**	**5 368**
2100 Employees	..	..	..	1 446	2 488	2 736	2 767	2 698	2 637	2 777
2110 On a payroll basis	..	..	..	1 446	2 488	2 736	2 767	2 698	2 637	2 777
2120 On an income tax basis	..	..	..	0	0	0	0	0	0	0
2200 Employers	..	..	..	1 008	1 844	2 032	2 064	2 054	2 022	2 026
2210 On a payroll basis	..	..	..	1 008	1 844	2 032	2 064	2 054	2 022	2 026
2220 On an income tax basis	..	..	..	0	0	0	0	0	0	0
2300 Self-employed or non-employed	..	..	..	177	392	508	575	614	610	565
2310 On a payroll basis	..	..	..	177	392	508	575	614	610	565
2320 On an income tax basis	..	..	..	0	0	0	0	0	0	0
2400 Unallocable between 2100, 2200 and 2300	..	..	..	0	0	0	0	0	0	0
2410 On a payroll basis	..	..	..	..	..	..	..	..	..	..
2420 On an income tax basis	..	..	..	..	..	..	..	..	..	..
3000 Taxes on payroll and workforce	..	..	..	**289**	**418**	**27**	**29**	**26**	**23**	**20**
Payroll tax	..	..	..	272	391	0	0	0	0	0
Tax on work contracts	..	..	..	18	27	27	29	26	23	20
4000 Taxes on property	..	..	..	**120**	**206**	**210**	**219**	**227**	**232**	**233**
4100 Recurrent taxes on immovable property	..	..	..	81	140	169	177	188	199	193
4110 Households	..	..	..	17	38	46	46	54	61	56
Property tax on weekend cottages	..	..	..	1	1	1	1	1	1	1
Compensation on the use of building ground - paid by individuals	..	..	..	16	37	45	45	52	48	54
Tax on immovable property of higher value	..	..	..	0	0	0	0	1	13	2
4120 Others	..	..	..	65	102	123	131	135	138	137
Property tax on buildings	..	..	..	2	3	3	4	4	4	2
Compensation on the use of building ground - paid by legal entities	..	..	..	63	100	120	127	131	134	135
4200 Recurrent taxes on net wealth	..	..	..	4	0	0	0	0	0	0
4210 Individual	..	..	..	0	..	..	..	..	..	..
4220 Corporate	..	..	..	4	..	..	..	..	..	..
Tax on balance wealth paid by banks	..	..	..	4	..	..	..	..	..	..
4300 Estate, inheritance and gift taxes	..	..	..	2	9	11	10	9	8	7
4310 Estate and inheritance taxes	..	..	..	..	..	..	..	..	..	..
4320 Gift taxes	..	..	..	..	..	..	..	..	..	..
4400 Taxes on financial and capital transactions	..	..	..	23	57	30	29	27	23	25
Taxes on the sale of immovable property - from legal entities	..	..	..	11	19	7	6	5	5	5
Taxes on the sale of immovable property - from individuals	..	..	..	12	38	22	23	21	18	21
4500 Non-recurrent taxes	..	..	..	10	0	0	4	2	1	7
4510 On net wealth	..	..	..	0	..	..	0	0	0	0
4520 Other non-recurrent taxes	..	..	..	10	..	..	4	2	1	7
Payments for the change of use of agricultural and forest land	..	..	..	10	..	..	2	0	1	3
Granting of easements and the creation of building rights	..	..	..	0	..	..	2	2	1	5
4600 Other recurrent taxes on property	..	..	..	0	0	0	0	0	0	0
Property tax on boats	..	..	..	0	0	0	0	0	0	0
5000 Taxes on goods and services	..	..	..	**2 602**	**4 556**	**4 804**	**5 070**	**5 099**	**5 336**	**5 501**
5100 Taxes on production, sale, transfer, etc	..	..	..	2 481	4 341	4 597	4 850	4 853	4 996	5 152
5110 General taxes	..	..	..	1 641	2 916	2 862	2 995	2 889	3 048	3 158
5111 Value added taxes	..	..	..	1 610	2 916	2 862	2 995	2 889	3 048	3 158
Value added tax	..	..	..	1 598	2 898	2 849	2 994	2 886	3 044	3 153
Negative compensation of farmers in a VAT flat rate system	..	..	..	12	18	13	1	3	4	5

StatLink http://dx.doi.org/10.1787/888933416942

Table 4.29. **Slovenia/Slovénie** *(cont./suite)*

Details of tax revenue/Recettes fiscales détaillées

Million EUR

	1965	1980	1990	2000	2007	2009	2011	2012	2013	2014
5112 Sales tax	..	..	..	31	0	0	0	0	0	0
Turnover tax on goods	..	..	..	11	..	..	..	..	..	..
Turnover tax on services	..	..	..	12	..	..	..	..	..	..
Special turnover tax on alcohol	..	..	..	0	..	..	..	..	..	..
Customs duties paid by individuals	..	..	..	1	..	..	..	..	..	..
Special import duties and customs charges	..	..	..	7	..	..	..	..	..	..
5113 Other	..	..	..	0	0	0	0	0	0	0
5120 Taxes on specific goods and services	..	..	..	841	1 425	1 735	1 855	1 964	1 948	1 994
5121 Excises	..	..	..	581	1 196	1 502	1 548	1 637	1 579	1 598
Alcohol and alcoholic drinks	..	..	..	39	71	86	92	93	96	102
Mineral oil and gas	..	..	..	405	758	1 005	955	1 035	998	1 015
Tobacco	..	..	..	97	301	363	429	442	425	420
Duty free shops - alcohol and alcoholic drinks	..	..	..	3	0	0	0	0	0	0
Duty free shops - tobacco	..	..	..	17	0	0	0	0	0	0
Electric power and coal	..	..	..	0	4	7	33	33	31	34
Tax on the sales of new motor vehicles	..	..	..	18	60	41	38	34	26	23
Tax on the sales of used motor vehicles	..	..	..	2	2	0	0	0	0	0
Additional tax on motor vehicles	..	..	..	0	0	0	0	1	3	4
5122 Profits of fiscal monopolies	..	..	..	0	0	0	0	0	0	0
5123 Customs and import duties	..	..	..	158	0	0	0	0	0	0
Import duties	..	..	..	151	..	..	..	..	..	..
Levies on imported agricultural products	..	..	..	7	..	..	..	..	..	..
5124 Taxes on exports	..	..	..	0	0	0	0	0	0	0
5125 Taxes on investment goods	..	..	..	0	0	0	0	0	0	0
5126 Taxes on specific services	..	..	..	102	230	233	308	327	369	396
Tax on special gambling (gambling in casinos)	..	..	..	25	64	57	51	45	41	43
Tax on classical gambling (lottery...)	..	..	..	1	3	4	3	4	3	3
Special tax on slot machines	..	..	..	4	0	0	0	0	0	0
Tax on insurance services	..	..	..	37	65	69	71	70	65	63
Sojourn tax	..	..	..	3	7	7	7	8	8	8
Concessions	..	..	..	1	29	40	42	60	90	83
Concessions duties on special gambling (gambling in casinos)	..	..	..	26	55	49	45	41	38	37
Fire protection tax	..	..	..	4	6	7	8	8	8	8
Tax on lottery tickets	..	..	..	0	0	0	0	0	3	17
Tax on financial services	..	..	..	0	0	0	0	0	32	44
FIHO, FSO	..	..	..	0	0	0	23	37	26	26
SOS	..	..	..	0	0	0	27	17	10	12
Tax on balace wealth paid by banks	..	..	..	0	0	0	0	7	18	26
Commodity reserve fund	..	..	..	0	0	0	31	31	27	27
5127 Other taxes on internat. trade and transactions	..	..	..	0	0	0	0	0	0	0
5128 Other taxes	..	..	..	0	0	0	0	0	0	0
Sugar levy	..	..	..	..	0	..	..	..	..	..
5130 Unallocable between 5110 and 5120	..	..	..	0	0	0	0	0	0	0
5200 Taxes on use of goods and perform activities	..	..	..	121	215	207	220	245	340	349
5210 Recurrent taxes	..	..	..	121	215	207	220	245	323	332
5211 Paid by households: motor vehicles	..	..	..	49	87	83	87	88	109	117
Registration fees on motor vehicles, boats and airplanes paid by individuals	..	..	..	49	87	83	87	88	109	117
5212 Paid by others: motor vehicles	..	..	..	12	21	22	20	20	24	26
Registration fees on motor vehicles, boats and airplanes paid by legal entities	..	..	..	12	21	22	20	20	24	26
Registration fees on tractors	..	..	..	0	0	0	0	0	0	0
5213 Paid in respect of other goods	..	..	..	59	107	102	113	137	189	189
Charges on the use of water	..	..	..	4	22	22	25	26	29	29
Taxes on waste pollution	..	..	..	7	10	4	4	4	4	2
Taxes on air pollution - caused by gas and hard fuels	..	..	..	3	8	9	10	8	10	12
Contribution of Nuclear power plant to finance its de-composition	..	..	..	16	8	8	9	8	8	9
Indemnity for the restricted use of area on the territory of Nuclear power plant	..	..	..	0	7	7	11	11	11	12
Taxes on air pollution	..	..	..	29	21	23	21	49	98	98
Special water tax	..	..	..	0	30	29	33	30	29	28
5220 Non-recurrent taxes	..	..	..	0	0	0	0	0	18	17
Emission permits	..	..	..	0	0	0	0	0	18	17
5300 Unallocable between 5100 and 5200	..	..	..	0	0	0	0	0	0	0
6000 Other taxes	**..**	**..**	**..**	**0**	**0**	**0**	**0**	**0**	**0**	**0**
6100 Paid solely by business	..	..	..	..	..	..	..	..	..	..
6200 Other	..	..	..	..	..	..	..	..	..	..
Custom duties collected for the EU	**..**	**..**	**..**	**..**	**85**	**57**	**62**	**54**	**52**	**52**
Total tax revenue on cash basis	**..**	**..**	**..**	**6 990**	**12 937**	**13 344**	**13 690**	**13 614**	**13 129**	**13 702**

StatLink http://dx.doi.org/10.1787/888933416942

Table 4.29. **Slovenia/Slovénie** *(cont./suite)*

Details of tax revenue/Recettes fiscales détaillées

Million EUR

	1965	1980	1990	2000	2007	2009	2011	2012	2013	2014
Total tax revenue on accrual basis	..	..	..	**6 924**	**13 030**	**13 096**	**13 458**	**13 265**	**13 198**	**13 612**
Conciliation with National Accounts										
Additional taxes included in National Accounts	..	..	..	0	0	85	81	92	90	93
Radio and television licence fee	..	..	..	..	..	85	81	92	90	93
Taxes excluded from National Accounts	..	..	..	0	0	0	0	0	0	0
Difference in treatment of tax credits	..	..	..	0	0	0	0	0	0	0
Capital transfer for uncollected revenue	..	..	..	0	0	0	0	0	0	0
Voluntary social security contributions	..	..	..	0	0	0	0	0	0	0
Miscellaneous differences	..	..	..	0	0	0	0	0	0	0
National Accounts: Taxes and actual social contributions	..	..	..	6 924	13 030	13 181	13 539	13 357	13 288	13 705
Imputed social contributions	..	..	..	39	80	97	101	101	97	95
National Accounts: Taxes and all social contributions	..	..	..	6 962	13 110	13 278	13 641	13 457	13 385	13 800

Notes : Year ending 31st December.

Data are on accrual basis.

Source : Statistical Office of the Republic of Slovenia.

StatLink http://dx.doi.org/10.1787/888933416942

Table 4.30. **Spain/Espagne**

Details of tax revenue/Recettes fiscales détaillées

Million EUR

	1965	1980	1990	2000	2007	2009	2011	2012	2013	2014
Total tax revenue	**1 238**	**22 002**	**103 662**	**219 347**	**399 659**	**332 587**	**345 436**	**346 247**	**349 394**	**356 700**
Total tax revenue exclusive of custom duties	..	..	..	**218 377**	**397 937**	**331 259**	**343 882**	**344 811**	**348 078**	**355 188**
1000 Taxes on income, profits and capital gains	**304**	**5 714**	**31 763**	**62 162**	**133 841**	**99 661**	**100 125**	**103 646**	**102 130**	**102 469**
1100 Of individuals	177	4 481	22 527	41 851	81 510	73 126	78 807	79 281	78 625	79 655
1110 On income and profits	169	4 393	22 527	41 851	81 510	73 126	78 807	79 281	78 625	79 655
Personal income tax	..	..	22 527	40 969	80 757	72 590	78 297	78 893	78 321	79 383
Non-resident (individuals)	..	..	0	882	753	536	510	388	304	272
1120 On capital gains	8	88	0	0	0	0	0	0	0	0
1200 Corporate	114	1 119	9 146	19 918	51 642	25 777	20 490	23 491	22 589	21 831
1210 On profits	114	1 089	9 146	19 918	51 642	25 777	20 490	23 491	22 589	21 831
Tax on commercial activity	33	5	0	0	0	0	0	0	0	0
Special tax 4 percent	0	0	0	0	0	0	0	0	0	0
Taxes on profits	81	1 084	0	0	0	0	0	0	0	0
Corporate income tax	0	0	9 146	19 616	49 750	23 832	18 853	22 098	21 465	20 688
Non-Resident (legal persons)	0	0	0	302	1 892	1 945	1 637	1 393	1 124	1 143
1220 On capital gains	0	29	0	0	0	0	0	0	0	0
1300 Unallocable between 1100 and 1200	13	114	91	393	689	758	828	874	916	983
Local taxes	13	114	0	0	0	0	0	0	0	0
Other taxes	0	0	91	393	689	758	828	874	916	983
2000 Social security contributions	**350**	**10 682**	**36 722**	**76 421**	**129 170**	**131 510**	**129 535**	**123 967**	**120 728**	**122 664**
2100 Employees	81	2 376	5 976	12 336	20 582	20 599	20 491	19 393	18 821	19 374
2110 On a payroll basis	..	..	5 976	12 336	20 582	20 599	20 491	19 393	18 821	19 374
2120 On an income tax basis	..	..	0	0	0	0	0	0	0	0
2200 Employers	269	8 306	26 385	55 090	94 102	91 710	90 875	85 700	83 464	85 928
2210 On a payroll basis	..	..	26 385	55 090	94 102	91 710	90 875	85 700	83 464	85 928
2220 On an income tax basis	..	..	0	0	0	0	0	0	0	0
2300 Self-employed or non-employed	0	0	4 361	8 995	14 486	19 201	18 169	18 874	18 443	17 362
Self-employment	..	..	2 492	7 037	10 335	10 535	10 632	10 713	10 639	10 952
Unemployment	..	..	1 869	1 958	4 151	8 666	7 537	8 161	7 804	6 410
2310 On a payroll basis	..	..	..	..	..	..	..	..	..	..
2320 On an income tax basis	..	..	..	..	..	..	..	..	..	..
2400 Unallocable between 2100, 2200 and 2300	0	0	0	0	0	0	0	0	0	0
2410 On a payroll basis	..	..	..	..	..	..	..	..	..	..
2420 On an income tax basis	..	..	..	..	..	..	..	..	..	..
3000 Taxes on payroll and workforce	**0**	**0**	**0**	**0**	**0**	**0**	**0**	**0**	**0**	**0**
4000 Taxes on property	**79**	**1 004**	**5 718**	**13 819**	**32 084**	**21 755**	**20 702**	**21 623**	**23 263**	**25 018**
4100 Recurrent taxes on immovable property	6	41	1 478	3 990	7 274	8 861	10 176	11 182	11 763	12 478
4110 Households	..	40	1 478	3 990	7 274	8 861	10 176	11 182	11 763	12 478
Real State tax	..	..	1 478	3 990	7 274	8 861	10 176	11 182	11 763	12 478
Real State tax. Surchage	..	..	0	0	0	0	0	0	0	0
4120 Others	..	1	0	0	0	0	0	0	0	0
4200 Recurrent taxes on net wealth	0	107	637	1 200	2 059	93	56	784	1 370	1 168
4210 Individual	..	107	637	1 200	2 059	93	56	784	1 370	1 168
Wealth tax	..	..	637	1 200	2 059	93	56	784	1 370	1 168
4220 Corporate	..	0	0	0	0	0	0	0	0	0
4300 Estate, inheritance and gift taxes	13	90	440	1 381	2 905	2 667	2 220	2 285	2 515	2 704
4310 Estate and inheritance taxes	..	90	440	1 381	2 905	2 667	2 220	2 285	2 515	2 704
Inheritance and gift tax	..	..	440	1 381	2 905	2 667	2 220	2 285	2 515	2 704
4320 Gift taxes	..	0	0	0	0	0	0	0	0	0
4400 Taxes on financial and capital transactions	60	767	2 478	6 140	17 399	8 483	6 574	5 777	5 657	6 384
Taxes on property transactions	60	767	2 478	6 140	17 399	8 483	6 574	5 777	5 657	6 384
4500 Non-recurrent taxes	0	0	646	1 108	2 447	1 651	1 676	1 595	1 958	2 284
4510 On net wealth	..	..	467	705	1 911	1 290	1 357	1 382	1 801	2 159
Tax on land holding gains	..	..	467	705	1 911	1 290	1 357	1 382	1 801	2 159
4520 Other non-recurrent taxes	..	..	179	403	536	361	319	213	157	125
Special duties	..	..	179	180	168	135	134	94	86	76
Land development contributions	..	..	0	223	368	226	185	119	71	49
4600 Other recurrent taxes on property	0	0	38	0	0	0	0	0	0	0
5000 Taxes on goods and services	**506**	**4 553**	**29 437**	**64 649**	**100 739**	**75 405**	**89 714**	**92 117**	**98 261**	**101 506**
5100 Taxes on production, sale, transfer, etc	503	4 552	27 508	59 582	93 943	69 526	83 650	86 363	92 414	95 607
5110 General taxes	275	2 234	16 611	38 546	63 943	41 782	56 733	57 584	62 058	64 688
5111 Value added taxes	0	0	16 304	38 546	63 943	41 782	56 733	57 584	62 058	64 688
Value added tax (VAT)	..	..	16 304	37 806	62 672	41 045	55 904	56 652	60 951	63 422
Canary Islands general indirect tax	..	..	0	740	1 271	737	829	932	1 107	1 266
5112 Sales tax	0	0	0	0	0	0	0	0	0	0
5113 Other	275	2 234	307	0	0	0	0	0	0	0
Cascade tax	118	1 483	197	..	..	..	..	..	..	..
Excises on luxury expenditure	96	939	15	..	..	..	..	..	..	..
Other import duties	94	832	128	..	..	..	..	..	..	..
Refund of internal taxes	-33	-1 020	-33	..	..	..	..	..	..	..

StatLink http://dx.doi.org/10.1787/888933416956

Table 4.30. **Spain/Espagne** *(cont./suite)*

Details of tax revenue/Recettes fiscales détaillées

Million EUR

	1965	1980	1990	2000	2007	2009	2011	2012	2013	2014
5120 Taxes on specific goods and services	228	2 317	10 896	21 036	30 000	27 744	26 917	28 779	30 356	30 919
5121 Excises	69	1 239	6 048	16 489	23 176	22 634	22 256	21 711	24 218	24 173
Special excises	69	1 239	10	0	0	0	0	0	0	0
On beer	0	0	87	202	307	299	302	303	302	311
On wine	0	0	0	0	0	0	0	0	0	0
On alcohol	0	0	481	821	1 032	907	830	827	779	828
On hydrocarbon	0	0	4 222	9 997	11 785	10 859	10 226	9 460	11 918	12 087
On tobacco	0	0	1 123	4 505	7 250	7 717	7 845	7 737	7 126	7 153
On electricity bills	0	0	0	703	1 153	1 363	1 499	1 632	1 560	1 506
On carbon	0	0	0	0	0	0	0	0	148	268
Tax on retail sales of specific hydrocarbons	0	0	0	0	1 356	1 232	1 315	1 489	499	6
Tax on oil derived fuels	0	0	120	237	263	227	216	240	267	286
Petrol tax	0	0	0	6	5	6	5	4	13	19
Production and storage of electricity	0	0	0	0	0	0	0	0	1 587	1 657
Tax Greenhouse Effect Flourinated	0	0	0	0	2	0	0	1	0	31
Other taxes	0	0	5	18	23	24	18	18	19	21
5122 Profits of fiscal monopolies	66	132	546	0	0	0	0	0	0	0
Tobacco	21	77	0	..	..	..	..	..	..	..
Petroleum	45	55	546	..	..	..	..	..	..	..
5123 Customs and import duties	87	561	2 078	103	145	120	127	118	124	132
Import duties	87	561	1 394	0	0	0	0	0	0	0
Canary Islands taxes on imported products	0	0	137	33	51	36	48	46	45	60
Taxes on imported products in Ceuta and Melilla	0	0	36	41	42	39	41	28	39	42
Customs duties paid to EU	0	0	511	0	0	0	0	0	0	0
Special duties and other taxes on importes products	0	0	0	29	52	45	38	44	40	30
5124 Taxes on exports	0	0	0	0	0	0	0	0	0	0
5125 Taxes on investment goods	0	0	0	0	0	0	0	0	0	0
5126 Taxes on specific services	7	385	2 203	2 913	4 326	3 997	3 779	6 368	5 504	6 083
Taxes on betting and gambling	0	232	1 307	1 699	2 062	1 747	1 475	1 495	1 282	1 225
Taxes on other specific services	6	153	120	0	0	0	0	0	0	0
Taxes on insurance premiums	0	0	0	849	1 581	1 498	1 517	1 473	1 417	1 407
Compensation for local taxes	0	0	86	140	176	178	158	144	129	125
Parafiscal taxes	0	0	690	225	492	552	486	467	629	707
Deposit Guarantee Fund (DGF)	0	0	0	0	15	22	143	2 789	2 047	2 619
5127 Other taxes on internat. trade and transactions	0	0	0	0	0	0	0	0	0	0
5128 Other taxes	0	0	22	1 531	2 353	993	755	582	510	531
Duty on specific means of transport	..	..	0	1 323	2 159	819	563	426	325	322
Canary Islands taxes on national products	..	..	0	51	86	63	76	72	75	95
Taxes on national products in Ceuta and Melilla	..	..	0	108	110	103	109	73	103	112
Duty on the production of sugar	..	..	22	49	-2	8	7	11	7	2
5130 Unallocable between 5110 and 5120	0	0	0	0	0	0	0	0	0	0
5200 Taxes on use of goods and perform activities	3	1	1 857	5 032	6 721	5 443	5 235	5 047	5 313	5 408
5210 Recurrent taxes	3	1	1 530	3 464	4 004	4 205	4 242	4 382	4 499	4 503
5211 Paid by households: motor vehicles	..	0	461	1 129	1 698	1 800	1 799	1 805	1 876	1 728
Car registration tax	..	..	461	1 129	1 698	1 800	1 799	1 805	1 876	1 728
5212 Paid by others: motor vehicles	..	0	117	286	430	456	456	457	475	437
Car registration tax	..	..	117	286	430	456	456	457	475	437
5213 Paid in respect of other goods	..	1	952	2 049	1 876	1 949	1 987	2 120	2 148	2 338
Hunting and fishing taxes	..	..	0	28	28	29	30	30	34	34
Economic activity tax	..	..	925	1 934	1 635	1 790	1 732	1 764	1 701	1 838
Economic activity tax. Surchage	..	..	0	0	0	0	0	0	0	0
Advertising	..	..	27	0	0	0	0	0	0	0
Tax on environment and pollution	..	..	0	0	0	0	0	0	0	0
Other taxes on environment	..	..	0	42	131	80	151	233	316	329
Tax on effluent, use of hydrocarbon and mines	..	..	0	45	82	50	74	93	97	137
5220 Non-recurrent taxes	0	0	327	1 568	2 717	1 238	993	665	814	905
Tax and building permits	..	..	327	1 117	2 227	988	773	500	519	484
Urban licenses	..	..	0	451	490	250	220	165	157	173
Greenhouse gas emission trading	..	..	0	0	0	0	0	0	138	248
5300 Unallocable between 5100 and 5200	0	0	72	35	75	436	829	707	534	491
6000 Other taxes	**0**	**49**	**22**	**1 326**	**2 103**	**2 928**	**3 806**	**3 458**	**3 696**	**3 531**
6100 Paid solely by business	..	49	0	510	886	958	1 211	1 258	1 274	1 256
Municipal fees for private use of public space	..	..	..	510	886	958	1 211	1 258	1 274	1 256
6200 Other	..	0	22	816	1 217	1 970	2 595	2 200	2 422	2 275
Custom duties collected for the EU	..	..	..	**970**	**1 722**	**1 328**	**1 554**	**1 436**	**1 316**	**1 512**

StatLink http://dx.doi.org/10.1787/888933416956

Table 4.30. **Spain/Espagne** *(cont./suite)*

Details of tax revenue/Recettes fiscales détaillées

Million EUR

	1965	1980	1990	2000	2007	2009	2011	2012	2013	2014
Non-wastable tax credits										
Non-wastable tax credits against 1110	..	..	..	..	1 044	1 760	852	687	625	582
Tax expenditure component	..	..	..	..	..	..	..	..	..	..
Transfer component	..	..	..	..	..	..	..	..	..	..
Non-wastable tax credits against 1210	..	..	..	..	0	0	0	0	0	0
Tax expenditure component	..	..	..	..	..	..	..	..	..	..
Transfer component	..	..	..	..	..	..	..	..	..	..
Total tax revenue on cash basis	**1 238**	**22 002**	**103 662**	**215 212**	**394 169**	**321 507**	**335 671**	**339 131**	**345 877**	**353 563**
Total tax revenue on accrual basis	**..**	**..**	**..**	**219 347**	**399 659**	**332 587**	**345 436**	**346 247**	**349 394**	**356 700**
Conciliation with National Accounts										
Additional taxes included in National Accounts	..	..	..	0	0	0	0	0	0	0
Taxes excluded from National Accounts	..	..	..	-2 201	-3 334	-3 518	-4 029	-4 226	-4 128	-4 173
Fines and penalties	..	..	..	-1 182	-1 614	-2 182	-2 468	-2 779	-2 805	-2 659
VAT for EU	..	..	..	0	0	0	0	0	0	0
Duty on the production of sugar	..	..	..	-49	2	-8	-7	-11	-7	-2
Customs duties collected for the EU	..	..	..	-970	-1 722	-1 328	-1 554	-1 436	-1 316	-1 512
Difference in treatment of tax credits	..	..	..	0	0	0	0	0	0	0
Capital transfer for uncollected revenue	..	..	..	-3 454	-4 837	-9 351	-8 811	-7 955	-6 501	-4 306
Voluntary social security contributions	..	..	..	0	0	0	0	0	0	0
Miscellaneous differences	..	..	..	0	0	0	0	0	0	0
National Accounts: Taxes and actual social contributions	..	..	..	213 692	391 488	319 718	332 596	334 976	339 127	347 313
Imputed social contributions	..	..	..	5 379	7 702	8 767	8 814	8 534	8 012	7 984
National Accounts: Taxes and all social contributions	..	..	..	219 071	399 190	328 485	341 410	343 510	347 139	355 297

Notes : Year ending 31st December.

From 2000, data are on accrual basis.

From 1981, the figures take into account the classification procedures set out in the *OECD Interpretative Guide*. Consequently, they are not completely comparable with the figures for earlier years though the amounts involved are quite small.

Heading 1000: Includes a tax on property «Contribucion Rustica», which would be more appropriately classified in 4110, and the «Licencia fiscal industrial and professionals», which, because it is a tax levied by reference to the size of the firm, energy input, etc, would be more appropriately classified in 6000. The data necessary to provide a breakdown is not available.

All subdivisions are estimated.

Heading 2300: Contributions paid by self-employed were shown under heading 2100 until 1982.

Heading 4100: Most of these receipts fall under 4110.

Heading 4400: In 1988, revenues from taxes on legal Acts issued by Autonomous Communities (Local) are included in 4400.

Heading 5121 comprises certain local levies which may include non-tax revenues.

Source : Informacion Estatistica del Ministerio de Hacienda (for national taxes); Cuentas de las Administraciones Publicas (for local taxes and social security) both published by Secretaria General Tecnica del Ministerio de Hacienda.

StatLink http://dx.doi.org/10.1787/888933416956

Table 4.31. **Sweden/Suède**

Details of tax revenue/Recettes fiscales détaillées

Million SEK

	1965	1980	1990	2000	2007	2009	2011	2012	2013	2014
Total tax revenue	**40 003**	**259 216**	**755 953**	**1 166 006**	**1 482 649**	**1 449 712**	**1 554 311**	**1 568 247**	**1 617 799**	**1 676 380**
Total tax revenue exclusive of custom duties	..	..	..	**1 162 556**	**1 477 550**	**1 444 948**	**1 548 912**	**1 563 252**	**1 612 823**	**1 670 643**
1000 Taxes on income, profits and capital gains	**21 956**	**112 730**	**314 797**	**475 304**	**573 698**	**510 372**	**540 942**	**534 404**	**559 026**	**585 570**
1100 Of individuals	19 500	106 376	291 146	387 531	457 760	417 337	427 894	439 623	459 078	479 463
1110 On income and profits	19 390	105 866	289 598	353 106	408 054	392 416	399 118	411 899	426 777	431 484
Coupon tax	9	44	233	2 040	6 306	3 063	4 536	3 722	4 108	4 189
Duties on foreign artists	4	3	3	50	86	127	85	6	-1	0
National income tax individual	8 676	31 682	70 755	32 486	44 326	39 935	44 636	44 080	44 664	47 766
Local income tax individual	9 294	78 134	220 072	336 304	479 068	511 150	538 227	560 766	581 934	602 652
Tax reduction individual	0	-3 997	-1 465	-18 872	-122 029	-162 550	-189 120	-197 423	-204 632	-223 791
Other	1 407	0	0	1 098	296	690	753	748	704	669
1120 On capital gains	110	510	1 548	34 425	49 707	24 921	28 776	27 724	32 301	47 979
Lottery prize tax	110	510	1 548	60	0	0	0	0	0	0
1200 Corporate	2 456	6 354	23 651	87 772	115 937	93 035	113 048	94 781	99 948	106 107
1210 On profits	2 456	6 354	23 651	87 772	115 937	93 035	113 048	94 781	99 948	106 107
Tax on profits not distributed	1	10	3	0	0	0	0	0	0	0
National income tax b.c. list	1 425	2 078	19 774	74 501	103 150	80 718	101 186	84 635	93 097	95 858
Local income tax b.c. list	1 030	4 266	0	0	0	0	0	0	0	0
Special tax on profits	0	0	3 874	0	0	0	0	0	0	0
Taxes on pension insurance savings	0	0	0	13 271	12 787	12 317	11 862	10 146	6 850	10 249
1220 On capital gains	0	0	0	0	0	0	0	0	0	0
1300 Unallocable between 1100 and 1200	0	0	0	0	0	0	0	0	0	0
2000 Social security contributions	**4 851**	**74 647**	**205 867**	**306 974**	**388 505**	**357 289**	**361 987**	**375 628**	**376 684**	**388 651**
2100 Employees	743	254	823	63 074	81 088	86 845	93 500	97 561	100 861	103 955
Health insurance fees	743	9	5	0	0	0	0	0	0	0
Unemployment insurance fees	0	245	818	0	0	0	0	0	0	0
Pension fees	0	0	0	63 074	81 088	86 845	93 500	97 561	100 861	103 955
2110 On a payroll basis	..	..	..	63 074	81 088	86 845	93 500	97 561	100 861	103 955
2120 On an income tax basis	..	..	..	0	0	0	0	0	0	0
2200 Employers	3 568	71 602	196 905	237 527	300 010	264 807	263 272	272 511	271 449	280 085
Survivors pension fees	0	20 343	44 181	14 847	19 611	19 905	14 771	15 250	15 693	16 216
Health insurance fees	717	26 005	58 334	74 097	100 979	78 631	63 318	65 434	58 365	60 287
Unemployment insurance fees	0	0	0	0	0	28 325	0	0	0	0
Labour market fees	0	982	12 516	45 975	48 471	7 964	36 752	37 919	39 007	39 366
Industrial injury insurance fees	132	1 201	4 663	12 030	7 844	0	8 571	3 914	4 022	4 151
Seamen's pension fees	0	10	26	30	0	0	0	0	0	0
Part pension fees	0	1 119	2 897	0	0	0	0	0	0	0
Supplementary pension fees	2 719	21 458	73 129	71 335	97 748	104 219	112 130	116 116	119 508	124 027
Parent insurance fees	0	484	1 159	19 215	25 356	25 764	27 729	33 878	34 854	36 038
2210 On a payroll basis	..	..	..	237 527	300 010	264 807	263 272	272 511	271 449	280 085
2220 On an income tax basis	..	..	..	0	0	0	0	0	0	0
2300 Self-employed or non-employed	540	2 791	8 139	5 618	8 391	7 721	6 252	5 881	5 607	5 038
Survivors pension fees	0	943	1 580	451	662	643	482	452	442	443
Health insurance fees	260	992	1 702	1 988	3 297	2 609	840	751	550	290
Industrial injury insurance fees	0	64	191	365	264	258	279	116	113	104
Parent insurance fees	0	58	106	573	856	834	903	1 008	960	597
Supplementary pension fees	280	734	4 560	2 241	3 312	3 377	3 747	3 554	3 542	3 604
Reduction	0	0	0	0	0	0	0	0	0	0
2310 On a payroll basis	..	..	..	5 618	8 391	7 721	6 252	5 881	5 607	5 038
2320 On an income tax basis	..	..	..	0	0	0	0	0	0	0
2400 Unallocable between 2100, 2200 and 2300	0	0	0	756	-984	-2 084	-1 036	-324	-1 233	-427
2410 On a payroll basis	..	..	..	756	-984	-2 084	-1 036	-324	-1 233	-427
2420 On an income tax basis	..	..	..	0	0	0	0	0	0	0
3000 Taxes on payroll and workforce	**13**	**6 759**	**18 686**	**50 106**	**83 279**	**122 591**	**155 341**	**160 326**	**172 170**	**177 412**
Special wage tax	0	61	0	22 391	30 225	32 462	36 218	37 400	36 832	37 022
Child care fees	0	4 740	13 080	0	0	0	0	0	0	0
Adult education fees	0	614	1 555	0	0	0	0	0	0	0
Building research fees	13	105	0	0	0	0	0	0	0	0
Labour welfare fees	0	257	2 033	0	0	0	0	0	0	0
Labour education fees	0	982	0	0	0	0	0	0	0	0
Labour market fees	0	0	0	112	156	189	14	2	7	6
General wage fees	0	0	2 018	27 603	52 898	89 939	119 109	122 924	135 331	140 384
4000 Taxes on property	**712**	**2 424**	**26 630**	**39 890**	**36 228**	**34 288**	**36 529**	**37 558**	**41 182**	**41 935**
4100 Recurrent taxes on immovable property	10	16	8 946	23 286	25 899	25 352	27 584	28 743	31 596	32 005
4110 Households	0	0	3 877	13 321	13 474	11 571	11 866	13 071	13 422	13 048
Special tax on real estate	..	..	3 877	13 321	13 474	11 571	11 866	13 071	13 422	13 048
4120 Others	10	16	5 069	9 965	12 424	13 781	15 718	15 672	18 174	18 957
Forestry levy	10	16	423	22	34	25	44	51	37	21
Special tax on real estate	0	0	4 646	9 943	12 390	13 756	15 673	15 621	18 137	18 935
4200 Recurrent taxes on net wealth	366	717	3 200	8 223	0	0	0	0	0	0

StatLink http://dx.doi.org/10.1787/888933416965

Table 4.31. **Sweden/Suède** (*cont./suite*)

Details of tax revenue/Recettes fiscales détaillées

Million SEK

	1965	1980	1990	2000	2007	2009	2011	2012	2013	2014
4210 Individual	361	702	3 135	8 043	..	..	..	..	..	..
4220 Corporate	5	15	65	180	..	..	..	..	..	..
4300 Estate, inheritance and gift taxes	155	545	1 433	2 549	23	2	4	-5	-4	1
4310 Estate and inheritance taxes	143	495	1 118	2 088	15	2	4	-5	-4	1
4320 Gift taxes	12	50	315	460	8	0	0	0	0	0
4400 Taxes on financial and capital transactions	181	1 146	13 051	5 833	10 305	8 934	8 942	8 819	9 590	9 929
Taxes on financial and capital transactions	181	1 146	6 946	4 878	9 414	8 064	7 989	7 961	8 913	9 261
Turnover tax on securities	0	0	6 105	0	0	0	0	0	0	0
Tax on life group insurances	0	0	0	955	891	870	953	859	678	667
4500 Non-recurrent taxes	0	0	0	0	0	0	0	0	0	0
4510 On net wealth	..	..	..	..	..	..	..	..	..	..
4520 Other non-recurrent taxes	..	..	..	..	..	..	..	..	..	..
4600 Other recurrent taxes on property	0	0	0	0	0	0	0	0	0	0
5000 Taxes on goods and services	**12 471**	**62 234**	**188 709**	**288 803**	**394 073**	**418 419**	**452 359**	**453 503**	**461 955**	**475 716**
5100 Taxes on production, sale, transfer, etc	11 808	58 474	181 587	281 370	380 990	402 042	436 635	437 900	445 453	458 909
5110 General taxes	4 147	34 643	112 399	199 606	286 211	303 095	334 708	333 342	341 952	357 385
5111 Value added taxes	0	34 643	112 399	197 483	282 586	299 452	330 769	329 311	337 822	353 439
5112 Sales tax	4 147	0	0	0	0	0	0	0	0	0
5113 Other	0	0	0	2 123	3 625	3 643	3 939	4 031	4 130	3 946
5120 Taxes on specific goods and services	7 661	23 831	69 188	81 764	94 779	98 947	101 927	104 558	103 500	101 524
5121 Excises	5 953	19 941	55 332	70 313	84 818	89 173	89 715	89 772	88 485	86 879
Taxes on petrol and fuel	1 420	4 229	17 171	39 011	44 501	46 274	45 723	45 099	43 869	42 603
Special sales tax	390	585	1 098	0	0	0	0	0	0	0
Sales tax on motor vehicles	325	553	1 983	195	3	0	0	0	0	0
Tobacco tax	1 150	3 087	5 636	7 747	9 742	10 604	11 261	11 799	11 136	11 376
Tax on spirits	1 548	4 431	6 205	4 902	4 249	4 437	4 349	4 328	4 001	4 092
Tax on wine	149	930	2 922	3 567	4 001	4 449	4 678	4 767	4 887	5 197
Tax on beer and soft drinks	242	964	2 532	2 355	2 773	3 271	3 186	3 237	3 329	3 509
Tax on energy consumption	729	5 162	16 352	11 451	18 939	19 949	20 314	20 343	21 144	19 962
Taxes on electricity from certain sources	0	0	1 018	0	0	0	0	0	0	0
Tax on wastes	0	0	0	1 085	609	189	205	198	119	140
Tax on cassette tapes	0	0	194	0	0	0	0	0	0	0
Tax on videorecorders	0	0	221	0	0	0	0	0	0	0
5122 Profits of fiscal monopolies	72	204	332	3 641	3 952	4 822	5 165	5 227	5 385	5 013
Alcohol monopoly wholesale	23	116	98	0	0	0	0	0	0	0
Alcohol monopoly retailing	49	88	234	80	296	345	159	90	116	251
Gaming monopoly retailing	0	0	0	3 561	3 657	4 477	5 006	5 137	5 269	4 762
5123 Customs and import duties	1 419	2 433	8 308	0	0	0	0	0	0	0
Customs	1 080	1 300	3 115	..	..	..	..	..	..	..
Agricultural levies	339	1 133	5 193	..	..	..	..	..	..	..
5124 Taxes on exports	0	0	0	0	0	0	0	0	0	0
5125 Taxes on investment goods	0	0	40	0	0	0	0	0	0	0
Investment tax	..	..	40	..	..	..	..	..	..	..
5126 Taxes on specific services	217	1 253	5 176	6 472	4 341	4 075	6 224	8 915	9 072	9 200
Betting tax	79	223	616	0	0	0	0	0	0	0
Advertisement tax	0	202	1 073	1 116	657	292	390	290	244	225
Tax on gambling	0	69	88	1 245	1 315	1 370	1 411	1 335	1 309	1 320
Other specific services	138	656	2 938	4 111	2 369	2 412	4 422	7 291	7 520	7 655
Tax on charter travelling	0	103	461	0	0	0	0	0	0	0
5127 Other taxes on internat. trade and transactions	0	0	0	0	0	0	0	0	0	0
5128 Other taxes	0	0	0	1 339	1 668	878	824	644	559	432
5130 Unallocable between 5110 and 5120	0	0	0	0	0	0	0	0	0	0
5200 Taxes on use of goods and perform activities	663	3 760	7 122	7 433	13 083	16 376	15 724	15 603	16 502	16 807
5210 Recurrent taxes	663	3 760	7 122	7 433	13 083	16 376	15 724	15 603	16 502	16 807
5211 Paid by households: motor vehicles	336	1 241	2 003	4 969	7 451	8 411	8 090	8 058	8 275	9 493
5212 Paid by others: motor vehicles	313	2 476	5 055	2 464	5 632	7 965	7 633	7 545	8 227	7 314
5213 Paid in respect of other goods	14	43	64	0	0	0	0	0	0	0
5220 Non-recurrent taxes	0	0	0	0	0	0	0	0	0	0
5300 Unallocable between 5100 and 5200	0	0	0	0	0	0	0	0	0	0
6000 Other taxes	**0**	**422**	**1 264**	**1 479**	**1 768**	**1 990**	**1 754**	**1 832**	**1 806**	**1 360**
6100 Paid solely by business	..	0	0	0	0	0	0	0	0	0
6200 Other	..	422	1 264	1 479	1 768	1 990	1 754	1 832	1 806	1 360
Custom duties collected for the EU	**..**	**..**	**..**	**3 450**	**5 099**	**4 764**	**5 399**	**4 995**	**4 976**	**5 737**
Total tax revenue on cash basis	**40 003**	**259 216**	**755 953**	**1 144 233**	**1 465 382**	**1 437 531**	**1 574 357**	**1 584 780**	**1 611 798**	**1 661 413**
Total tax revenue on accrual basis	**..**	**..**	**..**	**1 166 006**	**1 482 649**	**1 449 712**	**1 554 311**	**1 568 247**	**1 617 799**	**1 676 380**

StatLink http://dx.doi.org/10.1787/888933416965

Table 4.31. **Sweden/Suède** *(cont./suite)*

Details of tax revenue/Recettes fiscales détaillées

Million SEK

	1965	1980	1990	2000	2007	2009	2011	2012	2013	2014
Conciliation with National Accounts										
Additional taxes included in National Accounts	..	..	..	0	0	0	0	0	0	0
Taxes excluded from National Accounts	..	..	..	0	0	0	0	0	0	0
Difference in treatment of tax credits	..	..	..	0	0	0	0	0	0	0
Capital transfer for uncollected revenue	..	..	..	0	0	0	0	0	0	0
Voluntary social security contributions	..	..	..	14 336	24 420	27 282	29 719	28 803	30 013	31 228
Miscellaneous differences	..	..	..	0	0	0	0	0	0	0
National Accounts: Taxes and actual social contributions	..	..	..	1 180 342	1 507 069	1 476 994	1 584 030	1 597 050	1 647 812	1 707 608
Imputed social contributions	..	..	..	0	0	0	0	0	0	0
National Accounts: Taxes and all social contributions	..	..	..	1 180 342	1 507 069	1 476 994	1 584 030	1 597 050	1 647 812	1 707 608

Notes : Year ending 31st December.
From 2000, data are on accrual basis.
Figures prior to 1970 are not strictly comparable with those of later years, though the amounts involved are insignificant.
Heading 1000: Receipts are on accrual and not on a cash basis for all years.
Heading 2000 includes some voluntary contributions.
Source : Monthly reports of central Government Revenues (unpublished) National Audit Bureau, Stockholm; Local Government Finance (SOS), Tax assessment statistics (SOS), National Central Bureau of Statistics, Stockholm.National Accounts (Statistical Reports), National Bureau of Statistics, Stockholm.

StatLink http://dx.doi.org/10.1787/888933416965

Table 4.32. **Switzerland/Suisse**

Details of tax revenue/Recettes fiscales détaillées

Million CHF

	1965	1980	1990	2000	2007	2009	2011	2012	2013	2014
Recettes fiscales totales	**11 237**	**46 385**	**84 401**	**125 916**	**149 750**	**158 780**	**167 003**	**167 067**	**170 659**	**173 585**
1000 Impôts sur revenu, bénéfices et gains en capital	**4 616**	**21 022**	**39 998**	**55 819**	**69 184**	**73 702**	**76 739**	**75 837**	**77 789**	**79 257**
1100 Des personnes physiques	3 748	18 056	27 661	37 467	47 445	50 526	51 753	52 796	53 205	53 757
1110 Sur le revenu et les bénéfices	3 547	17 622	27 661	37 467	47 445	50 526	51 753	52 796	53 205	53 757
Impôt fédéral direct	245	2 525	4 432	5 713	8 529	9 791	9 574	9 754	9 655	9 487
Taxe d'exemption service militaire	35	103	135	163	138	148	157	161	163	174
Impôt cantonal personnes physiques	1 473	7 510	12 773	17 308	22 792	23 891	25 072	25 718	25 918	26 298
Impôt communal personnes physiques	1 322	6 235	10 321	14 283	15 986	16 696	16 949	17 164	17 469	17 798
Impôt anticipé	358	1 249	0	0	0	0	0	0	0	0
Coupons	114	0	0	0	0	0	0	0	0	0
1120 Sur les gains en capital	201	434	0	0	0	0	0	0	0	0
Impôt cantonal personnes physiques	84	229	..	..	..	..	..	..	..	..
Impôt communal personnes physiques	112	190	..	..	..	..	..	..	..	..
Impôt fédéral direct	5	15	..	..	..	..	..	..	..	..
1200 Des sociétés	868	2 966	10 316	17 428	20 332	16 554	17 417	17 411	17 760	18 075
1210 Sur les bénéfices	801	2 818	10 316	17 428	20 332	16 554	17 417	17 411	17 760	18 075
Impôt fédéral direct	153	781	2 214	4 928	6 860	8 157	8 396	8 659	8 769	8 559
Impôt cantonal personnes morales	363	1 230	2 559	3 925	6 018	5 500	5 795	5 664	5 908	6 195
Impôt communal personnes morales	285	807	1 498	2 373	3 225	2 897	3 225	3 088	3 082	3 321
Impôt anticipé	0	0	4 044	6 202	4 230	0	0	0	0	0
1220 Sur les gains en capital	67	148	0	0	0	0	0	0	0	0
Impôt sur gains personnes morales	2	7	..	..	..	..	..	..	..	..
Impôt cantonal personnes morales	28	77	..	..	..	..	..	..	..	..
Impôt communal personnes morales	37	64	..	..	..	..	..	..	..	..
1300 Non-ventilables entre 1100 et 1200	0	0	2 021	924	1 406	6 623	7 570	5 630	6 825	7 425
Impôt anticipé	..	..	0	0	0	5 280	5 961	3 835	5 119	5 469
Impôt sur les gains immobiliers	..	..	2 021	924	1 406	1 436	1 690	1 883	2 006	1 978
Autre	..	..	0	0	0	-93	-81	-88	-301	-22
2000 Cotisations de sécurité sociale	**1 670**	**10 844**	**19 862**	**30 628**	**34 841**	**37 978**	**40 837**	**41 801**	**42 518**	**43 152**
2100 A la charge des salariés	716	4 833	9 305	14 350	16 322	17 413	18 847	19 363	19 672	19 991
2110 Sur la base du salaire	716	4 833	9 305	14 350	16 322	17 413	18 847	19 363	19 672	19 991
2120 Sur la base de l'impôt sur les revenus	0	0	0	0	0	0	0	0	0	0
2200 A la charge des employeurs	747	4 897	9 313	14 363	16 336	17 442	18 878	19 393	19 705	20 024
2210 Sur la base du salaire	747	4 897	9 313	14 363	16 336	17 442	18 878	19 393	19 705	20 024
2220 Sur la base de l'impôt sur les revenus	0	0	0	0	0	0	0	0	0	0
2300 A charge des travailleurs indép. ou sans emploi	208	1 046	1 245	1 915	2 183	3 124	3 113	3 046	3 141	3 137
2310 Sur la base du salaire	209	1 046	1 245	1 915	2 183	3 124	3 113	3 046	3 141	3 137
2320 Sur la base de l'impôt sur les revenus	0	0	0	0	0	0	0	0	0	0
2400 Non-ventilables entre 2100, 2200 et 2300	0	68	0	0	0	0	0	0	0	0
2410 Sur la base du salaire	..	68	..	..	..	..	..	..	..	..
2420 Sur la base de l'impôt sur les revenus	..	0	..	..	..	..	..	..	..	..
3000 Sur salaires ou main d'oeuvre	**0**	**0**	**0**	**0**	**0**	**0**	**0**	**0**	**0**	**0**
4000 Impôts sur le patrimoine	**1 108**	**3 830**	**6 856**	**11 390**	**11 812**	**11 183**	**11 086**	**10 447**	**10 912**	**11 513**
4100 Impôts périodiques sur la propriété immobilière	78	304	447	735	895	936	967	1 027	1 052	1 044
4110 Ménages	78	304	447	735	895	936	967	1 027	1 052	1 044
Impôt sur immeubles canton	20	71	125	187	265	265	266	315	303	264
Impôt sur immeubles commune	58	233	322	548	630	671	701	712	748	780
4120 Autres agents	0	0	0	0	0	0	0	0	0	0
4200 Impôts périodiques sur l'actif net	692	2 201	3 382	5 254	7 002	7 061	7 011	7 004	7 403	7 806
4210 Personnes physiques	420	1 383	2 194	3 972	5 309	5 623	5 498	5 540	5 785	6 346
Impôt fortune canton	206	739	1 232	2 241	3 145	3 314	3 360	3 397	3 532	3 864
Impôt fortune commune	214	644	962	1 731	2 164	2 309	2 138	2 144	2 253	2 483
4220 Sociétés	272	818	1 188	1 282	1 693	1 437	1 513	1 463	1 617	1 459
Impôt capital fédéral direct	21	92	0	0	0	0	0	0	0	0
Impôt capital canton	142	436	760	821	1 107	923	972	957	1 032	943
Impôt capital commune	109	290	428	461	586	515	540	506	585	517
4300 Impôts sur mut. par décès, succ. et donations	142	393	890	1 196	858	974	848	885	952	1 163
4310 Impôts sur mut. par décès et successions	142	393	890	1 196	858	974	848	885	952	1 163
Impôt successions cantons	128	361	815	1 100	764	890	762	772	842	1 061
Impôt successions commune	14	32	75	96	95	84	87	114	110	102
4320 Impôts sur les donations	0	0	0	0	0	0	0	0	0	0
4400 Impôts sur transact. mobilières et immob.	196	932	2 137	4 205	3 057	2 212	2 260	1 531	1 505	1 501
Impôt mutations canton	48	245	34	43	55	55	59	56	55	52
Impôt mutations commune	21	103	12	16	13	13	15	15	16	15
Emissions de titres	99	175	0	0	0	672	874	353	182	177
Négociation de titres	19	409	0	0	0	1 472	1 312	1 107	1 253	1 256
Effets de change	9	0	0	0	0	0	0	0	0	0
Emissions et négociation de titres	0	0	2 091	4 146	2 990	0	0	0	0	0
4500 Impôts non-périodiques	0	0	0	0	0	0	0	0	0	0
4510 Sur l'actif net	..	..	..	..	..	..	..	..	..	..

StatLink http://dx.doi.org/10.1787/888933416976

Table 4.32. **Switzerland/Suisse** *(cont./suite)*

Details of tax revenue/Recettes fiscales détaillées

Million CHF

	1965	1980	1990	2000	2007	2009	2011	2012	2013	2014
4520 Autres non-périodiques	..	..	..	..	..	..	..	..	..	..
4600 Autres impôts périodiques sur patrimoine	0	0	0	0	0	0	0	0	0	0
5000 Impôts sur les biens et services	**3 843**	**10 689**	**17 546**	**27 864**	**33 664**	**35 328**	**37 743**	**38 375**	**38 777**	**38 941**
5100 Impôts sur production, vente, transfert, etc.	3 582	9 863	15 975	25 302	29 613	30 835	32 788	33 319	33 712	33 751
5110 Impôts généraux	1 191	4 772	9 871	16 917	19 830	19 969	21 865	22 214	22 717	22 728
5111 Taxes sur la valeur ajoutée	0	0	9 871	16 594	19 472	19 657	21 456	21 802	22 348	22 375
5112 Impôts sur les ventes	1 191	4 772	0	323	358	312	408	412	369	354
Impôt sur les automobiles	..	..	..	323	358	312	408	412	369	354
Autres impôt sur les ventes	..	..	..	0	0	0	0	0	0	0
5113 Autres impôts	0	0	0	0	0	0	0	0	0	0
5120 Impôts sur biens et services déterminés	2 391	5 091	6 058	8 337	9 739	10 829	10 881	11 063	10 936	10 963
5121 Accises	1 016	3 427	1 538	6 810	7 525	7 941	8 021	8 233	8 099	8 097
Impôt sur bière	26	33	0	0	0	110	113	113	113	113
Impôt sur tabac	190	634	15	32	60	2 032	2 265	2 459	2 354	2 315
Supplément de prix autres	104	542	1 503	6 736	7 383	4	0	0	0	3
Droits carburants	467	955	12	25	48	3 129	3 041	3 051	3 034	3 017
Droits supplémentaires carburants	229	1 263	8	17	32	2 100	2 036	2 038	2 025	2 013
Taxes routières	0	0	0	0	0	0	0	0	0	0
Impôt sur les huiles minérales grèvant les combustibles	0	0	0	0	0	24	19	20	23	17
Impôt sur les automobiles	0	0	0	0	0	0	0	0	0	0
Impôt boissons distillées	0	0	0	1	1	292	293	296	292	285
Taxe sur la consommation d'électricité	0	0	0	0	0	249	255	256	258	334
5122 Bénéfices des monopoles fiscaux	158	472	0	0	0	0	0	0	0	0
Monopole d'alcool	111	354	..	..	..	..	..	..	..	..
Régale des sels	16	25	..	..	..	..	..	..	..	..
Régale des eaux	30	90	..	..	..	..	..	..	..	..
Autres	1	3	..	..	..	..	..	..	..	..
5123 Droits de douane et droits à l'importation	1 104	953	4 267	1 096	1 040	1 033	1 046	1 044	1 059	1 068
Droits d'entrée	972	923	4 267	1 096	1 040	1 033	1 046	1 044	1 059	1 068
Droits tabac	114	6	0	0	0	0	0	0	0	0
Autres droits supplémentaires	18	24	0	0	0	0	0	0	0	0
5124 Taxes à l'exportation	0	0	0	0	0	0	0	0	0	0
5125 Impôts sur biens d'équipement	0	0	0	0	0	0	0	0	0	0
5126 Impôts sur services déterminés	113	239	253	431	1 173	1 855	1 813	1 786	1 778	1 798
Jeux dans kursaals confédération	2	2	2	37	449	415	376	329	308	285
Impôt sur divertissement canton	17	37	23	27	39	126	93	87	73	68
Impôt sur divertissement commune	11	19	46	26	18	17	16	15	15	16
Autres impôts dépenses canton	24	63	0	0	0	0	0	0	0	0
Autres impôts dépenses commune	19	6	0	0	0	0	0	0	0	0
Quittances de primes	40	112	0	0	0	662	671	675	700	711
Impôts loteries	0	0	181	320	474	454	445	462	466	478
Autres	0	0	0	20	193	182	213	217	216	239
5127 Autres impôts sur commerce et transact. internat.	0	0	0	0	0	0	0	0	0	0
5128 Autres impôts	0	0	0	0	0	0	0	0	0	0
5130 Non-ventilables entre 5110 et 5120	0	0	46	47	44	36	42	43	59	59
5200 Impôts sur utilisation des biens et exerc. activités	261	826	1 570	2 562	4 050	4 494	4 955	5 056	5 065	5 190
5210 Impôts périodiques	261	826	1 570	2 562	4 050	4 494	4 955	5 056	5 065	5 190
5211 A la charge des ménages : véhicules à moteur	152	501	1 075	1 573	1 845	1 924	1 999	2 030	1 977	2 025
A la charge des ménages : véhicules à moteur	..	..	921	1 336	1 580	1 638	1 704	1 741	1 685	1 726
A la charge des ménages : vignette autoroutière	..	..	154	237	265	286	295	289	292	299
5212 A la charge autres agents : véhicules à moteur	76	251	431	799	1 895	2 040	2 132	2 114	2 089	2 076
A la charge des autres agents : véhicules à moteur	..	..	367	686	1 722	409	426	435	421	432
A la charge des autres agents : vignette autoroutière	..	..	39	59	66	72	74	72	73	75
A la charge autres agents : redevance trafic poids lourds	..	..	25	54	107	1 559	1 632	1 607	1 594	1 570
5213 Autres impôts périodiques	33	74	64	190	311	529	825	912	999	1 089
Chasse et pêche	9	20	0	0	0	0	0	0	0	0
Impôt sur chiens canton	3	9	6	9	8	8	9	9	10	9
Impôt sur chiens commune	2	8	14	21	25	28	31	31	33	34
Auberges canton	12	24	0	0	0	0	0	0	0	0
Patentes canton	5	12	0	0	0	0	0	0	0	0
Autres	2	1	0	33	47	33	30	30	31	23
Taxes d'incitation, protection de l'environnement	0	0	3	73	166	380	669	730	833	931
Patentes et concessions	0	0	42	53	64	81	86	111	93	91
5220 Impôts non-périodiques	0	0	0	0	0	0	0	0	0	0
5300 Non-ventilables entre 5100 et 5200	0	0	0	0	0	0	0	0	0	0
6000 Autres impôts	**0**	**0**	**140**	**215**	**249**	**588**	**598**	**606**	**663**	**723**
6100 A la charge exclusive des entreprises	..	..	0	0	0	222	211	202	218	247
6200 A la charge d'autres agents	..	..	140	215	249	366	387	404	445	476
Taxe de compensation	..	..	140	215	249	269	269	253	271	271
Autres	..	..	0	0	0	97	118	151	173	205

StatLink http://dx.doi.org/10.1787/888933416976

Table 4.32. **Switzerland/Suisse** *(cont./suite)*

Details of tax revenue/Recettes fiscales détaillées

Million CHF

	1965	1980	1990	2000	2007	2009	2011	2012	2013	2014
Recettes fiscales totales sur la base d'encaissements	**11 237**	**46 385**	**84 401**	**125 916**	**149 750**	**158 780**	**167 003**	**167 067**	**170 659**	**173 585**
Recettes fiscales totales sur la base des droits constatés	..	..	..	..	..	..	..	..	..	..
Conciliation avec les comptes nationaux										
Impôts additionnels inclus dans les comptes nationaux	..	..	0	0	0	0	0	0	0	0
Impôt exclus des comptes nationaux	..	..	0	0	0	0	0	0	0	0
Différence dans les traitements des crédits d'impôts	..	..	0	0	0	0	0	0	0	0
Transfert en capital des recettes non collectées	..	..	0	0	0	0	0	0	0	0
Cotisations de sécurité sociale volontaires	..	..	0	0	0	0	0	0	0	0
Différences diverses	..	..	0	0	0	0	0	0	0	0
Comptes nationaux: impôts et cotisations sociales effectives	..	..	84 401	125 916	149 750	158 780	167 003	167 067	170 659	173 585
Cotisations sociales imputées	..	..	398	503	555	497	521	575	589	480
Comptes nationaux: impôts et toutes les cotisations sociales	..	..	84 800	126 419	150 305	159 277	167 524	167 642	171 249	174 066

Notes : Année civile se terminant le 31 décembre.

Les données sont sur la base des encaissements.

Les chiffres antérieurs à 1970 ne sont pas strictement comparables avec ceux des années suivantes qui ont été légèrement révisés.

À compter de 1985, les « Impôts paroissiaux » ne sont plus reportés dans ces statistiques.

À la rubrique 1100 : les paiements effectués en contrepartie de l'exemption du service militaire pourraient être classés dans les recettes non fiscales.

La rubrique 2000 (Cotisations de sécurité sociale) a été révisée depuis 1985 pour tenir compte de la sectorisation des administrations publiques retenue dans le cadre du passage aux Comptes nationaux SEC95. De ce fait, les cotisations à l'assurance maladie et à la Caisse nationale suisse contre les accidents sont maintenant exclues de la rubrique 2000.

Source : Statistique financière, Administration fédérale des finances.

StatLink http://dx.doi.org/10.1787/888933416976

Table 4.33. **Turkey/Turquie**

Details of tax revenue/Recettes fiscales détaillées

Million TRY

	1965	1980	1990	2000	2007	2009	2011	2012	2013	2014
Total tax revenue	**0**	**1**	**79**	**40 263**	**203 053**	**234 669**	**361 153**	**391 572**	**458 698**	**502 571**
1000 Taxes on income, profits and capital gains	**0**	**0**	**26**	**11 890**	**48 197**	**56 469**	**75 800**	**85 511**	**92 749**	**106 207**
1100 Of individuals	0	0	21	8 954	34 447	38 446	48 807	56 494	63 761	73 902
1110 On income and profits	0	0	21	8 954	34 447	38 446	48 807	56 494	63 761	73 902
Income tax	0	0	21	8 954	34 447	38 446	48 807	56 494	63 761	73 902
1120 On capital gains	0	0	0	0	0	0	0	0	0	0
1200 Corporate	0	0	5	2 935	13 751	18 023	26 993	29 017	28 988	32 305
1210 On profits	0	0	5	2 935	13 751	18 023	26 993	29 017	28 988	32 305
Corporation tax	0	0	5	2 935	13 751	18 023	26 993	29 017	28 988	32 305
1220 On capital gains	0	0	0	0	0	0	0	0	0	0
1300 Unallocable between 1100 and 1200	0	0	0	0	0	0	0	0	0	0
Fiscal balance tax	..	0	..	..	..	..	..	..	..	..
Capital gains tax on real estate sales	..	0	..	..	..	..	..	..	..	..
2000 Social security contributions	**0**	**0**	**15**	**7 543**	**44 052**	**57 595**	**100 687**	**106 405**	**125 871**	**143 400**
2100 Employees	0	0	6	2 712	17 867	21 059	36 230	40 714	49 831	54 281
2110 On a payroll basis	..	..	..	2 712	17 867	21 059	36 230	40 714	49 831	54 281
2120 On an income tax basis	..	..	..	0	0	0	0	0	0	0
2200 Employers	0	0	9	3 619	20 442	31 477	53 162	58 272	71 184	80 028
2210 On a payroll basis	..	..	..	3 619	20 442	31 477	53 162	58 272	71 184	80 028
2220 On an income tax basis	..	..	..	0	0	0	0	0	0	0
2300 Self-employed or non-employed	0	0	1	1 211	5 743	5 059	11 295	7 419	4 856	9 091
2310 On a payroll basis	..	..	..	1 211	5 743	5 059	11 295	7 419	4 856	9 091
2320 On an income tax basis	..	..	..	0	0	0	0	0	0	0
2400 Unallocable between 2100, 2200 and 2300	0	0	0	0	0	0	0	0	0	0
2410 On a payroll basis	..	..	..	..	..	..	..	..	..	..
2420 On an income tax basis	..	..	..	..	..	..	..	..	..	..
3000 Taxes on payroll and workforce	**0**	**0**	**0**	**0**	**0**	**0**	**0**	**0**	**0**	**0**
4000 Taxes on property	**0**	**0**	**2**	**1 272**	**7 621**	**8 518**	**14 661**	**16 511**	**21 280**	**24 473**
4100 Recurrent taxes on immovable property	0	0	0	191	1 464	1 854	3 464	3 528	3 847	4 993
Real estate tax	0	0	..	191	1 464	1 854	3 464	3 528	3 847	4 993
4110 Households	..	..	..	..	..	..	..	..	..	..
4120 Others	..	..	..	..	..	..	..	..	..	..
4200 Recurrent taxes on net wealth	0	0	0	0	0	0	0	0	0	0
4210 Individual	..	..	..	..	..	..	..	..	..	..
4220 Corporate	..	..	..	..	..	..	..	..	..	..
4300 Estate, inheritance and gift taxes	0	0	0	15	125	168	253	293	340	428
Gift and inheritance tax	0	0	0	15	125	168	253	293	340	428
4310 Estate and inheritance taxes	..	..	..	..	..	..	..	..	..	..
4320 Gift taxes	..	..	..	..	..	..	..	..	..	..
4400 Taxes on financial and capital transactions	0	0	2	1 065	6 032	6 496	10 943	12 690	17 093	19 052
Stamp tax	0	0	2	818	3 642	4 169	6 464	7 360	9 416	10 325
Real estate purchase tax	0	0	0	0	0	0	0	0	0	0
Title deed fees	0	0	0	207	2 000	1 889	4 042	4 844	7 072	8 066
Notary fees	0	0	0	40	389	437	437	486	606	661
4500 Non-recurrent taxes	0	0	0	0	0	0	0	0	0	0
4510 On net wealth	..	..	..	..	..	..	..	..	..	..
4520 Other non-recurrent taxes	..	..	..	..	..	..	..	..	..	..
4600 Other recurrent taxes on property	0	0	0	0	0	0	0	0	0	0
5000 Taxes on goods and services	**0**	**0**	**22**	**16 901**	**96 766**	**107 128**	**163 347**	**176 305**	**211 257**	**221 642**
5100 Taxes on production, sale, transfer, etc	0	0	22	16 328	92 605	102 384	156 944	169 226	203 364	213 257
5110 General taxes	0	0	16	9 735	43 285	46 987	78 642	81 572	100 723	102 533
5111 Value added taxes	..	..	14	9 735	43 285	46 987	78 642	81 572	100 723	102 533
5112 Sales tax	..	..	0	0	0	0	0	0	0	0
5113 Other	..	..	1	0	0	0	0	0	0	0
5120 Taxes on specific goods and services	0	0	6	6 593	49 320	55 397	78 302	87 653	102 641	110 725
5121 Excises	0	0	1	4 718	39 111	43 620	64 189	71 706	85 462	91 095
Sales taxes	0	0	0	0	0	0	0	0	0	0
Domestic production tax	0	0	0	0	0	0	0	0	0	0
Domestic production tax on petrol	0	0	0	0	0	0	0	0	0	0
Production tax on monopoly goods	0	0	0	0	0	0	0	0	0	0
Sugar consumption taxes	0	0	0	0	0	0	0	0	0	0
Motor vehicles purchase tax (Total)	0	0	1	916	4 293	3 353	8 568	8 409	10 565	12 851
Motor vehicles purchase tax	0	0	0	498	4 293	3 353	8 568	8 409	10 565	12 851
Additional motor vehicle purchase tax	0	0	0	418	0	0	0	0	0	0
Revenue from other excises	0	0	0	533	12 765	14 742	22 048	27 362	29 739	32 616
Petroleum consumption tax	0	0	0	3 269	22 052	25 525	33 573	35 935	45 158	45 628
5122 Profits of fiscal monopolies	0	0	0	0	0	0	0	0	0	0

StatLink http://dx.doi.org/10.1787/888933416982

Table 4.33. **Turkey/Turquie** *(cont./suite)*

Details of tax revenue/Recettes fiscales détaillées

Million TRY

	1965	1980	1990	2000	2007	2009	2011	2012	2013	2014
5123 Customs and import duties	0	0	4	462	2 478	2 517	4 767	5 310	5 542	6 733
Customs duty	0	0	1	449	2 441	2 466	4 653	5 195	5 409	6 543
Customs duty on petrol	0	0	0	0	0	0	0	0	0	0
Production tax on imports	0	0	0	0	0	0	0	0	0	0
Production tax on petrol imports	0	0	0	0	0	0	0	0	0	0
Stamp duty on imports	0	0	2	0	0	0	0	0	0	0
Wharf duty	0	0	1	0	0	0	0	0	0	0
Other	0	0	0	13	37	51	113	115	133	190
5124 Taxes on exports	0	0	0	0	0	0	0	0	0	0
5125 Taxes on investment goods	0	0	0	0	0	0	0	0	0	0
5126 Taxes on specific services	0	0	1	997	7 686	4 399	4 816	6 086	6 853	8 255
Bank, insurance transaction tax	0	0	1	997	3 149	4 003	4 288	5 471	6 160	7 487
Transportation tax	0	0	0	0	0	0	0	0	0	0
PTT service tax	0	0	0	0	4 211	0	0	0	0	0
Tax on football pool	0	0	0	0	0	0	0	0	0	0
Lottery tax	0	0	0	0	327	396	528	616	692	768
5127 Other taxes on internat. trade and transactions	0	0	0	0	0	0	0	0	0	0
Foreign travel expenditures tax	0	0	..	..	..	..	..	..	..	..
5128 Other taxes	0	0	0	416	46	4 861	4 531	4 551	4 785	4 643
5130 Unallocable between 5110 and 5120	0	0	0	0	0	0	0	0	0	0
5200 Taxes on use of goods and perform activities	0	0	0	572	4 161	4 744	6 403	7 079	7 894	8 385
5210 Recurrent taxes	0	0	0	359	4 161	4 744	6 403	7 079	7 894	8 385
Motor vehicles tax	0	0	0	359	0	4 744	6 403	7 079	7 894	8 385
5211 Paid by households: motor vehicles	..	..	..	0	0	0	0	0	0	0
5212 Paid by others: motor vehicles	..	..	..	359	4 161	4 744	6 403	7 079	7 894	8 385
Motor vehicles tax	..	..	..	302	3 521	4 496	6 004	6 716	7 353	7 787
Traffic fees	..	..	..	58	640	248	399	363	540	598
5213 Paid in respect of other goods	..	..	..	0	0	0	0	0	0	0
5220 Non-recurrent taxes	0	0	0	213	0	0	0	0	0	0
Building construction tax	..	0	..	..	..	..	..	..	..	..
5300 Unallocable between 5100 and 5200	0	0	0	0	0	0	0	0	0	0
6000 Other taxes	**0**	**0**	**13**	**2 658**	**6 417**	**4 959**	**6 658**	**6 840**	**7 541**	**6 849**
6100 Paid solely by business	..	0	0	0	0	0	0	0	0	0
6200 Other	..	0	13	2 658	6 417	4 959	6 658	6 840	7 541	6 849
Funds	..	..	..	1 938	0	0	0	0	0	0
Vocatial Train Pro.F.	..	..	..	67	0	0	0	0	0	0
Tax penalties and fines	..	..	..	548	4 191	3 037	3 221	3 119	3 175	2 551
Municipalities revenue	..	..	..	106	2 227	1 922	3 437	3 722	4 366	4 299
Total tax revenue on cash basis	**0**	**1**	**79**	**40 263**	**203 053**	**234 669**	**361 153**	**391 572**	**458 698**	**502 571**
Total tax revenue on accrual basis	..	..	..	..	..	..	..	..	..	..
Conciliation with National Accounts										
Additional taxes included in National Accounts	..	..	..	..	..	..	..	..	..	..
Taxes excluded from National Accounts	..	..	..	..	..	..	..	..	..	..
Difference in treatment of tax credits	..	..	..	..	..	..	..	..	..	..
Capital transfer for uncollected revenue	..	..	..	..	..	..	..	..	..	..
Voluntary social security contributions	..	..	..	..	..	..	..	..	..	..
Miscellaneous differences	..	..	..	..	..	..	..	..	..	..
National Accounts: Taxes and actual social contributions	..	..	..	..	..	..	..	..	..	..
Imputed social contributions	..	..	..	..	..	..	..	..	..	..
National Accounts: Taxes and all social contributions	..	..	..	..	..	..	..	..	..	..

Notes : From 1982, the data are based on the fiscal year ending 31st December. Before that, the data are on a fiscal year basis beginning 1st March.

Revenue is reported on a cash basis, except for social security contributions which are reported on an assessment basis.

The figures under the local tax collections include taxes under «'Municipalities Revenues Law» and Property tax. They also include transfers to the local authorities from central budget tax revenues under the revenue sharing system.

Heading 2000: Before 2003, contributions to some private social security schemes are included in this heading.

Source : Bulletin of national accounts and the Budget revenue Bulletin.

StatLink http://dx.doi.org/10.1787/888933416982

Table 4.34. **United Kingdom/Royaume-Uni**

Details of tax revenue/Recettes fiscales détaillées

Million GBP

	1965	1980	1990	2000	2007	2009	2011	2012	2013	2014
Total tax revenue	**10 945**	**81 153**	**202 414**	**354 948**	**505 013**	**479 368**	**543 877**	**547 750**	**564 763**	**584 469**
Total tax revenue exclusive of custom duties	..	..	..	**353 148**	**502 939**	**476 933**	**540 952**	**544 865**	**561 849**	**581 520**
1000 Taxes on income, profits and capital gains	**4 050**	**30 651**	**79 576**	**138 591**	**198 985**	**184 531**	**199 356**	**195 025**	**199 887**	**204 008**
1100 Of individuals	3 618	23 868	59 506	104 136	151 219	145 779	152 692	150 454	156 299	160 293
1110 On income and profits	3 615	23 376	57 614	101 925	147 371	137 964	149 092	146 120	152 397	156 379
Income tax	..	23 370	57 614	101 925	147 371	137 964	149 092	146 120	152 397	156 379
Surtax	..	6	0	0	0	0	0	0	0	0
1120 On capital gains	3	492	1 892	2 211	3 848	7 815	3 600	4 334	3 902	3 914
1200 Corporate	484	6 783	20 070	34 455	47 766	38 752	46 664	44 571	43 588	43 715
1210 On profits	484	6 510	18 994	32 087	44 403	37 461	45 762	43 082	41 487	40 886
Petroleum revenue tax	..	1 799	941	1 540	1 387	1 047	1 775	2 106	1 296	568
Supplementary petroleum duty	..	0	0	0	0	0	0	0	0	0
Corporation tax	..	4 712	18 053	30 547	42 302	35 718	43 362	40 349	39 524	39 739
Corporation tax overspill relief	..	-1	0	0	0	0	0	0	0	0
Profits tax	..	0	0	0	0	0	0	0	0	0
Windfall tax	..	0	0	0	0	0	0	0	0	0
Betting tax	..	0	0	0	590	543	539	565	605	532
Non fossil fuel obligation levy	..	0	0	0	124	153	86	62	62	47
1220 On capital gains	0	273	1 076	2 368	3 363	1 291	902	1 489	2 101	2 829
1300 Unallocable between 1100 and 1200	-52	0	0	0	0	0	0	0	0	0
2000 Social security contributions	**1 685**	**13 531**	**34 457**	**60 252**	**93 210**	**94 445**	**101 441**	**104 319**	**106 085**	**109 120**
2100 Employees	770	5 228	13 296	24 175	36 585	37 184	40 626	41 118	41 587	42 604
2110 On a payroll basis	..	..	13 296	24 175	36 585	37 184	40 626	41 118	41 587	42 604
2120 On an income tax basis	..	..	0	0	0	0	0	0	0	0
2200 Employers	831	8 210	19 984	34 028	53 765	54 411	58 174	60 638	61 912	63 844
2210 On a payroll basis	..	..	19 984	34 028	53 765	54 411	58 174	60 638	61 912	63 844
2220 On an income tax basis	..	..	0	0	0	0	0	0	0	0
2300 Self-employed or non-employed	75	317	1 177	2 049	2 860	2 850	2 641	2 563	2 586	2 672
2310 On a payroll basis	..	..	1 177	2 049	2 860	2 850	2 641	2 563	2 586	2 672
2320 On an income tax basis	..	..	0	0	0	0	0	0	0	0
2400 Unallocable between 2100, 2200 and 2300	9	-224	0	0	0	0	0	0	0	0
2410 On a payroll basis	..	..	..	..	..	..	..	..	..	..
2420 On an income tax basis	..	..	..	..	..	..	..	..	..	..
3000 Taxes on payroll and workforce	**0**	**3 498**	**0**	**0**	**0**	**0**	**0**	**0**	**0**	**0**
Selective employment tax	..	0	..	..	..	..	..	..	..	..
National insurance surcharge	..	3 498	..	..	..	..	..	..	..	..
4000 Taxes on property	**1 591**	**9 774**	**16 538**	**41 134**	**63 378**	**58 370**	**63 239**	**65 028**	**69 790**	**74 227**
4100 Recurrent taxes on immovable property	1 228	8 665	13 462	30 552	44 877	48 828	51 472	52 977	54 833	56 170
4110 Households	539	3 687	2 373	14 205	23 609	25 402	26 263	26 610	27 624	28 515
Northern Ireland rates paid to CG	..	37	113	141	265	355	391	416	406	404
Council tax	..	0	0	13 991	23 217	24 916	25 715	26 030	27 048	27 935
Rates paid to LA	..	3 650	2 260	73	127	131	157	164	170	176
4120 Others	689	4 978	11 089	16 347	21 268	23 426	25 209	26 367	27 209	27 655
National non-domestic rates	..	0	7 542	14 966	19 344	21 361	22 444	23 535	24 364	24 771
Rates paid to LA	..	4 925	2 869	149	267	317	548	561	554	559
Northern Ireland rates paid to CG	..	53	115	207	353	325	368	366	373	378
London Regional Transport levy	..	0	47	0	0	0	0	0	0	0
LA payments of NNDR	..	0	469	889	1 111	1 189	1 356	1 389	1 389	1 389
NPISH payments of NNDR	..	0	47	136	193	234	281	299	325	352
Crossrail Business rates supplement	..	0	0	0	0	0	212	217	204	206
4200 Recurrent taxes on net wealth	0	0	0	0	0	0	0	0	0	0
4210 Individual	..	..	..	..	..	..	..	..	..	..
4220 Corporate	..	..	..	..	..	..	..	..	..	..
4300 Estate, inheritance and gift taxes	287	479	1 321	2 215	3 867	2 401	2 936	3 129	3 379	3 886
4310 Estate and inheritance taxes	287	479	1 321	2 215	3 867	2 401	2 936	3 129	3 379	3 886
Death duties	..	423	1 278	2 156	3 764	2 305	2 856	3 041	3 293	3 702
Development land tax	..	42	6	0	0	0	0	0	0	0
Taxes on other capital transfers	..	14	37	59	50	50	50	50	50	50
Special tax on bank deposits	..	0	0	0	0	0	0	0	0	0
Betterment duty	..	0	0	0	0	0	0	0	0	0
Special charges	..	0	0	0	0	0	0	0	0	0
Special contribution	..	0	0	0	0	0	0	0	0	0
Equal pay on capital transfers	..	0	0	0	53	46	30	38	36	134
4320 Gift taxes	0	0	0	0	0	0	0	0	0	0
4400 Taxes on financial and capital transactions	76	630	1 755	8 367	14 634	7 141	8 831	8 918	11 540	14 067
Stamp duties	..	630	1 755	8 367	14 634	7 141	8 831	8 918	11 540	14 067
4500 Non-recurrent taxes	0	0	0	0	0	0	0	4	38	104
4510 On net wealth	..	..	..	..	..	..	..	0	0	0
4520 Other non-recurrent taxes	..	..	..	..	..	..	..	4	38	104
4600 Other recurrent taxes on property	0	0	0	0	0	0	0	0	0	0

StatLink http://dx.doi.org/10.1787/888933416999

Table 4.34. **United Kingdom/Royaume-Uni** *(cont./suite)*

Details of tax revenue/Recettes fiscales détaillées

Million GBP

	1965	1980	1990	2000	2007	2009	2011	2012	2013	2014
5000 Taxes on goods and services	**3 619**	**23 699**	**62 826**	**113 171**	**147 366**	**139 587**	**176 900**	**180 477**	**186 074**	**194 153**
5100 Taxes on production, sale, transfer, etc	3 406	22 677	59 425	108 188	141 400	132 707	170 004	173 439	178 828	186 966
5110 General taxes	647	11 897	34 136	64 202	92 025	79 862	111 461	113 862	118 044	124 211
5111 Value added taxes	0	11 897	34 136	64 202	92 025	79 862	111 461	113 862	118 044	124 211
Value added tax	..	11 893	33 620	64 202	92 025	79 862	111 437	113 859	118 234	124 211
Adj. to VAT contribution	..	4	516	0	0	0	24	3	-190	0
Purchase tax	..	0	0	0	0	0	0	0	0	0
5112 Sales tax	647	0	0	0	0	0	0	0	0	0
5113 Other	0	0	0	0	0	0	0	0	0	0
5120 Taxes on specific goods and services	2 759	10 780	25 289	43 986	49 375	52 845	58 543	59 577	60 784	62 755
5121 Excises	2 383	8 616	19 707	37 271	40 424	43 867	46 152	46 800	46 577	47 114
Beer	..	1 029	2 220	2 813	3 042	3 189	3 429	3 425	3 337	3 337
Wines, spirits, cider and perry	..	1 513	2 627	3 751	5 008	5 728	6 439	6 775	7 063	7 246
Tobacco	..	2 735	5 541	7 666	7 862	9 056	9 361	9 897	9 479	9 436
Hydrocarbon oil	..	3 327	9 302	23 041	24 512	25 894	26 923	26 703	26 698	27 095
Other excise duties	..	12	17	0	0	0	0	0	0	0
5122 Profits of fiscal monopolies	0	0	0	0	0	0	0	0	0	0
5123 Customs and import duties	343	1 109	1 837	286	519	462	235	259	204	313
Custom duties	..	0	0	0	0	0	0	0	0	0
Import duties	..	855	1 722	0	0	0	0	0	0	0
Agricultural levies	..	254	115	286	338	210	0	0	0	0
Temporary charges of import	..	0	0	0	0	0	0	0	0	0
British Transport Police	..	0	0	0	181	252	235	259	204	313
5124 Taxes on exports	0	-1	36	0	0	0	0	0	0	0
Levies on exports	..	-1	36	..	..	..	..	..	..	..
5125 Taxes on investment goods	0	0	0	0	0	0	0	0	0	0
5126 Taxes on specific services	33	456	1 022	5 826	6 523	6 696	10 089	10 523	11 420	12 326
Betting and gaming	..	456	1 022	1 522	959	1 013	1 206	1 207	1 538	1 708
National Lottery contributions to fund	..	0	0	1 590	1 310	1 553	1 793	1 832	1 644	1 721
Air passenger duty	..	0	0	940	1 883	1 800	2 605	2 766	2 960	3 154
Insurance premium tax	..	0	0	1 707	2 306	2 259	2 942	3 022	3 018	2 964
Bank Levy - Stability Fee Scheme	..	0	0	0	0	0	1 454	1 609	2 171	2 693
Light Dues	..	0	0	67	65	71	89	87	89	86
5127 Other taxes on internat. trade and transactions	0	0	0	0	0	0	0	0	0	0
5128 Other taxes	0	600	2 687	603	1 909	1 820	2 067	1 995	2 583	3 002
Fossil fuel levy	..	0	875	56	0	0	0	0	0	0
Sugar levy	..	21	46	44	3	10	12	13	12	11
European coal and steel levy	..	12	11	0	0	0	0	0	0	0
Gas levy	..	83	291	0	0	0	0	0	0	0
Car tax	..	484	1 464	0	0	0	0	0	0	0
Landfill tax	..	0	0	461	877	842	1 090	1 094	1 191	1 143
Climate change levy	..	0	0	0	690	693	675	624	1 098	1 506
Aggregates levy	..	0	0	0	339	275	290	264	282	342
Hydro benefit	..	0	0	42	0	0	0	0	0	0
Renewable energy obligations	..	0	0	0	0	0	0	0	0	0
Channel 4 advertising formula	..	0	0	0	0	0	0	0	0	0
Milk super levy	..	0	0	0	0	0	0	0	0	0
5130 Unallocable between 5110 and 5120	0	0	0	0	0	0	0	0	0	0
5200 Taxes on use of goods and perform activities	212	1 378	3 401	4 983	5 966	6 880	6 896	7 038	7 246	7 187
5210 Recurrent taxes	212	1 378	3 401	4 983	5 966	6 880	6 896	7 038	7 246	7 187
5211 Paid by households: motor vehicles	118	729	1 841	3 195	4 506	4 722	4 889	4 933	5 124	4 900
Motor vehicle duty	..	726	1 837	3 191	4 506	4 722	4 889	4 933	5 124	4 900
Boat licences	..	3	4	4	0	0	0	0	0	0
5212 Paid by others: motor vehicles	74	588	1 134	1 415	878	908	931	940	977	1 075
Motor vehicle levy	..	588	1 134	1 415	878	908	931	940	977	1 075
5213 Paid in respect of other goods	20	61	426	373	582	1 250	1 076	1 165	1 145	1 212
IBA levy	..	..	134	0	0	0	0	0	0	0
Telecommunications regulator fees	..	..	7	12	17	12	12	3	0	0
Gas regulator fees	..	..	2	0	0	0	0	0	0	0
Electricity regulator fees	..	..	5	0	0	0	0	0	0	0
Water regulator fees	..	..	6	11	11	12	21	24	24	33
Rail regulator fees	..	..	0	14	12	12	12	12	12	12
Company registration surplus fees	..	..	12	0	0	0	0	0	0	0
Consumer and credit act fees	..	..	163	119	281	435	480	480	480	480
Levy funded bodies	..	..	97	217	261	746	508	600	585	630
1936 Tithe Act payments	..	..	0	0	0	0	0	0	0	0
Air travel organiser license fees	..	0	0	0	0	33	43	46	44	57
5220 Non-recurrent taxes	0	0	0	0	0	0	0	0	0	0
5300 Unallocable between 5100 and 5200	1	-356	0	0	0	0	0	0	0	0
6000 Other taxes	**0**	**0**	**9 017**	**0**	**0**	**0**	**16**	**16**	**13**	**12**

StatLink http://dx.doi.org/10.1787/888933416999

Table 4.34. **United Kingdom/Royaume-Uni** *(cont./suite)*

Details of tax revenue/Recettes fiscales détaillées

Million GBP

	1965	1980	1990	2000	2007	2009	2011	2012	2013	2014
6100 Paid solely by business	..	..	0	..	..	..	0	0	0	0
6200 Other	..	..	9 017	..	..	..	16	16	13	12
Community charge	..	..	9 017	..	..	..	..	..	..	..
Custom duties collected for the EU	..	..	..	**1 800**	**2 074**	**2 435**	**2 925**	**2 885**	**2 914**	**2 949**
Non-wastable tax credits										
Non-wastable tax credits against 1110	..	..	7 454	4 651	19 586	26 935	29 615	29 934	29 833	29 560
Tax expenditure component	..	..	6 973	1 233	4 352	5 659	4 973	3 338	2 809	2 486
Transfer component	..	..	481	3 418	15 234	21 276	24 642	26 596	27 024	27 074
Non-wastable tax credits against 1210	..	..	0	1	762	1 079	1 309	1 349	1 470	1 872
Tax expenditure component	..	..	..	0	549	778	973	869	979	941
Transfer component	..	..	..	1	213	301	336	480	491	931
Total tax revenue on cash basis	**10 945**	**81 153**	**202 400**	**351 778**	**509 064**	**483 721**	**540 461**	**542 974**	**561 137**	**577 475**
Total tax revenue on accrual basis	..	..	**202 414**	**354 948**	**505 013**	**479 368**	**543 877**	**547 750**	**564 763**	**584 469**
Conciliation with National Accounts										
Additional taxes included in National Accounts	..	..	1 323	2 062	4 072	4 459	4 879	5 321	5 816	6 441
Taxes excluded from National Accounts	..	..	0	0	0	0	0	0	0	0
Difference in treatment of tax credits	..	..	308	1 204	575	795	982	877	987	948
Capital transfer for uncollected revenue	..	..	0	0	0	0	0	0	0	0
Voluntary social security contributions	..	..	3 288	5 305	13 645	15 218	15 937	16 763	18 420	19 135
Miscellaneous differences	..	..	0	0	0	0	0	0	0	0
National Accounts: Taxes and actual social contributions	..	..	207 333	363 519	523 305	499 840	565 675	570 711	589 986	610 993
Imputed social contributions	..	..	3 966	8 337	8 489	10 156	9 958	9 654	9 462	9 552
National Accounts: Taxes and all social contributions	..	..	211 299	371 856	531 794	509 996	575 633	580 365	599 448	620 545

Notes : Year ending 31st December.

From 1990, data are on accrual basis.

Heading 1210: The corporate tax figures include company income tax from 1990 onwards.

Heading 2000: Includes some voluntary contributions which cannot be separately identified.

Heading 6200: The community charge replaced domestic rates in Scotland in April 1989 and was extended to England and Wales in April 1990. This tax has been classified in heading 6200 as it is a lump-sum tax levied on each adult in a household (domestic rates are classified in heading 4100).

Headings for non-wastable tax credits 1110 and 1210 are consistent with the guidelines, and the figures in the data are treated accordingly. The following method is adopted separately for Working Families «Tax Credit and Disabled Persons Tax Credit» paid from 1999 to 2003. For each calendar, a random sample of awards over-lapping the quarter is taken. Each recipient family's income tax liability for the fiscal year within which the quarter falls is calculated, based on the earned income reported for the award (uprated to the middle of the overlap period). And the result multiplied by the number of days in the overlap period divided by 365. The tax expenditure component is defined as the minimum of this amount and the total amount of award paid in the overlap period. The total amount of award paid and the tax expenditure component are each summed over the sample cases, and the ratio is taken as the tax expenditure ration for the quarter. From 2003, the equivalent breakdown for Child and Working tax credits is based on household survey data. Survey data is used to estimate the breakdown into the tax expenditure and the transfer components for the other smaller tax credits.

Source : National Income and Expenditure; Central Statistical Office; Annual reports of Her Majesty's Revenue and Customs.

StatLink http://dx.doi.org/10.1787/888933416999

Table 4.35. **United States/État-Unis**

Details of tax revenue/Recettes fiscales détaillées

Million USD

	1965	1980	1990	2000	2007	2009	2011	2012	2013	2014
Total tax revenue	**167 022**	**730 672**	**1 552 413**	**2 900 519**	**3 867 405**	**3 318 696**	**3 708 707**	**3 888 470**	**4 283 029**	**4 500 530**
1000 Taxes on income, profits and capital gains	**80 284**	**364 137**	**701 731**	**1 453 865**	**1 867 486**	**1 337 382**	**1 712 859**	**1 824 353**	**2 014 211**	**2 147 832**
1100 Of individuals	52 894	285 513	584 733	1 224 538	1 481 367	1 138 824	1 438 703	1 497 167	1 659 113	1 768 531
1110 On income and profits	50 401	272 879	552 859	1 088 967	1 328 809	1 102 302	1 375 320	1 392 359	1 551 385	1 612 717
Individual income tax federal	46 492	233 269	449 239	895 677	1 062 955	851 119	1 095 349	1 100 079	1 234 186	1 293 644
Individual income tax state and local govt.	3 909	39 610	103 620	193 290	265 854	251 183	279 971	292 280	317 199	319 072
1120 On capital gains	2 493	12 634	31 874	135 571	152 558	36 522	63 383	104 808	107 728	155 815
Capital gains federal	2 300	10 800	25 900	111 507	122 036	28 200	50 480	82 807	85 702	124 987
Capital gains tax state and local govt.	193	1 834	5 974	24 064	30 522	8 322	12 903	22 001	22 026	30 828
1200 Corporate	27 390	78 624	116 998	229 327	386 119	198 558	274 157	327 186	355 098	379 301
1210 On profits	26 745	73 586	106 134	170 835	330 596	179 866	239 513	288 000	315 749	330 146
Corporate income tax federal	24 861	60 525	85 736	144 590	281 040	138 562	195 653	241 800	266 405	279 404
Corporate income tax state and local govt.	1 884	13 061	20 398	26 245	49 556	41 304	43 860	46 200	49 344	50 742
1220 On capital gains	645	5 038	10 864	58 492	55 523	18 692	34 644	39 186	39 349	49 155
Capital gains tax corp. federal	600	4 143	8 776	49 506	47 200	14 400	28 300	32 900	33 200	41 600
Capital gains tax corp. state and local govt.	45	895	2 088	8 986	8 323	4 292	6 344	6 286	6 149	7 555
1300 Unallocable between 1100 and 1200	0	0	0	0	0	0	0	0	0	0
2000 Social security contributions	**22 192**	**159 763**	**396 972**	**683 104**	**907 433**	**902 632**	**848 299**	**881 327**	**1 032 550**	**1 082 386**
2100 Employees	8 459	67 022	173 860	305 555	400 940	401 239	315 703	327 794	457 136	479 451
Federal insurance contribution Act tax	8 084	66 221	..	..	..	..	..	..	..	..
Less refund federal	-192	-507	..	..	..	..	..	..	..	..
Railroad retirement taxes federal	322	590	..	..	..	..	..	..	..	..
Fed. hosp. insur. recpts from railroad retir.	0	111	..	..	..	..	..	..	..	..
Unemployment state tax federal	20	127	..	..	..	..	..	..	..	..
Temp. disability insurance state and local	225	480	..	..	..	..	..	..	..	..
2110 On a payroll basis	..	..	..	..	..	..	..	..	..	..
2120 On an income tax basis	..	..	..	..	..	..	..	..	..	..
2200 Employers	12 703	87 019	204 102	343 184	456 655	451 475	485 865	506 386	520 162	540 101
Federal insurance contributions act tax	7 802	64 768	..	..	..	..	..	..	..	..
Railroad retirement taxes federal	314	1 722	..	..	..	..	..	..	..	..
Fed. hosp. insur. recpts from railroad retir.	0	111	..	..	..	..	..	..	..	..
Military service credit federal	14	652	..	..	..	..	..	..	..	..
Old-age dis. hosp. insur. fed. employer contr.	282	1 453	..	..	..	..	..	..	..	..
Unemployment state tax federal	3 032	11 788	..	..	..	..	..	..	..	..
Federal unemployment tax Act	615	3 246	..	..	..	..	..	..	..	..
Railroad unempl. insurance Act tax federal	152	175	..	..	..	..	..	..	..	..
Workmen's compensation state and local	484	3 039	..	..	..	..	..	..	..	..
Temp. disability insurance state and local	8	65	..	..	..	..	..	..	..	..
2210 On a payroll basis	..	..	..	..	..	..	..	..	..	..
2220 On an income tax basis	..	..	..	..	..	..	..	..	..	..
2300 Self-employed or non-employed	1 030	5 722	19 010	34 365	49 838	49 918	46 731	47 147	55 252	62 834
Federal old-age survivors trust	0	4 250	..	..	..	..	..	..	..	..
Federal disability insurance trust	1 030	733	..	..	..	..	..	..	..	..
Federal hospital insurance trust	0	739	..	..	..	..	..	..	..	..
2310 On a payroll basis	..	..	..	..	..	..	..	..	..	..
2320 On an income tax basis	..	..	..	..	..	..	..	..	..	..
2400 Unallocable between 2100, 2200 and 2300	0	0	0	0	0	0	0	0	0	0
2410 On a payroll basis	..	..	..	..	..	..	..	..	..	..
2420 On an income tax basis	..	..	..	..	..	..	..	..	..	..
3000 Taxes on payroll and workforce	**0**	**0**	**0**	**0**	**0**	**0**	**0**	**0**	**0**	**0**
4000 Taxes on property	**26 529**	**77 913**	**180 260**	**295 157**	**442 276**	**467 458**	**460 902**	**468 495**	**483 072**	**487 096**
4100 Recurrent taxes on immovable property	22 918	68 499	161 533	254 669	403 828	435 104	439 178	442 198	449 533	455 578
4110 Households	8 548	28 975	..	..	..	..	..	..	..	..
Property tax state and local	8 548	28 975	..	..	..	..	..	..	..	..
Other	0	0	..	..	..	..	..	..	..	..
4120 Others	14 370	39 524	..	..	..	..	..	..	..	..
Property tax state and local	14 370	39 524	..	..	..	..	..	..	..	..
Other	0	0	..	..	..	..	..	..	..	..
4200 Recurrent taxes on net wealth	0	0	0	0	0	0	0	0	0	0
4210 Individual	..	..	..	..	..	..	..	..	..	..
4220 Corporate	..	..	..	..	..	..	..	..	..	..
4300 Estate, inheritance and gift taxes	3 447	8 425	15 755	35 640	31 509	24 917	14 379	18 995	25 982	23 791
4310 Estate and inheritance taxes	3 080	8 149	..	..	..	..	..	..	..	..
Estate tax less refund federal	2 427	6 181	..	..	..	..	..	..	..	..
Estate tax state and local govt.	653	1 968	..	..	..	..	..	..	..	..
4320 Gift taxes	367	276	..	..	..	..	..	..	..	..
Gift tax less refund federal	289	209	..	..	..	..	..	..	..	..
Gift tax calculate state and local govt.	78	67	..	..	..	..	..	..	..	..

StatLink http://dx.doi.org/10.1787/888933417005

Table 4.35. **United States/État-Unis** *(cont./suite)*

Details of tax revenue/Recettes fiscales détaillées

Million USD

	1965	1980	1990	2000	2007	2009	2011	2012	2013	2014
4400 Taxes on financial and capital transactions	164	989	0	0	0	0	0	0	0	0
Interest equalisation tax federal	15	0	..	..	..	..	..	..	..	..
Document and stock transfer state and local	149	989	..	..	..	..	..	..	..	..
4500 Non-recurrent taxes	0	0	0	0	0	0	0	0	0	0
4510 On net wealth	..	..	..	..	..	..	..	..	..	..
4520 Other non-recurrent taxes	..	..	..	..	..	..	..	..	..	..
4600 Other recurrent taxes on property	0	0	2 972	4 848	6 939	7 437	7 345	7 302	7 557	7 727
5000 Taxes on goods and services	**38 017**	**128 844**	**273 450**	**468 393**	**650 209**	**611 223**	**686 647**	**714 295**	**753 196**	**783 216**
5100 Taxes on production, sale, transfer, etc	33 300	111 810	235 203	404 065	542 829	514 619	574 656	597 263	632 418	662 097
5110 General taxes	8 016	51 328	125 575	221 358	305 524	281 577	308 257	319 663	338 537	353 947
5111 Value added taxes	0	0	0	0	0	0	0	0	0	0
5112 Sales tax	8 016	51 328	125 575	221 358	305 524	281 577	308 257	319 663	338 537	353 947
General sales - general receipts state and local	7 981	51 328	125 575	221 358	305 524	281 577	308 257	319 663	338 537	353 947
Other state and local	35	0	0	0	0	0	0	0	0	0
5113 Other	0	0	0	0	0	0	0	0	0	0
5120 Taxes on specific goods and services	25 284	60 482	109 628	182 707	237 305	233 042	266 399	277 600	293 881	308 150
5121 Excises	21 209	45 471	64 953	108 600	137 346	142 125	146 549	154 131	153 362	154 825
Alcohol taxes federal govt.	3 689	5 601	5 228	7 281	8 571	8 645	9 010	9 423	9 025	9 978
Tobacco taxes federal govt.	2 142	2 443	4 217	6 741	8 377	16 309	16 959	16 592	15 830	15 029
Airport, airway, highway federal	3 559	6 411	0	0	0	0	0	0	0	0
Manufacturer's excise taxes federal govt.	2 867	6 122	0	0	0	0	0	0	0	0
Sugar tax federal govt.	97	0	0	0	0	0	0	0	0	0
Other taxes excise federal govt.	889	2	0	0	0	0	0	0	0	0
Undistributed tax deposits federal government	-11	152	0	0	0	0	0	0	0	0
Other taxes excise and undist. fed.govt. -	0	0	13 316	32 005	31 747	28 008	26 779	33 767	33 712	34 299
Less special tax liquor occupations federal	-22	-21	0	0	0	0	0	0	0	0
Other federal (refunds)	-7	-32	0	0	0	0	0	0	0	0
Alcohol taxes state and local govt.	949	2 642	3 577	4 485	5 677	5 941	6 273	6 580	6 752	6 756
Tobacco taxes state and local govt.	1 386	3 874	6 009	8 726	16 435	16 954	17 634	17 585	17 555	17 440
Public utilities state and local govt.	871	5 888	11 814	17 989	27 863	28 501	28 661	28 512	28 252	28 074
Motor fuel taxes state and local govt.	4 331	9 822	20 792	31 373	38 676	37 767	41 233	41 672	42 236	43 249
Other state and local taxes	469	2 295	0	0	0	0	0	0	0	0
Coal tonnage tax federal govt.	0	272	0	0	0	0	0	0	0	0
Hazardous substances tax federal	0	0	0	0	0	0	0	0	0	0
Transportation fuels tax federal	0	0	0	0	0	0	0	0	0	0
Boat fuels and equipment tax federal	0	0	0	0	0	0	0	0	0	0
Waste site deposits tax federal	0	0	0	0	0	0	0	0	0	0
Leaking underground storage federal	0	0	0	0	0	0	0	0	0	0
Vaccine injury compens. federal	0	0	0	0	0	0	0	0	0	0
Ozone depletion tax federal	0	0	0	0	0	0	0	0	0	0
Oil spill liability federal	0	0	0	0	0	0	0	0	0	0
Luxury tax federal govt.	0	0	0	0	0	0	0	0	0	0
5122 Profits of fiscal monopolies	275	608	0	0	0	0	0	0	0	0
Liquor store revenue state and local govt.	1 447	3 200	..	..	..	..	..	..	..	..
Liquor store expend. state and local govt.	-1 172	-2 592	..	..	..	..	..	..	..	..
5123 Customs and import duties	1 442	7 436	17 490	21 123	28 773	23 062	31 870	33 481	35 425	37 342
Custom duties federal	1 442	7 436	17 490	21 123	28 773	23 062	31 870	33 481	35 425	37 342
Petroleum import fees federal govt.	0	0	0	0	0	0	0	0	0	0
5124 Taxes on exports	0	0	0	0	0	0	0	0	0	0
5125 Taxes on investment goods	0	0	0	0	0	0	0	0	0	0
5126 Taxes on specific services	2 358	6 967	7 535	9 835	15 472	15 544	16 436	16 802	18 066	19 419
Amusements state and local govt.	23	234	0	0	0	0	0	0	0	0
Parimutuels state and local govt.	386	731	0	0	0	0	0	0	0	0
Transportation of persons federal	126	1 601	0	0	0	0	0	0	0	0
Transport of property	0	92	0	0	0	0	0	0	0	0
General and toll telephone federal	1 079	1 118	0	0	0	0	0	0	0	0
Foreign insurance policies federal	0	75	0	0	0	0	0	0	0	0
Insurance state and local govt.	744	3 113	7 535	9 835	15 472	15 544	16 436	16 802	18 066	19 419
Employee pension plans federal	0	3	0	0	0	0	0	0	0	0
Inland waterway tax federal	0	0	0	0	0	0	0	0	0	0
Ship departure tax federal	0	0	0	0	0	0	0	0	0	0
5127 Other taxes on internat. trade and transactions	0	0	0	0	0	0	0	0	0	0
5128 Other taxes	0	0	19 650	43 149	55 714	52 311	71 544	73 186	87 028	96 564
5130 Unallocable between 5110 and 5120	0	0	0	0	0	0	0	0	0	0
5200 Taxes on use of goods and perform activities	4 717	17 034	38 247	64 328	107 380	96 604	111 991	117 032	120 778	121 119
5210 Recurrent taxes	3 490	9 501	30 655	55 139	86 725	80 471	87 852	92 446	95 097	96 012
5211 Paid by households: motor vehicles	1 211	3 370	8 104	11 408	14 990	15 391	16 967	17 763	17 930	18 161
Motor vehicle regis. license st. and loc.	1 056	2 981	..	..	..	..	..	..	..	..
Motor vehicle oper. license st. and loc.	152	389	..	..	..	..	..	..	..	..
Other motor vehicle	3	0	..	..	..	..	..	..	..	..

StatLink http://dx.doi.org/10.1787/888933417005

Table 4.35. **United States/État-Unis** *(cont./suite)*

Details of tax revenue/Recettes fiscales détaillées

Million USD

	1965	1980	1990	2000	2007
5212 Paid by others: motor vehicles	937	2 343	3 564	6 689	8 478
Motor vehicle regis. license st. and loc.	937	2 343	..	..	..
Motor vehicle oper. license st. and loc.	0	0	..	..	..
5213 Paid in respect of other goods	1 342	3 788	18 987	37 042	63 257
Misc. fees permit license federal	19	0	0	0	0
Special tax liquor occupations federal	22	21	0	0	0
Use tax of certain vehicles federal	99	277	0	0	0
Use of internat. travel facilities federal	0	92	0	0	0
Use tax of aircraft federal	0	21	0	0	0
Corporation in general license st. and loc.	528	1 388	0	0	0
Alcoholic beverage license tax st. and loc.	133	179	0	0	0
Public utilities license tax st. and loc.	30	130	0	0	0
Amusements license taxes st. and loc.	7	69	0	0	0
Occupation and business license st. and loc.	349	1 113	0	0	0
Wagering occupation tax federal	7	12	0	0	0
Other license taxes st. and loc.	10	69	18 987	37 042	63 257
Hunting and fishing license taxes st. and loc.	138	417	0	0	0
Other	0	0	0	0	0
5220 Non-recurrent taxes	1 227	7 533	7 592	9 189	20 655
Severance state and local govt.	503	4 167	5 224	5 285	12 898
Poll taxes state and local govt.	9	0	0	0	0
Other taxes state and local govt.	715	3 366	2 368	3 904	7 757
5300 Unallocable between 5100 and 5200	0	0	0	0	0
6000 Other taxes	**0**	**15**	**0**	**0**	**0**
6100 Paid solely by business	..	0	..	..	..
6200 Other	..	15	..	..	..
Non-wastable tax credits					
Non-wastable tax credits against 1110	..	..	..	36 511	90 439
Tax expenditure component	..	..	..	9 602	35 910
Transfer component	..	..	..	26 909	54 529
Non-wastable tax credits against 1210	..	..	..	0	0
Tax expenditure component	..	..	..	..	..
Transfer component	..	..	..	..	..
Unallocable transfer component	..	..	..	..	..
Total tax revenue on cash basis	**167 022**	**730 672**	**1 518 943**	**2 870 276**	**3 839 516**
Total tax revenue on accrual basis	..	..	**1 552 413**	**2 900 519**	**3 867 405**
Conciliation with National Accounts					
Additional taxes included in National Accounts	..	..	23 608	25 344	34 598
Taxes excluded from National Accounts	..	..	0	0	0
Difference in treatment of tax credits	..	..	0	0	0
Capital transfer for uncollected revenue	..	..	0	0	0
Voluntary social security contributions	..	..	11 719	22 562	51 617
Miscellaneous differences	..	..	0	0	0
National Accounts: Taxes and actual social contributions	..	..	1 564 132	2 923 081	3 919 022
Imputed social contributions	..	..	3 384	3 727	7 077
National Accounts: Taxes and all social contributions	..	..	1 567 516	2 926 808	3 926 099

	2009	2011	2012	2013	2014
5212 Paid by others: motor vehicles	8 666	9 541	10 016	10 180	10 349
Motor vehicle regis. license st. and loc.	..	..	..	..	..
Motor vehicle oper. license st. and loc.	..	..	..	..	..
5213 Paid in respect of other goods	56 414	61 344	64 667	66 987	67 502
Misc. fees permit license federal	0	0	0	0	0
Special tax liquor occupations federal	0	0	0	0	0
Use tax of certain vehicles federal	0	0	0	0	0
Use of internat. travel facilities federal	0	0	0	0	0
Use tax of aircraft federal	0	0	0	0	0
Corporation in general license st. and loc.	0	0	0	0	0
Alcoholic beverage license tax st. and loc.	0	0	0	0	0
Public utilities license tax st. and loc.	0	0	0	0	0
Amusements license taxes st. and loc.	0	0	0	0	0
Occupation and business license st. and loc.	0	0	0	0	0
Wagering occupation tax federal	0	0	0	0	0
Other license taxes st. and loc.	56 414	61 344	64 667	66 987	67 502
Hunting and fishing license taxes st. and loc.	0	0	0	0	0
Other	0	0	0	0	0
5220 Non-recurrent taxes	16 133	24 139	24 586	25 681	25 107
Severance state and local govt.	8 675	16 581	17 086	18 266	17 648
Poll taxes state and local govt.	0	0	0	0	0
Other taxes state and local govt.	7 458	7 558	7 500	7 415	7 459
5300 Unallocable between 5100 and 5200	0	0	0	0	0
6000 Other taxes	**0**	**0**	**0**	**0**	**0**
6100 Paid solely by business	..	..	..	..	..
6200 Other	..	..	..	..	..
Non-wastable tax credits					
Non-wastable tax credits against 1110	103 974	162 586	124 532	158 160	144 200
Tax expenditure component	39 610	65 860	40 392	42 560	44 440
Transfer component	64 364	96 726	84 140	116 600	99 760
Non-wastable tax credits against 1210	40	6 400	7 720	630	440
Tax expenditure component	40	6 390	7 700	610	390
Transfer component	0	10	20	20	50
Unallocable transfer component	20	7 330	4 470	4 280	4 760
Total tax revenue on cash basis	**3 382 562**	**3 567 004**	**3 765 763**	**4 152 597**	**4 416 457**
Total tax revenue on accrual basis	**3 318 696**	**3 708 707**	**3 888 470**	**4 283 029**	**4 500 530**
Conciliation with National Accounts					
Additional taxes included in National Accounts	47 430	75 424	88 418	79 633	96 902
Taxes excluded from National Accounts	0	0	0	0	0
Difference in treatment of tax credits	0	0	0	0	0
Capital transfer for uncollected revenue	0	0	0	0	0
Voluntary social security contributions	57 954	63 761	64 680	69 939	72 440
Miscellaneous differences	0	0	0	0	0
National Accounts: Taxes and actual social contributions	3 376 650	3 772 468	3 953 150	4 352 968	4 572 970
Imputed social contributions	8 779	10 148	10 179	9 476	9 233
National Accounts: Taxes and all social contributions	3 385 429	3 782 616	3 963 329	4 362 444	4 582 203

Notes : From 1990, data are on a year ending 31st December basis. For years up to and including 1976, the dated covered fiscal years ending 30th June. Between 1977 and 1989, Federal government data covered fiscal years ending 30th September and State & Local government data covered fiscal years ending 30th June.

From 1990, data are on accrual basis. There are no separate estimates for the State and Local capital gains tax revenues.

Heading 5121: In 1994 through 1996, some Federal excise taxes formerly shown separately were included in «Other taxes,excises and undistributed, Federal government».

Source : Federal estimates are derived from the US Budget, the Final Monthly Treasury Statement and the Annual Report of the US Treasury Department; the State and Local estimates are derived from Government Finances, published by the Bureau of the Census.

StatLink *http://dx.doi.org/10.1787/888933417005*

4.2. Financing social benefits/Le financement des prestations sociales

Table 4.36. **Financing social benefits/Le financement des prestations sociales**

Memorandum item : on the financing of social security benefits/Pour mémoire : le financement des systèmes de sécurité sociale

	1965	1980	1990	2000	2007	2009	2011	2012	2013	2014
Australia, million AUD										
Contribution under 2000 heading	..	..	..	..	..	..	..	..	..	..
Other taxes	..	..	..	..	..	..	..	..	..	..
Voluntary contributions to government	..	..	..	..	..	..	..	..	..	..
Compulsory contributions to private sector	..	..	..	..	..	..	..	..	..	..
Total	**0**	**0**	**0**	**0**	**0**	**0**	**0**	**0**	**0**	**0**
Austria, million EUR										
Contribution under 2000 heading	1 548	9 200	17 763	30 613	38 583	40 771	43 486	45 058	46 988	48 454
Other taxes	0	0	0	0	0	0	0	0	0	0
Voluntary contributions to government	32	135	141	206	256	300	343	310	299	311
Compulsory contributions to private sector	0	0	0	0	0	0	0	0	0	0
Total	**1 580**	**9 335**	**17 904**	**30 820**	**38 839**	**41 070**	**43 828**	**45 368**	**47 286**	**48 765**
Belgique, millions EUR										
Impôts de la série 2000	2 018	10 798	23 386	34 636	45 659	49 315	52 971	55 066	56 362	57 026
Autres impôts	0	171	644	5 375	13 659	15 344	19 635	18 009	18 320	18 823
Contributions volontaires au gouvernement	0	41	52	54	55	62	67	71	75	74
Contributions obligatoires au secteur privé	0	0	0	0	0	0	0	0	0	0
Total	**2 018**	**11 009**	**24 082**	**40 065**	**59 372**	**64 721**	**72 672**	**73 145**	**74 756**	**75 922**
Canada, million CAD										
Contribution under 2000 heading	854	10 649	29 653	53 109	73 722	76 386	80 513	85 866	89 589	93 576
Other taxes	1 199	0	0	0	0	0	0	0	0	0
Voluntary contributions to government	0	0	0	0	0	0	0	0	0	0
Compulsory contributions to private sector	0	0	0	0	0	0	0	0	0	0
Total	**2 053**	**10 649**	**29 653**	**53 109**	**73 722**	**76 386**	**80 513**	**85 866**	**89 589**	**93 576**
Chile, million CLP										
Contribution under 2000 heading	..	..	159 559	576 758	1 148 647	1 371 750	1 623 818	1 802 468	1 968 973	2 110 087
Other taxes	..	..	0	0	0	0	0	0	0	0
Voluntary contributions to government	..	..	0	0	0	0	0	0	0	0
Compulsory contributions to private sector	..	..	328 102	2 021 631	3 808 658	4 832 756	6 103 523	6 843 561	7 583 251	8 195 259
Total	**..**	**..**	**487 661**	**2 598 389**	**4 957 305**	**6 204 506**	**7 727 341**	**8 646 029**	**9 552 224**	**10 305 346**
Czech Republic, million CZK										
Contribution under 2000 heading	..	..	..	341 544	573 417	557 702	588 996	596 841	603 072	625 508
Other taxes	..	..	..	0	0	0	0	0	0	0
Voluntary contributions to government	..	..	..	1 099	974	635	423	313	326	350
Compulsory contributions to private sector	..	..	..	2 837	5 757	6 140	6 286	6 408	6 424	6 482
Total	**..**	**..**	**..**	**345 480**	**580 148**	**564 477**	**595 705**	**603 562**	**609 822**	**632 340**
Denmark, million DKK										
Contribution under 2000 heading	690	710	101	8 453	1 286	1 018	2 040	1 824	1 618	1 451
Other taxes	0	0	0	0	0	0	0	0	0	0
Voluntary contributions to government	0	1 673	8 087	16 633	17 061	16 816	17 610	16 320	14 655	14 718
Compulsory contributions to private sector	145	554	1 278	1 445	4 526	4 368	3 584	3 458	3 068	2 994
Total	**835**	**2 937**	**9 466**	**26 531**	**22 873**	**22 202**	**23 234**	**21 602**	**19 341**	**19 163**
Estonia, million EUR										
Contribution under 2000 heading	..	..	..	674	1 683	1 819	1 935	2 000	2 077	2 178
Other taxes	..	..	..	0	0	0	0	0	0	0
Voluntary contributions to government	..	..	..	0	0	0	0	0	0	0
Compulsory contributions to private sector	..	..	..	1	341	119	129	272	280	492
Total	**..**	**..**	**..**	**674**	**2 024**	**1 939**	**2 064**	**2 273**	**2 358**	**2 670**
Finland, million EUR										
Contribution under 2000 heading	93	2 776	10 012	15 756	21 384	22 055	23 776	25 261	25 632	26 011
Other taxes	47	22	0	404	0	0	0	0	0	0
Voluntary contributions to government	0	262	632	236	228	220	261	267	270	277
Compulsory contributions to private sector	0	123	426	508	631	599	626	666	668	638
Total	**140**	**3 183**	**11 070**	**16 904**	**22 243**	**22 874**	**24 663**	**26 194**	**26 570**	**26 926**

StatLink http://dx.doi.org/10.1787/888933417015

Table 4.36. **Financing social benefits/Le financement des prestations sociales** *(cont./suite)*

Memorandum item : on the financing of social security benefits/Pour mémoire : le financement des systèmes de sécurité sociale

	1965	1980	1990	2000	2007	2009	2011	2012	2013	2014
France, millions EUR										
Impôts de la série 2000	8 804	76 235	191 141	231 875	307 663	317 560	336 595	346 137	356 934	366 338
Autres impôts	0	895	2 950	81 001	127 511	136 019	151 201	158 663	162 838	167 667
Contributions volontaires au gouvernement	0	0	0	0	0	0	0	0	0	0
Contributions obligatoires au secteur privé	0	0	0	0	0	0	0	0	0	0
Total	**8 804**	**77 130**	**194 091**	**312 876**	**435 174**	**453 579**	**487 796**	**504 800**	**519 772**	**534 005**
Germany, million EUR										
Contribution under 2000 heading	19 876	98 659	170 449	299 440	320 594	342 658	372 025	383 489	392 290	407 726
Other taxes	0	0	0	0	0	0	0	0	0	0
Voluntary contributions to government	1 946	8 441	13 002	23 329	20 930	7 763	6 237	6 913	7 353	7 744
Compulsory contributions to private sector	107	690	1 462	6 120	8 243	8 904	9 615	9 957	10 326	10 597
Total	**21 929**	**107 791**	**184 914**	**328 889**	**349 767**	**359 325**	**387 877**	**400 359**	**409 969**	**426 067**
Greece, million EUR										
Contribution under 2000 heading	37	485	3 466	14 299	24 941	24 453	22 410	20 988	19 537	18 234
Other taxes	8	0	0	0	0	0	0	0	0	0
Voluntary contributions to government	0	0	0	0	0	0	0	0	0	0
Compulsory contributions to private sector	0	0	0	0	0	0	0	0	0	0
Total	**44**	**485**	**3 466**	**14 299**	**24 941**	**24 453**	**22 410**	**20 988**	**19 537**	**18 234**
Hungary, million HUF										
Contribution under 2000 heading	..	..	..	1 506 755	3 402 194	3 334 455	3 495 557	3 607 882	3 745 638	4 025 298
Other taxes	..	..	..	188 413	158 212	163 436	122 613	177 266	173 751	174 489
Voluntary contributions to government	..	..	..	1 273	1 762	1 626	1 676	1 590	1 503	1 335
Compulsory contributions to private sector	..	..	..	62 836	190 331	318 563	3 127	0	0	0
Total	**..**	**..**	**..**	**1 759 277**	**3 752 499**	**3 818 080**	**3 622 973**	**3 786 738**	**3 920 892**	**4 201 122**
Iceland, million ISK										
Contribution under 2000 heading	5	102	3 607	19 680	39 594	45 912	66 820	64 882	69 899	73 432
Other taxes	0	1 047	20 571	26 732	52 444	98 224	87 142	92 338	90 895	95 960
Voluntary contributions to government	0	0	0	0	0	0	0	0	0	0
Compulsory contributions to private sector	0	459	13 454	48 847	118 117	93 146	103 363	109 865	117 903	125 889
Total	**5**	**1 608**	**37 632**	**95 260**	**210 155**	**237 283**	**257 325**	**267 086**	**278 697**	**295 281**
Ireland, million EUR										
Contribution under 2000 heading	21	578	1 729	3 941	8 118	8 795	9 039	8 482	9 020	9 581
Other taxes	0	0	0	0	0	0	0	0	0	0
Voluntary contributions to government	0	0	0	0	0	0	0	0	0	0
Compulsory contributions to private sector	0	0	0	0	0	0	0	0	0	0
Total	**21**	**578**	**1 729**	**3 941**	**8 118**	**8 795**	**9 039**	**8 482**	**9 020**	**9 581**
Israel, million ILS										
Contribution under 2000 heading	..	..	..	27 565	37 909	41 227	48 759	50 296	53 364	56 130
Other taxes	..	..	..	0	0	0	0	0	0	0
Voluntary contributions to government	..	..	..	0	0	0	0	0	0	0
Compulsory contributions to private sector	..	..	..	0	0	5 300	13 200	17 700	22 500	27 500
Total	**..**	**..**	**..**	**27 565**	**37 909**	**46 527**	**61 959**	**67 996**	**75 864**	**83 630**
Italie, millions EUR										
Impôts de la série 2000	1 881	22 976	87 256	143 629	200 772	207 635	211 637	210 897	210 462	209 653
Autres impôts	0	0	0	0	0	0	0	0	0	0
Contributions volontaires au gouvernement	0	0	0	464	567	531	579	836	738	739
Contributions obligatoires au secteur privé	0	0	0	0	0	0	0	0	0	0
Total	**1 881**	**22 976**	**87 256**	**144 093**	**201 339**	**208 166**	**212 216**	**211 733**	**211 200**	**210 392**
Japan, billion JPY										
Contribution under 2000 heading	1 344	18 178	34 593	47 857	53 321	52 342	56 321	58 068	59 800	62 232
Other taxes	0	0	0	0	0	0	0	0	0	0
Voluntary contributions to government	0	0	0	0	0	0	0	0	0	0
Compulsory contributions to private sector	0	0	0	0	0	0	0	0	0	0
Total	**1 344**	**18 178**	**34 593**	**47 857**	**53 321**	**52 342**	**56 321**	**58 068**	**59 800**	**62 232**

StatLink http://dx.doi.org/10.1787/888933417015

Table 4.36. **Financing social benefits/Le financement des prestations sociales** *(cont./suite)*

Memorandum item : on the financing of social security benefits/Pour mémoire : le financement des systèmes de sécurité sociale

	1965	1980	1990	2000	2007	2009	2011	2012	2013	2014
Korea, billion KRW										
Contribution under 2000 heading	..	73	3 760	22 759	53 588	63 939	77 234	84 380	91 596	98 184
Other taxes	..	0	0	0	0	0	0	0	0	0
Voluntary contributions to government	..	0	0	0	0	0	0	0	0	0
Compulsory contributions to private sector	..	0	0	0	0	0	0	0	0	0
Total	**..**	**73**	**3 760**	**22 759**	**53 588**	**63 939**	**77 234**	**84 380**	**91 596**	**98 184**
Latvia, millions EUR										
Impôts de la série 2000	..	..	..	669	1 774	1 742	1 763	1 903	1 933	1 982
Autres impôts	..	..	..	12	51	64	31	45	59	71
Contributions volontaires au gouvernement	..	..	..	0	0	0	0	0	0	0
Contributions obligatoires au secteur privé	..	..	..	0	0	0	0	0	0	0
Total	**..**	**..**	**..**	**682**	**1 825**	**1 806**	**1 795**	**1 948**	**1 992**	**2 054**
Luxembourg, millions EUR										
Impôts de la série 2000	86	443	1 011	2 223	3 704	4 231	4 669	4 926	5 128	5 388
Autres impôts	0	0	0	0	0	0	0	0	0	0
Contributions volontaires au gouvernement	0	0	4	18	18	25	30	33	34	36
Contributions obligatoires au secteur privé	0	0	0	0	0	0	0	0	0	0
Total	**86**	**443**	**1 015**	**2 240**	**3 722**	**4 256**	**4 699**	**4 959**	**5 162**	**5 424**
Mexico, million MXN										
Contribution under 2000 heading	..	109	17 165	167 292	307 026	346 031	411 289	454 778	490 918	538 213
Other taxes	..	0	0	0	0	0	0	0	0	0
Voluntary contributions to government	..	0	0	0	0	0	0	0	0	0
Compulsory contributions to private sector	..	25	3 840	67 352	144 331	129 207	154 996	160 669	168 111	190 376
Total	**..**	**134**	**21 005**	**234 644**	**451 357**	**475 238**	**566 285**	**615 447**	**659 029**	**728 589**
Netherlands, million EUR										
Contribution under 2000 heading	3 342	26 641	39 075	64 522	77 072	78 839	88 470	94 844	97 372	98 616
Other taxes	0	0	0	0	0	0	0	0	0	0
Voluntary contributions to government	168	1 139	163	0	0	0	0	0	0	0
Compulsory contributions to private sector	1 266	7 642	5 727	37 088	..	..	..	..	..	..
Total	**4 776**	**35 422**	**44 965**	**101 610**	**..**	**..**	**..**	**..**	**..**	**..**
New Zealand, million NZD										
Contribution under 2000 heading	..	..	..	..	..	..	..	..	..	..
Other taxes	..	..	..	..	..	..	..	..	..	..
Voluntary contributions to government	..	..	..	..	..	..	..	..	..	..
Compulsory contributions to private sector	..	..	..	..	..	..	..	..	..	..
Total	**0**	**0**	**0**	**0**	**0**	**0**	**0**	**0**	**0**	**0**
Norway, million NOK										
Contribution under 2000 heading	2 009	28 205	79 362	132 170	206 314	233 083	258 760	276 790	292 278	312 942
Other taxes	1 305	4 256	0	0	0	0	0	0	0	0
Voluntary contributions to government	0	0	0	0	0	0	0	0	0	0
Compulsory contributions to private sector	0	242	339	0	0	0	0	0	0	0
Total	**3 314**	**32 703**	**79 701**	**132 170**	**206 314**	**233 083**	**258 760**	**276 790**	**292 278**	**312 942**
Poland, million PLN										
Contribution under 2000 heading	..	..	..	96 386	140 086	152 032	174 212	194 720	202 629	209 902
Other taxes	..	..	..	0	0	0	0	0	0	0
Voluntary contributions to government	..	..	..	0	0	0	0	0	0	0
Compulsory contributions to private sector	..	..	..	0	0	0	0	0	0	0
Total	**..**	**..**	**..**	**96 386**	**140 086**	**152 032**	**174 212**	**194 720**	**202 629**	**209 902**
Portugal, million EUR										
Contribution under 2000 heading	22	531	4 026	10 168	14 274	14 998	15 671	14 621	15 139	15 544
Other taxes	0	1	29	434	658	689	715	892	970	976
Voluntary contributions to government	0	0	0	0	0	0	0	0	0	0
Compulsory contributions to private sector	0	0	0	0	0	0	0	0	0	0
Total	**22**	**532**	**4 055**	**10 602**	**14 932**	**15 687**	**16 386**	**15 513**	**16 109**	**16 520**

StatLink http://dx.doi.org/10.1787/888933417015

Table 4.36. **Financing social benefits/Le financement des prestations sociales** *(cont./suite)*

Memorandum item : on the financing of social security benefits/Pour mêmoire : le financement des systèmes de sécurité sociale

	1965	1980	1990	2000	2007	2009	2011	2012	2013	2014
Slovak Republic, million EUR										
Contribution under 2000 heading	..	..	..	4 409	7 192	7 858	8 479	8 907	9 783	10 125
Other taxes	..	..	..	0	0	0	0	0	0	0
Voluntary contributions to government	..	..	..	0	22	26	34	22	17	13
Compulsory contributions to private sector	..	..	..	0	701	690	756	645	385	406
Total	**..**	**..**	**..**	**4 409**	**7 915**	**8 574**	**9 270**	**9 574**	**10 186**	**10 544**
Slovenia, million EUR										
Contribution under 2000 heading	..	..	..	2 631	4 724	5 276	5 407	5 365	5 269	5 368
Other taxes	..	..	..	0	0	0	0	0	0	0
Voluntary contributions to government	..	..	..	0	0	0	0	0	0	0
Compulsory contributions to private sector	..	..	..	0	0	0	0	0	0	0
Total	**..**	**..**	**..**	**2 631**	**4 724**	**5 276**	**5 407**	**5 365**	**5 269**	**5 368**
Spain, million EUR										
Contribution under 2000 heading	350	10 682	36 722	76 421	129 170	131 510	129 535	123 967	120 728	122 664
Other taxes	0	49	0	0	0	0	0	0	0	0
Voluntary contributions to government	0	0	0	0	0	0	0	0	0	0
Compulsory contributions to private sector	0	0	0	0	0	0	0	0	0	0
Total	**350**	**10 731**	**36 722**	**76 421**	**129 170**	**131 510**	**129 535**	**123 967**	**120 728**	**122 664**
Sweden, million SEK										
Contribution under 2000 heading	4 851	74 647	205 867	306 974	388 505	357 289	361 987	375 628	376 684	388 651
Other taxes	1 407	0	0	0	0	0	0	0	0	0
Voluntary contributions to government	0	0	0	14 336	24 420	27 282	29 719	28 803	30 013	31 228
Compulsory contributions to private sector	0	0	0	0	0	0	0	0	0	0
Total	**6 258**	**74 647**	**205 867**	**321 310**	**412 925**	**384 571**	**391 706**	**404 431**	**406 697**	**419 879**
Suisse, millions CHF										
Impôts de la série 2000	1 670	10 844	19 862	30 628	34 841	37 978	40 837	41 801	42 518	43 152
Autres impôts	336	778	1 185	1 918	4 919	6 152	7 601	8 094	7 850	7 845
Contributions volontaires au gouvernement	95	431	0	0	0	0	0	0	0	0
Contributions obligatoires au secteur privé	2 505	9 674	20 797	29 532	41 478	43 072	47 330	48 399	49 473	51 821
Total	**4 606**	**21 727**	**41 843**	**62 079**	**81 239**	**87 202**	**95 769**	**98 294**	**99 841**	**102 818**
Turkey, million TRY										
Contribution under 2000 heading	0	0	15	7 543	44 052	57 595	100 687	106 405	125 871	143 400
Other taxes	0	0	0	0	0	0	0	0	0	0
Voluntary contributions to government	0	0	0	0	0	0	0	0	0	0
Compulsory contributions to private sector	0	0	0	0	0	0	0	0	0	0
Total	**0**	**0**	**15**	**7 543**	**44 052**	**57 595**	**100 687**	**106 405**	**125 871**	**143 400**
United Kingdom, million GBP										
Contribution under 2000 heading	1 685	13 531	34 457	60 252	93 210	94 445	101 441	104 319	106 085	109 120
Other taxes	0	0	0	0	0	0	0	0	0	0
Voluntary contributions to government	0	11	3 288	5 305	13 645	15 218	15 937	16 763	18 420	19 135
Compulsory contributions to private sector	1 148	13 350	7 945	8 308	9 969	9 545	9 706	8 848	6 592	5 872
Total	**2 833**	**26 892**	**45 690**	**73 865**	**116 824**	**119 208**	**127 084**	**129 930**	**131 097**	**134 127**
United States, million USD										
Contribution under 2000 heading	22 192	159 763	396 972	683 104	907 433	902 632	848 299	881 327	1 032 550	1 082 386
Other taxes	0	0	0	0	0	0	0	0	0	0
Voluntary contributions to government	488	3 407	11 719	22 562	51 617	57 954	63 761	64 680	69 939	72 440
Compulsory contributions to private sector	0	0	0	0	0	0	0	0	0	0
Total	**22 680**	**163 170**	**408 691**	**705 666**	**959 050**	**960 586**	**912 060**	**946 007**	**1 102 489**	**1 154 826**

StatLink http://dx.doi.org/10.1787/888933417015

4.3. Social security contributions and payroll taxes paid by Government

During the revision of the Interpretative Guide in 1984, the question arose of how to treat taxes paid by government. The two most prominent examples of such taxes are social security contributions and payroll taxes paid by government in respect of its employees. After a long discussion, it was decided that the data shown in this publication should continue to include taxes paid by government (see §5 of the *Interpretative Guide* in Annex A).

Whilst it was recognised that for certain purposes (e.g. to show the cash flow to the government sector from the private sector) it would be appropriate to eliminate taxes paid by one sector of government to another or tax payments between different units of the same sector of government, the view was taken that to record tax flows in the context of the economy as a whole required that taxes paid by government should be included in the data. This treatment ensures that the different resource flows of an economy, including the calculation of the output of government, are measured consistently in after-tax units. Nevertheless, it was decided that data on identifiable taxes paid by government should be separately identified in a memorandum item and this is the purpose of the country tables which follow.

The data that are reproduced in the following tables refer to actual compulsory payments made by general government in respect of their employees. Fictive, voluntary and imputed contributions are excluded from these data. The definitions of social security contributions, payroll taxes and general government are those set out in §35 to §41, §42 and §3 to §4 of the *Interpretative Guide*. Information on the other taxes paid by government (namely property taxes and consumption taxes) is not available in most countries, although it is believed that in all countries taxes based upon payroll are the most important taxes paid by government. In many cases, the data are estimates and are not always constructed on a basis consistent with that used in the main tables.

4.3. Les cotisations de sécurité sociale et impôts sur les salaires payés par les administrations publiques

Lors de la révision du *Guide d'interprétation* en 1984, la question s'est posée de savoir comment il convenait de traiter les impôts acquittés par les administrations. Les deux exemples les plus marquants d'impôts de ce type sont les cotisations de sécurité sociale et les impôts sur les salaires acquittés par les administrations au titre de leurs agents. Après un échange de vues approfondi, il a été décidé que les données présentées dans cette publication continueraient d'inclure les impôts acquittés par les administrations (voir le §5 du *Guide d'interprétation* dans l'Annexe A).

Alors qu'il a été admis qu'à certaines fins (par exemple, pour mesurer le flux de paiements allant du secteur privé au secteur des administrations), il conviendrait d'exclure les impôts payés par un secteur de l'administration à un autre ou les impôts acquittés entre les différentes unités d'un même secteur de l'administration, il a été décidé que les impôts acquittés par les administrations devaient être inclus dans les données lorsque l'on comptabilise tous les flux d'impôts de l'ensemble de l'économie. Cette prise en compte permet d'être sûr que les différents flux de ressources d'une économie, y compris la valeur de la production des administrations, sont bien mesurés de façon cohérente nette d'impôt.

Il a été toutefois décidé que les données sur les impôts acquittés par les administrations et que l'on pouvait identifier isolément seraient présentées séparément dans un poste pour mémoire et c'est l'objet des tableaux par pays qui suivent.

Les données reproduites dans les tableaux suivants ont trait aux montants effectifs versés par les administrations publiques au titre de leurs agents. Les cotisations fictives, volontaires et imputées sont exclues de ces données. Les définitions des cotisations de sécurité sociale, des impôts sur les salaires et des administrations publiques correspondent aux définitions données aux §35 à §41, §42, et §3 à §4 du *Guide d'interprétation*. Les informations sur les autres impôts payés par les administrations (à savoir impôts sur la propriété et impôts sur la consommation) ne sont pas disponibles pour la plupart des pays, même s'il semble bien que, dans tous les pays, les impôts assis sur les salaires sont les impôts les plus importants qu'acquittent les administrations. Dans beaucoup de cas, les données sont estimées et ne sont pas toujours établies sur une base compatible avec celle utilisée dans les tableaux principaux.

Table 4.37. **Social security contributions and payroll taxes paid by government/Les cotisations de sécurité sociale et impôts sur les salaires payés par les administrations publiques**

	1965	1980	1990	2000	2007	2009	2011	2012	2013	2014
Australia, million AUD										
2000 Social security contributions										
Federal or Central government	..	..	..	..	..	..	..	..	..	..
State/Regional	..	..	..	..	..	..	..	..	..	..
Local government	..	..	..	..	..	..	..	..	..	..
Social Security Funds	..	..	..	..	..	..	..	..	..	..
Total	**0**	**0**	**0**	**0**	**0**	**0**	**0**	**0**	**0**	**0**
3000 Taxes on payroll and workforce										
Federal or Central government	0	4	0	0	0	0	0	0	0	0
State/Regional	15	302	0	0	0	0	0	0	0	0
Local government	0	0	2	19	41	34	30	36	37	37
Social Security Funds	0	0	0	0	0	0	0	0	0	0
Multi-jurisdictional (University) sector[1]	0	0	90	282	455	520	585	634	665	708
Total	**15**	**306**	**92**	**301**	**496**	**554**	**615**	**670**	**702**	**745**
2000+3000 Total	**15**	**306**	**92**	**301**	**496**	**554**	**615**	**670**	**702**	**745**
Austria, million EUR[2]										
2000 Social security contributions										
Federal or Central government	48	230	337	536	1 161	1 368	1 414	1 493	1 586	1 646
State/Regional	13	166	337	692	988	1 179	1 221	1 244	1 255	1 291
Local government	17	145	292	699	1 036	1 216	1 290	1 341	1 379	1 444
Social Security Funds	11	79	48	176	203	224	232	240	250	257
Total	**88**	**619**	**1 015**	**2 102**	**3 388**	**3 988**	**4 157**	**4 319**	**4 469**	**4 638**
3000 Taxes on payroll and workforce										
Federal or Central government	0	49	134	165	314	501	532	550	535	542
State/Regional	0	48	74	232	351	453	470	480	485	491
Local government	1	29	79	301	262	355	364	381	396	404
Social Security Funds	0	0	39	44	51	55	56	59	61	63
Total	**1**	**125**	**326**	**742**	**977**	**1 365**	**1 423**	**1 470**	**1 477**	**1 501**
2000+3000 Total	**89**	**745**	**1 341**	**2 844**	**4 366**	**5 352**	**5 580**	**5 789**	**5 946**	**6 138**
Belgique, millions EUR										
2000 Cotisations de sécurité sociale										
Administration fédérale ou centrale	..	536	211	259	434	490	507	519	531	524
Administration d'un Etat/Länder	..	0	614	1 218	1 600	1 739	1 889	1 905	1 984	2 035
Administrations locales	..	434	768	1 376	2 151	2 455	2 777	3 284	3 601	3 832
Administrations de sécurite sociale	..	89	176	252	308	349	398	408	418	423
Total	..	**1 059**	**1 769**	**3 105**	**4 493**	**5 032**	**5 571**	**6 115**	**6 533**	**6 814**
3000 Impôts sur les salaires										
Administration fédérale ou centrale	..	..	..	..	..	..	..	..	..	..
Administration d'un Etat/Länder	..	..	..	..	..	..	..	..	..	..
Administrations locales	..	..	..	..	..	..	..	..	..	..
Administrations de sécurite sociale	..	..	..	..	..	..	..	..	..	..
Total	..	**0**	**0**	**0**	**0**	**0**	**0**	**0**	**0**	**0**
2000+3000 Total	..	**1 059**	**1 769**	**3 105**	**4 493**	**5 032**	**5 571**	**6 115**	**6 533**	**6 814**
Canada, million CAD										
2000 Social security contributions										
Federal or Central government	..	..	..	944	1 130	1 302	1 408	1 452	1 501	1 451
State/Regional	..	..	..	3 023	4 269	4 970	5 348	5 562	5 723	5 775
Local government	..	..	..	2 225	2 806	3 396	3 548	3 742	3 912	3 948
Social Security Funds	..	..	..	0	0	0	0	0	0	0
Total	..	..	..	**6 192**	**8 205**	**9 667**	**10 304**	**10 755**	**11 136**	**11 173**
3000 Taxes on payroll and workforce										
Federal or Central government	..	..	..	0	0	0	0	0	0	0
State/Regional	..	..	..	173	234	330	350	354	363	346
Local government	..	..	..	0	0	0	0	0	0	0
Social Security Funds	..	..	..	0	0	0	0	0	0	0
Total	..	..	..	**173**	**234**	**330**	**350**	**354**	**363**	**346**
2000+3000 Total	..	..	..	**6 365**	**8 439**	**9 997**	**10 654**	**11 109**	**11 499**	**11 519**

StatLink http://dx.doi.org/10.1787/888933417027

Table 4.37. **Social security contributions and payroll taxes paid by government/Les cotisations de sécurité sociale et impôts sur les salaires payés par les administrations publiques** *(cont./suite)*

	1965	1980	1990	2000	2007	2009	2011	2012	2013	2014
Chile, million CLP										
2000 Social security contributions										
Federal or Central government	..	..	..	43 210	107 911	125 449	169 141	177 036	186 652	191 812
State/Regional	..	..	..	..	..	..	..	..	..	..
Local government	..	..	..	11 317	30 218	35 262	45 580	48 269	51 114	56 151
Social Security Funds	..	..	..	106	263	297	467	500	550	564
Total	..	..	..	**54 633**	**138 392**	**161 008**	**215 188**	**225 805**	**238 315**	**248 527**
3000 Taxes on payroll and workforce										
Federal or Central government	..	..	..	..	..	..	..	..	..	..
State/Regional	..	..	..	..	..	..	..	..	..	..
Local government	..	..	..	..	..	..	..	..	..	..
Social Security Funds	..	..	..	..	..	..	..	..	..	..
Total	..	..	..	..	..	..	..	..	..	..
2000+3000 Total	..	..	..	**54 633**	**138 392**	**161 008**	**215 188**	**225 805**	**238 315**	**248 527**
Czech Republic, million CZK										
2000 Social security contributions										
Federal or Central government	..	..	..	28 050	44 437	46 351	43 857	45 424	46 360	47 666
State/Regional	..	..	..	..	..	..	..	..	..	..
Local government	..	..	..	5 660	8 253	8 917	9 268	9 124	9 448	9 890
Social Security Funds	..	..	..	510	791	908	935	894	881	929
Total	..	..	..	**34 220**	**53 481**	**56 177**	**54 060**	**55 442**	**56 689**	**58 485**
3000 Taxes on payroll and workforce										
Federal or Central government	..	..	..	..	..	..	..	..	..	..
State/Regional	.	..	..	..	..	..	..	..	..	..
Local government	..	..	..	..	..	..	..	..	..	..
Social Security Funds	..	..	..	..	..	..	..	..	..	..
Total	..	..	..	**0**	**0**	**0**	**0**	**0**	**0**	**0**
2000+3000 Total	..	..	..	**34 220**	**53 481**	**56 177**	**54 060**	**55 442**	**56 689**	**58 485**
Denmark, million DKK										
2000 Social security contributions										
Federal or Central government	..	179	..	..	..	..	..	..	..	..
State/Regional	..	..	..	..	..	..	..	..	..	..
Local government	..	0	..	..	..	..	..	..	..	..
Social Security Funds	..	0	..	..	..	..	..	..	..	..
Total	..	**179**	**0**	**0**	**0**	**0**	**0**	**0**	**0**	**0**
3000 Taxes on payroll and workforce										
Federal or Central government	..	..	..	..	..	..	..	..	..	..
State/Regional	..	..	..	..	..	..	..	..	..	..
Local government	..	..	..	..	..	..	..	..	..	..
Social Security Funds	..	..	..	..	..	..	..	..	..	..
Total	..	**0**	**0**	**0**	**0**	**0**	**0**	**0**	**0**	**0**
2000+3000 Total	..	**179**	**0**	**0**	**0**	**0**	**0**	**0**	**0**	**0**
Estonia, million EUR										
2000 Social security contributions										
Federal or Central government	..	..	..	129	257	325	332	347	368	405
State/Regional	..	..	..	..	..	..	..	..	..	..
Local government	..	..	..	48	156	184	180	184	206	220
Social Security Funds	..	..	..	0	3	38	32	25	24	22
Total	..	..	..	**177**	**417**	**547**	**543**	**556**	**598**	**647**
3000 Taxes on payroll and workforce										
Federal or Central government	..	..	..	..	..	..	..	..	..	..
State/Regional	..	..	..	..	..	..	..	..	..	..
Local government	..	..	..	..	..	..	..	..	..	..
Social Security Funds	..	..	..	..	..	..	..	..	..	..
Total	..	..	..	**0**	**0**	**0**	**0**	**0**	**0**	**0**
2000+3000 Total	..	..	..	**177**	**417**	**547**	**543**	**556**	**598**	**647**

StatLink http://dx.doi.org/10.1787/888933417027

Table 4.37. Social security contributions and payroll taxes paid by government/Les cotisations de sécurité sociale et impôts sur les salaires payés par les administrations publiques *(cont./suite)*

	1965	1980	1990	2000	2007	2009	2011	2012	2013	2014
Finland, million EUR										
2000 Social security contributions										
Federal or Central government	..	61	196	908	1 057	1 140	1 134	1 174	1 226	1 279
State/Regional	..	..	..	..	..	..	..	..	..	..
Local government	..	170	1 709	2 786	4 061	4 318	4 568	4 755	4 881	4 871
Social Security Funds	..	9	33	75	88	90	93	97	102	107
Total	..	**239**	**1 938**	**3 769**	**5 206**	**5 548**	**5 795**	**6 026**	**6 209**	**6 257**
3000 Taxes on payroll and workforce										
Federal or Central government	..	1	..	..	..	..	..	..	..	..
State/Regional	..	..	..	..	..	..	..	..	..	..
Local government	..	4	..	..	..	..	..	..	..	..
Social Security Funds	..	0	..	..	..	..	..	..	..	..
Total	..	**5**	**0**	**0**	**0**	**0**	**0**	**0**	**0**	**0**
2000+3000 Total	..	**245**	**1 938**	**3 769**	**5 206**	**5 548**	**5 795**	**6 026**	**6 209**	**6 257**
France, millions EUR										
2000 Cotisations de sécurité sociale										
Administration fédérale ou centrale	..	3 816	8 063	10 474	12 438	12 608	12 781	12 800	12 845	12 893
Administration d'un Etat/Länder	..	..	..	..	..	..	..	..	..	..
Administrations locales	..	2 369	5 542	10 364	15 913	17 568	18 349	18 935	20 030	21 049
Administrations de sécurite sociale	..	2 594	6 940	10 827	14 035	15 117	15 857	16 131	16 614	17 235
Total	..	**8 779**	**20 545**	**31 665**	**42 386**	**45 293**	**46 987**	**47 866**	**49 489**	**51 177**
3000 Impôts sur les salaires										
Administration fédérale ou centrale	..	836	494	854	1 558	1 568	1 639	1 653	1 697	1 729
Administration d'un Etat/Länder	..	..	..	..	..	..	..	..	..	..
Administrations locales	..	27	107	324	549	675	721	750	791	821
Administrations de sécurite sociale	..	629	2 234	3 413	4 531	4 910	5 115	5 156	5 374	5 500
Total	..	**1 492**	**2 835**	**4 591**	**6 638**	**7 153**	**7 475**	**7 559**	**7 862**	**8 050**
2000+3000 Total	..	**10 271**	**23 380**	**36 256**	**49 024**	**52 446**	**54 462**	**55 425**	**57 351**	**59 227**
Germany, million EUR										
2000 Social security contributions										
Federal or Central government	775	1 324	2 376	1 615	1 203	1 263	1 336	1 375	1 367	1 428
State/Regional	293	2 611	4 647	7 645	5 314	5 554	5 967	6 183	6 126	6 410
Local government	325	3 140	5 791	10 561	9 940	10 372	11 132	11 548	11 378	11 921
Social Security Funds	1 495	456	767	1 884	2 283	2 374	2 548	2 637	2 650	2 762
Total	**2 887**	**7 531**	**13 581**	**21 705**	**18 740**	**19 563**	**20 983**	**21 743**	**21 521**	**22 521**
3000 Taxes on payroll and workforce										
Federal or Central government	..	..	..	..	..	..	..	..	..	..
State/Regional	..	..	..	..	..	..	..	..	..	..
Local government	..	..	..	..	..	..	..	..	..	..
Social Security Funds	..	..	..	..	..	..	..	..	..	..
Total	**0**	**0**	**0**	**0**	**0**	**0**	**0**	**0**	**0**	**0**
2000+3000 Total	**2 887**	**7 531**	**13 581**	**21 705**	**18 740**	**19 563**	**20 983**	**21 743**	**21 521**	**22 521**
Greece, million EUR										
2000 Social security contributions										
Federal or Central government	..	..	124	1 542	2 888	3 403	3 695	3 283	2 956	2 946
State/Regional	..	..	..	..	..	..	..	..	..	..
Local government	..	..	0	0	0	0	0	0	0	0
Social Security Funds	..	..	0	200	440	502	346	401	347	290
Total	..	..	**124**	**1 742**	**3 328**	**3 905**	**4 041**	**3 684**	**3 303**	**3 236**
3000 Taxes on payroll and workforce										
Federal or Central government	..	..	..	..	..	..	..	..	..	..
State/Regional	..	..	..	..	..	..	..	..	..	..
Local government	..	..	..	..	..	..	..	..	..	..
Social Security Funds	..	..	..	..	..	..	..	..	..	..
Total	..	..	**0**	**0**	**0**	**0**	**0**	**0**	**0**	**0**
2000+3000 Total	..	..	**124**	**1 742**	**3 328**	**3 905**	**4 041**	**3 684**	**3 303**	**3 236**

StatLink http://dx.doi.org/10.1787/888933417027

Table 4.37. Social security contributions and payroll taxes paid by government/Les cotisations de sécurité sociale et impôts sur les salaires payés par les administrations publiques *(cont./suite)*

	1965	1980	1990	2000	2007	2009	2011	2012	2013	2014
Hungary, million HUF										
2000 Social security contributions										
Federal or Central government	..	..	..	148 251	293 684	266 442	243 241	320 040	449 428	480 327
State/Regional	..	..	..	..	..	..	..	..	..	..
Local government	..	..	..	173 475	343 306	307 680	260 764	208 411	124 111	137 504
Social Security Funds	..	..	..	4 936	8 052	7 547	3 016	2 992	2 781	2 674
Total	**..**	**..**	**..**	**326 661**	**645 042**	**581 669**	**507 021**	**531 444**	**576 320**	**620 505**
3000 Taxes on payroll and workforce										
Federal or Central government	..	..	..	13 901	7 287	6 913	7 979	9 140	12 435	13 706
State/Regional	..	..	..	..	..	..	..	..	..	..
Local government	..	..	..	25 990	11 928	11 175	10 656	10 382	4 224	3 345
Social Security Funds	..	..	..	406	162	171	13	119	101	112
Total	**..**	**..**	**..**	**40 297**	**19 377**	**18 259**	**18 649**	**19 641**	**16 760**	**17 163**
2000+3000 Total	**..**	**..**	**..**	**366 958**	**664 420**	**599 927**	**525 670**	**551 085**	**593 080**	**637 668**
Iceland, million ISK										
2000 Social security contributions										
Federal or Central government	..	..	..	..	..	..	..	..	..	..
State/Regional	..	..	..	..	..	..	..	..	..	..
Local government	..	..	..	..	..	..	..	..	..	..
Social Security Funds	..	..	..	..	..	..	..	..	..	..
Total	**..**	**..**	**..**	**..**	**..**	**..**	**..**	**..**	**..**	**..**
3000 Taxes on payroll and workforce										
Federal or Central government	..	..	..	..	..	..	..	..	..	..
State/Regional	..	..	..	..	..	..	..	..	..	..
Local government	..	..	..	..	..	..	..	..	..	..
Social Security Funds	..	..	..	..	..	..	..	..	..	..
Total	**..**	**..**	**..**	**..**	**..**	**..**	**..**	**..**	**..**	**..**
2000+3000 Total	**..**	**..**	**..**	**..**	**..**	**..**	**..**	**..**	**..**	**..**
Ireland, million EUR										
2000 Social security contributions										
Federal or Central government	..	21	65	166	460	422	429	401	426	465
State/Regional	..	..	..	..	..	..	..	..	..	..
Local government	..	25	83	277	862	792	805	751	799	873
Social Security Funds	..	0	1	4	6	6	6	6	6	6
Total	**..**	**46**	**149**	**447**	**1 328**	**1 220**	**1 240**	**1 158**	**1 231**	**1 344**
3000 Taxes on payroll and workforce										
Federal or Central government	..	..	..	..	..	..	..	..	..	..
State/Regional	..	..	..	..	..	..	..	..	..	..
Local government	..	..	..	..	..	..	..	..	..	..
Social Security Funds	..	..	..	..	..	..	..	..	..	..
Total	**..**	**0**	**0**	**0**	**0**	**0**	**0**	**0**	**0**	**0**
2000+3000 Total	**..**	**46**	**149**	**447**	**1 328**	**1 220**	**1 240**	**1 158**	**1 231**	**1 344**
Israel, million ILS										
2000 Social security contributions										
Federal or Central government	..	..	..	840	1 030	1 060	1 320	1 370	1 550	1 660
State/Regional	..	..	..	..	..	..	..	..	..	..
Local government	..	..	..	280	340	350	440	450	510	550
Social Security Funds	..	..	..	0	0	0	0	0	0	0
Total	**..**	**..**	**..**	**1 120**	**1 370**	**1 410**	**1 760**	**1 820**	**2 060**	**2 210**
3000 Taxes on payroll and workforce										
Federal or Central government	..	..	..	2 330	3 600	3 970	4 400	4 680	4 930	5 460
State/Regional	..	..	..	..	..	..	..	..	..	..
Local government	..	..	..	780	1 120	910	1 010	1 070	1 130	1 250
Social Security Funds	..	..	..	0	0	0	0	0	0	0
Total	**..**	**..**	**..**	**3 110**	**4 720**	**4 880**	**5 410**	**5 750**	**6 060**	**6 710**
2000+3000 Total	**..**	**..**	**..**	**4 230**	**6 090**	**6 290**	**7 170**	**7 570**	**8 120**	**8 920**

StatLink http://dx.doi.org/10.1787/888933417027

Table 4.37. **Social security contributions and payroll taxes paid by government/Les cotisations de sécurité sociale et impôts sur les salaires payés par les administrations publiques** *(cont./suite)*

	1965	1980	1990	2000	2007	2009	2011	2012	2013	2014
Italie, millions EUR										
2000 Cotisations de sécurité sociale										
Administration fédérale ou centrale	..	..	..	0	0	0	0	0	0	0
Administration d'un Etat/Länder	..	..	..	..	..	..	..	..	..	..
Administrations locales	..	..	..	0	0	0	0	0	0	0
Administrations de sécurite sociale	..	..	..	36 679	47 394	49 734	50 701	50 131	49 827	49 571
Total	..	..	..	**36 679**	**47 394**	**49 734**	**50 701**	**50 131**	**49 827**	**49 571**
3000 Impôts sur les salaires										
Administration fédérale ou centrale	..	..	..	..	..	..	..	..	..	..
Administration d'un Etat/Länder	..	..	..	..	..	..	..	..	..	..
Administrations locales	..	..	..	..	..	..	..	..	..	..
Administrations de sécurite sociale	..	..	..	..	..	..	..	..	..	..
Total	..	..	..	**0**	**0**	**0**	**0**	**0**	**0**	**0**
2000+3000 Total	..	..	..	**36 679**	**47 394**	**49 734**	**50 701**	**50 131**	**49 827**	**49 571**
Japan, billion JPY										
2000 Social security contributions										
Federal or Central government	..	..	507	732	766	816	776	778	810	858
State/Regional	..	..	..	..	..	..	..	..	..	..
Local government	..	..	1 510	2 168	2 216	2 203	2 387	2 406	2 392	2 513
Social Security Funds	..	..	0	0	0	0	0	0	0	0
Total	..	..	**2 017**	**2 900**	**2 982**	**3 019**	**3 163**	**3 184**	**3 202**	**3 371**
3000 Taxes on payroll and workforce										
Federal or Central government	..	..	..	..	..	..	..	..	..	..
State/Regional	..	..	..	..	..	..	..	..	..	..
Local government	..	..	..	..	..	..	..	..	..	..
Social Security Funds	..	..	..	..	..	..	..	..	..	..
Total	..	..	**0**	**0**	**0**	**0**	**0**	**0**	**0**	**0**
2000+3000 Total	..	..	**2 017**	**2 900**	**2 982**	**3 019**	**3 163**	**3 184**	**3 202**	**3 371**
Korea, billion KRW										
2000 Social security contributions										
Federal or Central government	..	..	..	..	..	..	..	..	..	..
State/Regional	..	..	..	..	..	..	..	..	..	..
Local government	..	..	..	..	..	..	..	..	..	..
Social Security Funds	..	..	..	..	..	..	..	..	..	..
Total	..	..	..	..	..	..	..	..	..	..
3000 Taxes on payroll and workforce										
Federal or Central government	..	..	..	..	..	..	..	..	..	..
State/Regional	..	..	..	..	..	..	..	..	..	..
Local government	..	..	..	..	..	..	..	..	..	..
Social Security Funds	..	..	..	..	..	..	..	..	..	..
Total	..	..	..	..	..	..	..	..	..	..
2000+3000 Total	..	..	..	..	..	..	..	..	..	..
Latvia, millions EUR										
2000 Cotisations de sécurité sociale										
Administration fédérale ou centrale	..	..	..	..	..	..	..	..	..	..
Administration d'un Etat/Länder	..	..	..	..	..	..	..	..	..	..
Administrations locales	..	..	..	..	..	..	..	..	..	..
Administrations de sécurite sociale	..	..	..	..	..	..	..	..	..	..
Total	..	..	**0**	**40**	**156**	**183**	**189**	**206**	**228**	**248**
3000 Impôts sur les salaires										
Administration fédérale ou centrale	..	..	..	..	..	..	..	..	..	..
Administration d'un Etat/Länder	..	..	..	..	..	..	..	..	..	..
Administrations locales	..	..	..	..	..	..	..	..	..	..
Administrations de sécurite sociale	..	..	..	..	..	..	..	..	..	..
Total	..	..	**0**	**0**	**0**	**0**	**0**	**0**	**0**	**0**
2000+3000 Total	..	..	**0**	**40**	**156**	**183**	**189**	**206**	**228**	**248**

StatLink http://dx.doi.org/10.1787/888933417027

Table 4.37. **Social security contributions and payroll taxes paid by government/Les cotisations de sécurité sociale et impôts sur les salaires payés par les administrations publiques** *(cont./suite)*

	1965	1980	1990	2000	2007	2009	2011	2012	2013	2014
Luxembourg, millions EUR										
2000 Cotisations de sécurité sociale										
Administration fédérale ou centrale	..	..	..	..	..	..	..	..	..	..
Administration d'un Etat/Länder	..	..	..	..	..	..	..	..	..	..
Administrations locales	..	..	..	..	..	..	..	..	..	..
Administrations de sécurite sociale	..	..	..	..	..	..	..	..	..	..
Total	**..**	**..**	**..**	**..**	**..**	**..**	**..**	**..**	**..**	**..**
3000 Impôts sur les salaires										
Administration fédérale ou centrale	..	..	..	..	..	..	..	..	..	..
Administration d'un Etat/Länder	..	..	..	..	..	..	..	..	..	..
Administrations locales	..	..	..	..	..	..	..	..	..	..
Administrations de sécurite sociale	..	..	..	..	..	..	..	..	..	..
Total	**..**	**..**	**..**	**..**	**..**	**..**	**..**	**..**	**..**	**..**
2000+3000 Total	**..**	**..**	**..**	**..**	**..**	**..**	**..**	**..**	**..**	**..**
Mexico, million MXN										
2000 Social security contributions										
Federal or Central government	..	25	2 952	73 948	140 647	167 568	199 488	224 566	243 849	271 202
State/Regional	..	0	0	0	0	0	0	0	0	0
Local government	..	0	0	0	0	0	0	0	0	0
Social Security Funds	..	0	0	0	0	0	0	0	0	0
Total	**..**	**25**	**2 952**	**73 948**	**140 647**	**167 568**	**199 488**	**224 566**	**243 849**	**271 202**
3000 Taxes on payroll and workforce										
Federal or Central government	..	..	..	..	..	..	..	..	..	..
State/Regional	..	..	..	..	..	..	..	..	..	..
Local government	..	..	..	..	..	..	..	..	..	..
Social Security Funds	..	..	..	..	..	..	..	..	..	..
Total	**..**	**0**	**0**	**0**	**0**	**0**	**0**	**0**	**0**	**0**
2000+3000 Total	**..**	**25**	**2 952**	**73 948**	**140 647**	**167 568**	**199 488**	**224 566**	**243 849**	**271 202**
Netherlands, million EUR										
2000 Social security contributions										
Federal or Central government	63	1 366	286	..	..	..	..	..	..	..
State/Regional	..	..	..	..	..	..	..	..	..	..
Local government	0	0	0	..	..	..	..	..	..	..
Social Security Funds	7	91	59	..	..	..	..	..	..	..
Total	**70**	**1 457**	**345**	**2 006**	**4 310**	**4 802**	**..**	**..**	**..**	**..**
3000 Taxes on payroll and workforce										
Federal or Central government	..	..	..	..	..	..	..	..	..	..
State/Regional	..	..	..	..	..	..	..	..	..	..
Local government	..	..	..	..	..	..	..	..	..	..
Social Security Funds	..	..	..	..	..	..	..	..	..	..
Total	**0**	**0**	**0**	**0**	**0**	**0**	**0**	**0**	**0**	**0**
2000+3000 Total	**70**	**1 457**	**345**	**2 006**	**4 310**	**4 802**	**0**	**0**	**0**	**0**
New Zealand, million NZD										
2000 Social security contributions										
Federal or Central government	..	..	..	..	..	..	..	..	..	..
State/Regional	..	..	..	..	..	..	..	..	..	..
Local government	..	..	..	..	..	..	..	..	..	..
Social Security Funds	..	..	..	..	..	..	..	..	..	..
Total	**0**	**0**	**0**	**0**	**0**	**0**	**0**	**0**	**0**	**0**
3000 Taxes on payroll and workforce										
Federal or Central government	..	..	..	..	..	..	..	..	..	..
State/Regional	..	..	..	..	..	..	..	..	..	..
Local government	..	..	..	..	..	..	..	..	..	..
Social Security Funds	..	..	..	..	..	..	..	..	..	..
Total	**0**	**0**	**0**	**0**	**0**	**0**	**0**	**0**	**0**	**0**
2000+3000 Total	**0**	**0**	**0**	**0**	**0**	**0**	**0**	**0**	**0**	**0**

StatLink http://dx.doi.org/10.1787/888933417027

Table 4.37. **Social security contributions and payroll taxes paid by government/Les cotisations de sécurité sociale et impôts sur les salaires payés par les administrations publiques** *(cont./suite)*

	1965	1980	1990	2000	2007	2009	2011	2012	2013	2014
Norway, million NOK										
2000 Social security contributions										
Federal or Central government	..	1 242	2 859	11 895	30 530	34 502	38 808	42 711	44 540	48 643
State/Regional	..	..	..	..	..	..	..	..	..	..
Local government	..	4 538	11 964	24 831	32 096	39 310	44 646	48 329	53 062	58 040
Social Security Funds	..	1 222	3 064	0	0	0	0	0	0	0
Total	..	**7 002**	**17 887**	**36 726**	**62 626**	**73 812**	**83 454**	**91 040**	**97 602**	**106 683**
3000 Taxes on payroll and workforce										
Federal or Central government	..	..	..	..	..	..	..	..	..	..
State/Regional	..	..	..	..	..	..	..	..	..	..
Local government	..	..	..	..	..	..	..	..	..	..
Social Security Funds	..	..	..	..	..	..	..	..	..	..
Total	..	**0**	**0**	**0**	**0**	**0**	**0**	**0**	**0**	**0**
2000+3000 Total	..	**7 002**	**17 887**	**36 726**	**62 626**	**73 812**	**83 454**	**91 040**	**97 602**	**106 683**
Poland, million PLN										
2000 Social security contributions										
Federal or Central government	..	..	..	2 834	5 801	6 403	6 733	7 634	8 172	8 645
State/Regional	..	..	..	..	..	..	..	..	..	..
Local government	..	..	..	5 204	9 654	10 795	11 946	13 152	13 402	13 752
Social Security Funds	..	..	..	943	382	881	440	498	507	512
Total	..	..	..	**8 981**	**15 837**	**18 079**	**19 119**	**21 284**	**22 081**	**22 909**
3000 Taxes on payroll and workforce										
Federal or Central government	..	..	..	..	..	..	..	..	..	..
State/Regional	..	..	..	..	..	..	..	..	..	..
Local government	..	..	..	..	..	..	..	..	..	..
Social Security Funds	..	..	..	..	..	..	..	..	..	..
Total	..	..	..	**0**	**0**	**0**	**0**	**0**	**0**	**0**
2000+3000 Total	..	..	..	**8 981**	**15 837**	**18 079**	**19 119**	**21 284**	**22 081**	**22 909**
Portugal, million EUR										
2000 Social security contributions										
Federal or Central government	..	0	0	0	..	..	..	..	..	..
State/Regional	..	..	..	..	..	..	..	..	..	..
Local government	..	0	33	197	..	..	..	..	..	..
Social Security Funds	..	4	0	0	..	..	..	..	..	..
Total	..	**4**	**33**	**197**	**0**	**0**	**0**	**0**	**0**	**0**
3000 Taxes on payroll and workforce										
Federal or Central government	..	..	..	..	..	..	..	..	..	..
State/Regional	..	..	..	..	..	..	..	..	..	..
Local government	..	..	..	..	..	..	..	..	..	..
Social Security Funds	..	..	..	..	..	..	..	..	..	..
Total	..	**0**	**0**	**0**	**0**	**0**	**0**	**0**	**0**	**0**
2000+3000 Total	..	**4**	**33**	**197**	**0**	**0**	**0**	**0**	**0**	**0**
Slovak Republic, million EUR										
2000 Social security contributions										
Federal or Central government	..	..	..	489	587	765	864	859	929	979
State/Regional	..	..	..	..	..	..	..	..	..	..
Local government	..	..	..	130	427	490	511	521	562	609
Social Security Funds	..	..	..	22	26	29	30	31	32	34
Total	..	..	..	**642**	**1 040**	**1 283**	**1 405**	**1 411**	**1 523**	**1 622**
3000 Taxes on payroll and workforce										
Federal or Central government	..	..	..	..	..	..	..	..	..	..
State/Regional	..	..	..	..	..	..	..	..	..	..
Local government	..	..	..	..	..	..	..	..	..	..
Social Security Funds	..	..	..	..	..	..	..	..	..	..
Total	..	..	..	**0**	**0**	**0**	**0**	**0**	**0**	**0**
2000+3000 Total	..	..	..	**642**	**1 040**	**1 283**	**1 405**	**1 411**	**1 523**	**1 622**

StatLink http://dx.doi.org/10.1787/888933417027

Table 4.37. **Social security contributions and payroll taxes paid by government/Les cotisations de sécurité sociale et impôts sur les salaires payés par les administrations publiques** *(cont./suite)*

	1965	1980	1990	2000	2007	2009	2011	2012	2013	2014
Slovenia, million EUR										
2000 Social security contributions										
Federal or Central government	..	..	..	161	333	395	421	412	402	365
State/Regional	..	..	..	..	..	..	..	..	..	..
Local government	..	..	..	86	175	188	198	196	197	187
Social Security Funds	..	..	..	3	7	8	8	8	7	7
Total	..	..	..	**250**	**515**	**590**	**627**	**616**	**606**	**559**
3000 Taxes on payroll and workforce										
Federal or Central government	..	..	..	55	76	6	6	7	7	7
State/Regional	..	..	..	..	..	..	..	..	..	..
Local government	..	..	..	29	36	3	3	4	4	4
Social Security Funds	..	..	..	1	2	0	0	0	0	0
Total	..	..	..	**85**	**114**	**9**	**9**	**11**	**11**	**11**
2000+3000 Total	..	..	..	**335**	**629**	**600**	**636**	**626**	**617**	**570**
Spain, million EUR										
2000 Social security contributions										
Federal or Central government	..	387	989	1 401	1 960	2 150	2 128	1 983	2 008	2 064
State/Regional	..	2	0	4 411	9 426	11 135	11 224	10 553	10 218	10 743
Local government	..	252	1 819	2 524	4 098	4 638	4 819	4 655	4 617	4 560
Social Security Funds	..	396	1 202	1 284	484	555	515	503	498	498
Total	..	**1 037**	**4 010**	**9 620**	**15 968**	**18 478**	**18 686**	**17 694**	**17 341**	**17 865**
3000 Taxes on payroll and workforce										
Federal or Central government	..	..	..	..	..	..	..	..	..	..
State/Regional	..	..	..	..	..	..	..	..	..	..
Local government	..	..	..	..	..	..	..	..	..	..
Social Security Funds	..	..	..	..	..	..	..	..	..	..
Total	..	**0**	**0**	**0**	**0**	**0**	**0**	**0**	**0**	**0**
2000+3000 Total	..	**1 037**	**4 010**	**9 620**	**15 968**	**18 478**	**18 686**	**17 694**	**17 341**	**17 865**
Sweden, million SEK										
2000 Social security contributions										
Federal or Central government	..	7 543	12 430	21 153	25 164	23 277	23 022	24 298	24 595	25 161
State/Regional	..	..	..	..	..	..	..	..	..	..
Local government	..	18 149	49 298	66 215	83 877	77 634	75 358	77 840	78 774	81 524
Social Security Funds	..	0	0	0	0	0	0	0	0	0
Total	..	**25 692**	**61 728**	**87 367**	**109 040**	**100 912**	**98 380**	**102 138**	**103 370**	**106 686**
3000 Taxes on payroll and workforce										
Federal or Central government	..	..	1 527	3 453	5 394	7 987	9 880	10 371	11 242	11 486
State/Regional	..	..	..	..	..	..	..	..	..	..
Local government	..	..	6 060	10 808	17 980	26 637	32 339	33 224	36 005	37 214
Social Security Funds	..	..	0	0	0	0	0	0	0	0
Total	..	**0**	**7 587**	**14 261**	**23 374**	**34 624**	**42 218**	**43 595**	**47 247**	**48 700**
2000+3000 Total	..	**25 692**	**69 315**	**101 628**	**132 414**	**135 536**	**140 599**	**145 733**	**150 616**	**155 386**
Suisse, millions CHF										
2000 Cotisations de sécurité sociale										
Administration fédérale ou centrale	13	91	379	414	391	438	479	497	619	539
Administration d'un Etat/Länder	34	380	850	1 100	1 431	1 613	1 710	1 790	1 832	1 846
Administrations locales	22	270	522	650	808	873	914	913	932	951
Administrations de sécurite sociale	2	21	4	14	19	20	24	24	26	26
Total	**71**	**762**	**1 755**	**2 178**	**2 649**	**2 945**	**3 127**	**3 224**	**3 408**	**3 363**
3000 Impôts sur les salaires										
Administration fédérale ou centrale	..	..	..	..	..	..	..	..	..	..
Administration d'un Etat/Länder	..	..	..	..	..	..	..	..	..	..
Administrations locales	..	..	..	..	..	..	..	..	..	..
Administrations de sécurite sociale	..	..	..	..	..	..	..	..	..	..
Total	**0**	**0**	**0**	**0**	**0**	**0**	**0**	**0**	**0**	**0**
2000+3000 Total	**71**	**762**	**1 755**	**2 178**	**2 649**	**2 945**	**3 127**	**3 224**	**3 408**	**3 363**

StatLink http://dx.doi.org/10.1787/888933417027

Table 4.37. **Social security contributions and payroll taxes paid by government/Les cotisations de sécurité sociale et impôts sur les salaires payés par les administrations publiques** *(cont./suite)*

	1965	1980	1990	2000	2007	2009	2011	2012	2013	2014
Turkey, million TRY										
2000 Social security contributions										
Federal or Central government	..	..	9	3 619	20 442	31 477	53 162	58 272	71 184	80 028
State/Regional	..	..	..	..	..	..	..	..	..	..
Local government	..	..	0	0	0	0	0	0	0	0
Social Security Funds	..	..	0	0	0	0	0	0	0	0
Total	**..**	**..**	**9**	**3 619**	**20 442**	**31 477**	**53 162**	**58 272**	**71 184**	**80 028**
3000 Taxes on payroll and workforce										
Federal or Central government	..	..	..	..	..	..	..	..	..	..
State/Regional	..	..	..	..	..	..	..	..	..	..
Local government	..	..	..	..	..	..	..	..	..	..
Social Security Funds	..	..	..	..	..	..	..	..	..	..
Total	**..**	**..**	**0**	**0**	**0**	**0**	**0**	**0**	**0**	**0**
2000+3000 Total	**..**	**..**	**9**	**3 619**	**20 442**	**31 477**	**53 162**	**58 272**	**71 184**	**80 028**
United Kingdom, million GBP										
2000 Social security contributions										
Federal or Central government	87	920	2 134	3 110	5 843	6 114	6 674	7 115	7 049	7 527
State/Regional	..	..	..	..	..	..	..	..	..	..
Local government	83	926	1 957	2 943	4 996	5 266	5 307	5 122	4 798	4 710
Social Security Funds	0	0	0	0	0	0	0	0	0	0
Total	**170**	**1 846**	**4 091**	**6 053**	**10 839**	**11 380**	**11 981**	**12 237**	**11 847**	**12 237**
3000 Taxes on payroll and workforce										
Federal or Central government	..	360	..	..	..	..	..	..	..	..
State/Regional	..	..	..	..	..	..	..	..	..	..
Local government	..	410	..	..	..	..	..	..	..	..
Social Security Funds	..	0	..	..	..	..	..	..	..	..
Total	**0**	**770**	**0**	**0**	**0**	**0**	**0**	**0**	**0**	**0**
2000+3000 Total	**170**	**2 616**	**4 091**	**6 053**	**10 839**	**11 380**	**11 981**	**12 237**	**11 847**	**12 237**
United States, million USD										
2000 Social security contributions										
Federal or Central government	301	2 053	9 055	11 320	19 590	23 391	26 364	26 648	25 725	25 555
State/Regional	699	7 585	19 802	32 815	43 624	46 367	45 688	45 839	46 332	47 136
Local government	0	0	0	0	0	0	0	0	0	0
Social Security Funds	0	0	0	0	0	0	0	0	0	0
Total	**1 000**	**9 638**	**28 857**	**44 135**	**63 214**	**69 758**	**72 052**	**72 487**	**72 057**	**72 691**
3000 Taxes on payroll and workforce										
Federal or Central government	..	..	..	..	..	..	..	..	..	..
State/Regional	..	..	..	..	..	..	..	..	..	..
Local government	..	..	..	..	..	..	..	..	..	..
Social Security Funds	..	..	..	..	..	..	..	..	..	..
Total	**0**	**0**	**0**	**0**	**0**	**0**	**0**	**0**	**0**	**0**
2000+3000 Total	**1 000**	**9 638**	**28 857**	**44 135**	**63 214**	**69 758**	**72 052**	**72 487**	**72 057**	**72 691**

1. The multi-jurisdictional sector contains units where jurisdiction is shared between two or more governments, or classification of a unit to a jurisdiction is otherwise unclear. The main type of units currently falling into this category is public universities.
2. There is a break in the series in 1990. The data are based on ESA 2010 from that year onwards.
1. Le secteur multi-juridictionnel contient des unités où la juridiction est partagée entre deux administrations publiques au moins, ou contient des unités dont le classement dans une juridiction n'est pas clair. Les universités publiques sont le principal type d'unités appartenant actuellement à cette catégorie.
2. Il y a une rupture dans les séries en 1990. À partir de cette année, les données se fondent sur le SEC 2010.

StatLink http://dx.doi.org/10.1787/888933417027

Revenue Statistics 2016
Statistiques des recettes publiques 2016

Chapter 5

Tax revenues by subsectors of general government

Chapitre 5

Recettes fiscales par sous-secteur d'administration

The tax data presented in this part of the Report have been attributed to the subsectors of general government identified in Section A.12 of the Interpretative guide (see Annex A) and the attribution criteria used are those set out in that guide.

The column «supranational» reports the customs duties collected by the twenty-one EU member states on behalf of the European Union.

Les données présentées dans cette partie ont été réparties entre les sous-secteurs d'administration identifiés dans la section A.12 du Guide d'interprétation (voir Annexe A) et les critères d'attribution utilisés sont ceux indiqués dans cette annexe.

La colonne « supranationale » indique les droits de douane collectés par les vingt et un pays membres pour le compte de l'Union européenne.

5.1. Comparative figures 2014/Graphiques comparatifs 2014

Figure 5.1. **The structure of central government tax receipts**
Graphique 5.1. **Structure des recettes fiscales des administrations centrales 2014**

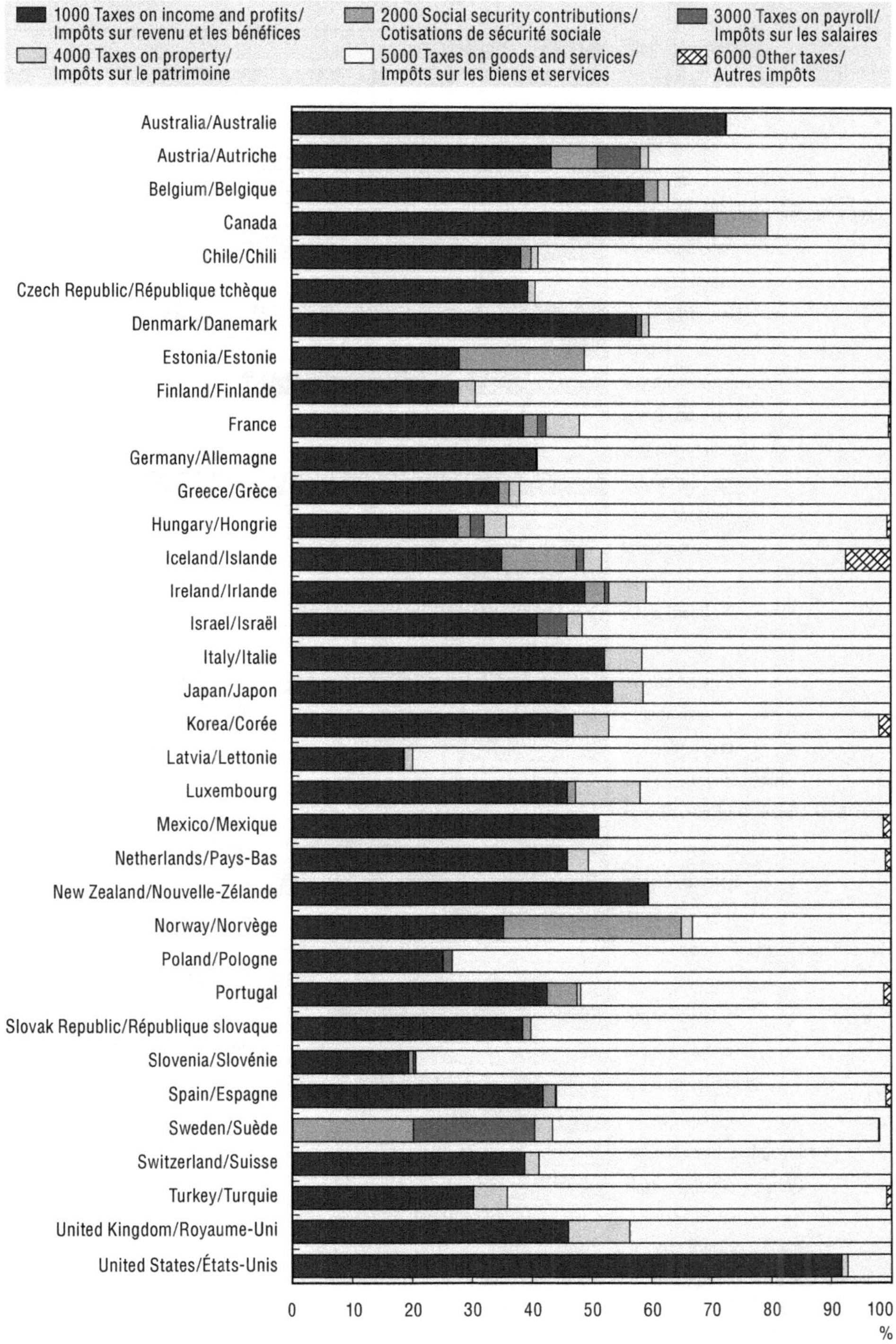

Note : This refers to only those taxes which are classified as central government taxes. Social security contributions paid to social security funds are excluded./Ceci ne tient compte que des impôts des administrations centrales. Les cotisations de sécurité sociale versées au profit des administrations de sécurité sociale sont exclues.

StatLink http://dx.doi.org/10.1787/888933416145

Figure 5.2. **The structure of state, regional and local government tax receipts**
Graphique 5.2. **Structure des recettes fiscales des administrations d'État, régionales et locales, 2014**

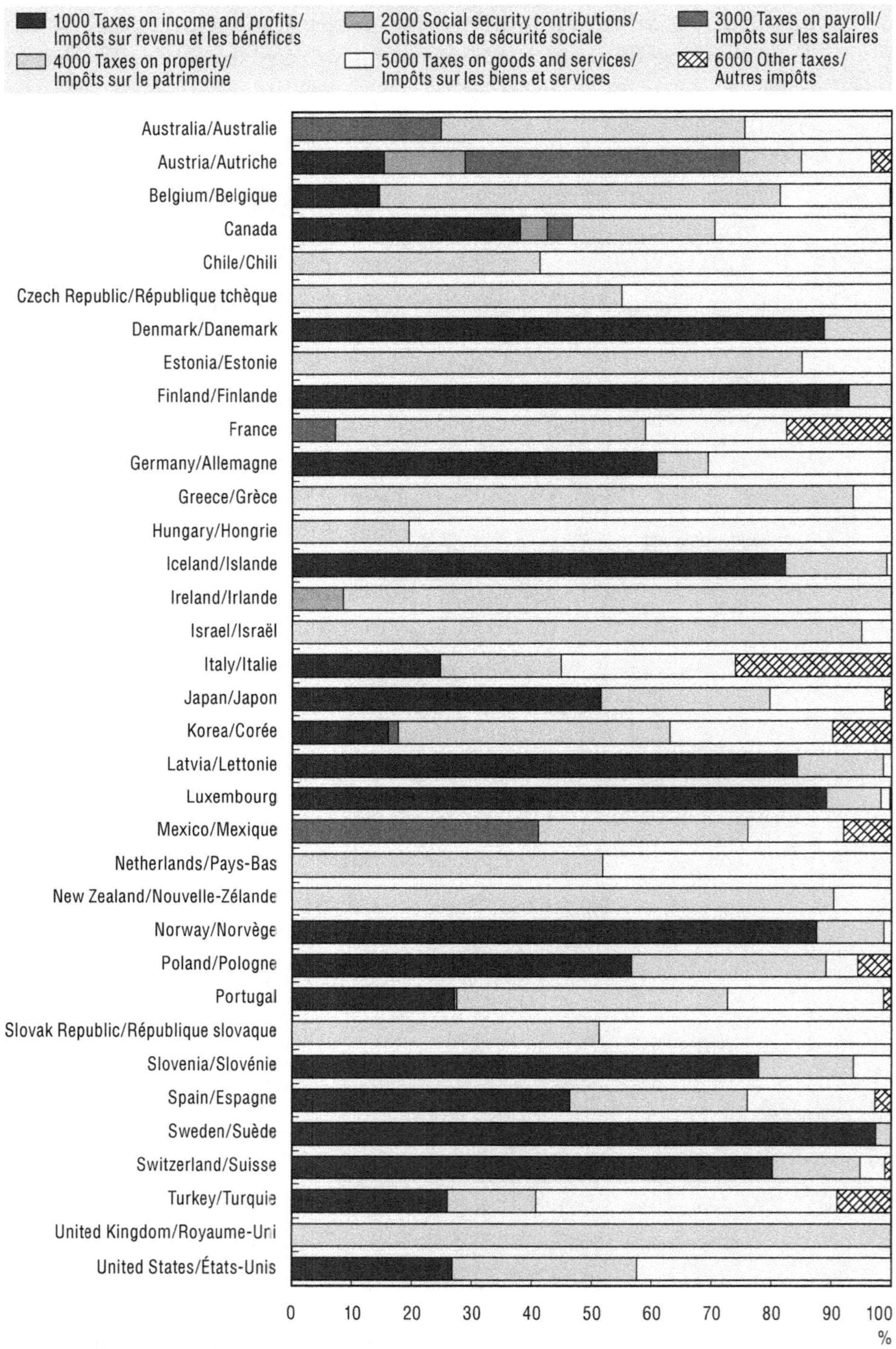

Note: This refers to only those taxes which are classified as sub-central government taxes. Social security contributions paid to social security funds are excluded./Ceci ne tient compte que des impôts des administrations infranationales. Les cotisations de sécurité sociale versées au profit des administrations de sécurité sociale sont exclues.

StatLink http://dx.doi.org/10.1787/888933416153

5.2. Comparative tables 1975, 1995, 2000 and 2014/Tableaux comparatifs 1975, 1995, 2000 et 2014

Table 5.1. Tax revenues of sub-sectors of general government as % of total tax revenue (Federal/regional countries)

Tableau 5.1. Recettes fiscales des sous-secteurs de l'administration en % du total des recettes fiscales (Pays fédéraux/régionaux)

	Total				Supranational / Supranationale			
	1975	1995	2000	2014	1975	1995	2000	2014
Federal countries / Pays fédéraux								
Australia / Australie	100.0	100.0	100.0	100.0	..	..	..	..
Austria / Autriche	100.0	100.0	100.0	100.0	..	0.0	0.5	0.3
Belgium / Belgique	100.0	100.0	100.0	100.0	1.4	1.0	0.9	0.7
Canada	100.0	100.0	100.0	100.0	..	..	..	..
Germany / Allemagne	100.0	100.0	100.0	100.0	1.2	0.6	0.5	0.4
Mexico / Mexique	..	100.0	100.0	100.0	..	..	..	..
Switzerland / Suisse	100.0	100.0	100.0	100.0	..	..	..	..
United States / États-Unis	100.0	100.0	100.0	100.0	..	..	..	..
Unweighted average / Moyenne non pondérée	100.0	100.0	100.0	100.0	1.3	0.6	0.6	0.5
Regional country / Pays régional								
Spain / Espagne[1,2]	100.0	100.0	100.0	100.0	..	0.5	0.4	0.4

	Central government / Administration centrale				State or Regional government / Administration d'un État/Région			
	1975	1995	2000	2014	1975	1995	2000	2014
Federal countries / Pays fédéraux								
Australia / Australie	80.1	77.5	81.8	80.0	15.7	19.0	15.2	16.5
Austria / Autriche	51.7	64.8	66.7	66.5	10.6	1.8	1.6	1.6
Belgium / Belgique	65.3	60.1	61.8	57.4	..	1.8	2.2	5.3
Canada	47.6	39.1	47.3	41.4	32.5	37.1	38.0	39.1
Germany / Allemagne	33.5	31.4	30.6	31.2	22.3	21.6	22.4	22.0
Mexico / Mexique	..	73.9	76.5	73.3	..	2.8	2.5	4.4
Switzerland / Suisse	30.7	31.6	37.2	35.2	27.0	23.8	22.4	24.7
United States / États-Unis	45.4	41.4	45.4	42.1	19.5	20.0	18.9	19.7
Unweighted average / Moyenne non pondérée	50.6	52.5	55.9	53.4	21.3	16.0	15.4	16.7
Regional country / Pays régional								
Spain / Espagne[1,2]	48.2	50.4	49.0	42.3	..	4.8	7.7	13.6

	Local government / Administrations locales				Social Security Funds / Administrations de sécurité sociale			
	1975	1995	2000	2014	1975	1995	2000	2014
Federal countries / Pays fédéraux								
Australia / Australie	4.2	3.4	3.0	3.5	0.0	0.0	0.0	0.0
Austria / Autriche	12.4	4.1	3.6	3.2	25.3	29.3	27.6	28.5
Belgium / Belgique	4.4	4.8	4.1	4.6	28.8	32.2	31.1	31.9
Canada	9.9	9.8	8.1	10.3	10.0	14.0	6.7	9.2
Germany / Allemagne	9.0	7.4	7.4	8.2	34.0	39.0	39.0	38.1
Mexico / Mexique	..	1.5	1.0	1.6	..	21.8	20.1	20.6
Switzerland / Suisse	20.3	17.6	16.1	15.3	22.0	27.0	24.3	24.9
United States / États-Unis	14.7	13.3	12.2	14.1	20.5	25.2	23.6	24.1
Unweighted average / Moyenne non pondérée	10.7	7.7	6.9	7.6	20.1	23.6	21.5	22.2
Regional country / Pays régional								
Spain / Espagne[1,2]	4.3	8.5	9.1	10.0	47.5	35.8	33.8	33.6

1. The total tax revenue has been reduced by the amount of any capital transfer that represents uncollected taxes. The capital transfer has been allocated between tax headings in proportion to the reported tax revenue./Le total des recettes fiscales a été diminué du montant de tout transfert en capital représentant les impôts non perçus. Le transfert en capital a été réparti entre les différentes rubriques en proportion des recettes fiscales.
2. Spain is constitutionally a non-federal country but has a highly decentralised political structure./L'Espagne est constitutionnellement un pays non fédéral mais avec une structure politique très décentralisée.

StatLink http://dx.doi.org/10.1787/888933417030

Table 5.2. **Tax revenues of sub-sectors of general government as % of total tax revenue (Unitary countries)**

Tableau 5.2. **Recettes fiscales des sous-secteurs de l'administration en % du total des recettes fiscales (Pays unitaires)**

	Supranational / Supranationale				Central government / Administration centrale			
	1975	1995	2000	2014	1975	1995	2000	2014
Chile / Chili	..	..	..	..	..	89.9	87.8	86.7
Czech Republic / République tchèque	..	..	..	0.5	..	57.7	54.9	54.5
Denmark / Danemark[1]	1.1	0.5	0.4	0.3	68.9	68.2	67.6	74.6
Estonia / Estonie	..	..	..	0.5	..	84.3	84.6	82.0
Finland / Finlande	..	0.4	0.2	0.2	56.0	46.6	53.0	47.4
France[1]	0.7	0.4	0.3	0.2	51.2	42.3	41.9	33.1
Greece / Grèce[1]	..	0.6	0.5	0.2	67.1	66.8	68.9	68.6
Hungary / Hongrie	..	..	..	0.3	..	63.8	64.5	60.8
Iceland / Islande	..	..	..	..	81.3	79.2	76.7	75.5
Ireland / Irlande	2.3	1.5	0.6	0.5	77.4	83.1	86.2	82.4
Israel / Israël	..	..	..	..	..	79.7	78.6	75.6
Italy / Italie	..	0.4	0.3	0.3	53.2	62.7	55.8	53.4
Japan / Japon	..	..	..	..	45.4	41.2	38.7	36.9
Korea / Corée	..	..	..	..	89.0	69.2	68.2	56.2
Latvia / Lettonie	..	..	..	0.5	..	43.5	49.5	50.8
Luxembourg	0.8	0.4	0.3	0.1	63.6	66.5	68.6	68.8
Netherlands / Pays-Bas	1.5	1.3	1.0	1.0	58.9	56.0	57.0	55.6
New Zealand / Nouvelle-Zélande	..	..	..	..	92.3	94.7	94.3	93.3
Norway / Norvège	..	..	..	..	50.6	58.4	84.9	86.1
Poland / Pologne	..	..	..	0.3	..	61.9	51.6	48.2
Portugal	..	0.8	0.5	0.3	65.4	72.3	69.7	67.8
Slovak Republic / République slovaque	..	..	..	0.5	..	62.5	58.0	54.6
Slovenia / Slovénie	..	..	..	0.4	..	51.8	55.1	50.0
Sweden / Suède	..	0.4	0.3	0.3	51.3	46.9	60.0	50.0
Turkey / Turquie	..	..	..	..	..	75.1	72.4	62.0
United Kingdom / Royaume-Uni	1.0	1.0	0.6	0.6	70.5	77.5	78.4	75.8
Unweighted average / Moyenne non pondérée	1.2	0.7	0.5	0.4	65.1	65.5	66.4	63.5

	Local government / Administrations locales				Social Security Funds / Administrations de sécurité sociale			
	1975	1995	2000	2014	1975	1995	2000	2014
Chile / Chili	..	6.5	7.9	7.6	..	3.6	4.4	5.8
Czech Republic / République tchèque	..	0.9	0.9	1.2	..	41.4	44.3	43.8
Denmark / Danemark[1]	30.0	31.3	30.8	25.0	0.1	0.0	1.1	0.1
Estonia / Estonie	..	0.8	1.6	1.1	..	14.9	13.8	16.5
Finland / Finlande	23.5	22.3	21.6	23.5	20.4	30.8	25.2	28.9
France[1]	7.6	11.0	10.1	13.0	40.6	46.3	47.7	53.7
Greece / Grèce[1]	3.4	0.9	0.8	3.0	29.5	31.7	29.8	28.2
Hungary / Hongrie	..	2.5	5.2	5.7	..	33.6	30.3	33.2
Iceland / Islande	18.7	20.8	23.3	24.5	0.0	0.0	0.0	0.0
Ireland / Irlande	7.3	2.7	2.0	2.8	13.1	12.7	11.2	14.3
Israel / Israël	..	6.4	6.7	8.0	..	13.9	14.7	16.4
Italy / Italie	0.9	5.4	15.3	16.5	45.9	31.5	28.5	29.8
Japan / Japon	25.6	25.3	26.1	23.5	29.0	33.5	35.2	39.7
Korea / Corée	10.1	18.7	15.1	16.9	0.9	12.1	16.7	26.9
Latvia / Lettonie	..	19.5	16.9	19.5	..	36.9	33.5	29.1
Luxembourg	6.7	6.5	5.8	3.3	29.0	26.6	25.3	27.8
Netherlands / Pays-Bas	1.2	3.1	3.3	3.8	38.4	39.5	38.7	39.6
New Zealand / Nouvelle-Zélande	7.7	5.3	5.7	6.7	0.0	0.0	0.0	0.0
Norway / Norvège	22.4	19.6	15.1	13.9	27.0	22.0	0.0	0.0
Poland / Pologne	..	8.3	9.2	13.4	..	29.8	39.2	38.1
Portugal	0.0	5.4	6.3	7.2	34.6	21.5	23.5	24.7
Slovak Republic / République slovaque	..	1.3	1.4	2.7	..	36.2	40.6	42.1
Slovenia / Slovénie	..	6.3	7.3	10.6	..	41.9	37.6	39.0
Sweden / Suède	29.2	30.9	28.8	36.9	19.5	21.8	10.9	12.7
Turkey / Turquie	..	12.8	8.9	9.4	..	12.1	18.7	28.5
United Kingdom / Royaume-Uni	11.1	3.7	4.0	5.0	17.5	17.8	17.0	18.7
Unweighted average / Moyenne non pondérée	12.8	10.7	10.8	11.7	21.6	23.5	22.6	24.5

1. The total tax revenue has been reduced by the amount of any capital transfer that represents uncollected taxes. The capital transfer has been allocated between tax headings in proportion to the reported tax revenue./Le total des recettes fiscales a été diminué du montant de tout transfert en capital représentant les impôts non perçus. Le transfert en capital a été réparti entre les différentes rubriques en proportion des recettes fiscales.

StatLink http://dx.doi.org/10.1787/888933417049

Table 5.3. **Main central government tax revenues as % of GDP at market prices (Federal/regional countries)**

Tableau 5.3. **Principales recettes fiscales de l'administration centrale en % du PIB aux prix du marché (Pays fédéraux/régionaux)**

	1000 Income & profits / Revenu & bénéfices			2000+3000 Social security & payroll / Sécurité sociale & salaires[3]			4000 Property / Patrimoine		
	1975	1995	2014	1975	1995	2014	1975	1995	2014
Federal countries / Pays fédéraux									
Australia / Australie	14.2	15.6	16.1	0.1	0.6	0.0	0.1	0.0	0.0
Austria / Autriche	6.1	10.5	12.3	3.1	4.3	4.2	0.6	0.4	0.4
Belgium / Belgique	14.2	14.6	15.2	0.5	0.6	0.6	1.0	0.6	0.5
Canada	10.4	9.9	9.1	0.0	0.0	1.2	0.0	0.0	0.0
Germany / Allemagne	4.9	4.8	4.7	0.0	0.0	0.0	0.2	0.0	0.0
Mexico / Mexique	..	3.7	5.7	..	0.0	0.0	..	0.0	0.0
Switzerland / Suisse	2.1	2.6	3.7	0.0	0.0	0.0	0.3	0.4	0.2
United States / États-Unis	9.7	9.8	10.0	0.0	0.0	0.0	0.3	0.2	0.1
Unweighted average / Moyenne non pondérée	8.8	8.9	9.6	0.5	0.7	0.8	0.3	0.2	0.2
Regional country / Pays régional									
Spain / Espagne[1,2]	3.5	8.5	6.0	0.0	0.1	0.3	1.1	0.1	0.0

	5110 General taxes / Impôts généraux			5120 Specific goods and services / Biens et services déterminés			Other taxes / Autres impôts		
	1975	1995	2014	1975	1995	2014	1975	1995	2014
Federal countries / Pays fédéraux									
Australia / Australie	1.7	2.5	3.6	4.2	3.1	2.2	0.0	0.1	0.3
Austria / Autriche	5.0	7.6	7.7	3.9	3.1	3.1	0.1	0.7	0.8
Belgium / Belgique	6.3	6.5	6.9	3.0	2.8	2.7	0.4	0.6	0.0
Canada	1.9	2.3	1.8	2.5	1.4	0.8	0.1	0.0	0.0
Germany / Allemagne	3.4	3.5	3.7	3.1	3.1	2.7	0.0	0.0	0.4
Mexico / Mexique	..	2.5	3.9	..	1.8	1.1	..	0.4	0.5
Switzerland / Suisse	2.0	3.1	3.5	2.6	1.8	1.6	0.0	0.1	0.5
United States / États-Unis	0.0	0.0	0.0	1.2	1.0	0.8	0.0	0.0	0.0
Unweighted average / Moyenne non pondérée	2.9	3.5	3.9	2.9	2.3	1.9	0.1	0.2	0.3
Regional country / Pays régional									
Spain / Espagne[1,2]	2.5	4.4	5.4	1.5	2.6	2.4	0.0	0.0	0.2

Notes : Excluding social security contributions accruing to social security funds./Sont exclues les cotisations de sécurité sociale versées aux administrations de sécurité sociale.

1. The total tax revenue has been reduced by the amount of any capital transfer that represents uncollected taxes. The capital transfer has been allocated between tax headings in proportion to the reported tax revenue./Le total des recettes fiscales a été diminué du montant de tout transfert en capital représentant les impôts non perçus. Le transfert en capital a été réparti entre les différentes rubriques en proportion des recettes fiscales.
2. Spain is constitutionally a non-federal country but has a highly decentralised political structure./L'Espagne est constitutionnellement un pays non fédéral mais avec une structure politique très décentralisée.
3. These comprise only social security contributions accruing to central government./Ne sont incluses que les cotisations de sécurité sociale versées à l'administration centrale.

StatLink http://dx.doi.org/10.1787/888933417057

Table 5.4. **Main central government tax revenues as % of GDP at market prices (Unitary countries)**

Tableau 5.4. **Principales recettes fiscales de l'administration centrale en % du PIB aux prix du marché (Pays unitaires)**

	1000 Income & profits / Revenu & bénéfices			2000+3000 Social security & payroll / Sécurité sociale & salaires[2]			4000 Property / Patrimoine		
	1975	1995	2014	1975	1995	2014	1975	1995	2014
Chile / Chili	..	4.6	6.5	..	0.5	0.3	..	0.6	0.2
Czech Republic / République tchèque	..	8.7	7.1	..	0.0	0.0	..	0.2	0.2
Denmark / Danemark[1]	12.3	15.8	21.2	0.1	0.3	0.4	0.8	0.7	0.5
Estonia / Estonie	..	10.8	7.4	..	6.9	5.6	..	0.1	0.0
Finland / Finlande	7.1	6.6	5.8	0.8	0.0	0.0	0.7	0.5	0.6
France[1]	5.5	5.6	5.8	0.7	1.1	0.6	0.6	0.6	0.8
Greece / Grèce	2.4	6.2	8.5	0.0	0.4	0.4	1.8	0.9	0.4
Hungary / Hongrie	..	8.6	6.4	..	1.3	1.0	..	0.2	0.9
Iceland / Islande	3.1	5.8	10.3	2.0	2.5	4.0	0.7	1.5	0.9
Ireland / Irlande	8.4	12.8	11.6	0.2	0.5	1.0	0.7	0.7	1.5
Israel / Israël	..	12.4	9.7	..	1.7	1.2	..	1.3	0.6
Italy / Italie	5.1	13.0	12.2	0.0	0.1	0.0	0.8	1.4	1.4
Japan / Japon	6.2	6.6	6.3	0.0	0.0	0.0	0.6	1.1	0.6
Korea / Corée	3.3	5.4	6.5	0.0	0.0	0.0	0.6	0.6	0.8
Latvia / Lettonie	..	1.7	2.7	..	0.0	0.0	..	0.1	0.2
Luxembourg	12.0	11.9	12.1	0.1	0.1	0.3	1.4	2.4	2.9
Netherlands / Pays-Bas	13.2	10.3	9.6	0.0	0.0	0.0	0.7	0.9	0.7
New Zealand / Nouvelle-Zélande	18.3	21.8	18.0	0.0	0.0	0.0	0.7	0.2	0.0
Norway / Norvège	3.8	7.0	11.7	0.8	0.6	9.9	0.4	0.4	0.6
Poland / Pologne	..	9.5	3.9	..	0.2	0.2	..	0.0	0.0
Portugal	3.3	7.4	9.9	0.5	1.8	1.2	0.5	0.3	0.1
Slovak Republic / République slovaque	..	10.1	6.5	..	0.4	0.2	..	0.1	0.0
Slovenia / Slovénie	..	4.5	3.5	..	0.5	0.2	..	0.0	0.0
Sweden / Suède	8.3	3.8	-0.4	1.7	3.6	9.0	0.4	1.2	0.7
Turkey / Turquie	..	4.2	5.4	..	0.0	0.0	..	0.5	1.0
United Kingdom / Royaume-Uni	15.3	11.0	11.2	0.0	0.0	0.0	0.6	1.9	2.5
Unweighted average / Moyenne non pondérée	8.0	8.7	8.4	0.4	0.9	1.4	0.7	0.7	0.7

	5110 General taxes / Impôts généraux			5120 Specific goods and services / Biens et services déterminés			Other taxes / Autres impôts		
	1975	1995	2014	1975	1995	2014	1975	1995	2014
Chile / Chili	..	7.5	8.2	..	3.3	1.8	..	-0.1	0.1
Czech Republic / République tchèque	..	5.8	7.4	..	4.5	2.9	..	0.9	0.4
Denmark / Danemark[1]	6.5	9.0	9.5	5.2	5.3	4.3	0.7	0.7	1.2
Estonia / Estonie	..	9.6	8.6	..	2.8	4.4	..	0.2	0.6
Finland / Finlande	5.6	7.7	9.2	5.8	5.4	4.7	0.1	0.4	0.5
France[1]	8.1	7.3	6.3	2.8	3.0	1.4	0.2	0.1	0.1
Greece / Grèce	3.4	6.3	7.3	4.3	4.3	4.4	0.7	0.5	3.5
Hungary / Hongrie	..	7.3	10.0	..	8.5	4.5	..	0.2	0.4
Iceland / Islande	8.4	9.1	8.1	9.4	4.3	3.4	0.2	0.9	2.7
Ireland / Irlande	4.1	6.7	6.0	7.6	5.0	2.9	0.6	0.6	0.8
Israel / Israël	..	10.8	9.7	..	1.5	1.8	..	0.7	0.7
Italy / Italie	3.5	5.3	5.6	3.4	4.0	3.9	0.3	0.4	0.1
Japan / Japon	0.0	1.4	3.3	2.3	1.6	1.5	0.2	0.2	0.1
Korea / Corée	1.9	3.4	3.8	6.9	3.4	2.4	0.6	0.5	0.3
Latvia / Lettonie	..	8.4	7.7	..	2.7	3.4	..	0.0	0.7
Luxembourg	3.8	4.3	7.5	2.4	4.3	3.3	0.2	0.2	0.2
Netherlands / Pays-Bas	5.5	6.1	6.4	2.5	3.0	3.3	0.6	0.8	0.8
New Zealand / Nouvelle-Zélande	2.5	8.1	9.7	3.7	3.0	2.0	0.3	0.6	0.6
Norway / Norvège	8.0	8.5	7.8	6.2	6.2	2.8	0.5	0.7	0.5
Poland / Pologne	..	6.1	7.1	..	7.3	4.1	..	0.2	0.1
Portugal	2.1	6.2	7.5	5.5	5.3	3.7	0.5	0.3	0.8
Slovak Republic / République slovaque	..	8.2	6.6	..	4.9	3.1	..	0.9	0.5
Slovenia / Slovénie	..	11.3	8.5	..	3.2	5.2	..	0.3	0.8
Sweden / Suède	4.7	8.8	9.1	4.1	3.6	2.6	0.7	0.3	0.5
Turkey / Turquie	..	4.6	5.2	..	0.9	5.7	..	2.6	0.6
United Kingdom / Royaume-Uni	3.2	5.7	6.8	4.6	4.0	3.4	0.4	0.5	0.4
Unweighted average / Moyenne non pondérée	4.4	7.1	7.4	4.8	4.1	3.3	0.4	0.5	0.7

Notes : Excluding social security contributions accruing to social security funds./Sont exclues les cotisations de sécurité sociale versées aux administrations de sécurité sociale.

1. The total tax revenue has been reduced by the amount of any capital transfer that represents uncollected taxes. The capital transfer has been allocated between tax headings in proportion to the reported tax revenue./Le total des recettes fiscales a été diminué du montant de tout transfert en capital représentant les impôts non perçus. Le transfert en capital a été réparti entre les différentes rubriques en proportion des recettes fiscales.
2. These comprise only social security contributions accruing to central government./Ne sont incluses que les cotisations de sécurité sociale versées à l'administration centrale.

StatLink http://dx.doi.org/10.1787/888933417060

Table 5.5. Main central government taxes as % of total tax revenues of central government (Federal/regional countries)

Tableau 5.5. Principales recettes de l'administration centrale en % du total des recettes fiscales de l'administration centrale (Pays fédéraux/régionaux)

	1000 Income & profits / Revenu & bénéfices			1100 Individuals / Personnes physiques			1200 Corporate / Sociétés			2000+3000 Social security & payroll / Sécurité sociale & salaires[3]		
	1975	1995	2014	1975	1995	2014	1975	1995	2014	1975	1995	2014
Federal countries / Pays fédéraux												
Australia / Australie	69.9	71.4	72.4	54.5	52.4	51.3	15.5	19.0	21.0	0.3	2.6	0.2
Austria / Autriche	32.2	39.4	43.3	25.0	31.2	34.6	6.9	4.8	7.3	16.5	16.3	14.9
Belgium / Belgique	56.0	57.0	58.8	45.5	47.9	46.3	10.5	9.0	12.5	2.0	2.2	2.2
Canada	69.4	72.5	70.5	46.7	57.7	52.0	20.9	13.0	15.8	0.0	0.0	8.9
Germany / Allemagne	42.3	41.9	40.7	37.0	38.7	36.6	5.2	3.2	4.1	0.0	0.0	0.0
Mexico / Mexique	..	44.1	51.2	..	..	26.9	..	..	23.1	..	0.0	0.0
Switzerland / Suisse	30.2	32.3	38.7	24.0	17.6	15.8	6.3	14.6	14.0	0.0	0.0	0.0
United States / États-Unis	86.5	89.2	91.7	64.9	70.7	74.8	21.6	18.5	16.9	0.0	0.0	0.0
Unweighted average / Moyenne non pondérée	55.2	56.0	58.4	42.5	45.2	42.3	12.4	11.7	14.3	2.7	2.6	3.3
Regional country / Pays régional												
Spain / Espagne[1,2]	40.6	53.8	41.8	26.3	43.3	28.2	14.3	10.1	13.4	0.0	0.8	2.1

	4000 Property / Patrimoine			5110 General taxes / Impôts généraux			5120 Specific goods and services / Biens et services déterminés			Other taxes / Autres impôts		
	1975	1995	2014	1975	1995	2014	1975	1995	2014	1975	1995	2014
Federal countries / Pays fédéraux												
Australia / Australie	0.6	0.0	0.0	8.3	11.2	16.2	20.8	14.4	9.9	0.1	0.3	1.4
Austria / Autriche	3.0	1.4	1.4	26.7	28.7	27.1	20.9	11.7	10.8	0.7	2.6	2.7
Belgium / Belgique	3.8	2.5	1.9	24.8	25.3	26.6	11.7	10.8	10.4	1.7	2.2	0.0
Canada	0.0	0.0	0.0	12.8	16.9	14.1	17.0	10.6	6.4	0.7	0.0	0.0
Germany / Allemagne	1.9	0.1	0.2	29.1	31.1	32.5	26.7	26.9	23.4	0.0	0.0	3.2
Mexico / Mexique	..	0.0	0.0	..	30.0	34.9	..	21.2	9.5	..	4.8	4.4
Switzerland / Suisse	4.1	5.3	2.3	28.3	38.3	37.2	37.3	22.6	17.0	0.0	1.5	4.7
United States / États-Unis	2.4	1.8	1.0	0.0	0.0	0.0	10.8	9.0	7.3	0.2	0.0	0.0
Unweighted average / Moyenne non pondérée	2.3	1.4	0.9	18.6	22.7	23.6	20.8	15.9	11.8	0.5	1.4	2.0
Regional country / Pays régional												
Spain / Espagne[1,2]	12.3	0.6	0.1	29.0	28.1	37.8	17.8	16.4	16.8	0.3	0.3	1.4

Notes : Excluding social security contributions accruing to social security funds./Sont exclues les cotisations de sécurité sociale versées aux administrations de sécurité sociale.

1. The total tax revenue has been reduced by the amount of any capital transfer that represents uncollected taxes. The capital transfer has been allocated between tax headings in proportion to the reported tax revenue./Le total des recettes fiscales a été diminué du montant de tout transfert en capital représentant les impôts non perçus. Le transfert en capital a été réparti entre les différentes rubriques en proportion des recettes fiscales.
2. Spain is constitutionally a non-federal country but has a highly decentralised political structure./L'Espagne est constitutionnellement un pays non fédéral mais avec une structure politique très décentralisée.
3. These comprise only social security contributions accruing to central government./Ne sont incluses que les cotisations de sécurité sociale versées à l'administration centrale.

StatLink http://dx.doi.org/10.1787/888933417079

Table 5.6. **Main central government taxes as % of total tax revenues of central government (Unitary countries)**

Tableau 5.6. **Principales recettes de l'administration centrale en % du total des recettes fiscales de l'administration centrale (Pays unitaires)**

	1000 Income & profits / Revenu & bénéfices			1100 Individuals / Personnes physiques			1200 Corporate / Sociétés			2000+3000 Social security & payroll / Sécurité sociale & salaires[2]		
	1975	1995	2014	1975	1995	2014	1975	1995	2014	1975	1995	2014
Chile / Chili	..	28.1	38.1	..	5.8	8.4	..	17.3	24.5	..	3.2	1.7
Czech Republic / République tchèque	..	43.3	39.3	..	22.1	19.8	..	21.2	19.5	..	0.0	0.0
Denmark / Danemark[1]	48.1	49.8	57.4	43.4	37.6	42.8	4.7	7.2	7.1	0.2	0.9	1.0
Estonia / Estonie	..	35.6	27.9	..	27.7	21.4	..	7.9	6.5	..	22.6	20.9
Finland / Finlande	35.3	32.0	27.7	31.0	26.0	21.8	4.3	6.0	6.0	4.1	0.1	0.0
France[1]	31.0	31.6	38.6	20.7	20.1	23.2	10.1	11.5	15.4	3.8	6.4	3.9
Greece / Grèce	18.9	33.3	34.5	12.7	18.0	24.0	5.0	9.5	7.7	0.3	2.2	1.7
Hungary / Hongrie	..	32.8	27.7	..	25.3	21.4	..	7.0	6.3	..	4.9	4.4
Iceland / Islande	13.1	24.2	35.0	10.6	20.4	19.6	2.5	3.8	11.4	8.5	10.2	13.8
Ireland / Irlande	38.8	48.6	48.9	32.5	38.5	38.8	6.2	10.1	10.1	0.9	2.0	4.0
Israel / Israël	..	43.8	40.9	..	33.2	24.5	..	10.0	13.5	..	5.9	5.0
Italy / Italie	39.0	53.9	52.2	27.7	41.4	41.3	11.3	13.8	8.9	0.0	0.5	0.0
Japan / Japon	67.2	60.5	53.6	37.8	35.5	29.6	29.4	25.0	24.0	0.0	0.0	0.0
Korea / Corée	24.7	40.5	46.9	9.6	24.2	26.0	10.0	15.8	20.9	0.0	0.0	0.0
Latvia / Lettonie	..	12.9	18.5	..	0.0	8.0	..	12.9	10.5	..	0.0	0.1
Luxembourg	60.0	51.3	46.0	43.2	33.2	33.6	16.8	18.0	12.3	0.7	0.6	1.3
Netherlands / Pays-Bas	58.7	48.7	46.0	45.6	34.2	33.7	13.1	14.5	12.3	0.0	0.0	0.0
New Zealand / Nouvelle-Zélande	72.1	64.7	59.4	58.8	47.5	41.4	12.8	12.5	14.1	0.0	0.0	0.0
Norway / Norvège	19.2	30.0	35.2	16.1	16.9	15.3	3.2	13.0	19.9	4.0	2.7	29.8
Poland / Pologne	..	40.7	25.1	..	29.7	16.3	..	11.0	8.9	..	1.0	1.5
Portugal	26.7	34.8	42.5	..	24.9	31.2	..	9.9	11.3	3.8	8.3	5.0
Slovak Republic / République slovaque	..	40.9	38.4	..	14.3	17.6	..	23.9	19.4	..	1.7	1.4
Slovenia / Slovénie	..	22.9	19.3	..	19.8	11.5	..	2.6	7.8	..	2.5	1.1
Sweden / Suède	41.7	17.9	-2.0	37.9	5.6	-14.7	3.8	12.4	12.7	8.5	17.0	42.0
Turkey / Turquie	..	32.9	30.1	..	25.1	21.0	..	7.8	9.1	..	0.0	0.0
United Kingdom / Royaume-Uni	63.5	47.7	46.0	56.8	37.2	36.2	8.8	10.4	9.9	0.0	0.0	0.0
Unweighted average / Moyenne non pondérée	41.1	38.6	37.4	32.3	25.5	23.6	9.5	12.1	12.7	2.2	3.6	5.3

	4000 Property / Patrimoine			5110 General taxes / Impôts généraux			5120 Specific goods and services / Biens et services déterminés			Other taxes / Autres impôts		
	1975	1995	2014	1975	1995	2014	1975	1995	2014	1975	1995	2014
Chile / Chili	..	3.7	1.3	..	45.1	48.0	..	20.3	10.5	..	-0.4	0.4
Czech Republic / République tchèque	..	1.2	1.2	..	28.8	41.1	..	22.4	16.1	..	4.2	2.3
Denmark / Danemark[1]	3.0	2.1	1.3	25.4	28.5	25.6	20.5	16.6	11.6	2.8	2.2	3.2
Estonia / Estonie	..	0.3	0.0	..	31.5	32.2	..	9.3	16.7	..	0.6	2.2
Finland / Finlande	3.4	2.6	2.8	27.9	37.3	44.4	28.5	26.0	22.4	0.7	1.9	2.6
France[1]	3.2	3.4	5.5	45.1	41.0	42.0	15.5	16.9	9.0	1.4	0.8	0.9
Greece / Grèce	14.1	4.9	1.7	26.9	33.8	29.8	33.9	23.3	17.8	5.9	2.5	14.4
Hungary / Hongrie	..	0.8	3.8	..	27.9	42.8	..	32.6	19.5	..	0.9	1.9
Iceland / Islande	2.8	6.4	3.0	35.1	37.8	27.5	39.5	17.6	11.6	1.0	3.8	9.2
Ireland / Irlande	3.2	2.6	6.2	19.0	25.4	25.2	35.4	19.1	12.1	2.8	2.4	3.6
Israel / Israël	..	4.5	2.5	..	38.0	40.9	..	5.5	7.7	..	2.4	3.0
Italy / Italie	5.9	5.7	6.2	26.9	22.0	24.2	26.2	16.5	16.8	2.0	1.5	0.6
Japan / Japon	6.0	10.1	5.0	0.0	13.2	27.7	24.7	14.3	12.5	2.1	1.9	1.1
Korea / Corée	4.7	4.4	6.0	14.2	25.8	27.8	51.8	25.6	17.3	4.6	3.7	2.0
Latvia / Lettonie	..	0.8	1.5	..	65.3	52.5	..	21.0	22.9	..	0.1	4.5
Luxembourg	7.1	10.2	10.8	19.1	18.6	28.5	11.9	18.6	12.6	1.2	0.8	0.7
Netherlands / Pays-Bas	3.0	4.2	3.4	24.4	28.8	30.9	11.1	14.4	15.9	2.8	3.8	3.8
New Zealand / Nouvelle-Zélande	2.6	0.7	0.1	9.8	24.0	32.1	14.4	8.9	6.4	1.2	1.7	2.0
Norway / Norvège	2.3	1.6	1.8	40.5	36.3	23.3	31.7	26.5	8.3	2.4	3.0	1.6
Poland / Pologne	..	0.0	0.0	..	26.2	46.1	..	31.2	26.4	..	1.0	0.8
Portugal	3.8	1.2	0.6	17.1	29.1	32.5	44.3	25.0	16.1	4.4	1.6	3.3
Slovak Republic / République slovaque	..	0.5	0.0	..	33.2	38.9	..	20.0	18.1	..	3.6	3.2
Slovenia / Slovénie	..	0.2	0.1	..	57.0	46.4	..	15.9	28.6	..	1.5	4.5
Sweden / Suède	2.2	5.8	3.1	23.4	41.3	42.6	20.7	16.6	12.1	3.6	1.4	2.2
Turkey / Turquie	..	3.7	5.6	..	36.1	29.2	..	7.0	31.9	..	20.3	3.2
United Kingdom / Royaume-Uni	2.4	8.1	10.2	13.4	24.6	28.0	19.0	17.4	14.1	1.8	2.2	1.6
Unweighted average / Moyenne non pondérée	4.4	3.4	3.2	23.0	32.9	35.0	26.8	18.8	16.0	2.5	2.7	3.0

Notes : Excluding social security contributions accruing to social security funds./Sont exclues les cotisations de sécurité sociale versées aux administrations de sécurité sociale.

1. The total tax revenue has been reduced by the amount of any capital transfer that represents uncollected taxes. The capital transfer has been allocated between tax headings in proportion to the reported tax revenue./Le total des recettes fiscales a été diminué du montant de tout transfert en capital représentant les impôts non perçus. Le transfert en capital a été réparti entre les différentes rubriques en proportion des recettes fiscales.
2. These comprise only social security contributions accruing to central government./Ne sont incluses que les cotisations de sécurité sociale versées à l'administration centrale.

StatLink http://dx.doi.org/10.1787/888933417087

Table 5.7. **Main state government tax revenues as % of GDP at market prices (Federal/regional countries)**

Tableau 5.7. **Principales recettes fiscales des administrations d'états en % du PIB aux prix du marché (Pays fédéraux/régionaux)**

	1000 Income & profits / Revenu & bénéfices			2000 Social security / Sécurité sociale			3000 Payroll / Salaires			4000 Property / Patrimoine		
	1975	1995	2014	1975	1995	2014	1975	1995	2014	1975	1995	2014
Federal countries / Pays fédéraux												
Australia / Australie	0.0	0.0	0.0	0.0	0.0	0.0	1.4	1.3	1.4	1.1	1.5	1.8
Austria / Autriche	1.7	0.3	0.3	0.1	0.2	0.2	0.0	0.1	0.1	0.1	0.0	0.0
Belgium / Belgique[1]	..	0.0	0.0	..	0.0	0.0	..	0.0	0.0	..	0.6	1.7
Canada	4.5	6.3	5.9	0.0	0.0	0.7	0.0	0.8	0.6	0.2	0.8	0.5
Germany / Allemagne[1]	4.8	4.1	4.3	0.0	0.0	0.0	0.0	0.0	0.0	0.5	0.5	0.5
Mexico / Mexique	..	0.0	0.0	..	0.0	0.0	..	0.1	0.4	..	0.1	0.1
Switzerland / Suisse	4.7	4.7	5.2	0.0	0.0	0.0	0.0	0.0	0.0	0.9	0.9	1.0
United States / États-Unis	1.5	2.1	2.1	0.0	0.0	0.0	0.0	0.0	0.0	0.2	0.2	0.1
Unweighted average / Moyenne non pondérée	2.9	2.2	2.2	0.0	0.0	0.1	0.2	0.3	0.3	0.5	0.6	0.7
Regional country / Pays régional												
Spain / Espagne[1,2,3]	..	0.1	3.1	..	0.0	0.0	..	0.0	0.0	..	0.8	0.9

	5110 General taxes / Impôts généraux			5120 Specific goods and services / Biens et services déterminés			5200 Taxes on use of goods / Impôts sur utilisation des biens			6000 Other taxes / Autres impôts		
	1975	1995	2014	1975	1995	2014	1975	1995	2014	1975	1995	2014
Federal countries / Pays fédéraux												
Australia / Australie	0.0	0.0	0.0	0.6	0.9	0.7	0.9	1.6	0.7	0.0	0.0	0.0
Austria / Autriche	1.3	0.0	0.0	0.5	0.1	0.1	0.2	0.0	0.0	0.0	0.0	0.0
Belgium / Belgique[1]	..	0.0	0.0	..	0.0	0.0	..	0.2	0.6	..	0.0	0.0
Canada	2.0	2.6	2.5	1.7	2.0	1.6	1.8	0.5	0.4	0.0	0.0	0.0
Germany / Allemagne[1]	1.7	2.8	3.1	0.2	0.1	0.1	0.5	0.4	0.0	0.0	0.0	0.0
Mexico / Mexique	..	0.0	0.0	..	0.0	0.0	..	0.0	0.1	..	0.0	0.0
Switzerland / Suisse	0.0	0.0	0.0	0.1	0.1	0.1	0.4	0.4	0.3	0.0	0.0	0.0
United States / États-Unis	1.5	1.8	1.6	1.1	0.9	0.8	0.5	0.4	0.5	0.0	0.0	0.0
Unweighted average / Moyenne non pondérée	1.1	0.9	0.9	0.7	0.5	0.4	0.7	0.4	0.3	0.0	0.0	0.0
Regional country / Pays régional												
Spain / Espagne[1,2,3]	..	0.1	0.2	..	0.4	0.3	..	0.0	0.0	..	0.0	0.0

1. Payments to the European Union are excluded from these comparisons./Les versements à L'Union européenne ne sont pas retenus dans ces comparaisons.
2. The total tax revenue has been reduced by the amount of any capital transfer that represents uncollected taxes. The capital transfer has been allocated between tax headings in proportion to the reported tax revenue./Le total des recettes fiscales a été diminué du montant de tout transfert en capital représentant les impôts non perçus. Le transfert en capital a été réparti entre les différentes rubriques en proportion des recettes fiscales.
3. Spain is constitutionally a non-federal country but has a highly decentralised political structure./L'Espagne est constitutionnellement un pays non fédéral mais avec une structure politique très décentralisée.

StatLink http://dx.doi.org/10.1787/888933417094

Table 5.8. **Main local government tax revenues as % of GDP at market prices (Federal/regional countries)**

Tableau 5.8. **Principales recettes fiscales des administrations locales en % du PIB aux prix du marché (Pays fédéraux/régionaux)**

	1000 Income & profits / Revenu & bénéfices			2000 Social security / Sécurité sociale			3000 Payroll / Salaires			4000 Property / Patrimoine		
	1975	1995	2014	1975	1995	2014	1975	1995	2014	1975	1995	2014
Federal countries / Pays fédéraux												
Australia / Australie	0.0	0.0	0.0	0.0	0.0	0.0	0.0	0.0	0.0	1.1	1.0	1.0
Austria / Autriche	1.8	0.0	0.0	0.1	0.1	0.1	0.5	0.8	0.9	0.5	0.2	0.2
Belgium / Belgique[1]	1.1	1.4	0.6	0.0	0.0	0.0	0.0	0.0	0.0	0.3	0.4	1.3
Canada	0.0	0.0	0.0	0.0	0.0	0.0	0.0	0.0	0.0	2.7	2.9	3.1
Germany / Allemagne[1]	2.1	2.1	2.4	0.0	0.0	0.0	0.3	0.0	0.0	0.6	0.5	0.4
Mexico / Mexique	..	0.0	0.0	..	0.0	0.0	..	0.0	0.0	..	0.1	0.2
Switzerland / Suisse	3.9	3.8	3.4	0.0	0.0	0.0	0.0	0.0	0.0	0.7	0.6	0.6
United States / États-Unis	0.2	0.2	0.2	0.0	0.0	0.0	0.0	0.0	0.0	3.0	2.6	2.6
Unweighted average / Moyenne non pondérée	1.3	1.0	0.8	0.0	0.0	0.0	0.1	0.1	0.1	1.3	1.0	1.2
Regional country / Pays régional												
Spain / Espagne[1,2,3]	0.4	0.5	0.6	0.0	0.0	0.0	0.0	0.0	0.0	0.1	0.8	1.5

	5110 General taxes / Impôts généraux			5120 Specific goods and services / Biens et services déterminés			5200 Taxes on use of goods / Impôts sur utilisation des biens			6000 Other taxes / Autres impôts		
	1975	1995	2014	1975	1995	2014	1975	1995	2014	1975	1995	2014
Federal countries / Pays fédéraux												
Australia / Australie	0.0	0.0	0.0	0.0	0.0	0.0	0.0	0.0	0.0	0.0	0.0	0.0
Austria / Autriche	0.9	0.0	0.0	0.6	0.3	0.0	0.0	0.1	0.1	0.1	0.0	0.0
Belgium / Belgique[1]	0.0	0.0	0.0	0.3	0.1	0.2	0.0	0.0	0.0	0.0	0.0	0.0
Canada	0.0	0.0	0.0	0.0	0.0	0.0	0.1	0.0	0.1	0.3	0.4	0.0
Germany / Allemagne[1]	0.0	0.0	0.1	0.0	0.0	0.0	0.0	0.0	0.0	0.0	0.0	0.0
Mexico / Mexique	..	0.0	0.0	..	0.0	0.0	..	0.0	0.0	..	0.0	0.0
Switzerland / Suisse	0.0	0.0	0.0	0.0	0.0	0.0	0.0	0.0	0.0	0.0	0.0	0.1
United States / États-Unis	0.3	0.4	0.5	0.1	0.2	0.2	0.1	0.2	0.2	0.0	0.0	0.0
Unweighted average / Moyenne non pondérée	0.2	0.0	0.1	0.2	0.1	0.1	0.0	0.0	0.0	0.1	0.1	0.0
Regional country / Pays régional												
Spain / Espagne[1,2,3]	0.2	0.4	0.5	0.0	0.1	0.2	0.0	0.7	0.4	0.0	0.1	0.2

1. Payments to the European Union are excluded from these comparisons./Les versements à L'Union européenne ne sont pas retenus dans ces comparaisons.
2. The total tax revenue has been reduced by the amount of any capital transfer that represents uncollected taxes. The capital transfer has been allocated between tax headings in proportion to the reported tax revenue./Le total des recettes fiscales a été diminué du montant de tout transfert en capital représentant les impôts non perçus. Le transfert en capital a été réparti entre les différentes rubriques en proportion des recettes fiscales.
3. Spain is constitutionally a non-federal country but has a highly decentralised political structure./L'Espagne est constitutionnellement un pays non fédéral mais avec une structure politique très décentralisée.

StatLink http://dx.doi.org/10.1787/888933417100

Table 5.9. **Main state government taxes as % of total tax revenues of state government (Federal/regional countries)**

Tableau 5.9. **Principaux impôts des administrations d'états en % du total des recettes fiscales des administrations d'états (Pays fédéraux/régionaux)**

	1000 Income & profits / Revenu & bénéfices			2000 Social security / Sécurité sociale			3000 Payroll / Salaires			4000 Property / Patrimoine		
	1975	1995	2014	1975	1995	2014	1975	1995	2014	1975	1995	2014
Federal countries / Pays fédéraux												
Australia / Australie	0.0	0.0	0.0	0.0	0.0	0.0	35.3	25.1	30.2	26.6	28.1	40.0
Austria / Autriche	44.2	42.3	46.3	1.8	24.0	22.2	0.0	10.2	8.7	1.8	2.4	2.0
Belgium / Belgique[1]	..	4.7	0.0	..	0.0	0.2	..	0.0	0.0	..	70.4	72.3
Canada	43.6	48.7	48.1	0.0	0.0	5.7	0.0	6.0	5.2	2.3	6.0	4.4
Germany / Allemagne[1]	62.8	51.9	53.9	0.0	0.0	0.0	0.0	0.0	0.0	6.2	6.1	6.3
Mexico / Mexique	..	0.0	0.0	..	0.0	0.0	..	45.3	56.4	..	44.5	16.8
Switzerland / Suisse	77.7	78.2	78.6	0.0	0.0	0.0	0.0	0.0	0.0	14.3	14.8	14.4
United States / États-Unis	31.6	38.8	41.7	0.0	0.0	0.0	0.0	0.0	0.0	4.1	3.6	2.1
Unweighted average / Moyenne non pondérée	43.3	33.1	33.6	0.3	3.0	3.5	5.9	10.8	12.6	9.2	22.0	19.8
Regional country / Pays régional												
Spain / Espagne[1,2,3]	..	8.5	67.4	..	0.0	0.0	..	0.0	0.0	..	55.9	19.9

	5110 General taxes / Impôts généraux			5120 Specific goods and services / Biens et services déterminés			5200 Taxes on use of goods / Impôts sur utilisation des biens			6000 Other taxes / Autres impôts		
	1975	1995	2014	1975	1995	2014	1975	1995	2014	1975	1995	2014
Federal countries / Pays fédéraux												
Australia / Australie	0.0	0.0	0.0	16.0	17.3	15.1	22.0	29.5	14.7	0.0	0.0	0.0
Austria / Autriche	33.9	0.0	0.0	13.5	12.2	9.1	4.4	5.0	6.7	0.4	4.0	4.9
Belgium / Belgique[1]	..	0.0	0.0	..	3.5	1.8	..	21.4	25.3	..	0.0	0.5
Canada	19.6	19.9	20.3	16.8	15.5	13.2	17.8	3.8	3.1	0.0	0.0	0.0
Germany / Allemagne[1]	21.8	35.4	38.5	2.8	1.8	1.2	6.4	4.7	0.0	0.0	0.0	0.0
Mexico / Mexique	..	0.0	0.0	..	0.3	3.1	..	6.4	17.8	..	3.5	5.9
Switzerland / Suisse	0.0	0.0	0.0	1.5	1.0	1.3	6.4	5.9	5.2	0.0	0.1	0.4
United States / États-Unis	30.8	33.2	31.0	23.6	16.1	15.9	10.0	8.3	9.2	0.0	0.0	0.0
Unweighted average / Moyenne non pondérée	17.7	11.1	11.2	12.4	8.5	7.6	11.2	10.6	10.3	0.1	0.9	1.5
Regional country / Pays régional												
Spain / Espagne[1,2,3]	..	9.2	3.6	..	23.6	7.1	..	0.6	1.0	..	2.2	1.0

1. Payments to the European Union are excluded from these comparisons./Les versements à L'Union européenne ne sont pas retenus dans ces comparaisons.
2. The total tax revenue has been reduced by the amount of any capital transfer that represents uncollected taxes. The capital transfer has been allocated between tax headings in proportion to the reported tax revenue./Le total des recettes fiscales a été diminué du montant de tout transfert en capital représentant les impôts non perçus. Le transfert en capital a été réparti entre les différentes rubriques en proportion des recettes fiscales.
3. Spain is constitutionally a non-federal country but has a highly decentralised political structure./L'Espagne est constitutionnellement un pays non fédéral mais avec une structure politique très décentralisée.

StatLink http://dx.doi.org/10.1787/888933417110

Table 5.10. **Main local government taxes as % of total tax revenues of local governments (Federal/regional countries)**

Tableau 5.10. **Principaux impôts locaux en % du total des recettes fiscales des administrations locales (Pays fédéraux/régionaux)**

	1000 Income & profits / Revenu & bénéfices			2000 Social security / Sécurité sociale			3000 Payroll / Salaires			4000 Property / Patrimoine		
	1975	1995	2014	1975	1995	2014	1975	1995	2014	1975	1995	2014
Federal countries / Pays fédéraux												
Australia / Australie	0.0	0.0	0.0	0.0	0.0	0.0	0.0	0.0	0.0	100.0	100.0	100.0
Austria / Autriche	38.9	1.5	0.0	1.3	8.6	9.1	11.5	50.0	64.1	11.2	13.2	14.6
Belgium / Belgique[1]	66.3	71.3	30.9	2.6	1.9	0.3	0.0	0.0	0.0	15.0	19.0	60.6
Canada	0.0	0.0	0.0	0.0	0.0	0.0	0.0	0.0	0.0	88.3	85.7	97.2
Germany / Allemagne[1]	69.4	79.5	79.4	0.0	0.0	0.0	9.0	0.0	0.0	20.3	19.3	14.5
Mexico / Mexique	..	0.5	0.0	..	0.0	0.0	..	0.2	0.0	..	77.5	83.5
Switzerland / Suisse	85.5	85.2	82.8	0.0	0.0	0.0	0.0	0.0	0.0	14.3	13.4	14.7
United States / États-Unis	4.3	5.8	6.1	0.0	0.0	0.0	0.0	0.0	0.0	81.9	72.9	70.7
Unweighted average / Moyenne non pondérée	37.8	30.5	24.9	0.5	1.3	1.2	2.9	6.3	8.0	47.3	50.1	57.0
Regional country / Pays régional												
Spain / Espagne[1,2,3]	57.3	19.8	17.9	0.0	0.0	0.0	0.0	0.0	0.0	8.5	29.6	42.9

	5110 General taxes / Impôts généraux			5120 Specific goods and services / Biens et services déterminés			5200 Taxes on use of goods / Impôts sur utilisation des biens			6000 Other taxes / Autres impôts		
	1975	1995	2014	1975	1995	2014	1975	1995	2014	1975	1995	2014
Federal countries / Pays fédéraux												
Australia / Australie	0.0	0.0	0.0	0.0	0.0	0.0	0.0	0.0	0.0	0.0	0.0	0.0
Austria / Autriche	19.7	0.0	0.0	14.1	19.5	3.2	1.0	5.2	6.4	2.4	2.0	2.7
Belgium / Belgique[1]	0.0	0.0	0.0	14.6	6.9	8.0	1.5	0.9	0.2	0.0	0.0	0.0
Canada	0.2	0.1	0.0	0.2	0.0	0.1	2.1	1.2	1.6	9.2	12.9	1.2
Germany / Allemagne[1]	0.0	0.0	4.7	0.5	0.5	0.9	0.4	0.3	0.4	0.4	0.3	0.2
Mexico / Mexique	..	0.0	0.0	..	16.4	2.9	..	0.2	0.1	..	5.1	13.6
Switzerland / Suisse	0.0	0.0	0.0	0.2	0.2	0.1	0.1	0.2	0.3	0.0	0.9	2.1
United States / États-Unis	7.1	10.8	12.4	3.6	4.8	4.6	3.1	5.7	6.2	0.0	0.0	0.0
Unweighted average / Moyenne non pondérée	3.8	1.4	2.1	4.7	6.0	2.5	1.2	1.7	1.9	1.7	2.6	2.5
Regional country / Pays régional												
Spain / Espagne[1,2,3]	31.0	14.8	15.4	3.2	4.1	5.7	0.0	26.9	13.1	0.0	4.7	5.0

1. Payments to the European Union are excluded from these comparisons./Les versements à L'Union européenne ne sont pas retenus dans ces comparaisons.
2. The total tax revenue has been reduced by the amount of any capital transfer that represents uncollected taxes. The capital transfer has been allocated between tax headings in proportion to the reported tax revenue./Le total des recettes fiscales a été diminué du montant de tout transfert en capital représentant les impôts non perçus. Le transfert en capital a été réparti entre les différentes rubriques en proportion des recettes fiscales.
3. Spain is constitutionally a non-federal country but has a highly decentralised political structure./L'Espagne est constitutionnellement un pays non fédéral mais avec une structure politique très décentralisée.

StatLink http://dx.doi.org/10.1787/888933417123

Table 5.11. **Main local government tax revenues as % of GDP at market prices (Unitary countries)**
Tableau 5.11. **Principaux impôts locaux en % du PIB aux prix du marché (Pays unitaires)**

	1000 Income & profits / Revenu & bénéfices			4000 Property / Patrimoine			5110 General taxes / Impôts généraux		
	1975	1995	2014	1975	1995	2014	1975	1995	2014
Chile / Chili	..	0.0	0.0	..	0.5	0.6	..	0.0	0.0
Czech Republic / République tchèque[1]	..	0.0	0.0	..	0.2	0.2	..	0.0	0.0
Denmark / Danemark[1,2]	9.6	13.6	11.0	1.5	1.0	1.4	0.0	0.0	0.0
Estonia / Estonie[1]	..	0.0	0.0	..	0.3	0.3	..	0.0	0.0
Finland / Finlande[1]	8.5	9.5	9.6	0.0	0.4	0.7	0.0	0.0	0.0
France[1,2]	0.0	0.0	0.0	1.2	2.2	3.1	0.0	0.0	0.0
Greece / Grèce	0.1	0.0	0.0	0.0	0.1	1.0	0.1	0.0	0.0
Hungary / Hongrie[1]	..	0.0	0.0	..	0.3	0.4	..	0.7	1.6
Iceland / Islande	3.6	4.6	7.9	0.8	1.2	1.6	0.0	0.6	0.0
Ireland / Irlande[1]	0.0	0.0	0.0	2.0	0.7	0.7	0.0	0.0	0.0
Israel / Israël	..	0.0	0.0	..	2.1	2.4	..	0.0	0.0
Italy / Italie[1]	0.2	0.6	1.8	0.0	0.8	1.5	0.0	0.0	0.4
Japan / Japon	2.9	3.5	3.9	1.3	2.1	2.1	0.0	0.0	0.6
Korea / Corée	0.3	0.4	0.7	0.8	2.1	1.9	0.0	0.0	0.4
Latvia / Lettonie	..	4.9	4.8	..	0.9	0.8	..	0.0	0.0
Luxembourg[1]	1.6	2.1	1.1	0.2	0.1	0.1	0.0	0.0	0.0
Netherlands / Pays-Bas[1]	0.1	0.0	0.0	0.2	0.7	0.7	0.0	0.0	0.0
New Zealand / Nouvelle-Zélande	0.0	0.0	0.0	1.9	1.7	2.0	0.0	0.0	0.0
Norway / Norvège	8.0	7.1	4.7	0.4	0.8	0.6	0.0	0.0	0.0
Poland / Pologne[1]	..	1.4	2.4	..	1.3	1.4	..	0.0	0.0
Portugal[1]	0.0	0.3	0.7	0.0	0.7	1.1	0.0	0.4	0.4
Slovak Republic / République slovaque[1]	..	0.0	0.0	..	0.4	0.4	..	0.0	0.0
Slovenia / Slovénie[1]	..	1.8	3.0	..	0.5	0.6	..	0.0	0.0
Sweden / Suède[1]	11.3	14.1	15.4	0.0	0.0	0.4	0.0	0.0	0.0
Turkey / Turquie	..	0.6	0.7	..	0.0	0.4	..	0.7	0.7
United Kingdom / Royaume-Uni[1]	0.0	0.0	0.0	3.8	1.1	1.6	0.0	0.0	0.0
Unweighted average / Moyenne non pondérée	2.9	2.5	2.6	0.9	0.9	1.1	0.0	0.1	0.2

	5120 Specific goods and services / Biens et services déterminés			5200 Taxes on use of goods / Impôts sur utilisation des biens			Other taxes / Autres impôts		
	1975	1995	2014	1975	1995	2014	1975	1995	2014
Chile / Chili	..	0.2	0.2	..	0.5	0.6	..	0.0	0.0
Czech Republic / République tchèque[1]	..	0.0	0.0	..	0.1	0.2	..	0.0	0.0
Denmark / Danemark[1,2]	0.0	0.0	0.0	0.0	0.0	0.0	0.0	0.0	0.0
Estonia / Estonie[1]	..	0.0	0.0	..	0.0	0.0	..	0.0	0.0
Finland / Finlande[1]	0.0	0.0	0.0	0.0	0.0	0.0	0.0	0.0	0.0
France[1,2]	0.1	0.3	1.2	0.1	0.3	0.2	1.2	1.8	1.5
Greece / Grèce	0.2	0.1	0.1	0.1	0.0	0.0	0.1	0.0	0.0
Hungary / Hongrie[1]	..	0.0	0.0	..	0.0	0.1	..	0.0	0.0
Iceland / Islande	0.4	0.0	0.0	0.0	0.0	0.1	0.6	0.0	0.0
Ireland / Irlande[1]	0.0	0.0	0.0	0.0	0.0	0.0	0.0	0.1	0.1
Israel / Israël	..	0.0	0.0	..	0.1	0.1	..	0.0	0.0
Italy / Italie[1]	0.0	0.2	0.5	0.0	0.3	0.6	0.0	0.3	2.5
Japan / Japon	0.8	0.6	0.4	0.3	0.3	0.4	0.0	0.1	0.1
Korea / Corée	0.2	0.6	0.3	0.2	0.4	0.5	0.0	0.1	0.5
Latvia / Lettonie	..	0.0	0.0	..	0.0	0.0	..	0.0	0.0
Luxembourg[1]	0.0	0.0	0.0	0.0	0.0	0.0	0.3	0.0	0.0
Netherlands / Pays-Bas[1]	0.0	0.0	0.0	0.1	0.5	0.7	0.0	0.0	0.0
New Zealand / Nouvelle-Zélande	0.1	0.0	0.0	0.1	0.2	0.2	0.0	0.0	0.0
Norway / Norvège	0.0	0.0	0.0	0.0	0.0	0.1	0.3	0.0	0.0
Poland / Pologne[1]	..	0.0	0.0	..	0.4	0.2	..	0.0	0.2
Portugal[1]	0.0	0.1	0.1	0.0	0.1	0.2	0.0	0.0	0.0
Slovak Republic / République slovaque[1]	..	0.1	0.0	..	0.0	0.2	..	0.0	0.2
Slovenia / Slovénie[1]	..	0.1	0.1	..	0.0	0.1	..	0.0	0.0
Sweden / Suède[1]	0.0	0.0	0.0	0.0	0.0	0.0	0.0	0.0	0.0
Turkey / Turquie	..	0.1	0.7	..	0.0	0.1	..	0.7	0.2
United Kingdom / Royaume-Uni[1]	0.0	0.0	0.0	0.0	0.0	0.0	0.0	0.0	0.0
Unweighted average / Moyenne non pondérée	0.1	0.1	0.1	0.1	0.1	0.2	0.2	0.1	0.2

1. Payments to the European Union are excluded from these comparisons./Les versements à l'Union européenne ne sont pas retenus dans ces comparaisons.
2. The total tax revenue has been reduced by the amount of any capital transfer that represents uncollected taxes. The capital transfer has been allocated between tax headings in proportion to the reported tax revenue./Le total des recettes fiscales a été diminué du montant de tout transfert en capital représentant les impôts non perçus. Le transfert en capital a été réparti entre les différentes rubriques en proportion des recettes fiscales.

StatLink http://dx.doi.org/10.1787/888933417134

Table 5.12. **Main local government taxes as % of total tax revenues of local governments (Unitary countries)**

Tableau 5.12. **Principaux impôts locaux en % du total des recettes fiscales des administrations locales (Pays unitaires)**

	1000 Income & profits / Revenu & bénéfices			1100 Of individuals / Personnes physiques			1200 Corporate / Sociétés			4000 Property / Patrimoine		
	1975	1995	2014	1975	1995	2014	1975	1995	2014	1975	1995	2014
Chile / Chili	..	0.0	0.0	..	0.0	0.0	..	0.0	0.0	..	45.0	41.3
Czech Republic / République tchèque[1]	..	0.0	0.0	..	0.0	0.0	..	0.0	0.0	..	76.7	55.0
Denmark / Danemark[1,2]	86.3	93.3	88.7	86.3	93.3	88.7	0.0	0.0	0.0	13.7	6.7	11.3
Estonia / Estonie[1]	..	0.0	0.0	..	0.0	0.0	..	0.0	0.0	..	90.5	85.1
Finland / Finlande[1]	99.8	95.4	92.8	89.9	85.2	86.1	9.9	10.2	6.7	0.0	4.5	7.1
France[1,2]	0.0	0.0	0.0	0.0	0.0	0.0	0.0	0.0	0.0	46.0	47.8	51.8
Greece / Grèce	16.5	0.0	0.0	11.0	0.0	0.0	0.0	0.0	0.0	6.6	55.0	93.6
Hungary / Hongrie[1]	..	0.0	0.0	..	0.0	0.0	..	0.0	0.0	..	28.9	19.5
Iceland / Islande	65.1	71.9	82.3	62.0	71.9	82.3	3.1	0.0	0.0	15.3	19.3	17.0
Ireland / Irlande[1]	0.0	0.0	0.0	0.0	0.0	0.0	0.0	0.0	0.0	100.0	87.9	91.5
Israel / Israël	..	0.0	0.0	..	0.0	0.0	..	0.0	0.0	..	94.1	95.0
Italy / Italie[1]	80.0	27.5	24.7	48.0	0.7	23.2	32.0	0.5	1.4	17.5	38.6	20.2
Japan / Japon	54.8	52.7	51.5	26.3	30.5	34.0	28.5	22.2	17.5	24.9	31.6	28.2
Korea / Corée	23.0	11.1	16.0	0.0	7.4	9.7	0.0	3.7	6.3	54.5	58.5	45.3
Latvia / Lettonie	..	83.8	84.3	..	83.8	84.3	..	0.0	0.0	..	15.5	14.4
Luxembourg[1]	74.6	92.8	89.1	0.0	0.0	0.0	74.6	92.8	89.1	9.3	5.9	9.1
Netherlands / Pays-Bas[1]	15.4	0.0	0.0	15.4	0.0	0.0	0.0	0.0	0.0	54.2	60.0	51.8
New Zealand / Nouvelle-Zélande	0.0	0.0	0.0	0.0	0.0	0.0	0.0	0.0	0.0	89.1	89.9	90.3
Norway / Norvège	91.9	89.7	87.5	86.3	81.6	87.5	5.7	8.2	0.0	5.2	9.7	11.2
Poland / Pologne[1]	..	45.5	56.7	..	41.1	47.9	..	4.4	8.8	..	40.6	32.4
Portugal[1]	50.0	21.8	27.1	..	11.1	18.3	..	10.7	8.8	0.0	42.5	45.2
Slovak Republic / République slovaque[1]	..	0.0	0.0	..	0.0	0.0	..	0.0	0.0	..	83.4	51.3
Slovenia / Slovénie[1]	..	75.8	77.9	..	74.9	77.9	..	0.0	0.0	..	20.7	15.8
Sweden / Suède[1]	99.6	99.7	97.5	91.5	99.7	97.5	8.2	0.0	0.0	0.0	0.0	2.5
Turkey / Turquie	..	28.1	26.0	..	21.4	17.8	..	6.7	8.1	..	2.0	14.8
United Kingdom / Royaume-Uni[1]	0.0	0.0	0.0	0.0	0.0	0.0	0.0	0.0	0.0	100.0	100.0	100.0
Unweighted average / Moyenne non pondérée	47.3	34.2	34.7	34.4	27.0	29.1	10.8	6.1	5.6	33.5	44.4	42.3

	5110 General taxes / Impôts généraux			5120 Specific goods and services / Biens et services déterminés			5200 Taxes on use of goods / Impôts sur utilisation des biens			Other taxes / Autres impôts		
	1975	1995	2014	1975	1995	2014	1975	1995	2014	1975	1995	2014
Chile / Chili	..	0.0	0.0	..	15.1	15.7	..	40.0	42.9	..	0.0	0.0
Czech Republic / République tchèque[1]	..	0.0	0.0	..	2.5	1.6	..	20.8	43.4	..	0.0	0.0
Denmark / Danemark[1,2]	0.0	0.0	0.0	0.0	0.0	0.0	0.0	0.0	0.0	0.0	0.0	0.0
Estonia / Estonie[1]	..	2.0	0.0	..	0.9	5.8	..	6.7	9.1	..	0.0	0.0
Finland / Finlande[1]	0.0	0.0	0.0	0.1	0.0	0.0	0.1	0.1	0.0	0.0	0.0	0.1
France[1,2]	0.0	0.0	0.0	4.8	7.4	20.5	3.2	6.9	3.1	46.0	37.9	24.7
Greece / Grèce	9.0	2.9	1.0	32.9	24.4	5.0	18.7	17.6	0.5	16.3	0.0	0.0
Hungary / Hongrie[1]	..	63.5	74.9	..	1.3	1.3	..	4.5	4.3	..	1.8	0.0
Iceland / Islande	0.0	8.8	0.0	7.9	0.0	0.0	0.0	0.0	0.8	11.7	0.0	0.0
Ireland / Irlande[1]	0.0	0.0	0.0	0.0	0.0	0.0	0.0	0.0	0.0	0.0	12.1	8.5
Israel / Israël	..	0.0	0.0	..	0.0	0.0	..	5.9	5.0	..	0.0	0.0
Italy / Italie[1]	0.0	0.0	5.3	0.0	7.3	6.8	2.5	13.8	8.0	0.0	12.7	35.0
Japan / Japon	0.0	0.0	8.4	15.1	9.6	6.0	4.9	5.0	4.8	0.2	1.0	1.1
Korea / Corée	0.0	0.0	9.5	11.7	16.1	6.5	10.8	11.5	11.2	0.0	2.8	11.5
Latvia / Lettonie	..	0.0	0.0	..	0.0	0.5	..	0.7	0.8	..	0.0	0.0
Luxembourg[1]	0.0	0.0	0.0	0.9	0.9	1.3	0.0	0.2	0.2	15.2	0.2	0.2
Netherlands / Pays-Bas[1]	0.0	0.0	0.0	2.7	1.4	1.9	27.7	38.7	46.3	0.0	0.0	0.0
New Zealand / Nouvelle-Zélande	0.0	0.0	0.0	6.7	1.8	0.6	4.2	8.3	9.0	0.0	0.0	0.0
Norway / Norvège	0.0	0.0	0.0	0.0	0.0	0.0	0.0	0.6	1.3	2.9	0.0	0.0
Poland / Pologne[1]	..	0.0	0.0	..	0.0	0.0	..	12.4	5.3	..	1.5	5.6
Portugal[1]	0.0	22.5	14.7	0.0	8.8	5.1	50.0	4.0	6.2	0.0	0.4	1.7
Slovak Republic / République slovaque[1]	..	0.0	0.0	..	10.2	1.4	..	1.0	24.1	..	5.5	23.2
Slovenia / Slovénie[1]	..	0.0	0.0	..	2.8	3.6	..	0.0	2.8	..	0.8	0.0
Sweden / Suède[1]	0.0	0.0	0.0	0.3	0.3	0.0	0.1	0.0	0.0	0.0	0.0	0.0
Turkey / Turquie	..	30.8	24.3	..	6.0	24.0	..	0.5	1.9	..	32.7	9.1
United Kingdom / Royaume-Uni[1]	0.0	0.0	0.0	0.0	0.0	0.0	0.0	0.0	0.0	0.0	0.0	0.0
Unweighted average / Moyenne non pondérée	0.6	5.0	5.3	5.2	4.5	4.1	7.6	7.7	8.9	5.8	4.2	4.6

1. Payments to the European Union are excluded from these comparisons./Les versements à L'Union européenne ne sont pas retenus dans ces comparaisons.
2. The total tax revenue has been reduced by the amount of any capital transfer that represents uncollected taxes. The capital transfer has been allocated between tax headings in proportion to the reported tax revenue./Le total des recettes fiscales a été diminué du montant de tout transfert en capital représentant les impôts non perçus. Le transfert en capital a été réparti entre les différentes rubriques en proportion des recettes fiscales.

StatLink http://dx.doi.org/10.1787/888933417145

5.3. Country tables, 1975, 1985, 1995, 2005 and 2014/Tableaux par pays, 1975, 1985, 1995, 2005 et 2014

Table 5.13. Australia, tax revenues by sub-sectors of government

Million AUD

	Federal government					State/Regional				
	1975	1985	1995	2005	2014	1975	1985	1995	2005	2014
1000 Taxes on income, profits and capital gains	**11 831**	**39 435**	**82 615**	**175 929**	**258 605**	**0**	**0**	**0**	**0**	**0**
1100 Of individuals	9 213	32 673	60 602	118 494	183 383	..	..	..	..	..
1200 Corporate	2 618	6 762	22 013	57 435	75 222	..	..	..	..	..
1300 Unallocable between 1100 and 1200	0	0	0	0	0	..	..	..	..	..
2000 Social security contributions	**0**	**0**	**0**	**0**	**0**	**0**	**0**	**0**	**0**	**0**
2100 Employees	..	..	..	..	..	..	..	..	..	..
2200 Employers	..	..	..	..	..	..	..	..	..	..
2300 Self-employed or non-employed	..	..	..	..	..	..	..	..	..	..
2400 Unallocable between 2100, 2200 and 2300	..	..	..	..	..	..	..	..	..	..
3000 Taxes on payroll and workforce	**54**	**56**	**3 065**	**369**	**735**	**1 171**	**3 364**	**7 120**	**13 095**	**22 250**
4000 Taxes on property	**103**	**260**	**8**	**14**	**15**	**883**	**2 770**	**7 988**	**16 923**	**29 466**
4100 Recurrent taxes on immovable property	12	31	0	0	0	217	706	1 840	4 559	9 283
4200 Recurrent taxes on net wealth	0	0	0	0	0	0	0	0	0	0
4300 Estate, inheritance and gift taxes	87	0	0	0	0	227	6	0	0	0
4400 Taxes on financial and capital transactions	4	229	8	14	15	439	2 058	6 148	12 364	20 183
4500 Non-recurrent taxes	0	0	0	0	0	0	0	0	0	0
4600 Other recurrent taxes on property	0	0	0	0	0	0	0	0	0	0
5000 Taxes on goods and services	**4 932**	**19 087**	**30 004**	**69 448**	**98 052**	**1 262**	**4 630**	**13 295**	**14 458**	**21 925**
5100 Taxes on production, sale, transfer, etc	4 919	18 890	29 613	67 822	93 120	532	1 783	4 923	8 166	11 105
5110 General taxes	1 408	5 728	12 970	40 086	57 830	0	0	0	0	0
5120 Taxes on specific goods and services	3 511	13 162	16 643	27 736	35 290	532	1 783	4 923	8 166	11 105
5130 Unallocable between 5110 and 5120	0	0	0	0	0	0	0	0	0	0
5200 Taxes on use of goods and perform activities	13	197	391	1 626	4 932	730	2 847	8 372	6 292	10 820
5300 Unallocable between 5100 and 5200	0	0	0	0	0	0	0	0	0	0
6000 Other taxes	**0**	**0**	**0**	**0**	**0**	**0**	**0**	**0**	**0**	**0**
6100 Paid solely by business	..	..	..	..	..	..	..	..	..	..
6200 Other	..	..	..	..	..	..	..	..	..	..
Total tax revenue	**16 920**	**58 838**	**115 692**	**245 760**	**357 407**	**3 316**	**10 764**	**28 403**	**44 476**	**73 641**

Million AUD

	Local government					Social Security Funds				
	1975	1985	1995	2005	2014	1975	1985	1995	2005	2014
1000 Taxes on income, profits and capital gains	**0**	**0**	**0**	**0**	**0**	**0**	**0**	**0**	**0**	**0**
1100 Of individuals	..	..	..	..	..	..	..	..	..	..
1200 Corporate	..	..	..	..	..	..	..	..	..	..
1300 Unallocable between 1100 and 1200	..	..	..	..	..	..	..	..	..	..
2000 Social security contributions	**0**	**0**	**0**	**0**	**0**	**0**	**0**	**0**	**0**	**0**
2100 Employees	..	..	..	..	..	..	..	..	..	..
2200 Employers	..	..	..	..	..	..	..	..	..	..
2300 Self-employed or non-employed	..	..	..	..	..	..	..	..	..	..
2400 Unallocable between 2100, 2200 and 2300	..	..	..	..	..	..	..	..	..	..
3000 Taxes on payroll and workforce	**0**	**0**	**0**	**0**	**0**	**0**	**0**	**0**	**0**	**0**
4000 Taxes on property	**883**	**2 627**	**5 134**	**8 726**	**15 779**	**0**	**0**	**0**	**0**	**0**
4100 Recurrent taxes on immovable property	883	2 627	5 134	8 726	15 779	..	..	..	..	..
4200 Recurrent taxes on net wealth	0	0	0	0	0	..	..	..	..	..
4300 Estate, inheritance and gift taxes	0	0	0	0	0	..	..	..	..	..
4400 Taxes on financial and capital transactions	0	0	0	0	0	..	..	..	..	..
4500 Non-recurrent taxes	0	0	0	0	0	..	..	..	..	..
4600 Other recurrent taxes on property	0	0	0	0	0	..	..	..	..	..
5000 Taxes on goods and services	**0**	**10**	**0**	**0**	**0**	**0**	**0**	**0**	**0**	**0**
5100 Taxes on production, sale, transfer, etc	0	0	0	0	0	0	0	0	0	0
5110 General taxes	0	0	0	0	0	0	0	0	0	0
5120 Taxes on specific goods and services	0	0	0	0	0	0	0	0	0	0
5130 Unallocable between 5110 and 5120	0	0	0	0	0	0	0	0	0	0
5200 Taxes on use of goods and perform activities	0	10	0	0	0	0	0	0	0	0
5300 Unallocable between 5100 and 5200	0	0	0	0	0	0	0	0	0	0
6000 Other taxes	**0**	**0**	**0**	**0**	**0**	**0**	**0**	**0**	**0**	**0**
6100 Paid solely by business	..	..	..	..	..	..	..	..	..	..
6200 Other	..	..	..	..	..	..	..	..	..	..
Total tax revenue	**883**	**2 637**	**5 134**	**8 726**	**15 779**	**0**	**0**	**0**	**0**	**0**

StatLink http://dx.doi.org/10.1787/888933417155

Table 5.14. **Austria, tax revenues by sub-sectors of government**

Million EUR

	Federal government					State/Regional				
	1975	1985	1995	2005	2014	1975	1985	1995	2005	2014
1000 Taxes on income, profits and capital gains	**3 064**	**6 436**	**18 452**	**28 781**	**40 692**	**865**	**2 927**	**547**	**742**	**1 041**
1100 Of individuals	2 381	5 389	14 649	22 126	32 526	834	2 738	459	637	903
1200 Corporate	655	1 032	2 267	5 341	6 873	31	189	88	104	138
1300 Unallocable between 1100 and 1200	27	15	1 536	1 313	1 294	0	0	0	0	0
2000 Social security contributions	**352**	**1 687**	**4 243**	**5 720**	**7 284**	**34**	**137**	**311**	**409**	**499**
2100 Employees	225	1 003	2 379	2 978	3 771	34	137	310	395	462
2200 Employers	127	684	1 830	2 498	3 226	0	0	0	0	0
2300 Self-employed or non-employed	0	0	34	243	286	0	0	1	14	37
2400 Unallocable between 2100, 2200 and 2300	0	0	0	0	0	0	0	0	0	0
3000 Taxes on payroll and workforce	**1 217**	**1 654**	**3 394**	**4 384**	**6 691**	**0**	**255**	**132**	**156**	**196**
4000 Taxes on property	**282**	**517**	**655**	**801**	**1 286**	**35**	**57**	**31**	**36**	**45**
4100 Recurrent taxes on immovable property	18	28	32	32	45	15	26	31	36	45
4200 Recurrent taxes on net wealth	226	388	58	0	0	10	9	0	0	0
4300 Estate, inheritance and gift taxes	24	49	82	140	4	10	21	0	0	0
4400 Taxes on financial and capital transactions	14	52	483	629	945	0	0	0	0	0
4500 Non-recurrent taxes	0	0	0	0	292	0	0	0	0	0
4600 Other recurrent taxes on property	0	0	0	0	0	0	0	0	0	0
5000 Taxes on goods and services	**4 554**	**10 021**	**19 830**	**29 148**	**37 835**	**1 013**	**2 142**	**222**	**234**	**356**
5100 Taxes on production, sale, transfer, etc	4 549	9 649	18 974	27 658	35 582	926	1 929	158	139	205
5110 General taxes	2 545	6 186	13 468	19 466	25 467	662	1 644	0	0	0
5120 Taxes on specific goods and services	1 991	3 424	5 462	8 148	10 116	264	285	158	139	205
5130 Unallocable between 5110 and 5120	14	38	44	45	0	0	0	0	0	0
5200 Taxes on use of goods and perform activities	5	372	856	1 489	2 253	87	213	64	95	151
5300 Unallocable between 5100 and 5200	0	0	0	0	0	0	0	0	0	0
6000 Other taxes	**52**	**328**	**305**	**436**	**272**	**8**	**20**	**51**	**64**	**109**
6100 Paid solely by business	..	..	..	..	..	..	..	..	..	..
6200 Other	..	..	..	..	..	..	..	..	..	..
Total tax revenue	**9 521**	**20 644**	**46 879**	**69 270**	**94 059**	**1 955**	**5 538**	**1 295**	**1 640**	**2 246**

Million EUR

	Local government					Social Security Funds[1]				
	1975	1985	1995	2005	2014	1975	1985	1995	2005	2014
1000 Taxes on income, profits and capital gains	**887**	**1 781**	**46**	**0**	**0**	**0**	**0**	**0**	**0**	**0**
1100 Of individuals	771	1 544	19	0	0	..	..	..	..	..
1200 Corporate	115	237	26	0	0	..	..	..	..	..
1300 Unallocable between 1100 and 1200	0	0	0	0	0	..	..	..	..	..
2000 Social security contributions	**29**	**102**	**258**	**393**	**409**	**4 667**	**11 489**	**21 173**	**28 912**	**40 262**
2100 Employees	29	102	207	297	307	1 840	4 315	8 110	10 751	14 972
2200 Employers	0	0	50	95	102	2 375	6 016	10 912	14 037	19 354
2300 Self-employed or non-employed	0	0	0	0	0	453	1 158	2 151	4 125	5 936
2400 Unallocable between 2100, 2200 and 2300	0	0	0	0	0	0	0	0	0	0
3000 Taxes on payroll and workforce	**262**	**495**	**1 492**	**2 035**	**2 892**	**0**	**0**	**0**	**0**	**0**
4000 Taxes on property	**254**	**457**	**395**	**539**	**659**	**0**	**0**	**0**	**0**	**0**
4100 Recurrent taxes on immovable property	139	253	395	539	659	..	..	..	..	..
4200 Recurrent taxes on net wealth	35	21	0	0	0	..	..	..	..	..
4300 Estate, inheritance and gift taxes	0	0	0	0	0	..	..	..	..	..
4400 Taxes on financial and capital transactions	81	183	0	0	0	..	..	..	..	..
4500 Non-recurrent taxes	0	0	0	0	0	..	..	..	..	..
4600 Other recurrent taxes on property	0	0	0	0	0	..	..	..	..	..
5000 Taxes on goods and services	**792**	**1 578**	**738**	**302**	**431**	**0**	**0**	**0**	**0**	**0**
5100 Taxes on production, sale, transfer, etc	769	1 510	582	134	144	..	..	..	..	..
5110 General taxes	448	1 026	0	0	0	..	..	..	..	..
5120 Taxes on specific goods and services	321	484	582	134	144	..	..	..	..	..
5130 Unallocable between 5110 and 5120	0	0	0	0	0	..	..	..	..	..
5200 Taxes on use of goods and perform activities	24	68	155	168	287	..	..	..	..	..
5300 Unallocable between 5100 and 5200	0	0	0	0	0	..	..	..	..	..
6000 Other taxes	**55**	**103**	**59**	**101**	**120**	**0**	**0**	**0**	**0**	**0**
6100 Paid solely by business	..	..	..	..	..	..	..	..	..	..
6200 Other	..	..	..	..	..	..	..	..	..	..
Total tax revenue	**2 279**	**4 516**	**2 986**	**3 369**	**4 511**	**4 667**	**11 489**	**21 173**	**28 912**	**40 262**

Note : Excluding customs duties collected on behalf of the European Union: 2014 = 369.4.

1. These include social security funds whose contributions are controlled by sub-central levels of government. They account for 1.9 per cent of contributions in 2014.

StatLink http://dx.doi.org/10.1787/888933417169

Tableau 5.15. **Belgique, recettes fiscales par sous-secteurs d'administration**

Million EUR

	Administration fédérale					Administration d'État/Régions				
	1975	1985	1995	2005	2014	1975	1985	1995	2005	2014
1000 Impôts sur revenu, bénéfices et gains en capital	**8 534**	**20 536**	**30 899**	**45 809**	**60 830**	..	..	**79**	**0**	**0**
1100 Des personnes physiques	6 929	17 821	25 973	35 956	47 884	..	..	79	..	..
1200 Des sociétés	1 596	2 706	4 885	9 811	12 891	..	..	0	..	..
1300 Non-ventilables entre 1100 et 1200	10	9	41	42	55	..	..	0	..	..
2000 Cotisations de sécurité sociale	**299**	**866**	**1 181**	**1 904**	**2 325**	..	..	**0**	**38**	**16**
2100 A la charge des salariés	264	716	854	1 125	1 397	..	..	..	10	8
2200 A la charge des employeurs	36	150	228	608	703	..	..	..	27	8
2300 A charge des travailleurs indép. ou sans emploi	0	0	99	171	226	..	..	..	0	0
2400 Non-ventilables entre 2100, 2200 et 2300	0	0	0	0	0	..	..	..	0	0
3000 Sur salaires ou main d'oeuvre	**0**	**0**	**0**	**0**	**0**	..	..	**0**	**0**	**0**
4000 Impôts sur le patrimoine	**583**	**1 090**	**1 340**	**873**	**1 952**	..	..	**1 168**	**4 669**	**6 938**
4100 Impôts périodiques sur la propriété immobilière	12	25	25	41	39	..	..	83	192	246
4200 Impôts périodiques sur l'actif net	0	0	8	189	625	..	..	0	0	0
4300 Impôts sur mut. par décès, succ. et donations	178	326	42	0	0	..	..	647	1 749	2 809
4400 Impôts sur transact. mobilières et immob.	393	739	1 193	521	483	..	..	438	2 728	3 598
4500 Impôts non-périodiques	0	0	73	123	804	..	..	0	0	286
4600 Autres impôts périodiques sur patrimoine	0	0	0	0	0	..	..	0	0	0
5000 Impôts sur les biens et services	**5 813**	**12 732**	**20 791**	**29 790**	**38 339**	..	..	**412**	**2 044**	**2 600**
5100 Impôts sur production, vente, transfert, etc.	5 562	11 990	19 607	29 548	38 317	..	..	58	76	172
5110 Impôts généraux	3 776	8 735	13 734	21 340	27 518	..	..	0	0	0
5120 Impôts sur biens et services déterminés	1 785	3 255	5 872	8 208	10 799	..	..	58	76	172
5130 Non-ventilables entre 5110 et 5120	0	0	0	0	0	..	..	0	0	0
5200 Impôts sur utilisation des biens et exerc. activites	249	740	1 178	234	16	..	..	355	1 968	2 428
5300 Non-ventilables entre 5100 et 5200	3	2	6	8	7	..	..	0	0	0
6000 Autres impôts	**0**	**0**	**0**	**0**	**0**	..	..	**0**	**68**	**43**
6100 A la charge exclusive des entreprises	..	..	..	..	..	..	..	..	0	0
6200 A la charge d'autres agents	..	..	..	..	..	..	..	..	68	43
Recettes fiscales totales	**15 230**	**35 224**	**54 211**	**78 376**	**103 446**	..	..	**1 659**	**6 819**	**9 598**

Million EUR

	Administrations locales					Administrations de sécurité sociale[1]				
	1975	1985	1995	2005	2014	1975	1985	1995	2005	2014
1000 Impôts sur revenu, bénéfices et gains en capital	**683**	**1 868**	**3 058**	**2 249**	**2 576**	**0**	**90**	**335**	**825**	**1 116**
1100 Des personnes physiques	675	1 868	3 058	2 249	2 576	..	90	335	825	1 116
1200 Des sociétés	8	0	0	0	0	..	0	0	0	0
1300 Non-ventilables entre 1100 et 1200	0	0	0	0	0	..	0	0	0	0
2000 Cotisations de sécurité sociale	**27**	**94**	**81**	**23**	**26**	**6 709**	**16 581**	**28 289**	**39 256**	**54 659**
2100 A la charge des salariés	27	94	81	20	20	1 749	4 870	8 268	11 558	15 262
2200 A la charge des employeurs	0	0	0	3	6	4 347	10 121	17 556	24 332	34 470
2300 A charge des travailleurs indép. ou sans emploi	0	0	0	0	0	612	1 590	2 465	3 366	4 927
2400 Non-ventilables entre 2100, 2200 et 2300	0	0	0	0	0	0	0	0	0	0
3000 Sur salaires ou main d'oeuvre	**0**	**0**	**0**	**0**	**0**	**0**	**0**	**0**	**5**	**8**
4000 Impôts sur le patrimoine	**154**	**377**	**815**	**3 599**	**5 058**	**0**	**80**	**121**	**229**	**309**
4100 Impôts périodiques sur la propriété immobilière	154	377	815	3 599	5 058	..	0	0	0	0
4200 Impôts périodiques sur l'actif net	0	0	0	0	0	..	0	0	0	0
4300 Impôts sur mut. par décès, succ. et donations	0	0	0	0	0	..	0	0	0	0
4400 Impôts sur transact. mobilières et immob.	0	0	0	0	0	..	0	0	0	0
4500 Impôts non-périodiques	0	0	0	0	0	..	0	0	0	0
4600 Autres impôts périodiques sur patrimoine	0	0	0	0	0	..	80	121	229	309
5000 Impôts sur les biens et services	**166**	**223**	**332**	**523**	**684**	**14**	**113**	**330**	**1 237**	**1 453**
5100 Impôts sur production, vente, transfert, etc.	150	206	295	437	671	14	113	330	1 237	1 453
5110 Impôts généraux	0	0	0	0	0	0	0	29	373	225
5120 Impôts sur biens et services déterminés	150	206	295	437	671	14	113	301	865	1 228
5130 Non-ventilables entre 5110 et 5120	0	0	0	0	0	0	0	0	0	0
5200 Impôts sur utilisation des biens et exerc. activites	16	17	37	87	13	0	0	0	0	0
5300 Non-ventilables entre 5100 et 5200	0	0	0	0	0	0	0	0	0	0
6000 Autres impôts	**0**	**0**	**0**	**0**	**0**	**0**	**0**	**0**	**0**	**0**
6100 A la charge exclusive des entreprises	..	..	..	..	..	..	..	..	..	..
6200 A la charge d'autres agents	..	..	..	..	..	..	..	..	..	..
Recettes fiscales totales	**1 029**	**2 562**	**4 286**	**6 394**	**8 344**	**6 723**	**16 863**	**29 075**	**41 552**	**57 544**

Note : À l'exclusion des droits de douane perçus pour le compte de l'Union européenne : 2014 = 1 256.7.

1. Y compris les administrations de sécurité sociale dont les cotisations sont contrôlées par les sous-secteurs de l'administration centrale. Leur montant est de 0.1 pour cent des cotisations en 2014.

StatLink http://dx.doi.org/10.1787/888933417177

Table 5.16. **Canada, tax revenues by sub-sectors of government**

Million CAD

	Federal government					State/Regional				
	1975	1985	1995	2005	2014	1975	1985	1995	2005	2014
1000 Taxes on income, profits and capital gains	**19 047**	**44 908**	**82 237**	**140 013**	**180 385**	**8 165**	**25 979**	**52 373**	**78 331**	**116 262**
1100 Of individuals	12 822	34 676	65 384	102 366	133 114	6 074	21 904	43 428	62 435	91 562
1200 Corporate	5 741	9 176	14 739	32 197	40 451	2 091	4 075	8 944	15 896	24 700
1300 Unallocable between 1100 and 1200	484	1 056	2 114	5 450	6 820	0	0	0	0	0
2000 Social security contributions	**0**	**0**	**0**	**17 936**	**22 896**	**0**	**0**	**0**	**11 759**	**13 800**
2100 Employees	..	..	..	7 429	9 478	..	..	..	1 858	1 048
2200 Employers	..	..	..	10 507	13 418	..	..	..	9 901	12 752
2300 Self-employed or non-employed	..	..	..	0	0	..	..	..	0	0
2400 Unallocable between 2100, 2200 and 2300	..	..	..	0	0	..	..	..	0	0
3000 Taxes on payroll and workforce	**0**	**0**	**0**	**0**	**0**	**0**	**0**	**6 498**	**9 230**	**12 595**
4000 Taxes on property	**13**	**0**	**0**	**0**	**0**	**428**	**2 292**	**6 492**	**9 298**	**10 737**
4100 Recurrent taxes on immovable property	0	..	..	..	..	85	1 112	2 960	2 934	5 556
4200 Recurrent taxes on net wealth	0	..	..	..	..	200	1 139	2 914	3 456	375
4300 Estate, inheritance and gift taxes	13	..	..	..	..	143	41	3	0	220
4400 Taxes on financial and capital transactions	0	..	..	..	..	0	0	0	1 965	3 076
4500 Non-recurrent taxes	0	..	..	..	..	0	0	615	943	1 510
4600 Other recurrent taxes on property	0	..	..	..	..	0	0	0	0	0
5000 Taxes on goods and services	**8 180**	**21 212**	**31 160**	**48 551**	**52 655**	**10 128**	**29 639**	**42 076**	**67 537**	**88 388**
5100 Taxes on production, sale, transfer, etc	8 180	21 212	31 136	48 506	52 616	6 800	20 727	37 961	61 316	80 881
5110 General taxes	3 504	9 383	19 167	35 069	36 130	3 664	11 741	21 328	33 353	49 049
5120 Taxes on specific goods and services	4 676	11 829	11 969	13 437	16 486	3 136	8 986	16 633	27 963	31 832
5130 Unallocable between 5110 and 5120	0	0	0	0	0	0	0	0	0	0
5200 Taxes on use of goods and perform activities	0	0	24	45	39	3 328	8 912	4 115	6 221	7 507
5300 Unallocable between 5100 and 5200	0	0	0	0	0	0	0	0	0	0
6000 Other taxes	**198**	**-10**	**0**	**0**	**0**	**0**	**0**	**0**	**0**	**0**
6100 Paid solely by business	0	0	..	..	..	..	..	..	..	..
6200 Other	198	-10	..	..	..	..	..	..	..	..
Total tax revenue	**27 438**	**66 110**	**113 397**	**206 500**	**255 936**	**18 721**	**57 910**	**107 439**	**176 156**	**241 782**

Million CAD

	Local government					Social Security Funds[1]				
	1975	1985	1995	2005	2014	1975	1985	1995	2005	2014
1000 Taxes on income, profits and capital gains	**0**	**0**	**0**	**0**	**0**	**0**	**0**	**0**	**0**	**0**
1100 Of individuals	..	..	..	..	..	..	..	..	..	..
1200 Corporate	..	..	..	..	..	..	..	..	..	..
1300 Unallocable between 1100 and 1200	..	..	..	..	..	..	..	..	..	..
2000 Social security contributions	**0**	**0**	**0**	**0**	**0**	**5 787**	**21 648**	**40 559**	**38 834**	**56 880**
2100 Employees	..	..	..	..	..	2 142	7 516	15 028	18 328	26 843
2200 Employers	..	..	..	..	..	3 527	13 858	24 765	18 328	26 843
2300 Self-employed or non-employed	..	..	..	..	..	118	274	766	2 177	3 194
2400 Unallocable between 2100, 2200 and 2300	..	..	..	..	..	0	0	0	0	0
3000 Taxes on payroll and workforce	**0**	**0**	**0**	**0**	**0**	**0**	**0**	**0**	**0**	**0**
4000 Taxes on property	**5 018**	**12 699**	**24 415**	**40 495**	**61 854**	**0**	**0**	**0**	**0**	**0**
4100 Recurrent taxes on immovable property	4 770	11 900	23 150	37 409	54 277	..	..	..	..	..
4200 Recurrent taxes on net wealth	0	0	0	0	0	..	..	..	..	..
4300 Estate, inheritance and gift taxes	0	0	0	0	0	..	..	..	..	..
4400 Taxes on financial and capital transactions	0	0	0	375	953	..	..	..	..	..
4500 Non-recurrent taxes	248	799	1 265	2 711	6 624	..	..	..	..	..
4600 Other recurrent taxes on property	0	0	0	0	0	..	..	..	..	..
5000 Taxes on goods and services	**142**	**247**	**406**	**833**	**1 031**	**0**	**0**	**0**	**0**	**0**
5100 Taxes on production, sale, transfer, etc	22	52	51	104	32	..	..	..	..	..
5110 General taxes	10	25	40	88	0	..	..	..	..	..
5120 Taxes on specific goods and services	12	27	11	16	32	..	..	..	..	..
5130 Unallocable between 5110 and 5120	0	0	0	0	0	..	..	..	..	..
5200 Taxes on use of goods and perform activities	120	195	355	729	999	..	..	..	..	..
5300 Unallocable between 5100 and 5200	0	0	0	0	0	..	..	..	..	..
6000 Other taxes	**525**	**2 036**	**3 662**	**1 483**	**734**	**0**	**0**	**0**	**0**	**0**
6100 Paid solely by business	437	1 507	2 946	541	0	..	..	..	..	..
6200 Other	88	529	716	942	734	..	..	..	..	..
Total tax revenue	**5 685**	**14 982**	**28 483**	**42 811**	**63 619**	**5 787**	**21 648**	**40 559**	**38 834**	**56 880**

1. These include social security funds whose contributions are controlled by sub-central levels of government. They account for 14.7 per cent of contributions in 2014.

StatLink http://dx.doi.org/10.1787/888933417185

Table 5.17. **Chile, tax revenues by sub-sectors of government**

Million CLP

	Central government					State/Regional				
	1975	1985	1995	2005	2014					
1000 Taxes on income, profits and capital gains	..	..	**1 359 694**	**5 171 293**	**9 628 037**	..	..	..	..	..
1100 Of individuals	..	..	281 293	738 620	2 114 296	..	..	..	..	..
1200 Corporate	..	..	836 725	3 155 480	6 196 077	..	..	..	..	..
1300 Unallocable between 1100 and 1200	..	..	241 676	1 277 193	1 317 664	..	..	..	..	..
2000 Social security contributions	..	..	**155 855**	**287 422**	**430 968**	..	..	..	..	..
2100 Employees	..	..	142 001	249 526	365 237	..	..	..	..	..
2200 Employers	..	..	13 854	37 896	65 731	..	..	..	..	..
2300 Self-employed or non-employed	..	..	0	0	0	..	..	..	..	..
2400 Unallocable between 2100, 2200 and 2300	..	..	0	0	0	..	..	..	..	..
3000 Taxes on payroll and workforce	..	..	**0**	**0**	**0**	..	..	..	..	..
4000 Taxes on property	..	..	**181 432**	**490 120**	**318 726**	..	..	..	..	..
4100 Recurrent taxes on immovable property	..	..	13 044	4 909	13 827	..	..	..	..	..
4200 Recurrent taxes on net wealth	..	..	0	0	0	..	..	..	..	..
4300 Estate, inheritance and gift taxes	..	..	13 245	23 184	31 340	..	..	..	..	..
4400 Taxes on financial and capital transactions	..	..	155 143	462 027	273 559	..	..	..	..	..
4500 Non-recurrent taxes	..	..	0	0	0	..	..	..	..	..
4600 Other recurrent taxes on property	..	..	0	0	0	..	..	..	..	..
5000 Taxes on goods and services	..	..	**3 179 304**	**6 831 482**	**14 835 858**	..	..	..	..	..
5100 Taxes on production, sale, transfer, etc	..	..	3 169 645	6 811 389	14 785 410	..	..	..	..	..
5110 General taxes	..	..	2 187 602	5 391 285	12 133 710	..	..	..	..	..
5120 Taxes on specific goods and services	..	..	982 043	1 420 104	2 651 700	..	..	..	..	..
5130 Unallocable between 5110 and 5120	..	..	0	0	0	..	..	..	..	..
5200 Taxes on use of goods and perform activities	..	..	9 659	20 094	50 448	..	..	..	..	..
5300 Unallocable between 5100 and 5200	..	..	0	0	0	..	..	..	..	..
6000 Other taxes	..	..	**-29 554**	**-85 954**	**50 293**	..	..	..	..	..
6100 Paid solely by business	..	..	0	0	0	..	..	..	..	..
6200 Other	..	..	-29 554	-85 954	50 293	..	..	..	..	..
Total tax revenue	..	..	**4 846 730**	**12 694 362**	**25 263 882**	..	..	..	..	..

Million CLP

	Local government					Social Security Funds				
	1975	1985	1995	2005	2014	1975	1985	1995	2005	2014
1000 Taxes on income, profits and capital gains	..	..	**0**	**0**	**0**	..	..	**0**	**0**	**0**
1100 Of individuals	..	..	0	0	0	..	..	0	0	0
1200 Corporate	..	..	0	0	0	..	..	0	0	0
1300 Unallocable between 1100 and 1200	..	..	0	0	0	..	..	0	0	0
2000 Social security contributions	..	..	**0**	**0**	**0**	..	..	**193 269**	**644 295**	**1 679 119**
2100 Employees	..	..	..	..	..	..	..	193 269	644 295	1 679 119
2200 Employers	..	..	..	..	..	..	..	0	0	0
2300 Self-employed or non-employed	..	..	..	..	..	..	..	0	0	0
2400 Unallocable between 2100, 2200 and 2300	..	..	..	..	..	..	..	0	0	0
3000 Taxes on payroll and workforce	..	..	**0**	**0**	**0**	..	..	**0**	**0**	**0**
4000 Taxes on property	..	..	**157 193**	**411 656**	**910 235**	..	..	**0**	**0**	**0**
4100 Recurrent taxes on immovable property	..	..	157 193	411 656	910 235	..	..	..	..	..
4200 Recurrent taxes on net wealth	..	..	0	0	0	..	..	..	..	..
4300 Estate, inheritance and gift taxes	..	..	0	0	0	..	..	..	..	..
4400 Taxes on financial and capital transactions	..	..	0	0	0	..	..	..	..	..
4500 Non-recurrent taxes	..	..	0	0	0	..	..	..	..	..
4600 Other recurrent taxes on property	..	..	0	0	0	..	..	..	..	..
5000 Taxes on goods and services	..	..	**192 325**	**514 952**	**1 291 983**	..	..	**0**	**0**	**0**
5100 Taxes on production, sale, transfer, etc	..	..	52 690	140 703	346 251	..	..	..	..	..
5110 General taxes	..	..	0	0	0	..	..	..	..	..
5120 Taxes on specific goods and services	..	..	52 690	140 703	346 251	..	..	..	..	..
5130 Unallocable between 5110 and 5120	..	..	0	0	0	..	..	..	..	..
5200 Taxes on use of goods and perform activities	..	..	139 635	374 249	945 732	..	..	..	..	..
5300 Unallocable between 5100 and 5200	..	..	0	0	0	..	..	..	..	..
6000 Other taxes	..	..	**0**	**0**	**0**	..	..	**0**	**0**	**0**
6100 Paid solely by business	..	..	..	..	..	..	..	..	..	..
6200 Other	..	..	..	..	..	..	..	..	..	..
Total tax revenue	..	..	**349 518**	**926 608**	**2 202 218**	..	..	**193 269**	**644 295**	**1 679 119**

StatLink http://dx.doi.org/10.1787/888933417198

Table 5.18. Czech Republic, tax revenues by sub-sectors of government

Million CZK

	Central government[1]					State/Regional				
	1975	1985	1995	2005	2014					
1000 Taxes on income, profits and capital gains	..	..	**137 616**	**273 549**	**305 712**	..	..	..	..	..
1100 Of individuals	..	..	70 361	137 937	153 763	..	..	..	..	..
1200 Corporate	..	..	67 255	135 611	151 950	..	..	..	..	..
1300 Unallocable between 1100 and 1200	..	..	0	0	0	..	..	..	..	..
2000 Social security contributions	..	..	**0**	**0**	**0**	..	..	..	..	..
2100 Employees	..	..	..	..	..	..	..	..	..	..
2200 Employers	..	..	..	..	..	..	..	..	..	..
2300 Self-employed or non-employed	..	..	..	..	..	..	..	..	..	..
2400 Unallocable between 2100, 2200 and 2300	..	..	..	..	..	..	..	..	..	..
3000 Taxes on payroll and workforce	..	..	**0**	**0**	**0**	..	..	..	..	..
4000 Taxes on property	..	..	**3 857**	**8 050**	**9 627**	..	..	..	..	..
4100 Recurrent taxes on immovable property	..	..	0	5	21	..	..	..	..	..
4200 Recurrent taxes on net wealth	..	..	0	0	0	..	..	..	..	..
4300 Estate, inheritance and gift taxes	..	..	393	728	0	..	..	..	..	..
4400 Taxes on financial and capital transactions	..	..	3 464	7 317	9 606	..	..	..	..	..
4500 Non-recurrent taxes	..	..	0	0	0	..	..	..	..	..
4600 Other recurrent taxes on property	..	..	0	0	0	..	..	..	..	..
5000 Taxes on goods and services	..	..	**175 869**	**343 554**	**462 009**	..	..	..	..	..
5100 Taxes on production, sale, transfer, etc	..	..	162 913	325 662	444 381	..	..	..	..	..
5110 General taxes	..	..	91 673	215 118	319 485	..	..	..	..	..
5120 Taxes on specific goods and services	..	..	71 240	110 544	124 896	..	..	..	..	..
5130 Unallocable between 5110 and 5120	..	..	0	0	0	..	..	..	..	..
5200 Taxes on use of goods and perform activities	..	..	12 956	17 892	17 628	..	..	..	..	..
5300 Unallocable between 5100 and 5200	..	..	0	0	0	..	..	..	..	..
6000 Other taxes	..	..	**545**	**55**	**92**	..	..	..	..	..
6100 Paid solely by business	..	..	0	0	0	..	..	..	..	..
6200 Other	..	..	545	55	92	..	..	..	..	..
Total tax revenue	..	..	**317 887**	**625 207**	**777 440**	..	..	..	..	..

Million CZK

	Local government					Social Security Funds				
	1975	1985	1995	2005	2014	1975	1985	1995	2005	2014
1000 Taxes on income, profits and capital gains	..	..	**0**	**0**	**0**	..	..	**0**	**0**	**0**
1100 Of individuals	..	..	0	0	0	..	..	0	0	0
1200 Corporate	..	..	0	0	0	..	..	0	0	0
1300 Unallocable between 1100 and 1200	..	..	0	0	0	..	..	0	0	0
2000 Social security contributions	..	..	**0**	**0**	**0**	..	..	**227 871**	**481 626**	**625 508**
2100 Employees	..	..	..	..	..	..	..	54 536	108 316	126 894
2200 Employers	..	..	..	..	..	..	..	148 342	307 618	395 998
2300 Self-employed or non-employed	..	..	..	..	..	..	..	24 993	65 692	102 616
2400 Unallocable between 2100, 2200 and 2300	..	..	..	..	..	..	..	0	0	0
3000 Taxes on payroll and workforce	..	..	**0**	**0**	**0**	..	..	**0**	**0**	**0**
4000 Taxes on property	..	..	**3 778**	**4 987**	**9 541**	..	..	**0**	**0**	**0**
4100 Recurrent taxes on immovable property	..	..	3 778	4 987	9 541	..	..	..	..	..
4200 Recurrent taxes on net wealth	..	..	0	0	0	..	..	..	..	..
4300 Estate, inheritance and gift taxes	..	..	0	0	0	..	..	..	..	..
4400 Taxes on financial and capital transactions	..	..	0	0	0	..	..	..	..	..
4500 Non-recurrent taxes	..	..	0	0	0	..	..	..	..	..
4600 Other recurrent taxes on property	..	..	0	0	0	..	..	..	..	..
5000 Taxes on goods and services	..	..	**1 150**	**7 395**	**7 817**	..	..	**0**	**0**	**0**
5100 Taxes on production, sale, transfer, etc	..	..	124	199	279	..	..	..	..	..
5110 General taxes	..	..	0	0	0	..	..	..	..	..
5120 Taxes on specific goods and services	..	..	124	199	279	..	..	..	..	..
5130 Unallocable between 5110 and 5120	..	..	0	0	0	..	..	..	..	..
5200 Taxes on use of goods and perform activities	..	..	1 026	7 196	7 538	..	..	..	..	..
5300 Unallocable between 5100 and 5200	..	..	0	0	0	..	..	..	..	..
6000 Other taxes	..	..	**0**	**0**	**0**	..	..	**0**	**0**	**0**
6100 Paid solely by business	..	..	..	..	..	..	..	..	..	..
6200 Other	..	..	..	..	..	..	..	..	..	..
Total tax revenue	..	..	**4 928**	**12 382**	**17 358**	..	..	**227 871**	**481 626**	**625 508**

Note : Excluding customs duties collected on behalf of the European Union: 2014 = 6 968.2.

1. Tax revenues of the regions are reported under the heading of central government up to and including 1995 and under local government thereafter.

StatLink http://dx.doi.org/10.1787/888933417204

Table 5.19. **Denmark, tax revenues by sub-sectors of government**

Million DKK

	Central government					State/Regional				
	1975	1985	1995	2005	2014					
1000 Taxes on income, profits and capital gains	**28 694**	**94 221**	**164 962**	**258 922**	**417 070**	..	..	..	..	..
1100 Of individuals	25 904	73 303	124 613	167 082	310 788	..	..	..	..	..
1200 Corporate	2 790	14 473	23 803	54 597	51 892	..	..	..	..	..
1300 Unallocable between 1100 and 1200	0	6 445	16 546	37 244	54 391	..	..	..	..	..
2000 Social security contributions	**143**	**3 626**	**562**	**1 180**	**727**	..	..	..	..	..
2100 Employees	0	1	559	1 177	714	..	..	..	..	..
2200 Employers	142	3 625	3	3	13	..	..	..	..	..
2300 Self-employed or non-employed	0	0	0	0	0	..	..	..	..	..
2400 Unallocable between 2100, 2200 and 2300	0	0	0	0	0	..	..	..	..	..
3000 Taxes on payroll and workforce	**0**	**2 162**	**2 262**	**2 907**	**6 343**	..	..	..	..	..
4000 Taxes on property	**1 779**	**7 222**	**7 094**	**11 801**	**9 135**	..	..	..	..	..
4100 Recurrent taxes on immovable property	16	152	170	0	0	..	..	..	..	..
4200 Recurrent taxes on net wealth	414	1 408	930	0	0	..	..	..	..	..
4300 Estate, inheritance and gift taxes	336	1 418	2 372	3 154	3 848	..	..	..	..	..
4400 Taxes on financial and capital transactions	936	4 208	3 584	8 613	5 253	..	..	..	..	..
4500 Non-recurrent taxes	77	36	38	34	34	..	..	..	..	..
4600 Other recurrent taxes on property	0	0	0	0	0	..	..	..	..	..
5000 Taxes on goods and services	**29 014**	**100 038**	**156 578**	**253 352**	**293 268**	..	..	..	..	..
5100 Taxes on production, sale, transfer, etc	27 338	96 828	149 393	239 951	270 441	..	..	..	..	..
5110 General taxes	15 117	60 462	94 368	154 654	186 261	..	..	..	..	..
5120 Taxes on specific goods and services	12 221	36 365	55 026	85 298	84 180	..	..	..	..	..
5130 Unallocable between 5110 and 5120	0	0	0	0	0	..	..	..	..	..
5200 Taxes on use of goods and perform activities	1 676	3 210	4 739	9 379	15 972	..	..	..	..	..
5300 Unallocable between 5100 and 5200	0	0	2 446	4 021	6 855	..	..	..	..	..
6000 Other taxes	**0**	**0**	**0**	**203**	**220**	..	..	..	..	..
6100 Paid solely by business	..	..	..	203	220	..	..	..	..	..
6200 Other	..	..	..	0	0	..	..	..	..	..
Total tax revenue	**59 630**	**207 268**	**331 457**	**528 366**	**726 763**	..	..	..	..	..

Million DKK

	Local government					Social Security Funds				
	1975	1985	1995	2005	2014	1975	1985	1995	2005	2014
1000 Taxes on income, profits and capital gains	**22 171**	**76 364**	**140 762**	**214 581**	**214 095**	**0**	**0**	**0**	**0**	**0**
1100 Of individuals	22 170	76 358	140 758	214 581	214 095	..	..	..	..	..
1200 Corporate	1	5	5	0	0	..	..	..	..	..
1300 Unallocable between 1100 and 1200	0	0	0	0	0	..	..	..	..	..
2000 Social security contributions	**0**	**0**	**0**	**0**	**0**	**58**	**72**	**0**	**529**	**724**
2100 Employees	..	..	..	..	0	0	0	..	0	0
2200 Employers	..	..	..	..	0	58	72	..	529	724
2300 Self-employed or non-employed	..	..	..	..	0	0	0	..	0	0
2400 Unallocable between 2100, 2200 and 2300	..	..	..	..	0	0	0	..	0	0
3000 Taxes on payroll and workforce	**0**	**0**	**0**	**0**	**0**	**0**	**0**	**0**	**0**	**0**
4000 Taxes on property	**3 518**	**5 451**	**10 155**	**17 466**	**27 156**	**0**	**0**	**0**	**0**	**0**
4100 Recurrent taxes on immovable property	3 518	5 451	10 155	17 466	27 156	..	..	..	..	..
4200 Recurrent taxes on net wealth	0	0	0	0	0	..	..	..	..	..
4300 Estate, inheritance and gift taxes	0	0	0	0	0	..	..	..	..	..
4400 Taxes on financial and capital transactions	0	0	0	0	0	..	..	..	..	..
4500 Non-recurrent taxes	0	0	0	0	0	..	..	..	..	..
4600 Other recurrent taxes on property	0	0	0	0	0	..	..	..	..	..
5000 Taxes on goods and services	**0**	**0**	**0**	**0**	**0**	**0**	**0**	**0**	**0**	**0**
5100 Taxes on production, sale, transfer, etc	0	0	0	0	0	..	..	..	..	..
5110 General taxes	0	0	0	0	0	..	..	..	..	..
5120 Taxes on specific goods and services	0	0	0	0	0	..	..	..	..	..
5130 Unallocable between 5110 and 5120	0	0	0	0	0	..	..	..	..	..
5200 Taxes on use of goods and perform activities	0	0	0	0	0	..	..	..	..	..
5300 Unallocable between 5100 and 5200	0	0	0	0	0	..	..	..	..	..
6000 Other taxes	**0**	**0**	**0**	**0**	**0**	**0**	**0**	**0**	**0**	**0**
6100 Paid solely by business	..	..	..	..	..	..	..	..	..	..
6200 Other	..	..	..	..	..	..	..	..	..	..
Total tax revenue	**25 689**	**81 814**	**150 918**	**232 047**	**241 251**	**58**	**72**	**0**	**529**	**724**

Note : Excluding customs duties collected on behalf of the European Union: 2014 = 3 000.6.

StatLink http://dx.doi.org/10.1787/888933417211

Table 5.20. **Estonia, tax revenues by sub-sectors of government**

Million EUR

	Central government					State/Regional				
	1975	1985	1995	2005	2014					
1000 Taxes on income, profits and capital gains	..	..	**301**	**782**	**1 479**	..	..	..	..	..
1100 Of individuals	..	..	234	622	1 134	..	..	..	..	..
1200 Corporate	..	..	67	160	345	..	..	..	..	..
1300 Unallocable between 1100 and 1200	..	..	0	0	0	..	..	..	..	..
2000 Social security contributions	..	..	**191**	**636**	**1 111**	..	..	..	..	..
2100 Employees	..	..	0	0	0	..	..	..	..	..
2200 Employers	..	..	191	636	1 099	..	..	..	..	..
2300 Self-employed or non-employed	..	..	0	0	12	..	..	..	..	..
2400 Unallocable between 2100, 2200 and 2300	..	..	0	0	0	..	..	..	..	..
3000 Taxes on payroll and workforce	..	..	**0**	**0**	**0**	..	..	..	..	..
4000 Taxes on property	..	..	**3**	**0**	**0**	..	..	..	..	..
4100 Recurrent taxes on immovable property	..	..	3	..	..	..	..	..	..	..
4200 Recurrent taxes on net wealth	..	..	0	..	..	..	..	..	..	..
4300 Estate, inheritance and gift taxes	..	..	0	..	..	..	..	..	..	..
4400 Taxes on financial and capital transactions	..	..	0	..	..	..	..	..	..	..
4500 Non-recurrent taxes	..	..	0	..	..	..	..	..	..	..
4600 Other recurrent taxes on property	..	..	0	..	..	..	..	..	..	..
5000 Taxes on goods and services	..	..	**350**	**1 385**	**2 717**	..	..	..	..	..
5100 Taxes on production, sale, transfer, etc	..	..	345	1 348	2 598	..	..	..	..	..
5110 General taxes	..	..	266	908	1 711	..	..	..	..	..
5120 Taxes on specific goods and services	..	..	79	440	887	..	..	..	..	..
5130 Unallocable between 5110 and 5120	..	..	0	0	0	..	..	..	..	..
5200 Taxes on use of goods and perform activities	..	..	5	37	119	..	..	..	..	..
5300 Unallocable between 5100 and 5200	..	..	0	0	0	..	..	..	..	..
6000 Other taxes	..	..	**0**	**0**	**0**	..	..	..	..	..
6100 Paid solely by business	..	..	..	..	..	..	..	..	..	..
6200 Other	..	..	..	..	..	..	..	..	..	..
Total tax revenue	..	..	**845**	**2 803**	**5 307**	..	..	..	..	..

Million EUR

	Local government					Social Security Funds				
	1975	1985	1995	2005	2014	1975	1985	1995	2005	2014
1000 Taxes on income, profits and capital gains	..	..	**0**	**0**	**0**	..	..	**0**	**0**	**0**
1100 Of individuals	..	..	0	0	0	..	..	..	..	..
1200 Corporate	..	..	0	0	0	..	..	..	..	..
1300 Unallocable between 1100 and 1200	..	..	0	0	0	..	..	..	..	..
2000 Social security contributions	..	..	**0**	**0**	**0**	..	..	**149**	**511**	**1 067**
2100 Employees	..	..	..	..	..	..	..	0	31	114
2200 Employers	..	..	..	..	..	..	..	143	466	946
2300 Self-employed or non-employed	..	..	..	..	..	..	..	6	14	8
2400 Unallocable between 2100, 2200 and 2300	..	..	..	..	..	..	..	0	0	0
3000 Taxes on payroll and workforce	..	..	**0**	**0**	**0**	..	..	**0**	**0**	**0**
4000 Taxes on property	..	..	**7**	**32**	**59**	..	..	**0**	**0**	**0**
4100 Recurrent taxes on immovable property	..	..	7	32	59	..	..	..	..	..
4200 Recurrent taxes on net wealth	..	..	0	0	0	..	..	..	..	..
4300 Estate, inheritance and gift taxes	..	..	0	0	0	..	..	..	..	..
4400 Taxes on financial and capital transactions	..	..	0	0	0	..	..	..	..	..
4500 Non-recurrent taxes	..	..	0	0	0	..	..	..	..	..
4600 Other recurrent taxes on property	..	..	0	0	0	..	..	..	..	..
5000 Taxes on goods and services	..	..	**1**	**7**	**10**	..	..	**0**	**0**	**0**
5100 Taxes on production, sale, transfer, etc	..	..	0	2	4	..	..	..	..	..
5110 General taxes	..	..	0	0	0	..	..	..	..	..
5120 Taxes on specific goods and services	..	..	0	2	4	..	..	..	..	..
5130 Unallocable between 5110 and 5120	..	..	0	0	0	..	..	..	..	..
5200 Taxes on use of goods and perform activities	..	..	1	5	6	..	..	..	..	..
5300 Unallocable between 5100 and 5200	..	..	0	0	0	..	..	..	..	..
6000 Other taxes	..	..	**0**	**0**	**0**	..	..	**0**	**0**	**0**
6100 Paid solely by business	..	..	..	..	..	..	..	..	..	..
6200 Other	..	..	..	..	..	..	..	..	..	..
Total tax revenue	..	..	**8**	**40**	**69**	..	..	**149**	**511**	**1 067**

Note: Excluding customs duties collected on behalf of the European Union: 2014 = 30.3.

StatLink http://dx.doi.org/10.1787/888933417224

Table 5.21. **Finland, tax revenues by sub-sectors of government**

Million EUR

	Central government					State/Regional				
	1975	1985	1995	2005	2014					
1000 Taxes on income, profits and capital gains	**1 304**	**4 255**	**6 538**	**12 885**	**11 834**	..	..	..	..	..
1100 Of individuals	1 146	3 875	5 320	8 791	9 290	..	..	..	..	..
1200 Corporate	157	380	1 219	4 094	2 544	..	..	..	..	..
1300 Unallocable between 1100 and 1200	0	0	0	0	0	..	..	..	..	..
2000 Social security contributions	**0**	**0**	**25**	**0**	**0**	..	..	..	..	..
2100 Employees	..	..	0	..	..	..	..	..	..	..
2200 Employers	..	..	25	..	..	..	..	..	..	..
2300 Self-employed or non-employed	..	..	0	..	..	..	..	..	..	..
2400 Unallocable between 2100, 2200 and 2300	..	..	0	..	..	..	..	..	..	..
3000 Taxes on payroll and workforce	**153**	**113**	**0**	**0**	**0**	..	..	..	..	..
4000 Taxes on property	**127**	**572**	**534**	**1 169**	**1 207**	..	..	..	..	..
4100 Recurrent taxes on immovable property	0	0	0	0	0	..	..	..	..	..
4200 Recurrent taxes on net wealth	33	47	35	129	0	..	..	..	..	..
4300 Estate, inheritance and gift taxes	14	62	167	486	499	..	..	..	..	..
4400 Taxes on financial and capital transactions	80	463	331	554	708	..	..	..	..	..
4500 Non-recurrent taxes	0	0	0	0	0	..	..	..	..	..
4600 Other recurrent taxes on property	0	0	0	0	0	..	..	..	..	..
5000 Taxes on goods and services	**2 099**	**7 724**	**13 239**	**21 768**	**29 569**	..	..	..	..	..
5100 Taxes on production, sale, transfer, etc	2 082	7 630	12 936	21 178	28 520	..	..	..	..	..
5110 General taxes	1 030	4 173	7 621	13 748	18 948	..	..	..	..	..
5120 Taxes on specific goods and services	1 052	3 457	5 314	7 430	9 572	..	..	..	..	..
5130 Unallocable between 5110 and 5120	0	0	0	0	0	..	..	..	..	..
5200 Taxes on use of goods and perform activities	16	93	304	590	1 049	..	..	..	..	..
5300 Unallocable between 5100 and 5200	0	0	0	0	0	..	..	..	..	..
6000 Other taxes	**10**	**42**	**91**	**68**	**76**	..	..	..	..	..
6100 Paid solely by business	0	0	0	0	0	..	..	..	..	..
6200 Other	10	42	91	68	76	..	..	..	..	..
Total tax revenue	**3 693**	**12 706**	**20 427**	**35 890**	**42 686**	..	..	..	..	..

Million EUR

	Local government					Social Security Funds				
	1975	1985	1995	2005	2014	1975	1985	1995	2005	2014
1000 Taxes on income, profits and capital gains	**1 547**	**5 049**	**9 313**	**13 574**	**19 645**	**0**	**0**	**0**	**0**	**0**
1100 Of individuals	1 393	4 646	8 320	12 420	18 233	..	..	..	..	..
1200 Corporate	154	403	994	1 154	1 412	..	..	..	..	..
1300 Unallocable between 1100 and 1200	0	0	0	0	0	..	..	..	..	..
2000 Social security contributions	**0**	**0**	**0**	**23**	**15**	**1 347**	**5 005**	**13 492**	**18 856**	**25 996**
2100 Employees	..	..	..	4	4	278	849	2 536	3 460	6 097
2200 Employers	..	..	..	19	11	990	3 787	9 447	14 108	17 874
2300 Self-employed or non-employed	..	..	..	0	0	79	369	1 509	1 288	2 025
2400 Unallocable between 2100, 2200 and 2300	..	..	..	0	0	0	0	0	0	0
3000 Taxes on payroll and workforce	**0**	**0**	**0**	**0**	**0**	**0**	**0**	**0**	**0**	**0**
4000 Taxes on property	**0**	**49**	**441**	**725**	**1 512**	**0**	**0**	**0**	**0**	**0**
4100 Recurrent taxes on immovable property	0	49	441	725	1 512	..	..	..	..	..
4200 Recurrent taxes on net wealth	0	0	0	0	0	..	..	..	..	..
4300 Estate, inheritance and gift taxes	0	0	0	0	0	..	..	..	..	..
4400 Taxes on financial and capital transactions	0	0	0	0	0	..	..	..	..	..
4500 Non-recurrent taxes	0	0	0	0	0	..	..	..	..	..
4600 Other recurrent taxes on property	0	0	0	0	0	..	..	..	..	..
5000 Taxes on goods and services	**3**	**3**	**7**	**8**	**2**	**0**	**0**	**0**	**0**	**0**
5100 Taxes on production, sale, transfer, etc	1	0	1	4	1	..	..	..	..	..
5110 General taxes	0	0	0	0	0	..	..	..	..	..
5120 Taxes on specific goods and services	1	0	1	4	1	..	..	..	..	..
5130 Unallocable between 5110 and 5120	0	0	0	0	0	..	..	..	..	..
5200 Taxes on use of goods and perform activities	2	3	6	4	1	..	..	..	..	..
5300 Unallocable between 5100 and 5200	0	0	0	0	0	..	..	..	..	..
6000 Other taxes	**0**	**0**	**0**	**0**	**0**	**0**	**0**	**0**	**0**	**0**
6100 Paid solely by business	..	..	..	..	..	..	..	..	..	..
6200 Other	..	..	..	..	..	..	..	..	..	..
Total tax revenue	**1 550**	**5 102**	**9 761**	**14 330**	**21 174**	**1 347**	**5 005**	**13 492**	**18 856**	**25 996**

Note : Excluding customs duties collected on behalf of the European Union: 2014 = 170.0.

StatLink http://dx.doi.org/10.1787/888933417236

Tableau 5.22. **France, recettes fiscales par sous-secteurs d'administration**

Million EUR

	Administration centrale					Administration d'État/Régions				
	1975	1985	1995	2005	2014					
1000 Impôts sur revenu, bénéfices et gains en capital	**13 106**	**50 864**	**69 134**	**98 623**	**125 357**	..	..	..	..	..
1100 Des personnes physiques	8 743	36 441	43 963	56 862	75 364	..	..	..	..	..
1200 Des sociétés	4 282	14 180	25 172	41 761	49 993	..	..	..	..	..
1300 Non-ventilables entre 1100 et 1200	80	244	0	0	0	..	..	..	..	..
2000 Cotisations de sécurité sociale	**419**	**1 984**	**3 733**	**5 796**	**7 775**	..	..	..	..	..
2100 A la charge des salariés	419	1 984	3 733	4 812	5 783	..	..	..	..	..
2200 A la charge des employeurs	0	0	0	984	1 992	..	..	..	..	..
2300 A charge des travailleurs indép. ou sans emploi	0	0	0	0	0	..	..	..	..	..
2400 Non-ventilables entre 2100, 2200 et 2300	0	0	0	0	0	..	..	..	..	..
3000 Sur salaires ou main d'oeuvre	**1 194**	**4 570**	**10 299**	**13 117**	**4 821**	..	..	..	..	..
4000 Impôts sur le patrimoine	**1 372**	**5 315**	**7 356**	**13 945**	**18 022**	..	..	..	..	..
4100 Impôts périodiques sur la propriété immobilière	26	70	9	30	64	..	..	..	..	..
4200 Impôts périodiques sur l'actif net	0	2 021	1 309	3 053	5 182	..	..	..	..	..
4300 Impôts sur mut. par décès, succ. et donations	616	1 932	4 261	9 006	10 273	..	..	..	..	..
4400 Impôts sur transact. mobilières et immob.	731	1 291	1 777	1 856	2 503	..	..	..	..	..
4500 Impôts non-périodiques	0	0	0	0	0	..	..	..	..	..
4600 Autres impôts périodiques sur patrimoine	0	0	0	0	0	..	..	..	..	..
5000 Impôts sur les biens et services	**26 154**	**87 164**	**127 617**	**165 674**	**167 846**	..	..	..	..	..
5100 Impôts sur production, vente, transfert, etc.	25 618	86 328	126 699	163 729	165 956	..	..	..	..	..
5110 Impôts généraux	19 077	62 687	89 768	127 096	136 582	..	..	..	..	..
5120 Impôts sur biens et services déterminés	6 540	23 641	36 931	36 633	29 374	..	..	..	..	..
5130 Non-ventilables entre 5110 et 5120	0	0	0	0	0	..	..	..	..	..
5200 Impôts sur utilisation des biens et exerc. activites	536	836	918	1 945	1 890	..	..	..	..	..
5300 Non-ventilables entre 5100 et 5200	0	0	0	0	0	..	..	..	..	..
6000 Autres impôts	**49**	**595**	**924**	**3 522**	**1 060**	..	..	..	..	..
6100 A la charge exclusive des entreprises	32	595	871	3 502	1 054	..	..	..	..	..
6200 A la charge d'autres agents	17	0	53	21	6	..	..	..	..	..
Recettes fiscales totales	**42 294**	**150 491**	**219 063**	**300 677**	**324 881**	..	..	..	..	..

Million EUR

	Administrations locales					Administrations de sécurité sociale				
	1975	1985	1995	2005	2014	1975	1985	1995	2005	2014
1000 Impôts sur revenu, bénéfices et gains en capital	**0**	**0**	**0**	**0**	**16**	**0**	**33**	**14 997**	**80 173**	**108 240**
1100 Des personnes physiques	0	0	0	0	10	..	33	14 997	80 173	108 240
1200 Des sociétés	0	0	0	0	6	..	0	0	0	0
1300 Non-ventilables entre 1100 et 1200	0	0	0	0	0	..	0	0	0	0
2000 Cotisations de sécurité sociale	**0**	**0**	**0**	**0**	**0**	**33 089**	**136 004**	**217 995**	**275 433**	**358 563**
2100 A la charge des salariés	..	..	..	..	..	6 683	35 579	65 964	65 369	85 274
2200 A la charge des employeurs	..	..	..	..	..	24 236	89 322	135 892	190 090	244 359
2300 A charge des travailleurs indép. ou sans emploi	..	..	..	..	..	2 170	11 103	16 139	19 975	28 930
2400 Non-ventilables entre 2100, 2200 et 2300	..	..	..	..	..	0	0	0	0	0
3000 Sur salaires ou main d'oeuvre	**299**	**1 377**	**2 529**	**5 437**	**9 088**	**107**	**606**	**36**	**1 767**	**20 525**
4000 Impôts sur le patrimoine	**2 876**	**13 078**	**27 105**	**44 534**	**65 571**	**0**	**0**	**0**	**0**	**0**
4100 Impôts périodiques sur la propriété immobilière	2 626	11 085	23 117	35 989	55 429	..	..	..	..	..
4200 Impôts périodiques sur l'actif net	0	0	0	0	0	..	..	..	..	..
4300 Impôts sur mut. par décès, succ. et donations	0	0	0	0	0	..	..	..	..	..
4400 Impôts sur transact. mobilières et immob.	250	1 994	3 988	8 545	10 142	..	..	..	..	..
4500 Impôts non-périodiques	0	0	0	0	0	..	..	..	..	..
4600 Autres impôts périodiques sur patrimoine	0	0	0	0	0	..	..	..	..	..
5000 Impôts sur les biens et services	**496**	**3 625**	**8 056**	**14 708**	**29 804**	**301**	**1 850**	**5 708**	**12 776**	**38 421**
5100 Impôts sur production, vente, transfert, etc.	297	1 417	4 168	12 233	25 919	301	1 810	5 429	12 393	37 342
5110 Impôts généraux	0	0	0	0	0	248	873	1 810	4 271	17 903
5120 Impôts sur biens et services déterminés	297	1 417	4 168	12 233	25 919	53	937	3 620	8 122	19 439
5130 Non-ventilables entre 5110 et 5120	0	0	0	0	0	0	0	0	0	0
5200 Impôts sur utilisation des biens et exerc. activites	198	2 208	3 888	2 475	3 885	0	40	279	383	1 079
5300 Non-ventilables entre 5100 et 5200	0	0	0	0	0	0	0	0	0	0
6000 Autres impôts	**2 577**	**9 612**	**18 971**	**22 334**	**22 198**	**0**	**0**	**0**	**0**	**481**
6100 A la charge exclusive des entreprises	2 577	9 612	18 970	22 334	22 198	..	..	..	..	481
6200 A la charge d'autres agents	0	0	1	0	0	..	..	..	..	0
Recettes fiscales totales	**6 248**	**27 693**	**56 661**	**87 013**	**126 677**	**33 497**	**138 493**	**238 737**	**370 149**	**526 230**

Note : À l'exclusion des droits de douane perçus pour le compte de l'Union européenne : 2014 = 1 827.0.

StatLink http://dx.doi.org/10.1787/888933417243

Table 5.23. **Germany, tax revenues by sub-sectors of government**

Million EUR

	Federal government					State/Regional				
	1975	1985	1995	2005	2014	1975	1985	1995	2005	2014
1000 Taxes on income, profits and capital gains	**26 782**	**49 039**	**90 688**	**89 383**	**136 005**	**26 428**	**49 034**	**77 258**	**83 503**	**126 797**
1100 Of individuals	23 469	40 497	83 710	77 468	122 326	23 267	40 497	71 598	70 916	112 048
1200 Corporate	3 314	8 542	6 978	11 915	13 679	3 160	8 537	5 659	12 587	14 749
1300 Unallocable between 1100 and 1200	0	0	0	0	0	0	0	0	0	0
2000 Social security contributions	**0**	**0**	**0**	**0**	**0**	**0**	**0**	**0**	**0**	**0**
2100 Employees	..	..	..	..	..	..	..	..	..	..
2200 Employers	..	..	..	..	..	..	..	..	..	..
2300 Self-employed or non-employed	..	..	..	..	..	..	..	..	..	..
2400 Unallocable between 2100, 2200 and 2300	..	..	..	..	..	..	..	..	..	..
3000 Taxes on payroll and workforce	**0**	**0**	**0**	**0**	**0**	**0**	**0**	**0**	**0**	**0**
4000 Taxes on property	**1 225**	**836**	**175**	**0**	**684**	**2 606**	**4 192**	**9 080**	**8 985**	**14 789**
4100 Recurrent taxes on immovable property	0	0	0	..	0	0	0	0	0	0
4200 Recurrent taxes on net wealth	920	127	147	..	684	1 993	2 318	4 163	97	-2
4300 Estate, inheritance and gift taxes	0	0	0	..	0	271	773	1 815	4 097	5 452
4400 Taxes on financial and capital transactions	305	709	28	..	0	342	1 100	3 102	4 791	9 339
4500 Non-recurrent taxes	0	0	0	..	0	0	0	0	0	0
4600 Other recurrent taxes on property	0	0	0	..	0	0	0	0	0	0
5000 Taxes on goods and services	**35 370**	**62 539**	**125 377**	**147 967**	**197 399**	**13 082**	**24 754**	**62 564**	**75 007**	**93 490**
5100 Taxes on production, sale, transfer, etc	35 370	62 539	125 377	147 967	187 064	10 371	20 996	55 506	66 334	93 490
5110 General taxes	18 458	36 780	67 178	74 361	108 708	9 194	19 373	52 783	62 851	90 593
5120 Taxes on specific goods and services	16 913	25 759	58 200	73 170	78 072	1 177	1 623	2 723	3 483	2 897
5130 Unallocable between 5110 and 5120	0	0	0	436	284	0	0	0	0	0
5200 Taxes on use of goods and perform activities	0	0	0	0	10 335	2 711	3 758	7 058	8 673	0
5300 Unallocable between 5100 and 5200	0	0	0	0	0	0	0	0	0	0
6000 Other taxes	**0**	**0**	**0**	**-1**	**0**	**0**	**0**	**0**	**0**	**0**
6100 Paid solely by business	..	..	..	0	..	..	..	..	..	..
6200 Other	..	..	..	-1	..	..	..	..	..	..
Total tax revenue	**63 378**	**112 414**	**216 240**	**237 349**	**334 088**	**42 116**	**77 980**	**148 902**	**167 495**	**235 076**

Million EUR

	Local government					Social Security Funds				
	1975	1985	1995	2005	2014	1975	1985	1995	2005	2014
1000 Taxes on income, profits and capital gains	**11 819**	**25 467**	**40 295**	**46 725**	**69 747**	**0**	**0**	**0**	**0**	**0**
1100 Of individuals	9 931	20 805	33 761	31 261	47 211	..	..	..	..	..
1200 Corporate	1 888	4 662	6 534	15 464	22 536	..	..	..	..	..
1300 Unallocable between 1100 and 1200	0	0	0	0	0	..	..	..	..	..
2000 Social security contributions	**0**	**0**	**0**	**0**	**0**	**64 290**	**129 761**	**268 052**	**310 301**	**407 726**
2100 Employees	..	..	..	..	..	28 106	56 247	117 916	135 775	181 608
2200 Employers	..	..	..	..	..	34 609	67 255	133 120	149 191	191 409
2300 Self-employed or non-employed	..	..	..	..	..	1 575	6 258	17 016	25 335	34 709
2400 Unallocable between 2100, 2200 and 2300	..	..	..	..	..	0	0	0	0	0
3000 Taxes on payroll and workforce	**1 533**	**0**	**0**	**0**	**0**	**0**	**0**	**0**	**0**	**0**
4000 Taxes on property	**3 461**	**5 705**	**9 794**	**10 247**	**12 690**	**0**	**0**	**0**	**0**	**0**
4100 Recurrent taxes on immovable property	2 122	3 766	7 027	10 247	12 690	..	..	..	..	..
4200 Recurrent taxes on net wealth	911	1 477	2 615	0	0	..	..	..	..	..
4300 Estate, inheritance and gift taxes	0	0	0	0	0	..	..	..	..	..
4400 Taxes on financial and capital transactions	428	462	151	0	0	..	..	..	..	..
4500 Non-recurrent taxes	0	0	0	0	0	..	..	..	..	..
4600 Other recurrent taxes on property	0	0	0	0	0	..	..	..	..	..
5000 Taxes on goods and services	**162**	**238**	**448**	**3 395**	**5 203**	**0**	**0**	**0**	**0**	**0**
5100 Taxes on production, sale, transfer, etc	94	112	271	3 136	4 884	..	..	..	..	..
5110 General taxes	0	0	0	2 909	4 100	..	..	..	..	..
5120 Taxes on specific goods and services	94	112	271	227	784	..	..	..	..	..
5130 Unallocable between 5110 and 5120	0	0	0	0	0	..	..	..	..	..
5200 Taxes on use of goods and perform activities	68	126	176	259	319	..	..	..	..	..
5300 Unallocable between 5100 and 5200	0	0	0	0	0	..	..	..	..	..
6000 Other taxes	**67**	**64**	**130**	**79**	**172**	**0**	**0**	**0**	**0**	**0**
6100 Paid solely by business	0	0	0	0	0	..	..	..	..	..
6200 Other	67	64	130	79	172	..	..	..	..	..
Total tax revenue	**17 042**	**31 475**	**50 666**	**60 446**	**87 812**	**64 290**	**129 761**	**268 052**	**310 301**	**407 726**

Note : Excluding customs duties collected on behalf of the European Union: 2014 = 4 608.0.

StatLink http://dx.doi.org/10.1787/888933417259

Table 5.24. **Greece, tax revenues by sub-sectors of government**

Million EUR

	Central government					State/Regional				
	1975	1985	1995	2005	2014					
1000 Taxes on income, profits and capital gains	**64**	**826**	**5 756**	**15 725**	**15 023**	..	..	..	..	..
1100 Of individuals	43	654	3 112	9 090	10 438	..	..	..	..	..
1200 Corporate	17	130	1 635	6 402	3 344	..	..	..	..	..
1300 Unallocable between 1100 and 1200	4	42	1 010	233	1 241	..	..	..	..	..
2000 Social security contributions	**0**	**14**	**373**	**1 033**	**741**	..	..	..	..	..
2100 Employees	..	12	354	1 026	740	..	..	..	..	..
2200 Employers	..	1	10	7	1	..	..	..	..	..
2300 Self-employed or non-employed	..	0	9	0	0	..	..	..	..	..
2400 Unallocable between 2100, 2200 and 2300	..	1	0	0	0	..	..	..	..	..
3000 Taxes on payroll and workforce	**1**	**44**	**0**	**0**	**0**	..	..	..	..	..
4000 Taxes on property	**47**	**123**	**854**	**1 975**	**754**	..	..	..	..	..
4100 Recurrent taxes on immovable property	1	8	10	0	0	..	..	..	..	..
4200 Recurrent taxes on net wealth	0	0	0	0	0	..	..	..	..	..
4300 Estate, inheritance and gift taxes	5	45	250	258	111	..	..	..	..	..
4400 Taxes on financial and capital transactions	41	69	594	1 469	513	..	..	..	..	..
4500 Non-recurrent taxes	0	1	0	0	0	..	..	..	..	..
4600 Other recurrent taxes on property	0	0	0	248	130	..	..	..	..	..
5000 Taxes on goods and services	**224**	**1 967**	**10 296**	**21 233**	**27 038**	..	..	..	..	..
5100 Taxes on production, sale, transfer, etc	205	1 845	9 865	19 433	24 836	..	..	..	..	..
5110 General taxes	90	815	5 845	13 686	12 994	..	..	..	..	..
5120 Taxes on specific goods and services	114	936	4 020	5 679	7 770	..	..	..	..	..
5130 Unallocable between 5110 and 5120	0	94	95	68	4 072	..	..	..	..	..
5200 Taxes on use of goods and perform activities	20	122	432	1 725	1 732	..	..	..	..	..
5300 Unallocable between 5100 and 5200	0	0	0	75	470	..	..	..	..	..
6000 Other taxes	**0**	**3**	**0**	**0**	**0**	..	..	..	..	..
6100 Paid solely by business	.	0	..	..	..	..	..	..	..	..
6200 Other	..	3	..	..	..	..	..	..	..	..
Total tax revenue	**337**	**2 976**	**17 280**	**39 966**	**43 556**	..	..	..	..	..

Million EUR

	Local government					Social Security Funds				
	1975	1985	1995	2005	2014	1975	1985	1995	2005	2014
1000 Taxes on income, profits and capital gains	**3**	**6**	**0**	**0**	**0**	**0**	**0**	**0**	**0**	**0**
1100 Of individuals	2	6	0	0	0	0	0	0	0	0
1200 Corporate	0	0	0	0	0	0	0	0	0	0
1300 Unallocable between 1100 and 1200	1	0	0	0	0	0	0	0	0	0
2000 Social security contributions	**0**	**0**	**0**	**0**	**0**	**148**	**1 679**	**8 003**	**20 873**	**17 493**
2100 Employees	..	..	..	..	..	62	742	3 073	7 667	6 749
2200 Employers	..	..	..	..	..	62	709	3 810	9 934	7 955
2300 Self-employed or non-employed	..	..	..	..	..	0	0	1 120	3 272	2 789
2400 Unallocable between 2100, 2200 and 2300	..	..	..	..	..	24	229	0	0	0
3000 Taxes on payroll and workforce	**0**	**26**	**0**	**0**	**0**	**0**	**0**	**0**	**0**	**0**
4000 Taxes on property	**1**	**6**	**131**	**258**	**1 772**	**0**	**0**	**67**	**360**	**26**
4100 Recurrent taxes on immovable property	0	3	109	111	755	..	..	33	83	0
4200 Recurrent taxes on net wealth	0	0	14	127	1 017	..	..	0	0	0
4300 Estate, inheritance and gift taxes	0	0	0	0	0	..	..	0	0	0
4400 Taxes on financial and capital transactions	0	2	8	20	0	..	..	34	277	26
4500 Non-recurrent taxes	0	1	0	0	0	..	..	0	0	0
4600 Other recurrent taxes on property	0	1	0	0	0	..	..	0	0	0
5000 Taxes on goods and services	**10**	**26**	**107**	**215**	**122**	**0**	**0**	**124**	**250**	**395**
5100 Taxes on production, sale, transfer, etc	7	18	65	188	112	..	..	101	195	374
5110 General taxes	2	2	7	29	18	..	..	85	85	324
5120 Taxes on specific goods and services	6	17	58	159	94	..	..	16	110	50
5130 Unallocable between 5110 and 5120	0	0	0	0	0	..	..	0	0	0
5200 Taxes on use of goods and perform activities	3	7	42	27	10	..	..	23	55	21
5300 Unallocable between 5100 and 5200	0	0	0	0	0	..	..	0	0	0
6000 Other taxes	**0**	**0**	**0**	**0**	**0**	**0**	**0**	**0**	**0**	**0**
6100 Paid solely by business	..	..	..	..	..	..	..	..	..	..
6200 Other	..	..	..	..	..	..	..	..	..	..
Total tax revenue	**17**	**64**	**238**	**473**	**1 894**	**148**	**1 679**	**8 194**	**21 483**	**17 914**

Note : Excluding customs duties collected on behalf of the European Union: 2014 = 148.0.

StatLink http://dx.doi.org/10.1787/888933417264

Table 5.25. **Hungary, tax revenues by sub-sectors of government**

Million HUF

	Central government					State/Regional				
	1975	1985	1995	2005	2014					
1000 Taxes on income, profits and capital gains	..	..	**498 608**	**1 915 178**	**2 069 915**	..	..	..	..	..
1100 Of individuals	..	..	383 744	1 449 552	1 597 988	..	..	..	..	..
1200 Corporate	..	..	106 259	465 626	471 927	..	..	..	..	..
1300 Unallocable between 1100 and 1200	..	..	8 605	0	0	..	..	..	..	..
2000 Social security contributions	..	..	**69 554**	**235 148**	**155 609**	..	..	..	..	..
2100 Employees	..	..	18 468	53 611	135 621	..	..	..	..	..
2200 Employers	..	..	51 086	175 013	19 988	..	..	..	..	..
2300 Self-employed or non-employed	..	..	0	0	0	..	..	..	..	..
2400 Unallocable between 2100, 2200 and 2300	..	..	0	6 524	0	..	..	..	..	..
3000 Taxes on payroll and workforce	..	..	**5 474**	**39 459**	**170 715**	..	..	..	..	..
4000 Taxes on property	..	..	**11 463**	**63 007**	**281 220**	..	..	..	..	..
4100 Recurrent taxes on immovable property	..	..	0	0	55 021	..	..	..	..	..
4200 Recurrent taxes on net wealth	..	..	0	0	138 141	..	..	..	..	..
4300 Estate, inheritance and gift taxes	..	..	1 364	7 678	6 179	..	..	..	..	..
4400 Taxes on financial and capital transactions	..	..	10 099	55 329	81 879	..	..	..	..	..
4500 Non-recurrent taxes	..	..	0	0	0	..	..	..	..	..
4600 Other recurrent taxes on property	..	..	0	0	0	..	..	..	..	..
5000 Taxes on goods and services	..	..	**924 906**	**2 869 329**	**4 759 546**	..	..	..	..	..
5100 Taxes on production, sale, transfer, etc	..	..	919 500	2 853 878	4 662 543	..	..	..	..	..
5110 General taxes	..	..	423 954	1 972 998	3 204 649	..	..	..	..	..
5120 Taxes on specific goods and services	..	..	495 546	880 880	1 457 894	..	..	..	..	..
5130 Unallocable between 5110 and 5120	..	..	0	0	0	..	..	..	..	..
5200 Taxes on use of goods and perform activities	..	..	5 406	15 451	97 003	..	..	..	..	..
5300 Unallocable between 5100 and 5200	..	..	0	0	0	..	..	..	..	..
6000 Other taxes	..	..	**8 901**	**44 873**	**45 445**	..	..	..	..	..
6100 Paid solely by business	..	..	..	..	..	..	..	..	..	..
6200 Other	..	..	..	..	..	..	..	..	..	..
Total tax revenue	..	..	**1 518 905**	**5 166 993**	**7 482 450**	..	..	..	..	..

Million HUF

	Local government					Social Security Funds				
	1975	1985	1995	2005	2014	1975	1985	1995	2005	2014
1000 Taxes on income, profits and capital gains	..	..	**0**	**173**	**42**	..	..	**0**	**26 307**	**107 082**
1100 Of individuals	..	..	0	173	42	..	..	0	26 307	107 082
1200 Corporate	..	..	0	0	0	..	..	0	0	0
1300 Unallocable between 1100 and 1200	..	..	0	0	0	..	..	0	0	0
2000 Social security contributions	..	..	**0**	**0**	**0**	..	..	**778 467**	**2 452 562**	**3 869 689**
2100 Employees	..	..	..	..	..	..	..	116 824	530 098	1 524 879
2200 Employers	..	..	..	..	..	..	..	632 478	1 894 306	2 317 153
2300 Self-employed or non-employed	..	..	..	..	..	..	..	27 466	2 080	0
2400 Unallocable between 2100, 2200 and 2300	..	..	..	..	..	..	..	1 699	26 078	27 657
3000 Taxes on payroll and workforce	..	..	**1 075**	**1 153**	**0**	..	..	**0**	**44 397**	**9 749**
4000 Taxes on property	..	..	**17 531**	**123 929**	**136 159**	..	..	**0**	**0**	**0**
4100 Recurrent taxes on immovable property	..	..	6 068	58 836	136 159	..	..	..	..	..
4200 Recurrent taxes on net wealth	..	..	0	0	0	..	..	..	..	..
4300 Estate, inheritance and gift taxes	..	..	1 364	7 932	0	..	..	..	..	..
4400 Taxes on financial and capital transactions	..	..	10 099	57 162	0	..	..	..	..	..
4500 Non-recurrent taxes	..	..	0	0	0	..	..	..	..	..
4600 Other recurrent taxes on property	..	..	0	0	0	..	..	..	..	..
5000 Taxes on goods and services	..	..	**41 970**	**388 385**	**562 262**	..	..	**0**	**0**	**86 555**
5100 Taxes on production, sale, transfer, etc	..	..	39 240	337 935	532 251	..	..	..	..	86 555
5110 General taxes	..	..	38 472	334 077	523 125	..	..	..	..	20 390
5120 Taxes on specific goods and services	..	..	768	3 858	9 126	..	..	..	..	66 165
5130 Unallocable between 5110 and 5120	..	..	0	0	0	..	..	..	..	0
5200 Taxes on use of goods and perform activities	..	..	2 730	50 450	30 011	..	..	..	..	0
5300 Unallocable between 5100 and 5200	..	..	0	0	0	..	..	..	..	0
6000 Other taxes	..	..	**0**	**0**	**0**	..	..	**21 605**	**9 616**	**15 395**
6100 Paid solely by business	..	..	..	..	..	..	..	..	..	..
6200 Other	..	..	..	..	..	..	..	..	..	..
Total tax revenue	..	..	**60 576**	**513 641**	**698 463**	..	..	**800 072**	**2 532 882**	**4 088 470**

Note : Excluding customs duties collected on behalf of the European Union: 2014 = 31 927.0.

StatLink http://dx.doi.org/10.1787/888933417275

Table 5.26. **Iceland, tax revenues by sub-sectors of government**

Million ISK

	Central government					State/Regional				
	1975	1985	1995	2005	2014					
1000 Taxes on income, profits and capital gains	**68**	**3 741**	**27 156**	**105 705**	**204 260**	..	..	..	..	..
1100 Of individuals	55	3 183	22 914	70 944	114 369	..	..	..	..	..
1200 Corporate	13	558	4 242	20 297	66 803	..	..	..	..	..
1300 Unallocable between 1100 and 1200	0	0	0	14 464	23 088	..	..	..	..	..
2000 Social security contributions	**17**	**841**	**11 452**	**32 777**	**73 432**	..	..	..	..	..
2100 Employees	0	56	460	..	..	..	..	..	..	..
2200 Employers	17	785	10 992	..	..	..	..	..	..	..
2300 Self-employed or non-employed	0	0	0	..	..	..	..	..	..	..
2400 Unallocable between 2100, 2200 and 2300	0	0	0	32 777	73 432	..	..	..	..	..
3000 Taxes on payroll and workforce	**27**	**1 233**	**0**	**324**	**6 994**	..	..	..	..	..
4000 Taxes on property	**15**	**1 534**	**7 198**	**13 340**	**17 455**	..	..	..	..	..
4100 Recurrent taxes on immovable property	0	89	47	0	165	..	..	..	..	..
4200 Recurrent taxes on net wealth	5	588	3 191	2 887	10 751	..	..	..	..	..
4300 Estate, inheritance and gift taxes	0	67	389	866	2 507	..	..	..	..	..
4400 Taxes on financial and capital transactions	9	790	3 571	9 073	3 485	..	..	..	..	..
4500 Non-recurrent taxes	0	0	0	248	237	..	..	..	..	..
4600 Other recurrent taxes on property	0	0	0	266	311	..	..	..	..	..
5000 Taxes on goods and services	**392**	**20 639**	**66 356**	**168 295**	**238 467**	..	..	..	..	..
5100 Taxes on production, sale, transfer, etc	387	20 109	62 140	157 941	228 715	..	..	..	..	..
5110 General taxes	182	11 360	42 358	113 897	160 871	..	..	..	..	..
5120 Taxes on specific goods and services	205	8 749	19 782	44 044	67 844	..	..	..	..	..
5130 Unallocable between 5110 and 5120	0	0	0	0	0	..	..	..	..	..
5200 Taxes on use of goods and perform activities	5	530	4 216	10 354	9 752	..	..	..	..	..
5300 Unallocable between 5100 and 5200	0	0	0	0	0	..	..	..	..	..
6000 Other taxes	**0**	**0**	**0**	**1 504**	**43 814**	..	..	..	..	..
6100 Paid solely by business	..	..	..	565	37 762	..	..	..	..	..
6200 Other	..	..	..	939	6 052	..	..	..	..	..
Total tax revenue	**519**	**27 988**	**112 162**	**321 944**	**584 423**	..	..	..	..	..

Million ISK

	Local government					Social Security Funds				
	1975	1985	1995	2005	2014	1975	1985	1995	2005	2014
1000 Taxes on income, profits and capital gains	**78**	**4 055**	**21 170**	**74 455**	**156 214**	**0**	**0**	**0**	**0**	**0**
1100 Of individuals	74	3 532	21 170	74 455	156 214	..	..	..	..	..
1200 Corporate	4	523	0	0	0	..	..	..	..	..
1300 Unallocable between 1100 and 1200	0	0	0	0	0	..	..	..	..	..
2000 Social security contributions	**0**	**0**	**0**	**0**	**0**	**0**	**0**	**0**	**0**	**0**
2100 Employees	..	..	..	..	..	..	..	..	..	..
2200 Employers	..	..	..	..	..	..	..	..	..	..
2300 Self-employed or non-employed	..	..	..	..	..	..	..	..	..	..
2400 Unallocable between 2100, 2200 and 2300	..	..	..	..	..	..	..	..	..	..
3000 Taxes on payroll and workforce	**0**	**0**	**0**	**0**	**0**	**0**	**0**	**0**	**0**	**0**
4000 Taxes on property	**18**	**979**	**5 674**	**13 931**	**32 179**	**0**	**0**	**0**	**0**	**0**
4100 Recurrent taxes on immovable property	18	979	5 674	13 931	32 179	..	..	..	..	..
4200 Recurrent taxes on net wealth	0	0	0	0	0	..	..	..	..	..
4300 Estate, inheritance and gift taxes	0	0	0	0	0	..	..	..	..	..
4400 Taxes on financial and capital transactions	0	0	0	0	0	..	..	..	..	..
4500 Non-recurrent taxes	0	0	0	0	0	..	..	..	..	..
4600 Other recurrent taxes on property	0	0	0	0	0	..	..	..	..	..
5000 Taxes on goods and services	**9**	**351**	**2 585**	**6 904**	**1 447**	**0**	**0**	**0**	**0**	**0**
5100 Taxes on production, sale, transfer, etc	9	351	2 585	0	0	..	..	..	..	..
5110 General taxes	0	0	2 585	0	0	..	..	..	..	..
5120 Taxes on specific goods and services	9	351	0	0	0	..	..	..	..	..
5130 Unallocable between 5110 and 5120	0	0	0	0	0	..	..	..	..	..
5200 Taxes on use of goods and perform activities	0	0	0	6 904	1 447	..	..	..	..	..
5300 Unallocable between 5100 and 5200	0	0	0	0	0	..	..	..	..	..
6000 Other taxes	**14**	**1 002**	**0**	**93**	**0**	**0**	**0**	**0**	**0**	**0**
6100 Paid solely by business	14	1 002	..	93	..	..	..	..	..	..
6200 Other	0	0	..	0	..	..	..	..	..	..
Total tax revenue	**119**	**6 387**	**29 429**	**95 383**	**189 840**	**0**	**0**	**0**	**0**	**0**

StatLink http://dx.doi.org/10.1787/888933417286

Table 5.27. **Ireland, tax revenues by sub-sectors of government**

Million EUR

	Central government					State/Regional				
	1975	1985	1995	2005	2014					
1000 Taxes on income, profits and capital gains	**456**	**2 963**	**7 022**	**20 080**	**22 349**	..	..	..	..	..
1100 Of individuals	382	2 686	5 563	14 568	17 727	..	..	..	..	..
1200 Corporate	73	276	1 458	5 511	4 618	..	..	..	..	..
1300 Unallocable between 1100 and 1200	0	0	0	0	4	..	..	..	..	..
2000 Social security contributions	**11**	**96**	**87**	**217**	**1 503**	..	..	..	..	..
2100 Employees	10	89	87	217	1 503	..	..	..	..	..
2200 Employers	0	0	0	0	0	..	..	..	..	..
2300 Self-employed or non-employed	1	7	0	0	0	..	..	..	..	..
2400 Unallocable between 2100, 2200 and 2300	0	0	0	0	0	..	..	..	..	..
3000 Taxes on payroll and workforce	**0**	**201**	**209**	**332**	**338**	..	..	..	..	..
4000 Taxes on property	**37**	**148**	**370**	**2 741**	**2 839**	..	..	..	..	..
4100 Recurrent taxes on immovable property	0	32	15	0	493	..	..	..	..	..
4200 Recurrent taxes on net wealth	5	0	0	0	743	..	..	..	..	..
4300 Estate, inheritance and gift taxes	17	26	76	255	359	..	..	..	..	..
4400 Taxes on financial and capital transactions	15	90	279	2 486	1 245	..	..	..	..	..
4500 Non-recurrent taxes	0	0	0	0	0	..	..	..	..	..
4600 Other recurrent taxes on property	0	0	0	0	0	..	..	..	..	..
5000 Taxes on goods and services	**671**	**3 638**	**6 763**	**19 122**	**18 645**	..	..	..	..	..
5100 Taxes on production, sale, transfer, etc	639	3 481	6 419	18 107	17 028	..	..	..	..	..
5110 General taxes	223	1 768	3 666	12 373	11 521	..	..	..	..	..
5120 Taxes on specific goods and services	416	1 713	2 753	5 733	5 507	..	..	..	..	..
5130 Unallocable between 5110 and 5120	0	0	0	0	0	..	..	..	..	..
5200 Taxes on use of goods and perform activities	33	157	344	1 015	1 618	..	..	..	..	..
5300 Unallocable between 5100 and 5200	0	0	0	0	0	..	..	..	..	..
6000 Other taxes	**0**	**0**	**0**	**0**	**23**	..	..	..	..	..
6100 Paid solely by business	..	..	..	..	0	..	..	..	..	..
6200 Other	..	..	..	..	23	..	..	..	..	..
Total tax revenue	**1 175**	**7 046**	**14 451**	**42 492**	**45 698**	..	..	..	..	..

Million EUR

	Local government					Social Security Funds				
	1975	1985	1995	2005	2014	1975	1985	1995	2005	2014
1000 Taxes on income, profits and capital gains	**0**	**0**	**0**	**0**	**0**	**0**	**0**	**0**	**0**	**0**
1100 Of individuals	0	0	0	0	0	0	0	0	0	0
1200 Corporate	0	0	0	0	0	0	0	0	0	0
1300 Unallocable between 1100 and 1200	0	0	0	0	0	0	0	0	0	0
2000 Social security contributions	**0**	**0**	**56**	**90**	**130**	**198**	**1 170**	**2 215**	**6 205**	**7 947**
2100 Employees	..	..	56	90	130	73	362	576	1 389	1 724
2200 Employers	..	..	0	0	0	125	809	1 528	4 427	5 817
2300 Self-employed or non-employed	..	..	0	0	0	0	0	111	388	406
2400 Unallocable between 2100, 2200 and 2300	..	..	0	0	0	0	0	0	0	0
3000 Taxes on payroll and workforce	**0**	**0**	**0**	**0**	**0**	**0**	**0**	**0**	**0**	**0**
4000 Taxes on property	**110**	**195**	**408**	**1 020**	**1 403**	**0**	**0**	**0**	**0**	**0**
4100 Recurrent taxes on immovable property	110	195	408	1 020	1 403	..	..	..	..	..
4200 Recurrent taxes on net wealth	0	0	0	0	0	..	..	..	..	..
4300 Estate, inheritance and gift taxes	0	0	0	0	0	..	..	..	..	..
4400 Taxes on financial and capital transactions	0	0	0	0	0	..	..	..	..	..
4500 Non-recurrent taxes	0	0	0	0	0	..	..	..	..	..
4600 Other recurrent taxes on property	0	0	0	0	0	..	..	..	..	..
5000 Taxes on goods and services	**0**	**0**	**0**	**0**	**0**	**0**	**0**	**0**	**0**	**0**
5100 Taxes on production, sale, transfer, etc	0	0	0	0	0	0	0	0	0	0
5110 General taxes	0	0	0	0	0	0	0	0	0	0
5120 Taxes on specific goods and services	0	0	0	0	0	0	0	0	0	0
5130 Unallocable between 5110 and 5120	0	0	0	0	0	0	0	0	0	0
5200 Taxes on use of goods and perform activities	0	0	0	0	0	0	0	0	0	0
5300 Unallocable between 5100 and 5200	0	0	0	0	0	0	0	0	0	0
6000 Other taxes	**0**	**0**	**0**	**0**	**0**	**0**	**0**	**0**	**0**	**0**
6100 Paid solely by business	..	..	..	..	..	..	..	..	..	..
6200 Other	..	..	..	..	..	..	..	..	..	..
Total tax revenue	**110**	**195**	**464**	**1 110**	**1 533**	**198**	**1 170**	**2 215**	**6 205**	**7 947**

Note : Excluding customs duties collected on behalf of the European Union: 2014 = 274.7.
The data for personal income tax revenues differs from the ESA2010 presentation as payable tax credits are excluded in accordance with the presentation in earlier editions of the publication.

StatLink http://dx.doi.org/10.1787/888933417290

Table 5.28. **Israel, tax revenues by sub-sectors of government**

Million ILS

	Central government					State/Regional				
	1975	1985	1995	2005	2014					
1000 Taxes on income, profits and capital gains	..	..	**37 422**	**73 082**	**105 628**	..	..	..	..	..
1100 Of individuals	..	..	28 399	47 062	63 402	..	..	..	..	..
1200 Corporate	..	..	8 514	21 909	34 957	..	..	..	..	..
1300 Unallocable between 1100 and 1200	..	..	509	4 111	7 269	..	..	..	..	..
2000 Social security contributions	..	..	**0**	**0**	**0**	..	..	..	..	..
2100 Employees	..	..	..	..	..	..	..	..	..	..
2200 Employers	..	..	..	..	..	..	..	..	..	..
2300 Self-employed or non-employed	..	..	..	..	..	..	..	..	..	..
2400 Unallocable between 2100, 2200 and 2300	..	..	..	..	..	..	..	..	..	..
3000 Taxes on payroll and workforce	..	..	**5 007**	**9 920**	**12 967**	..	..	..	..	..
4000 Taxes on property	..	..	**3 811**	**5 140**	**6 526**	..	..	..	..	..
4100 Recurrent taxes on immovable property	..	..	786	322	95	..	..	..	..	..
4200 Recurrent taxes on net wealth	..	..	0	0	0	..	..	..	..	..
4300 Estate, inheritance and gift taxes	..	..	0	0	0	..	..	..	..	..
4400 Taxes on financial and capital transactions	..	..	1 738	3 184	3 727	..	..	..	..	..
4500 Non-recurrent taxes	..	..	1 287	1 634	2 704	..	..	..	..	..
4600 Other recurrent taxes on property	..	..	0	0	0	..	..	..	..	..
5000 Taxes on goods and services	..	..	**39 207**	**75 932**	**133 204**	..	..	..	..	..
5100 Taxes on production, sale, transfer, etc.	..	..	37 172	70 741	125 577	..	..	..	..	..
5110 General taxes	..	..	32 510	59 374	105 700	..	..	..	..	..
5120 Taxes on specific goods and services	..	..	4 662	11 367	19 877	..	..	..	..	..
5130 Unallocable between 5110 and 5120	..	..	0	0	0	..	..	..	..	..
5200 Taxes on use of goods and perform activities	..	..	2 035	5 192	7 628	..	..	..	..	..
5300 Unallocable between 5100 and 5200	..	..	0	0	0	..	..	..	..	..
6000 Other taxes	..	..	**0**	**0**	**0**	..	..	..	..	..
6100 Paid solely by business	..	..	..	..	..	..	..	..	..	..
6200 Other	..	..	..	..	..	..	..	..	..	..
Total tax revenue	..	..	**85 447**	**164 074**	**258 325**	..	..	..	..	..

Million ILS

	Local government					Social Security Funds				
	1975	1985	1995	2005	2014	1975	1985	1995	2005	2014
1000 Taxes on income, profits and capital gains	..	..	**0**	**0**	**0**	..	..	**0**	**0**	**0**
1100 Of individuals	..	..	0	0	0	..	..	0	0	0
1200 Corporate	..	..	0	0	0	..	..	0	0	0
1300 Unallocable between 1100 and 1200	..	..	0	0	0	..	..	0	0	0
2000 Social security contributions	..	..	**0**	**0**	**0**	..	..	**14 958**	**34 597**	**56 130**
2100 Employees	..	..	..	..	..	..	..	8 905	22 135	36 546
2200 Employers	..	..	..	..	..	..	..	4 672	10 679	16 163
2300 Self-employed or non-employed	..	..	..	..	..	..	..	1 381	1 783	3 421
2400 Unallocable between 2100, 2200 and 2300	..	..	..	..	..	..	..	0	0	0
3000 Taxes on payroll and workforce	..	..	**0**	**0**	**0**	..	..	**0**	**0**	**0**
4000 Taxes on property	..	..	**6 445**	**15 689**	**25 890**	..	..	**0**	**0**	**0**
4100 Recurrent taxes on immovable property	..	..	5 489	13 962	22 381	..	..	..	..	..
4200 Recurrent taxes on net wealth	..	..	0	0	0	..	..	..	..	..
4300 Estate, inheritance and gift taxes	..	..	0	0	0	..	..	..	..	..
4400 Taxes on financial and capital transactions	..	..	0	0	0	..	..	..	..	..
4500 Non-recurrent taxes	..	..	956	1 727	3 509	..	..	..	..	..
4600 Other recurrent taxes on property	..	..	0	0	0	..	..	..	..	..
5000 Taxes on goods and services	..	..	**401**	**763**	**1 369**	..	..	**0**	**0**	**0**
5100 Taxes on production, sale, transfer, etc	..	..	0	0	0	..	..	..	..	..
5110 General taxes	..	..	0	0	0	..	..	..	..	..
5120 Taxes on specific goods and services	..	..	0	0	0	..	..	..	..	..
5130 Unallocable between 5110 and 5120	..	..	0	0	0	..	..	..	..	..
5200 Taxes on use of goods and perform activities	..	..	401	763	1 369	..	..	..	..	..
5300 Unallocable between 5100 and 5200	..	..	0	0	0	..	..	..	..	..
6000 Other taxes	..	..	**0**	**0**	**0**	..	..	**0**	**0**	**0**
6100 Paid solely by business	..	..	..	..	..	..	..	..	..	..
6200 Other	..	..	..	..	..	..	..	..	..	..
Total tax revenue	..	..	**6 846**	**16 452**	**27 259**	..	..	**14 958**	**34 597**	**56 130**

Note : The statistical data for Israel are supplied by and under the responsibility of the relevant Israeli authorities. The use of such data by the OECD is without prejudice to the status of the Golan Heights, East Jerusalem and Israeli settlements in the West Bank under the terms of international law.

StatLink http://dx.doi.org/10.1787/888933417304

Table 5.29. Italy, tax revenues by sub-sectors of government

Million EUR

	Central government					State/Regional				
	1975	1985	1995	2005	2014					
1000 Taxes on income, profits and capital gains	**3 897**	**50 995**	**128 458**	**165 580**	**196 396**	..	..	..	..	..
1100 Of individuals	2 767	38 086	98 695	131 047	155 183	..	..	..	..	..
1200 Corporate	1 131	13 011	32 890	31 969	33 599	..	..	..	..	..
1300 Unallocable between 1100 and 1200	0	-101	-3 127	2 564	7 614	..	..	..	..	..
2000 Social security contributions	**0**	**0**	**0**	**0**	**0**	..	..	..	..	..
2100 Employees	..	..	..	..	..	..	..	..	..	..
2200 Employers	..	..	..	..	..	..	..	..	..	..
2300 Self-employed or non-employed	..	..	..	..	..	..	..	..	..	..
2400 Unallocable between 2100, 2200 and 2300	..	..	..	..	..	..	..	..	..	..
3000 Taxes on payroll and workforce	**0**	**815**	**1 136**	**0**	**0**	..	..	..	..	..
4000 Taxes on property	**587**	**3 635**	**13 546**	**15 717**	**23 231**	..	..	..	..	..
4100 Recurrent taxes on immovable property	4	0	0	0	3 937	..	..	..	..	..
4200 Recurrent taxes on net wealth	0	0	4 494	0	829	..	..	..	..	..
4300 Estate, inheritance and gift taxes	39	332	587	56	581	..	..	..	..	..
4400 Taxes on financial and capital transactions	544	3 303	8 464	13 794	16 990	..	..	..	..	..
4500 Non-recurrent taxes	0	0	0	1 322	124	..	..	..	..	..
4600 Other recurrent taxes on property	0	0	0	545	770	..	..	..	..	..
5000 Taxes on goods and services	**5 506**	**34 640**	**95 323**	**123 870**	**156 381**	..	..	..	..	..
5100 Taxes on production, sale, transfer, etc.	5 306	32 897	92 042	121 824	154 030	..	..	..	..	..
5110 General taxes	2 685	20 957	52 531	80 619	90 826	..	..	..	..	..
5120 Taxes on specific goods and services	2 621	11 914	39 245	41 205	63 204	..	..	..	..	..
5130 Unallocable between 5110 and 5120	0	122	323	0	0	..	..	..	..	..
5200 Taxes on use of goods and perform activities	200	1 682	2 802	1 535	2 064	..	..	..	..	..
5300 Unallocable between 5100 and 5200	0	61	479	511	287	..	..	..	..	..
6000 Other taxes	**1**	**0**	**0**	**0**	**0**	..	..	..	..	..
6100 Paid solely by business	0	..	..	..	..	..	..	..	..	..
6200 Other	1	..	..	..	..	..	..	..	..	..
Total tax revenue	**9 991**	**90 086**	**238 462**	**305 167**	**376 008**	..	..	..	..	..

Million EUR

	Local government					Social Security Funds				
	1975	1985	1995	2005	2014	1975	1985	1995	2005	2014
1000 Taxes on income, profits and capital gains	**134**	**2 234**	**5 658**	**18 494**	**28 779**	**0**	**0**	**0**	**0**	**0**
1100 Of individuals	81	535	145	16 995	27 093	..	..	..	..	..
1200 Corporate	54	357	97	1 491	1 647	..	..	..	..	..
1300 Unallocable between 1100 and 1200	0	1 342	5 416	8	39	..	..	..	..	..
2000 Social security contributions	**0**	**0**	**0**	**0**	**0**	**8 607**	**50 156**	**119 612**	**179 362**	**209 653**
2100 Employees	..	..	..	..	..	1 692	9 772	23 036	31 998	38 616
2200 Employers	..	..	..	..	..	6 915	35 788	79 716	125 099	140 608
2300 Self-employed or non-employed	..	..	..	..	..	0	4 595	16 860	22 265	30 429
2400 Unallocable between 2100, 2200 and 2300	..	..	..	..	..	0	0	0	0	0
3000 Taxes on payroll and workforce	**0**	**0**	**0**	**0**	**0**	**0**	**0**	**0**	**0**	**0**
4000 Taxes on property	**29**	**0**	**7 915**	**13 484**	**23 531**	**0**	**0**	**0**	**0**	**0**
4100 Recurrent taxes on immovable property	29	..	7 449	11 736	21 262	..	..	..	..	..
4200 Recurrent taxes on net wealth	0	..	0	0	0	..	..	..	..	..
4300 Estate, inheritance and gift taxes	0	..	0	5	40	..	..	..	..	..
4400 Taxes on financial and capital transactions	0	..	466	904	1 000	..	..	..	..	..
4500 Non-recurrent taxes	0	..	0	481	7	..	..	..	..	..
4600 Other recurrent taxes on property	0	..	0	358	1 222	..	..	..	..	..
5000 Taxes on goods and services	**4**	**1 113**	**6 941**	**30 231**	**33 839**	**0**	**0**	**0**	**0**	**0**
5100 Taxes on production, sale, transfer, etc.	0	341	1 505	17 114	14 121	..	..	..	..	..
5110 General taxes	0	0	0	4 698	6 215	..	..	..	..	..
5120 Taxes on specific goods and services	0	341	1 505	12 416	7 906	..	..	..	..	..
5130 Unallocable between 5110 and 5120	0	0	0	0	0	..	..	..	..	..
5200 Taxes on use of goods and perform activities	4	11	2 838	7 512	9 277	..	..	..	..	..
5300 Unallocable between 5100 and 5200	0	761	2 597	5 605	10 441	..	..	..	..	..
6000 Other taxes	**0**	**0**	**0**	**34 690**	**30 385**	**0**	**0**	**0**	**0**	**0**
6100 Paid solely by business	..	..	..	34 690	30 385	..	..	..	..	..
6200 Other	..	..	..	0	0	..	..	..	..	..
Total tax revenue	**168**	**3 347**	**20 514**	**96 899**	**116 534**	**8 607**	**50 156**	**119 612**	**179 362**	**209 653**

Note : Excluding customs duties collected on behalf of the European Union: 2014 = 2 022.0.

StatLink http://dx.doi.org/10.1787/888933417317

Table 5.30. **Japan, tax revenues by sub-sectors of government**

Billion JPY

	Central government					State/Regional				
	1975	1985	1995	2005	2014					
1000 Taxes on income, profits and capital gains	**9 747**	**27 456**	**33 255**	**29 975**	**30 999**	**..**	**..**	**..**	**..**	**..**
1100 Of individuals	5 482	15 435	19 515	16 702	17 139	..	..	..	..	..
1200 Corporate	4 265	12 021	13 740	13 274	13 860	..	..	..	..	..
1300 Unallocable between 1100 and 1200	0	0	0	0	0	..	..	..	..	..
2000 Social security contributions	**0**	**0**	**0**	**0**	**0**	**..**	**..**	**..**	**..**	**..**
2100 Employees	..	..	..	..	..	..	..	..	..	..
2200 Employers	..	..	..	..	..	..	..	..	..	..
2300 Self-employed or non-employed	..	..	..	..	..	..	..	..	..	..
2400 Unallocable between 2100, 2200 and 2300	..	..	..	..	..	..	..	..	..	..
3000 Taxes on payroll and workforce	**0**	**0**	**0**	**0**	**0**	**..**	**..**	**..**	**..**	**..**
4000 Taxes on property	**871**	**3 156**	**5 561**	**2 735**	**2 918**	**..**	**..**	**..**	**..**	**..**
4100 Recurrent taxes on immovable property	0	0	406	0	0	..	..	..	..	..
4200 Recurrent taxes on net wealth	0	0	0	0	0	..	..	..	..	..
4300 Estate, inheritance and gift taxes	310	1 061	2 690	1 566	1 883	..	..	..	..	..
4400 Taxes on financial and capital transactions	561	2 095	2 464	1 169	1 035	..	..	..	..	..
4500 Non-recurrent taxes	0	0	0	0	0	..	..	..	..	..
4600 Other recurrent taxes on property	0	0	0	0	0	..	..	..	..	..
5000 Taxes on goods and services	**3 888**	**8 540**	**16 147**	**19 580**	**23 932**	**..**	**..**	**..**	**..**	**..**
5100 Taxes on production, sale, transfer, etc	3 579	7 918	15 083	18 424	23 281	..	..	..	..	..
5110 General taxes	0	0	7 238	10 583	16 029	..	..	..	..	..
5120 Taxes on specific goods and services	3 579	7 918	7 845	7 840	7 252	..	..	..	..	..
5130 Unallocable between 5110 and 5120	0	0	0	0	0	..	..	..	..	..
5200 Taxes on use of goods and perform activities	309	622	1 065	1 157	651	..	..	..	..	..
5300 Unallocable between 5100 and 5200	0	0	0	0	0	..	..	..	..	..
6000 Other taxes	**0**	**0**	**0**	**0**	**0**	**..**	**..**	**..**	**..**	**..**
6100 Paid solely by business	..	..	..	..	..	..	..	..	..	..
6200 Other	..	..	..	..	..	..	..	..	..	..
Total tax revenue	**14 504**	**39 150**	**54 963**	**52 291**	**57 849**	**..**	**..**	**..**	**..**	**..**

Billion JPY

	Local government					Social Security Funds				
	1975	1985	1995	2005	2014	1975	1985	1995	2005	2014
1000 Taxes on income, profits and capital gains	**4 472**	**13 534**	**17 752**	**16 655**	**18 940**	**0**	**0**	**0**	**0**	**0**
1100 Of individuals	2 147	6 733	10 283	8 520	12 516	..	..	..	..	..
1200 Corporate	2 325	6 801	7 470	8 135	6 424	..	..	..	..	..
1300 Unallocable between 1100 and 1200	0	0	0	0	0	..	..	..	..	..
2000 Social security contributions	**0**	**0**	**0**	**0**	**0**	**9 253**	**27 121**	**44 639**	**50 844**	**62 232**
2100 Employees	..	..	..	..	..	3 436	9 668	18 347	20 980	27 146
2200 Employers	..	..	..	..	..	4 825	13 841	21 333	23 151	28 394
2300 Self-employed or non-employed	..	..	..	..	..	992	3 612	4 958	6 712	6 693
2400 Unallocable between 2100, 2200 and 2300	..	..	..	..	..	0	0	0	0	0
3000 Taxes on payroll and workforce	**0**	**0**	**0**	**0**	**0**	**0**	**0**	**0**	**0**	**0**
4000 Taxes on property	**2 029**	**5 537**	**10 653**	**10 593**	**10 388**	**0**	**0**	**0**	**0**	**0**
4100 Recurrent taxes on immovable property	1 848	5 102	9 865	10 116	10 016	..	..	..	..	..
4200 Recurrent taxes on net wealth	0	0	0	0	0	..	..	..	..	..
4300 Estate, inheritance and gift taxes	0	0	0	0	0	..	..	..	..	..
4400 Taxes on financial and capital transactions	181	435	788	477	372	..	..	..	..	..
4500 Non-recurrent taxes	0	0	0	0	0	..	..	..	..	..
4600 Other recurrent taxes on property	0	0	0	0	0	..	..	..	..	..
5000 Taxes on goods and services	**1 636**	**4 013**	**4 941**	**7 206**	**7 059**	**0**	**0**	**0**	**0**	**0**
5100 Taxes on production, sale, transfer, etc	1 234	2 899	3 245	5 299	5 306	..	..	..	..	..
5110 General taxes	0	0	0	2 551	3 106	..	..	..	..	..
5120 Taxes on specific goods and services	1 234	2 899	3 245	2 747	2 200	..	..	..	..	..
5130 Unallocable between 5110 and 5120	0	0	0	0	0	..	..	..	..	..
5200 Taxes on use of goods and perform activities	402	1 114	1 697	1 907	1 753	..	..	..	..	..
5300 Unallocable between 5100 and 5200	0	0	0	0	0	..	..	..	..	..
6000 Other taxes	**20**	**232**	**329**	**351**	**399**	**0**	**0**	**0**	**0**	**0**
6100 Paid solely by business	15	197	307	297	356	..	..	..	..	..
6200 Other	5	35	22	54	43	..	..	..	..	..
Total tax revenue	**8 155**	**23 317**	**33 675**	**34 804**	**36 786**	**9 253**	**27 121**	**44 639**	**50 844**	**62 232**

StatLink http://dx.doi.org/10.1787/888933417326

Table 5.31. **Korea, tax revenues by sub-sectors of government**

Billion KRW

	Central government					State/Regional				
	1975	1985	1995	2005	2014					
1000 Taxes on income, profits and capital gains	**344**	..	**23 000**	**55 109**	**96 454**	..	..	..	..	..
1100 Of individuals	134	..	13 713	24 766	53 440	..	..	..	..	..
1200 Corporate	139	..	8 988	30 343	43 014	..	..	..	..	..
1300 Unallocable between 1100 and 1200	71	..	300	0	0	..	..	..	..	..
2000 Social security contributions	**0**	..	**0**	**0**	**0**	..	..	..	..	..
2100 Employees	..	..	..	..	..	..	..	..	..	..
2200 Employers	..	..	..	..	..	..	..	..	..	..
2300 Self-employed or non-employed	..	..	..	..	..	..	..	..	..	..
2400 Unallocable between 2100, 2200 and 2300	..	..	..	..	..	..	..	..	..	..
3000 Taxes on payroll and workforce	**0**	..	**0**	**0**	**0**	..	..	..	..	..
4000 Taxes on property	**65**	..	**2 482**	**6 769**	**12 347**	..	..	..	..	..
4100 Recurrent taxes on immovable property	0	..	106	535	1 572	..	..	..	..	..
4200 Recurrent taxes on net wealth	0	..	0	0	0	..	..	..	..	..
4300 Estate, inheritance and gift taxes	11	..	1 029	1 873	4 625	..	..	..	..	..
4400 Taxes on financial and capital transactions	49	..	1 258	4 363	6 150	..	..	..	..	..
4500 Non-recurrent taxes	5	..	89	-2	0	..	..	..	..	..
4600 Other recurrent taxes on property	0	..	0	0	0	..	..	..	..	..
5000 Taxes on goods and services	**920**	..	**29 170**	**63 480**	**92 669**	..	..	..	..	..
5100 Taxes on production, sale, transfer, etc	920	..	29 170	63 480	92 669	..	..	..	..	..
5110 General taxes	198	..	14 637	36 118	57 139	..	..	..	..	..
5120 Taxes on specific goods and services	722	..	14 533	27 362	35 530	..	..	..	..	..
5130 Unallocable between 5110 and 5120	0	..	0	0	0	..	..	..	..	..
5200 Taxes on use of goods and perform activities	0	..	0	0	0	..	..	..	..	..
5300 Unallocable between 5100 and 5200	0	..	0	0	0	..	..	..	..	..
6000 Other taxes	**64**	..	**2 121**	**2 108**	**4 049**	..	..	..	..	..
6100 Paid solely by business	0	..	0	0	0	..	..	..	..	..
6200 Other	64	..	2 121	2 108	4 049	..	..	..	..	..
Total tax revenue	**1 393**	..	**56 774**	**127 466**	**205 519**	..	..	..	..	..

Billion KRW

	Local government					Social Security Funds				
	1975	1985	1995	2005	2014	1975	1985	1995	2005	2014
1000 Taxes on income, profits and capital gains	**36**	..	**1 704**	**5 500**	**9 899**	**0**	..	**0**	**0**	**0**
1100 Of individuals	0	..	1 137	2 804	6 017	..	..	..	..	..
1200 Corporate	0	..	565	2 696	3 882	..	..	..	..	..
1300 Unallocable between 1100 and 1200	36	..	3	0	0	..	..	..	..	..
2000 Social security contributions	**0**	..	**0**	**0**	**0**	**13**	..	**9 913**	**43 902**	**98 184**
2100 Employees	..	..	..	..	..	0	..	4 539	17 632	41 355
2200 Employers	..	..	..	..	..	13	..	3 918	18 486	44 806
2300 Self-employed or non-employed	..	..	..	..	..	0	..	1 456	7 784	12 023
2400 Unallocable between 2100, 2200 and 2300	..	..	..	..	..	0	..	0	0	0
3000 Taxes on payroll and workforce	**0**	..	**237**	**514**	**1 042**	**0**	..	**0**	**0**	**0**
4000 Taxes on property	**87**	..	**8 960**	**17 928**	**27 958**	**0**	..	**0**	**0**	**0**
4100 Recurrent taxes on immovable property	45	..	2 636	4 495	10 082	..	..	..	..	..
4200 Recurrent taxes on net wealth	0	..	0	0	0	..	..	..	..	..
4300 Estate, inheritance and gift taxes	0	..	0	0	0	..	..	..	..	..
4400 Taxes on financial and capital transactions	42	..	6 324	13 433	17 876	..	..	..	..	..
4500 Non-recurrent taxes	0	..	0	0	0	..	..	..	..	..
4600 Other recurrent taxes on property	0	..	0	0	0	..	..	..	..	..
5000 Taxes on goods and services	**36**	..	**4 218**	**7 561**	**16 782**	**0**	..	**0**	**0**	**0**
5100 Taxes on production, sale, transfer, etc	19	..	2 464	5 589	9 862	..	..	..	..	..
5110 General taxes	0	..	0	0	5 836	..	..	..	..	..
5120 Taxes on specific goods and services	19	..	2 464	5 589	4 026	..	..	..	..	..
5130 Unallocable between 5110 and 5120	0	..	0	0	0	..	..	..	..	..
5200 Taxes on use of goods and perform activities	17	..	1 754	1 972	6 920	..	..	..	..	..
5300 Unallocable between 5100 and 5200	0	..	0	0	0	..	..	..	..	..
6000 Other taxes	**0**	..	**198**	**4 474**	**6 044**	**0**	..	**0**	**0**	**0**
6100 Paid solely by business	..	..	0	0	0	..	..	..	..	..
6200 Other	..	..	198	4 474	6 044	..	..	..	..	..
Total tax revenue	**159**	..	**15 316**	**35 977**	**61 725**	**13**	..	**9 913**	**43 902**	**98 184**

StatLink http://dx.doi.org/10.1787/888933417337

Table 5.32. **Latvia, tax revenues by sub-sectors of government**

Million EUR

	Central government					State/Regional				
	1975	1985	1995	2005	2014					
1000 Taxes on income, profits and capital gains	..	..	**68**	**453**	**641**	..	..	..	..	..
1100 Of individuals	..	..	0	195	277	..	..	..	..	..
1200 Corporate	..	..	68	258	364	..	..	..	..	..
1300 Unallocable between 1100 and 1200	..	..	0	0	0	..	..	..	..	..
2000 Social security contributions	..	..	**0**	**0**	**0**	..	..	..	..	..
2100 Employees	..	..	..	..	..	..	..	..	..	..
2200 Employers	..	..	..	..	..	..	..	..	..	..
2300 Self-employed or non-employed	..	..	..	..	..	..	..	..	..	..
2400 Unallocable between 2100, 2200 and 2300	..	..	..	..	..	..	..	..	..	..
3000 Taxes on payroll and workforce	..	..	**0**	**4**	**3**	..	..	..	..	..
4000 Taxes on property	..	..	**4**	**48**	**52**	..	..	..	..	..
4100 Recurrent taxes on immovable property	..	..	0	0	0	..	..	..	..	..
4200 Recurrent taxes on net wealth	..	..	0	0	0	..	..	..	..	..
4300 Estate, inheritance and gift taxes	..	..	0	0	2	..	..	..	..	..
4400 Taxes on financial and capital transactions	..	..	4	48	49	..	..	..	..	..
4500 Non-recurrent taxes	..	..	0	0	0	..	..	..	..	..
4600 Other recurrent taxes on property	..	..	0	0	0	..	..	..	..	..
5000 Taxes on goods and services	..	..	**453**	**1 537**	**2 765**	..	..	..	..	..
5100 Taxes on production, sale, transfer, etc	..	..	453	1 494	2 609	..	..	..	..	..
5110 General taxes	..	..	343	1 002	1 818	..	..	..	..	..
5120 Taxes on specific goods and services	..	..	110	493	791	..	..	..	..	..
5130 Unallocable between 5110 and 5120	..	..	0	0	0	..	..	..	..	..
5200 Taxes on use of goods and perform activities	..	..	1	43	157	..	..	..	..	..
5300 Unallocable between 5100 and 5200	..	..	0	0	0	..	..	..	..	..
6000 Other taxes	..	..	**0**	**0**	**0**	..	..	..	..	..
6100 Paid solely by business	..	..	..	..	..	..	..	..	..	..
6200 Other	..	..	..	..	..	..	..	..	..	..
Total tax revenue	..	..	**525**	**2 043**	**3 461**	..	..	..	..	..

Million EUR

	Local government					Social Security Funds				
	1975	1985	1995	2005	2014	1975	1985	1995	2005	2014
1000 Taxes on income, profits and capital gains	..	..	**197**	**538**	**1 120**	..	..	**0**	**0**	**0**
1100 Of individuals	..	..	197	538	1 120	..	..	..	..	..
1200 Corporate	..	..	0	0	0	..	..	..	..	..
1300 Unallocable between 1100 and 1200	..	..	0	0	0	..	..	..	..	..
2000 Social security contributions	..	..	**0**	**0**	**0**	..	..	**445**	**1 079**	**1 982**
2100 Employees	..	..	..	..	..	..	..	12	292	607
2200 Employers	..	..	..	..	..	..	..	433	781	1 364
2300 Self-employed or non-employed	..	..	..	..	..	..	..	1	7	12
2400 Unallocable between 2100, 2200 and 2300	..	..	..	..	..	..	..	0	0	0
3000 Taxes on payroll and workforce	..	..	**0**	**0**	**0**	..	..	**0**	**0**	**0**
4000 Taxes on property	..	..	**37**	**88**	**191**	..	..	**0**	**0**	**0**
4100 Recurrent taxes on immovable property	..	..	37	88	191	..	..	..	..	..
4200 Recurrent taxes on net wealth	..	..	0	0	0	..	..	..	..	..
4300 Estate, inheritance and gift taxes	..	..	0	0	0	..	..	..	..	..
4400 Taxes on financial and capital transactions	..	..	0	0	0	..	..	..	..	..
4500 Non-recurrent taxes	..	..	0	0	0	..	..	..	..	..
4600 Other recurrent taxes on property	..	..	0	0	0	..	..	..	..	..
5000 Taxes on goods and services	..	..	**2**	**8**	**17**	..	..	**0**	**0**	**0**
5100 Taxes on production, sale, transfer, etc	..	..	0	5	7	..	..	..	..	..
5110 General taxes	..	..	0	0	0	..	..	..	..	..
5120 Taxes on specific goods and services	..	..	0	5	7	..	..	..	..	..
5130 Unallocable between 5110 and 5120	..	..	0	0	0	..	..	..	..	..
5200 Taxes on use of goods and perform activities	..	..	2	3	10	..	..	..	..	..
5300 Unallocable between 5100 and 5200	..	..	0	0	0	..	..	..	..	..
6000 Other taxes	..	..	**0**	**0**	**0**	..	..	**0**	**0**	**0**
6100 Paid solely by business	..	..	..	..	..	..	..	..	..	..
6200 Other	..	..	..	..	..	..	..	..	..	..
Total tax revenue	..	..	**236**	**634**	**1 329**	..	..	**445**	**1 079**	**1 982**

Note : Excluding customs duties collected on behalf of the European Union: 2014 = 35.7.

StatLink http://dx.doi.org/10.1787/888933417348

Tableau 5.33. **Luxembourg, recettes fiscales par sous-secteurs d'administration**

Million EUR

	Administration centrale					Administration d'État/Régions				
	1975	1985	1995	2005	2014					
1000 Impôts sur revenu, bénéfices et gains en capital	**353**	**992**	**1 873**	**3 454**	**5 938**	..	..	..	..	..
1100 Des personnes physiques	254	672	1 214	2 162	4 344	..	..	..	..	..
1200 Des sociétés	99	320	659	1 293	1 594	..	..	..	..	..
1300 Non-ventilables entre 1100 et 1200	0	0	0	0	0	..	..	..	..	..
2000 Cotisations de sécurité sociale	**4**	**11**	**20**	**89**	**170**	..	..	..	..	..
2100 A la charge des salariés	3	8	15	89	170	..	..	..	..	..
2200 A la charge des employeurs	0	0	0	0	0	..	..	..	..	..
2300 A charge des travailleurs indép. ou sans emploi	1	3	5	0	0	..	..	..	..	..
2400 Non-ventilables entre 2100, 2200 et 2300	0	0	0	0	0	..	..	..	..	..
3000 Sur salaires ou main d'oeuvre	**0**	**0**	**0**	**0**	**0**	..	..	..	..	..
4000 Impôts sur le patrimoine	**42**	**134**	**371**	**928**	**1 399**	..	..	..	..	..
4100 Impôts périodiques sur la propriété immobilière	0	0	0	0	0	..	..	..	..	..
4200 Impôts périodiques sur l'actif net	21	83	268	698	1 077	..	..	..	..	..
4300 Impôts sur mut. par décès, succ. et donations	3	7	15	44	74	..	..	..	..	..
4400 Impôts sur transact. mobilières et immob.	18	44	88	186	249	..	..	..	..	..
4500 Impôts non-périodiques	0	0	0	0	0	..	..	..	..	..
4600 Autres impôts périodiques sur patrimoine	0	0	0	0	0	..	..	..	..	..
5000 Impôts sur les biens et services	**189**	**632**	**1 384**	**3 255**	**5 386**	..	..	..	..	..
5100 Impôts sur production, vente, transfert, etc.	182	620	1 361	3 216	5 307	..	..	..	..	..
5110 Impôts généraux	112	337	680	1 826	3 684	..	..	..	..	..
5120 Impôts sur biens et services déterminés	70	283	680	1 390	1 623	..	..	..	..	..
5130 Non-ventilables entre 5110 et 5120	0	0	0	0	0	..	..	..	..	..
5200 Impôts sur utilisation des biens et exerc. activites	7	13	23	39	79	..	..	..	..	..
5300 Non-ventilables entre 5100 et 5200	0	0	0	0	0	..	..	..	..	..
6000 Autres impôts	**0**	**0**	**6**	**11**	**17**	..	..	..	..	..
6100 A la charge exclusive des entreprises	..	0	6	10	16	..	..	..	..	..
6200 A la charge d'autres agents	..	0	0	0	0	..	..	..	..	..
Recettes fiscales totales	**588**	**1 769**	**3 655**	**7 737**	**12 911**	..	..	..	..	..

Million EUR

	Administrations locales					Administrations de sécurité sociale				
	1975	1985	1995	2005	2014	1975	1985	1995	2005	2014
1000 Impôts sur revenu, bénéfices et gains en capital	**46**	**145**	**331**	**460**	**546**	**0**	**0**	**0**	**0**	**0**
1100 Des personnes physiques	0	0	0	0	0	..	..	..	..	..
1200 Des sociétés	46	145	331	460	546	..	..	..	..	..
1300 Non-ventilables entre 1100 et 1200	0	0	0	0	0	..	..	..	..	..
2000 Cotisations de sécurité sociale	**0**	**0**	**0**	**0**	**0**	**268**	**679**	**1 464**	**3 084**	**5 218**
2100 A la charge des salariés	..	..	..	..	..	102	247	578	1 321	2 291
2200 A la charge des employeurs	..	..	..	..	..	150	339	685	1 375	2 280
2300 A charge des travailleurs indép. ou sans emploi	..	..	..	..	..	16	94	200	388	647
2400 Non-ventilables entre 2100, 2200 et 2300	..	..	..	..	..	0	0	0	0	0
3000 Sur salaires ou main d'oeuvre	**9**	**14**	**0**	**0**	**0**	**0**	**0**	**0**	**0**	**0**
4000 Impôts sur le patrimoine	**6**	**13**	**21**	**35**	**56**	**0**	**0**	**0**	**0**	**0**
4100 Impôts périodiques sur la propriété immobilière	6	13	17	26	34	..	..	..	..	..
4200 Impôts périodiques sur l'actif net	0	0	0	0	0	..	..	..	..	..
4300 Impôts sur mut. par décès, succ. et donations	0	0	0	0	0	..	..	..	..	..
4400 Impôts sur transact. mobilières et immob.	0	0	4	10	21	..	..	..	..	..
4500 Impôts non-périodiques	0	0	0	0	0	..	..	..	..	..
4600 Autres impôts périodiques sur patrimoine	0	0	0	0	0	..	..	..	..	..
5000 Impôts sur les biens et services	**1**	**2**	**4**	**8**	**9**	**0**	**0**	**0**	**0**	**0**
5100 Impôts sur production, vente, transfert, etc.	1	2	3	7	8	..	..	..	..	..
5110 Impôts généraux	0	0	0	0	0	..	..	..	..	..
5120 Impôts sur biens et services déterminés	1	2	3	7	8	..	..	..	..	..
5130 Non-ventilables entre 5110 et 5120	0	0	0	0	0	..	..	..	..	..
5200 Impôts sur utilisation des biens et exerc. activites	0	0	1	1	1	..	..	..	..	..
5300 Non-ventilables entre 5100 et 5200	0	0	0	0	0	..	..	..	..	..
6000 Autres impôts	**0**	**0**	**1**	**2**	**1**	**0**	**0**	**0**	**0**	**0**
6100 A la charge exclusive des entreprises	..	..	1	2	1	..	..	..	..	..
6200 A la charge d'autres agents	..	..	0	0	0	..	..	..	..	..
Recettes fiscales totales	**62**	**174**	**357**	**505**	**613**	**268**	**679**	**1 464**	**3 084**	**5 218**

Note : À l'exclusion des droits de douane perçus pour le compte de l'Union européenne : 2014 = 18.9.

StatLink http://dx.doi.org/10.1787/888933417353

Table 5.34. **Mexico, tax revenues by sub-sectors of government**

Million MXN

	Federal government					State/Regional				
	1975	1985	1995	2005	2014	1975	1985	1995	2005	2014
1000 Taxes on income, profits and capital gains	..	1 899	76 148	402 036	979 251	..	0	1	0	0
1100 Of individuals	..	..	..	195 869	514 208	..	..	..	..	..
1200 Corporate	..	..	..	135 840	441 317	..	..	..	..	..
1300 Unallocable between 1100 and 1200	..	1 899	76 148	70 327	23 726	..	..	1	..	..
2000 Social security contributions	..	0	0	0	0	..	0	0	0	0
2100 Employees	..	..	..	..	..	..	..	..	..	..
2200 Employers	..	..	..	..	..	..	..	..	..	..
2300 Self-employed or non-employed	..	..	..	..	..	..	..	..	..	..
2400 Unallocable between 2100, 2200 and 2300	..	..	..	..	..	..	..	..	..	..
3000 Taxes on payroll and workforce	..	49	0	0	0	..	20	2 976	20 429	64 711
4000 Taxes on property	..	0	0	0	0	..	3	2 927	10 905	19 324
4100 Recurrent taxes on immovable property	..	..	..	..	..	..	0	2 198	6 544	11 850
4200 Recurrent taxes on net wealth	..	..	..	..	..	..	0	0	0	0
4300 Estate, inheritance and gift taxes	..	..	..	..	..	..	0	2	0	0
4400 Taxes on financial and capital transactions	..	..	..	..	..	..	3	727	4 361	7 474
4500 Non-recurrent taxes	..	..	..	..	..	..	0	0	0	0
4600 Other recurrent taxes on property	..	..	..	..	..	..	0	0	0	0
5000 Taxes on goods and services	..	5 539	91 452	467 019	908 631	..	4	441	2 124	23 932
5100 Taxes on production, sale, transfer, etc	..	5 517	88 372	401 580	849 408	..	1	22	1 364	3 546
5110 General taxes	..	1 365	51 785	318 432	667 085	..	1	0	0	0
5120 Taxes on specific goods and services	..	4 152	36 587	83 148	182 323	..	0	22	1 364	3 546
5130 Unallocable between 5110 and 5120	..	0	0	0	0	..	0	0	0	0
5200 Taxes on use of goods and perform activities	..	22	3 080	65 439	59 223	..	3	419	760	20 386
5300 Unallocable between 5100 and 5200	..	0	0	0	0	..	0	0	0	0
6000 Other taxes	..	24	5 149	8 616	24 221	..	8	228	1 537	6 762
6100 Paid solely by business	..	0	0	0	0	..	0	0	0	0
6200 Other	..	24	5 149	8 616	24 221	..	8	228	1 537	6 762
Total tax revenue (collecting government)	..	7 511	172 749	877 671	1 912 103	..	35	6 573	34 995	114 729
Adjustment[1]	..	-1 336	-49 115	-278 892	-584 904	..	1 094	39 225	218 291	456 326
Total tax revenue (beneficiary government)	..	6 175	123 634	598 779	1 327 199	..	1 129	45 798	253 286	571 055

Million MXN

	Local government					Social Security Funds				
	1975	1985	1995	2005	2014	1975	1985	1995	2005	2014
1000 Taxes on income, profits and capital gains	..	0	16	0	0	..	0	0	0	0
1100 Of individuals	..	..	..	..	..	..	..	..	..	..
1200 Corporate	..	..	..	..	..	..	..	..	..	..
1300 Unallocable between 1100 and 1200	..	..	16	..	..	..	..	..	..	..
2000 Social security contributions	..	0	0	0	0	..	968	50 871	261 673	538 213
2100 Employees	..	..	..	..	..	..	..	..	..	..
2200 Employers	..	..	..	..	..	..	..	..	..	..
2300 Self-employed or non-employed	..	..	..	..	..	..	..	..	..	..
2400 Unallocable between 2100, 2200 and 2300	..	..	..	..	..	..	968	50 871	261 673	538 213
3000 Taxes on payroll and workforce	..	0	6	32	2	..	0	0	0	0
4000 Taxes on property	..	39	2 702	15 891	35 596	..	0	0	0	0
4100 Recurrent taxes on immovable property	..	29	1 854	10 098	25 843	..	..	..	..	..
4200 Recurrent taxes on net wealth	..	0	0	0	0	..	..	..	..	..
4300 Estate, inheritance and gift taxes	..	0	0	0	0	..	..	..	..	..
4400 Taxes on financial and capital transactions	..	10	848	5 793	9 753	..	..	..	..	..
4500 Non-recurrent taxes	..	0	0	0	0	..	..	..	..	..
4600 Other recurrent taxes on property	..	0	0	0	0	..	..	..	..	..
5000 Taxes on goods and services	..	7	582	288	1 269	..	0	0	0	0
5100 Taxes on production, sale, transfer, etc	..	7	575	214	1 235	..	..	..	..	..
5110 General taxes	..	0	0	0	0	..	..	..	..	..
5120 Taxes on specific goods and services	..	7	572	214	1 235	..	..	..	..	..
5130 Unallocable between 5110 and 5120	..	0	3	0	0	..	..	..	..	..
5200 Taxes on use of goods and perform activities	..	0	7	74	33	..	..	..	..	..
5300 Unallocable between 5100 and 5200	..	0	0	0	0	..	..	..	..	..
6000 Other taxes	..	5	179	1 539	5 784	..	0	0	0	0
6100 Paid solely by business	..	0	0	0	0	..	..	..	..	..
6200 Other	..	5	179	1 539	5 784	..	..	..	..	..
Total tax revenue (collecting government)	..	51	3 485	17 750	42 651	..	968	50 871	261 673	538 213
Adjustment[1]	..	242	9 890	60 601	128 578	..	0	0	0	0
Total tax revenue (beneficiary government)	..	293	13 375	78 351	171 229	..	968	50 871	261 673	538 213

1. This adjustment is for taxes collected by Federal government in which States and Local governments have a share. Sub-central government's shares cannot be identified by type of tax.

StatLink http://dx.doi.org/10.1787/888933417363

Table 5.35. **Netherlands, tax revenues by sub-sectors of government**

Million EUR

	Central government					State/Regional				
	1975	1985	1995	2005	2014					
1000 Taxes on income, profits and capital gains	**15 075**	**22 453**	**33 520**	**52 640**	**63 671**	..	..	..	..	..
1100 Of individuals	11 713	16 527	23 557	33 905	46 581	..	..	..	..	..
1200 Corporate	3 361	5 926	9 963	18 735	17 090	..	..	..	..	..
1300 Unallocable between 1100 and 1200	0	0	0	0	0	..	..	..	..	..
2000 Social security contributions	**0**	**0**	**0**	**0**	**0**	..	..	..	..	..
2100 Employees	..	..	..	..	..	..	..	..	..	..
2200 Employers	..	..	..	..	..	..	..	..	..	..
2300 Self-employed or non-employed	..	..	..	..	..	..	..	..	..	..
2400 Unallocable between 2100, 2200 and 2300	..	..	..	..	..	..	..	..	..	..
3000 Taxes on payroll and workforce	**0**	**0**	**0**	**0**	**0**	..	..	..	..	..
4000 Taxes on property	**767**	**1 429**	**2 880**	**6 235**	**4 770**	..	..	..	..	..
4100 Recurrent taxes on immovable property	50	0	0	0	1 679	..	..	..	..	..
4200 Recurrent taxes on net wealth	231	427	671	60	0	..	..	..	..	..
4300 Estate, inheritance and gift taxes	163	372	773	1 709	1 525	..	..	..	..	..
4400 Taxes on financial and capital transactions	323	631	1 436	4 466	1 566	..	..	..	..	..
4500 Non-recurrent taxes	0	0	0	0	0	..	..	..	..	..
4600 Other recurrent taxes on property	0	0	0	0	0	..	..	..	..	..
5000 Taxes on goods and services	**9 716**	**20 075**	**31 898**	**57 126**	**68 745**	..	..	..	..	..
5100 Taxes on production, sale, transfer, etc	9 113	18 669	29 758	54 716	64 691	..	..	..	..	..
5110 General taxes	6 257	13 790	19 838	36 960	42 741	..	..	..	..	..
5120 Taxes on specific goods and services	2 856	4 878	9 920	17 756	21 950	..	..	..	..	..
5130 Unallocable between 5110 and 5120	0	0	0	0	0	..	..	..	..	..
5200 Taxes on use of goods and perform activities	604	1 407	2 140	2 410	4 054	..	..	..	..	..
5300 Unallocable between 5100 and 5200	0	0	0	0	0	..	..	..	..	..
6000 Other taxes	**109**	**195**	**491**	**989**	**1 233**	..	..	..	..	..
6100 Paid solely by business	109	195	448	372	33	..	..	..	..	..
6200 Other	0	0	43	617	1 200	..	..	..	..	..
Total tax revenue	**25 667**	**44 153**	**68 789**	**116 990**	**138 419**	..	..	..	..	..

Million EUR

	Local government					Social Security Funds				
	1975	1985	1995	2005	2014	1975	1985	1995	2005	2014
1000 Taxes on income, profits and capital gains	**77**	**0**	**0**	**0**	**0**	**0**	**0**	**0**	**0**	**0**
1100 Of individuals	77	0	0	0	0	0	0	0	0	0
1200 Corporate	0	0	0	0	0	0	0	0	0	0
1300 Unallocable between 1100 and 1200	0	0	0	0	0	0	0	0	0	0
2000 Social security contributions	**0**	**0**	**0**	**0**	**0**	**16 732**	**37 709**	**48 532**	**66 547**	**98 616**
2100 Employees	..	..	..	..	..	7 139	16 835	32 795	35 383	48 351
2200 Employers	..	..	..	..	..	7 687	15 093	5 941	20 595	34 996
2300 Self-employed or non-employed	..	..	..	..	..	1 905	5 781	9 796	10 569	15 269
2400 Unallocable between 2100, 2200 and 2300	..	..	..	..	..	0	0	0	0	0
3000 Taxes on payroll and workforce	**0**	**0**	**0**	**0**	**0**	**0**	**0**	**0**	**0**	**0**
4000 Taxes on property	**272**	**1 529**	**2 287**	**4 341**	**4 836**	**0**	**0**	**0**	**0**	**0**
4100 Recurrent taxes on immovable property	272	1 529	2 287	4 341	4 836	..	..	..	..	..
4200 Recurrent taxes on net wealth	0	0	0	0	0	..	..	..	..	..
4300 Estate, inheritance and gift taxes	0	0	0	0	0	..	..	..	..	..
4400 Taxes on financial and capital transactions	0	0	0	0	0	..	..	..	..	..
4500 Non-recurrent taxes	0	0	0	0	0	..	..	..	..	..
4600 Other recurrent taxes on property	0	0	0	0	0	..	..	..	..	..
5000 Taxes on goods and services	**153**	**508**	**1 527**	**3 320**	**4 502**	**0**	**0**	**0**	**0**	**0**
5100 Taxes on production, sale, transfer, etc	14	23	53	108	180	..	..	..	..	..
5110 General taxes	0	0	0	0	0	..	..	..	..	..
5120 Taxes on specific goods and services	14	23	53	108	180	..	..	..	..	..
5130 Unallocable between 5110 and 5120	0	0	0	0	0	..	..	..	..	..
5200 Taxes on use of goods and perform activities	139	486	1 474	3 212	4 322	..	..	..	..	..
5300 Unallocable between 5100 and 5200	0	0	0	0	0	..	..	..	..	..
6000 Other taxes	**0**	**0**	**0**	**0**	**0**	**0**	**0**	**0**	**0**	**0**
6100 Paid solely by business	..	..	..	..	..	..	..	..	..	..
6200 Other	..	..	..	..	..	..	..	..	..	..
Total tax revenue	**502**	**2 037**	**3 814**	**7 661**	**9 338**	**16 732**	**37 709**	**48 532**	**66 547**	**98 616**

Note : Excluding customs duties collected on behalf of the European Union: 2014 = 2 046.0.

StatLink http://dx.doi.org/10.1787/888933417371

Table 5.36. New Zealand, tax revenues by sub-sectors of government

Million NZD

	Central government					State/Regional				
	1975	1985	1995	2005	2014					
1000 Taxes on income, profits and capital gains	**2 296**	**10 567**	**21 253**	**37 379**	**43 161**	..	..	..	..	..
1100 Of individuals	1 874	9 212	15 626	24 373	30 069	..	..	..	..	..
1200 Corporate	407	1 270	4 122	9 957	10 250	..	..	..	..	..
1300 Unallocable between 1100 and 1200	16	86	1 505	3 049	2 842	..	..	..	..	..
2000 Social security contributions	**0**	**0**	**0**	**0**	**0**	..	..	..	..	..
2100 Employees	..	..	..	..	..	..	..	..	..	..
2200 Employers	..	..	..	..	..	..	..	..	..	..
2300 Self-employed or non-employed	..	..	..	..	..	..	..	..	..	..
2400 Unallocable between 2100, 2200 and 2300	..	..	..	..	..	..	..	..	..	..
3000 Taxes on payroll and workforce	**0**	**0**	**0**	**0**	**0**	..	..	..	..	..
4000 Taxes on property	**83**	**211**	**218**	**86**	**100**	..	..	..	..	..
4100 Recurrent taxes on immovable property	3	56	-1	0	0	..	..	..	..	..
4200 Recurrent taxes on net wealth	0	0	0	0	0	..	..	..	..	..
4300 Estate, inheritance and gift taxes	54	28	3	3	0	..	..	..	..	..
4400 Taxes on financial and capital transactions	25	127	216	83	100	..	..	..	..	..
4500 Non-recurrent taxes	0	0	0	0	0	..	..	..	..	..
4600 Other recurrent taxes on property	0	0	0	0	0	..	..	..	..	..
5000 Taxes on goods and services	**807**	**3 457**	**11 395**	**18 744**	**29 440**	..	..	..	..	..
5100 Taxes on production, sale, transfer, etc	770	3 336	10 833	17 792	27 976	..	..	..	..	..
5110 General taxes	311	1 577	7 895	14 133	23 306	..	..	..	..	..
5120 Taxes on specific goods and services	459	1 758	2 938	3 659	4 670	..	..	..	..	..
5130 Unallocable between 5110 and 5120	0	0	0	0	0	..	..	..	..	..
5200 Taxes on use of goods and perform activities	37	122	562	952	1 464	..	..	..	..	..
5300 Unallocable between 5100 and 5200	0	0	0	0	0	..	..	..	..	..
6000 Other taxes	**0**	**0**	**0**	**14**	**2**	..	..	..	..	..
6100 Paid solely by business	..	..	..	0	0	..	..	..	..	..
6200 Other	..	..	..	14	2	..	..	..	..	..
Total tax revenue	**3 186**	**14 236**	**32 866**	**56 223**	**72 703**	..	..	..	..	..

Million NZD

	Local government					Social Security Funds				
	1975	1985	1995	2005	2014	1975	1985	1995	2005	2014
1000 Taxes on income, profits and capital gains	**0**	**0**	**0**	**0**	**0**	**0**	**0**	**0**	**0**	**0**
1100 Of individuals	0	0	0	0	0	0	0	0	0	0
1200 Corporate	0	0	0	0	0	0	0	0	0	0
1300 Unallocable between 1100 and 1200	0	0	0	0	0	0	0	0	0	0
2000 Social security contributions	**0**	**0**	**0**	**0**	**0**	**0**	**0**	**0**	**0**	**0**
2100 Employees	..	..	..	..	..	..	..	..	..	..
2200 Employers	..	..	..	..	..	..	..	..	..	..
2300 Self-employed or non-employed	..	..	..	..	..	..	..	..	..	..
2400 Unallocable between 2100, 2200 and 2300	..	..	..	..	..	..	..	..	..	..
3000 Taxes on payroll and workforce	**0**	**0**	**0**	**0**	**0**	**0**	**0**	**0**	**0**	**0**
4000 Taxes on property	**237**	**921**	**1 646**	**2 825**	**4 704**	**0**	**0**	**0**	**0**	**0**
4100 Recurrent taxes on immovable property	237	921	1 646	2 825	4 704	..	..	..	..	..
4200 Recurrent taxes on net wealth	0	0	0	0	0	..	..	..	..	..
4300 Estate, inheritance and gift taxes	0	0	0	0	0	..	..	..	..	..
4400 Taxes on financial and capital transactions	0	0	0	0	0	..	..	..	..	..
4500 Non-recurrent taxes	0	0	0	0	0	..	..	..	..	..
4600 Other recurrent taxes on property	0	0	0	0	0	..	..	..	..	..
5000 Taxes on goods and services	**29**	**66**	**184**	**310**	**504**	**0**	**0**	**0**	**0**	**0**
5100 Taxes on production, sale, transfer, etc	18	18	33	30	33	..	..	..	..	..
5110 General taxes	0	0	0	0	0	..	..	..	..	..
5120 Taxes on specific goods and services	18	18	33	30	33	..	..	..	..	..
5130 Unallocable between 5110 and 5120	0	0	0	0	0	..	..	..	..	..
5200 Taxes on use of goods and perform activities	11	48	151	280	471	..	..	..	..	..
5300 Unallocable between 5100 and 5200	0	0	0	0	0	..	..	..	..	..
6000 Other taxes	**0**	**0**	**0**	**0**	**0**	**0**	**0**	**0**	**0**	**0**
6100 Paid solely by business	..	..	..	..	..	..	..	..	..	..
6200 Other	..	..	..	..	..	..	..	..	..	..
Total tax revenue	**266**	**987**	**1 830**	**3 135**	**5 208**	**0**	**0**	**0**	**0**	**0**

StatLink http://dx.doi.org/10.1787/888933417388

Table 5.37. **Norway, tax revenues by sub-sectors of government**

Million NOK

	Central government[1]					State/Regional				
	1975	1985	1995	2005	2014					
1000 Taxes on income, profits and capital gains	**6 495**	**47 772**	**67 402**	**316 851**	**369 783**	..	..	..	..	..
1100 Of individuals	5 424	10 115	38 059	87 503	161 150	..	..	..	..	..
1200 Corporate	1 071	37 657	29 343	229 348	208 633	..	..	..	..	..
1300 Unallocable between 1100 and 1200	0	0	0	0	0	..	..	..	..	..
2000 Social security contributions	**1 341**	**2 854**	**6 013**	**173 151**	**312 942**	..	..	..	..	..
2100 Employees	331	569	1 233	58 320	107 875	..	..	..	..	..
2200 Employers	1 010	2 285	4 780	104 794	186 469	..	..	..	..	..
2300 Self-employed or non-employed	0	0	0	10 037	18 598	..	..	..	..	..
2400 Unallocable between 2100, 2200 and 2300	0	0	0	0	0	..	..	..	..	..
3000 Taxes on payroll and workforce	**0**	**0**	**0**	**0**	**0**	..	..	..	..	..
4000 Taxes on property	**771**	**1 800**	**3 497**	**11 406**	**19 266**	..	..	..	..	..
4100 Recurrent taxes on immovable property	0	0	0	228	1 536	..	..	..	..	..
4200 Recurrent taxes on net wealth	490	940	1 172	4 741	8 206	..	..	..	..	..
4300 Estate, inheritance and gift taxes	146	226	975	1 768	1 880	..	..	..	..	..
4400 Taxes on financial and capital transactions	135	634	1 350	4 669	7 644	..	..	..	..	..
4500 Non-recurrent taxes	0	0	0	0	0	..	..	..	..	..
4600 Other recurrent taxes on property	0	0	0	0	0	..	..	..	..	..
5000 Taxes on goods and services	**25 056**	**87 964**	**148 088**	**232 759**	**348 244**	..	..	..	..	..
5100 Taxes on production, sale, transfer, etc	24 367	85 468	141 408	220 835	331 701	..	..	..	..	..
5110 General taxes	13 670	42 889	81 772	153 820	244 767	..	..	..	..	..
5120 Taxes on specific goods and services	10 697	42 579	59 636	67 015	86 934	..	..	..	..	..
5130 Unallocable between 5110 and 5120	0	0	0	0	0	..	..	..	..	..
5200 Taxes on use of goods and perform activities	689	2 496	6 680	11 924	16 543	..	..	..	..	..
5300 Unallocable between 5100 and 5200	0	0	0	0	0	..	..	..	..	..
6000 Other taxes	**130**	**24**	**15**	**0**	**0**	..	..	..	..	..
6100 Paid solely by business	124	15	1	..	..	..	..	..	..	..
6200 Other	6	9	14	..	..	..	..	..	..	..
Total tax revenue	**33 793**	**140 414**	**225 015**	**734 167**	**1 050 235**	..	..	..	..	..

Million NOK

	Local government					Social Security Funds				
	1975	1985	1995	2005	2014	1975	1985	1995	2005	2014
1000 Taxes on income, profits and capital gains	**13 725**	**38 655**	**67 978**	**100 512**	**148 468**	**2 728**	**7 163**	**0**	**0**	**0**
1100 Of individuals	12 877	35 739	61 784	100 512	148 468	2 728	7 163	..	..	..
1200 Corporate	848	2 916	6 194	0	0	0	0	..	..	..
1300 Unallocable between 1100 and 1200	0	0	0	0	0	0	0	..	..	..
2000 Social security contributions	**0**	**0**	**0**	**0**	**0**	**15 224**	**46 106**	**84 563**	**0**	**0**
2100 Employees	..	..	..	..	..	2 949	12 623	30 417	..	..
2200 Employers	..	..	..	..	..	11 315	31 628	48 396	..	..
2300 Self-employed or non-employed	..	..	..	..	..	960	1 855	5 750	..	..
2400 Unallocable between 2100, 2200 and 2300	..	..	..	..	..	0	0	0	..	..
3000 Taxes on payroll and workforce	**0**	**0**	**0**	**0**	**0**	**0**	**0**	**0**	**0**	**0**
4000 Taxes on property	**772**	**2 755**	**7 352**	**10 283**	**19 022**	**0**	**0**	**0**	**0**	**0**
4100 Recurrent taxes on immovable property	278	1 072	2 792	4 324	9 626	..	..	..	..	..
4200 Recurrent taxes on net wealth	494	1 683	4 560	5 959	9 396	..	..	..	..	..
4300 Estate, inheritance and gift taxes	0	0	0	0	0	..	..	..	..	..
4400 Taxes on financial and capital transactions	0	0	0	0	0	..	..	..	..	..
4500 Non-recurrent taxes	0	0	0	0	0	..	..	..	..	..
4600 Other recurrent taxes on property	0	0	0	0	0	..	..	..	..	..
5000 Taxes on goods and services	**0**	**211**	**431**	**2 281**	**2 144**	**51**	**157**	**267**	**0**	**0**
5100 Taxes on production, sale, transfer, etc	0	0	0	0	0	51	157	267	..	..
5110 General taxes	0	0	0	0	0	0	0	0	..	..
5120 Taxes on specific goods and services	0	0	0	0	0	51	157	267	..	..
5130 Unallocable between 5110 and 5120	0	0	0	0	0	0	0	0	..	..
5200 Taxes on use of goods and perform activities	0	211	431	2 281	2 144	0	0	0	..	..
5300 Unallocable between 5100 and 5200	0	0	0	0	0	0	0	0	..	..
6000 Other taxes	**432**	**0**	**0**	**0**	**0**	**0**	**0**	**0**	**0**	**0**
6100 Paid solely by business	0	..	..	..	..	..	..	..	..	..
6200 Other	432	..	..	..	..	..	..	..	..	..
Total tax revenue	**14 929**	**41 621**	**75 761**	**113 076**	**169 634**	**18 003**	**53 426**	**84 830**	**0**	**0**

1. The Norwegian National Insurance has been integrated into the Central government sector from the year 2000 and onwards.

StatLink http://dx.doi.org/10.1787/888933417391

Table 5.38. **Poland, tax revenues by sub-sectors of government**

Million PLN

	Central government					State/Regional				
	1975	1985	1995	2005	2014					
1000 Taxes on income, profits and capital gains	..	..	**32 774**	**40 398**	**66 829**	..	..	..	..	..
1100 Of individuals	..	..	23 937	24 518	43 299	..	..	..	..	..
1200 Corporate	..	..	8 837	15 880	23 530	..	..	..	..	..
1300 Unallocable between 1100 and 1200	..	..	0	0	0	..	..	..	..	..
2000 Social security contributions	..	..	**0**	**0**	**0**	..	..	..	..	..
2100 Employees	..	..	..	..	..	..	..	..	..	..
2200 Employers	..	..	..	..	..	..	..	..	..	..
2300 Self-employed or non-employed	..	..	..	..	..	..	..	..	..	..
2400 Unallocable between 2100, 2200 and 2300	..	..	..	..	..	..	..	..	..	..
3000 Taxes on payroll and workforce	..	..	**831**	**2 555**	**4 042**	..	..	..	..	..
4000 Taxes on property	..	..	**0**	**0**	**0**	..	..	..	..	..
4100 Recurrent taxes on immovable property	..	..	..	..	..	..	..	..	..	..
4200 Recurrent taxes on net wealth	..	..	..	..	..	..	..	..	..	..
4300 Estate, inheritance and gift taxes	..	..	..	..	..	..	..	..	..	..
4400 Taxes on financial and capital transactions	..	..	..	..	..	..	..	..	..	..
4500 Non-recurrent taxes	..	..	..	..	..	..	..	..	..	..
4600 Other recurrent taxes on property	..	..	..	..	..	..	..	..	..	..
5000 Taxes on goods and services	..	..	**46 749**	**120 625**	**194 976**	..	..	..	..	..
5100 Taxes on production, sale, transfer, etc	..	..	46 129	120 223	192 900	..	..	..	..	..
5110 General taxes	..	..	21 051	75 783	122 671	..	..	..	..	..
5120 Taxes on specific goods and services	..	..	25 078	44 440	70 229	..	..	..	..	..
5130 Unallocable between 5110 and 5120	..	..	0	0	0	..	..	..	..	..
5200 Taxes on use of goods and perform activities	..	..	620	402	2 076	..	..	..	..	..
5300 Unallocable between 5100 and 5200	..	..	0	0	0	..	..	..	..	..
6000 Other taxes	..	..	**145**	**18**	**0**	..	..	..	..	..
6100 Paid solely by business	..	..	0	0	..	..	..	..	..	..
6200 Other	..	..	145	18	..	..	..	..	..	..
Total tax revenue	..	..	**80 499**	**163 596**	**265 847**	..	..	..	..	..

Million PLN

	Local government					Social Security Funds				
	1975	1985	1995	2005	2014	1975	1985	1995	2005	2014
1000 Taxes on income, profits and capital gains	..	..	**4 896**	**23 093**	**41 930**	..	..	**0**	**0**	**0**
1100 Of individuals	..	..	4 427	17 916	35 420	..	..	..	..	..
1200 Corporate	..	..	469	5 177	6 510	..	..	..	..	..
1300 Unallocable between 1100 and 1200	..	..	0	0	0	..	..	..	..	..
2000 Social security contributions	..	..	**0**	**0**	**0**	..	..	**38 808**	**120 296**	**209 902**
2100 Employees	..	..	..	..	..	..	..	15 801	47 110	78 494
2200 Employers	..	..	..	..	..	..	..	20 416	48 263	86 474
2300 Self-employed or non-employed	..	..	..	..	..	..	..	2 591	24 923	44 934
2400 Unallocable between 2100, 2200 and 2300	..	..	..	..	..	..	..	0	0	0
3000 Taxes on payroll and workforce	..	..	**0**	**0**	**0**	..	..	**0**	**0**	**0**
4000 Taxes on property	..	..	**4 370**	**14 723**	**23 991**	..	..	**0**	**0**	**0**
4100 Recurrent taxes on immovable property	..	..	3 579	12 718	21 423	..	..	..	..	..
4200 Recurrent taxes on net wealth	..	..	0	0	0	..	..	..	..	..
4300 Estate, inheritance and gift taxes	..	..	44	242	263	..	..	..	..	..
4400 Taxes on financial and capital transactions	..	..	747	1 763	2 305	..	..	..	..	..
4500 Non-recurrent taxes	..	..	0	0	0	..	..	..	..	..
4600 Other recurrent taxes on property	..	..	0	0	0	..	..	..	..	..
5000 Taxes on goods and services	..	..	**1 332**	**3 368**	**3 936**	..	..	**0**	**0**	**0**
5100 Taxes on production, sale, transfer, etc	..	..	0	0	0	..	..	..	..	..
5110 General taxes	..	..	0	0	0	..	..	..	..	..
5120 Taxes on specific goods and services	..	..	0	0	0	..	..	..	..	..
5130 Unallocable between 5110 and 5120	..	..	0	0	0	..	..	..	..	..
5200 Taxes on use of goods and perform activities	..	..	1 332	3 368	3 936	..	..	..	..	..
5300 Unallocable between 5100 and 5200	..	..	0	0	0	..	..	..	..	..
6000 Other taxes	..	..	**166**	**278**	**4 147**	..	..	**0**	**0**	**0**
6100 Paid solely by business	..	..	0	0	0	..	..	..	..	..
6200 Other	..	..	166	278	4 147	..	..	..	..	..
Total tax revenue	..	..	**10 764**	**41 462**	**74 004**	..	..	**38 808**	**120 296**	**209 902**

Note : Excluding customs duties collected on behalf of the European Union: 2014 = 1 791.0.

StatLink http://dx.doi.org/10.1787/888933417406

Table 5.39. **Portugal, tax revenues by sub-sectors of government**

Million EUR

	Central government					State/Regional				
	1975	1985	1995	2005	2014					
1000 Taxes on income, profits and capital gains	**81**	**1 306**	**6 557**	**11 506**	**17 086**	..	..	..	..	..
1100 Of individuals	..	..	4 691	7 757	12 535	..	..	..	..	..
1200 Corporate	..	..	1 866	3 705	4 551	..	..	..	..	..
1300 Unallocable between 1100 and 1200	81	1 306	0	43	0	..	..	..	..	..
2000 Social security contributions	**0**	**0**	**1 560**	**1 887**	**2 024**	..	..	..	..	..
2100 Employees	..	..	941	1 629	1 853	..	..	..	..	..
2200 Employers	..	..	619	259	171	..	..	..	..	..
2300 Self-employed or non-employed	..	..	0	0	0	..	..	..	..	..
2400 Unallocable between 2100, 2200 and 2300	..	..	0	0	0	..	..	..	..	..
3000 Taxes on payroll and workforce	**12**	**137**	**0**	**0**	**0**	..	..	..	..	..
4000 Taxes on property	**12**	**103**	**226**	**261**	**221**	..	..	..	..	..
4100 Recurrent taxes on immovable property	0	0	0	0	20	..	..	..	..	..
4200 Recurrent taxes on net wealth	0	0	0	0	0	..	..	..	..	..
4300 Estate, inheritance and gift taxes	4	45	57	25	0	..	..	..	..	..
4400 Taxes on financial and capital transactions	7	58	169	236	201	..	..	..	..	..
4500 Non-recurrent taxes	0	0	0	0	0	..	..	..	..	..
4600 Other recurrent taxes on property	0	0	0	0	0	..	..	..	..	..
5000 Taxes on goods and services	**198**	**2 362**	**10 402**	**19 638**	**20 356**	..	..	..	..	..
5100 Taxes on production, sale, transfer, etc	187	2 290	10 195	19 220	19 515	..	..	..	..	..
5110 General taxes	52	681	5 481	11 846	13 065	..	..	..	..	..
5120 Taxes on specific goods and services	135	1 609	4 714	7 374	6 450	..	..	..	..	..
5130 Unallocable between 5110 and 5120	0	0	0	0	0	..	..	..	..	..
5200 Taxes on use of goods and perform activities	12	72	178	375	817	..	..	..	..	..
5300 Unallocable between 5100 and 5200	0	0	30	43	24	..	..	..	..	..
6000 Other taxes	**2**	**15**	**98**	**252**	**476**	..	..	..	..	..
6100 Paid solely by business	1	11	18	160	249	..	..	..	..	..
6200 Other	0	4	81	92	227	..	..	..	..	..
Total tax revenue	**304**	**3 922**	**18 844**	**33 544**	**40 163**	..	..	..	..	..

Million EUR

	Local government					Social Security Funds				
	1975	1985	1995	2005	2014	1975	1985	1995	2005	2014
1000 Taxes on income, profits and capital gains	**0**	**126**	**307**	**725**	**1 161**	**0**	**0**	**0**	**0**	**0**
1100 Of individuals	..	..	156	298	783	..	..	..	..	..
1200 Corporate	..	..	151	427	378	..	..	..	..	..
1300 Unallocable between 1100 and 1200	0	126	0	0	0	..	..	..	..	..
2000 Social security contributions	**0**	**0**	**2**	**7**	**17**	**161**	**1 440**	**5 267**	**11 100**	**13 503**
2100 Employees	..	..	2	7	17	62	563	2 100	4 053	4 939
2200 Employers	..	..	0	0	0	97	827	3 167	7 047	8 563
2300 Self-employed or non-employed	..	..	0	0	0	2	32	0	0	0
2400 Unallocable between 2100, 2200 and 2300	..	..	0	0	0	0	18	0	0	0
3000 Taxes on payroll and workforce	**0**	**0**	**0**	**0**	**0**	**0**	**0**	**0**	**0**	**0**
4000 Taxes on property	**0**	**3**	**599**	**1 532**	**1 936**	**0**	**0**	**0**	**0**	**0**
4100 Recurrent taxes on immovable property	..	0	310	827	1 445	..	..	..	..	..
4200 Recurrent taxes on net wealth	..	0	0	0	0	..	..	..	..	..
4300 Estate, inheritance and gift taxes	..	1	0	1	0	..	..	..	..	..
4400 Taxes on financial and capital transactions	..	2	289	704	492	..	..	..	..	..
4500 Non-recurrent taxes	..	0	0	0	0	..	..	..	..	..
4600 Other recurrent taxes on property	..	0	0	0	0	..	..	..	..	..
5000 Taxes on goods and services	**0**	**68**	**499**	**971**	**1 116**	**0**	**0**	**335**	**823**	**1 150**
5100 Taxes on production, sale, transfer, etc	0	59	442	837	852	..	..	335	823	1 150
5110 General taxes	0	18	318	563	631	..	..	276	592	976
5120 Taxes on specific goods and services	0	41	124	273	221	..	..	59	231	174
5130 Unallocable between 5110 and 5120	0	0	0	0	0	..	..	0	0	0
5200 Taxes on use of goods and perform activities	0	8	57	133	264	..	..	0	0	0
5300 Unallocable between 5100 and 5200	0	0	0	1	0	..	..	0	0	0
6000 Other taxes	**0**	**0**	**3**	**28**	**55**	**0**	**0**	**1**	**3**	**9**
6100 Paid solely by business	..	0	0	25	9	..	..	0	0	0
6200 Other	..	0	3	3	46	..	..	1	3	9
Total tax revenue	**0**	**197**	**1 410**	**3 262**	**4 285**	**161**	**1 440**	**5 603**	**11 926**	**14 662**

Note : Excluding customs duties collected on behalf of the European Union: 2014 = 148.6.

StatLink http://dx.doi.org/10.1787/888933417410

Table 5.40. Slovak Republic, tax revenues by sub-sectors of government

Million EUR

	Central government					State/Regional				
	1975	1985	1995	2005	2014					
1000 Taxes on income, profits and capital gains	..	..	**1 993**	**2 968**	**4 949**	..	..	..	..	..
1100 Of individuals	..	..	695	1 496	2 275	..	..	..	..	..
1200 Corporate	..	..	1 166	1 345	2 498	..	..	..	..	..
1300 Unallocable between 1100 and 1200	..	..	132	128	175	..	..	..	..	..
2000 Social security contributions	..	..	**85**	**200**	**177**	..	..	..	..	..
2100 Employees	..	..	10	104	56	..	..	..	..	..
2200 Employers	..	..	75	95	120	..	..	..	..	..
2300 Self-employed or non-employed	..	..	0	0	1	..	..	..	..	..
2400 Unallocable between 2100, 2200 and 2300	..	..	0	0	0	..	..	..	..	..
3000 Taxes on payroll and workforce	..	..	**0**	**0**	**0**	..	..	..	..	..
4000 Taxes on property	..	..	**27**	**28**	**0**	..	..	..	..	..
4100 Recurrent taxes on immovable property	..	..	8	9	0	..	..	..	..	..
4200 Recurrent taxes on net wealth	..	..	0	0	0	..	..	..	..	..
4300 Estate, inheritance and gift taxes	..	..	2	1	0	..	..	..	..	..
4400 Taxes on financial and capital transactions	..	..	16	18	0	..	..	..	..	..
4500 Non-recurrent taxes	..	..	0	0	0	..	..	..	..	..
4600 Other recurrent taxes on property	..	..	0	0	0	..	..	..	..	..
5000 Taxes on goods and services	..	..	**2 766**	**5 994**	**7 766**	..	..	..	..	..
5100 Taxes on production, sale, transfer, etc	..	..	2 590	5 750	7 356	..	..	..	..	..
5110 General taxes	..	..	1 616	3 880	5 021	..	..	..	..	..
5120 Taxes on specific goods and services	..	..	973	1 870	2 335	..	..	..	..	..
5130 Unallocable between 5110 and 5120	..	..	0	0	0	..	..	..	..	..
5200 Taxes on use of goods and perform activities	..	..	177	243	410	..	..	..	..	..
5300 Unallocable between 5100 and 5200	..	..	0	2	0	..	..	..	..	..
6000 Other taxes	..	..	**0**	**0**	**0**	..	..	..	..	..
6100 Paid solely by business	..	..	..	..	..	..	..	..	..	..
6200 Other	..	..	..	..	..	..	..	..	..	..
Total tax revenue	..	..	**4 870**	**9 191**	**12 892**	..	..	..	..	..

Million EUR

	Local government					Social Security Funds				
	1975	1985	1995	2005	2014	1975	1985	1995	2005	2014
1000 Taxes on income, profits and capital gains	..	..	**0**	**0**	**0**	..	..	**0**	**0**	**0**
1100 Of individuals	..	..	0	0	0	..	..	0	0	0
1200 Corporate	..	..	0	0	0	..	..	0	0	0
1300 Unallocable between 1100 and 1200	..	..	0	0	0	..	..	0	0	0
2000 Social security contributions	..	..	**0**	**0**	**0**	..	..	**2 817**	**6 037**	**9 948**
2100 Employees	..	..	..	..	..	..	..	540	1 377	2 249
2200 Employers	..	..	..	..	..	..	..	1 774	3 356	5 642
2300 Self-employed or non-employed	..	..	..	..	..	..	..	503	1 304	2 057
2400 Unallocable between 2100, 2200 and 2300	..	..	..	..	..	..	..	0	0	0
3000 Taxes on payroll and workforce	..	..	**0**	**0**	**0**	..	..	**0**	**0**	**0**
4000 Taxes on property	..	..	**84**	**220**	**331**	..	..	**0**	**0**	**0**
4100 Recurrent taxes on immovable property	..	..	72	220	331	..	..	..	..	..
4200 Recurrent taxes on net wealth	..	..	0	0	0	..	..	..	..	..
4300 Estate, inheritance and gift taxes	..	..	0	0	0	..	..	..	..	..
4400 Taxes on financial and capital transactions	..	..	12	0	0	..	..	..	..	..
4500 Non-recurrent taxes	..	..	0	0	0	..	..	..	..	..
4600 Other recurrent taxes on property	..	..	0	0	0	..	..	..	..	..
5000 Taxes on goods and services	..	..	**17**	**198**	**314**	..	..	**0**	**0**	**0**
5100 Taxes on production, sale, transfer, etc	..	..	10	8	9	..	..	..	..	..
5110 General taxes	..	..	0	0	0	..	..	..	..	..
5120 Taxes on specific goods and services	..	..	10	8	9	..	..	..	..	..
5130 Unallocable between 5110 and 5120	..	..	0	0	0	..	..	..	..	..
5200 Taxes on use of goods and perform activities	..	..	1	95	156	..	..	..	..	..
5300 Unallocable between 5100 and 5200	..	..	6	95	150	..	..	..	..	..
6000 Other taxes	..	..	**0**	**0**	**0**	..	..	**0**	**0**	**0**
6100 Paid solely by business	..	..	..	..	..	..	..	..	..	..
6200 Other	..	..	..	..	..	..	..	..	..	..
Total tax revenue	..	..	**101**	**418**	**645**	..	..	**2 817**	**6 037**	**9 948**

Note : Excluding customs duties collected on behalf of the European Union: 2014 = 127.3.

StatLink http://dx.doi.org/10.1787/888933417427

Table 5.41. **Slovenia, tax revenues by sub-sectors of government**

Million EUR

	Central government					State/Regional				
	1975	1985	1995	2005	2014					
1000 Taxes on income, profits and capital gains	..	..	**479**	**1 828**	**1 310**	..	..	..	..	..
1100 Of individuals	..	..	413	1 029	779	..	..	..	..	..
1200 Corporate	..	..	54	795	529	..	..	..	..	..
1300 Unallocable between 1100 and 1200	..	..	12	5	2	..	..	..	..	..
2000 Social security contributions	..	..	**38**	**42**	**57**	..	..	..	..	..
2100 Employees	..	..	20	24	30	..	..	..	..	..
2200 Employers	..	..	17	15	22	..	..	..	..	..
2300 Self-employed or non-employed	..	..	1	3	5	..	..	..	..	..
2400 Unallocable between 2100, 2200 and 2300	..	..	0	0	0	..	..	..	..	..
3000 Taxes on payroll and workforce	..	..	**14**	**521**	**20**	..	..	..	..	..
4000 Taxes on property	..	..	**5**	**3**	**5**	..	..	..	..	..
4100 Recurrent taxes on immovable property	..	..	0	0	2	..	..	..	..	..
4200 Recurrent taxes on net wealth	..	..	0	3	0	..	..	..	..	..
4300 Estate, inheritance and gift taxes	..	..	0	0	0	..	..	..	..	..
4400 Taxes on financial and capital transactions	..	..	0	0	0	..	..	..	..	..
4500 Non-recurrent taxes	..	..	5	0	3	..	..	..	..	..
4600 Other recurrent taxes on property	..	..	0	0	0	..	..	..	..	..
5000 Taxes on goods and services	..	..	**1 554**	**3 805**	**5 409**	..	..	..	..	..
5100 Taxes on production, sale, transfer, etc	..	..	1 524	3 624	5 100	..	..	..	..	..
5110 General taxes	..	..	1 192	2 467	3 158	..	..	..	..	..
5120 Taxes on specific goods and services	..	..	332	1 156	1 942	..	..	..	..	..
5130 Unallocable between 5110 and 5120	..	..	0	0	0	..	..	..	..	..
5200 Taxes on use of goods and perform activities	..	..	31	181	309	..	..	..	..	..
5300 Unallocable between 5100 and 5200	..	..	0	0	0	..	..	..	..	..
6000 Other taxes	..	..	**0**	**0**	**0**	..	..	..	..	..
6100 Paid solely by business	..	..	..	..	..	..	..	..	..	..
6200 Other	..	..	..	..	..	..	..	..	..	..
Total tax revenue	..	..	**2 090**	**6 199**	**6 801**	..	..	..	..	..

Million EUR

	Local government					Social Security Funds				
	1975	1985	1995	2005	2014	1975	1985	1995	2005	2014
1000 Taxes on income, profits and capital gains	..	..	**194**	**559**	**1 127**	..	..	**0**	**0**	**0**
1100 Of individuals	..	..	192	556	1 127	..	..	..	..	..
1200 Corporate	..	..	0	0	0	..	..	..	..	..
1300 Unallocable between 1100 and 1200	..	..	2	2	0	..	..	..	..	..
2000 Social security contributions	..	..	**0**	**0**	**0**	..	..	**1 690**	**4 042**	**5 312**
2100 Employees	..	..	..	..	..	..	..	810	2 122	2 747
2200 Employers	..	..	..	..	..	..	..	802	1 572	2 004
2300 Self-employed or non-employed	..	..	..	..	..	..	..	78	348	561
2400 Unallocable between 2100, 2200 and 2300	..	..	..	..	..	..	..	0	0	0
3000 Taxes on payroll and workforce	..	..	**2**	**0**	**0**	..	..	**0**	**0**	**0**
4000 Taxes on property	..	..	**53**	**167**	**228**	..	..	**0**	**0**	**0**
4100 Recurrent taxes on immovable property	..	..	37	122	191	..	..	..	..	..
4200 Recurrent taxes on net wealth	..	..	0	0	0	..	..	..	..	..
4300 Estate, inheritance and gift taxes	..	..	1	5	7	..	..	..	..	..
4400 Taxes on financial and capital transactions	..	..	12	40	25	..	..	..	..	..
4500 Non-recurrent taxes	..	..	3	0	5	..	..	..	..	..
4600 Other recurrent taxes on property	..	..	0	0	0	..	..	..	..	..
5000 Taxes on goods and services	..	..	**7**	**91**	**92**	..	..	**0**	**0**	**0**
5100 Taxes on production, sale, transfer, etc	..	..	7	43	52	..	..	..	..	..
5110 General taxes	..	..	0	0	0	..	..	..	..	..
5120 Taxes on specific goods and services	..	..	7	43	52	..	..	..	..	..
5130 Unallocable between 5110 and 5120	..	..	0	0	0	..	..	..	..	..
5200 Taxes on use of goods and perform activities	..	..	0	48	40	..	..	..	..	..
5300 Unallocable between 5100 and 5200	..	..	0	0	0	..	..	..	..	..
6000 Other taxes	..	..	**0**	**0**	**0**	..	..	**0**	**0**	**0**
6100 Paid solely by business	..	..	..	..	..	..	..	..	..	..
6200 Other	..	..	..	..	..	..	..	..	..	..
Total tax revenue	..	..	**256**	**817**	**1 447**	..	..	**1 690**	**4 042**	**5 312**

Note : Excluding customs duties collected on behalf of the European Union: 2014 = 52.2.

StatLink http://dx.doi.org/10.1787/888933417438

Table 5.42. **Spain, tax revenues by sub-sectors of government**

Million EUR

	Federal government					State/Regional[1]				
	1975	1985	1995	2005	2014	1975	1985	1995	2005	2014
1000 Taxes on income, profits and capital gains	**1 388**	**11 321**	**38 969**	**73 127**	**63 481**	**..**	**126**	**584**	**19 504**	**32 676**
1100 Of individuals	897	8 800	31 410	38 390	42 826	..	112	459	19 104	32 441
1200 Corporate	490	2 410	7 338	34 493	20 426	..	14	125	399	235
1300 Unallocable between 1100 and 1200	1	111	221	244	229	..	0	0	1	0
2000 Social security contributions	**0**	**183**	**583**	**3 027**	**3 243**	**..**	**0**	**1**	**0**	**0**
2100 Employees	..	183	583	1 369	1 549	..	..	1	..	..
2200 Employers	..	0	0	1 658	1 694	..	..	0	..	..
2300 Self-employed or non-employed	..	0	0	0	0	..	..	0	..	..
2400 Unallocable between 2100, 2200 and 2300	..	0	0	0	0	..	..	0	..	..
3000 Taxes on payroll and workforce	**0**	**0**	**0**	**0**	**0**	**..**	**0**	**0**	**0**	**0**
4000 Taxes on property	**421**	**795**	**451**	**78**	**221**	**..**	**568**	**3 851**	**19 246**	**9 647**
4100 Recurrent taxes on immovable property	1	0	0	6	4	..	0	0	0	0
4200 Recurrent taxes on net wealth	0	58	166	37	30	..	88	417	1 251	985
4300 Estate, inheritance and gift taxes	56	60	1	25	182	..	131	713	2 315	2 409
4400 Taxes on financial and capital transactions	364	674	235	10	5	..	348	2 721	15 680	6 252
4500 Non-recurrent taxes	0	0	0	0	0	..	0	0	0	1
4600 Other recurrent taxes on property	0	3	48	0	0	..	0	0	0	0
5000 Taxes on goods and services	**1 609**	**11 013**	**32 482**	**72 406**	**83 706**	**..**	**1 050**	**2 304**	**7 367**	**5 678**
5100 Taxes on production, sale, transfer, etc	1 599	10 904	32 262	72 300	82 943	..	1 050	2 261	7 171	5 197
5110 General taxes	990	5 416	20 360	52 627	57 483	..	581	637	1 455	1 748
5120 Taxes on specific goods and services	608	5 488	11 902	19 673	25 460	..	469	1 624	5 716	3 449
5130 Unallocable between 5110 and 5120	0	0	0	0	0	..	0	0	0	0
5200 Taxes on use of goods and perform activities	10	3	2	50	307	..	0	43	196	481
5300 Unallocable between 5100 and 5200	0	106	218	56	456	..	0	0	0	0
6000 Other taxes	**0**	**0**	**-11**	**669**	**1 300**	**..**	**16**	**155**	**104**	**476**
6100 Paid solely by business	..	..	0	52	72	..	0	0	0	0
6200 Other	..	..	-11	617	1 228	..	16	155	104	476
Total tax revenue	**3 418**	**23 313**	**72 474**	**149 307**	**151 951**	**..**	**1 760**	**6 895**	**46 221**	**48 477**

Million EUR

	Local government					Social Security Funds				
	1975	1985	1995	2005	2014	1975	1985	1995	2005	2014
1000 Taxes on income, profits and capital gains	**175**	**825**	**2 431**	**5 216**	**6 312**	**0**	**0**	**0**	**0**	**0**
1100 Of individuals	131	703	2 051	3 426	4 388	..	..	..	..	..
1200 Corporate	0	122	349	1 466	1 170	..	..	..	..	..
1300 Unallocable between 1100 and 1200	44	0	31	324	754	..	..	..	..	..
2000 Social security contributions	**0**	**0**	**0**	**0**	**0**	**3 367**	**19 976**	**51 393**	**108 048**	**119 421**
2100 Employees	..	..	..	..	..	645	3 393	7 781	16 164	17 825
2200 Employers	..	..	..	..	..	2 722	15 152	35 929	78 925	84 234
2300 Self-employed or non-employed	..	..	..	..	..	0	1 432	7 684	12 959	17 362
2400 Unallocable between 2100, 2200 and 2300	..	..	..	..	..	0	0	0	0	0
3000 Taxes on payroll and workforce	**0**	**0**	**0**	**0**	**0**	**0**	**0**	**0**	**0**	**0**
4000 Taxes on property	**26**	**1 574**	**3 625**	**8 545**	**15 150**	**0**	**0**	**0**	**0**	**0**
4100 Recurrent taxes on immovable property	26	1 102	2 825	6 038	12 474	..	..	..	..	..
4200 Recurrent taxes on net wealth	0	10	42	107	153	..	..	..	..	..
4300 Estate, inheritance and gift taxes	0	12	18	79	113	..	..	..	..	..
4400 Taxes on financial and capital transactions	0	82	162	423	127	..	..	..	..	..
4500 Non-recurrent taxes	0	367	579	1 898	2 283	..	..	..	..	..
4600 Other recurrent taxes on property	0	1	0	0	0	..	..	..	..	..
5000 Taxes on goods and services	**104**	**1 989**	**5 619**	**12 749**	**12 122**	**0**	**0**	**0**	**0**	**0**
5100 Taxes on production, sale, transfer, etc	104	1 679	2 326	6 800	7 467	..	..	..	..	..
5110 General taxes	95	1 288	1 818	4 718	5 457	..	..	..	..	..
5120 Taxes on specific goods and services	10	391	508	2 082	2 010	..	..	..	..	..
5130 Unallocable between 5110 and 5120	0	0	0	0	0	..	..	..	..	..
5200 Taxes on use of goods and perform activities	0	301	3 294	5 937	4 620	..	..	..	..	..
5300 Unallocable between 5100 and 5200	0	9	0	12	35	..	..	..	..	..
6000 Other taxes	**0**	**16**	**576**	**866**	**1 755**	**0**	**0**	**0**	**0**	**0**
6100 Paid solely by business	..	6	457	691	1 184	..	..	..	..	..
6200 Other	..	10	118	175	571	..	..	..	..	..
Total tax revenue	**305**	**4 404**	**12 251**	**27 376**	**35 339**	**3 367**	**19 976**	**51 393**	**108 048**	**119 421**

Note : Excluding customs duties collected on behalf of the European Union: 2014 = 1 512.0.

1. Spain is constitutionally a non-federal country but has a highly decentralised political structure.

StatLink http://dx.doi.org/10.1787/888933417441

Table 5.43. **Sweden, tax revenues by sub-sectors of government**

Million SEK

	Central government					State/Regional				
	1975	1985	1995	2005	2014					
1000 Taxes on income, profits and capital gains	**28 216**	**51 824**	**72 342**	**94 015**	**-17 082**	..	..	..	..	..
1100 Of individuals	25 626	38 521	22 541	-7 974	-123 189	..	..	..	..	..
1200 Corporate	2 590	13 303	49 801	101 989	106 107	..	..	..	..	..
1300 Unallocable between 1100 and 1200	0	0	0	0	0	..	..	..	..	..
2000 Social security contributions[1]	**0**	**40 675**	**50 560**	**212 964**	**174 993**	..	..	..	..	..
2100 Employees	..	551	0	0	0	..	..	..	..	..
2200 Employers	..	38 386	49 222	209 370	173 508	..	..	..	..	..
2300 Self-employed or non-employed	..	1 738	1 338	4 639	1 913	..	..	..	..	..
2400 Unallocable between 2100, 2200 and 2300	..	0	0	-1 044	-427	..	..	..	..	..
3000 Taxes on payroll and workforce	**5 723**	**16 107**	**17 800**	**62 432**	**177 412**	..	..	..	..	..
4000 Taxes on property	**1 469**	**10 157**	**23 260**	**40 116**	**26 363**	..	..	..	..	..
4100 Recurrent taxes on immovable property	11	3 861	15 263	25 139	16 433	..	..	..	..	..
4200 Recurrent taxes on net wealth	647	1 871	3 583	4 998	0	..	..	..	..	..
4300 Estate, inheritance and gift taxes	335	1 114	1 388	1 092	1	..	..	..	..	..
4400 Taxes on financial and capital transactions	476	3 311	3 026	8 887	9 929	..	..	..	..	..
4500 Non-recurrent taxes	0	0	0	0	0	..	..	..	..	..
4600 Other recurrent taxes on property	0	0	0	0	0	..	..	..	..	..
5000 Taxes on goods and services	**31 985**	**114 957**	**237 720**	**353 031**	**475 646**	..	..	..	..	..
5100 Taxes on production, sale, transfer, etc	29 820	110 367	233 671	342 011	458 839	..	..	..	..	..
5110 General taxes	15 806	60 523	166 557	250 470	357 385	..	..	..	..	..
5120 Taxes on specific goods and services	14 014	49 844	67 114	91 541	101 454	..	..	..	..	..
5130 Unallocable between 5110 and 5120	0	0	0	0	0	..	..	..	..	..
5200 Taxes on use of goods and perform activities	2 165	4 590	4 049	11 019	16 807	..	..	..	..	..
5300 Unallocable between 5100 and 5200	0	0	0	0	0	..	..	..	..	..
6000 Other taxes	**260**	**623**	**1 438**	**1 347**	**1 360**	..	..	..	..	..
6100 Paid solely by business	0	0	0	0	0	..	..	..	..	..
6200 Other	260	623	1 438	1 347	1 360	..	..	..	..	..
Total tax revenue	**67 653**	**234 343**	**403 120**	**763 906**	**838 692**	..	..	..	..	..

Million SEK

	Local government					Social Security Funds				
	1975	1985	1995	2005	2014	1975	1985	1995	2005	2014
1000 Taxes on income, profits and capital gains	**38 415**	**131 242**	**265 068**	**435 577**	**602 652**	**0**	**0**	**0**	**0**	**0**
1100 Of individuals	35 269	129 401	265 068	435 577	602 652	..	..	..	..	..
1200 Corporate	3 146	1 841	0	0	0	..	..	..	..	..
1300 Unallocable between 1100 and 1200	0	0	0	0	0	..	..	..	..	..
2000 Social security contributions[1]	**0**	**0**	**0**	**0**	**0**	**25 756**	**67 531**	**186 992**	**151 019**	**213 657**
2100 Employees	..	..	..	..	..	0	2	28 989	74 178	103 955
2200 Employers	..	..	..	..	..	24 203	64 916	154 154	74 377	106 577
2300 Self-employed or non-employed	..	..	..	..	..	1 553	2 613	3 849	2 464	3 125
2400 Unallocable between 2100, 2200 and 2300	..	..	..	..	..	0	0	0	0	0
3000 Taxes on payroll and workforce	**0**	**0**	**0**	**0**	**0**	**0**	**0**	**0**	**0**	**0**
4000 Taxes on property	**0**	**0**	**0**	**0**	**15 571**	**0**	**0**	**0**	**0**	**0**
4100 Recurrent taxes on immovable property	..	..	..	..	15 571	..	..	..	..	..
4200 Recurrent taxes on net wealth	..	..	..	..	0	..	..	..	..	..
4300 Estate, inheritance and gift taxes	..	..	..	..	0	..	..	..	..	..
4400 Taxes on financial and capital transactions	..	..	..	..	0	..	..	..	..	..
4500 Non-recurrent taxes	..	..	..	..	0	..	..	..	..	..
4600 Other recurrent taxes on property	..	..	..	..	0	..	..	..	..	..
5000 Taxes on goods and services	**149**	**358**	**786**	**0**	**0**	**0**	**0**	**0**	**0**	**0**
5100 Taxes on production, sale, transfer, etc	119	290	732	0	0	0	0	0	0	0
5110 General taxes	0	0	0	0	0	0	0	0	0	0
5120 Taxes on specific goods and services	119	290	732	0	0	0	0	0	0	0
5130 Unallocable between 5110 and 5120	0	0	0	0	0	0	0	0	0	0
5200 Taxes on use of goods and perform activities	30	68	54	0	0	0	0	0	0	0
5300 Unallocable between 5100 and 5200	0	0	0	0	0	0	0	0	0	0
6000 Other taxes	**0**	**0**	**0**	**0**	**0**	**0**	**0**	**0**	**0**	**0**
6100 Paid solely by business	..	..	..	..	..	..	..	..	..	..
6200 Other	..	..	..	..	..	..	..	..	..	..
Total tax revenue	**38 564**	**131 600**	**265 854**	**435 577**	**618 223**	**25 756**	**67 531**	**186 992**	**151 019**	**213 657**

Note : Excluding customs duties collected on behalf of the European Union: 2014 = 5 737.0.

1. From 1985, social security contributions are classified using the SNA definition of Social security Funds which means that a proportion of these payments are shown under the heading of Central Government. Prior to that year, all such payments were classified under the heading of Social Security Funds.

StatLink http://dx.doi.org/10.1787/888933417450

Tableau 5.44. **Suisse, recettes fiscales par sous-secteurs d'administration**

Million CHF

	Administration fédérale					État/Régions				
	1975	1985	1995	2005	2014	1975	1985	1995	2005	2014
1000 Impôts sur revenu, bénéfices et gains en capital	**3 422**	**6 523**	**10 468**	**16 341**	**23 666**	**7 756**	**12 652**	**19 147**	**26 176**	**33 659**
1100 Des personnes physiques	2 712	5 330	5 699	7 823	9 661	6 342	10 770	15 964	20 994	26 298
1200 Des sociétés	710	1 193	4 725	8 519	8 559	1 414	1 882	2 593	4 562	6 195
1300 Non-ventilables entre 1100 et 1200	0	0	45	0	5 447	0	0	590	620	1 166
2000 Cotisations de sécurité sociale	**0**	**0**	**0**	**0**	**0**	**0**	**0**	**0**	**0**	**0**
2100 A la charge des salariés	..	..	..	..	..	..	..	..	..	..
2200 A la charge des employeurs	..	..	..	..	..	..	..	..	..	..
2300 A charge des travailleurs indép. ou sans emploi	..	..	..	..	..	..	..	..	..	..
2400 Non-ventilables entre 2100, 2200 et 2300	..	..	..	..	..	..	..	..	..	..
3000 Sur salaires ou main d'oeuvre	**0**	**0**	**0**	**0**	**0**	**0**	**0**	**0**	**0**	**0**
4000 Impôts sur le patrimoine	**463**	**1 877**	**1 703**	**2 703**	**1 434**	**1 428**	**2 543**	**3 620**	**4 772**	**6 183**
4100 Impôts périodiques sur la propriété immobilière	0	0	0	0	0	60	95	162	230	264
4200 Impôts périodiques sur l'actif net	89	175	0	0	0	988	1 442	2 467	3 683	4 806
4300 Impôts sur mut. par décès, succ. et donations	0	0	0	0	0	270	552	961	813	1 061
4400 Impôts sur transact. mobilières et immob.	374	1 702	1 703	2 703	1 434	110	454	31	47	52
4500 Impôts non-périodiques	0	0	0	0	0	0	0	0	0	0
4600 Autres impôts périodiques sur patrimoine	0	0	0	0	0	0	0	0	0	0
5000 Impôts sur les biens et services	**7 431**	**12 521**	**20 257**	**28 941**	**36 027**	**795**	**1 258**	**1 706**	**2 373**	**2 791**
5100 Impôts sur production, vente, transfert, etc.	7 431	12 521	19 763	27 114	33 129	154	213	266	447	567
5110 Impôts généraux	3 205	6 777	12 428	18 429	22 728	0	0	0	0	0
5120 Impôts sur biens et services déterminés	4 226	5 744	7 335	8 685	10 401	154	213	236	410	547
5130 Non-ventilables entre 5110 et 5120	0	0	0	0	0	0	0	29	37	21
5200 Impôts sur utilisation des biens et exerc. activites	0	0	494	1 827	2 898	641	1 045	1 440	1 927	2 223
5300 Non-ventilables entre 5100 et 5200	0	0	0	0	0	0	0	0	0	0
6000 Autres impôts	**0**	**0**	**0**	**0**	**0**	**0**	**0**	**19**	**23**	**177**
6100 A la charge exclusive des entreprises	..	..	..	..	..	..	..	0	0	40
6200 A la charge d'autres agents	..	..	..	..	..	..	..	19	23	137
Recettes fiscales totales	**11 316**	**20 921**	**32 428**	**47 986**	**61 127**	**9 979**	**16 453**	**24 492**	**33 344**	**42 810**

Million CHF

	Administrations locales					Administrations de sécurité sociale				
	1975	1985	1995	2005	2014	1975	1985	1995	2005	2014
1000 Impôts sur revenu, bénéfices et gains en capital	**6 403**	**9 842**	**15 369**	**17 790**	**21 931**	**0**	**0**	**0**	**0**	**0**
1100 Des personnes physiques	5 398	8 644	13 163	15 071	17 798	..	..	..	..	..
1200 Des sociétés	1 005	1 198	1 603	2 277	3 321	..	..	..	..	..
1300 Non-ventilables entre 1100 et 1200	0	0	603	442	812	..	..	..	..	..
2000 Cotisations de sécurité sociale	**0**	**0**	**0**	**0**	**0**	**8 111**	**14 344**	**27 743**	**32 193**	**43 152**
2100 A la charge des salariés	..	..	..	..	..	3 589	6 469	12 995	15 085	19 991
2200 A la charge des employeurs	..	..	..	..	..	3 618	6 503	13 007	15 099	20 024
2300 A charge des travailleurs indép. ou sans emploi	..	..	..	..	..	840	1 372	1 740	2 009	3 137
2400 Non-ventilables entre 2100, 2200 et 2300	..	..	..	..	..	64	0	0	0	0
3000 Sur salaires ou main d'oeuvre	**0**	**0**	**0**	**0**	**0**	**0**	**0**	**0**	**0**	**0**
4000 Impôts sur le patrimoine	**1 068**	**1 462**	**2 416**	**3 071**	**3 896**	**0**	**0**	**0**	**0**	**0**
4100 Impôts périodiques sur la propriété immobilière	182	240	443	588	780	..	..	..	..	..
4200 Impôts périodiques sur l'actif net	809	1 040	1 873	2 393	2 999	..	..	..	..	..
4300 Impôts sur mut. par décès, succ. et donations	27	44	88	78	102	..	..	..	..	..
4400 Impôts sur transact. mobilières et immob.	50	138	13	11	15	..	..	..	..	..
4500 Impôts non-périodiques	0	0	0	0	0	..	..	..	..	..
4600 Autres impôts périodiques sur patrimoine	0	0	0	0	0	..	..	..	..	..
5000 Impôts sur les biens et services	**22**	**39**	**97**	**78**	**123**	**0**	**0**	**0**	**0**	**0**
5100 Impôts sur production, vente, transfert, etc.	17	30	55	26	54	..	..	..	..	..
5110 Impôts généraux	0	0	0	0	0	..	..	..	..	..
5120 Impôts sur biens et services déterminés	17	30	29	20	16	..	..	..	..	..
5130 Non-ventilables entre 5110 et 5120	0	0	25	6	39	..	..	..	..	..
5200 Impôts sur utilisation des biens et exerc. activites	5	9	42	52	68	..	..	..	..	..
5300 Non-ventilables entre 5100 et 5200	0	0	0	0	0	..	..	..	..	..
6000 Autres impôts	**0**	**0**	**164**	**223**	**546**	**0**	**0**	**0**	**0**	**0**
6100 A la charge exclusive des entreprises	..	..	0	0	207	..	..	..	..	..
6200 A la charge d'autres agents	..	..	164	223	339	..	..	..	..	..
Recettes fiscales totales	**7 493**	**11 343**	**18 046**	**21 162**	**26 496**	**8 111**	**14 344**	**27 743**	**32 193**	**43 152**

StatLink http://dx.doi.org/10.1787/888933417461

Table 5.45. **Turkey, tax revenues by sub-sectors of government**

Million TRY

	Central government					State/Regional				
	1975	1985	1995	2005	2014					
1000 Taxes on income, profits and capital gains	..	**2**	**433**	**30 324**	**93 892**	..	..	..	..	..
1100 Of individuals	..	1	330	20 458	65 443	..	..	..	..	..
1200 Corporate	..	0	103	9 866	28 449	..	..	..	..	..
1300 Unallocable between 1100 and 1200	..	0	0	0	0	..	..	..	..	..
2000 Social security contributions	..	**0**	**0**	**0**	**0**	..	..	..	..	..
2100 Employees	..	..	..	..	..	..	..	..	..	..
2200 Employers	..	..	..	..	..	..	..	..	..	..
2300 Self-employed or non-employed	..	..	..	..	..	..	..	..	..	..
2400 Unallocable between 2100, 2200 and 2300	..	..	..	..	..	..	..	..	..	..
3000 Taxes on payroll and workforce	..	**0**	**0**	**0**	**0**	..	..	..	..	..
4000 Taxes on property	..	**0**	**49**	**3 626**	**17 458**	..	..	..	..	..
4100 Recurrent taxes on immovable property	..	0	0	0	0	..	..	..	..	..
4200 Recurrent taxes on net wealth	..	0	0	0	0	..	..	..	..	..
4300 Estate, inheritance and gift taxes	..	0	1	78	379	..	..	..	..	..
4400 Taxes on financial and capital transactions	..	0	29	3 548	17 080	..	..	..	..	..
4500 Non-recurrent taxes	..	0	19	0	0	..	..	..	..	..
4600 Other recurrent taxes on property	..	0	0	0	0	..	..	..	..	..
5000 Taxes on goods and services	..	**2**	**574**	**71 956**	**197 820**	..	..	..	..	..
5100 Taxes on production, sale, transfer, etc	..	2	567	69 266	190 326	..	..	..	..	..
5110 General taxes	..	1	475	30 343	90 988	..	..	..	..	..
5120 Taxes on specific goods and services	..	1	92	38 923	99 338	..	..	..	..	..
5130 Unallocable between 5110 and 5120	..	0	0	0	0	..	..	..	..	..
5200 Taxes on use of goods and perform activities	..	0	8	2 691	7 494	..	..	..	..	..
5300 Unallocable between 5100 and 5200	..	0	0	0	0	..	..	..	..	..
6000 Other taxes	..	**0**	**259**	**4 181**	**2 551**	..	..	..	..	..
6100 Paid solely by business	..	0	0	0	0	..	..	..	..	..
6200 Other	..	0	259	4 181	2 551	..	..	..	..	..
Total tax revenue	..	**4**	**1 316**	**110 088**	**311 721**	..	..	..	..	..

Million TRY

	Local government					Social Security Funds				
	1975	1985	1995	2005	2014	1975	1985	1995	2005	2014
1000 Taxes on income, profits and capital gains	..	**0**	**63**	**4 011**	**12 315**	..	**0**	**0**	**0**	**0**
1100 Of individuals	..	0	48	2 706	8 459	..	..	..	..	..
1200 Corporate	..	0	15	1 305	3 856	..	..	..	..	..
1300 Unallocable between 1100 and 1200	..	0	0	0	0	..	..	..	..	..
2000 Social security contributions	..	**0**	**0**	**0**	**0**	..	**1**	**212**	**35 321**	**143 400**
2100 Employees	..	..	..	..	..	..	0	82	12 128	54 281
2200 Employers	..	..	..	..	..	..	0	110	16 132	80 028
2300 Self-employed or non-employed	..	..	..	..	..	..	0	19	7 061	9 091
2400 Unallocable between 2100, 2200 and 2300	..	..	..	..	..	..	0	0	0	0
3000 Taxes on payroll and workforce	..	**0**	**0**	**0**	**0**	..	**0**	**0**	**0**	**0**
4000 Taxes on property	..	**0**	**4**	**1 627**	**7 015**	..	**0**	**0**	**0**	**0**
4100 Recurrent taxes on immovable property	..	0	0	1 148	4 993	..	..	..	..	..
4200 Recurrent taxes on net wealth	..	0	0	0	0	..	..	..	..	..
4300 Estate, inheritance and gift taxes	..	0	0	10	50	..	..	..	..	..
4400 Taxes on financial and capital transactions	..	0	4	469	1 972	..	..	..	..	..
4500 Non-recurrent taxes	..	0	0	0	0	..	..	..	..	..
4600 Other recurrent taxes on property	..	0	0	0	0	..	..	..	..	..
5000 Taxes on goods and services	..	**0**	**84**	**5 649**	**23 822**	..	**0**	**0**	**0**	**0**
5100 Taxes on production, sale, transfer, etc	..	0	82	5 295	22 932	..	..	..	..	..
5110 General taxes	..	0	69	4 014	11 545	..	..	..	..	..
5120 Taxes on specific goods and services	..	0	13	1 281	11 387	..	..	..	..	..
5130 Unallocable between 5110 and 5120	..	0	0	0	0	..	..	..	..	..
5200 Taxes on use of goods and perform activities	..	0	1	354	890	..	..	..	..	..
5300 Unallocable between 5100 and 5200	..	0	0	0	0	..	..	..	..	..
6000 Other taxes	..	**0**	**73**	**721**	**4 299**	..	**0**	**0**	**0**	**0**
6100 Paid solely by business	..	0	0	0	0	..	..	..	..	..
6200 Other	..	0	73	721	4 299	..	..	..	..	..
Total tax revenue	..	**1**	**224**	**12 008**	**47 450**	..	**1**	**212**	**35 321**	**143 400**

StatLink http://dx.doi.org/10.1787/888933417477

Table 5.46. **United Kingdom, tax revenues by sub-sectors of government**

Million GBP

	Central government					State/Regional				
	1975	1985	1995	2005	2014					
1000 Taxes on income, profits and capital gains	**16 716**	**51 674**	**92 147**	**171 995**	**204 008**	..	..	..	..	..
1100 Of individuals	14 936	34 820	71 973	130 216	160 293	..	..	..	..	..
1200 Corporate	2 310	16 854	20 174	41 779	43 715	..	..	..	..	..
1300 Unallocable between 1100 and 1200	-530	0	0	0	0	..	..	..	..	..
2000 Social security contributions	**0**	**0**	**0**	**0**	**0**	..	..	..	..	..
2100 Employees	..	..	..	..	..	..	..	..	..	..
2200 Employers	..	..	..	..	..	..	..	..	..	..
2300 Self-employed or non-employed	..	..	..	..	..	..	..	..	..	..
2400 Unallocable between 2100, 2200 and 2300	..	..	..	..	..	..	..	..	..	..
3000 Taxes on payroll and workforce	**-1**	**96**	**0**	**0**	**0**	..	..	..	..	..
4000 Taxes on property	**619**	**2 425**	**15 730**	**32 583**	**45 247**	..	..	..	..	..
4100 Recurrent taxes on immovable property	44	343	12 369	19 523	27 294	..	..	..	..	..
4200 Recurrent taxes on net wealth	0	0	0	0	0	..	..	..	..	..
4300 Estate, inheritance and gift taxes	307	923	1 441	3 150	3 886	..	..	..	..	..
4400 Taxes on financial and capital transactions	266	1 159	1 920	9 910	14 067	..	..	..	..	..
4500 Non-recurrent taxes	2	0	0	0	0	..	..	..	..	..
4600 Other recurrent taxes on property	0	0	0	0	0	..	..	..	..	..
5000 Taxes on goods and services	**8 982**	**40 673**	**85 507**	**135 276**	**193 829**	..	..	..	..	..
5100 Taxes on production, sale, transfer, etc	8 502	38 260	81 175	130 040	186 642	..	..	..	..	..
5110 General taxes	3 515	21 228	47 539	83 425	124 211	..	..	..	..	..
5120 Taxes on specific goods and services	4 987	17 032	33 636	46 615	62 431	..	..	..	..	..
5130 Unallocable between 5110 and 5120	0	0	0	0	0	..	..	..	..	..
5200 Taxes on use of goods and perform activities	698	2 413	4 332	5 236	7 187	..	..	..	..	..
5300 Unallocable between 5100 and 5200	-218	0	0	0	0	..	..	..	..	..
6000 Other taxes	**0**	**0**	**0**	**0**	**0**	..	..	..	..	..
6100 Paid solely by business	..	..	..	..	..	..	..	..	..	..
6200 Other	..	..	..	..	..	..	..	..	..	..
Total tax revenue	**26 316**	**94 868**	**193 384**	**339 854**	**443 084**	..	..	..	..	..

Million GBP

	Local government					Social Security Funds				
	1975	1985	1995	2005	2014	1975	1985	1995	2005	2014
1000 Taxes on income, profits and capital gains	**0**	**0**	**0**	**0**	**0**	**0**	**0**	**0**	**0**	**0**
1100 Of individuals	0	0	0	0	0	0	0	0	0	0
1200 Corporate	0	0	0	0	0	0	0	0	0	0
1300 Unallocable between 1100 and 1200	0	0	0	0	0	0	0	0	0	0
2000 Social security contributions	**0**	**0**	**0**	**0**	**0**	**6 540**	**23 769**	**44 397**	**84 459**	**109 120**
2100 Employees	..	..	..	..	..	2 562	11 220	18 646	35 159	42 604
2200 Employers	..	..	..	..	..	4 068	12 245	24 210	46 475	63 844
2300 Self-employed or non-employed	..	..	..	..	..	195	745	1 541	2 825	2 672
2400 Unallocable between 2100, 2200 and 2300	..	..	..	..	..	-285	-441	0	0	0
3000 Taxes on payroll and workforce	**0**	**0**	**0**	**0**	**0**	**0**	**0**	**0**	**0**	**0**
4000 Taxes on property	**4 127**	**13 582**	**9 303**	**21 255**	**28 980**	**0**	**0**	**0**	**0**	**0**
4100 Recurrent taxes on immovable property	3 978	13 582	9 303	21 255	28 876	..	..	..	..	..
4200 Recurrent taxes on net wealth	0	0	0	0	0	..	..	..	..	..
4300 Estate, inheritance and gift taxes	0	0	0	0	0	..	..	..	..	..
4400 Taxes on financial and capital transactions	0	0	0	0	0	..	..	..	..	..
4500 Non-recurrent taxes	0	0	0	0	104	..	..	..	..	..
4600 Other recurrent taxes on property	149	0	0	0	0	..	..	..	..	..
5000 Taxes on goods and services	**0**	**0**	**0**	**0**	**0**	**0**	**0**	**0**	**0**	**0**
5100 Taxes on production, sale, transfer, etc	0	0	0	0	0	0	0	0	0	0
5110 General taxes	0	0	0	0	0	0	0	0	0	0
5120 Taxes on specific goods and services	0	0	0	0	0	0	0	0	0	0
5130 Unallocable between 5110 and 5120	0	0	0	0	0	0	0	0	0	0
5200 Taxes on use of goods and perform activities	0	0	0	0	0	0	0	0	0	0
5300 Unallocable between 5100 and 5200	0	0	0	0	0	0	0	0	0	0
6000 Other taxes	**0**	**0**	**0**	**0**	**12**	**0**	**0**	**0**	**0**	**0**
6100 Paid solely by business	..	..	..	..	0	..	..	..	..	..
6200 Other	..	..	..	..	12	..	..	..	..	..
Total tax revenue	**4 127**	**13 582**	**9 303**	**21 255**	**28 992**	**6 540**	**23 769**	**44 397**	**84 459**	**109 120**

Note : Excluding customs duties collected on behalf of the European Union: 2014 = 2 949.0.

StatLink http://dx.doi.org/10.1787/888933417488

Table 5.47. **United States, tax revenues by sub-sectors of government**

Million USD

	Federal government					State/Regional				
	1975	1985	1995	2005	2014	1975	1985	1995	2005	2014
1000 Taxes on income, profits and capital gains	**163 072**	**396 098**	**750 144**	**1 268 412**	**1 739 635**	**25 509**	**81 281**	**157 598**	**278 072**	**369 491**
1100 Of individuals	122 386	334 625	594 213	948 922	1 418 631	..	63 644	128 429	228 997	320 905
1200 Corporate	40 686	61 473	155 931	319 490	321 004	..	17 637	29 169	49 075	48 586
1300 Unallocable between 1100 and 1200	0	0	0	0	0	..	0	0	0	0
2000 Social security contributions	**0**	**0**	**0**	**0**	**0**	**0**	**0**	**0**	**0**	**0**
2100 Employees	..	..	..	..	..	..	..	..	..	..
2200 Employers	..	..	..	..	..	..	..	..	..	..
2300 Self-employed or non-employed	..	..	..	..	..	..	..	..	..	..
2400 Unallocable between 2100, 2200 and 2300	..	..	..	..	..	..	..	..	..	..
3000 Taxes on payroll and workforce	**0**	**0**	**0**	**0**	**0**	**0**	**0**	**0**	**0**	**0**
4000 Taxes on property	**4 613**	**6 422**	**14 948**	**24 989**	**18 810**	**3 284**	**7 902**	**14 494**	**16 993**	**18 502**
4100 Recurrent taxes on immovable property	0	0	0	0	0	1 451	3 984	7 240	9 051	10 672
4200 Recurrent taxes on net wealth	0	0	0	0	0	0	0	0	0	0
4300 Estate, inheritance and gift taxes	4 611	6 422	14 948	24 989	18 810	1 418	2 328	5 061	5 200	4 597
4400 Taxes on financial and capital transactions	2	0	0	0	0	415	1 590	0	0	0
4500 Non-recurrent taxes	0	0	0	0	0	0	0	0	0	0
4600 Other recurrent taxes on property	0	0	0	0	0	0	0	2 193	2 742	3 233
5000 Taxes on goods and services	**20 773**	**48 027**	**75 553**	**99 393**	**137 841**	**52 032**	**126 501**	**234 419**	**390 979**	**497 776**
5100 Taxes on production, sale, transfer, etc	20 442	47 512	75 553	99 393	137 841	43 960	105 687	200 495	325 649	415 978
5110 General taxes	0	0	0	0	0	24 916	69 629	135 132	221 461	274 980
5120 Taxes on specific goods and services	20 442	47 512	75 553	99 393	137 841	19 044	36 058	65 363	104 188	140 998
5130 Unallocable between 5110 and 5120	0	0	0	0	0	0	0	0	0	0
5200 Taxes on use of goods and perform activities	331	515	0	0	0	8 072	20 814	33 924	65 330	81 798
5300 Unallocable between 5100 and 5200	0	0	0	0	0	0	0	0	0	0
6000 Other taxes	**0**	**16**	**0**	**0**	**0**	**0**	**0**	**0**	**0**	**0**
6100 Paid solely by business	..	0	..	..	..	..	..	..	..	..
6200 Other	..	16	..	..	..	..	..	..	..	..
Total tax revenue	**188 458**	**450 563**	**840 645**	**1 392 794**	**1 896 286**	**80 825**	**215 684**	**406 511**	**686 044**	**885 769**

Million USD

	Local government					Social Security Funds				
	1975	1985	1995	2005	2014	1975	1985	1995	2005	2014
1000 Taxes on income, profits and capital gains	**2 635**	**7 974**	**15 795**	**28 382**	**38 706**	**0**	**0**	**0**	**0**	**0**
1100 Of individuals	..	6 496	13 308	22 514	28 995	..	..	..	..	..
1200 Corporate	..	1 478	2 487	5 868	9 711	..	..	..	..	..
1300 Unallocable between 1100 and 1200	..	0	0	0	0	..	..	..	..	..
2000 Social security contributions	**0**	**0**	**0**	**0**	**0**	**85 039**	**269 144**	**510 476**	**831 410**	**1 082 386**
2100 Employees	..	..	..	..	..	36 382	112 114	221 800	362 834	479 451
2200 Employers	..	..	..	..	..	45 241	146 562	261 805	423 933	540 101
2300 Self-employed or non-employed	..	..	..	..	..	3 416	10 468	26 871	44 643	62 834
2400 Unallocable between 2100, 2200 and 2300	..	..	..	..	..	0	0	0	0	0
3000 Taxes on payroll and workforce	**0**	**0**	**0**	**0**	**0**	**0**	**0**	**0**	**0**	**0**
4000 Taxes on property	**50 040**	**99 772**	**197 342**	**345 840**	**449 784**	**0**	**0**	**0**	**0**	**0**
4100 Recurrent taxes on immovable property	50 040	99 772	195 339	342 267	444 906	..	..	..	..	..
4200 Recurrent taxes on net wealth	0	0	0	0	0	..	..	..	..	..
4300 Estate, inheritance and gift taxes	0	0	30	116	384	..	..	..	..	..
4400 Taxes on financial and capital transactions	0	0	0	0	0	..	..	..	..	..
4500 Non-recurrent taxes	0	0	0	0	0	..	..	..	..	..
4600 Other recurrent taxes on property	0	0	1 973	3 457	4 494	..	..	..	..	..
5000 Taxes on goods and services	**8 389**	**26 777**	**57 558**	**111 114**	**147 599**	**0**	**0**	**0**	**0**	**0**
5100 Taxes on production, sale, transfer, etc	6 518	21 007	42 240	76 369	108 278	..	..	..	..	..
5110 General taxes	4 322	14 663	29 316	53 838	78 967	..	..	..	..	..
5120 Taxes on specific goods and services	2 196	6 344	12 924	22 531	29 311	..	..	..	..	..
5130 Unallocable between 5110 and 5120	0	0	0	0	0	..	..	..	..	..
5200 Taxes on use of goods and perform activities	1 871	5 770	15 318	34 745	39 321	..	..	..	..	..
5300 Unallocable between 5100 and 5200	0	0	0	0	0	..	..	..	..	..
6000 Other taxes	**0**	**0**	**0**	**0**	**0**	**0**	**0**	**0**	**0**	**0**
6100 Paid solely by business	..	..	..	..	..	..	..	..	..	..
6200 Other	..	..	..	..	..	..	..	..	..	..
Total tax revenue	**61 064**	**134 523**	**270 695**	**485 336**	**636 089**	**85 039**	**269 144**	**510 476**	**831 410**	**1 082 386**

StatLink http://dx.doi.org/10.1787/888933417498

Revenue Statistics 2016
Statistiques des recettes publiques 2016

ANNEX A

The OECD classification of taxes and interpretative guide

Table of contents

A.1. The OECD Classification of taxes

1. 1000 Taxes on income, profits and capital gains
    - 1100 Taxes on income, profits and capital gains of individuals
        - 1110 On income and profits
        - 1120 On capital gains
    - 1200 Corporate taxes on income, profits and capital gains
        - 1210 On income and profits
        - 1220 On capital gains
    - 1300 Unallocable as between 1100 and 1200
2. 2000 Social security contributions
    - 2100 Employees
        - 2110 On a payroll basis
        - 2120 On an income tax basis
    - 2200 Employers
        - 2210 On a payroll basis
        - 2220 On an income tax basis
    - 2300 Self-employed or non-employed
        - 2310 On a payroll basis
        - 2320 On an income tax basis
    - 2400 Unallocable as between 2100, 2200 and 2300
        - 2410 On a payroll basis
        - 2420 On an income tax basis
3. 3000 Taxes on payroll and workforce
4. 4000 Taxes on property
    - 4100 Recurrent taxes on immovable property
        - 4110 Households
        - 4120 Other
    - 4200 Recurrent taxes on net wealth
        - 4210 Individual
        - 4220 Corporate
    - 4300 Estate, inheritance and gift taxes
        - 4310 Estate and inheritance taxes
        - 4320 Gift taxes
    - 4400 Taxes on financial and capital transactions
    - 4500 Other non-recurrent taxes on property
        - 4510 On net wealth
        - 4520 Other non-recurrent taxes
    - 4600 Other recurrent taxes on property
5. 5000 Taxes on goods and services

5100 Taxes on production, sale, transfer, leasing and delivery of goods and rendering of services

5110 General taxes

5111 Value added taxes

5112 Sales taxes

5113 Other general taxes on goods and services

5120 Taxes on specific goods and services

5121 Excises

5122 Profits of fiscal monopolies

5123 Customs and import duties

5124 Taxes on exports

5125 Taxes on investment goods

5126 Taxes on specific services

5127 Other taxes on international trade and transactions

5128 Other taxes on specific goods and services

5130 Unallocable as between 5110 and 5120

5200 Taxes on use of goods, or on permission to use goods or perform activities

5210 Recurrent taxes

5211 Paid by households in respect of motor vehicles

5212 Paid by others in respect of motor vehicles

5213 Other recurrent taxes

5220 Non-recurrent taxes

5300 Unallocable as between 5100 and 5200

6. 6000 Other taxes

6100 Paid solely by business

6200 Paid by other than business or unidentifiable

A.2. Coverage

General criteria

1. In the OECD classification the term "taxes" is confined to compulsory unrequited payments to general government. Taxes are unrequited in the sense that benefits provided by government to taxpayers are not normally in proportion to their payments.

2. The term "tax" does not include fines, penalties and compulsory loans paid to government. Borderline cases between tax and non-tax revenues in relation to certain fees and charges are discussed in §9-12.

3. General government consists of the central administration, agencies whose operations are under its effective control, state and local governments and their administrations, certain social security schemes and autonomous governmental entities, excluding public enterprises. This definition of government follows that of the 2008 *System of National Accounts* (SNA),[1] where the general government sector and its sub-sectors are defined in Chapter 4, Section F, pages 80-84.

4. Compulsory payments to supra-national bodies and their agencies are no longer included as taxes as from 1998, with some exceptions. However, custom duties collected by EU member states on behalf of the European Union are still identified as memorandum items and included in overall tax revenue amounts in the country tables (Chapter 4) of the country in which they are collected (see §94). In countries where the church forms part of general government church taxes are included, provided they meet the criteria set out in §1 above. As the data refer to receipts of general government, levies paid to non-government bodies, welfare agencies or social insurance schemes outside general government, trade unions or trade associations, even where such levies are compulsory, are excluded. Compulsory payments to general government earmarked for such bodies are, however, included, provided that the government is not simply acting in an agency capacity.[2] Profits from fiscal monopolies are distinguished from those of other public enterprises and are treated as taxes because they reflect the exercise of the taxing power of the state by the use of monopoly powers (see §61-63), as are profits received by the government from the purchase and sale of foreign exchange at different rates (see §69).

5. Taxes paid by governments (e.g., social security contributions and payroll taxes paid by governments in their capacity as an employer, consumption taxes on their purchases or taxes on their property) are not excluded from the data provided. However, where it is possible to identify the amounts of revenue involved,[3] they are shown in Section 4.3 of this Report.

6. The relationship between this classification and that of the System of National Accounts (SNA) is set out in Sections A.9 and A.11 below. Because of the differences between the two classifications, the data shown in national accounts are sometimes calculated or classified differently from the practice set out in this guide. These and other differences are mentioned where appropriate (e.g., in §25 below) but it is not possible to refer to all of them. There may also be some differences between this classification and that employed domestically by certain national administrations (e.g., see §10 below), so that OECD and national statistics data may not always be consistent: any such differences, however, are likely to be very slight in terms of amounts of revenues involved.

Social security contributions

7. Compulsory social security contributions, as defined in §34 below, paid to general government, are treated here as tax revenues. Being compulsory payments to general government they clearly resemble taxes. They may, however, differ from other taxes in that the receipt of social security benefits depends, in most countries, upon appropriate contributions having been made, although the size of the benefits is not necessarily related to the amount of the contributions. Better comparability between countries is obtained by treating social security contributions as taxes, but they are listed under a separate heading so that they can be distinguished in any analysis.

8. Social security contributions which are either voluntary or not payable to general government (see §1) are not treated as taxes, though in some countries, as indicated in the country footnotes, there are difficulties in eliminating voluntary contributions and certain compulsory payments to the private sector. Imputed social security contributions are also not treated as taxes.

Fees, user charges and licence fees

9. Apart from vehicle licence fees, which are universally regarded as taxes, it is not easy to distinguish between those fees and user charges which are to be treated as taxes

and those which are not, since, whilst a fee or charge is levied in connection with a specific service or activity, the strength of the link between the fee and the service provided may vary considerably, as may the relation between the amount of the fee and the cost of providing the service. Where the recipient of a service pays a fee clearly related to the cost of providing the service, the levy may be regarded as requited and under the definition of §1 would not be considered as a tax. In the following cases, however, a levy could be considered as "unrequited":

a) where the charge greatly exceeds the cost of providing the service;
b) where the payer of the levy is not the receiver of the benefit (e.g., a fee collected from slaughterhouses to finance a service which is provided to farmers);
c) where government is not providing a specific service in return for the levy which it receives even though a licence may be issued to the payer (e.g., where the government grants a hunting, fishing or shooting licence which is not accompanied by the right to use a specific area of government land);
d) where benefits are received only by those paying the levy but the benefits received by each individual are not necessarily in proportion to his payments (e.g., a milk marketing levy paid by dairy farmers and used to promote the consumption of milk).

10. In marginal cases, however, the application of the criteria set out in §1 can be particularly difficult. The solution adopted – given the desirability of international uniformity and the relatively small amounts of revenue usually involved – is to follow the predominant practice among tax administrations rather than to allow each country to adopt its own view as to whether such levies are regarded as taxes or as non-tax revenue.[4]

11. A list of the main fees and charges in question and their normal[5] treatment in this publication is as follows:

Non-tax revenues:	court fees; driving licence fees; harbour fees; passport fees; radio and television licence fees where public authorities provide the service.
Taxes within heading 5200:	permission to perform such activities as distributing films; hunting, fishing and shooting; providing entertainment or gambling facilities; selling alcohol or tobacco; permission to own dogs or to use or own motor vehicles or guns; severance taxes.

12. In practice, it may not always be possible to isolate tax receipts from non-tax revenue receipts when they are recorded together. If it is estimated that the bulk of the receipts derive from non-tax revenues, the whole amount involved is treated as a non-tax revenue; otherwise, such government receipts are included and classified according to the rules provided in §27.

Royalties

13. Royalty payments for the right to extract oil and gas or to exploit other mineral resources are normally regarded as non-tax revenues since they are property income from government-owned land or resources.

Fines and penalties

14. In principle, fines and penalties charged on overdue taxes or penalties imposed for the attempted evasion of taxes should not be recorded as tax revenues. However, it may not be possible to separate payments of fines or other penalties from the revenues from the

taxes to which they relate. In this case the fines and penalties relating to a particular tax are recorded together with the revenues from that tax and fines and penalties paid with revenue from unidentifiable taxes are classified as other taxes in category 6000. Fines not relating to tax offences (e.g., for parking offences), or not identifiable as relating to tax offences, are also not treated as tax revenues.

A.3. Basis of reporting

Accrual reporting

15. The data reported in this publication for recent years are predominantly recorded on an accrual basis, i.e. recorded at the time that the tax liability was created. Further information is provided in the footnotes to the country table in Chapter 4 of the Report.

16. However, data for earlier years are still predominantly recorded on a cash basis, i.e. at the time at which the payment was received by government. Thus, for example, taxes withheld by employers in one year but paid to the government in the following year and taxes due in one year, but actually paid in the following year are both included in the receipts of the second year. Corrective transactions, such as refunds, repayments and drawbacks, are deducted from gross revenues of the period in which they are made.

17. Data on tax revenues are recorded without offsets for the administrative expenses connected with tax collection. Similarly, where the proceeds of tax are used to subsidise particular members of the community, the subsidy is not deducted from the yield of the tax, though the tax may be shown net of subsidies in the national records of some countries.

18. As regards fiscal monopolies (heading 5122), only the amount actually transferred to the government is included in government revenues. However, if any expenditures of fiscal monopolies are considered to be government expenditures (e.g., social expenditures undertaken by fiscal monopolies at the direction of the government) they are added back for the purpose of arriving at tax revenue figures (see §61).

The distinction between tax and expenditure provisions[6]

19. Because this publication is concerned only with the revenue side of government operations, no account being taken of the expenditure side, a distinction has to be made between tax and expenditure provisions. Normally, there is no difficulty in making this distinction as expenditures are made outside the tax system and the tax accounts and under legislation separate from the tax legislation. In borderline cases, cash flow is used to distinguish between tax provisions and expenditure provisions. Insofar as a provision affects the flow of tax payments from the taxpayer to the government, it is regarded as a tax provision and is taken into account in the data shown in this publication. A provision which does not affect this flow is seen as an expenditure provision and is disregarded in the data recorded in this publication.

20. Tax allowances, exemptions and deductions against the tax base clearly affect the amount of tax paid to the government and are therefore considered as tax provisions. At the other extreme, those subsidies which cannot be offset against tax liability and which are clearly not connected with the assessment process, do not reduce tax revenues as recorded in this publication. Tax credits are amounts deductible from tax payable (as distinct from deductions from the tax base). Two types of tax credits are distinguished, those (referred to here as "wastable" tax credits) which are limited to the amount of the tax liability and therefore cannot give rise to a payment by the authorities to the taxpayer, and

those (referred to as "non-wastable" tax credits) which are not so limited, so that the excess of the credit over the tax liability can be paid to the taxpayer.[7] A wastable tax credit, like a tax allowance, clearly affects the amount of tax paid to the government, and is therefore considered as a tax provision. The practice followed for non-wastable tax credits[8] is to distinguish between the "tax expenditure component",[9] which is that portion of the credit that is used to reduce or eliminate a taxpayer's liability, and the "transfer component", which is the portion that exceeds the taxpayer's liability and is paid to that taxpayer. Reported tax revenues should be reduced by the amount of the tax expenditure component but not by the amount of the transfer component. In addition, the amounts of the tax expenditure and transfer components should be reported as memorandum items in the country tables. Countries that are unable to distinguish between the tax expenditure and transfer components should indicate whether or not the tax revenues have been reduced by the total of these components, and provide any available estimates of the amounts of the two components. Further information is given in Chapter 2 of the Report, which illustrates the effect of alternative treatments of non-wastable tax credits on Tax to GDP.

Calendar and fiscal years

21. National authorities whose fiscal years do not correspond to the calendar year show data, where possible, on a calendar year basis to permit maximum comparability with the data of other countries. There remain a few countries where data refer to fiscal years. For these the GDP data used in the comparative tables also correspond to the fiscal years.

A.4. General classification criteria

The main classification criteria

22. The classification of receipts among the main headings (1000, 2000, 3000, 4000, 5000 and 6000) is generally governed by the base on which the tax is levied: 1000 income, profits and capital gains; 2000 and 3000 earnings, payroll or number of employees; 4000 property; 5000 goods and services; 6000 multiple bases, other bases or unidentifiable bases. Where a tax is calculated on more than one base, the receipts are, where possible, split among the various headings (see §27 and §77). The headings 4000 and 5000 cover not only taxes where the tax base is the property, goods or services themselves but also certain related taxes. Thus, taxes on the transfer of property are included in 4400[10] and taxes on the use of goods or on permission to perform activities in 5200. In headings 4000 and 5000, a distinction is made in certain sub-headings between recurrent and non-recurrent taxes: recurrent taxes are defined as those levied at regular intervals (usually annually) and non-recurrent taxes are levied once and for all (see also §42 to §45, §48, §49 and §75 for particular applications of this distinction).

23. Earmarking of a tax for specific purposes does not affect the classification of tax receipts. However, as explained in §34 on the classification of social security contributions, the conferment of an entitlement to social benefits is crucial to the definition of the 2000 main heading.

24. The way that a tax is levied or collected (e.g., by use of stamps) does not affect classification.

Classification of taxpayers

25. In certain sub-headings distinctions are made between different categories of taxpayers. These distinctions vary from tax to tax:

a) Between individuals and corporations in relation to income and net wealth taxes

The basic distinction is that corporation income taxes, as distinct from individual income taxes, are levied on the corporation as an entity, not on the individuals who own it, and without regard to the personal circumstances of these individuals. The same distinction applies to net wealth taxes on corporations and those on individuals. Taxes paid on the profits of partnerships and the income of institutions, such as life insurance or pension funds, are classified according to the same rule. They are classified as corporate taxes (1200) if they are charged on the partnership or institution as an entity without regard to the personal circumstances of the owners. Otherwise, they are treated as individual taxes (1100). Usually, there is different legislation for the corporation taxes and for the individual taxes.[11] The distinction made here between individuals and corporations does not follow the sector classification between households, enterprises, and so on of the System of National Accounts for income and outlay accounts. The SNA classification requires certain unincorporated businesses[12] to be excluded from the household sector and included with non-financial enterprises and financial institutions. The tax on the profits of these businesses, however, cannot always be separated from the tax on the other income of their owners, or can be separated only on an arbitrary basis. No attempt at this separation is made here and the whole of the individual income tax is shown together without regard to the nature of the income chargeable.

b) Between households and others in relation to taxes on immovable property

Here the distinction is that adopted by the SNA for the production and consumption expenditure accounts. The distinction is between households as consumers (i.e. excluding non-incorporated business) on the one hand and producers on the other hand. However, taxes on dwellings occupied by households, whether paid by owner-occupiers, tenants or landlords, are classified under households. This follows the common distinction made between taxes on domestic property versus taxes on business property. Some countries are not, however, in a position to make this distinction.

c) Between households and others in relation to motor vehicle licences

Here the distinction is between households as consumers on the one hand and producers on the other, as in the production and consumption expenditure accounts of the SNA.

d) Between business and others in relation to the residual taxes (6000)

The distinction is the same as in *c)* above between producers on the one hand and households as consumers on the other hand. Taxes which are included under the heading 6000 because they involve more than one tax base or because the tax base does not fall within any of the previous categories but which are identifiable as levyable only on producers and not on households are included under "business". The rest of the taxes which are included under the heading 6000 are shown as 'other' or non-identified.

Surcharges

26. Receipts from surcharges in respect of particular taxes are usually classified with the receipts from the relevant tax whether or not the surcharge is temporary. If, however, the

surcharge has a characteristic which would render it classifiable in a different heading of the OECD list, receipts from the surcharge are classified under that heading separately from the relevant tax.

Unidentifiable tax receipts and residual sub-headings

27. A number of cases arise where taxes cannot be identified as belonging entirely to a heading or sub-heading of the OECD classification and the following practices are applied in such cases:

a) the heading is known, but it is not known how receipts should be allocated between sub-headings: receipts are classified in the appropriate residual sub-heading (1300, 2400, 4520, 4600, 5130, 5300 or 6200);

b) it is known that the bulk of receipts from a group of taxes (usually local taxes) is derived from taxes within a particular heading or sub-heading, but some of the taxes in the group whose amount cannot be precisely ascertained may be classifiable in other headings or sub-headings: receipts are shown in the heading or sub-heading under which most of the receipts fall;

c) neither the heading nor sub-heading of a tax (usually local) can be identified: the tax is classified in 6200 unless it is known that it is a tax on business in which case it is classified in 6100.

A.5. Commentaries on items of the list

1000 – Taxes on income, profits and capital gains

28. This heading covers taxes levied on the net income or profits (i.e. gross income minus allowable tax reliefs) of individuals and enterprises. Also covered are taxes levied on the capital gains of individuals and enterprises, and gains from gambling.

29. Included in the heading are:

a) taxes levied predominantly on income or profits, though partially on other bases. Taxes on various bases which are not predominantly income or profits are classified according to the principles laid down in §27 and §77;

b) taxes on property, which are levied on a presumed or estimated income as part of an income tax [see also §42a), c) and d)];

c) compulsory payments to social security fund contributions that are levied on income but do not confer an entitlement to social benefits; when such contributions do confer an entitlement to social benefits, they are included in heading 2000 (see §34);

d) receipts from integrated scheduler income tax systems are classified as a whole in this heading, even though certain of the scheduler taxes may be based upon gross income and may not take into account the personal circumstances of the taxpayer.

30. The main subdivision of this heading is between levies on individuals (1100) and those on corporate enterprises (1200). Under each subdivision a distinction is made between taxes on income and profits (1110 and 1210), and taxes on capital gains (1120 and 1220). If certain receipts cannot be identified as appropriate to either 1100 or 1200, or if in practice this distinction cannot be made (e.g., because there are no reliable data on the recipients of payments from which withholding taxes are deducted) they are classified in 1300 as not-allocable.

Treatment of credits under imputation systems

31. Under imputation systems of corporate income tax, a company's shareholders are wholly or partly relieved of their liability to income tax on dividends paid by the company out of income or profits liable to corporate income tax. In countries with such systems,[13] part of the tax on the company's profits is available to provide relief against the shareholders' own tax liability. The relief to the shareholder takes the form of a tax credit, the amount of which may be less than, equal to, or more than the shareholder's overall tax liability. If the tax credit exceeds this tax liability the excess may be payable to the shareholder. As this type of tax credit is an integral part of the imputation system of corporate income tax, any payment to the shareholders is treated as a repayment of tax and not as expenditure (compare the treatment of other tax credits described in §20).

32. As the tax credit under imputation systems (even when exceeding tax liability) is to be regarded as a tax provision, the question arises whether it should be deducted from individual income tax receipts (1110) or corporate income tax receipts (1210). In this Report, the full amount of corporate income tax paid is shown under 1210 and no imputed tax is included under 1110. Thus, the full amount of the credit reduces the amount of 1110 whether the credit results in a reduction of personal income tax liability or whether an actual refund is made because the credit exceeds the income tax liability (where, however, such tax credits are deducted from corporation tax in respect of dividends paid to corporations the amounts are deducted from the receipts of 1210).

1120 and 1220 – Taxes on capital gains

33. These sub-headings comprise taxes imposed on capital gains, 1120 covering those levied on the gains of individuals and 1220 those levied on the gains of corporate enterprises, where receipts from such taxes can be separately identified. In many countries this is not the case and the receipts from such taxes are then classified with those from the income tax. Heading 1120 also includes taxes on gains from gambling.

2000 – Social security contributions

34. Classified here are all compulsory payments that confer an entitlement to receive a (contingent) future social benefit. Such payments are usually earmarked to finance social benefits and are often paid to institutions of general government that provide such benefits. However, such earmarking is not part of the definition of social security contributions and is not required for a tax to be classified here. However, conferment of an entitlement is required for a tax to be classified under this heading. So, levies on income or payroll that are earmarked for social security funds but do not confer an entitlement to benefit are excluded from this heading and shown under personal income taxes (1100) or taxes on payroll and workforce (3000). Taxes on other bases, such as goods and services, which are earmarked for social security benefits are not shown here but are classified according to their respective bases because they generally confer no entitlement to social security benefits.

35. Contributions for the following types of social security benefits would, *inter alia*, be included: unemployment insurance benefits and supplements, accident, injury and sickness benefits, old-age, disability and survivors' pensions, family allowances, reimbursements for medical and hospital expenses or provision of hospital or medical services. Contributions may be levied on both employees and employers.

36. Contributions may be based on earnings or payroll ("on a payroll basis") or on net income after deductions and exemptions for personal circumstances ("on an income tax basis"), and the revenues from the two bases should be separately identified if possible. However, where contributions to a general social security scheme are on a payroll basis, but the contributions of particular groups (such as the self-employed) cannot be assessed on this basis and net income is used as a proxy for gross earnings, the receipts may still be classified as being on a payroll basis. In principle, this heading excludes voluntary contributions paid to social security schemes. When separately identifiable these are shown in the memorandum item on the financing of social security benefits. In practice, however, they cannot always be separately identified from compulsory contributions, in which case they are included in this heading.

37. Contributions to social insurance schemes which are not institutions of general government and to other types of insurance schemes, provident funds, pension funds, friendly societies or other saving schemes are not considered as social security contributions. Provident funds are arrangements under which the contributions of each employee and of the corresponding employer on his/her behalf are kept in a separate account earning interest and withdrawable under specific circumstances. Pension funds are separately organised schemes negotiated between employees and employers and carry provisions for different contributions and benefits, sometimes more directly tied to salary levels and length of service than under social security schemes. When contributions to these schemes are compulsory or quasi-compulsory (e.g., by virtue of agreement with professional and union organisations) they are shown in the memorandum item (refer to Section 4.2 in this Report).

38. Contributions by government employees and by governments in respect of their employees, to social security schemes classified within general government are included in this heading. Contributions to separate schemes for government employees, which can be regarded as replacing general social security schemes, are also regarded as taxes.[14] Where, however, a separate scheme is not seen as replacing a general scheme and has been negotiated between the government, in its role as an employer, and its employees, it is not regarded as social security and contributions to it are not regarded as taxes, even though the scheme may have been established by legislation.

39. This heading excludes "imputed" contributions, which correspond to social benefits paid directly by employers to their employees or former employees or to their representatives (e.g., when employers are legally obliged to pay sickness benefits for a certain period).

40. Contributions are divided into those of employees (2100), employers (2200), and self-employed or non-employed (2300), and then further sub-divided according to the basis on which they are levied. Employees are defined for this purpose as all persons engaged in activities of business units, government bodies, private non-profit institutions, or other paid employment, except the proprietors and their unpaid family members in the case of unincorporated businesses. Members of the armed forces are included, irrespective of the duration and type of their service, if they contribute to social security schemes. The contributions of employers are defined as their payments on account of their employees to social security schemes. Where employees or employers are required to continue the payment of social security contributions when the employee becomes unemployed these contributions, data permitting, are shown in 2100 and 2200 respectively. Accordingly, the

sub-heading 2300 is confined to contributions paid by the self-employed and by those outside of the labour force (e.g., disabled or retired individuals).

3000 – Taxes on payroll and workforce

41. This heading covers taxes paid by employers, employees or the self-employed either as a proportion of payroll or as a fixed amount per person, and which do not confer entitlement to social benefits. Examples of taxes classified here are the United Kingdom national insurance surcharge (introduced in 1977), the Swedish payroll tax (1969-79), and the Austrian Contribution to the Family Burden Equalisation Fund and Community Tax.

4000 – Taxes on property

42. This heading covers recurrent and non-recurrent taxes on the use, ownership or transfer of property. These include taxes on immovable property or net wealth, taxes on the change of ownership of property through inheritance or gift and taxes on financial and capital transactions. The following kinds of tax are excluded from this heading:

a) taxes on capital gains resulting from the sale of a property (1120 or 1220);

b) taxes on the use of goods or on permission to use goods or perform activities (5200) (see §72);

c) taxes on immovable property levied on the basis of a presumed net income which take into account the personal circumstances of the taxpayer; they are classified as income taxes along with taxes on income and capital gains derived from property (1100);

d) taxes on the use of property for residence, where the tax is payable by either proprietor or tenant and the amount payable is a function of the user's personal circumstances (pay, dependants, and so on); they are classified as taxes on income (1100);

e) taxes on building in excess of permitted maximum density, taxes on the enlargement, construction or alteration of certain buildings beyond a permitted value and taxes on building construction; they are classified as taxes on permission to perform activities (5200);

f) taxes on the use of one's own property for special trading purposes like selling alcohol, tobacco, meat or for exploitation of land resources (e.g., United States severance taxes); they are classified as taxes on permission to perform activities (5200).

4100 – Recurrent taxes on immovable property

43. This sub-heading covers taxes levied regularly in respect of the use or ownership of immovable property:

- these taxes are levied on land and buildings;
- they can be in the form of a percentage of an assessed property value based on a national rental income, sales price, or capitalised yield; or in terms of other characteristics of real property, (for example, size or location) from which a presumed rent or capital value can be derived;
- such taxes can be levied on proprietors, tenants, or both; they can also be paid by one level of government to another level of government in respect of property under the jurisdiction of the latter;
- debts are not taken into account in the assessment of these taxes, and they differ from taxes on net wealth in this respect.

44. Taxes on immovable property are further sub-divided into those paid by households (4110) and those paid by other entities (4120), according to the criteria set out in §25 b) above.

4200 – *Recurrent taxes on net wealth*

45. This sub-heading covers taxes levied regularly (in most cases annually) on net wealth, i.e. taxes on a wide range of movable and immovable property, net of debt. It is sub-divided into taxes paid by individuals (4210) and taxes paid by corporate enterprises (4220) according to the criteria set out in §25 a) above. If separate figures exist for receipts paid by institutions, the tax payments involved are added to those paid by corporations.

4300 – *Estate, inheritance and gift taxes*

46. This sub-heading is divided into taxes on estates and inheritances (4310) and taxes on gifts (4320).[15] Estate taxes are charged on the amount of the total estate whereas inheritance taxes are charged on the shares of the individual recipients; in addition the latter may take into account the relationship of the individual recipients to the deceased.

4400 – *Taxes on financial and capital transactions*

47. This sub-heading comprises, *inter alia*, taxes on the issue, transfer, purchase and sale of securities, taxes on cheques, and taxes levied on specific legal transactions such as validation of contracts and the sale of immovable property. The heading does not include:

a) taxes on the use of goods or property or permission to perform certain activities (5200);

b) fees paid to cover court charges, charges for birth, marriage or death certificates, which are normally regarded as non-tax revenues (see §9);

c) taxes on capital gains (1000);

d) recurrent taxes on immovable property (4100);

e) recurrent taxes on net wealth (4200);

f) once-and-for-all levies on property or wealth (4500).

4500 – *Other non-recurrent taxes on property*[16]

48. This sub-heading covers once-and-for-all, as distinct from recurrent, levies on property. It is divided into taxes on net wealth (4510) and other non-recurrent taxes on property (4520). Heading 4510 would include taxes levied to meet emergency expenditures, or for redistribution purposes. Heading 4520 would cover taxes levied to take account of increases in land value due to permission given to develop or provision of additional local facilities by general government, any taxes on the revaluation of capital and once-and-for-all taxes on particular items of property.

4600 – *Other recurrent taxes on property*

49. These rarely exist in OECD member countries, but the heading would include taxes on goods such as cattle, jewellery, windows, and other external signs of wealth.

5000 – *Taxes on goods and services*

50. All taxes and duties levied on the production, extraction, sale, transfer, leasing or delivery of goods, and the rendering of services (5100), or in respect of the use of goods or

permission to use goods or to perform activities (5200) are included here. The heading thus covers:

a) multi-stage cumulative taxes;

b) general sales taxes – whether levied at manufacture/production, wholesale or retail level;

c) value-added taxes;

d) excises;

e) taxes levied on the import and export of goods;

f) taxes levied in respect of the use of goods and taxes on permission to use goods, or perform certain activities;

g) taxes on the extraction, processing or production of minerals and other products.

51. Borderline cases between this heading and heading 4000 (taxes on property) and 6100 (other taxes on business) are referred to in §42, §47 and §74. Residual sub-headings (5300) and (5130) cover tax receipts which cannot be allocated between 5100 and 5200 and between 5110 and 5120, respectively; see §27.

5100 – *Taxes on the production, sale, transfer, leasing and delivery of goods and rendering of services*

52. This sub-heading consists of all taxes, levied on transactions in goods and services on the basis of their intrinsic characteristics (e.g., value, weight of tobacco, strength of alcohol, and so on) as distinct from taxes imposed on the use of goods, or permission to use goods or perform activities, which fall under 5200.

5110 – *General taxes on goods and services*

53. This sub-heading includes all taxes, other than import and export duties (5123 and 5124), levied on the production, leasing, transfer, delivery or sales of a wide range of goods and/or the rendering of a wide range of services, irrespective of whether they are domestically produced or imported and irrespective of the stage of production or distribution at which they are levied. It thus covers value-added taxes, sales taxes and multi-stage cumulative taxes. Receipts from border adjustments in respect of such taxes when goods are imported are added to gross receipts for this category, and repayments of such taxes when goods are exported are deducted. These taxes are subdivided into 5111 value-added taxes, 5112 sales taxes, 5113 other general taxes on goods and services.

54. Borderline cases arise between this heading and taxes on specific goods (5120) when taxes are levied on a large number of goods, for example, the United Kingdom purchase tax (repealed in 1973) and the Japanese commodity tax (repealed in 1988). In conformity with national views, the former United Kingdom purchase tax is classified as a general tax (5112) and the former Japanese commodity tax as excises (5121).

5111 – *Value-added taxes*

55. All general consumption taxes charged on value-added are classified in this sub-heading, irrespective of the method of deduction and the stages at which the taxes are levied. In practice, all OECD countries with value-added taxes normally allow immediate deduction of taxes on purchases by all but the final consumer and impose tax at all stages. In some countries the heading may include certain taxes, such as those on financial and

insurance activities, either because receipts from them cannot be identified separately from those from the value-added tax, or because they are regarded as an integral part of the value-added tax, even though similar taxes in other countries might be classified elsewhere (e.g., 5126 as taxes on services or 4400 as taxes on financial and capital transactions).

5112 – *Sales taxes*

56. All general taxes levied at one stage only, whether at manufacturing or production, wholesale or retail stage are classified here.

5113 – *Other general taxes on goods and services*

57. This sub-heading covers multi-stage cumulative taxes (also known as "cascade taxes") where tax is levied each time a transaction takes place without deduction for tax paid on inputs, and also those general consumption taxes where elements of value-added, sales or cascade taxes are combined.

5120 – *Taxes on specific goods and services*

58. Excises, profits generated and transferred from fiscal monopolies, and customs and imports duties as well as taxes on exports, foreign exchange transactions, investment goods and betting stakes and special taxes on services, which do not form part of a general tax of 5110, are included in this category.

5121 – *Excises*

59. Excises are taxes levied on particular products, or on a limited range of products, which are not classifiable under 5110 (general taxes), 5123 (import duties) and 5124 (export duties). They may be imposed at any stage of production or distribution and are usually assessed by reference to the weight or strength or quantity of the product, but sometimes by reference to value. Thus, special taxes on, for example, sugar, beetroot, matches, chocolates, and taxes at varying rates on a certain range of goods, as well as those levied in most countries on tobacco goods, alcoholic drinks and hydrocarbon oils and other energy sources, are included in this sub-heading.

60. Excises are distinguished from:

a) 5110 (general taxes): this is discussed in §53-54;

b) 5123 (import duties): if a tax collected principally on imported goods also applies, or would apply, under the law by which the tax is imposed to comparable home-produced goods, the receipts there from would be classified as excises (5121); this principle applies even if there is no comparable home production or no possibility of it (see also §64);

c) 5126 (taxes on services): the problem here arises in respect of taxes on electricity, gas and energy; all of these are regarded as taxes on goods and are included under 5121.

5122 – *Profits of fiscal monopolies*

61. This sub-heading covers that part of the profits of fiscal monopolies which is transferred to general government or which is used to finance any expenditures considered to be government expenditures (see §18). Amounts are shown when they are transferred to general government or used to make expenditures considered to be government expenditures.

62. Fiscal monopolies reflect the exercise of the taxing power of government by the use of monopoly powers. Fiscal monopolies are non-financial public enterprises exercising a monopoly in most cases over the production or distribution of tobacco, alcoholic beverages, salt, matches, playing cards and petroleum or agricultural products (i.e. on the kind of products which are likely to be, alternatively or additionally, subject to the excises of 5121), to raise the government revenues which in other countries are gathered through taxes on dealings in such commodities by private business units. The government monopoly may be at the production stage or, as in the case of government-owned and controlled liquor stores, at the distribution stage.

63. Fiscal monopolies are distinguished from public utilities such as rail transport, electricity, post offices, and other communications, which may enjoy a monopoly or quasi-monopoly position but where the primary purpose is normally to provide basic services rather than to raise revenue for government. Transfers from such other public enterprises to the government are considered as non-tax revenues. The traditional concept of fiscal monopoly is not generally extended to include state lotteries, the profits of which are usually accordingly regarded as non-tax revenues. However, they can be included as tax revenues if the prime reason for their operation is to raise revenues to finance government expenditure. Fiscal monopoly profits are distinguished from export and import monopoly profits (5127) transferred from marketing boards or other enterprises dealing with international trade.

5123 – *Customs and other import duties*

64. Taxes, stamp duties and surcharges restricted by law to imported products are included here. Also included are levies on imported agricultural products which are imposed in member countries of the European Union and amounts paid by certain of these countries under the Monetary Compensation Accounts (MCA) system.[16] Starting from 1998, customs duties collected by European Union member states on behalf of the European Union are no longer reported under this heading in the country tables (in Chapter 4 of the Report). Excluded here are taxes collected on imports as part of a general tax on goods and services, or an excise applicable to both imported and domestically produced goods.

5124 – *Taxes on exports*

65. In the 1970s, export duties were levied in Australia, Canada and Portugal as a regular measure and they have been used in Finland for counter-cyclical purposes. Some member countries of the European Union pay, as part of the MCA system, a levy on exports (see note 16 to §64). Where these amounts are identifiable, they are shown in this heading. This heading does not include repayments of general consumption taxes or excises or customs duties on exported goods, which should be deducted from the gross receipts under 5110, 5121 or 5123, as appropriate.

5125 – *Taxes on investment goods*

66. This sub-heading covers taxes on investment goods, such as machinery. These taxes may be imposed for a number of years or temporarily for counter-cyclical purposes. Taxes on industrial inputs which are also levied on consumers (e.g., the Swedish energy tax which is classified under 5121) are not included here.

5126 – *Taxes on specific services*

67. All taxes assessed on the payment for specific services, such as taxes on insurance premiums, banking services, gambling and betting stakes (e.g., from horse races, football pools, lottery tickets), transport, entertainment, restaurant and advertising charges, fall into this category. Taxes levied on the gross income of companies providing the service (e.g., gross insurance premiums or gambling stakes received by the company) are also classified under this heading. Tax revenues from bank levies and payments to deposit insurance and financial stability schemes are provisionally included here for the 2012 edition. The detailed classification is set out in paragraph 104.

68. Excluded from this sub-heading are:

a) taxes on services forming part of a general tax on goods and services (5110);

b) taxes on electricity, gas and energy (5121 as excises);

c) taxes on individual gains from gambling (1120 as taxes on capital gains of individuals and non-corporate enterprises) and lump-sum taxes on the transfer of private lotteries or on the permission to set up lotteries (5200);[17]

d) taxes on cheques and on the issue, transfer or redemption of securities (4400 as taxes on financial and capital transactions).

5127 – *Other taxes on international trade and transactions*

69. This sub-heading covers revenue received by the government from the purchase and sale of foreign exchange at different rates. When the government exercises monopoly powers to extract a margin between the purchase and sales price of foreign exchange, other than to cover administrative costs, the revenue derived constitutes a compulsory levy exacted in indeterminate proportions from both purchaser and seller of foreign exchange. It is the common equivalent of an import duty and export duty levied in a single exchange rate system or of a tax on the sale or purchase of foreign exchange. Like the profits of fiscal monopolies and import or export monopolies transferred to government, it represents the exercise of monopoly powers for tax purposes and is included in tax revenues.

70. The sub-heading covers also the profits of export or import monopolies, which do not however exist in OECD countries, taxes on purchase or sale of foreign exchange, and any other taxes levied specifically on international trade or transactions.

5128 – *Other taxes on specific goods and services*

71. This item includes taxes on the extraction of minerals, fossil fuels and other exhaustible resources from deposits owned privately or by another government together with any other unidentifiable receipts from taxes on specific goods and services. Taxes on the extraction of exhaustible resources are usually a fixed amount per unit of quality or weight, but can be a percentage of value. The taxes are recorded when the resources are extracted. Payments from the extraction of exhaustible resources from deposits owned by the government unit receiving the payment are classified as rent.

5200 – *Taxes on use of goods or on permission to use goods or perform activities*

72. This sub-heading covers taxes which are levied in respect of the use of goods as distinct from taxes on the goods themselves. Unlike the latter taxes – reported under 5100 – they are not assessed on the value of the goods but usually as fixed amounts. Taxes on permission to use goods or to perform activities are also included here, as are

pollution taxes not based upon the value of particular goods. It is sometimes difficult to distinguish between compulsory user charges and licence fees which are regarded as taxes and those which are excluded as non-tax revenues. The criteria which are employed are noted in §9-10.

73. Although the sub-heading refers to the "use" of goods, registration of ownership rather than use may be what generates liability to tax, so that the taxes of this heading may apply to the ownership of animals or goods rather than their use (e.g., race horses, dogs and motor vehicles) and may apply even to unusable goods (e.g., unusable motor vehicles or guns).

74. Borderline cases arise with:

a) taxes on the permission to perform business activities which are levied on a combined income, payroll or turnover base and, accordingly, are classified following the rules in §77;

b) taxes on the ownership or use of property of headings 4100, 4200 and 4600; the heading 4100 is confined to taxes on the ownership or tenancy of immovable property and – unlike the taxes of 5200 – they are related to the value of the property; the net wealth taxes and taxes on chattels of 4200 and 4600 respectively are confined to the ownership rather than the use of assets, apply to groups of assets rather than particular goods and again are related to the value of the assets.

5210 – *Recurrent taxes on use of goods and on permission to use goods or perform activities*

75. The principal characteristic of taxes classified here is that they are levied at regular intervals and that they are usually fixed amounts. The most important item in terms of revenue receipts is vehicle licence taxes. This sub-heading also covers taxes on permission to hunt, shoot, fish or to sell certain products and taxes on the ownership of dogs and on the performance of certain services, provided that they meet the criteria set out in §9-10. The sub-divisions of 5210 are user taxes on motor vehicles paid by households (5211) and those paid by others (5212).[18] Sub-heading 5213 covers dog licences and user charges for permission to perform activities such as selling meat or liquor when the levies are on a recurring basis. It also covers recurrent general licences for hunting, shooting and fishing where the right to carry out these activities is not granted as part of a normal commercial transaction (e.g., the granting of the licence is not accompanied by the right to use a specific area which is owned by government).

5220 – *Non-recurrent taxes on use of goods and on permission to use goods or perform activities*

76. This section covers non-recurrent taxes levied on the use of goods or on permission to use goods or perform activities and taxes levied each time goods are used. It includes taxes levied on the emission or discharge into the environment of noxious gases, liquids or other harmful substances.

- Payments for tradable emission permits issued by governments under cap and trade schemes should be recorded here at the time the emissions occur. *Les paiements au titre des permis d'émission négociables délivrés par les administrations publiques dans le cadre des dispositifs de plafonnement et d'échange doivent également être comptabilisés sous cette rubrique au moment où les émissions sont produites.* No revenue should be recorded for permits that governments issue free of charge.

- The accrual basis of recording means that there can be a timing difference between the cash being received by government for the permits and the time the emission occurs. In the national accounts, this timing gives rise to a financial liability for government during the period.
- Payments made for the collection and disposal of waste or noxious substances by public authorities should be excluded as they constitute a sale of services to enterprises.

77. Other taxes falling under heading 5200 that are not levied recurrently are also included here. Thus, once-and-for-all payments for permission to sell liquor or tobacco or to set up betting shops are included provided they meet the criteria set out in §9-10.

6000 – Other taxes

78. Taxes levied on a base, or bases, other than those described under headings 1000, 3000, 4000 and 5000, or on bases of which none could be regarded as being predominantly the same as that of any one of these headings, are covered here. As regards taxes levied on a multiple base, if it is possible to estimate receipts related to each base (e.g., the Austrian and German "*Gewerbesteuer*") this is done and the separate amounts included under the appropriate headings. If the separate amounts cannot be estimated, but it is known that most of the receipts are derived from one base, the whole of the receipts are classified according to that base. If neither of these procedures can be followed, they are classified here. The sub-headings may also include receipts from taxes which governments are unable to identify or isolate (see §27). Included here also are fines and penalties paid for infringement of regulations relating to taxes but not identifiable as relating to a particular category of taxes (see §14). A subdivision is made between taxes levied wholly or predominantly on business (6100) and those levied on others (6200).

A.6. Conciliation with National Accounts

79. This section of the tables provides a re-conciliation between the OECD calculation of total tax revenues and the total of all taxes and social contributions paid to general government as recorded in the country's National Accounts. Where the country is a member of the European Union (EU), the comparison is between the OECD calculation of total tax revenues and the sum of tax revenues and social contributions recorded in the combination of the general government and the institutions of the EU sectors of the National Accounts.

A.7. Memorandum item on the financing of social security benefits

80. In view of the varying relationship between taxation and social security contributions and the cases referred to in §34 to §40, a memorandum item collects together all payments earmarked for social security-type benefits, other than voluntary payments to the private sector. Data are presented as follows (refer Section 4.2 in this Report):

a) taxes of 2000 series;

b) taxes earmarked for social security benefits;

c) voluntary contributions to the government;

d) compulsory contributions to the private sector.

Guidance on the breakdown of a) to d) above is provided in §34 to §40.

A.8. Memorandum item on identifiable taxes paid by government

81. Identifiable taxes actually paid by government are presented in a memorandum item classified by the main headings of the OECD classification of taxes. In the vast majority of countries, only social security contributions and payroll taxes paid by government can be identified. These are, however, usually the most important taxes paid by governments (refer to Section 4.3 in the Report).

A.9. Relation of OECD classification of taxes to national accounting systems

82. A system of national accounts (SNA) seeks to provide a coherent framework for recording and presenting the main flows relating respectively to production, consumption, accumulation and external transactions of a given economic area, usually a country or a major region within a country. Government revenues are an important part of the transactions recorded in SNA. The final version of the 2008 SNA was jointly published by five international organisations: the United Nations, the International Monetary Fund, the European Union, the Organisation for Economic Co-Operation and Development, and the World Bank in August 2009. The *System* is a comprehensive, consistent and flexible set of macroeconomic accounts. It is designed for use in countries with market economies, whatever their stage of economic development, and also in countries in transition to market economies. The important parts of the SNA's conceptual framework and its definitions of the various sectors of the economy have been reflected in the OECD's classification of taxes.

83. There are, however, some differences between the OECD classification of taxes and SNA concepts that are listed below. They arise because the aim of the former is to provide the maximum disaggregation of statistical data on what are generally regarded as taxes by tax administrations.

a) OECD includes compulsory social security contributions paid to general government in total tax revenues; imputed and voluntary contributions plus those paid to private funds are not treated as taxes (§7 and §8 above);

b) there are different points of view on whether or not some levies and fees are classified as taxes (§9 and §10 above);

c) OECD excludes imputed taxes or subsidies resulting from the operation of official multiple exchange rates or from the central bank paying a rate of interest on required reserves that is different from other market rates;

d) there are differences in the treatment of non-wastable tax credits.

84. As noted in §1 and §2, headings 1000 to 6000 of the OECD list of taxes cover all unrequited payments to general government, other than compulsory loans and fines. Such unrequited payments including fines, but excluding compulsory loans can be obtained from adding together the following figures in the 2008 SNA:

- value-added type taxes (D.211);
- taxes and duties on imports, excluding VAT (D.212);
- export taxes (D.213);
- taxes on products, excluding VAT, import and export taxes (D.214);
- other taxes on production (D.29);
- taxes on income (D.51);

- other current taxes (D.59);
- social contributions (D.61), excluding voluntary contributions;
- capital taxes (D.91).

A.10. The OECD classification of taxes and the International Monetary Fund (GFS) system

85. The coverage and valuation of tax revenues in the GFS system and the 2008 SNA are very similar. Therefore, the differences between the OECD classification and that of the 2008 SNA (see §83 above) also apply to the GFS. In addition, the International Monetary Fund subdivides the OECD 5000 heading into Section IV (Domestic Taxes on Goods and Services) and Section V (Taxes on International Trade and Transactions). This reflects the fact that while the latter usually yield insignificant amounts of revenue in OECD countries, this is not the case in many non-OECD countries.

A.11. Comparison of the OECD classification of taxes with other international classifications

86. The table below describes an item-by-item comparison of the OECD classification of taxes and the classifications, used in the following:

i) System of National Accounts (2008 SNA);

ii) European System of Accounts (2010 ESA);

iii) IMF *Government Finance Statistics Manual* (GFSM 2014).

87. These comparisons represent those that would be expected to apply in the majority of cases. However in practice some flexibility should be used in their application. This is because in particular cases, countries can adopt varying approaches to the classification of revenues in National Accounts.

OECD Classification					2008 SNA	2010 ESA	GFSM 2014
1000				Taxes on income, profits and capital gains			
	1100			Individuals			
		1 110		Income and profits	D51-8.61a	D51A	1111
		1 120		Capital gains	D51-8.61c, d	D51C, D	1111
	1200			Corporations			
		1 210		Income and profits	D51-8.61b	D51B	1112
		1 220		Capital gains	D51-8.61c	D51C	1112
	1300			Unallocable as between 1100 and 1200			1113
2000				Social security contributions			
	2100			Employees	D613-8.85	D613	1211
	2200			Employers	D611-8.83	D611	1212
	2300			Self-employed, non-employed	D613-8.85	D613	1213
	2400			Unallocable as between 2100, 2200 and 2300			1214
3000				Taxes on payroll and workforce	D29-7.97a	D29C	112
4000				Taxes on property			
	4100			Recurrent taxes on immovable property			
		4110		Households	D59-8.63a	D59A	1131
		4120		Other	D29-7.97b	D29A	1131
	4200			Recurrent net wealth taxes			
		4210		Individual	D59-8.63b	D59A	1132
		4220		Corporations	D59-8.63b	D59A	1132
	4300			Estate, inheritance and gift taxes			
		4310		Estate and inheritance taxes	D91-10.207b	D91A	1133
		4320		Gift taxes	D91-10.207b	D91A	1133
	4400			Taxes on financial and capital transactions	D59-7.96d; D29-7.97e	D214B, C	114114; 1161
	4500			Other non-recurrent taxes on property	D91-10.207a	D91B	1135
	4600			Other recurrent taxes on property	D59-8.63c	D59A	1136
5000				Taxes on goods and services			
	5100			Taxes on production, sale and transfer of goods and services			
		5110		General taxes on goods and services			
			5111	Value-added taxes	D211-7.89	D211; D29G	11411
			5112	Sales taxes	D2122-7.94a; D214-7.96a	D21224; D214I	11412
			5113	Other general taxes on goods and services	D214-7.96a	D214I	11413
		5120		Taxes on specific goods and services			
			5121	Excises	D2122-7.94b; D214-7.96b	D21223; D214A, B, D	1142
			5122	Profits of fiscal monopolies	D214-7.96e	D214J	1143
			5123	Customs and other import duties	D2121-7.93	D2121; D21221, 2	1151
			5124	On exports	D213-7.95a	D214K	1152-4
			5125	On investment goods			
			5126	On specific services	D2122-7.94c; D214-7.96c	D21225; D214E, F, G; D29F	1144; 1156
			5127	Other taxes on international trade and transactions	D2122-7.94d D29-7.95b D29-7.97g D59-8.64d	D21226; D29D; D59E	1153; 1155-6
			5128	Other taxes on specific goods and services			1146
		5130		Unallocable between 5110 and 5120			
	5200			Taxes on use of goods and on permission to use goods or perform activities			
		5210		Recurrent taxes on use of goods and on permission to use goods or perform activities			
			5211	Motor vehicle taxes households	D59-8.64c	D59D	11451
			5212	Motor vehicles taxes others	D29-7.97d	D214D; D29B	11451
			5213	Other recurrent taxes on use of goods and on permission to use goods or perform activities	D29-7.97c, d, f D59-8.64c	D29B, E, F; D59D	11452
		5220		Non-recurrent taxes on permission to use goods or perform activities			11452
	5300			Unallocable as between 5100 and 5200			
6000				Other taxes			
	6100			Payable solely by business			1161
	6200			Payable by other than business, or unidentifiable	D59-8.64a, b	D59B, C	1162

A.12. Attribution of tax revenues by sub-sectors of general government

88. The OECD classification requires a breakdown of tax revenues by sub-sectors of government. The definition of each sub-sector and the criteria to be used to attribute tax revenues between these sub-sectors are set out below. They follow the guidance of the 2008 SNA and GFSM 2014.

Sub-sectors of general government to be identified

a) Central government

89. The central government sub-sector includes all governmental departments, offices, establishments and other bodies which are agencies or instruments of the central authority whose competence extends over the whole territory, with the exception of the administration of social security funds. Central government therefore has the authority to impose taxes on all resident and non-resident units engaged in economic activities within the country.

b) State, provincial or regional government

90. This sub-sector consists of intermediate units of government exercising a competence at a level below that of central government. It includes all such units operating independently of central government in a part of a country's territory encompassing a number of smaller localities, with the exception of the administration of social security funds. In unitary countries, regional governments may be considered to have a separate existence where they have substantial autonomy to raise a significant proportion of their revenues from sources within their control and their officers are independent of external administrative control in the actual operation of the unit's activities.

91. At present, federal countries comprise the majority of cases where revenues attributed to intermediate units of government are identified separately. Spain is the only unitary country in this position. In the remaining unitary countries, regional revenues are included with those of local governments.

c) Local government

92. This sub-sector includes all other units of government exercising an independent competence in part of the territory of a country, with the exception of the administration of social security funds. It encompasses various urban and/or rural jurisdictions (e.g., local authorities, municipalities, cities, boroughs, districts).

d) Social security funds

93. Social security funds form a separate sub-sector of general government. The social security sub-sector is defined in the 2008 SNA by the following extracts from paragraphs 4.124 to 4.126 and 4.147:

> "Social security schemes are social insurance schemes covering the community as a whole or large section of the community that are imposed and controlled by government units. The schemes cover a wide variety of programmes, providing benefits in cash or in kind for old age, invalidity or death, survivors, sickness and maternity, work injury, unemployment, family allowance, health care, etc. There is not necessarily a direct link between the amount of the contribution paid by an individual and the benefits he or she may receive." (Paragraph 4.124)

"When social security schemes are separately organised from the other activities of government units and hold their assets and liabilities separately from the latter and engage in financial transactions on their own account they qualify as institutional units that are described as social security funds." (Paragraph 4.125)

"The amounts raised, and paid out, in social security contributions and benefits may be deliberately varied in order to achieve objectives of government policy that have no direct connection with the concept of social security as a scheme to provide social benefits to members of the community. They may be raised or lowered in order to influence the level of aggregate demand in the economy, for example. Nevertheless, so long as they remain separately constituted funds, they must be treated as separate institutional units in the SNA." (Paragraph 4.126)

"The social security funds sub-sector (of general government) consists of the social security funds operating at all levels of government. Such funds are social insurance schemes covering the community as a whole or large section of the community that are imposed by government units." (Paragraph 4.147)

94. This definition of social security funds is followed in the OECD classification with the two following exceptions which are excluded:

- schemes imposed by government and operated by bodies outside the general government sector, as defined in §3 of this manual; and
- sqchemes to which all contributions are voluntary.

Supra-national Authorities

95. This sub-sector covers the revenue-raising operations of supra-national authorities within a country. In practice, the only relevant supra-national authority in the OECD area is that of the institutions of the European Union (EU). As from 1998, supra-national authorities are no longer included in the *Revenue Statistics*, to achieve consistency with the SNA definition of general government which excludes them. For example, income taxes and social security contributions collected by European Institutions and paid by European civil servants who are resident of EU member countries should not be included. However the specific levies paid by the member states of the EU continue to be included in total tax revenues and they are shown under this heading.

Criteria to be used for the attribution of tax revenues

96. When a government collects taxes and pays them over in whole or in part to other governments, it is necessary to determine whether the revenues should be considered to be those of the collecting government which it distributes to others as grants, or those of the beneficiary governments which the collecting government receives and passes on only as their agent. The criteria to be used in the attribution of revenues are set out in §97 to §100, which replicate Paragraphs 3.70 to 3.73 from the 2008 SNA.

97. In general, a tax is attributed to the government unit that:

a) exercises the authority to impose the tax (either as a principal or through the delegated authority of the principal);

b) has final discretion to set and vary the rate of the tax.

98. Where an amount is collected by one government for and on behalf of another government, and the latter government has the authority to impose the tax, and set and

vary its rate, then the former is acting as an agent for the latter and the tax is reassigned. Any amount retained by the collecting government as a collection charge should be treated as a payment for a service. Any other amount retained by the collecting government, such as under a tax-sharing arrangement, should be treated as a current grant. If the collecting government was delegated the authority to set and vary the rate, then the amount collected should be treated as tax revenue of this government.

99. Where different governments jointly and equally set the rate of a tax and jointly and equally decide on the distribution of the proceeds, with no individual government having ultimate overriding authority, then the tax revenues are attributed to each government according to its respective share of the proceeds. If an arrangement allows one government unit to exercise ultimate overriding authority, then all of the tax revenue is attributed to that unit.

100. There may also be the circumstance where a tax is imposed under the constitutional or other authority of one government, but other governments individually set the tax rate in their jurisdictions. The proceeds of the tax generated in each respective government's jurisdiction are attributed as tax revenues of that government.

Levies paid by member states of the European Union

101. The levies paid by the member states of the EU take the form specific levies which include:

a) custom duties and levies on agricultural goods (5123);

b) gross monetary compensation accounts (5123 if relating to imports and 5124 if relating to exports); and

c) steel, coal, sugar and milk levies (5128).

102. The custom duties collected by member states on behalf of the EU are recorded:

- on a gross of collection fee basis;
- using figures adjusted so that duties are shown on a "final destination" as opposed to a "country of first entry" basis where such adjustments can be made. These adjustments concern in particular duties collected at important (sea) ports. Although the EU duties are collected by the authorities of the country of first entry, when possible these duties should be excluded from the revenue of the collecting country and be included in the revenue of the country of final destination.

103. This is the specific EU levy that most clearly conforms to the attribution criterion described in §95 above. Consequently as from 1998, these amounts are footnoted as a "memorandum item" to the EU member state country tables (in Chapter 4) and no longer shown under heading 5123. However, the figures are included in the total tax revenue figures on the top line for all the relevant years shown in the tables.

A.13. Provisional classification of revenues from bank levies and payments to deposit insurance and financial stability schemes

104. The OECD have adopted the following interim approach to reporting revenue from bank levies plus deposit insurance and stability fees for the 2012 and subsequent editions of OECD *Revenue Statistics*. It is recommended that the amounts should be recorded under category 5126.

- Compulsory payments of stability fees, bank levies and deposit insurance should generally be treated as tax revenues where the payments are made to General Government and allocated to the governments' consolidated or general funds so that the Government is free to make immediate use of the money for the purposes that it chooses. This principle would apply regardless of whether the Government is promising to make payments to guarantee the banks' customer deposits in some future contingency.

- If the compulsory payments are made to general government and placed in funds that are earmarked to be entirely channelled back to the sector of the economy that comprises the companies that are subject to the payment, they would still generally be treated as tax revenues on the grounds that the funds would be available for the government and would reduce its budget deficit, the fee is unrequited for an individual entity and the amounts raised could be unrelated to any eventual pay out to depositors or expenditure on wider support for the financial sector.
- Payments to made to the smaller long-standing schemes for insuring "retail" deposits, where the payment levels are consistent with the costs of insurance, should be classified as fee for service.
- Any payments which involve governments realising the assets of a failed institution or receiving a priority claim on its assets in liquidation in order to fund payments of compensation to customers for their lost deposits would be treated as a fee for a service as opposed to tax revenues.
- Compulsory payments that are made to funds operated outside the government sector and non-state institutions backed by the deposit takers and all payments to voluntary schemes should not be treated as tax revenues.

Notes

1. All references to SNA are to the 2008 edition.
2. See Section A.12 of this *Guide* for a discussion of the concept of agency capacity.
3. It is usually possible to identify amounts of social security contributions and payroll taxes, but not other taxes paid by government.
4. If, however, a levy which is considered as non-tax revenue by most countries is regarded as a tax – or raises substantial revenue – in one or more countries, the amounts collected are footnoted at the end of the relevant country tables, even though the amounts are not included in total tax revenues.
5. Names, however, can frequently be misleading. For example, though a passport fee would normally be considered a non-tax revenue, if a supplementary levy on passports (as is the case in Portugal) were imposed in order to raise substantial amounts of revenue relative to the cost of providing the passport, the levy would be regarded as a tax under 5200.
6. A more detailed explanation of this distinction can be found in the special feature, "Current issues in reporting tax revenues", in the 2001 edition of the *Revenue Statistics*.
7. Sometimes the terms "non-refundable" and "refundable" are used, but it may be considered illogical to talk of "refundable" when nothing has been paid.
8. A different treatment, however, is accorded to non-wastable tax credits under imputation systems of corporate income tax (§31-33).
9. This is not strictly a true tax expenditure in the formal sense. Such tax expenditures require identification of a benchmark tax system for each country or, preferably, a common international benchmark. In practice it has not been possible to reach agreement on a common international benchmark.
10. Unless based on the profit made on a sale, in which case they would be classified as capital gains taxes under 1120 or 1220.

11. In some countries, the same legislation applies to both individual and corporate enterprises for particular taxes on income. However, the receipts from such taxes are usually allocable between individuals and enterprises and can therefore be shown in the appropriate sub-heading.
12. For example, "... sufficiently self-contained and independent that they behave in the same way as corporations [...] (including) keeping a complete set of accounts" (2008 SNA, Section 4.44).
13. In Canada – a country also referred to as having an imputation system – the (wastable) tax credit for the shareholder is in respect of domestic corporation tax deemed to have been paid whether or not a corporation tax liability has arisen. As there is no integral connection between the corporation tax liability and the credit given against income tax under such systems, these credits for dividends are treated, along with other tax credits, on the lines described in §20.
14. This may also apply where a scheme for government employees existed prior to the introduction of a general social security scheme.
15. In the 2008 SNA, these are regarded as capital transfers and not as taxes (see Section A.8).
16. This is the system by which the European Union adjusts for differences between the exchange rates used to determine prices under the Common Market Agricultural Policy and actual exchange rates. Payments under the system may relate to imports or exports and where these amounts are separately identifiable they are shown under the appropriate heading (5123 or 5124). In this Report, these amounts are shown gross (i.e. without deducting any subsidies paid out under the MCA system).
17. Transfers of profits of State lotteries are regarded as non-tax revenues (see also §63).
18. See §25 c) as regards this distinction.

Revenue Statistics 2016
Statistiques des recettes publiques 2016

ANNEXE A

Classification des impôts de l'OCDE et Guide d'interprétation

Table des matières

A.1. Classification des impôts de l'OCDE

1. 1000 Impôts sur le revenu, les bénéfices et les gains en capital
    - 1100 Impôts sur le revenu, les bénéfices et les gains en capital des personnes physiques
        - 1110 Sur le revenu et les bénéfices
        - 1120 Sur les gains en capital
    - 1200 Impôts sur le revenu, les bénéfices et les gains en capital des sociétés
        - 1210 Sur le revenu et les bénéfices
        - 1220 Sur les gains en capital
    - 1300 Non ventilables entres les rubriques 110 et 1200
2. 2000 Cotisations de sécurité sociale
    - 2100 A la charge des salariés
        - 2110 Sur la base du salaire
        - 2120 Sur la base de l'impôt sur le revenu
    - 2200 A la charge des employeurs
        - 2210 Sur la base du salaire
        - 2220 Sur la base de l'impôt sur le revenu
    - 2300 A la charge des travailleurs indépendants ou des personnes n'occupant pas d'emploi
        - 2310 Sur la base du salaire
        - 2320 Sur la base de l'impôt sur le revenu
    - 2400 Non ventilables entre les rubriques 2100, 2200 et 2300
        - 2410 Sur la base du salaire
        - 2420 Sur la base de l'impôt sur le revenu
3. 3000 Impôts sur les salaires et la main-d'œuvre
4. 4000 Impôts sur le patrimoine
    - 4100 Impôts périodiques sur la propriété immobilière
        - 4110 Ménages
        - 4120 Autres agents
    - 4200 Impôts périodiques sur l'actif net
        - 4210 Personnes physiques
        - 4220 Sociétés
    - 4300 Impôts sur les mutations par décès, les successions et les donations
        - 4310 Impôts sur les mutations par décès et les successions
        - 4320 Impôts sur les donations
    - 4400 Impôts sur les transactions mobilières et immobilières
    - 4500 Autres impôts non périodiques sur le patrimoine
        - 4510 Impôts sur l'actif net
        - 4520 Autres impôts non périodiques

4600 Autres impôts périodiques sur le patrimoine

5. 5000 Impôts sur les biens et services

5100 Impôts sur la production, la vente, le transfert, la location et la livraison des biens et la prestation de services

5110 Impôts généraux

5111 Taxes sur la valeur ajoutée

5112 Impôts sur les ventes

5113 Autres impôts généraux sur les biens et services

5120 Impôts sur des biens et des services déterminés

5121 Accises

5122 Bénéfices des monopoles fiscaux

5123 Droits de douane et droits à l'importation

5124 Taxes à l'exportation

5125 Impôts sur les biens d'équipement

5126 Impôts sur des services déterminés

5127 Autres impôts sur les transactions et les échanges internationaux

5128 Autres impôts sur des biens et services déterminés

5130 Non ventilables entre les rubriques 5110 et 5120

5200 Impôts sur l'utilisation des biens ou l'autorisation d'utiliser des biens ou d'exercer des activités

5210 Impôts périodiques

5211 À la charge des ménages au titre de véhicules à moteur

5212 À la charge d'autres agents au titre de véhicules à moteur

5213 Autres impôts périodiques

5220 Impôts non périodiques

5300 Non ventilables entre les rubriques 5100 et 5200

6. 6000 Autres impôts

6100 À la charge exclusive des entreprises

6200 À la charge d'autre agents que les entreprises ou non identifiables

A.2. Champ couvert

Principes généraux

1. Dans la classification de l'OCDE, le terme « impôts » désigne uniquement les versements obligatoires effectués sans contrepartie au profit des administrations publiques. Les impôts n'ont pas de contrepartie en ce sens que, normalement, les prestations fournies par les administrations au contribuable ne sont pas proportionnelles à ses versements.

2. Le terme « impôts » ne couvre pas les amendes, les pénalités, ni les prêts obligatoires aux administrations. Les cas dans lesquels la délimitation entre recettes fiscales et non

fiscales est délicate à tracer, pour certains droits et taxes d'utilisation, sont examinés dans les §9 à §12.

3. Les administrations publiques comprennent l'administration centrale et les organismes dont les opérations sont sous son contrôle effectif, les administrations régionales et locales et leurs services, les organismes de sécurité sociale et les entités publiques autonomes, à l'exception des entreprises publiques. Cette définition des administrations est calquée sur celle du *Système de comptabilité nationale* 2008 (SCN)[1], où les administrations publiques et leurs sous-secteurs sont décrits dans le Chapitre 4, Fection F, pages 80-84.

4. Les paiements obligatoires à des organismes supranationaux et aux organismes qui en dépendent ne sont plus compris depuis 1998 parmi les impôts sauf quelques exceptions. En effet, les droits de douane collectés par les États membres de l'Union européenne pour le compte de celle-ci sont toujours présentés à titre de rubrique « Pour mémoire » et compris dans le total des recettes fiscales, au chapitre 4, tableaux par pays (voir §94.). Dans les pays où les églises font partie des administrations publiques, les impôts sur les cultes sont inclus dans ces paiements, à condition qu'ils répondent aux critères énoncés au §1 ci-dessus. Comme les données se réfèrent aux montants encaissés par les administrations publiques, les contributions versées à des organismes privés, aux organismes sociaux ou régimes de sécurité sociale extérieurs aux administrations publiques, aux syndicats ou aux associations professionnelles sont exclues, même si elles sont obligatoires. Sont toutefois inclus les versements obligatoires aux administrations publiques dont le montant est affecté à ces organismes, à condition que l'administration ne fasse pas simplement office d'agent collecteur[2]. On a distingué les bénéfices des monopoles fiscaux de ceux d'autres entreprises publiques et on les a considérés comme des impôts parce qu'ils reflètent l'exercice du pouvoir d'imposition de l'État par l'intermédiaire du monopole (voir §61 à §63), comme le sont les bénéfices de l'État provenant de l'achat et de la vente de monnaies étrangères à des taux différents (voir §69).

5. Les impôts payés par les administrations elles-mêmes (tels que les cotisations de sécurité sociale et les impôts sur les salaires payés par les administrations en tant qu'employeurs (2200 et 3000), les impôts sur la consommation qu'elles acquittent à l'occasion de leurs achats ou les impôts sur leur patrimoine) sont inclus dans les données présentées. Toutefois, lorsqu'il est possible de les isoler, les montants provenant de ces impôts[3] sont indiqués dans la section 4.3 de cette publication.

6. Les rapports entre cette classification et celle du Système de comptabilité nationale (SCN) sont indiqués dans les sections A.9 et A.11. À cause des différences qui existent entre les deux classifications, les statistiques de la comptabilité nationale ne sont pas toujours établies ou classées suivant la pratique adoptée dans le présent guide. Ces différences et d'autres encore sont mentionnées dans les cas appropriés (voir par exemple §25), mais il est impossible de toutes les signaler. Il peut y avoir aussi certaines différences entre cette classification et celle utilisée par certaines administrations nationales (voir par exemple §10), aussi les statistiques nationales et celles de l'OCDE ne peuvent pas toujours être compatibles ; ces différences, cependant, sont vraisemblablement très insignifiantes dans les montants des recettes en cause.

Cotisations de sécurité sociale

7. Les cotisations de sécurité sociale, définies au §34, qui sont versées aux administrations publiques, font partie des recettes fiscales. Elles sont évidemment assimilables à des impôts puisqu'il s'agit de versements obligatoires à des administrations publiques. Mais elles peuvent différer toutefois des autres impôts du fait que le paiement des prestations de sécurité sociale dépend dans la plupart des pays du versement des cotisations appropriées, encore qu'il n'y ait pas forcément un lien entre l'importance des prestations et le montant des cotisations. La comparabilité entre les pays sera meilleure si on considère les cotisations de sécurité sociale comme des impôts ; elles figurent cependant sous une rubrique distincte de façon à permettre un traitement séparé pour n'importe quelle analyse.

8. Les cotisations de sécurité sociale qui sont volontaires ou qui ne sont pas versées à des administrations publiques (voir §1) ne sont pas considérées comme des impôts, bien que dans certains pays (comme il est indiqué dans les notes correspondantes) il soit difficile d'éliminer les cotisations volontaires et certains versements obligatoires au secteur privé. Les cotisations de sécurité sociale imputées ne sont pas considérées comme des impôts.

Droits, taxes d'utilisation et droits de licence

9. Si l'on excepte les droits perçus sur les permis de circulation des véhicules à moteur, qui sont universellement considérés comme des impôts, il n'est pas facile de distinguer les droits et taxes d'utilisation qui doivent être traitées comme des impôts de celles qui ne doivent pas l'être. Si, en effet, un droit ou une taxe est perçu au titre d'un service ou d'une activité déterminée, le lien entre ce prélèvement et la prestation fournie peut être plus ou moins important, de même que la relation entre le montant du prélèvement et le coût de la prestation. Lorsque le bénéficiaire d'une prestation acquitte un droit dont le montant est clairement lié au coût de la prestation fournie, on peut considérer que le prélèvement comporte une contrepartie, et d'après la définition donnée au §1, il ne sera pas traité comme un impôt. Toutefois, dans les cas suivants, les prélèvements seraient « sans contrepartie » :

a) lorsque le prélèvement est très supérieur au coût de la prestation fournie ;

b) lorsque le redevable de la contribution n'est pas le bénéficiaire de la prestation correspondante (par exemple, un droit perçu sur l'abattage du bétail pour financer un service qui est fourni aux agriculteurs) ;

c) lorsque l'État ne fournit pas un service déterminé en contrepartie du droit qu'il perçoit, même si un permis est délivré à celui qui acquitte le droit (par exemple, lorsque l'État délivre des permis de chasse, de pêche ou de port d'armes qui ne sont pas assortis du droit d'utiliser une parcelle déterminée de terres appartenant à l'État) ;

d) lorsque les bénéficiaires de la prestation sont les personnes qui ont acquitté le droit, mais que la prestation dont chacun bénéficie n'est pas nécessairement en rapport avec le montant de ses propres versements (par exemple, le droit de commercialisation du lait acquitté par les fermiers qui sert à promouvoir la consommation de lait.

10. Dans des cas limites, cependant, l'application des critères énoncés au §1 peut être particulièrement difficile. La solution adoptée, dans un souci d'uniformité entre les pays et eu égard aux montants relativement faibles des recettes en cause, consiste à s'en tenir à la pratique prépondérante des administrations fiscales plutôt que de laisser chaque pays décider si ces prélèvements sont des impôts ou des recettes non fiscales[4].

11. On trouvera ci-après la liste des principaux droits et taxes en question et leur traitement normal[5] dans la présente publication :

Recettes non fiscales :	frais de justice ; droits de délivrance de permis de conduire ; droits portuaires ; redevances de passeport ; redevances de radio et de télévision lorsque le service est assuré par les pouvoirs publics.
Impôts du sous-groupe 5200 :	autorisation d'exercer certaines activités telles que : distribution de films ; chasse, pêche et utilisation d'armes à feu ; organisation de spectacles ou de jeux et paris ; vente de boissons alcoolisées ou de tabacs ; autorisation de posséder des chiens et d'utiliser ou posséder des véhicules à moteur ou des armes à feu ; droit de lotissement.

12. Dans la pratique, il se peut qu'il ne soit pas toujours possible d'isoler les recettes fiscales des recettes non fiscales quand elles sont enregistrées ensemble. Si l'on estime qu'il s'agit surtout de recettes non fiscales, l'ensemble sera traité comme tel ; dans le cas contraire, les recettes seront comptabilisées et classées conformément aux règles énoncées au §27.

Redevances

13. Les redevances versées pour obtenir le droit d'extraire du pétrole et du gaz ou de mettre en valeur d'autres ressources minérales sont considérées normalement comme des recettes non fiscales, car il s'agit de revenus immobiliers procurés par des terres ou des ressources appartenant à l'État.

Amendes et pénalités

14. En principe, les amendes et pénalités portant sur les impôts impayés ou les pénalités appliquées en cas de tentative d'évasion fiscale ne doivent pas être enregistrées comme des recettes fiscales. Cependant, il se peut qu'il ne soit pas possible de séparer le versement des amendes et pénalités des recettes correspondant aux impôts auxquels ces amendes et pénalités se rattachent. Dans ce cas, les amendes et pénalités associés à un impôt particulier sont enregistrées avec les recettes correspondant à cet impôt alors que les amendes et pénalités liées à des recettes correspondant à des impôts non-identifiés sont classées comme autres impôts dans la catégorie 6000. Les amendes qui ne concernent pas des infractions fiscales (comme les infractions au stationnement), ou qui ne sont pas identifiables en tant que telles, ne sont pas non plus considérées comme des recettes fiscales.

A.3. Bases de comptabilisation

Droits constatés

15. Les données enregistrées dans cette publication pour les années récentes sont essentiellement indiquées en droits constatés, c'est-à-dire qu'elles sont enregistrées au moment du fait générateur de l'impôt. D'autres informations sont fournies dans les notes des tableaux par pays au chapitre 4 de ce Rapport.

16. Toutefois, les données des années antérieures sont encore principalement comptabilisées sur la base des décaissements, c'est-à-dire au moment où l'administration reçoit le versement. Ainsi, les impôts retenus à la source par les employeurs au cours d'un exercice, mais versés à l'administration au cours de l'exercice suivant, et les impôts dus au

titre d'une année mais effectivement versés l'année suivante, figurent les uns et les autres dans les recettes du second exercice. Les restitutions, remboursements et retraits résultant d'opérations rectificatives sont déduits des recettes brutes de la période au cours de laquelle ces opérations sont effectuées.

17. Les données relatives aux recettes fiscales sont comptabilisées, sans déduction compensatoire des dépenses administratives liées au recouvrement de l'impôt. De même, lorsque le produit d'un impôt sert à subventionner certains membres de la collectivité, la subvention n'est pas déduite du rendement de l'impôt, encore que certains pays fassent figurer dans leurs données l'impôt après déduction des subventions.

18. Pour les monopoles fiscaux (sous-groupe 5122), seul le montant effectivement transféré à l'État est inclus dans les recettes publiques. Toutefois, les dépenses des monopoles fiscaux qui sont considérées comme des dépenses publiques (par exemple, des dépenses de caractère social engagées par les monopoles fiscaux à l'instigation de l'État) sont ajoutées après coup pour calculer le montant des recettes fiscales (voir §61).

La distinction entre dispositions fiscales et dépenses directes[6]

19. Étant donné que la présente publication ne vise que les recettes publiques en faisant abstraction des dépenses, il convient de distinguer entre les dispositions fiscales et les dépenses directes. Normalement, cette distinction ne soulève aucune difficulté, car les dépenses directes sont effectuées en dehors du système fiscal et des comptes fiscaux et en vertu de dispositions législatives distinctes. Dans les cas limites, on recourt, pour établir la distinction, au principe de la comptabilisation sur la base des paiements. Dans la mesure où une disposition affecte le montant des paiements du contribuable à l'État, elle est considérée comme une disposition fiscale dont il est tenu compte dans les données figurant dans cette publication. Une disposition qui n'affecte pas ce montant est considérée comme une dépense directe dont il n'est pas tenu compte dans les données reproduites dans cette publication.

20. Il est clair que les abattements fiscaux, exonérations et déductions de l'assiette de l'impôt modifient le montant de l'impôt acquitté à l'État ; il s'agit donc de dispositions fiscales. Inversement, les formes d'aides qui ne sont pas imputables sur l'impôt et n'ont donc aucun lien avec le processus d'imposition, ne réduisent pas les recettes publiques qui sont consignées dans ce volume. Les crédits d'impôt sont des montants déductibles de l'impôt à acquitter (par opposition aux déductions, qui sont opérées sur l'assiette de l'impôt). On distingue deux catégories de crédits d'impôt : ceux (que l'on qualifiera ici de « non récupérables ») qui sont limités au montant de l'impôt à acquitter et ne peuvent donc donner lieu à un versement de l'administration au contribuable, et ceux (qualifiés ici de « récupérables ») qui n'ont pas cette limite, de sorte que l'excédent du crédit sur l'impôt peut être versé au contribuable[7]. Le crédit d'impôt non récupérable, comme un abattement fiscal, affecte évidemment le montant de l'impôt acquitté à l'État ; aussi est-il considéré comme une disposition fiscale. La solution adoptée pour les crédits d'impôts récupérables[8] consiste à distinguer l'élément de « dépense fiscale »[9], qui est la part du crédit utilisée pour réduire ou supprimer l'impôt dû par le contribuable, et « l'élément de transfert », qui correspond à la part excédant l'impôt dû par le contribuable et qui lui est reversée. Les recettes fiscales rapportées doivent être diminuées du montant de l'élément de dépense, mais non de l'élément de transfert. En outre, les montants de l'élément de dépense fiscale et de l'élément de transfert doivent être indiqués pour mémoire dans les tableaux par pays. Les pays qui ne sont pas en mesure de faire la distinction entre l'élément de dépense

fiscale et l'élément de transfert doivent indiquer si leurs recettes fiscales ont été ou non diminuées du montant total de ces éléments, et fournir toutes les estimations dont ils disposent concernant les montants de ces deux éléments. Des informations complémentaires figurent dans le chapitre 2 de ce Rapport, qui fait apparaître les effets des différents traitements possibles des crédits d'impôts récupérables sur les ratios impôt rapportant les impôts au PIB.

Année civile et année fiscale (exercice budgétaire)

21. Les autorités nationales dont l'exercice budgétaire ne correspond pas à l'année civile fournissent, autant que possible, leurs données sur la base de l'année civile afin de faciliter au maximum la comparaison avec les données des autres pays. Les données d'un petit nombre de pays se réfèrent à l'exercice budgétaire. Pour ceux-ci, les statistiques de PIB utilisées dans les tableaux comparatifs portent aussi sur les exercices budgétaires.

A.4. Principes généraux de classification

Les fondements essentiels de la classification

22. Les recettes sont classées par groupes principaux (1000, 2000, 3000, 4000, 5000, 6000) suivant l'assiette de l'impôt : 1000 revenus, bénéfices et gains en capital ; 2000 et 3000 salaires et nombre d'employés ; 4000 patrimoine ; 5000 biens et services ; 6000 assiettes diverses, autres ou non identifiables. Lorsqu'un impôt est calculé en fonction de plusieurs assiettes, les recettes sont, chaque fois que c'est possible, réparties entre les divers groupes (voir §27 et §77). Les groupes 4000 et 5000 ne comprennent pas seulement les impôts ayant pour assiette le patrimoine, les biens ou les services eux-mêmes, mais aussi certains impôts connexes. Ainsi, les impôts sur les mutations du patrimoine sont classés dans le groupe 4400[10] et les impôts sur l'utilisation des biens, ou l'autorisation d'exercer une activité, dans le groupe 5200. Dans les groupes 4000 et 5000, une distinction est faite dans certains sous-groupes entre impôts périodiques et impôts non périodiques : on entend par impôts périodiques ceux qui sont perçus à intervalles réguliers (ordinairement tous les ans) et par impôts non périodiques ceux qui ne sont perçus qu'une seule fois (voir aussi les §42 à §45, §48, §49 et §75 pour une application particulière de cette distinction).

23. L'affectation spéciale de certaines recettes fiscales n'influe pas sur leur classification. Toutefois comme explicité au §34 sur la classification des cotisations de sécurité sociale, l'octroi d'un droit aux prestations sociales est crucial dans la définition de la rubrique principale 2000.

24. La manière selon laquelle un impôt est perçu ou recouvré (par exemple, au moyen de timbres) n'affecte pas sa classification.

Classification des contribuables

25. Dans certains sous-groupes, des distinctions sont faites entre les différentes catégories de contribuables. Ces distinctions varient d'un impôt à l'autre :

a)Ventilation des impôts sur le revenu et sur l'actif net entre personnes physiques et sociétés

La distinction fondamentale entre les impôts sur le revenu des sociétés et les impôts sur le revenu des personnes physiques est que les premiers sont perçus sur la société en tant qu'entité et non sur les personnes physiques qui en sont propriétaires, donc sans tenir compte de la situation personnelle de celles-ci. La même distinction est applicable aux impôts sur l'actif net des sociétés et des personnes physiques. Les impôts perçus sur les bénéfices des sociétés de personnes et sur le revenu de certaines institutions comme les caisses d'assurance-vie ou de retraite, sont classés selon le même principe. Ils sont compris dans les impôts sur les sociétés (1200) lorsqu'ils sont perçus sur la société de personnes ou l'institution en tant qu'entité sans que la situation personnelle des propriétaires entre en ligne de compte ; dans les autres cas, ils sont considérés comme des impôts sur les personnes physiques (1100). Ordinairement, les impôts sur les sociétés et les impôts sur les personnes physiques sont régis par des dispositions législatives différentes[11]. La distinction qui est faite ici entre personnes physiques et sociétés ne reprend pas la classification par secteur (ménages, entreprises, etc.) adoptée dans les comptes de revenus et de dépenses du SCN. Cette dernière classification exclut du secteur des ménages certaines entreprises non constituées en sociétés[12] et les fait figurer parmi les entreprises non financières et les institutions financières. Toutefois, l'impôt sur les bénéfices de ces entreprises ne peut pas toujours être isolé de l'impôt sur les autres revenus des propriétaires de ces entreprises, ou ne peut l'être que d'une façon arbitraire. On n'a pas cherché ici à faire la distinction et l'impôt sur le revenu des personnes physiques figure globalement, quelle que soit la nature du revenu imposable.

b) Ventilation des impôts sur les biens immobiliers entre ménages et autres agents

En l'occurrence, la distinction est celle qui a été adoptée par le SCN dans les comptes de production et de consommation. On distingue, en effet, les ménages en tant que consommateurs d'une part (c'est-à-dire à l'exclusion des entreprises individuelles), et les producteurs d'autre part. Cependant, les impôts sur les logements occupés par les ménages, qu'ils soient à la charge des propriétaires qui les occupent, du locataire ou du propriétaire, sont classés comme étant à la charge des ménages. C'est la distinction faite habituellement entre les impôts sur les biens des personnes et les impôts sur les biens des entreprises. Toutefois, certains pays ne sont pas en mesure d'établir cette distinction.

c) Ventilation des permis de circuler des véhicules à moteur entre taxes à la charge des ménages et à la charge d'autres agents

On distingue ici les ménages en tant que consommateurs d'une part, et producteurs d'autre part, comme dans les comptes de production et de consommation du SCN.

d) Ventilation des autres impôts (6000) entre les entreprises et les autres agents

Il est fait la même distinction qu'au point c) ci-dessus entre les producteurs, d'une part, et les ménages consommateurs d'autre part. Les impôts qui figurent dans le groupe 6000 parce qu'ils ne comportent pas une assiette unique ou parce que leur assiette ne relève d'aucune des catégories précédentes, mais qui ne sont manifestement perçus que sur les producteurs et non sur les ménages, sont classés comme étant « à la charge des entreprises ». Les autres impôts du groupe 6000 figurent sous la rubrique « à la charge d'autres agents » ou « non identifiés ».

Surtaxes

26. Les recettes des surtaxes relatives à des impôts particuliers sont classées ordinairement avec les recettes de l'impôt correspondant, que la surtaxe ait ou non un caractère temporaire. Toutefois, si l'une des caractéristiques de la surtaxe permet de la classer sous une rubrique différente de la classification de l'OCDE, les recettes de cette surtaxe sont classées sous cette rubrique et non pas avec les recettes de l'impôt correspondant.

Recettes fiscales non identifiables et sous-groupes résiduels

27. Il arrive parfois qu'on ne puisse déterminer si des impôts relèvent entièrement d'un groupe ou d'un sous-groupe de la classification de l'OCDE ; dans ces cas on applique les méthodes suivantes :

a) le groupe est connu, mais on ne sait pas comment répartir les recettes entre les sous-groupes ; les recettes sont alors classées dans le sous-groupe résiduel approprié (1300, 2400, 4520, 4600, 5130, 5300 ou 6200) ;

b) on sait que l'ensemble des recettes d'un groupe d'impôts (ordinairement des impôts locaux) provient d'impôts relevant d'un groupe ou sous-groupe particulier, mais certains impôts du groupe, dont le montant ne peut être déterminé avec précision, peuvent être classés dans d'autres groupes ou sous-groupes ; dans ce cas les recettes sont comptabilisées dans le groupe ou sous-groupe dont relève l'essentiel des recettes ;

c) il est impossible d'identifier le groupe ou le sous-groupe d'un impôt (ordinairement un impôt local) ; l'impôt est alors classé dans le groupe 6200, à moins qu'il ne s'agisse d'un impôt manifestement à la charge des entreprises, auquel cas il est classé dans le sous-groupe 6100.

A.5. Commentaires sur les postes de la liste

1000 – Impôts sur le revenu, les bénéfices et les gains en capital

28. Ce groupe couvre les impôts prélevés sur le revenu ou le bénéfice net (c'est-à-dire le revenu brut déduction faite des abattements autorisés) des personnes physiques et des entreprises. Sont aussi couverts les impôts prélevés sur les gains en capital des personnes physiques et des entreprises et sur les gains provenant de jeux.

29. Ce groupe comprend :

a) les impôts perçus principalement sur les revenus ou les bénéfices, bien qu'ils puissent l'être partiellement sur d'autres bases ; les impôts qui ont une autre assiette principale que le revenu ou les bénéfices sont classés selon les principes énoncés aux §27 et §77 ;

b) les impôts sur la propriété immobilière, qui sont perçus sur la base d'un revenu présumé ou estimé faisant partie de l'assiette de l'impôt sur le revenu [voir aussi §42a), c) et d)] ;

c) les versements obligatoires aux caisses de sécurité sociale qui sont prélevés sur les revenus mais ne donnent pas droit à des prestations sociales ; lorsque ces contributions donnent droit à des prestations sociales, elles figurent à la rubrique 2000 (voir §34) ;

d) les recettes provenant d'impôts cédulaires sur le revenu intégrés dans le régime général qui sont globalement classés dans ce groupe, bien que certains de ces impôts soient sur le revenu brut et ne tiennent pas toujours compte de la situation personnelle du contribuable.

30. Les impôts figurant dans ce groupe sont subdivisés en deux grands sous-groupes, les impôts sur le revenu des personnes physiques (1100) et les impôts sur le revenu des sociétés (1200), une ventilation étant faite dans chacun d'eux entre les impôts sur le revenu et les bénéfices (1110 et 1210) et les impôts sur les gains en capital (1120 et 1220). Si certaines recettes ne peuvent être identifiées comme relevant soit du sous-groupe 1100, soit du sous-groupe 1200, ou si cette distinction ne peut être faite dans la pratique (parce qu'il n'y a pas de données fiables sur les bénéficiaires des paiements sur lesquels la retenue à la source est faite), elles sont classées dans le sous-groupe 1300 (non ventilables).

Traitement des crédits d'impôt dans les systèmes d'imputation

31. Dans les régimes d'imputation de l'impôt sur les bénéfices des sociétés, les actionnaires bénéficient d'une compensation totale ou partielle d'imposition sur les dividendes que la société leur a versés et pour lesquels elle a acquitté l'impôt sur le revenu des sociétés. Dans les pays[13] qui appliquent un tel régime, une fraction de l'impôt sur les bénéfices des sociétés sert à alléger l'impôt dû par l'actionnaire. Cet allégement prend la forme d'un crédit d'impôt, dont le montant peut être inférieur, égal ou supérieur au montant total de l'impôt dont il est redevable. Si le crédit d'impôt dépasse ce montant, l'excédent peut être versé à l'actionnaire. Comme ce type de crédit d'impôt fait partie intégrante des systèmes d'imputation de l'impôt sur le revenu des sociétés, tout paiement à l'actionnaire est considéré comme un remboursement d'impôt et non comme une dépense (se référer au traitement des autres crédits d'impôt exposé au §20).

32. Puisque, dans les systèmes d'imputation, le crédit d'impôt (même lorsqu'il dépasse l'impôt dû) est censé être une disposition fiscale, on peut se demander s'il doit être déduit des recettes de l'impôt sur le revenu des personnes physiques (1110) ou de celles de l'impôt sur les bénéfices de sociétés (1210). Dans ce Rapport, le montant intégral de l'impôt acquitté sur les bénéfices des sociétés figure sous le poste 1210 et aucun impôt imputé n'est inclus dans le poste 1110. Le montant total du crédit d'impôt réduit donc le montant des recettes du poste 1110, que ce crédit se traduise par une réduction de l'impôt dû sur le revenu des personnes physiques ou par un remboursement réel du fait que le crédit dépasse le montant de l'impôt (cependant, lorsque ces crédits sont déduits de l'impôt sur les sociétés au titre de dividendes versés à des sociétés, le montant est déduit des recettes du poste 1210).

1120 et 1220 – *Impôts sur les gains en capital*

33. Ces postes comprennent les impôts perçus sur les gains en capital, le sous-groupe 1120 comptabilisant les impôts prélevés sur les gains des personnes physiques et le sous-groupe 1220 ceux qui sont perçus sur les gains des entreprises constituées sous forme de sociétés, lorsque ces recettes peuvent être ventilées. Ce n'est pas le cas dans de nombreux pays et les recettes de ces impôts sont alors classées avec celles de l'impôt sur le revenu. Les impôts sur les gains provenant de jeux sont aussi classés sous le poste 1120.

2000 – *Cotisations de sécurité sociale*

34. Figurent dans ce groupe tous les versements obligatoires qui donnent le droit de bénéficier d'une prestation sociale future (éventuelle). Ces versements sont généralement affectés au financement de prestations sociales et souvent effectués au profit d'institutions ou d'administrations publiques qui fournissent de telles prestations. Cependant, cette affectation n'entre pas dans la définition des cotisations de sécurité sociale et n'est pas nécessaire pour qu'un impôt soit classé dans cette rubrique.

Cependant, il faut qu'un impôt confère un droit pour être classé dans cette rubrique. Par conséquent, les prélèvements sur les revenus ou la masse salariale qui sont affectés aux caisses de sécurité sociale mais ne donnent aucun droit à des prestations sont exclus de cette rubrique et figurent à celle des impôts sur le revenu des personnes physiques (1100) ou des impôts sur les salaires et la main-d'œuvre (3000). Les impôts assis sur d'autres bases, telles que les biens et services, qui sont affectés à des prestations de sécurité sociale, ne sont pas indiqués ici, mais sont classés en fonction de leurs bases respectives parce qu'en général ils ne donnent pas droit à des prestations de sécurité sociale.

35. Seraient entre autres incluses les cotisations au titre des catégories suivantes de prestations de sécurité sociale : les allocations d'assurance-chômage et les compléments, les allocations pour accidents, blessures et maladie, les pensions de retraite, d'invalidité et de survivant, les allocations familiales, les remboursements de dépenses médicales et d'hospitalisation ou la fourniture de services médicaux ou hospitaliers. Les cotisations peuvent être collectées à la fois auprès des employés et des employeurs.

36. Les cotisations peuvent être assises sur les gains ou la masse salariale (« sur la base du salaire ») ou sur le revenu net après déductions et exemptions en fonction de la situation personnelle (« sur la base de l'impôt sur le revenu ») et les recettes correspondant à ces deux bases doivent être identifiées séparément si possible. Cependant, lorsque les cotisations à un régime général de sécurité sociale sont assises sur la masse salariale, mais que les cotisations de groupes particuliers (tels que les travailleurs indépendants) ne peuvent être évaluées sur cette base et que le revenu net est utilisé comme valeur rapprochée des gains bruts, les recettes peuvent encore être considérées comme assises sur la masse salariale. En principe, cette rubrique exclut les contributions volontaires à des régimes de sécurité sociale. Lorsqu'elles peuvent être identifiées séparément, elles figurent pour mémoire dans le tableau indiquant le financement des prestations de sécurité sociale. Toutefois, en pratique, elles ne peuvent pas toujours être distinguées des cotisations volontaires, et dans ce cas elles figurent à cette rubrique.

37. Les cotisations à des régimes d'assurance sociale qui ne relèvent pas des pouvoirs publics et à d'autres régimes d'assurance ou de prévoyance, aux caisses de retraite, sociétés de secours mutuel ou autres systèmes d'épargne, ne sont pas considérées comme des cotisations de sécurité sociale. Les caisses de prévoyance résultant d'arrangements aux termes desquels les cotisations de chaque salarié et celles que l'employeur verse en son nom sont comptabilisées séparément dans un compte productif d'intérêts d'où elles peuvent être retirées dans des conditions biens déterminées. Les caisses de retraite sont des régimes autonomes organisés par négociations entre salariés et employeurs, qui comportent diverses contributions et prestations, parfois liées plus directement au salaire et à la durée d'activité que dans les régimes de sécurité sociale. Lorsque les cotisations à ces régimes sont obligatoires ou quasi obligatoires (par exemple en vertu d'un accord entre organisations professionnelles et syndicales), elles sont comptabilisées dans le poste pour mémoire (voir la section 4.2 de ce Rapport).

38. Les cotisations versées par les agents des administrations et par les administrations au titre de leurs agents à des régimes de sécurité sociale relevant des pouvoirs publics sont incluses dans ce groupe. Sont aussi assimilées à des impôts les cotisations à des régimes particuliers réservés aux agents des administrations qui sont censés remplacer un régime général de la sécurité sociale[14]. Par contre, lorsqu'un régime distinct n'est pas censé remplacer un régime général et résulte de négociations entre l'administration, agissant en

qualité d'employeur, et ses agents, il n'est pas considéré comme un régime de sécurité sociale et les cotisations à ce titre ne sont pas assimilées à des impôts, même si le régime a été institué par des dispositions législatives.

39. Cette rubrique ne comprend pas les cotisations « imputées », qui correspondent aux prestations sociales versées directement par les employeurs à leurs salariés, ou anciens salariés, ou à leurs représentants (par exemple, lorsque des employeurs sont légalement tenus de verser des prestations maladies pendant une certaine période).

40. Le groupe comprend les cotisations à la charge des salariés (2100), à la charge des employeurs (2200), et à la charge des travailleurs indépendants ou des personnes n'occupant pas d'emploi (2300). À cet effet, on entend par salariés toutes les personnes qui exercent une activité dans des entreprises, des administrations, des institutions privées sans but lucratif, ou qui occupent d'autres emplois rémunérés, à l'exception des propriétaires et des membres de leur famille non rémunérés dans le cas d'entreprises individuelles. Sont également compris les membres des forces armées, quelle que soit la durée et la nature de leurs services, s'ils cotisent à un régime de sécurité sociale. Par cotisations à la charge des employeurs, on entend les versements qu'ils effectuent au régime de sécurité sociale pour le compte de leurs salariés. Si, en cas de chômage, les salariés ou employeurs sont tenus de continuer à effectuer ces versements, ces derniers doivent figurer respectivement dans les sous-groupes 2100 et 2200. En conséquence, le sous-groupe 2300 est réservé aux cotisations versées par les travailleurs indépendants et par ceux qui n'appartiennent pas à la population active (comme les handicapés ou les retraités).

3000 – Impôts sur les salaires et la main-d'œuvre

41. Ce groupe couvre les impôts acquittés par les employeurs, les salariés et les travailleurs indépendants, en pourcentage du salaire ou d'après un montant forfaitaire par personne, qui ne sont pas affectés aux dépenses de sécurité sociale. Parmi les impôts classés ici, on peut citer l'impôt complémentaire d'assurance nationale sans affectation (institué en 1977) au Royaume-Uni, l'impôt sur la masse salariale en Suède (1969-79), la fraction du « *Gewerbesteuer* » autrichien et allemand qui reposait sur la masse salariale (1965-78).

4000 – Impôts sur le patrimoine

42. Ce groupe couvre les impôts périodiques et non périodiques sur l'utilisation, la propriété ou la mutation des biens. Sont comptabilisés ici les impôts sur la propriété immobilière et sur l'actif net, les impôts sur les mutations par décès, les successions et les donations, et les impôts sur les transactions mobilières et immobilières. Sont exclus de ce groupe :

a) les impôts sur les gains en capital provenant de la vente d'un bien (1120 ou 1220) ;

b) les impôts sur l'utilisation des biens ou l'autorisation d'utiliser des biens ou d'exercer des activités (5200) [voir §72] ;

c) les impôts immobiliers perçus sur la base d'un revenu net présumé qui tiennent compte de la situation personnelle du contribuable ; ces impôts sont classés dans le groupe 1100 en tant qu'impôts sur le revenu, avec les impôts sur le revenu et les gains en capital provenant des biens immobiliers ;

d) les impôts sur l'utilisation de biens immobiliers aux fins d'habitation qui sont à la charge du propriétaire ou du locataire et dont le montant est fonction de la situation personnelle de l'utilisateur (salaire, personnes à charge, etc.) ; ils sont classés dans le groupe 1100 en tant qu'impôts sur le revenu ;

e) les impôts sur les constructions dépassant la densité autorisée, les impôts sur l'extension, la construction ou la modification de certains immeubles au-delà d'une valeur autorisée et les impôts sur la construction d'immeubles ; ces impôts sont classés dans le poste 5200 en tant qu'impôts sur l'autorisation d'exercer certaines activités ;

f) les impôts sur l'utilisation de biens immobiliers par le propriétaire à des fins commerciales particulières, comme la vente de boissons alcoolisées, de tabac, de viande, ou pour l'exploitation de sols ou terrains (par exemple aux États-Unis, les taxes de lotissement) ; ils sont classés dans le poste 5200 en tant qu'impôts sur l'autorisation d'exercer certaines activités.

4100 – Impôts périodiques sur la propriété immobilière

43. Ce sous-groupe comprend les impôts prélevés régulièrement au titre de l'utilisation ou de la propriété de biens immobiliers :

- ces impôts sont prélevés sur les terrains et les bâtiments ;
- ces impôts sont calculés en pourcentage de la valeur du bien évalué d'après un revenu locatif fictif, le prix de vente ou le rendement capitalisé, ou en fonction d'autres caractéristiques du bien, comme sa dimension ou son emplacement, d'où l'on peut déduire une valeur locative présumée ou la valeur du capital ;
- ces impôts sont à la charge du propriétaire, du locataire ou des deux ; ils peuvent également être payés par une administration à une autre administration au titre d'un bien relevant de la compétence de cette dernière ;
- il n'est pas tenu compte des dettes pour la détermination de l'assiette de ces impôts, contrairement aux impôts sur l'actif net.

44. Les impôts sur la propriété immobilière sont en outre subdivisés en impôts acquittés par les ménages (4110) et impôts acquittés par d'autres agents (4120), suivant les critères exposés au §25 b) ci-dessus.

4200 – Impôts périodiques sur l'actif net

45. Ce sous-groupe comprend les impôts prélevés régulièrement (dans la plupart des cas annuellement) sur l'actif net, c'est-à-dire les impôts perçus sur un large éventail de biens mobiliers et immobiliers, endettement déduit. Il est subdivisé en impôts acquittés par des personnes physiques (4210), et en impôts acquittés par des sociétés (4220) selon les critères exposés plus haut au §25 a). Si les recettes provenant des institutions sont comptabilisées à part, elles doivent être ajoutées aux impôts des entreprises.

4300 – Impôts sur les mutations par décès, les successions et les donations

46. Ce sous-groupe comprend les impôts sur les mutations par décès et les successions (4310) et les impôts sur les donations (4320)[15]. Les impôts sur les mutations par décès sont calculés soit sur l'ensemble de la masse successorale, soit en fonction de la part de chacun des bénéficiaires (« part héréditaire ») ; en outre, ces derniers impôts peuvent tenir compte du degré de parenté entre chacun des bénéficiaires et le défunt.

4400 – Impôts sur les transactions mobilières et immobilières

47. Sont compris, entre autres, dans ce sous-groupe les impôts sur l'émission, le transfert, l'achat et la vente de valeurs mobilières, les impôts sur les chèques, ainsi que les

droits perçus à l'occasion d'actes juridiques déterminés, comme la validation de contrats et la vente de biens immobiliers. Sont exclus :

a) les impôts sur l'utilisation de biens, mobiliers ou immobiliers, ou l'autorisation d'exercer certaines activités (5200) ;

b) les droits acquittés au titre de frais de justice, ou pour la délivrance de certificats de naissance, de mariage ou de décès, car ces droits sont considérés comme des recettes non fiscales (voir §9) ;

c) les impôts sur les gains en capital (1000) ;

d) les impôts périodiques sur la propriété immobilière (4100) ;

e) les impôts périodiques sur l'actif net (4200) ;

f) les prélèvements sur le patrimoine ou sur l'actif net effectués une fois pour toutes (4500).

4500 – Autres impôts non périodiques sur le patrimoine[16]

48. Ce sous-groupe comprend les prélèvements sur le patrimoine effectués une fois pour toutes (par opposition aux prélèvements périodiques). Il est subdivisé en impôts sur l'actif net (4510) et en autres impôts non périodiques sur le patrimoine (4520). Le poste 4510 inclurait les impôts perçus pour couvrir des dépenses exceptionnelles ou à des fins de redistribution. Le poste 4520 comprendrait les impôts prélevés pour tenir compte d'une plus-value prise par les terrains du fait que les administrations publiques ont autorisé l'extension ou l'aménagement d'installations locales, ainsi que les impôts sur la réévaluation du capital ou les impôts perçus une seule fois sur certains biens déterminés.

4600 – Autres impôts périodiques sur le patrimoine

49. Ils sont rares dans des pays membres de l'OCDE ; ce sous-groupe comprendrait les impôts sur des biens tels que le cheptel, les bijoux, les fenêtres et les signes extérieurs de richesse.

5000 – Impôts sur les biens et services

50. Ce poste couvre tous les impôts et droits perçus sur la production, l'extraction, la vente, le transfert, la location ou la livraison de biens et la prestation de services (5100), ou sur l'utilisation ou l'autorisation d'utiliser des biens ou d'exercer des activités (5200). Ce groupe comprend donc :

a) les taxes cumulatives en cascade ;

b) les taxes générales sur les ventes – perçues au stade de la production ou de la fabrication, du gros ou du détail ;

c) les taxes sur la valeur ajoutée ;

d) les accises ;

e) les taxes perçues à l'importation et à l'exportation de biens ;

f) les impôts perçus sur l'utilisation de biens et sur l'autorisation d'utiliser des biens ou d'exercer certaines activités ;

g) les impôts sur l'extraction, le traitement ou la production de minéraux et autres produits.

51. Les cas douteux de délimitation entre ce groupe et le groupe 4000 (impôts sur le patrimoine) et le sous-groupe 6100 (autres impôts à la charge des entreprises) sont examinés au §42, §47 et §74. Des postes résiduels (5300 et 5130) ont été prévus pour

comptabiliser les recettes fiscales qui ne peuvent être ventilées respectivement entre les postes 5100 et 5200 et entre les postes 5110 et 5120 (voir §27).

5100 – *Impôts sur la production, la vente, le transfert, la location et la livraison de biens et la prestation de services*

52. Ce sous-groupe comprend tous les impôts perçus sur les transactions afférentes à des biens ou services, en fonction de leurs caractéristiques propres (comme la valeur, le poids du tabac, le degré d'alcool, etc.), à la différence des impôts perçus au titre de l'utilisation ou de l'autorisation d'utiliser des biens ou d'exercer des activités, qui entrent dans le sous-groupe 5200.

5110 – *Impôts généraux sur les biens et services*

53. Ce sous-groupe comprend tous les impôts, autres que les droits à l'importation et à l'exportation (5123 et 5124), perçus sur la production, la location, le transfert, la livraison ou la vente d'une gamme de biens ou la prestation d'une gamme de services, qu'ils soient produits dans le pays ou importés, et quel que soit le stade de la production ou de la distribution aux quel ils sont perçus. Il couvre ainsi les taxes sur la valeur ajoutée, les taxes sur les ventes et les taxes de caractère cumulatif en cascade. On a ajouté aux recettes brutes de cette catégorie les recettes provenant de la compensation à la frontière de ces impôts lorsque les biens sont importés, et déduit les remboursements d'impôts effectués lorsque les marchandises sont exportées. Ces impôts sont ventilés en : taxes sur la valeur ajoutée (5111), impôts sur les ventes (5112), autres impôts généraux sur les biens et services (5113).

54. Certains cas se trouvent à la limite entre ce sous-groupe et celui des impôts sur des biens et services déterminés (5120) lorsque ces impôts sont perçus sur un grand nombre de biens, comme dans le cas de la « purchase tax » au Royaume-Uni (abrogée en 1973) et l'impôt japonais sur les biens marchands (abrogé en 1988). Conformément aux options nationales, la « purchase tax » britannique est classée impôt général (5112) et l'impôt japonais dans les accises (5121).

5111 – *Taxes sur la valeur ajoutée*

55. Sont classés dans ce sous-groupe tous les impôts généraux sur la consommation prélevés sur la valeur ajoutée, quels que soient le mode de déduction et les stades auxquels ils sont perçus. En pratique, tous les pays de l'OCDE où existe une taxe sur la valeur ajoutée autorisent normalement la déduction immédiate des taxes sur les achats par tous les redevables, à l'exception du consommateur final, et imposent la taxe à tous les stades. Dans certains pays, le poste peut inclure aussi certains impôts, comme les taxes sur les activités financières et les assurances, soit parce que les recettes correspondantes ne peuvent être dissociées de celles de la taxe sur la valeur ajoutée, soit parce qu'elles sont considérées comme faisant partie intégrante de la taxe sur la valeur ajoutée, même si les taxes similaires qui existent dans d'autres pays peuvent être classées autrement (par exemple, sous le poste 5126 comme impôts sur les services ou sous le poste 4400 comme impôts sur les transactions mobilières et immobilières).

5112 – *Impôts sur les ventes*

56. Sont classés ici tous les impôts perçus à un stade unique, que ce soit celui de la fabrication, de la production, du gros ou du détail.

5113 – *Autres impôts généraux sur les biens et services*

57. Ce sous-groupe comprend les impôts cumulatifs, connus également sous le nom d'impôt en cascade, qui sont perçus sans déduction de l'impôt sur les moyens de production chaque fois qu'une opération a lieu, ainsi que les impôts généraux sur la consommation lorsqu'il s'y ajoute des éléments qui les font assimiler à la taxe sur la valeur ajoutée, à la taxe sur les ventes ou à des taxes en cascade.

5120 – *Impôts sur des biens et des services déterminés*

58. Ce sous-groupe couvre les accises, les bénéfices engendrés et transférés par les monopoles fiscaux, et les droits de douane et à l'importation, ainsi que les taxes à l'exportation, les opérations de change, les biens d'équipement et les paris, et aussi les impôts spéciaux sur les services qui ne font pas partie d'un impôt général du sous-groupe 5110.

5121 – *Accises*

59. Les accises sont perçues sur des produits particuliers, ou sur une gamme limitée de produits, qui ne peuvent être classés sous le poste 5110 (impôts généraux), 5123 (droits à l'importation) ou 5124 (droits à l'exportation). Elles peuvent être perçues à un stade quelconque de la production ou de la distribution et sont calculées ordinairement par référence au poids, au degré ou au volume du produit, mais parfois aussi à sa valeur. Cette subdivision couvre ainsi les impôts spéciaux, qui frappent notamment le sucre, la betterave, les allumettes, les chocolats, et les impôts auxquels sont soumis à des taux divers certains produits, comme ceux perçus dans la plupart des pays sur les tabacs, boissons alcoolisées, hydrocarbures et autres sources d'énergie.

60. Les accises sont à distinguer de :

a) 5110 (impôts généraux) ; ce cas est examiné aux §53 et §54 ;

b) 5123 (droits à l'importation) ; lorsqu'un impôt perçu principalement sur des biens importés s'applique, ou s'appliquerait, aussi légalement à un bien comparable produit dans le pays, les recettes procurées par cet impôt seront classées avec les accises (5121) ; ce principe s'applique même lorsqu'il n'y a pas de production locale, réelle ou potentielle, comparable (voir aussi §64) ;

c) 5126 (impôts sur les services) ; le problème ici concerne les impôts sur l'électricité, le gaz et l'énergie ; ils sont tous considérés comme des impôts sur les biens et inclus dans le poste 5121.

5122 – *Bénéfices des monopoles fiscaux*

61. Ce sous-groupe couvre la fraction des bénéfices des monopoles fiscaux qui est transférée aux administrations publiques ou qui sert à financer des dépenses considérées comme dépenses publiques (voir §18). Les montants sont comptabilisés lorsqu'ils sont transférés aux administrations publiques ou utilisés pour effectuer des dépenses considérées comme des dépenses publiques.

62. Les monopoles fiscaux reflètent l'exercice du pouvoir d'imposition de l'État par l'intermédiaire du monopole. Les monopoles fiscaux sont des entreprises publiques non financières, qui exercent dans la plupart des cas un monopole sur la production ou la distribution du tabac, des boissons alcoolisées, du sel, des allumettes, des cartes à jouer et des produits pétroliers ou agricoles (c'est-à-dire, sur le genre de produits qui peuvent être

soumis, principalement ou accessoirement, aux accises du poste 5121), pour procurer des recettes publiques qui, dans d'autres pays, sont obtenues par le biais d'impôts frappant les transactions sur ces produits d'entreprises privées. Le monopole d'État peut être exercé au stade de la production, ou au stade de la distribution comme dans le cas des magasins de vente de boissons alcoolisées qui appartiennent à l'État et sont contrôlés par lui.

63. Les monopoles fiscaux sont différents des services publics, comme les chemins de fer, l'électricité, les postes et autres moyens de communication, qui peuvent avoir une position de monopole ou de quasi-monopole, mais dont l'objet principal est, normalement, de fournir des services essentiels et non pas de procurer des recettes à l'État. Les transferts à l'administration de ces autres entreprises publiques sont considérés comme des recettes non fiscales. La notion traditionnelle de monopole fiscal n'a généralement pas été élargie pour inclure les loteries nationales, dont les bénéfices sont habituellement considérés comme des recettes non fiscales. Cependant, ces bénéfices peuvent être considérés comme des recettes fiscales quand la raison principale de la mise en œuvre de ces loteries est l'augmentation des recettes pour financer les dépenses publiques. On distingue les bénéfices des monopoles fiscaux des bénéfices des monopoles d'exportation et d'importation (5127), qui sont transférés des offices de commercialisation ou d'autres entreprises s'occupant du commerce international.

5123 – *Droits de douane et autres droits à l'importation*

64. Figurent ici les taxes, droits de timbre et surtaxes qui, selon la loi sont perçus exclusivement sur des produits importés. Sont aussi inclus dans ce poste les droits perçus sur l'importation de denrées agricoles dans les pays Membres de l'Union Européenne et les montants acquittés par certains de ces pays en vertu du Système de Montants Compensatoires[16]. À partir de 1998, les droits de douane collectés par les États membres de l'Union européenne pour le compte de l'Union européenne ne sont plus reportés sous cette rubrique dans les tableaux par pays (chapitre 4 de ce Rapport). Sont exclues ici les taxes perçues sur les importations au titre d'un impôt général sur les biens et les services ou d'une accise applicable aussi bien aux produits importés qu'aux produits fabriqués dans le pays.

5124 – *Taxes à l'exportation*

65. Pendant les années 70, les droits à l'exportation étaient perçus normalement en Australie, au Canada et au Portugal, et ils étaient utilisés en Finlande à des fins conjoncturelles. Certains pays Membres de l'Union Européenne acquittent, dans le cadre du système des montants compensatoires, une taxe sur les exportations (voir la note 16 du §64). Lorsque ces montants sont identifiables, ils sont inclus dans ce poste. Ce dernier ne comprend pas les remboursements effectués au titre d'impôts généraux sur la consommation d'accises ou de droits de douane sur des biens exportés, qui doivent être déduits des recettes brutes comptabilisées, selon le cas, sous le poste 5110, 5121 ou 5123.

5125 – *Impôts sur les biens d'équipement*

66. Ce sous-groupe comprend les impôts perçus sur les biens d'équipement, comme les machines. Ils peuvent exister depuis un certain nombre d'années ou avoir un caractère temporaire et être prélevés à des fins conjoncturelles. Ne sont pas inclus les impôts sur les « inputs » industriels qui frappent aussi les consommateurs (comme l'impôt suédois sur l'énergie qui est classé sous le poste 5121).

5126 – *Impôts sur des services déterminés*

67. Sous ce poste figurent tous les impôts calculés sur la rémunération de services spécifiques, comme les taxes sur les primes d'assurance, les taxes sur les services bancaires, sur les jeux et paris (par exemple : courses de chevaux, pronostics de football, billets de loterie nationale), les transports, les spectacles, les restaurants et la publicité. Les impôts prélevés sur le revenu brut des sociétés prestataires d'un service (exemple : primes d'assurance brutes, mises de jeux encaissées par les sociétés) sont classés sous ce poste. Les recettes fiscales provenant des prélèvements sur les banques et des contributions aux mécanismes de garantie des dépôts et de stabilité financière sont provisoirement classés ici pour l'édition 2012. La classification détaillée est présentée dans le paragraphe 104.

68. Ne figurent pas sous ce poste :

a) les impôts sur les services qui font partie d'un impôt général sur les biens et services et sont classés sous le poste 5110 ;

b) les taxes sur l'électricité, le gaz et l'énergie (classées sous le poste 5121 en tant qu'accises) ;

c) les taxes sur les gains personnels tirés de jeux et paris (qui sont classées sous le poste 1120, en tant qu'impôts sur les gains en capital des personnes physiques et entreprises individuelles) et les montants forfaitaires perçus sur le transfert de loteries privées ou sur l'autorisation de créer des loteries (5200)[17] ;

d) les impôts sur les chèques et sur l'émission, le transfert ou le remboursement de valeurs mobilières, (qui sont classés sous le poste 4400, en tant qu'impôts sur les transactions mobilières et immobilières).

5127 – *Autres impôts sur les transactions et les échanges internationaux*

69. Ce sous-groupe couvre les recettes perçues par l'État sur l'achat et la vente de monnaies étrangères à des taux différents. Lorsque l'État exerce le privilège exclusif dont il dispose pour s'assurer une marge entre le prix d'achat et le prix de vente de devises qui ne se réduit pas à la simple couverture des frais administratifs, ce bénéfice représente un prélèvement obligatoire imposé dans des proportions indéterminées à l'acheteur et au vendeur des monnaies étrangères. Il équivaut normalement au droit à l'importation et au droit à l'exportation perçus dans un système de taux de change unique, ou à une taxe sur la vente ou l'achat de monnaies étrangères. Comme les bénéfices des monopoles fiscaux et des monopoles d'importation ou d'exportation transférés à l'État, il représente l'exercice d'un monopole aux fins d'imposition et est inclus dans les recettes fiscales.

70. Ce sous-groupe comprend aussi les bénéfices des monopoles d'exportation ou d'importation, bien qu'il n'en existe pas dans les pays de l'OCDE, les impôts sur l'achat ou la vente de devises et tous les autres impôts perçus spécifiquement sur les opérations ou les échanges internationaux.

5128 – *Autres impôts sur des biens et services déterminés*

71. Cette rubrique comprend les impôts sur l'extraction de minéraux, combustibles fossiles et autres ressources non renouvelables provenant de gisements privés ou détenus par une autre administration, ainsi que toute autre recette non ventilable provenant des impôts sur des biens et services déterminés. Les impôts sur l'extraction de ressources non renouvelables correspondent généralement à un montant forfaitaire par unité de qualité ou de poids, mais peuvent être calculés ad valorem. Les impôts sont comptabilisés à la date

d'extraction des ressources. Les versements tirés de l'extraction de ressources non renouvelables issues de gisements appartenant à l'administration publique qui perçoit ces versements sont classés en tant que loyers.

5200 – Impôts sur l'utilisation des biens ou l'autorisation d'utiliser des biens ou d'exercer des activités

72. Ce sous-groupe comprend les taxes prélevées en raison de l'utilisation de biens, indépendamment des impôts frappant les biens eux-mêmes. Contrairement à ceux-ci (5100), les impôts du sous-groupe 5200 ne sont pas calculés d'après la valeur des biens, mais ordinairement d'après un montant forfaitaire. Sont aussi couverts les impôts perçus au titre du droit d'utiliser des biens ou d'exercer des activités, comme les taxes sur la pollution qui ne reposent pas sur la valeur de biens déterminés. Il est parfois difficile de distinguer les taxes d'utilisation et droits de licence obligatoires, qui sont considérés comme des impôts, de ceux qui ne le sont pas parce qu'ils sont assimilés à des recettes non fiscales ; les critères appliqués sont ceux indiqués aux §9 et §10.

73. Bien que le sous-groupe se réfère à l'utilisation des biens, le fait générateur de l'impôt peut être aussi bien l'enregistrement de la propriété, de sorte que les impôts relevant de ce sous-groupe peuvent viser la possession d'animaux ou de biens plutôt que leur utilisation (par exemple, les chevaux de course, les chiens, les véhicules à moteur) et même s'appliquer à des biens inutilisables (comme les véhicules à moteur ou les fusils inutilisables).

74. Les cas limites concernent :

a) les impôts sur l'autorisation d'exercer des activités commerciales, qui sont classés selon les règles exposées au §77 lorsqu'ils ont une assiette mixte associant le revenu, les salaires versés ou le chiffre d'affaires ;

b) les impôts sur la propriété ou l'utilisation de la propriété de biens visés par les postes 4100, 4200 et 4600 ; le poste 4100 ne vise que les impôts sur la propriété ou la location de biens immobiliers et, contrairement aux impôts du sous-groupe 5200, ils sont fonction de la valeur du bien ; les impôts sur l'actif net et les impôts sur les biens meubles des sous-groupes 4200 et 4600 visent la propriété et non pas l'utilisation des biens, couvrent un groupe d'actifs et non pas de biens particuliers et sont aussi fonction de la valeur du bien.

5210 – Impôts périodiques sur l'utilisation de biens ou sur l'autorisation d'utiliser des biens ou d'exercer certaines activités

75. Ces impôts ont pour principale caractéristique d'être perçus à intervalles réguliers et de représenter ordinairement des montants forfaitaires. Le poste le plus important, du point de vue du volume des recettes, est constitué par les permis de circulation des véhicules. Ce sous-groupe inclut aussi les taxes perçues lors de la délivrance de permis de chasse, de tir ou de pêche, ou l'autorisation de vendre certains produits, ainsi que les taxes sur la possession de chiens et sur la prestation de certains services à condition qu'elles répondent aux critères définis aux §9 et §10. Les subdivisions du poste 5210 comprennent les taxes d'utilisation de véhicules à moteur à la charge des ménages (5211) et à la charge d'autres agents (5212)[18]. Le poste 5213 couvre les plaques de chiens et les taxes perçues pour l'autorisation d'exercer certaines activités, comme la vente de viande et d'alcool, lorsque les prélèvements ont un caractère périodique. Il couvre aussi les permis généraux de chasse, de port d'armes et de pêche, lorsque le droit d'exercer ces activités n'est pas accordé au titre d'une opération

commerciale normale (par exemple, la délivrance du permis ne comporte pas le droit d'utiliser une parcelle déterminée de terrain appartenant à l'État).

5220 – Impôts non périodiques sur l'utilisation de biens ou sur l'autorisation d'utiliser des biens ou d'exercer certaines activités

76. Cette rubrique recouvre les taxes non périodiques perçues sur l'utilisation de biens ou sur l'autorisation d'utiliser des biens ou d'exercer certaines activités et celles qui sont prélevées chaque fois que des biens sont utilisés.

- Les impôts prélevés sur l'émission ou le rejet dans l'environnement de gaz toxiques, liquides nocifs ou autres substances dangereuses figurent ici. Les paiements au titre des permis d'émission négociables délivrés par les administrations publiques dans le cadre des dispositifs de plafonnement et d'échange doivent également être comptabilisés sous cette rubrique au moment où les émissions sont produites. Les permis délivrés gratuitement par les administrations ne donnent lieu à aucun enregistrement comptable de recettes.
- La comptabilisation en droits constatés implique un éventuel délai entre la date à laquelle l'administration perçoit le règlement des permis et la date à laquelle les émissions sont produites. Dans les comptes nationaux, ce délai se traduit pour l'administration par un engagement financier sur la période.
- Il convient d'exclure les paiements effectués au titre de la collecte et de l'élimination de déchets ou de substances nocives par les autorités publiques, étant donné qu'il s'agit là de vente de services aux entreprises.

77. D'autres impôts non périodiques qui relèvent du poste 5200 sont aussi classés dans cette rubrique. Ainsi figurent les paiements uniques effectués au titre de l'autorisation de vendre des boissons alcoolisées ou des tabacs ou d'ouvrir des guichets de « paris mutuels », à condition qu'ils répondent aux critères définis aux §9 et §10.

6000 – Autres impôts

78. Ce groupe couvre les impôts prélevés sur une ou plusieurs bases différentes de celles qui sont indiquées pour les groupes 1000, 3000, 4000 et 5000, ou sur des bases dont aucune ne pourrait être considérée comme étant essentiellement la même que l'une de celles afférentes à ces groupes. Quant aux impôts perçus sur plusieurs bases différentes, il convient si possible d'évaluer les recettes liées à chaque base de perception (par exemple, pour l'impôt allemand « *Gewerbesteuer* ») et d'inclure les montants séparés dans le groupe approprié. S'il est impossible d'évaluer les montants séparés, mais si l'on sait que la plus grande partie des recettes provient de l'impôt perçu sur une même base, la totalité des recettes sont classées en fonction de cette base. Si aucune de ces procédures ne peut être appliquée, les impôts sont classés dans le présent groupe. Les sous-groupes peuvent comprendre également les recettes provenant d'impôts que les administrations ne sont pas en mesure d'identifier ou d'isoler (voir §27). Figurent aussi dans ce groupe les recettes provenant d'amendes et de pénalités acquittées pour infraction aux réglementations fiscales, mais qui ne peuvent être identifiées comme se rapportant à une catégorie particulière d'impôts (voir §14). Ce poste est divisé en impôts exclusivement ou principalement à la charge des entreprises (6100) et en impôts à la charge d'autres contribuables (6200).

A.6. Conciliation avec les comptes nationaux

79. Cette section des tableaux permet de concilier les calculs des recettes fiscales totales de l'OCDE et l'ensemble des impôts et cotisations sociales versés aux administrations publiques qui sont enregistrés dans les comptes nationaux par pays. Lorsque le pays en question est membre de l'Union européenne (UE) la comparaison est effectuée entre les calculs des recettes fiscales totales des pays de l'OCDE et la somme des recettes fiscales et cotisations de sécurité sociale perçues par les administrations publiques et les institutions des secteurs de l'Union européenne des comptes nationaux.

A.7. Poste pour mémoire relatif au financement des prestations de sécurité sociale

80. Le rapport entre les impôts et les cotisations de sécurité sociale étant variable, et en raison des problèmes évoqués aux §34 et §40, on a réuni dans un poste pour mémoire l'ensemble des versements affectés à des prestations du type sécurité sociale, en dehors des versements volontaires au secteur privé. Les données sont présentées de la façon suivante (voir la section 4.2) :

a) impôts du groupe 2000 ;

b) impôts affectés aux prestations de sécurité sociale ;

c) cotisations volontaires à l'administration ;

d) cotisations obligatoires au secteur privé.

Les §34 et §40 ci-dessus contiennent des directives pour la ventilation entre ces quatre catégories.

A.8. Poste pour mémoire relatif aux impôts identifiables payés par les administrations

81. Les impôts effectivement payés par les administrations elles-mêmes et que l'on peut identifier sont indiqués dans un poste pour mémoire et classés suivant les grandes rubriques de la classification des impôts de l'OCDE. Dans la très grande majorité des pays, seuls peuvent être identifiées en l'occurrence les cotisations de sécurité sociale et les impôts sur les salaires, mais il s'agit là en général des impôts les plus importants acquittés par les administrations (voir la section 4.3 de cette publication).

A.9. Rapport de la classification des impôts de l'OCDE avec les systèmes nationaux de comptabilité nationale

82. Un système de comptabilité nationale (SCN) tend à fournir un cadre cohérent pour enregistrer et présenter les principaux flux relatifs à la production, à la consommation, à l'accumulation et aux transactions extérieures d'une zone économique donnée, d'ordinaire un pays ou une grande région d'un pays. Les recettes publiques sont une partie importante des transactions enregistrées dans le SCN. La version finale du SCN 2008 a été diffusée conjointement par cinq organisations internationales : les Nations Unies, le Fonds Monétaire International, l'Union européenne, l'Organisation de Coopération et de Développement Économiques et la Banque Mondiale, en août 2009. Le *Système* est un ensemble complet, cohérent et souple de comptes macro-économiques. Il est élaboré pour être utilisé dans les pays à économie de marché quel que soit leur niveau de développement économique ainsi que dans les pays en transition vers l'économie de

marché. De larges extraits du cadre théorique ainsi que les définitions des divers secteurs de l'économie du SCN figurent dans la classification des impôts de l'OCDE.

83. Il existe cependant un certain nombre de différences entre la classification des impôts de l'OCDE et les concepts du SCN qui sont indiqués ci-dessous. Ils proviennent du fait que l'objectif de cette classification est de permettre une ventilation aussi large que possible des données statistiques pour ce que les administrations fiscales conviennent de considérer de manière générale comme des impôts :

a) l'OCDE inclut les cotisations obligatoires de sécurité sociale payées aux administrations publiques dans les recettes fiscales totales ; les cotisations sociales volontaires et imputées ainsi que celles versées aux caisses privées ne sont pas considérées comme des impôts (§7 et §8 ci-dessus) ;

b) les avis diffèrent sur la question de savoir s'il y a lieu de classer certains prélèvements et redevances dans les impôts (§9 et §10 ci-dessus) ;

c) l'OCDE exclut les impôts imputés ou les subventions résultant d'opérations de taux de change officiels multiples et ceux résultant du fait que la banque centrale paye un taux d'intérêt sur les réserves obligatoires différent des autres taux du marché ;

d) il existe des différences dans le traitement des crédits d'impôt récupérables.

84. Comme on l'a noté aux §1 et §2, les groupes 1000 à 6000 de la classification de l'OCDE comprennent tous les versements sans contrepartie aux administrations publiques, à l'exclusion des prêts obligatoires et des amendes. On peut obtenir le total de ces versements sans contrepartie, amendes incluses, mais prêts obligatoires exclus, en additionnant les postes suivants du SCN 2008 :

- impôts du type valeur ajoutée (D.211) ;
- droits et taxes sur les importations à l'exclusion de la TVA (D.212) ;
- droits sur les exportations (D.213) ;
- taxes sur les produits, à l'exclusion de la TVA, des droits sur les importations et les exportations (D.214) ;
- autres impôts sur la production (D.29) ;
- impôts sur le revenu (D.51) ;
- autres impôts périodiques (D.59) ;
- cotisations de sécurité sociale (D.61) à l'exclusion des cotisations volontaires ;
- impôts sur le capital (D.91).

A.10. La classification des impôts de l'OCDE et le système du Fonds monétaire international (GFS)

85. Le champ d'application et l'évaluation des recettes fiscales dans le système GFS et dans le système SCN 2008 sont très proches. Par conséquent, les différences entre la classification de l'OCDE et celle du SCN 2008 (voir §83 ci-dessus) sont également valables pour le GFS. En outre, le Fonds monétaire international subdivise le groupe 5000 de la classification de l'OCDE en une Section IV (Taxes intérieures sur les biens et services) et une Section V (Taxes sur les transactions et les échanges internationaux). Cela tient à ce que le rendement de ces dernières taxes représente généralement des sommes infimes dans les pays de l'OCDE ce qui n'est pas le cas dans beaucoup de pays non membres.

A.11. Comparaison de la classification des impôts de l'OCDE et des autres classifications internationales des recettes publiques

86. Le tableau ci-dessous décrit point par point la comparaison entre la classification des impôts de l'OCDE et les classifications suivantes :

i) système des comptes nationaux (SCN 2008) ;

ii) système européen des comptes (SEC 2010) ;

iii) manuel de statistiques des finances publiques du Fonds monétaire international (MSFP 2014).

87. Ces comparaisons correspondent à celles qui devraient s'appliquer dans la majorité des cas. Toutefois, en pratique il faut faire preuve d'une certaine souplesse dans leur application. En effet, dans certains cas, les pays peuvent adopter des méthodes diverses de classification des recettes dans les comptes nationaux.

OECD Classification		2008 SNA	2010 ESA	GFSM 2014
1000	Impôts sur le revenu, les bénéfices et les gains en capital			
1100	Personnes physiques			
1110	Sur le revenu et les bénéfices	D51-8.61a	D51A	1111
1120	Sur les gains en capital	D51-8.61c, d	D51C, D	1111
1200	Sociétés			
1210	Sur le revenu et les bénéfices	D51-8.61b	D51B	1112
1220	Sur les gains en capital	D51-8.61c	D51C	1112
1300	Non ventilables entre les rubriques 1100 et 1200			1113
2000	Cotisations de sécurité sociale			
2100	Salariés	D613-8.85	D613	1211
2200	Employeurs	D611-8.83	D611	1212
2300	À la charge des travailleurs indépendants ou des personnes sans occupation	D613-8.85	D613	1213
2400	Non ventilables entre les rubriques 2100, 2200 et 2300			1214
3000	Impôts sur les salaires et la main-d'œuvre	D29-7.97a	D29C	112
4000	Impôts sur le patrimoine			
4100	Impôts périodiques sur la propriété immobilière			
4110	Ménages	D59-8.63a	D59A	1131
4120	Autres agents	D29-7.97b	D29A	1131
4200	Impôts périodiques sur l'actif net			
4210	Personnes physiques	D59-8.63b	D59A	1132
4220	Sociétés	D59-8.63b	D59A	1132
4300	Impôts sur les mutations par décès, les successions et les donations			
4310	Impôts sur les mutations par décès et les successions	D91-10.207b	D91A	1133
4320	Impôts sur les donations	D91-10.207b	D91A	1133
4400	Impôts sur les transactions mobilières et immobilières	D59-7.96d ; D29-7.97e	D214B, C	11411 ; 1161
4500	Autres impôts non périodiques sur le patrimoine	D91-10.207a	D91B	1135
4600	Autres impôts périodiques sur le patrimoine	D59-8.63c	D59A	1136
5000	Impôts sur les biens et services			
5100	Impôts sur les biens et services			
5110	Impôts généraux sur les biens et services			
5111	Taxes sur la valeur ajoutée	D211-7.89	D211 ; D29G	11411
5112	Impôts sur les ventes	D2122-7.94a ; D214-7.96a	D2122 ; D214I	11412
5113	Autres impôts généraux sur les biens et services	D214-7.96a	D214I	11413
5120	Impôts sur des biens et services déterminés			
5121	Accises	D2122-7.94b ; D214-7.96b	D21223 ; D214A, B, D	1142
5122	Bénéfices des monopoles fiscaux	D214-7.96e	D214J	1143
5123	Droits de douane et autres droits à l'importation	D2121-7.93	D2121 ; D21221, 2	1151
5124	Taxes à l'exportation	D213-7.95a	D214K	1152-4
5125	Impôts sur les biens d'équipements			
5126	Impôts sur les services déterminés	D2122-7.94c ; D214-7.96c	D21225 ; D214E, F, G ; D29F	114 ; 1156
5127	Autres impôts sur les transactions et les échanges internationaux	D2122-7.94d D29-7.95b D29-7.97g D59-8.64d	D21226 ; D29D ; D59E	1153 ; 1155-6
5128	Autres impôts sur des et services déterminés			1146
5130	Non ventilable entre les rubriques 5110 et 5120			
5200	Impôts sur l'utilisation des biens ou l'autorisation d'utiliser des biens ou d'exercer des activités			
5210	Impôts périodiques sur l'utilisation des biens ou l'autorisation d'utiliser des biens ou d'exercer des activités			
5211	À la charge des ménages au titre de véhicules à moteurs	D59-8.64c	D59D	11451
5212	À la charge d'autres agents au titre de véhicules à moteurs	D29-7.97d	D214D ; D29B	11451
5213	Autres impôts périodiques sur l'utilisation des biens ou l'autorisation d'utiliser des biens ou d'exercer des activités	D29-7.97c, d, f D59-8.64c	D29B, E, F ; D59D	11452
5220	Impôts non périodiques			11452
5300	Non ventilable entre les rubriques 5100 et 5200			
6000	Autres impôts			
6100	À la charge exclusive des entreprises			1161
6200	À la charge d'autres agents que les entreprises ou non identifiables	D59-8.64a, b	D59B, C	1162

A.12. Répartition des recettes fiscales par sous-secteurs d'administration publique

88. La classification de l'OCDE appelle une ventilation des recettes fiscales par sous-secteurs d'administration. On trouvera ci-après la définition de chaque sous-secteur et les critères à utiliser pour répartir entre eux les recettes fiscales. Ces définitions et critères suivent les orientations qui figurent dans le SCN 2008 et le MSFP 2014.

Sous-secteurs des administrations publiques à identifier

a) Administration centrale

89. Le sous-secteur des administrations centrales groupe tous les ministères, bureaux, établissements et autres organismes qui sont des services ou des moyens d'action du pouvoir central et dont la compétence s'étend à la totalité du territoire, à l'exception de l'administration des caisses de sécurité sociale. L'administration centrale a donc le pouvoir de prélever des impôts sur toutes les unités résidentes et non résidentes exerçant des activités économiques à l'intérieur du pays.

b) Administration d'un État fédéré, d'une province ou d'une région

90. Ce sous-secteur comprend les unités administratives intermédiaires et inclut toutes les unités administratives dont la compétence s'exerce indépendamment de l'Administration centrale sur une partie du territoire englobant un certain nombre de petites localités, à l'exception des caisses de sécurité sociale. Dans les pays unitaires, les administrations régionales peuvent être considérées comme dotées d'une existence distincte lorsqu'elles disposent d'une autonomie substantielle pour percevoir une part importante de leurs recettes de sources placées sous leur contrôle et lorsque leurs agents ne sont pas soumis à un contrôle administratif externe dans l'exercice des activités de l'unité.

91. Actuellement, les pays à structure fédérale représentent la majorité des cas dans lesquels les recettes attribuées aux unités administratives intermédiaires sont identifiées séparément. L'Espagne est le seul pays à structure unitaire qui se trouve dans cette situation. Dans les autres pays unitaires, les recettes des administrations régionales sont incluses dans celles des administrations locales.

c) Collectivités locales

92. Ce sous-secteur comprend toutes les autres unités administratives exerçant une compétence indépendante sur une partie du territoire d'un pays, à l'exception des administrations des caisses de sécurité sociale. Il englobe les diverses circonscriptions urbaines et/ou rurales (par exemple les collectivités locales, les municipalités, les villes, les bourgs ou les districts).

d) Caisses de sécurité sociale

93. Les caisses de sécurité sociale constituent un sous-secteur distinct des administrations publiques. Le sous-secteur de la sécurité sociale est défini dans le SCN de 2008 par les extraits suivants des paragraphes 4.124 à 4.126 et 4.147 :

« Les systèmes de sécurité sociale sont des systèmes d'assurance sociale qui couvrent l'ensemble de la collectivité ou d'importants sous-ensembles de la collectivité : ces systèmes sont imposés et contrôlés par les administrations publiques. Ces systèmes couvrent une grande variété de programmes qui consistent à fournir des prestations, en espèces ou en nature, au titre des circonstances suivantes : vieillesse, invalidité ou décès, survie, maladie et maternité, accident du travail, chômage, allocations familiales, soins de santé, etc. Il n'existe pas nécessairement de lien direct entre le montant de la cotisation versée par un particulier et les prestations qu'il est susceptible de recevoir » (paragraphe 4.124).

« Lorsque les systèmes de sécurité sociale ont une organisation distincte des autres activités des administrations publiques et détiennent des actifs et des engagements indépendamment de ces dernières et effectuent des opérations financières pour leur propre compte, ils peuvent être considérés comme des unités institutionnelles désignées sous le nom de caisses de sécurité sociale » (paragraphe 4.125).

« Il est possible de faire varier de façon discrétionnaire les montants prélevés et versés sous forme de cotisations de sécurité sociale et de prestations afin d'atteindre des objectifs de politique publique qui n'ont pas de lien direct avec la notion de sécurité sociale en tant que système visant à fournir des prestations à des membres de la collectivité. Ainsi, ces cotisations ou prestations peuvent être augmentées ou diminuées afin d'influer sur le niveau de la demande globale au sein de l'économie. Néanmoins, tant que ces caisses restent indépendantes, elles doivent être traitées comme des unités institutionnelles distinctes dans le SCN » (paragraphe 4.126).

« Le sous-secteur des administrations de sécurité sociale comprend les administrations de sécurité sociale opérant à tous les niveaux des administrations publiques. Les administrations de sécurité sociale sont des systèmes couvrant l'ensemble de la collectivité ou d'importants sous-ensembles de la collectivité qui sont rendus obligatoires et contrôlés par des administrations publiques » (paragraphe 4.147).

94. Cette définition des administrations de sécurité sociale est suivie dans la classification de l'OCDE à l'exception des régimes suivants :

- les régimes imposés par l'administration et exploités par des organismes extérieurs au secteur des administrations publiques, tel qu'il est défini au §3 de ce manuel ; et
- les régimes qui perçoivent des cotisations volontaires.

Autorités supranationales

95. Ce sous-secteur s'applique aux activités de collecte de recettes publiques des autorités supranationales sur le territoire d'un pays. En pratique, le seul cas d'autorité supranationale de la zone de l'OCDE est celui des institutions de l'Union européenne (UE). Depuis 1998, les autorités supranationales ne figurent plus dans les *Statistiques des recettes publiques* dans un souci de cohérence avec la définition du SCN des administrations publiques qui les exclut. Par exemple, les impôts sur le revenu et des contributions de sécurité sociale rassemblées par des Institutions européennes et payé par les fonctionnaires européens qui sont résidents de pays membres de l'Union européenne ne devraient pas être inclus. Toutefois, les prélèvements spécifiques versés par les États membres à l'Union européenne continuent à être inclus dans les recettes fiscales totales et ils sont indiqués sous cette rubrique.

Critères à utiliser pour l'attribution des recettes fiscales

96. Lorsqu'une administration collecte l'impôt et le reverse, en totalité ou en partie, à d'autres administrations, il est nécessaire de déterminer si ces recettes doivent être considérées comme étant celles de l'administration qui les perçoit et les répartit entre

d'autres administrations ou celles des administrations bénéficiaires auxquelles l'administration qui les a perçues les a transférées en simple qualité d'agent. Les critères à utiliser dans l'attribution des recettes sont indiqués aux paragraphes 97 à 100, qui reprennent les paragraphes 3.70 à 3.73 du SCN 2008.

97. En général, un impôt est attribué à l'Unité administrative qui :

a) exerce le pouvoir de percevoir l'impôt (soit en tant que détenteur de ce pouvoir soit par délégation de l'autorité qui le détient) ;

b) dispose du pouvoir discrétionnaire final de fixer et de faire varier le taux de l'impôt.

98. Lorsqu'une somme est collectée par une administration au profit d'une autre administration et en son nom, et que cette dernière a le pouvoir de percevoir l'impôt et de fixer et de faire varier son taux, la première intervient comme agent pour le compte de la dernière et l'impôt est réaffecté. Toute somme retenue par l'administration collectrice au titre des frais de recouvrement doit être considérée comme la rémunération d'un service rendu. Toute autre somme conservée par l'administration collectrice, notamment dans le cadre d'un accord de partage d'impôt, doit être considérée comme une subvention courante. Si l'administration collectrice s'est vu déléguer le pouvoir de fixer et de faire varier le taux, le montant recouvré doit être considéré comme une recette fiscale de cette administration.

99. Lorsque des administrations différentes fixent conjointement et sur un pied d'égalité la répartition du produit de cet impôt, aucune administration ne disposant d'un pouvoir prépondérant en dernier ressort, les recettes fiscales sont attribuées à chaque administration en fonction de sa part respective du produit de l'impôt. Si un accord permet à une unité administrative d'exercer un pouvoir prépondérant en dernier ressort, la totalité des recettes fiscales est attribuée à cette unité.

100. Dans certains cas aussi, un impôt est perçu dans le cadre des compétences d'une administration qui résulte de la constitution ou d'autres dispositions mais d'autres administrations fixent individuellement le taux d'imposition sur leurs territoires. Le produit de l'impôt généré sur les territoires respectifs de chaque administration est attribué à l'administration en question comme constituant ses recettes fiscales.

Versements effectués par les États membres de l'Union européenne

101. Les versements effectués par les États membres de l'Union européenne prennent la forme de prélèvements spécifiques qui comprennent :

a) les droits de douane et les prélèvements agricoles (5123) ;

b) les montants compensatoires monétaires bruts (5123 si relatifs aux importations et 5124 si relatifs aux exportations) ; et

c) les prélèvements de la CECA, les cotisations sucre et les taxes de co-responsabilité sur le lait (5128).

102. Les droits de douane collectés par les États membres pour le compte de l'Union européenne sont comptabilisés :

- sur une base qui ne tient pas compte des droits d'encaissement ;
- en utilisant des chiffres corrigés de manière à exprimer les droits sur la base de la « destination finale » et non du « pays de première entrée » lorsque de telles corrections sont possibles ; ces corrections concernent en particulier les droits prélevés dans des ports (maritimes) importants ; bien que les droits de l'UE soient prélevés par les autorités du

pays de première entrée, ces droits doivent être dans la mesure du possible déduits des recettes du pays qui les recouvre et inclus dans les recettes du pays de destination finale.

103. Ces droits de l'UE sont le plus clairement conformes au critère d'attribution décrit au §95 ci-dessus. En conséquence, à partir de 1998, ces montants sont mentionnés dans une note de bas de page à titre de rubrique « Pour mémoire » dans les tableaux des États membres de l'UE (chapitre 4 du Rapport) et ne figurent plus sous la rubrique 5123. Toutefois, ces montants sont inclus dans les grands totaux des recettes fiscales à la ligne supérieure pour toutes les années indiquées dans les tableaux.

A.13. Classification provisoire des recettes provenant des prélèvements sur les banques et des contributions aux mécanismes de garantie des dépôts et de stabilité financière

104. L'OCDE a provisoirement adopté, depuis l'édition 2012 de ses *Statistiques des recettes publiques*, le principe suivant concernant l'enregistrement comptable des recettes issues des prélèvements sur les banques ainsi que des redevances acquittées au titre de la garantie des dépôts et de la stabilité financière. Il est recommandé que les montants concernés soient comptabilisés à la rubrique 5126.

- Les redevances de stabilité, les prélèvements sur les banques et les contributions à la garantie des dépôts, qu'il est obligatoire d'acquitter, doivent généralement être traitées comme des recettes fiscales lorsque les versements sont effectués au profit de l'administration publique et affectés au budget consolidé ou général des administrations de sorte que les pouvoirs publics soient libres d'utiliser les fonds sans délai aux fins qu'ils jugent opportunes. Ce principe s'appliquerait indépendamment du fait que l'administration promette ou non d'effectuer des versements pour garantir les dépôts des clients des établissements bancaires si la situation l'exigeait à l'avenir.
- Si les paiements obligatoires sont effectués au profit de l'administration publique et imputés à des budgets dont les ressources doivent être entièrement réaffectées au secteur de l'économie qui englobe les entreprises assujetties à ces paiements, ceux-ci seront toujours traités, en règle générale, comme des recettes fiscales étant donné que les fonds seraient disponibles pour l'administration et réduiraient son déficit budgétaire, que la redevance est sans contrepartie pour les entités individuelles et que les montants collectés pourraient être dissociés de tout versement en faveur des déposants ou de toute dépense visant à soutenir plus largement le secteur financier.
- Les contributions aux mécanismes traditionnels de moindre envergure destinés à garantir les dépôts de « détail », contributions dont le montant est aligné sur le coût de la garantie, doivent être classées en tant que redevances pour services rendus.
- Tout versement au titre de la réalisation par une administration des actifs d'un établissement en faillite ou du recouvrement par cette administration d'une créance prioritaire sur les actifs de l'établissement en cours de liquidation, effectué en vue de financer l'indemnisation des clients ayant perdu leurs dépôts, serait traité comme une redevance par opposition aux recettes fiscales.
- Les contributions obligatoires aux fonds administrés en-dehors du secteur public et aux organismes non étatiques bénéficiant du soutien des institutions collectrices de dépôts ainsi que toutes les contributions aux mécanismes volontaires ne doivent pas être traitées comme des recettes fiscales.

Notes

1. Toutes les références au SCN concernent l'édition de 2008.
2. Se reporter à la section A.12 de ce manuel pour l'examen de cette notion.
3. Il est en général possible d'identifier les montants des cotisations de sécurité sociale et les impôts sur les salaires, mais pas les autres impôts payés par les administrations.
4. En revanche, si un ou plusieurs pays considèrent comme un impôt, un droit que la plupart des pays font entrer dans les recettes non fiscales ou qui procure des recettes substantielles, les montants ainsi perçus figureront dans une note de renvoi à la fin des tableaux par pays correspondants, même s'ils ne sont pas inclus dans le total des recettes fiscales.
5. Les appellations peuvent cependant être souvent trompeuses. Ainsi, une redevance de passeport sera normalement considérée comme une recette non fiscale, alors qu'un prélèvement additionnel sur les passeports (comme c'est le cas au Portugal), qui a pour but de procurer un montant substantiel de recettes eu égard au coût de délivrance du passeport, sera considéré comme un impôt du sous-groupe 5200.
6. On trouvera des précisions sur cette distinction dans l'étude spéciale intitulée « L'information sur les recettes fiscales : Problèmes actuels », de l'édition de 2001 des *Statistiques des recettes publiques.*
7. On utilise parfois les expressions « non remboursable » et « remboursable », mais il peut paraître illogique de parler de « remboursement » lorsque rien n'a été versé.
8. Toutefois, dans les systèmes d'imputation de l'impôt sur les sociétés, les crédits d'impôts récupérables sont traités différemment (§31-33).
9. Il ne s'agit pas d'une véritable dépense fiscale au sens strict. De telles dépenses fiscales supposent que l'on identifie un système fiscal de référence pour chaque pays ou, de préférence, une norme internationale commune. En pratique, il n'a pas été possible de parvenir à un accord sur une norme internationale commune.
10. Sauf s'ils sont calculés sur le bénéfice résultant de la vente, auquel cas ils seraient classés parmi les impôts sur les gains en capital dans le sous-groupe 1120 ou 1220.
11. Dans certains pays, la même législation est applicable aux personnes physiques et aux entreprises dans le cas d'impôts sur le revenu particuliers. Cependant, les recettes procurées par ces impôts peuvent, en général, être ventilées et figurent donc dans les deux sous-groupes appropriés.
12. Ainsi, « celles qui sont suffisamment autonomes et indépendantes pour que leur fonctionnement soit comparable à celui d'une société [...] (y compris) la tenue de comptes complets » (SCN 2008, Section 4.44).
13. Au Canada – pays généralement considéré comme appliquant un système d'imputation – le crédit d'impôt (non récupérable) offert à l'actionnaire concerne l'impôt national sur les sociétés censé avoir été acquitté, qu'un impôt sur les sociétés soit ou ne soit pas dû. Comme, dans ces systèmes, il n'y a aucun lien complet entre le montant de l'impôt sur le revenu, ces crédits pour les dividendes sont traités, comme les autres crédits d'impôt, selon les principes exposés au §20.
14. Il peut en être ainsi lorsqu'un régime en faveur des administrations existait avant l'instauration d'un régime général de sécurité sociale.
15. Dans le SCN 2008, ils sont considérés comme des transferts en capital et non pas comme des impôts (voir section A.8).
16. Système selon lequel l'Union Européenne ajuste les effets des différences entre les taux de change utilisés pour fixer les prix des produits agricoles dans le cadre de la politique agricole commune, et le taux de change réel. Les paiements effectués selon ce système portent sur les importations ou les exportations; lorsqu'ils sont identifiables, ces montants figurent dans la rubrique appropriée (5123 ou 5124). Dans ce *Guide*, sont inclus les montants bruts, c'est-à-dire sans déduction d'aucune prime payée par le SMC.
17. Les transferts de bénéfices de loteries d'État sont considérés comme des recettes non fiscales (voir aussi §63).
18. Voir à ce sujet le §25 c).

ORGANISATION FOR ECONOMIC CO-OPERATION AND DEVELOPMENT

The OECD is a unique forum where governments work together to address the economic, social and environmental challenges of globalisation. The OECD is also at the forefront of efforts to understand and to help governments respond to new developments and concerns, such as corporate governance, the information economy and the challenges of an ageing population. The Organisation provides a setting where governments can compare policy experiences, seek answers to common problems, identify good practice and work to co-ordinate domestic and international policies.

The OECD member countries are: Australia, Austria, Belgium, Canada, Chile, the Czech Republic, Denmark, Estonia, Finland, France, Germany, Greece, Hungary, Iceland, Ireland, Israel, Italy, Japan, Korea, Latvia, Luxembourg, Mexico, the Netherlands, New Zealand, Norway, Poland, Portugal, the Slovak Republic, Slovenia, Spain, Sweden, Switzerland, Turkey, the United Kingdom and the United States. The European Union takes part in the work of the OECD.

OECD Publishing disseminates widely the results of the Organisation's statistics gathering and research on economic, social and environmental issues, as well as the conventions, guidelines and standards agreed by its members.

ORGANISATION DE COOPÉRATION ET DE DÉVELOPPEMENT ÉCONOMIQUES

L'OCDE est un forum unique en son genre où les gouvernements œuvrent ensemble pour relever les défis économiques, sociaux et environnementaux que pose la mondialisation. L'OCDE est aussi à l'avant-garde des efforts entrepris pour comprendre les évolutions du monde actuel et les préoccupations qu'elles font naître. Elle aide les gouvernements à faire face à des situations nouvelles en examinant des thèmes tels que le gouvernement d'entreprise, l'économie de l'information et les défis posés par le vieillissement de la population. L'Organisation offre aux gouvernements un cadre leur permettant de comparer leurs expériences en matière de politiques, de chercher des réponses à des problèmes communs, d'identifier les bonnes pratiques et de travailler à la coordination des politiques nationales et internationales.

Les pays membres de l'OCDE sont : l'Allemagne, l'Australie, l'Autriche, la Belgique, le Canada, le Chili, la Corée, le Danemark, l'Espagne, l'Estonie, les États-Unis, la Finlande, la France, la Grèce, la Hongrie, l'Irlande, l'Islande, Israël, l'Italie, le Japon, le Luxembourg, le Mexique, la Norvège, la Nouvelle-Zélande, les Pays-Bas, la Pologne, le Portugal, la République slovaque, la République tchèque, le Royaume-Uni, la Slovénie, la Suède, la Suisse et la Turquie. L'Union européenne participe aux travaux de l'OCDE.

Les Éditions OCDE assurent une large diffusion aux travaux de l'Organisation. Ces derniers comprennent les résultats de l'activité de collecte de statistiques, les travaux de recherche menés sur des questions économiques, sociales et environnementales, ainsi que les conventions, les principes directeurs et les modèles développés par les pays membres.

OECD PUBLISHING, 2, rue André-Pascal, 75775 PARIS CEDEX 16
(23 2016 36 3 P) ISBN 978-92-64-26511-0 – 20156

www.ingramcontent.com/pod-product-compliance
Lightning Source LLC
Chambersburg PA
CBHW061156240926
51846CB00006B/1028
9789264265103